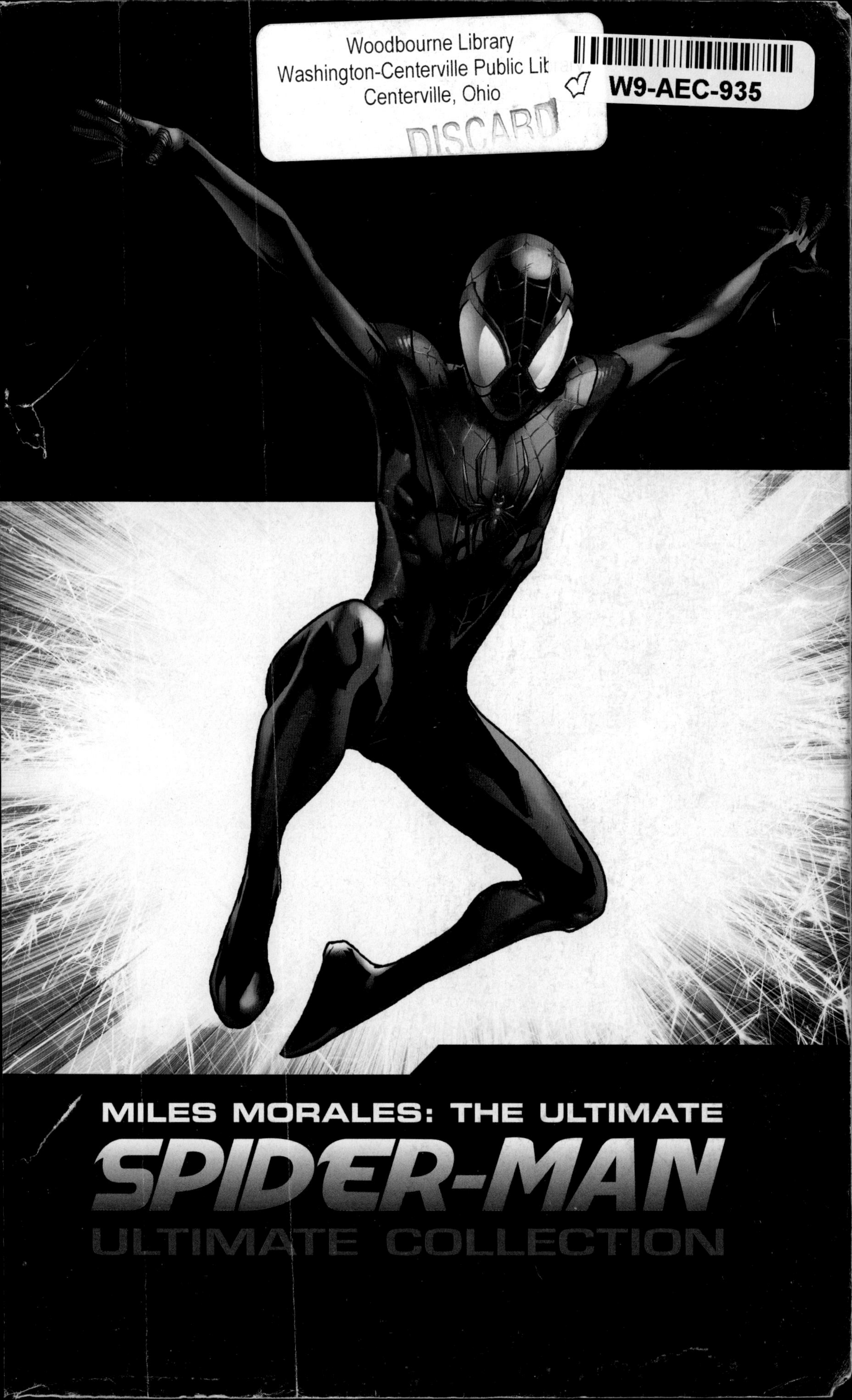

MILES MORALES: THE ULTIMATE

SPIDER-MAN

ULTIMATE COLLECTION

ULTIMATE COMICS SPIDER-MAN #1–12
& MATERIAL FROM *ULTIMATE FALLOUT #4*

WRITER: **BRIAN MICHAEL BENDIS**

ARTISTS: **SARA PICHELLI** (#1–5, #8 & ULTIMATE FALLOUT #4),
CHRIS SAMNEE (#6–7) & **DAVID MARQUEZ** (#9–12)

FINISHES, #5: **DAVID MESSINA**

COLORIST: **JUSTIN PONSOR**

LETTERER: **VC's CORY PETIT**

COVER ART: **KAARE ANDREWS** (#1–11) & **JORGE MOLINA** (#12)

SPIDER-MEN #1–5

ARTIST: **SARAH PICHELLI**

COLOR ARTIST: **JUSTIN PONSOR**

LETTERER: **CORY PETIT**

COVER ART: **JIM CHEUNG** & **JUSTIN PONSOR**

ASSISTANT EDITOR: **JON MOISAN**

ASSOCIATE EDITOR: **SANA AMANAT**

SENIOR EDITOR: **MARK PANICCIA**

SPIDER-MAN CREATED BY STAN LEE & STEVE DITKO

COLLECTION EDITOR: JENNIFER GRÜNWALD
ASSISTANT EDITOR: SARAH BRUNSTAD
ASSOCIATE MANAGING EDITOR: ALEX STARBUCK
EDITOR, SPECIAL PROJECTS: MARK D. BEAZLEY
SENIOR EDITOR, SPECIAL PROJECTS: JEFF YOUNGQUIST
SVP PRINT, SALES & MARKETING: DAVID GABRIEL
BOOK DESIGNER: ADAM DEL RE

EDITOR IN CHIEF: AXEL ALONSO
CHIEF CREATIVE OFFICER: JOE QUESADA
PUBLISHER: DAN BUCKLEY
EXECUTIVE PRODUCER: ALAN FINE

SPIDER-MAN ULTIMATE COLLECTION BOOK 1. Contains material originally published in magazine form as ULTIMATE FALLOUT #4, ULTIMATE COMICS SPIDER-MAN #1-12 and SPIDER-
5. ISBN# 978-0-7851-9778-2. Published by MARVEL WORLDWIDE, INC., a subsidiary of MARVEL ENTERTAINMENT, LLC. OFFICE OF PUBLICATION: 135 West 50th Street, New York, NY
ARVEL No similarity between any of the names, characters, persons, and/or institutions in this magazine with those of any living or dead person or institution is intended, and any such
purely coincidental. **Printed in the U.S.A.** ALAN FINE, President, Marvel Entertainment; DAN BUCKLEY, President, TV, Publishing and Brand Management; JOE QUESADA, Chief Creative
of Publishing; DAVID BOGART, SVP of Operations & Procurement, Publishing; C.B. CEBULSKI, VP of International Development & Brand Management; DAVID GABRIEL, SVP Print, Sales &
of Operations & Logistics; DAN CARR, Executive Director of Publishing Technology; SUSAN CRESPI, Editorial Operations Manager; ALEX MORALES, Publishing Operations Manager; STAN
information regarding advertising in Marvel Comics or on Marvel.com, please contact Jonathan Rheingold, VP of Custom Solutions & Ad Sales, at jrheingold@marvel.com. For Marvel
call 800-217-9158. **Manufactured between 6/5/2015 and 7/13/2015 by R.R. DONNELLEY, INC., SALEM, VA, USA.**

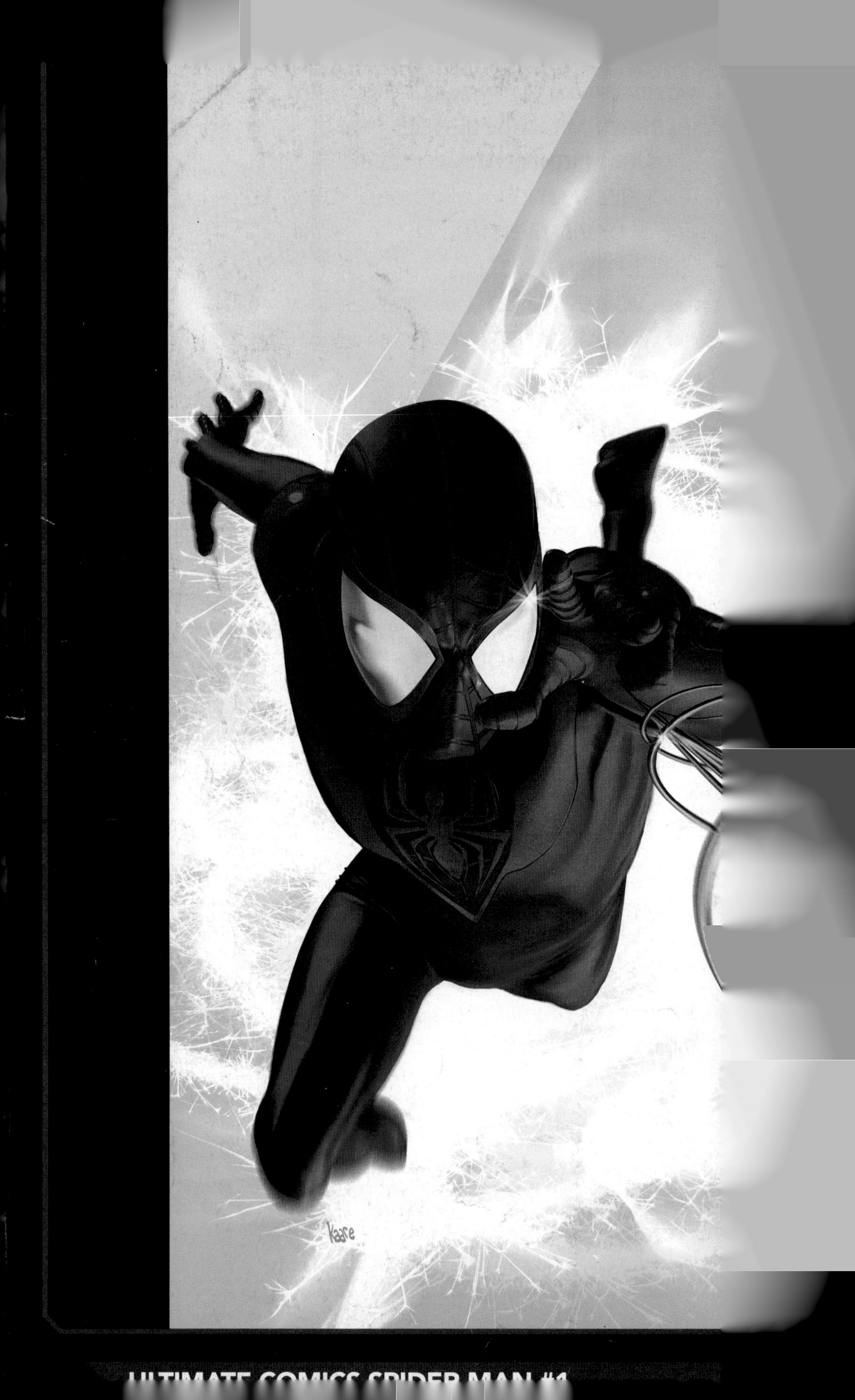

ULTIMATE COMICS SPIDER-MAN #1

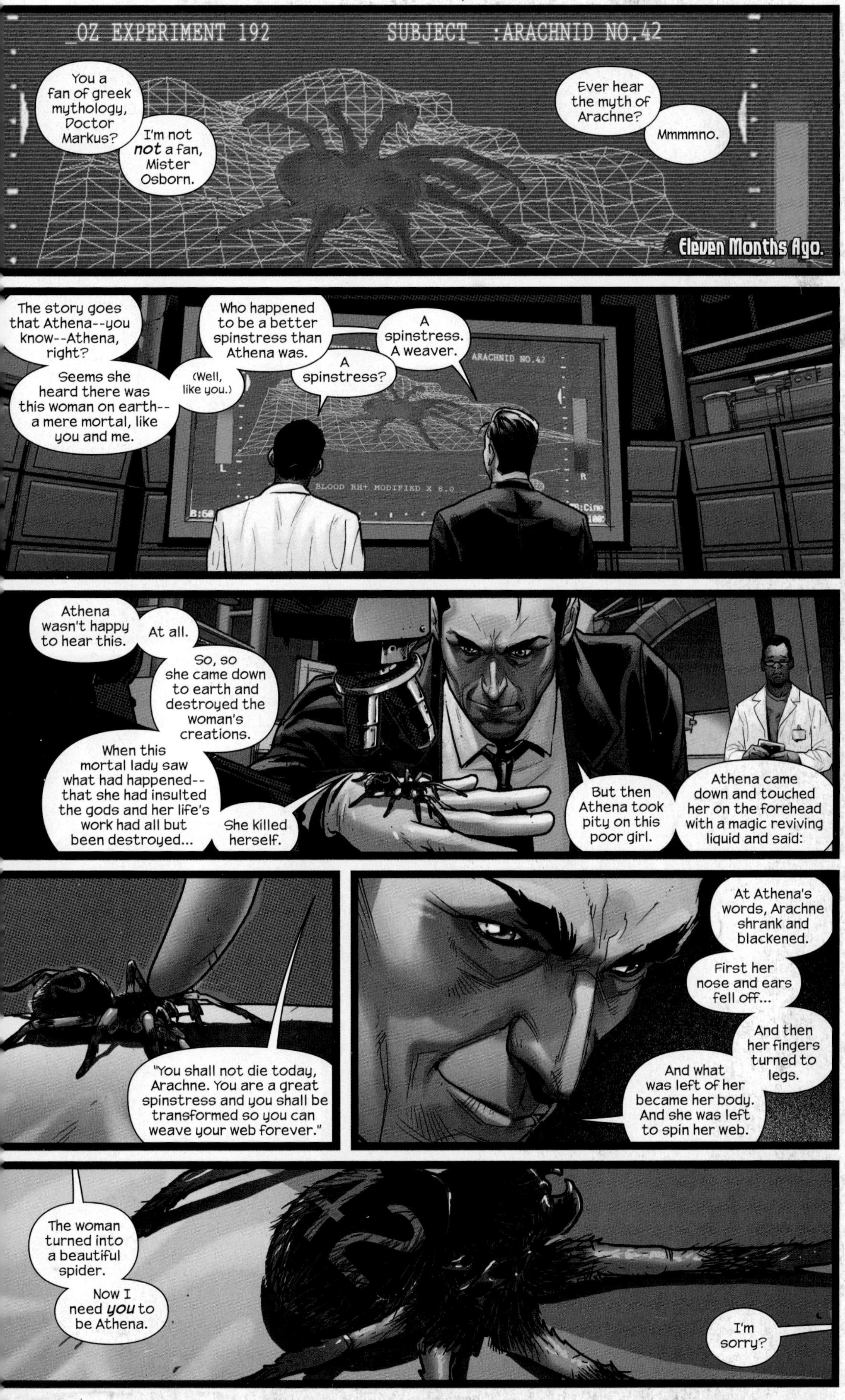
_OZ EXPERIMENT 192
SUBJECT_ :ARACHNID NO.42
Eleven Months Ago.
You a fan of greek mythology, Doctor Markus?
I'm not *not* a fan, Mister Osborn.
Ever hear the myth of Arachne?
Mmmmno.
The story goes that Athena--you know--Athena, right?
Seems she heard there was this woman on earth-- a mere mortal, like you and me.
(Well, like you.)
Who happened to be a better spinstress than Athena was.
A spinstress?
A spinstress. A weaver.
ARACHNID NO.42
BLOOD RH+ MODIFIED X 8.0
Athena wasn't happy to hear this.
At all.
So, so she came down to earth and destroyed the woman's creations.
When this mortal lady saw what had happened-- that she had insulted the gods and her life's work had all but been destroyed...
She killed herself.
But then Athena took pity on this poor girl.
Athena came down and touched her on the forehead with a magic reviving liquid and said:
"You shall not die today, Arachne. You are a great spinstress and you shall be transformed so you can weave your web forever."
At Athena's words, Arachne shrank and blackened.
First her nose and ears fell off...
And then her fingers turned to legs.
And what was left of her became her body. And she was left to spin her web.
The woman turned into a beautiful spider.
Now I need *you* to be Athena.
I'm sorry?

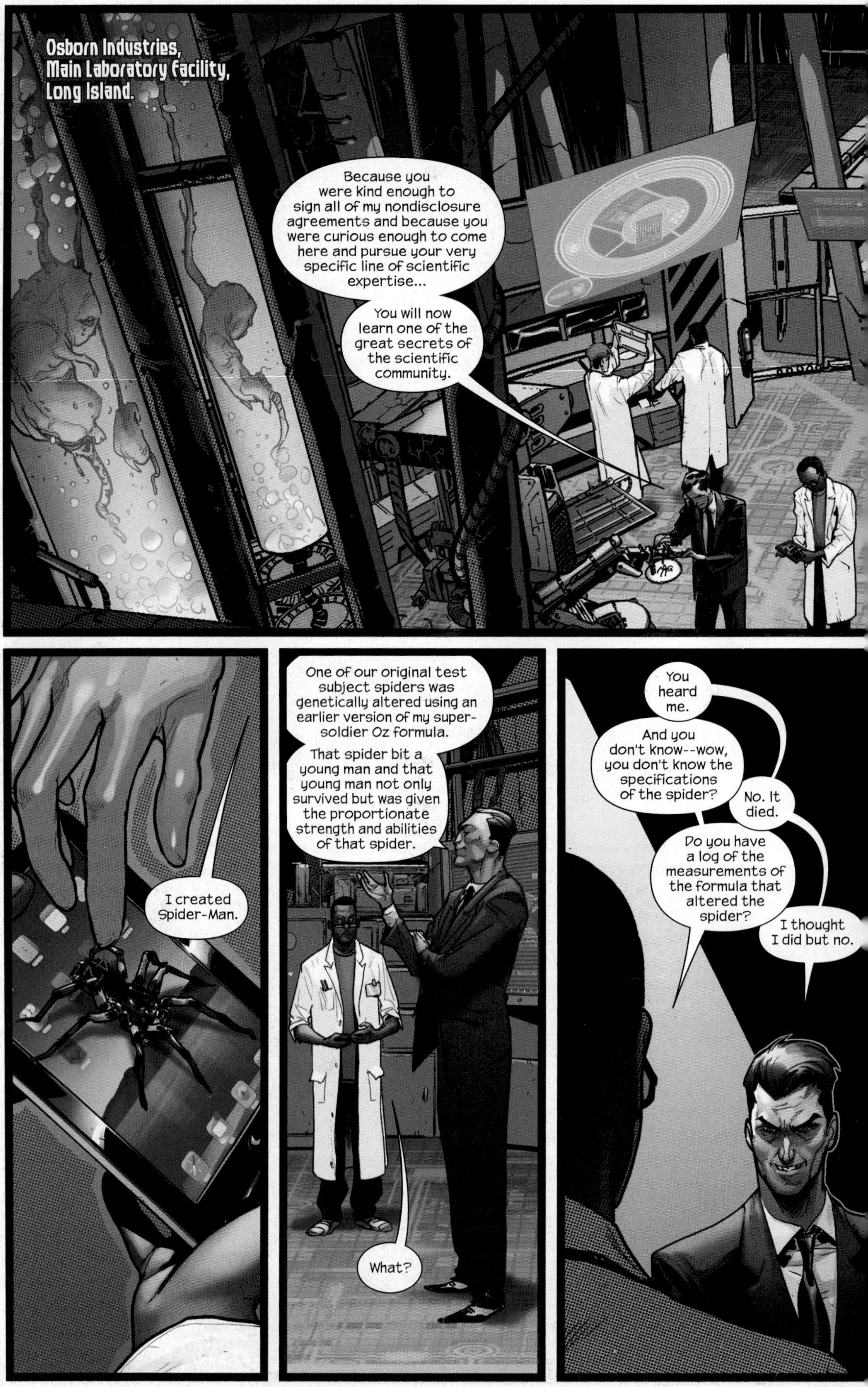
Osborn Industries, Main Laboratory Facility, Long Island.
Because you were kind enough to sign all of my nondisclosure agreements and because you were curious enough to come here and pursue your very specific line of scientific expertise...
You will now learn one of the great secrets of the scientific community.
I created Spider-Man.
One of our original test subject spiders was genetically altered using an earlier version of my super-soldier Oz formula.
That spider bit a young man and that young man not only survived but was given the proportionate strength and abilities of that spider.
What?
You heard me.
And you don't know--wow, you don't know the specifications of the spider?
No. It died.
Do you have a log of the measurements of the formula that altered the spider?
I thought I did but no.

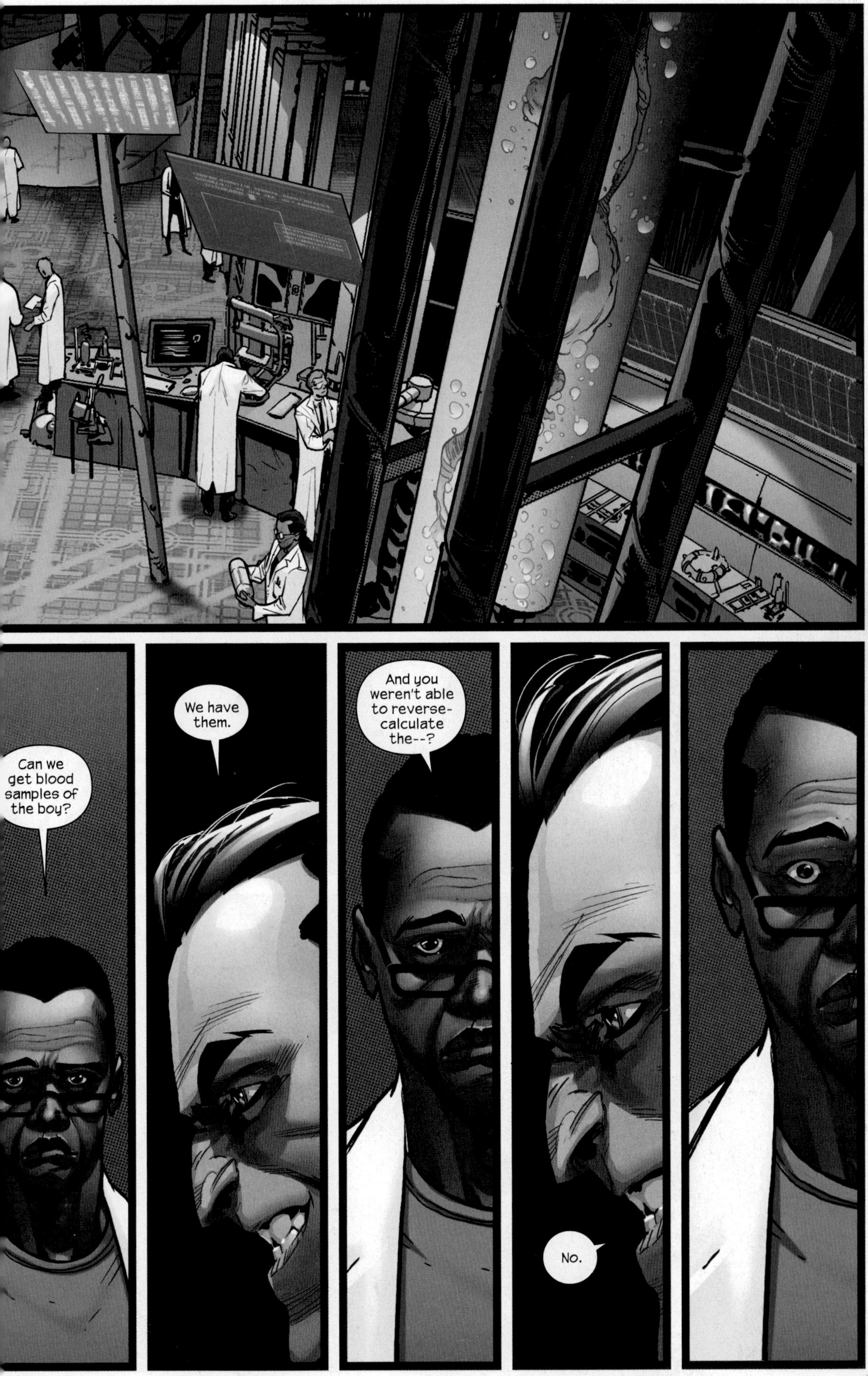
Can we get blood samples of the boy?
We have them.
And you weren't able to reverse-calculate the--?
No.

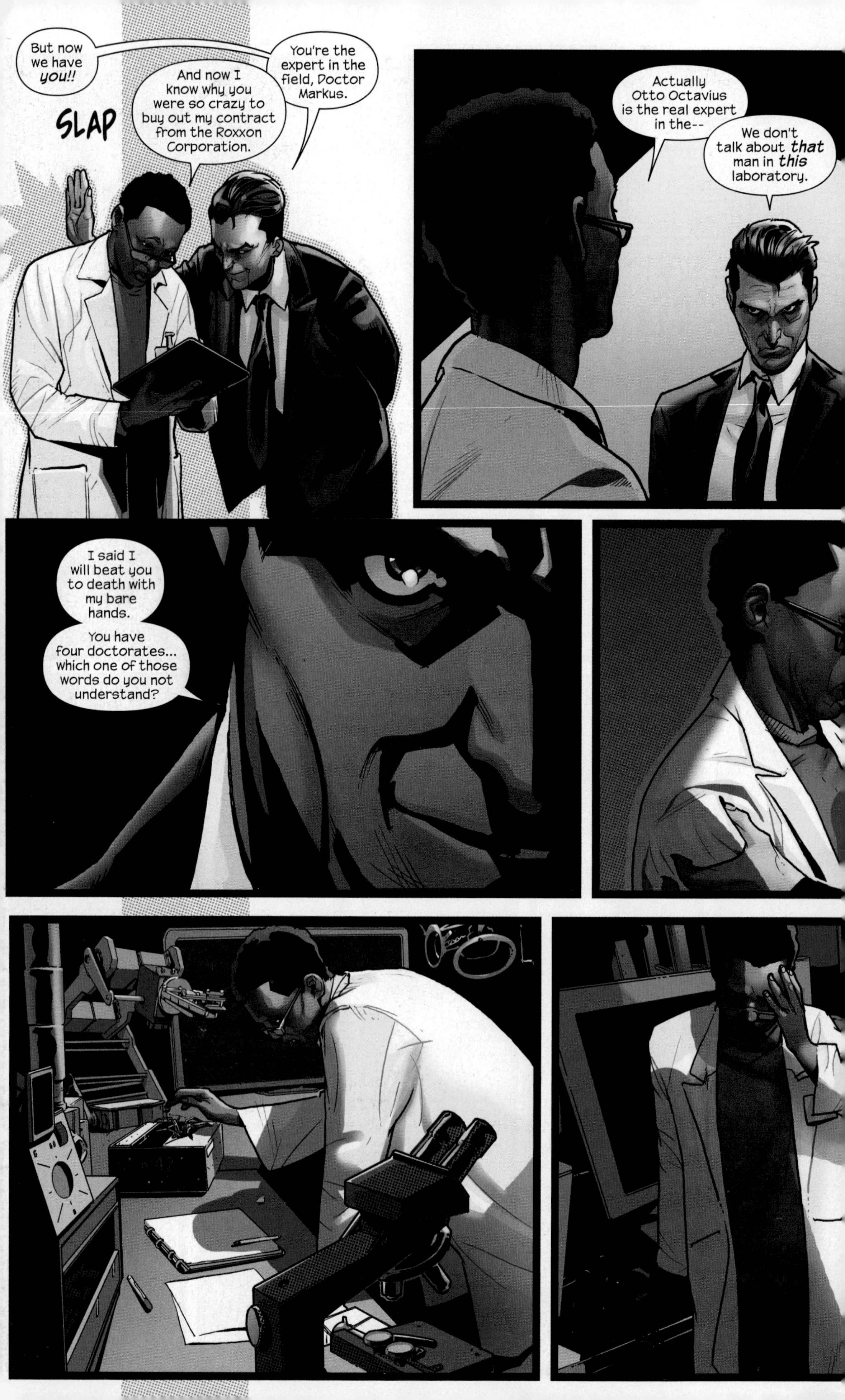

But now we have *you!!*
You're the expert in the field, Doctor Markus.
SLAP
And now I know why you were so crazy to buy out my contract from the Roxxon Corporation.
Actually Otto Octavius is the real expert in the--
We don't talk about *that* man in *this* laboratory.
I said I will beat you to death with my bare hands.
You have four doctorates... which one of those words do you not understand?

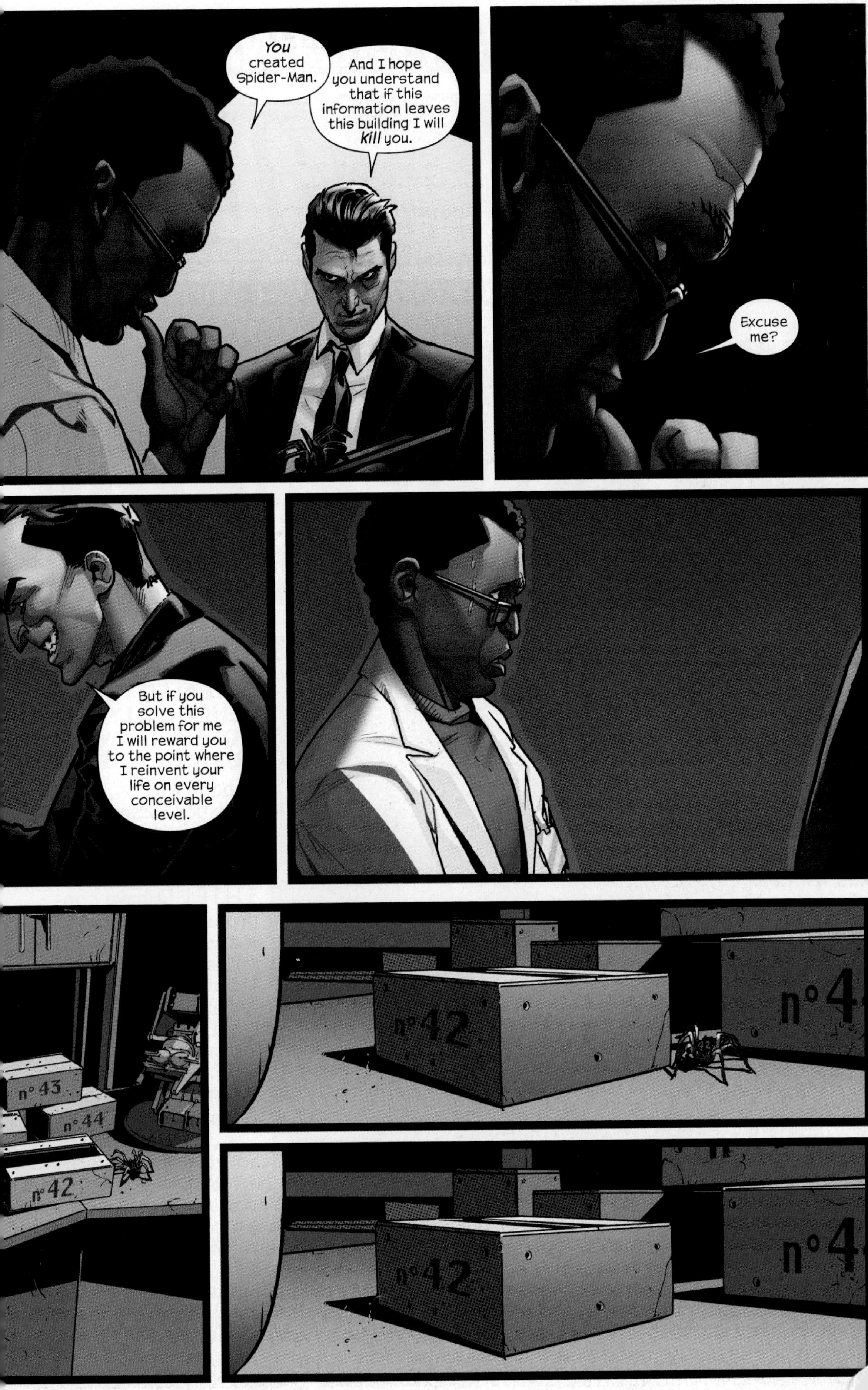
You created Spider-Man.
And I hope you understand that if this information leaves this building I will *kill* you.
Excuse me?
But if you solve this problem for me I will reward you to the point where I reinvent your life on every conceivable level.
n°43
n°44
n°42
n°42
n°4
n°42
n°4

DAILY BUGLE

NORMAN OSBORN IS THE GREEN GOBLIN!

CONTROVERSIAL INDUSTRIALIST IS REVEALED TO BE GENETICALLY ALTERED MONSTER NOW IN THE CUSTODY OF S.H.I.E.L.D.

Reporting by Frederick Fosswell

Agents of the world peacekeeping task force S.H.I.E.L.D. have confirmed to the Daily Bugle that controversial industrialist Norman Osborn had infected his own body with one of his experiments altering himself into what one of our S.H.I.E.L.D. sources are referring to as the Green Goblin.

Sources also confirm that this Green Goblin is the same one that attacked Midtown High School a few months ago, shutting the school down for weeks. It is also referred to as the public debut of the mystery man called Spider-Man. Whether or not there is a connection between Spider-Man and Norman Osborn's double life has yet to be revealed.

Speculation continues as to why Norman Osborn would break one of the cardinal rules of science by experimenting on himself. Sources close to Norman say that certain pressures to create a workable version of his experimental "super-soldier" formula led him to use the formula on himself.

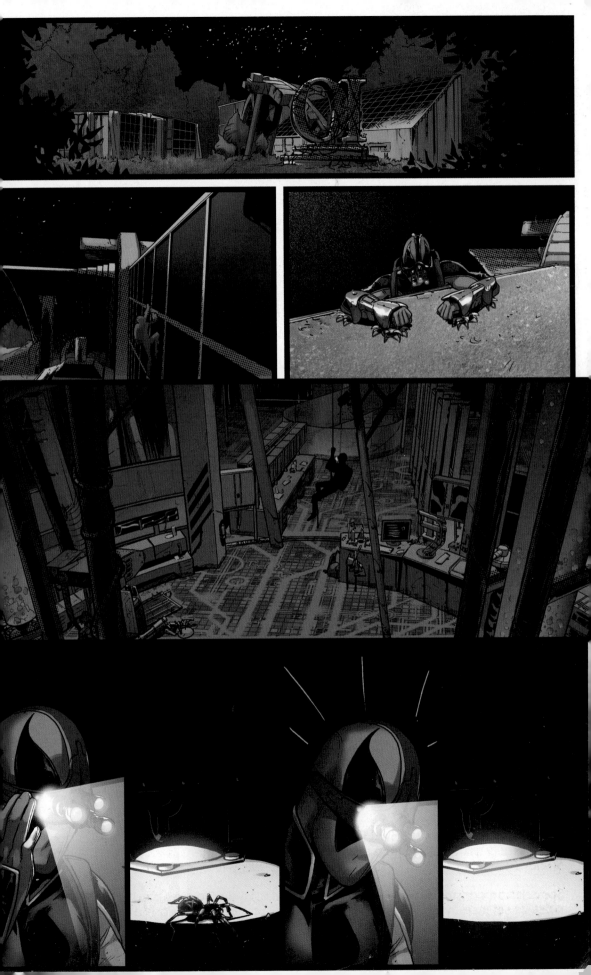

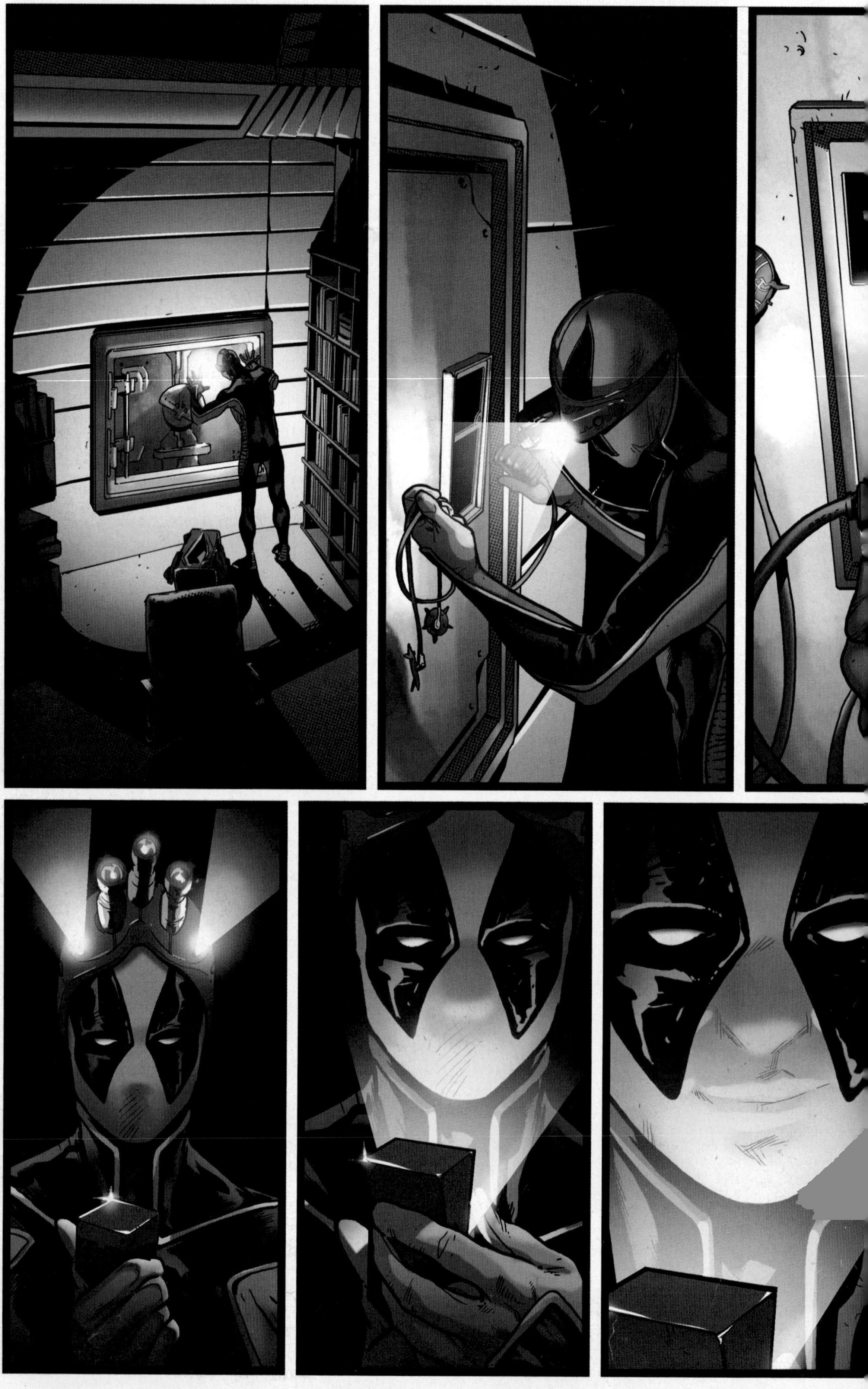

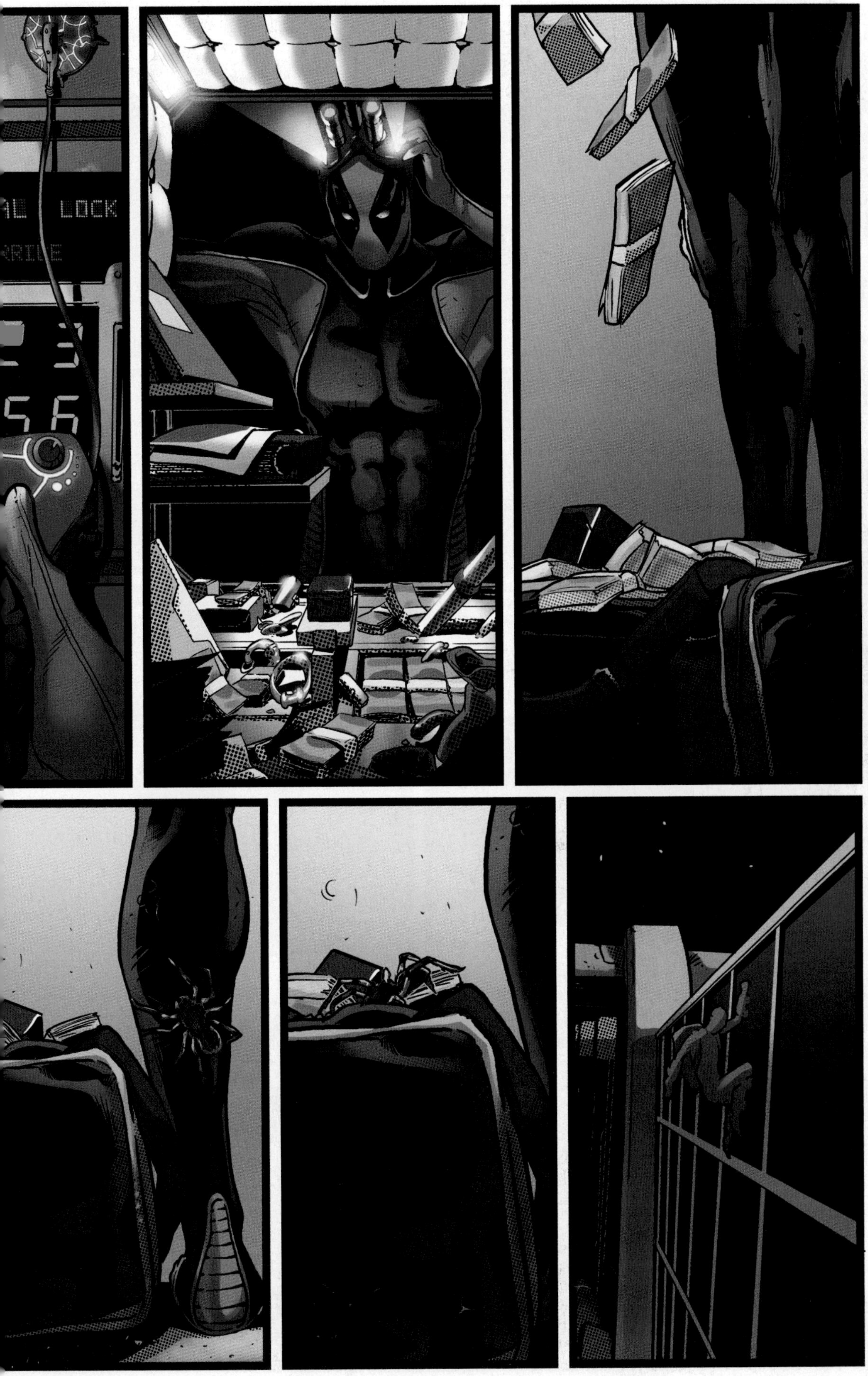
AL LOCK

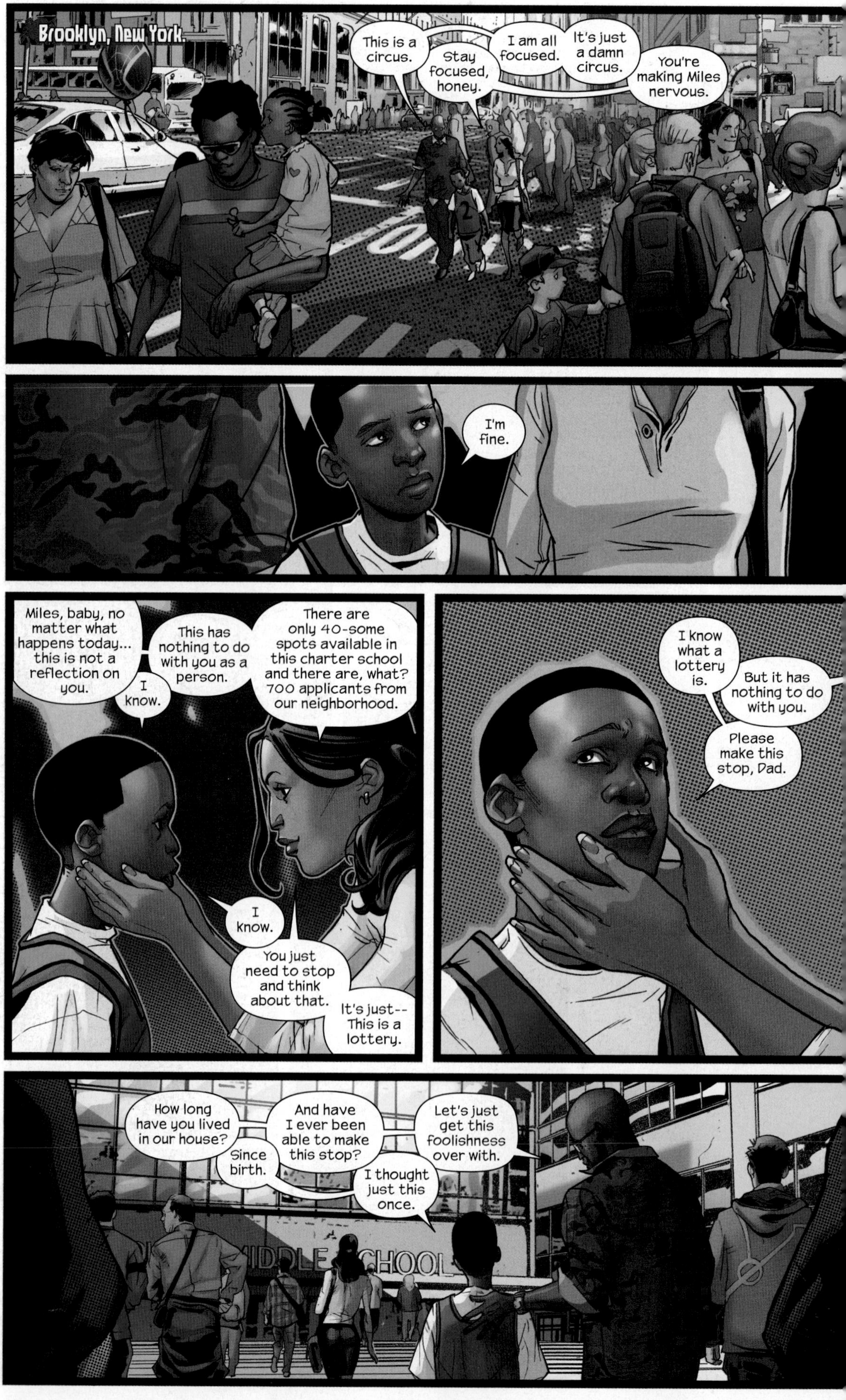
Brooklyn, New York.
This is a circus.
Stay focused, honey.
I am all focused.
It's just a damn circus.
You're making Miles nervous.
I'm fine.
Miles, baby, no matter what happens today... this is not a reflection on you.
I know.
This has nothing to do with you as a person.
There are only 40-some spots available in this charter school and there are, what? 700 applicants from our neighborhood.
I know.
You just need to stop and think about that.
It's just-- This is a lottery.
I know what a lottery is.
But it has nothing to do with you.
Please make this stop, Dad.
How long have you lived in our house?
Since birth.
And have I ever been able to make this stop?
I thought just this once.
Let's just get this foolishness over with.
MIDDLE SCHOOL

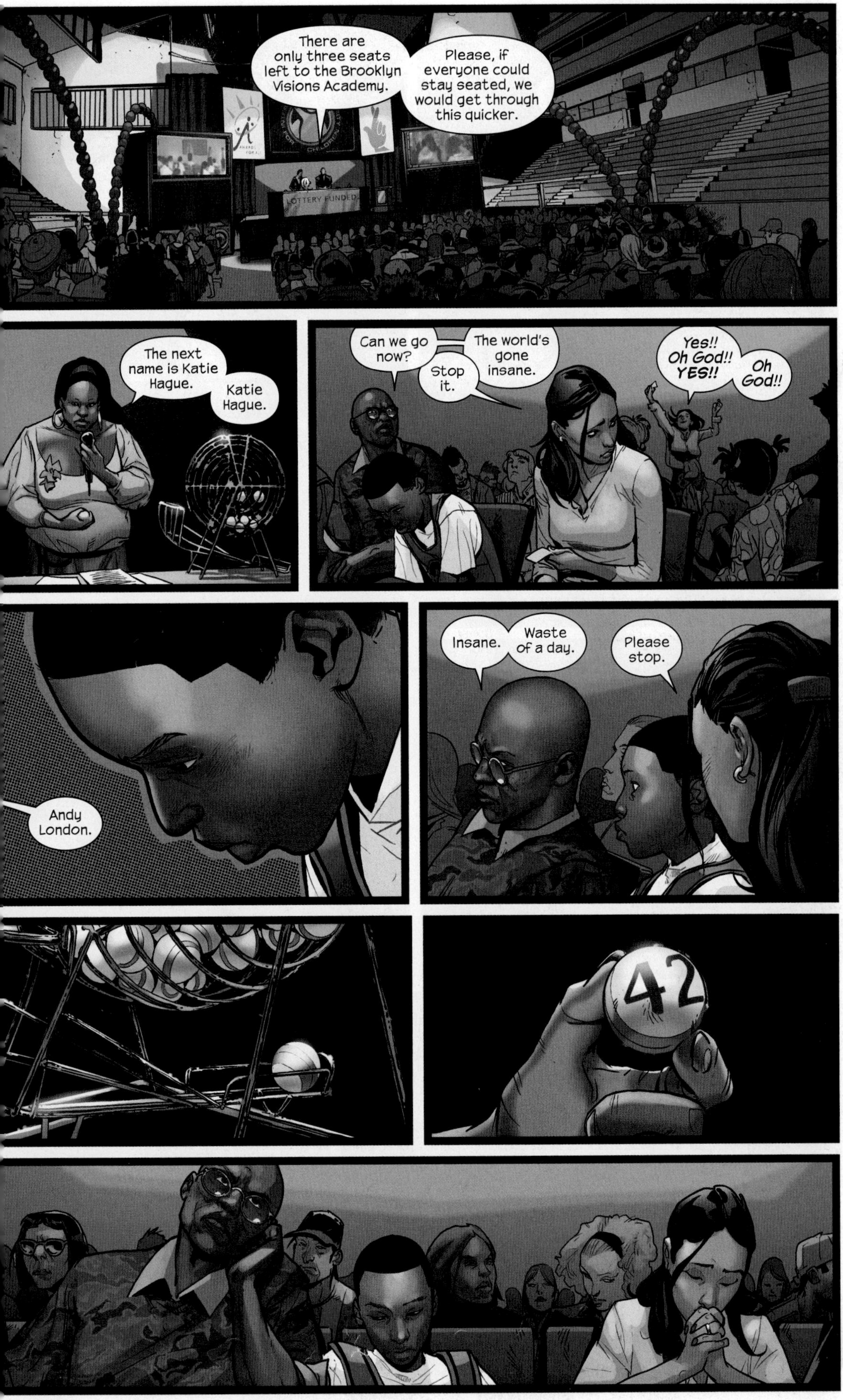
There are only three seats left to the Brooklyn Visions Academy.
Please, if everyone could stay seated, we would get through this quicker.
LOTTERY FUNDED
The next name is Katie Hague.
Katie Hague.
Can we go now?
The world's gone insane.
Stop it.
Yes!! Oh God!! YES!!
Oh God!!
Andy London.
Insane.
Waste of a day.
Please stop.
42

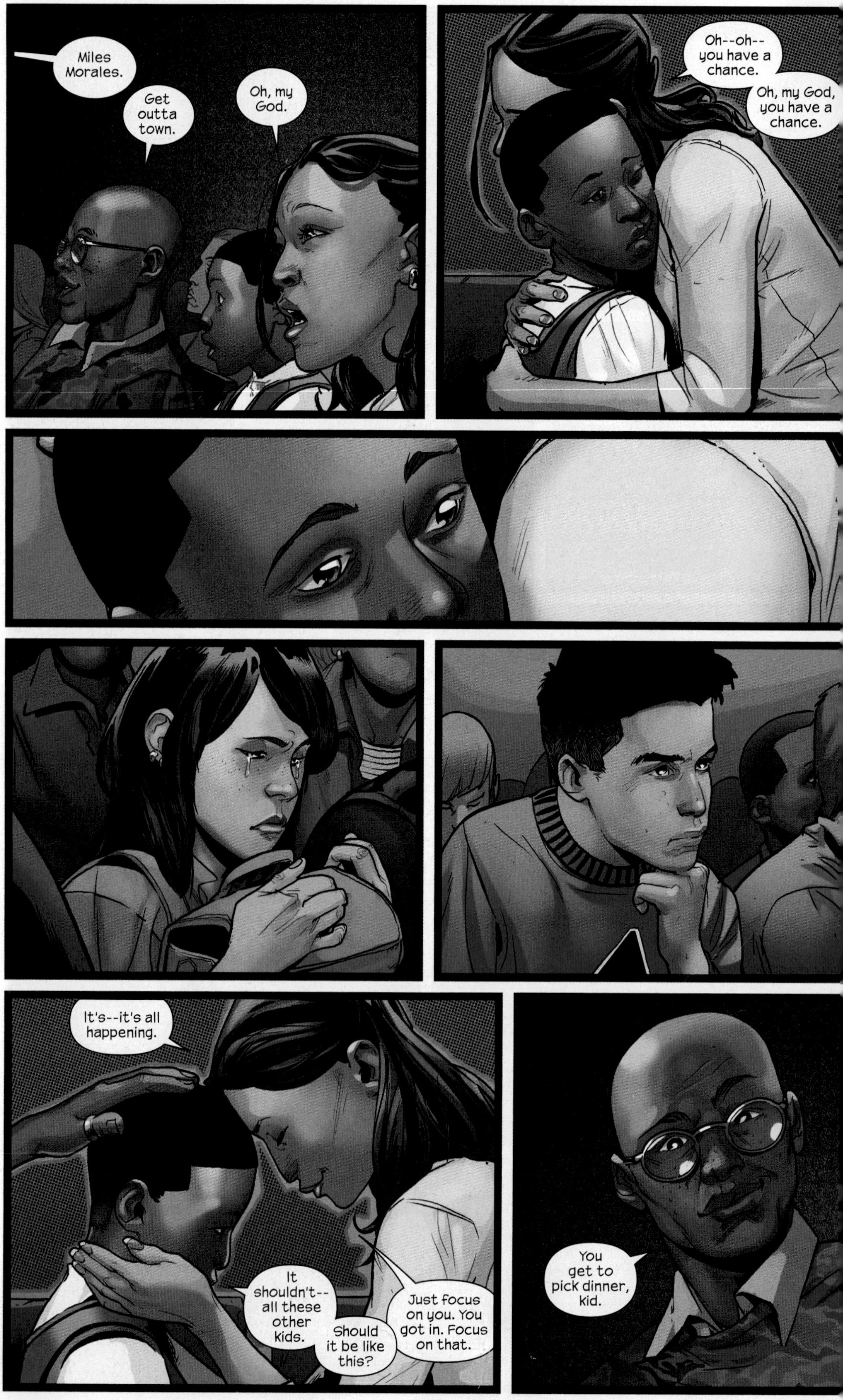
Miles Morales.
Get outta town.
Oh, my God.
Oh--oh-- you have a chance.
Oh, my God, you have a chance.
It's--it's all happening.
It shouldn't-- all these other kids.
Should it be like this?
Just focus on you. You got in. Focus on that.
You get to pick dinner, kid.

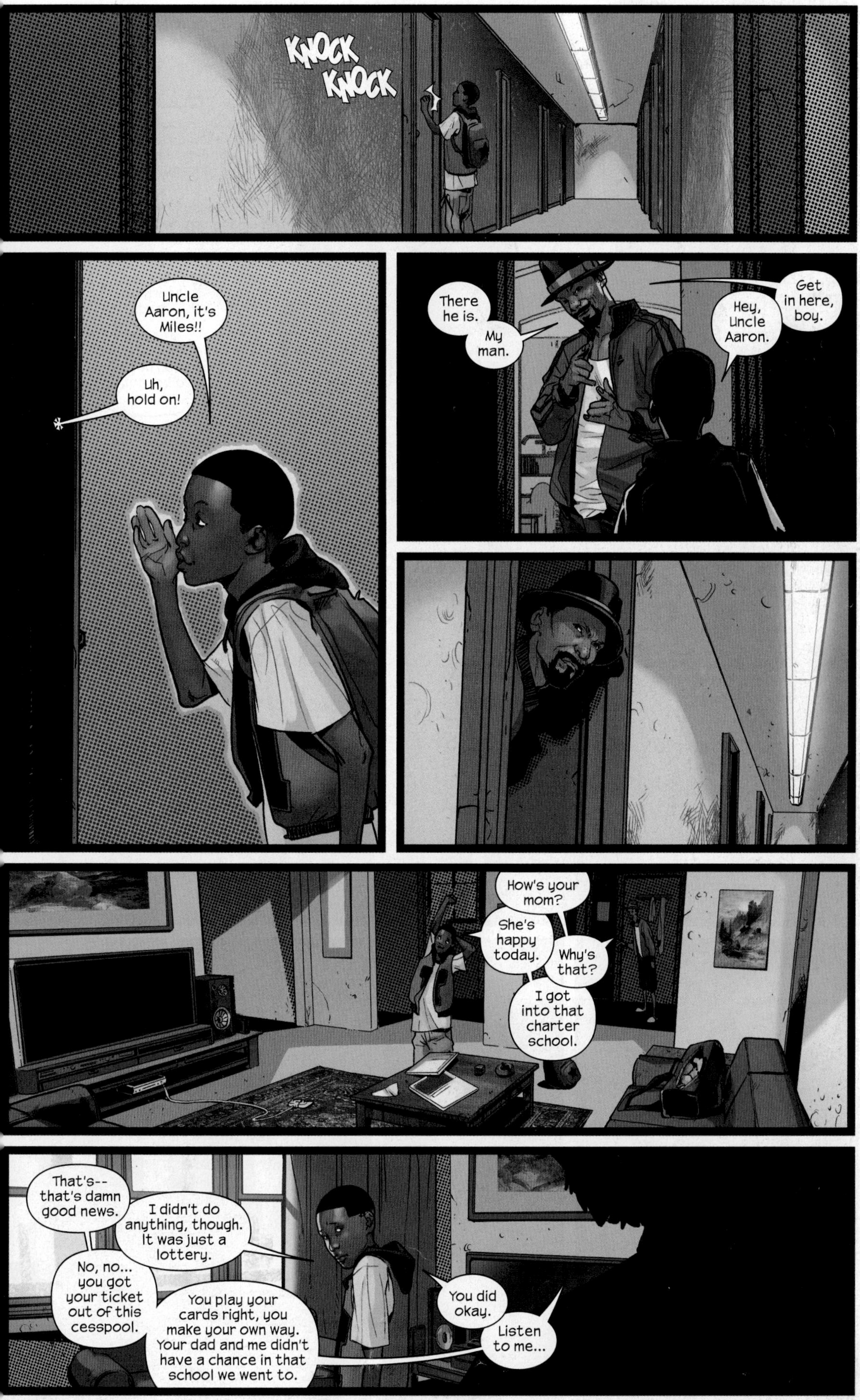
KNOCK KNOCK
Uncle Aaron, it's Miles!!
Uh, hold on!
There he is.
My man.
Hey, Uncle Aaron.
Get in here, boy.
How's your mom?
She's happy today.
Why's that?
I got into that charter school.
That's-- that's damn good news.
I didn't do anything, though. It was just a lottery.
No, no... you got your ticket out of this cesspool.
You play your cards right, you make your own way. Your dad and me didn't have a chance in that school we went to.
You did okay.
Listen to me...

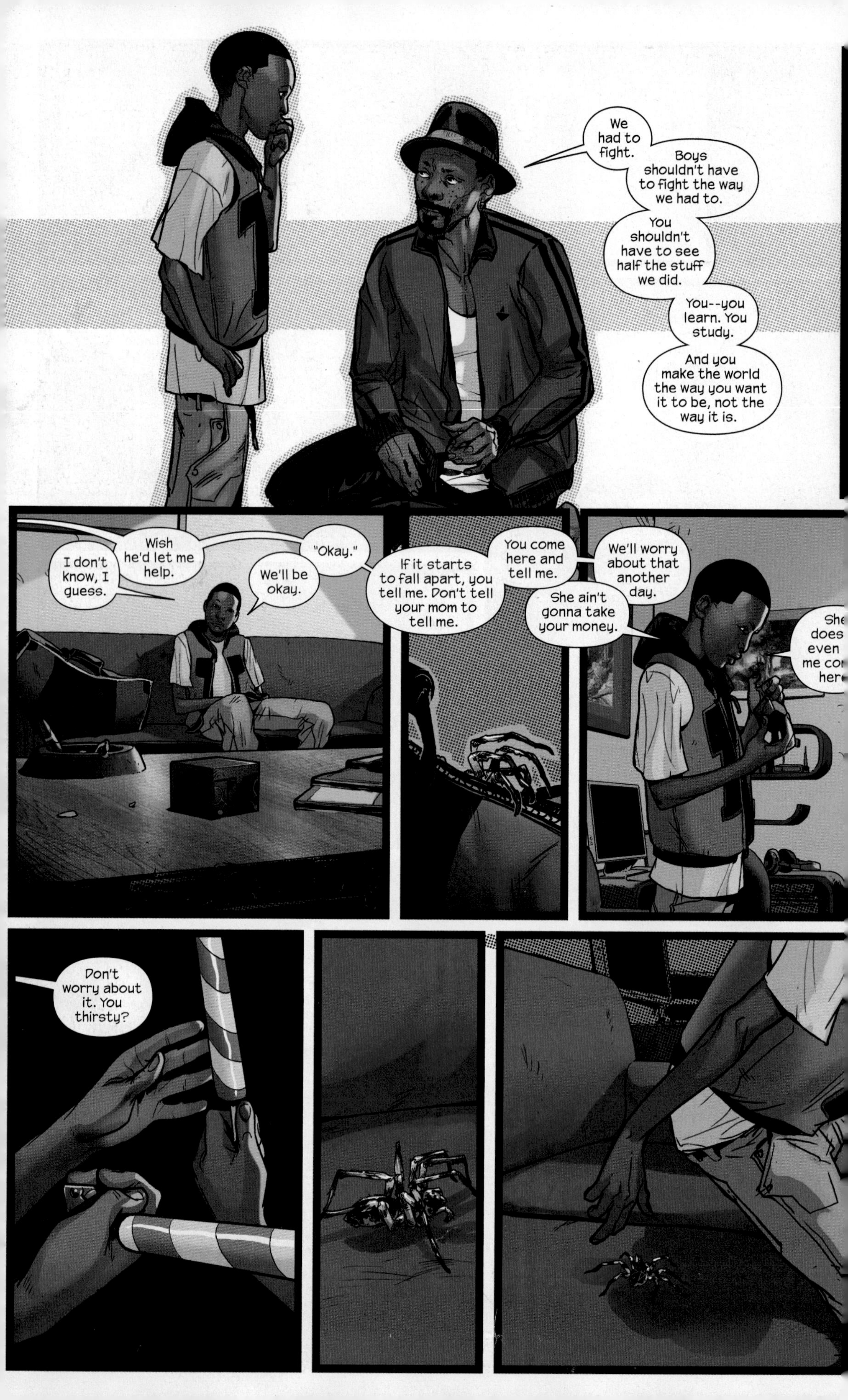
We had to fight.
Boys shouldn't have to fight the way we had to.
You shouldn't have to see half the stuff we did.
You--you learn. You study.
And you make the world the way you want it to be, not the way it is.
I don't know, I guess.
Wish he'd let me help.
We'll be okay.
"Okay."
If it starts to fall apart, you tell me. Don't tell your mom to tell me.
You come here and tell me.
We'll worry about that another day.
She ain't gonna take your money.
She does even me
Don't worry about it. You thirsty?

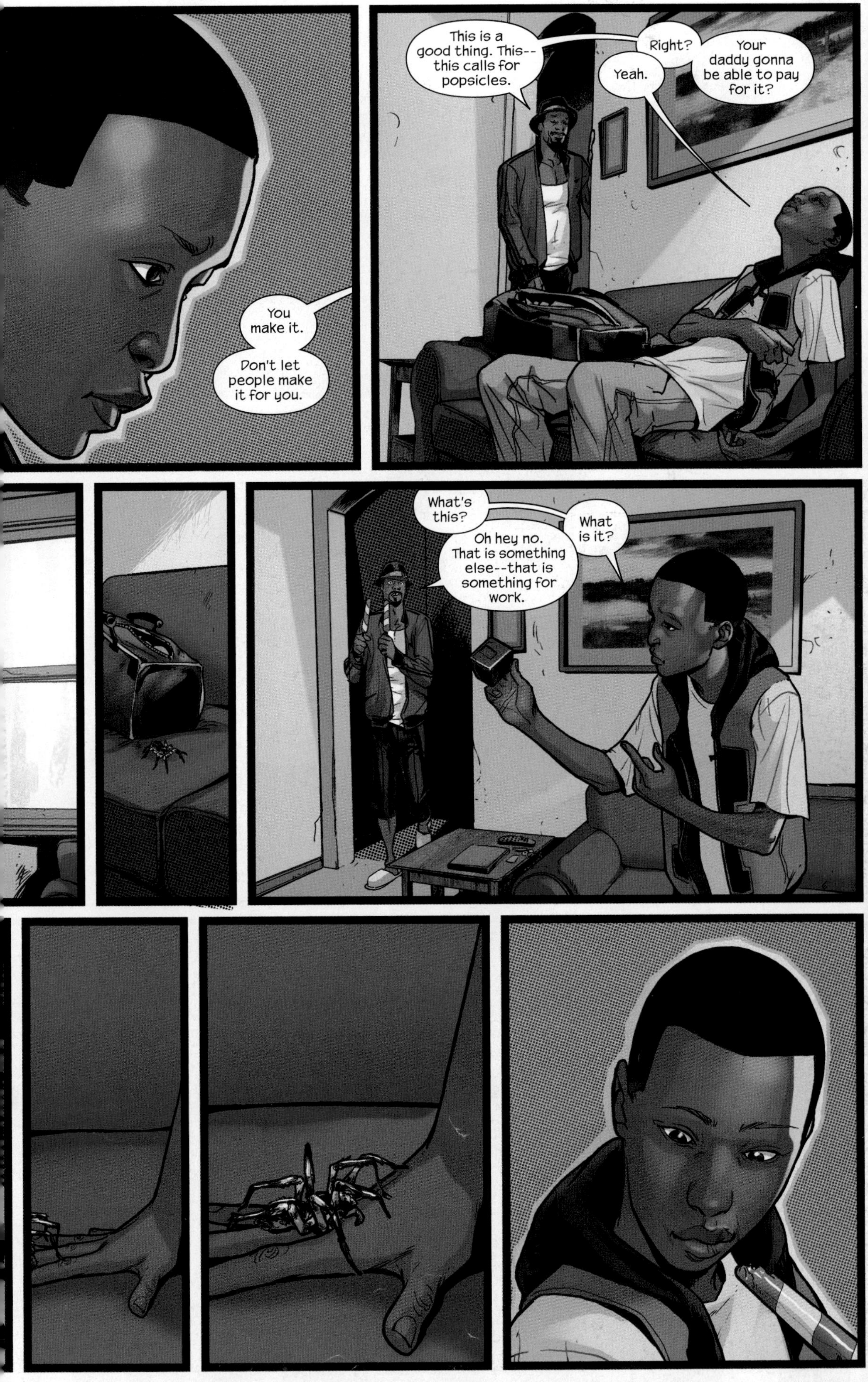

You make it.
Don't let people make it for you.
This is a good thing. This-- this calls for popsicles.
Right?
Yeah.
Your daddy gonna be able to pay for it?
What's this?
What is it?
Oh hey no. That is something else--that is something for work.

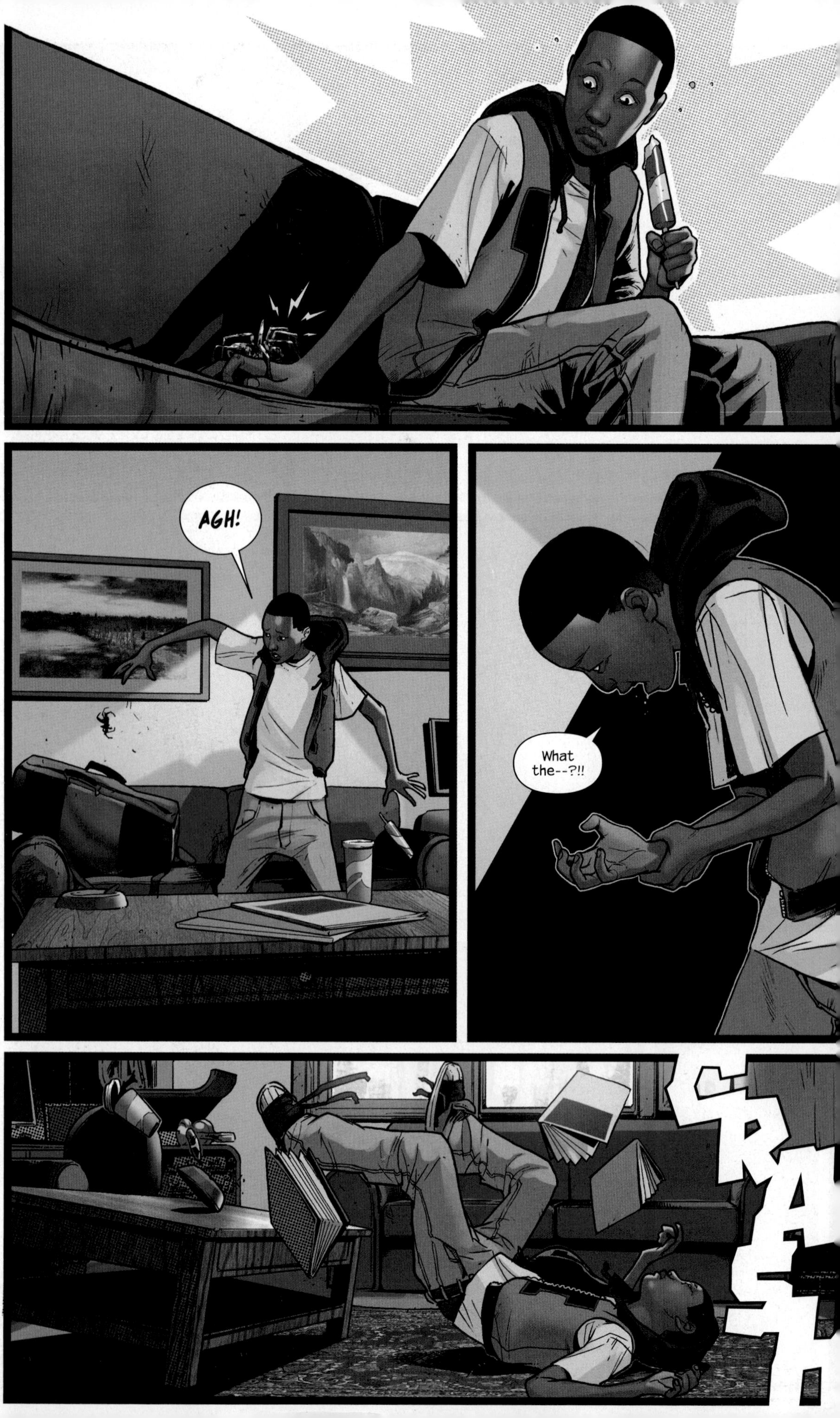
AGH!
What the--?!!
CRASH

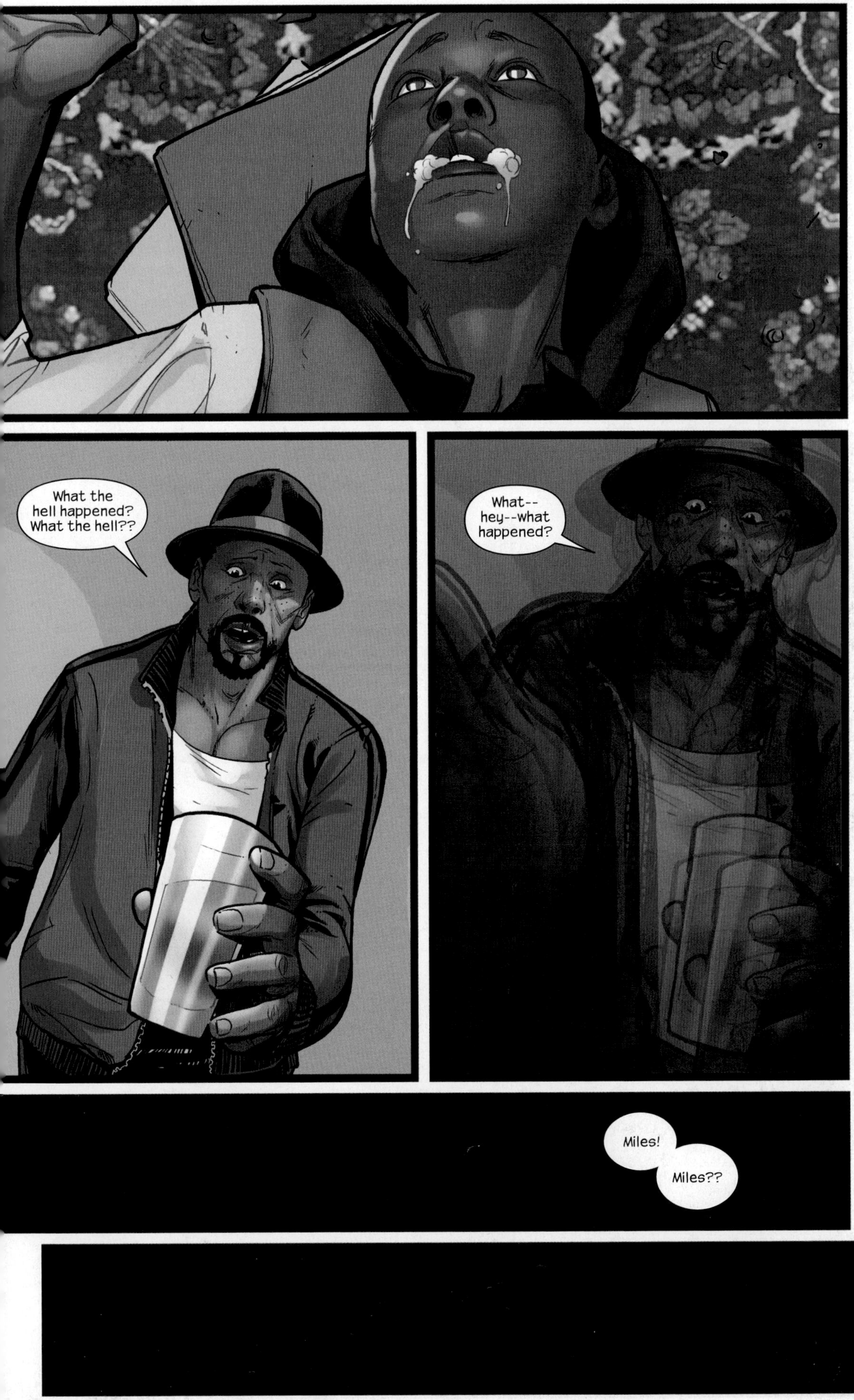

What the hell happened? What the hell??
What-- hey--what happened?
Miles!
Miles??

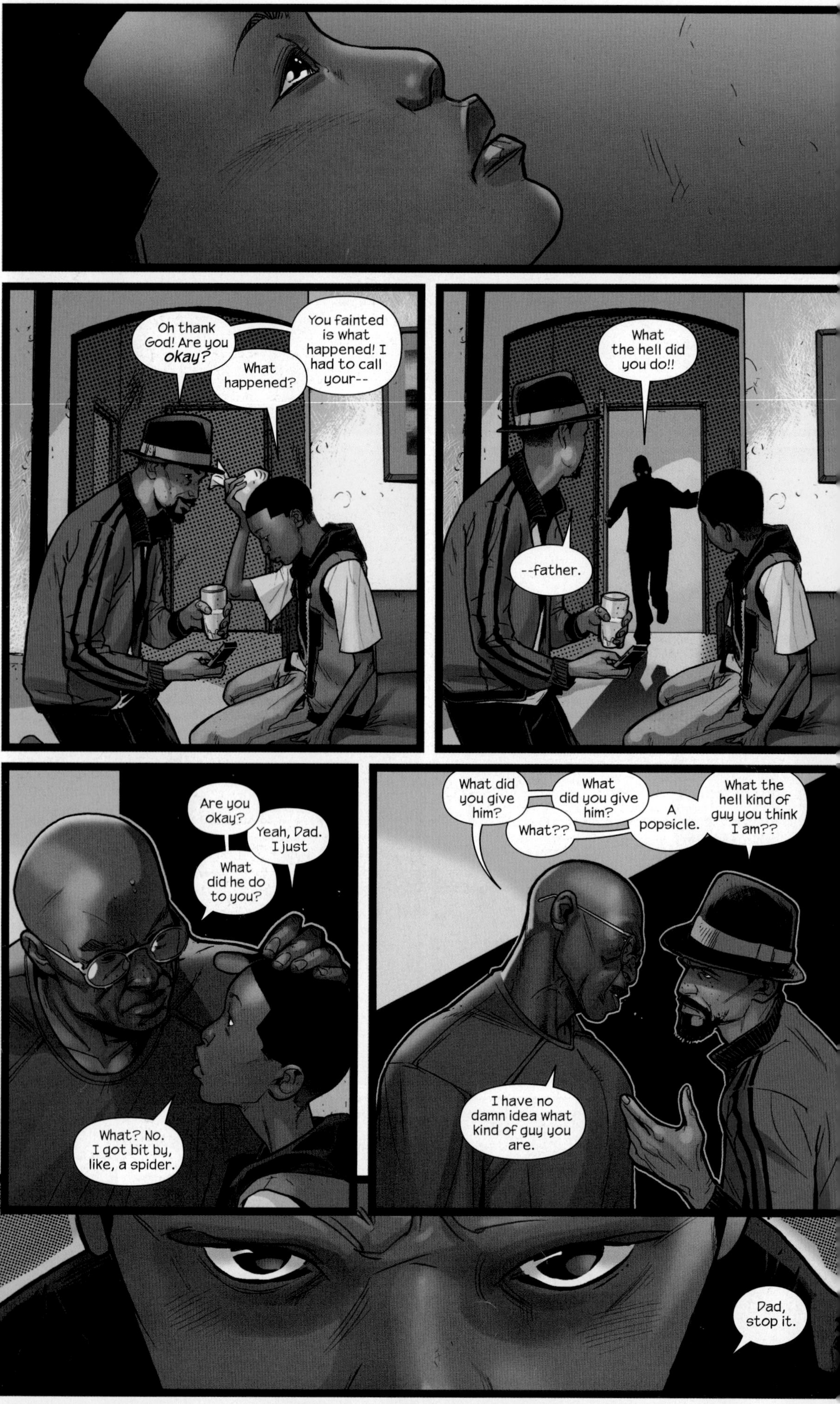
Oh thank God! Are you okay?
What happened?
You fainted is what happened! I had to call your--
What the hell did you do!!
--father.
Are you okay?
Yeah, Dad. I just
What did he do to you?
What? No. I got bit by, like, a spider.
What did you give him?
What??
What did you give him?
A popsicle.
What the hell kind of guy you think I am??
I have no damn idea what kind of guy you are.
Dad, stop it.

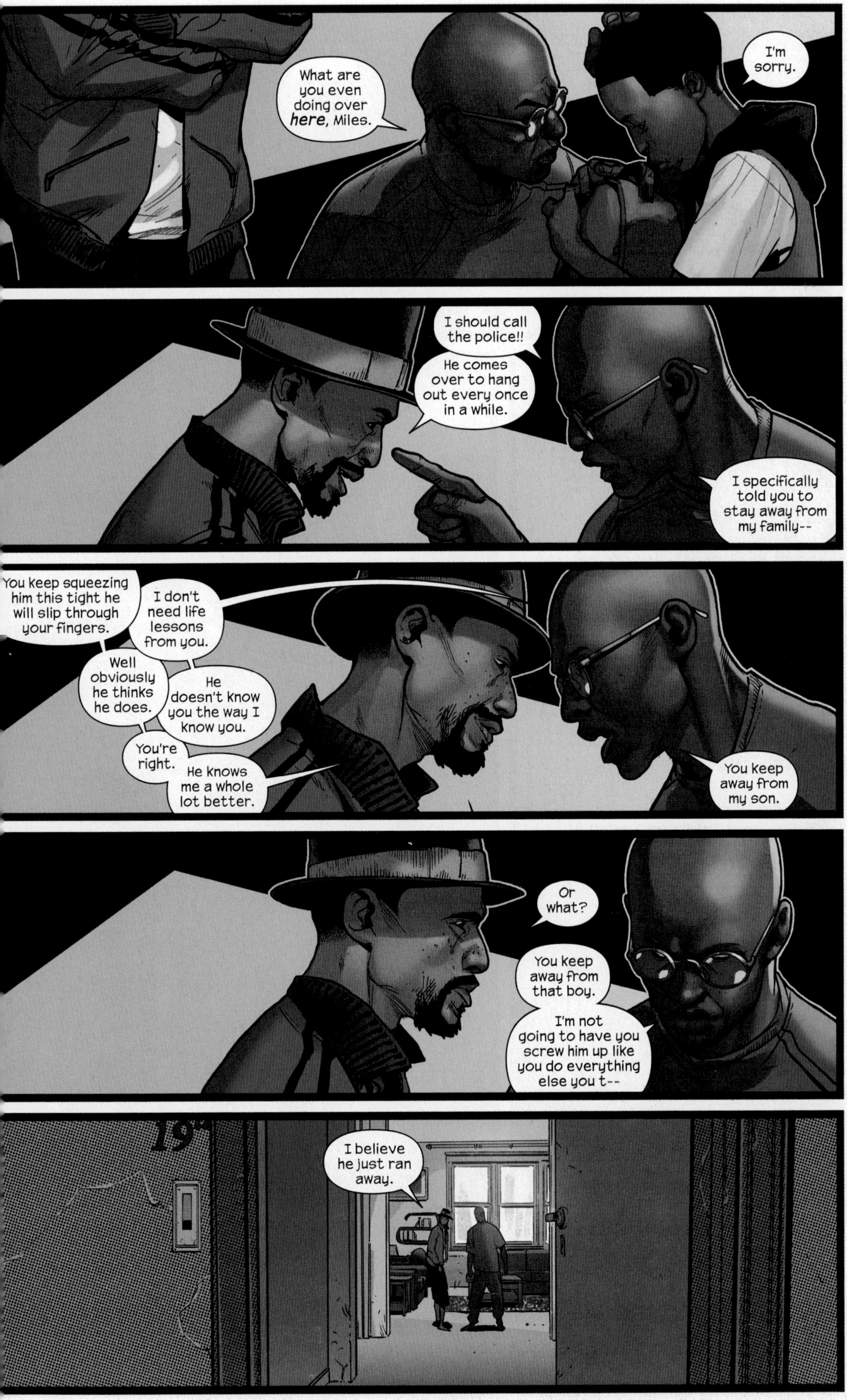
What are you even doing over *here*, Miles.
I'm sorry.
I should call the police!!
He comes over to hang out every once in a while.
I specifically told you to stay away from my family--
You keep squeezing him this tight he will slip through your fingers.
I don't need life lessons from you.
Well obviously he thinks he does.
He doesn't know you the way I know you.
You're right.
He knows me a whole lot better.
You keep away from my son.
Or what?
You keep away from that boy.
I'm not going to have you screw him up like you do everything else you t--
I believe he just ran away.

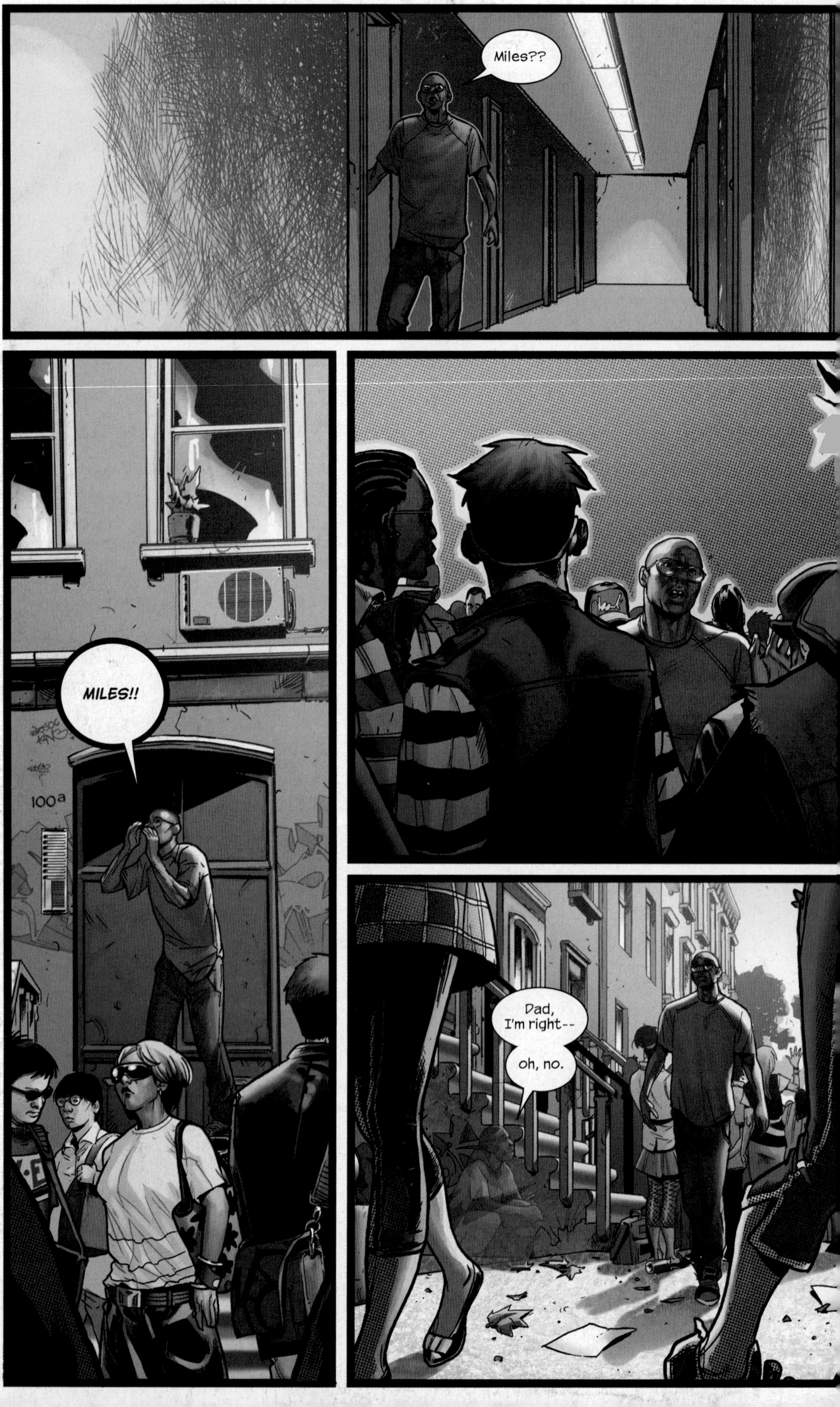
Miles??
MILES!!
100a
Dad,
I'm right--
oh, no.

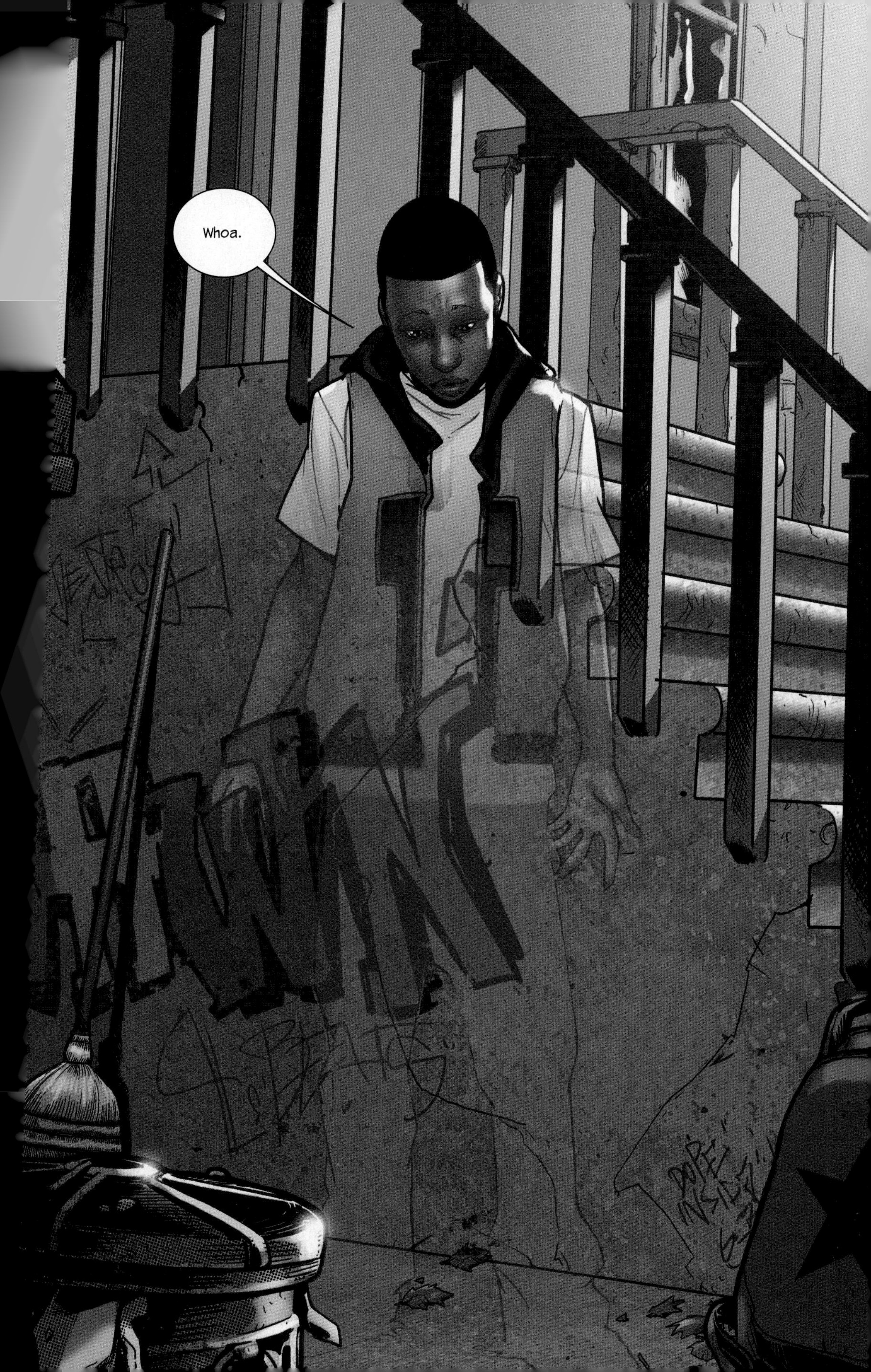
Whoa.

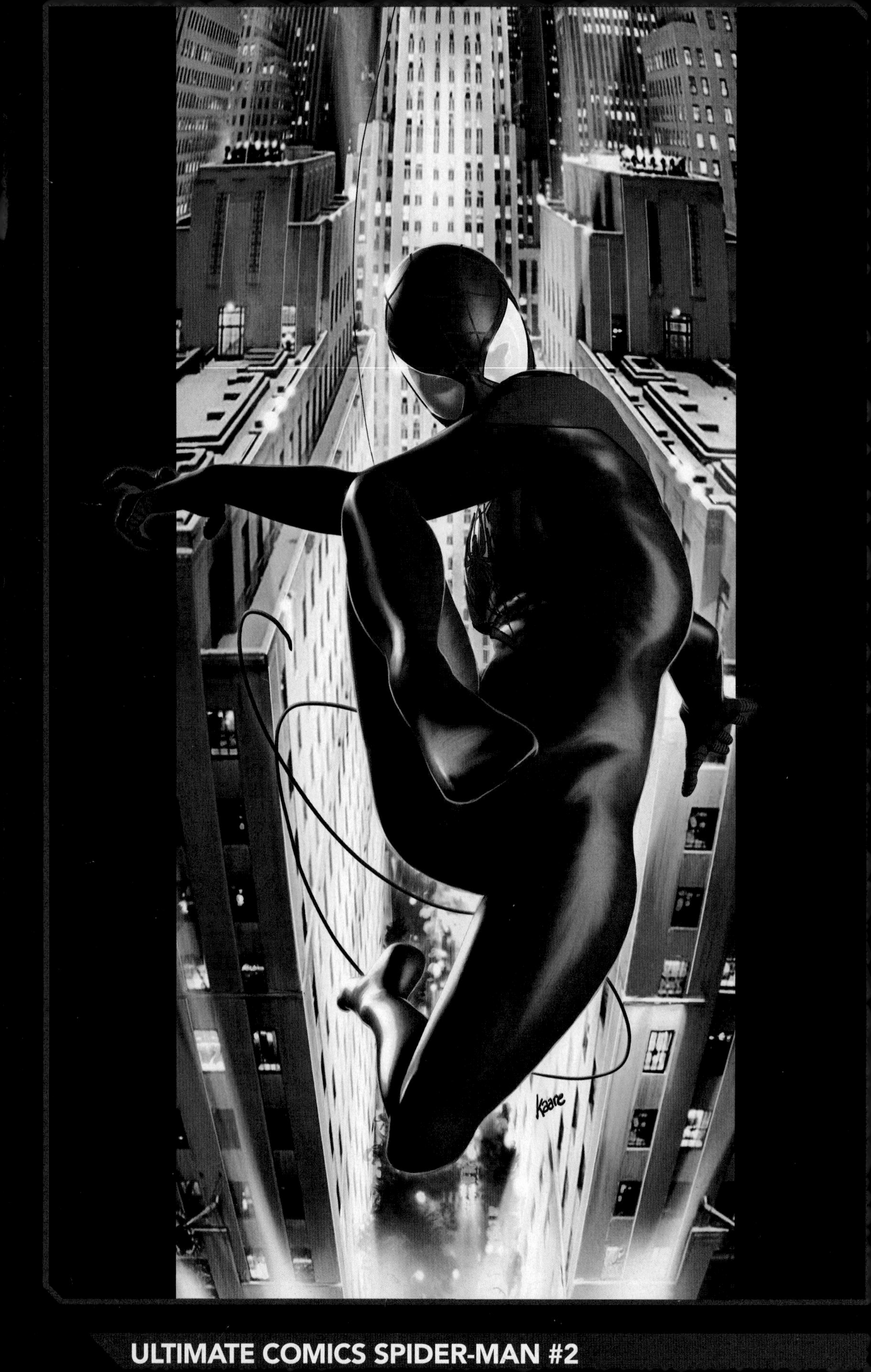
Kaare

ULTIMATE COMICS SPIDER-MAN #2

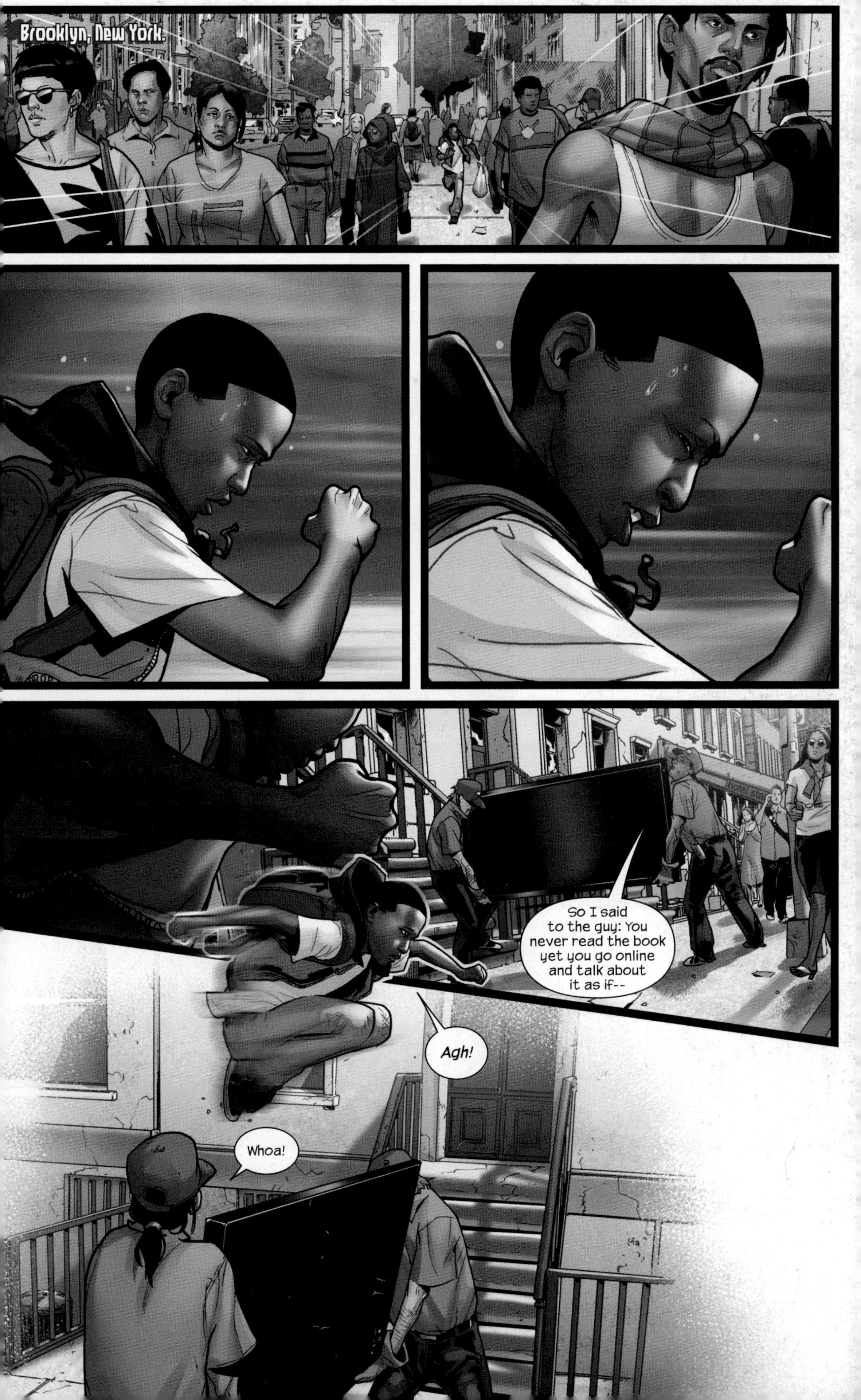
Brooklyn, New York.
So I said to the guy: You never read the book yet you go online and talk about it as if--
Agh!
Whoa!

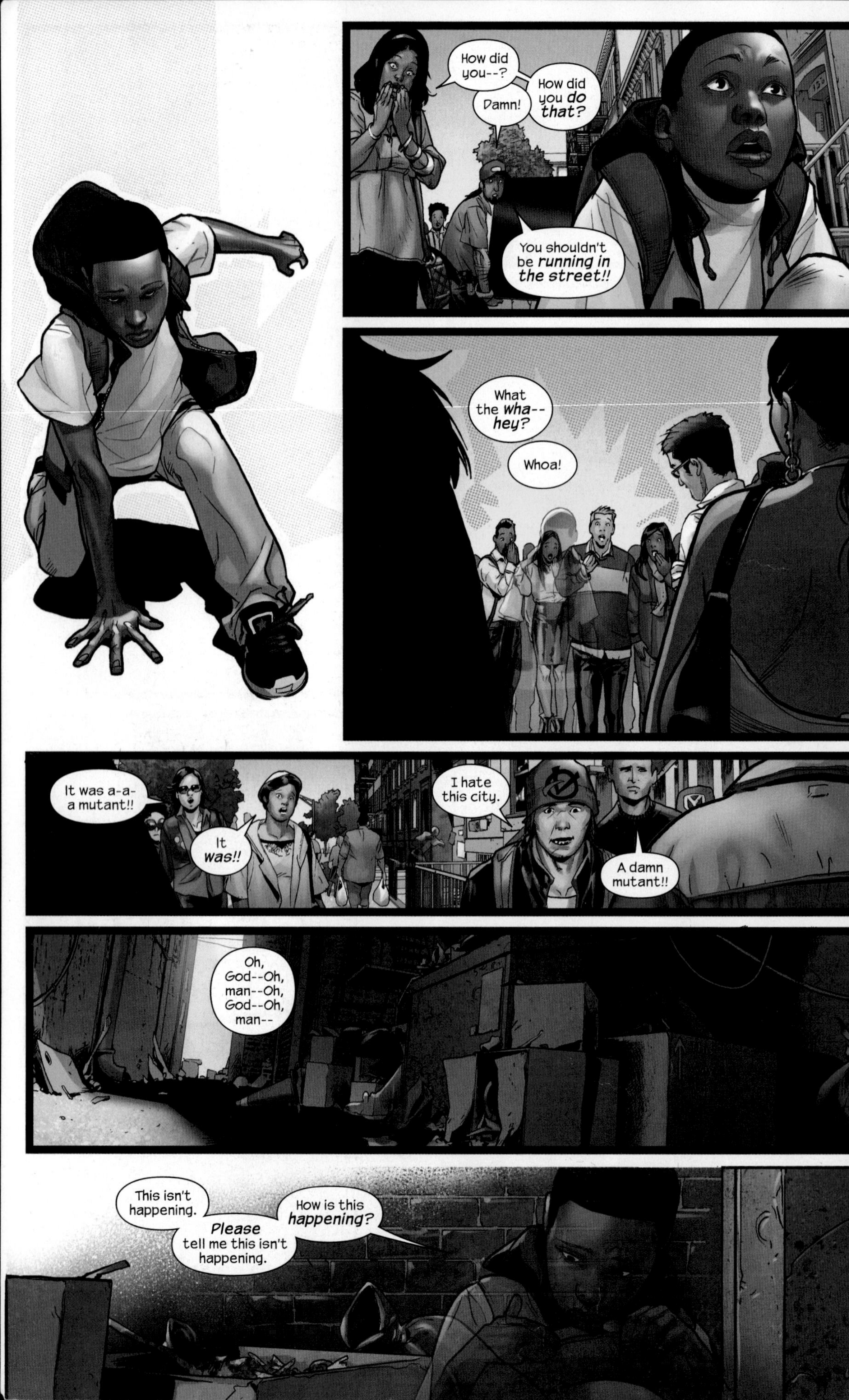

How did you--?
Damn!
How did you do that?
You shouldn't be running in the street!!
What the wha-- hey?
Whoa!
It was a-a-a mutant!!
It was!!
I hate this city.
A damn mutant!!
Oh, God--Oh, man--Oh, God--Oh, man--
This isn't happening.
Please tell me this isn't happening.
How is this happening?

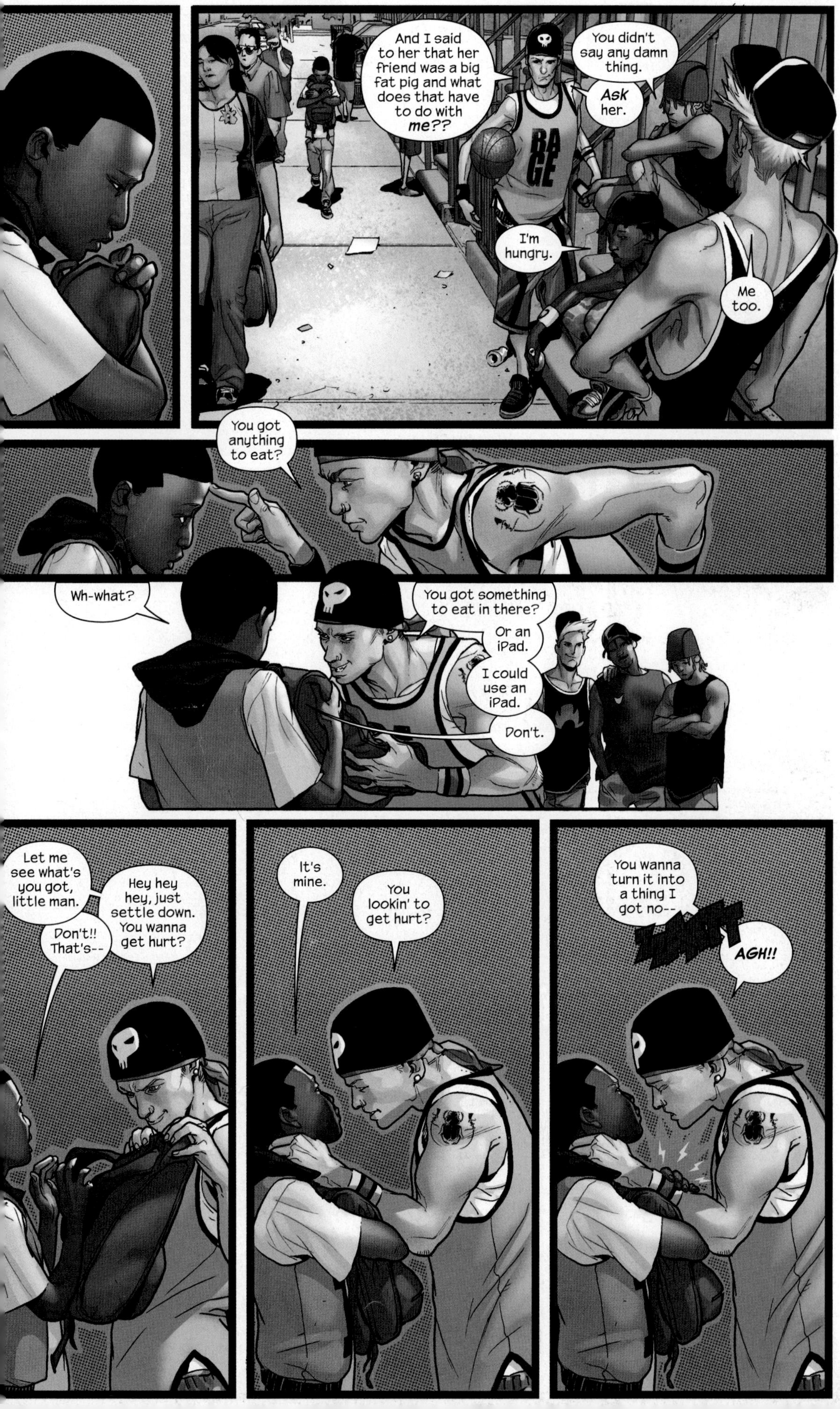
And I said to her that her friend was a big fat pig and what does that have to do with *me??*
You didn't say any damn thing.
Ask her.
I'm hungry.
Me too.
You got anything to eat?
Wh-what?
You got something to eat in there?
Or an iPad.
I could use an iPad.
Don't.
Let me see what's you got, little man.
Hey hey hey, just settle down. You wanna get hurt?
Don't!! That's--
It's mine.
You lookin' to get hurt?
You wanna turn it into a thing I got no--
AGH!!

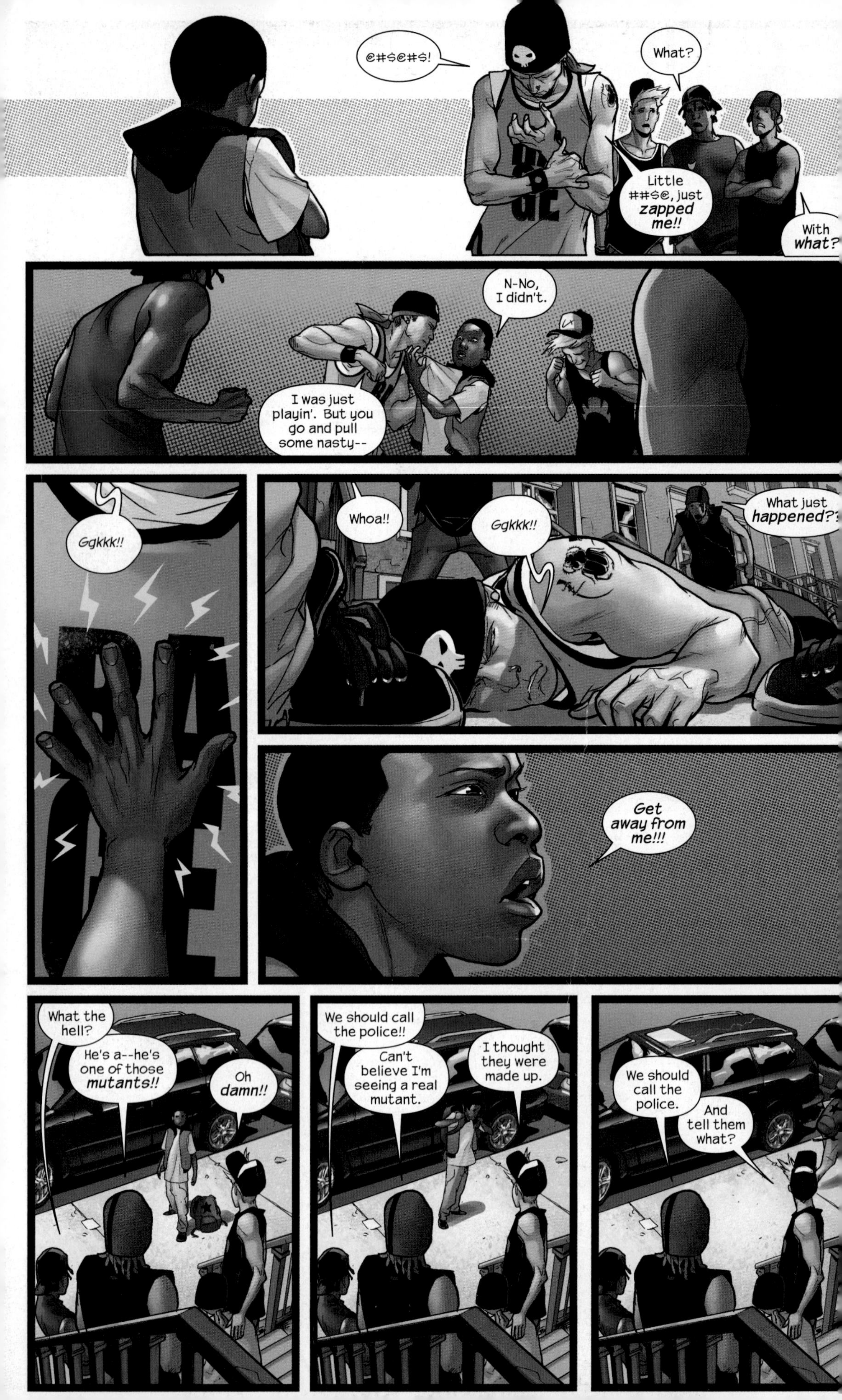

@#$@#$!
What?
Little ##$@, just *zapped* me!!
With *what?*
N-No, I didn't.
I was just playin'. But you go and pull some nasty--
Ggkkk!!
Whoa!!
Ggkkk!!
What just *happened?!*
Get away from me!!!
What the hell?
He's a--he's one of those *mutants!!*
Oh *damn!!*
We should call the police!!
Can't believe I'm seeing a real mutant.
I thought they were made up.
We should call the police.
And tell them what?

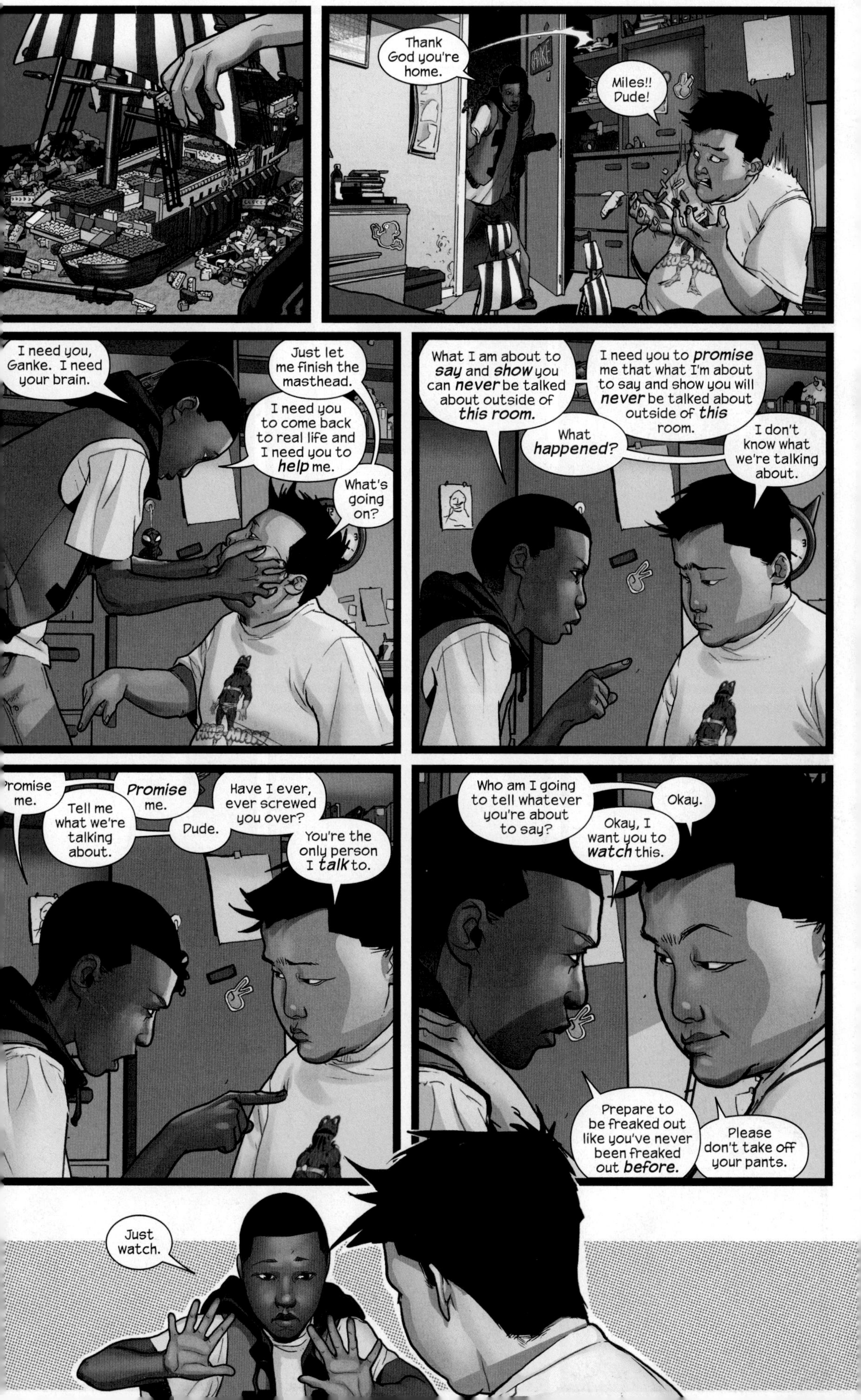
Thank God you're home.
Miles!! Dude!
I need you, Ganke. I need your brain.
Just let me finish the masthead.
I need you to come back to real life and I need you to help me.
What's going on?
What I am about to say and show you can never be talked about outside of this room.
I need you to promise me that what I'm about to say and show you will never be talked about outside of this room.
What happened?
I don't know what we're talking about.
Promise me.
Tell me what we're talking about.
Promise me.
Dude.
Have I ever, ever screwed you over?
You're the only person I talk to.
Who am I going to tell whatever you're about to say?
Okay.
Okay, I want you to watch this.
Prepare to be freaked out like you've never been freaked out before.
Please don't take off your pants.
Just watch.

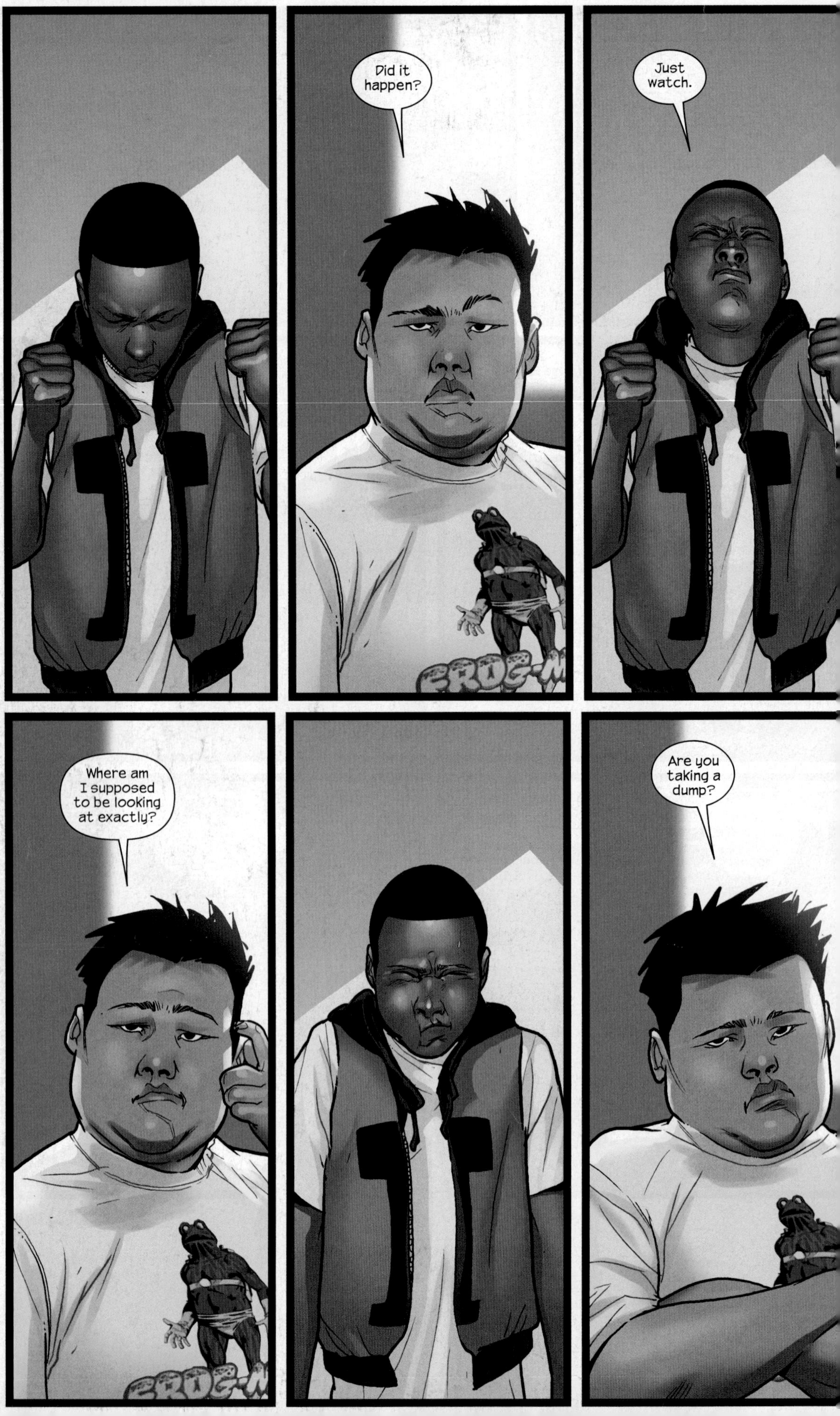

Did it happen?
Just watch.
Where am I supposed to be looking at exactly?
Are you taking a dump?

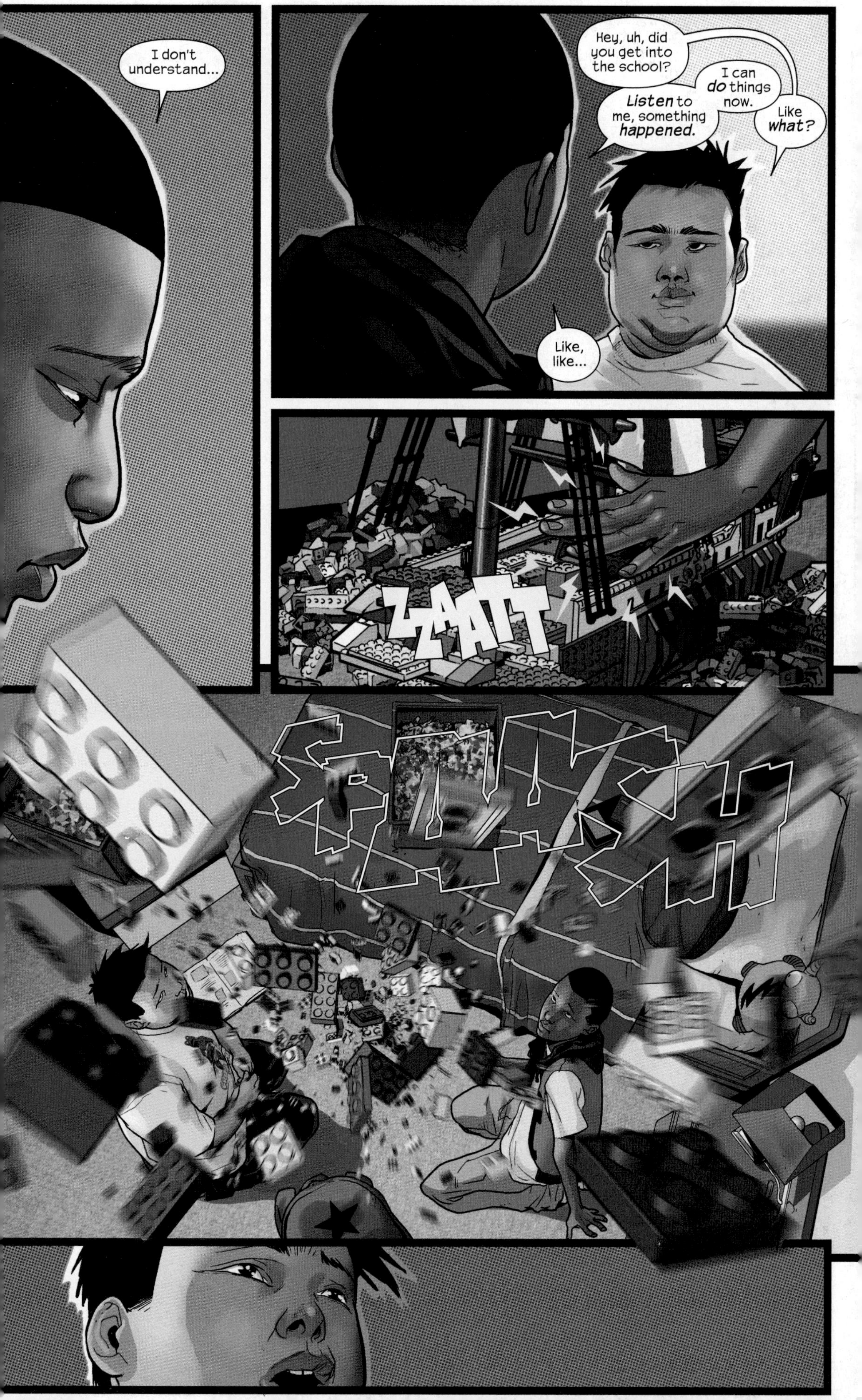
I don't understand...
Hey, uh, did you get into the school?
Listen to me, something happened.
I can do things now.
Like what?
Like, like...
ZZAATT
SPLUSH

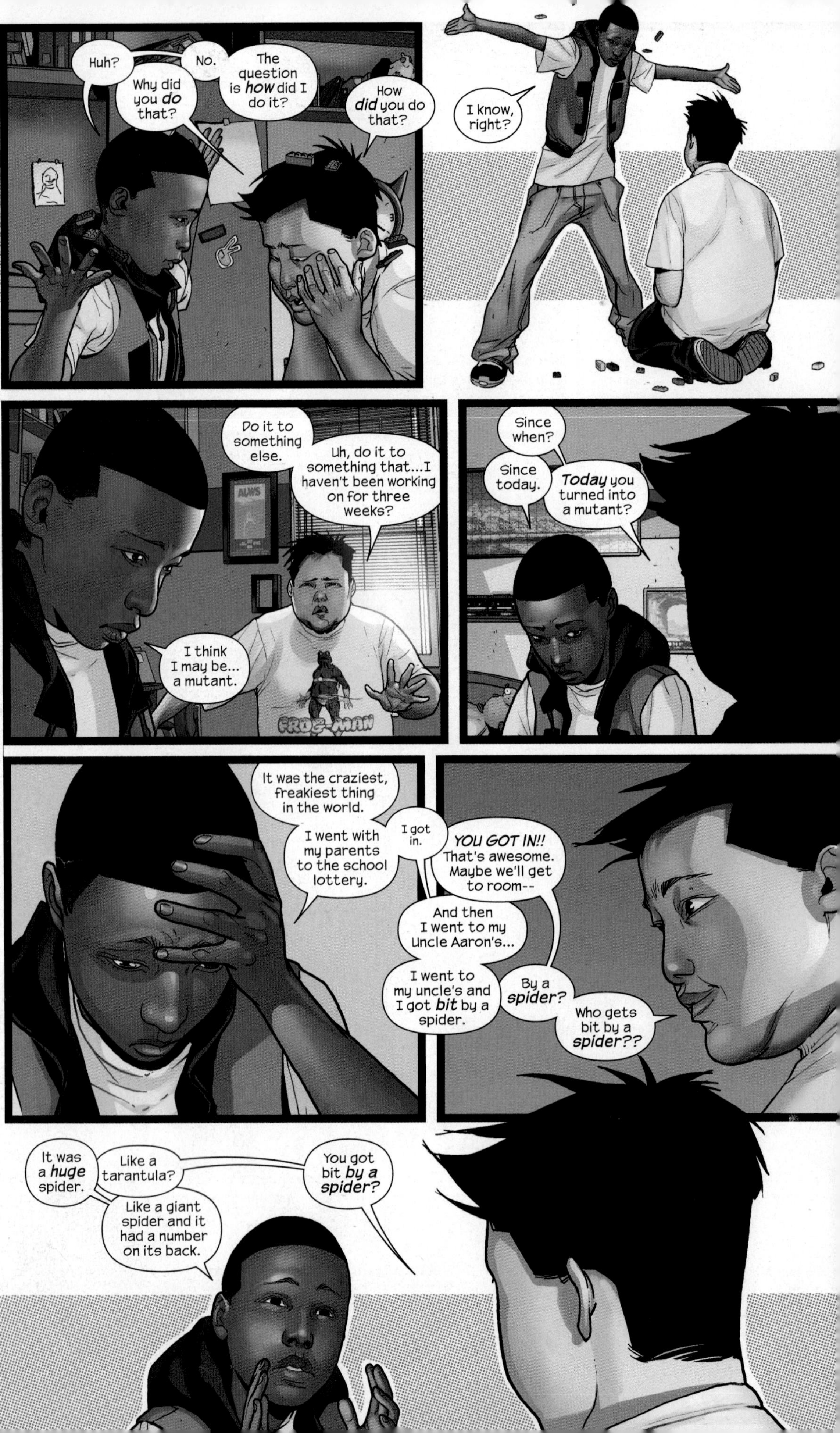

Huh?
Why did you *do* that?
No.
The question is *how* did I do it?
How *did* you do that?
I know, right?
Do it to something else.
Uh, do it to something that...I haven't been working on for three weeks?
I think I may be... a mutant.
Since when?
Since today.
Today you turned into a mutant?
It was the craziest, freakiest thing in the world.
I went with my parents to the school lottery.
I got in.
YOU GOT IN!! That's awesome. Maybe we'll get to room--
And then I went to my Uncle Aaron's...
I went to my uncle's and I got *bit* by a spider.
By a *spider?*
Who gets bit by a *spider??*
You got bit *by a spider?*
It was a *huge* spider.
Like a tarantula?
Like a giant spider and it had a number on its back.

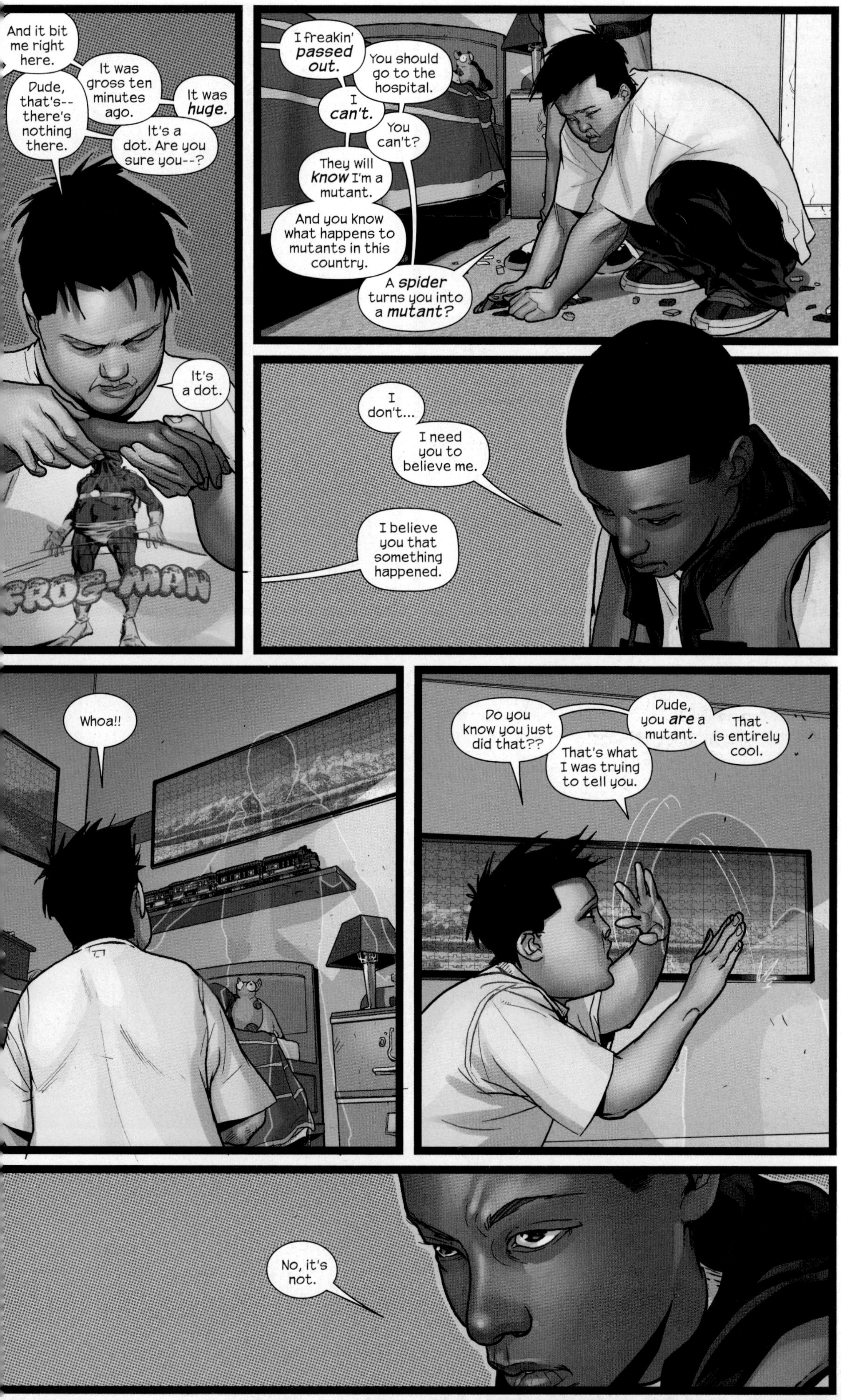
And it bit me right here.
It was gross ten minutes ago.
It was *huge.*
Dude, that's--there's nothing there.
It's a dot. Are you sure you--?
It's a dot.
FROG-MAN
I freakin' *passed out.*
You should go to the hospital.
I *can't.*
You can't?
They will *know* I'm a mutant.
And you know what happens to mutants in this country.
A *spider* turns you into a *mutant?*
I don't...
I need you to believe me.
I believe you that something happened.
Whoa!!
Do you know you just did that??
Dude, you *are* a mutant.
That is entirely cool.
That's what I was trying to tell you.
No, it's not.

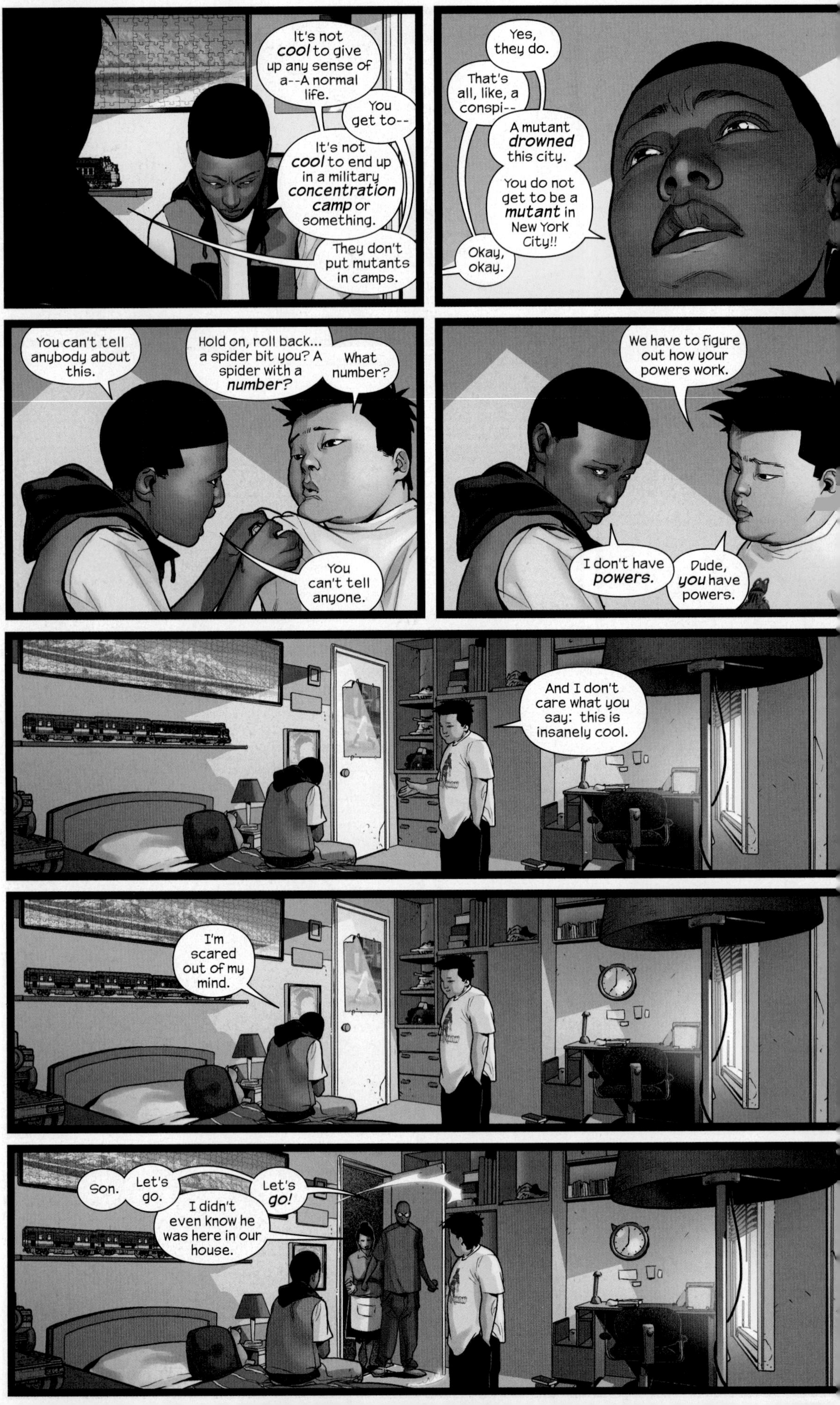
It's not cool to give up any sense of a--A normal life.
You get to--
It's not cool to end up in a military concentration camp or something.
They don't put mutants in camps.
Yes, they do.
That's all, like, a conspi--
A mutant drowned this city.
You do not get to be a mutant in New York City!!
Okay, okay.
You can't tell anybody about this.
Hold on, roll back... a spider bit you? A spider with a number?
What number?
You can't tell anyone.
We have to figure out how your powers work.
I don't have powers.
Dude, you have powers.
And I don't care what you say: this is insanely cool.
I'm scared out of my mind.
Son.
Let's go.
Let's go!
I didn't even know he was here in our house.

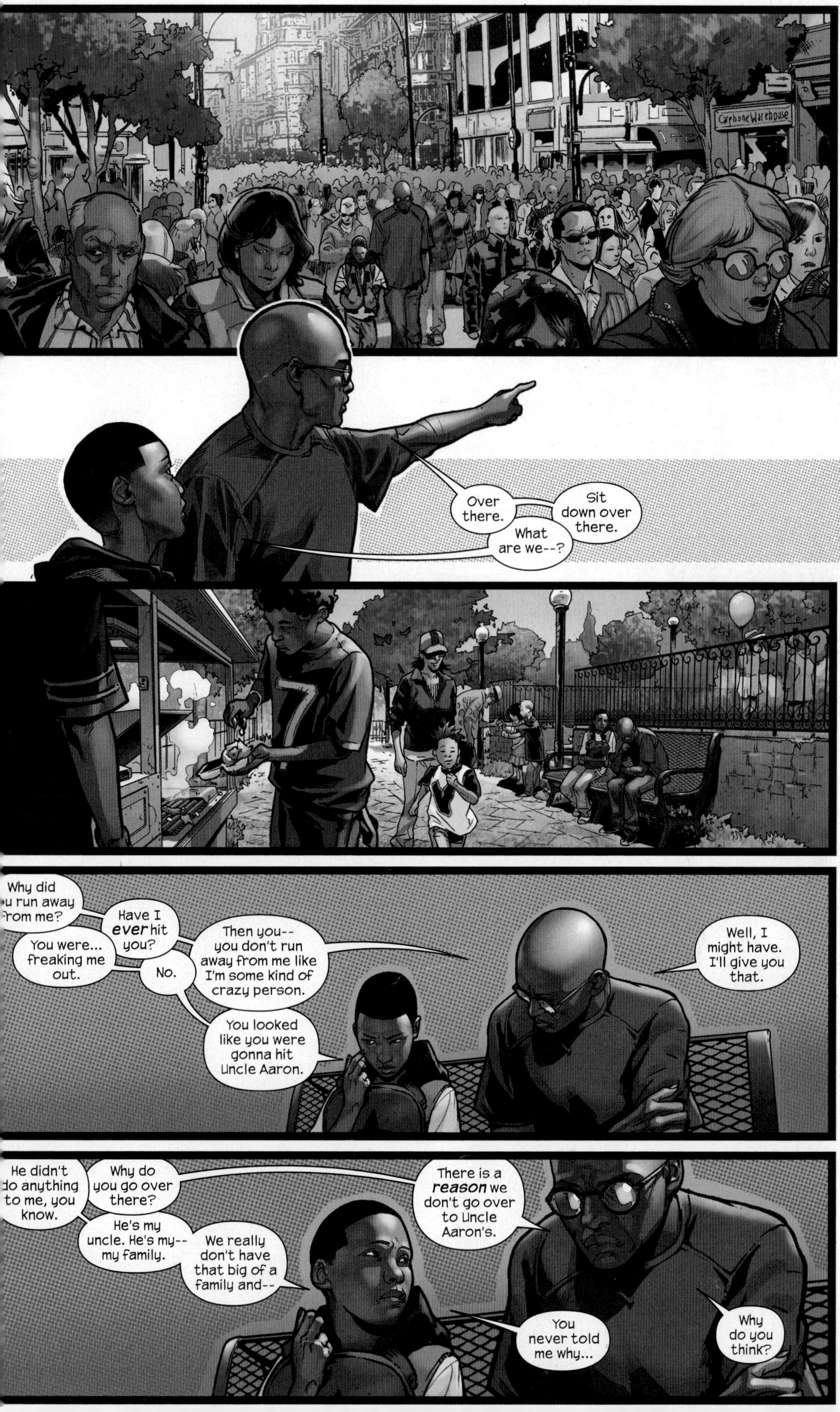

Carphone Warehouse
Over there.
What are we--?
Sit down over there.
Why did u run away rom me?
Have I *ever* hit you?
You were... freaking me out.
No.
Then you-- you don't run away from me like I'm some kind of crazy person.
You looked like you were gonna hit Uncle Aaron.
Well, I might have. I'll give you that.
He didn't lo anything to me, you know.
Why do you go over there?
He's my uncle. He's my-- my family.
We really don't have that big of a family and--
There is a *reason* we don't go over to Uncle Aaron's.
You never told me why...
Why do you think?

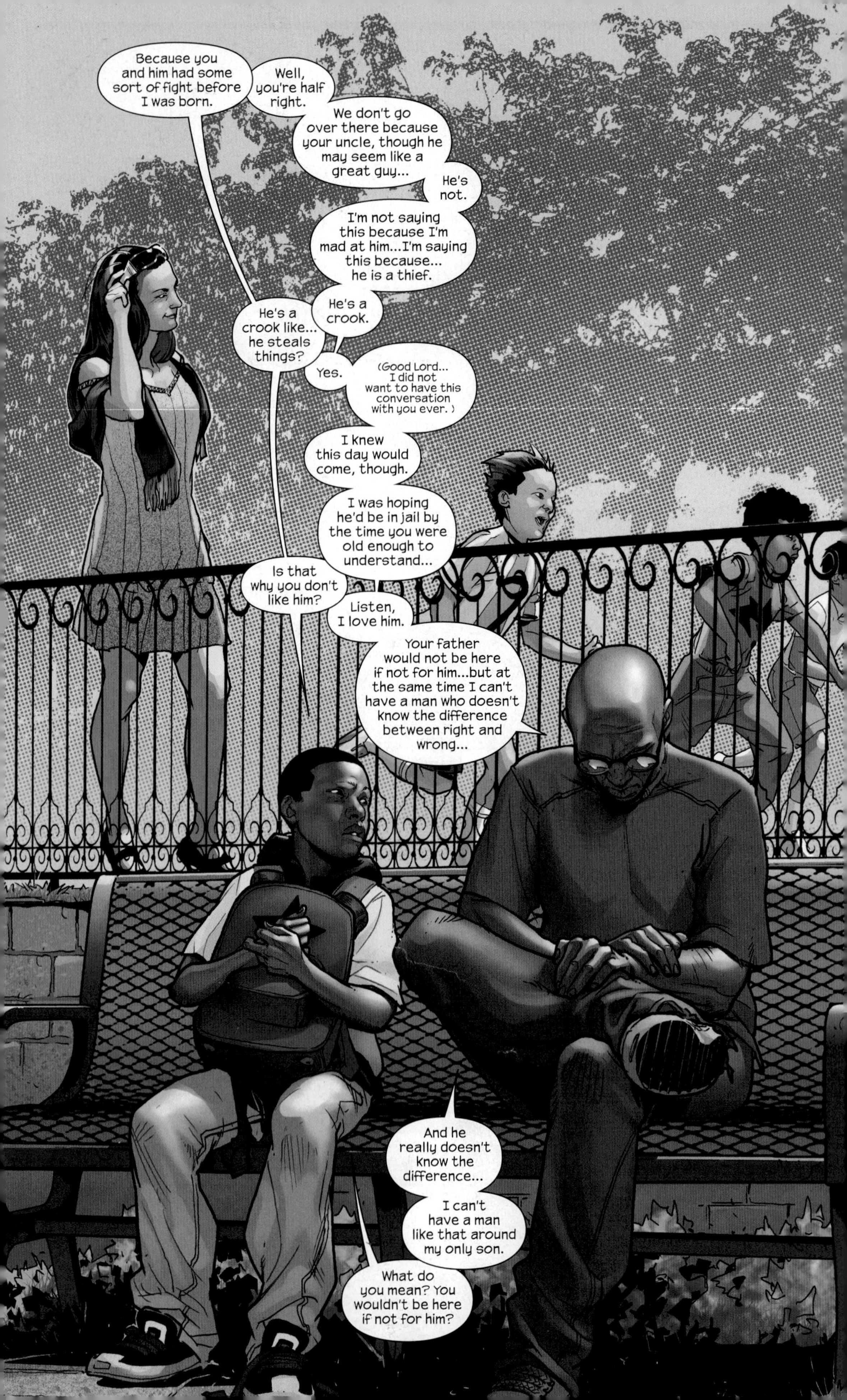
Because you and him had some sort of fight before I was born.
Well, you're half right.
We don't go over there because your uncle, though he may seem like a great guy...
He's not.
I'm not saying this because I'm mad at him...I'm saying this because... he is a thief.
He's a crook like... he steals things?
He's a crook.
Yes.
(Good Lord... I did not want to have this conversation with you ever.)
I knew this day would come, though.
I was hoping he'd be in jail by the time you were old enough to understand...
Is that why you don't like him?
Listen, I love him.
Your father would not be here if not for him...but at the same time I can't have a man who doesn't know the difference between right and wrong...
And he really doesn't know the difference...
I can't have a man like that around my only son.
What do you mean? You wouldn't be here if not for him?

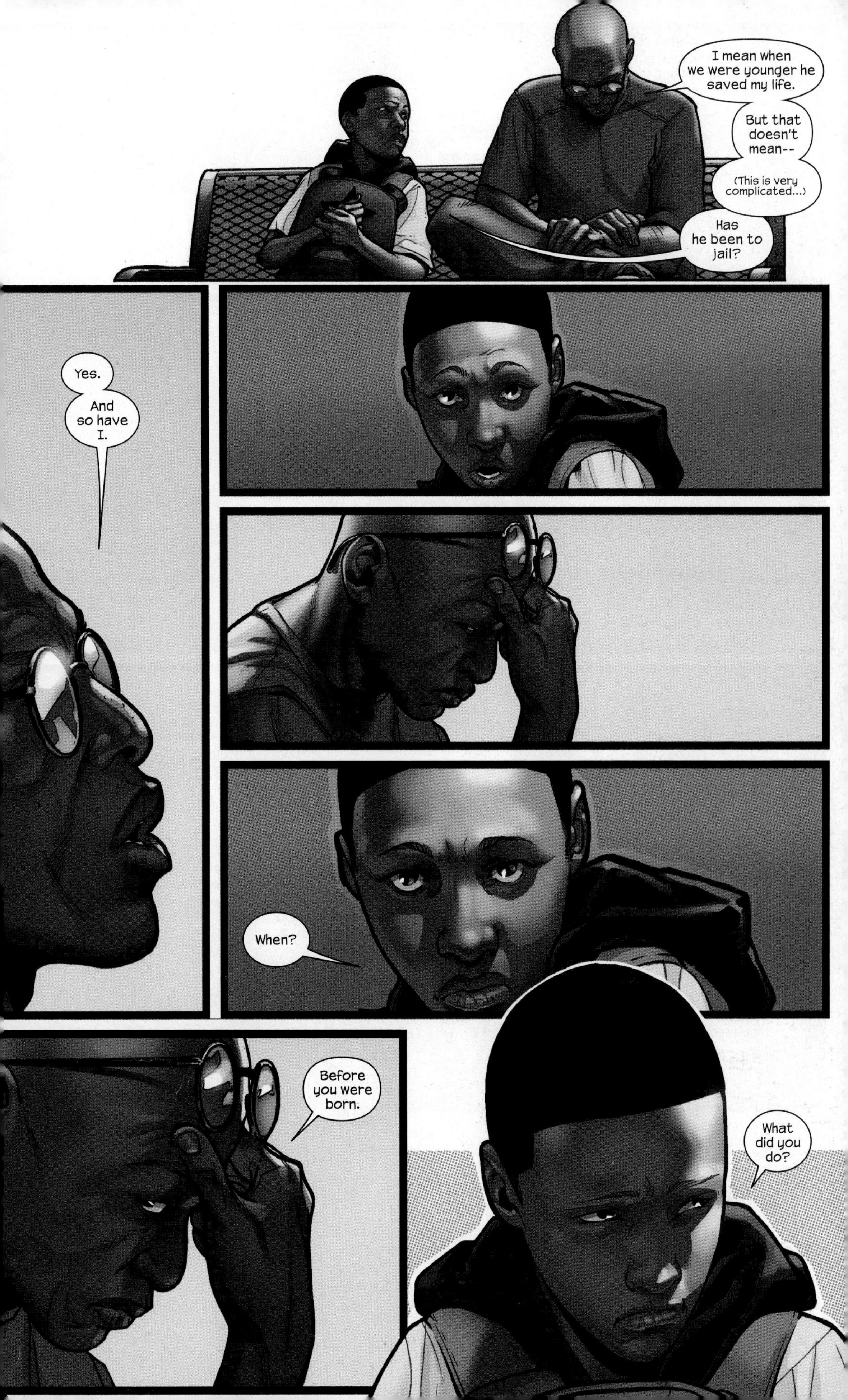
I mean when we were younger he saved my life.
But that doesn't mean--
(This is very complicated...)
Has he been to jail?
Yes.
And so have I.
When?
Before you were born.
What did you do?

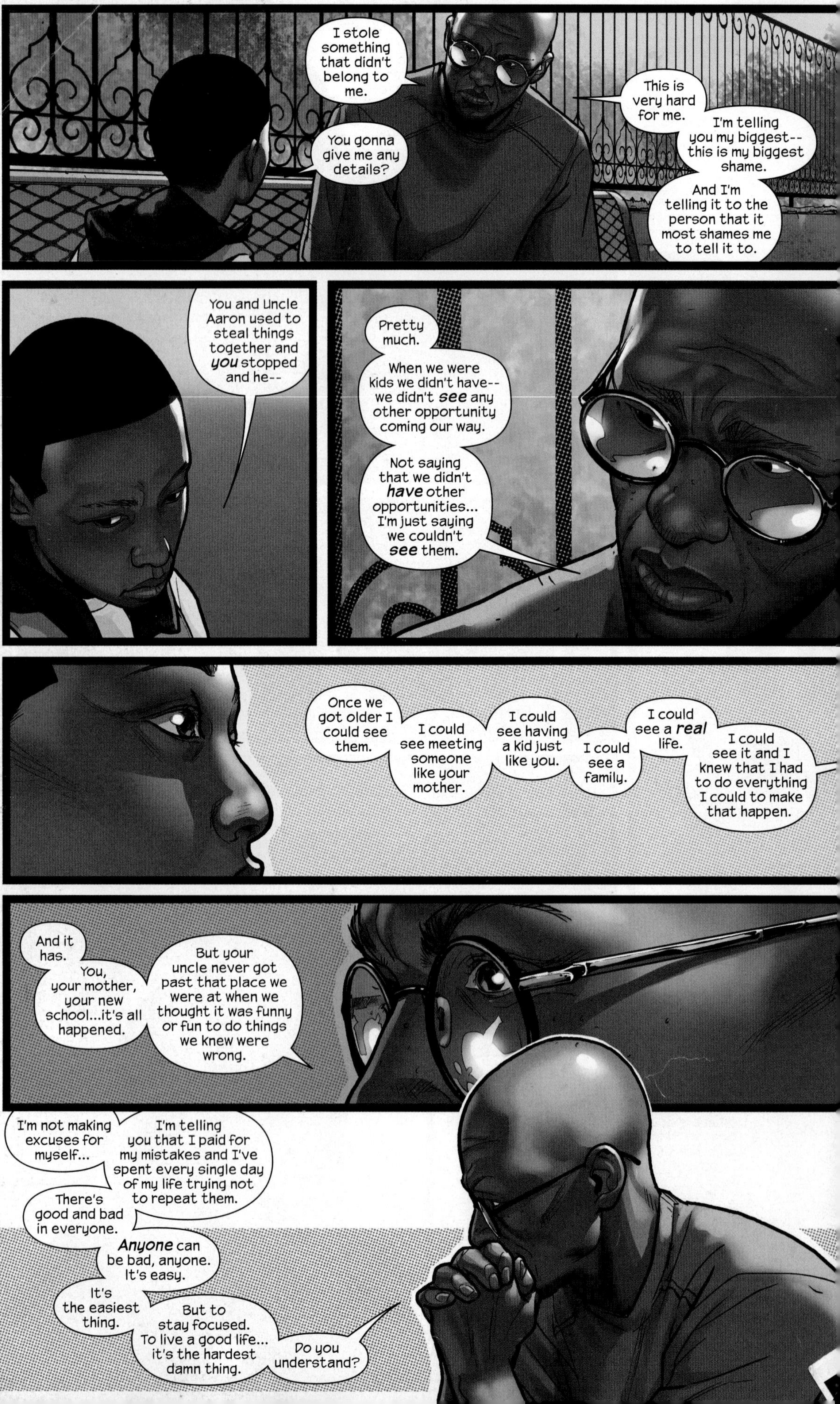

I stole something that didn't belong to me.
This is very hard for me.
I'm telling you my biggest-- this is my biggest shame.
You gonna give me any details?
And I'm telling it to the person that it most shames me to tell it to.
You and Uncle Aaron used to steal things together and *you* stopped and he--
Pretty much.
When we were kids we didn't have-- we didn't *see* any other opportunity coming our way.
Not saying that we didn't *have* other opportunities... I'm just saying we couldn't *see* them.
Once we got older I could see them.
I could see meeting someone like your mother.
I could see having a kid just like you.
I could see a family.
I could see a *real* life.
I could see it and I knew that I had to do everything I could to make that happen.
And it has.
You, your mother, your new school...it's all happened.
But your uncle never got past that place we were at when we thought it was funny or fun to do things we knew were wrong.
I'm not making excuses for myself...
I'm telling you that I paid for my mistakes and I've spent every single day of my life trying not to repeat them.
There's good and bad in everyone.
Anyone can be bad, anyone. It's easy.
It's the easiest thing.
But to stay focused. To live a good life... it's the hardest damn thing.
Do you understand?

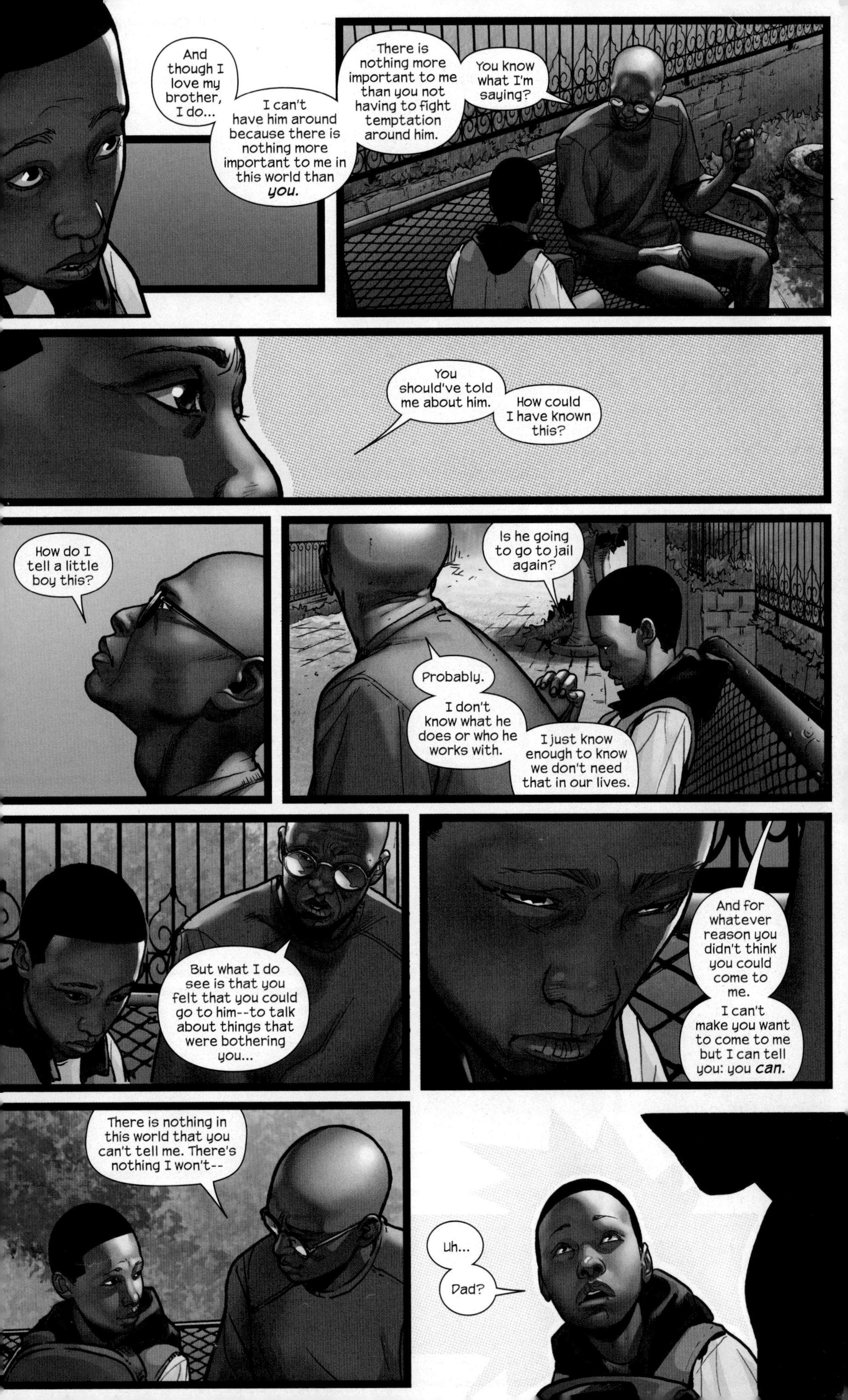
And though I love my brother, I do...
I can't have him around because there is nothing more important to me in this world than *you.*
There is nothing more important to me than you not having to fight temptation around him.
You know what I'm saying?
You should've told me about him.
How could I have known this?
How do I tell a little boy this?
Is he going to go to jail again?
Probably.
I don't know what he does or who he works with.
I just know enough to know we don't need that in our lives.
But what I do see is that you felt that you could go to him--to talk about things that were bothering you...
And for whatever reason you didn't think you could come to me.
I can't make you want to come to me but I can tell you: you *can.*
There is nothing in this world that you can't tell me. There's nothing I won't--
Uh...
Dad?

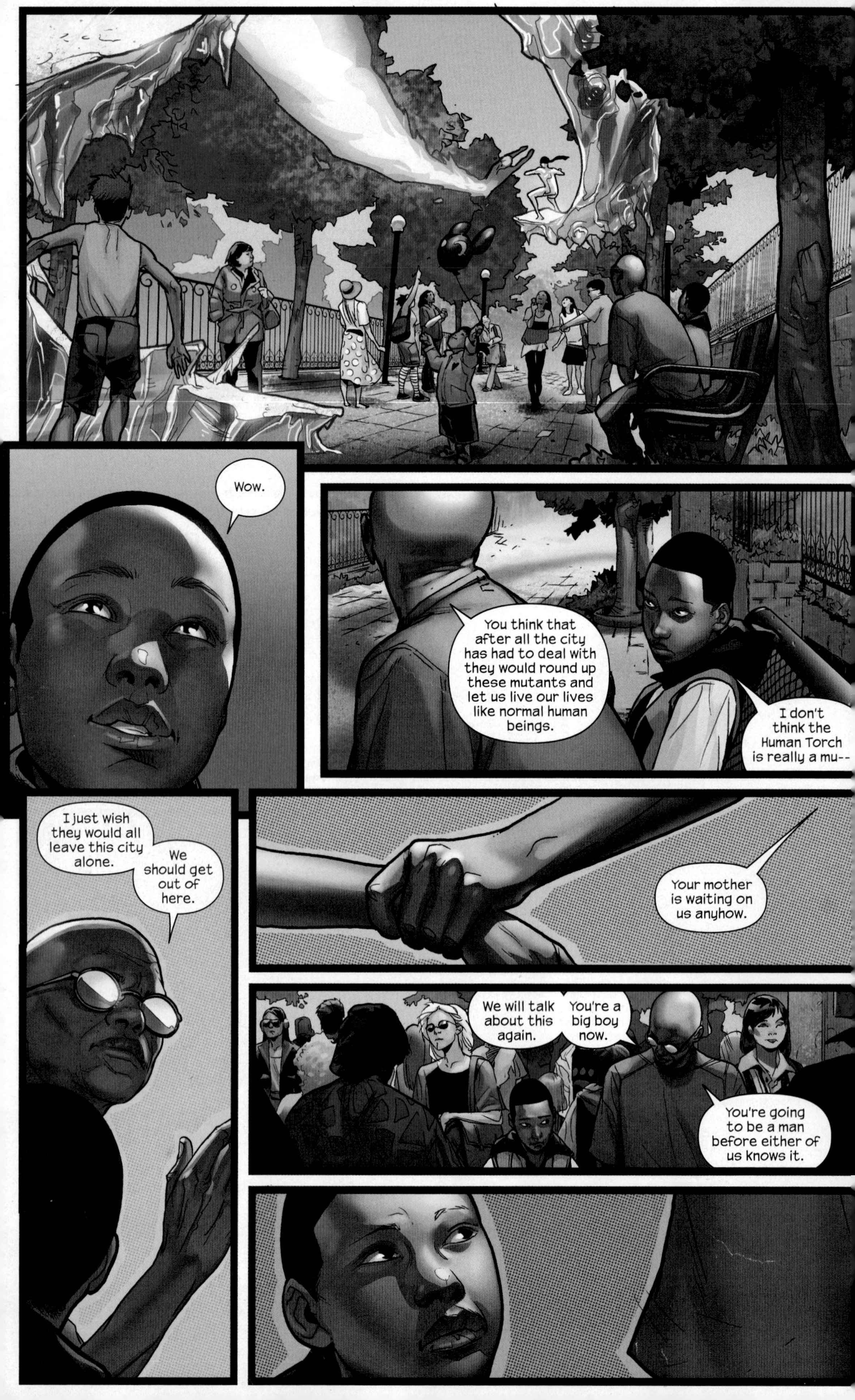
Wow.
You think that after all the city has had to deal with they would round up these mutants and let us live our lives like normal human beings.
I don't think the Human Torch is really a mu--
I just wish they would all leave this city alone.
We should get out of here.
Your mother is waiting on us anyhow.
We will talk about this again.
You're a big boy now.
You're going to be a man before either of us knows it.

STARPICS

Z100

Ganke THE AWESOME:
today,1:07 am
you're not a mutant.

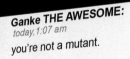

Ganke THE AWESOME:
today,1:07 am
you're not a mutant.

Ganke THE AWESOME:
today,1:08 am
u have chameleon like powers like some spiders do- & u have a venom strike, like some spiders have.

u have chameleon like powers like some spiders do- & u have a venom strike, like some spiders have.

Sir MILES:
today,1:09 am
what r u talking about?

today,1:09 am
what r u talking about?

Ganke THE AWESOME:
today,1:10 am
Spider-Man was bit by a spider too.

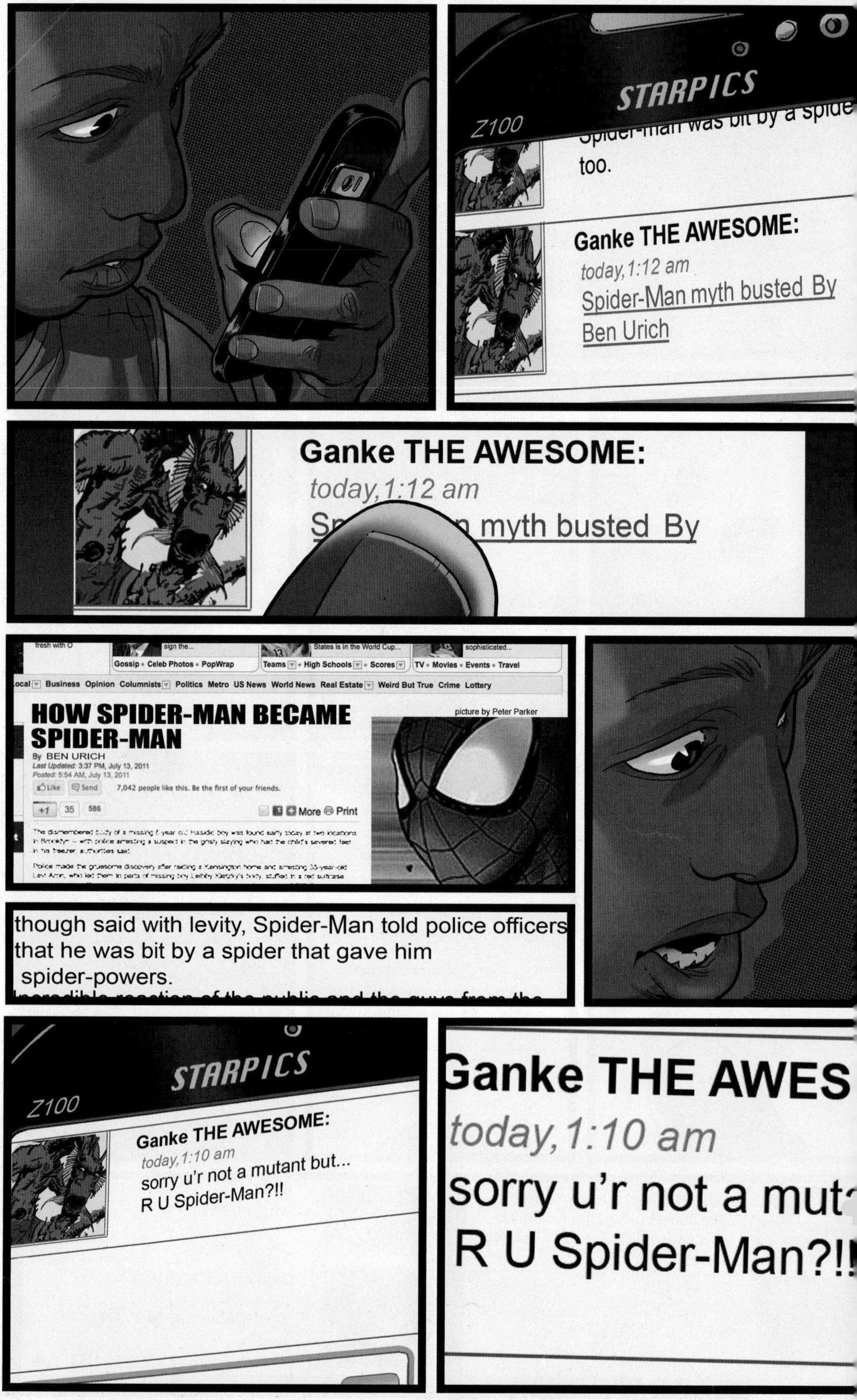

STARPICS
Z100
too.
Ganke THE AWESOME:
today,1:12 am
Spider-Man myth busted By Ben Urich
Ganke THE AWESOME:
today,1:12 am
myth busted By
Gossip • Celeb Photos • PopWrap
Teams • High Schools • Scores
TV • Movies • Events • Travel
Local Business Opinion Columnists Politics Metro US News World News Real Estate Weird But True Crime Lottery
HOW SPIDER-MAN BECAME SPIDER-MAN
picture by Peter Parker
By BEN URICH
Last Updated: 3:37 PM, July 13, 2011
Posted: 5:54 AM, July 13, 2011
Like Send 7,042 people like this. Be the first of your friends.
+1 35 586
More Print
though said with levity, Spider-Man told police officers that he was bit by a spider that gave him spider-powers.
STARPICS
Z100
Ganke THE AWESOME:
today,1:10 am
sorry u'r not a mutant but...
R U Spider-Man?!!
Ganke THE AWES
today,1:10 am
sorry u'r not a mut
R U Spider-Man?!!

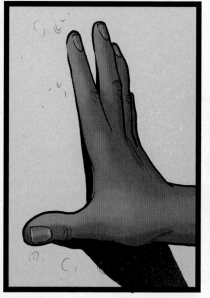
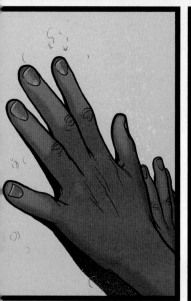
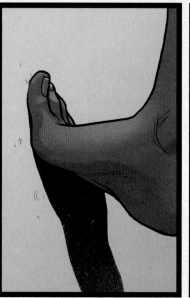

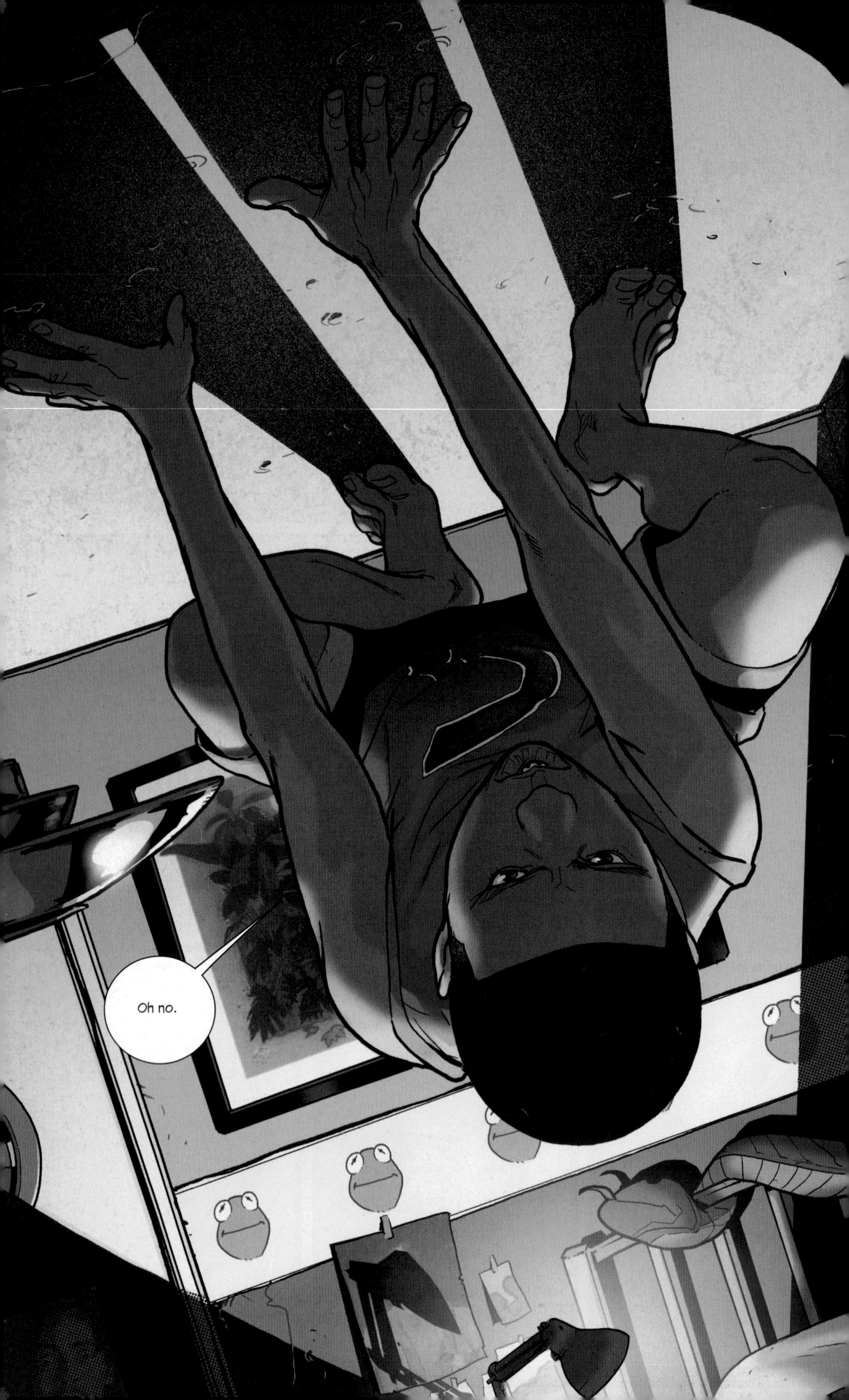
Oh no.

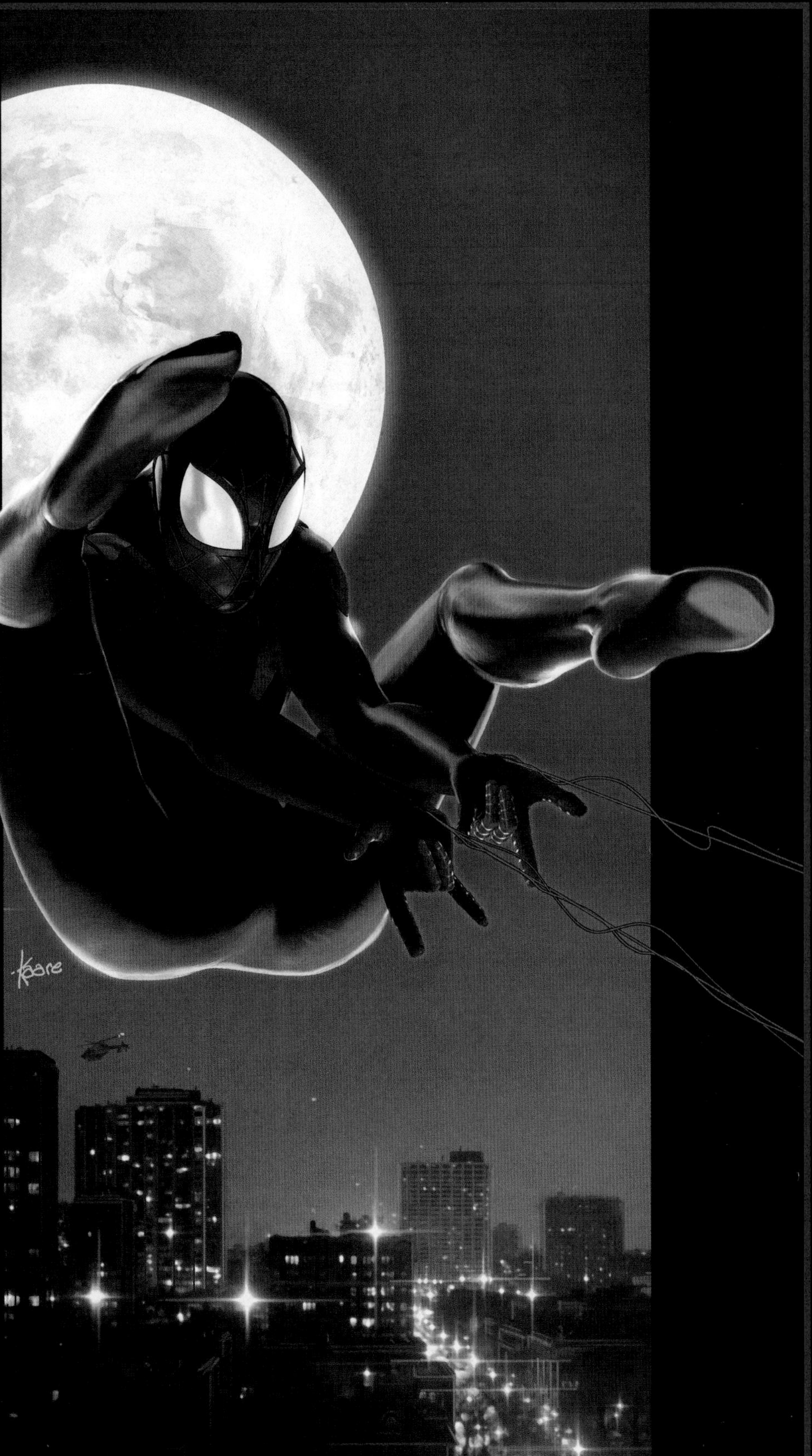
Kaare

ULTIMATE COMICS SPIDER-MAN #3

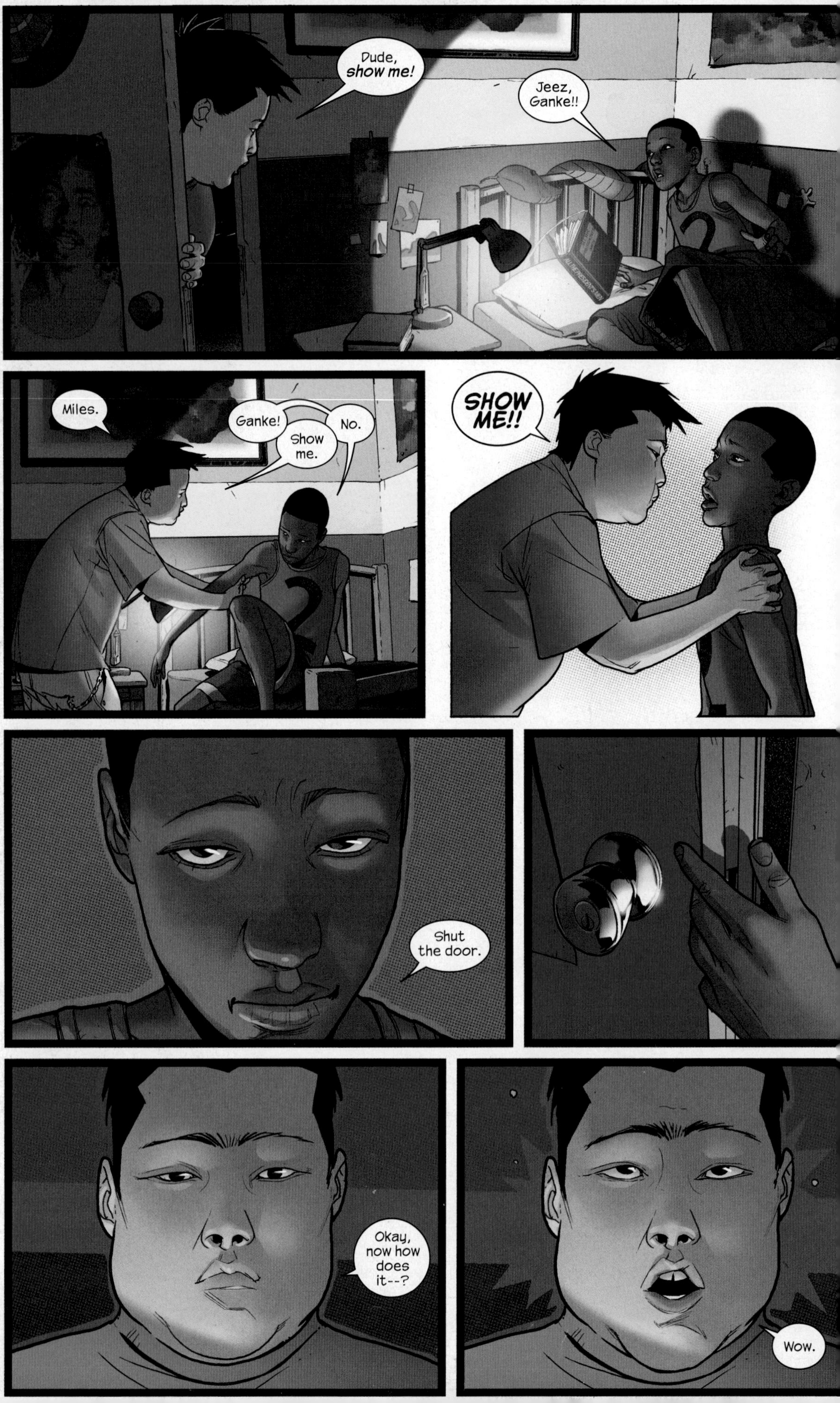

Dude, show me!
Jeez, Ganke!!
Miles.
Ganke!
Show me.
No.
SHOW ME!!
Shut the door.
Okay, now how does it--?
Wow.

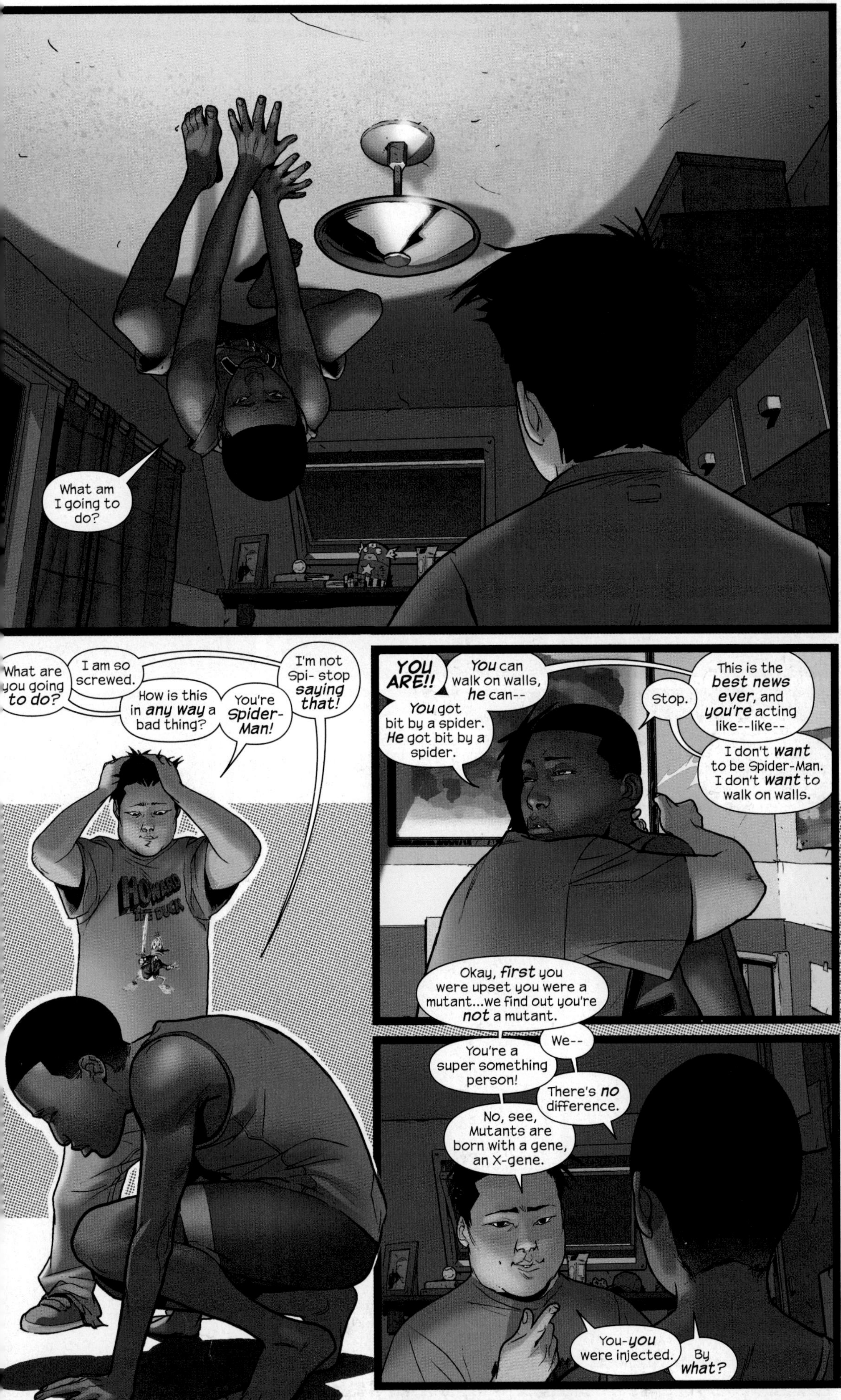

What am I going to do?
What are you going to do?
I am so screwed.
How is this in any way a bad thing?
You're Spider-Man!
I'm not Spi- stop saying that!
YOU ARE!!
You can walk on walls, he can--
You got bit by a spider. He got bit by a spider.
This is the best news ever, and you're acting like--like--
Stop.
I don't want to be Spider-Man. I don't want to walk on walls.
Okay, first you were upset you were a mutant...we find out you're not a mutant.
You're a super something person!
We--
There's no difference.
No, see, Mutants are born with a gene, an X-gene.
You-you were injected.
By what?

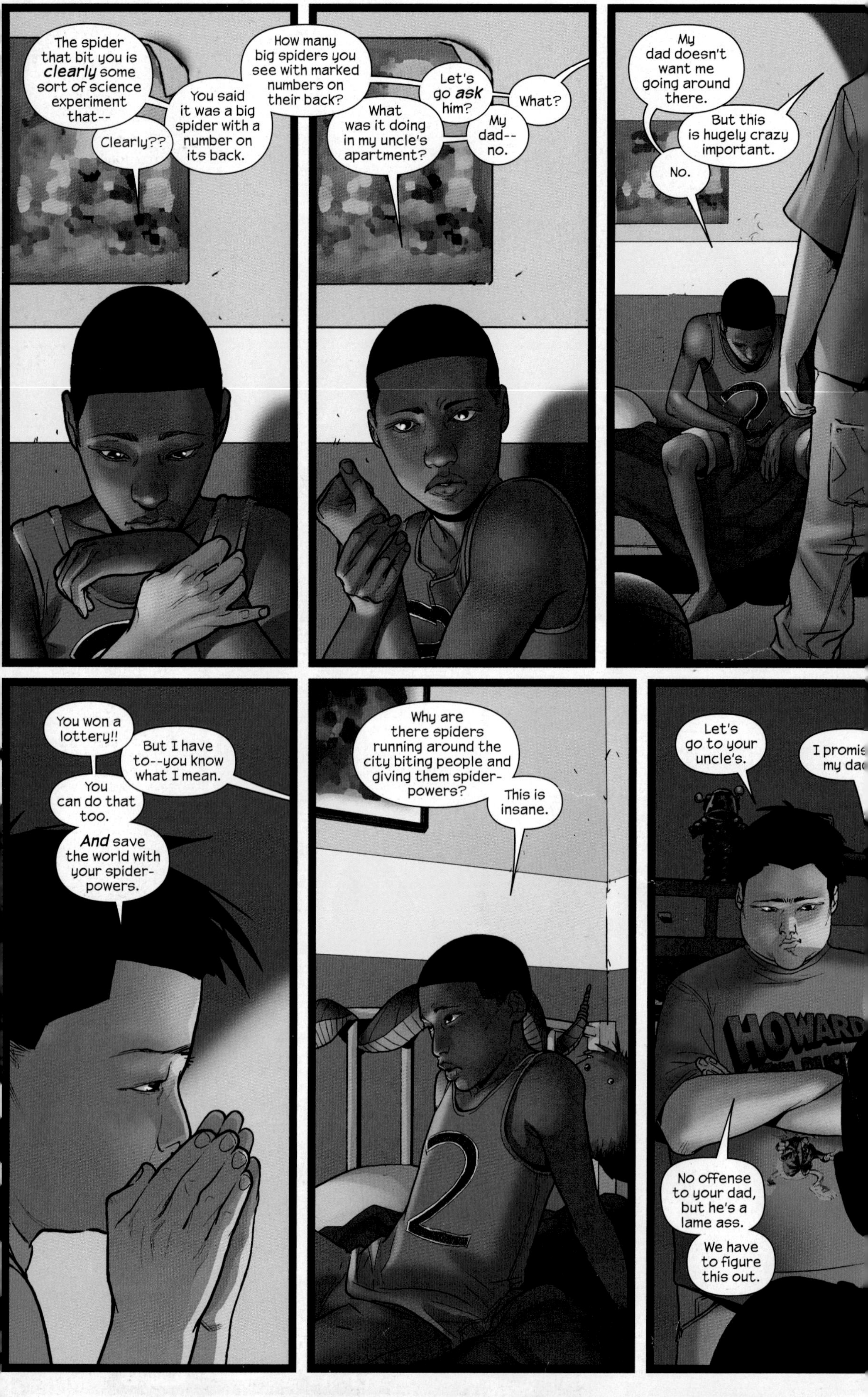
The spider that bit you is *clearly* some sort of science experiment that--
Clearly??
You said it was a big spider with a number on its back.
How many big spiders you see with marked numbers on their back?
What was it doing in my uncle's apartment?
Let's go *ask* him?
My dad-- no.
What?
My dad doesn't want me going around there.
No.
But this is hugely crazy important.
You won a lottery!!
You can do that too.
But I have to--you know what I mean.
And save the world with your spider-powers.
Why are there spiders running around the city biting people and giving them spider-powers?
This is insane.
Let's go to your uncle's.
I promis
my da
No offense to your dad, but he's a lame ass.
We have to figure this out.

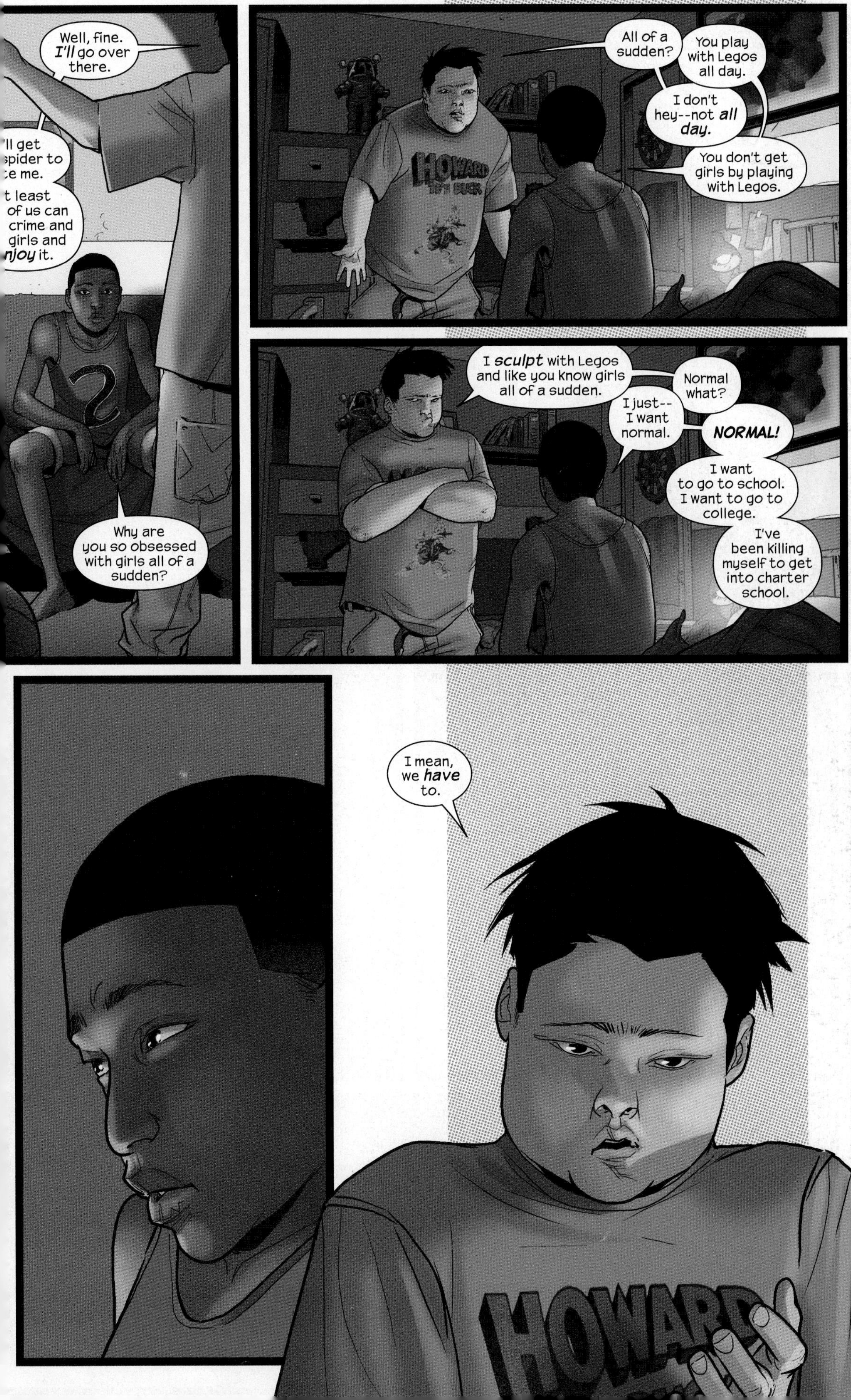
Well, fine. I'll go over there.
'll get spider to e me.
t least of us can crime and girls and njoy it.
Why are you so obsessed with girls all of a sudden?
All of a sudden?
You play with Legos all day.
I don't hey--not all day.
You don't get girls by playing with Legos.
I sculpt with Legos and like you know girls all of a sudden.
Normal what?
I just-- I want normal.
NORMAL!
I want to go to school. I want to go to college.
I've been killing myself to get into charter school.
I mean, we have to.

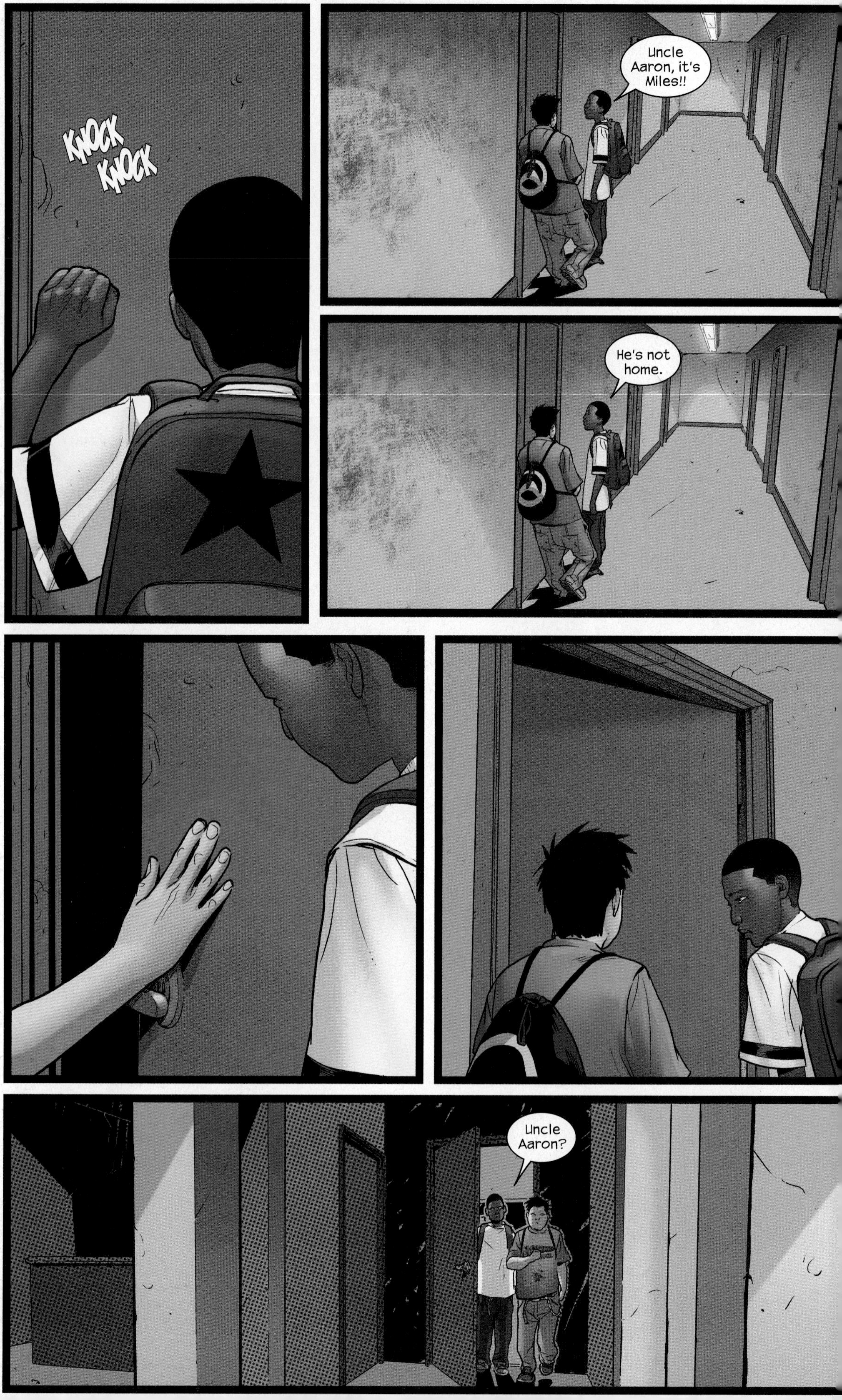
KNOCK
KNOCK
Uncle Aaron, it's Miles!!
He's not home.
Uncle Aaron?

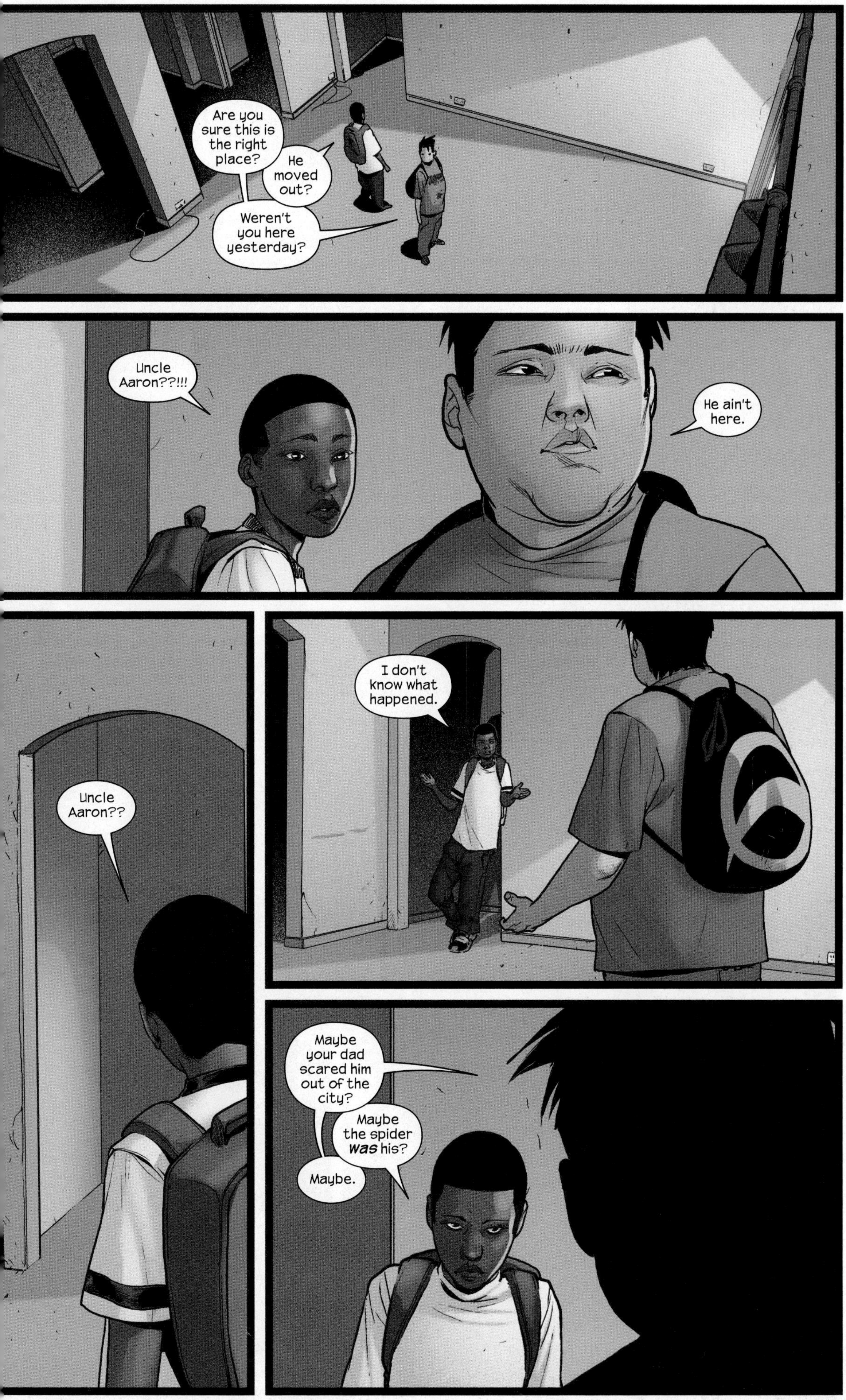

Are you sure this is the right place?
He moved out?
Weren't you here yesterday?
Uncle Aaron??!!!
He ain't here.
Uncle Aaron??
I don't know what happened.
Maybe your dad scared him out of the city?
Maybe the spider *was* his?
Maybe.

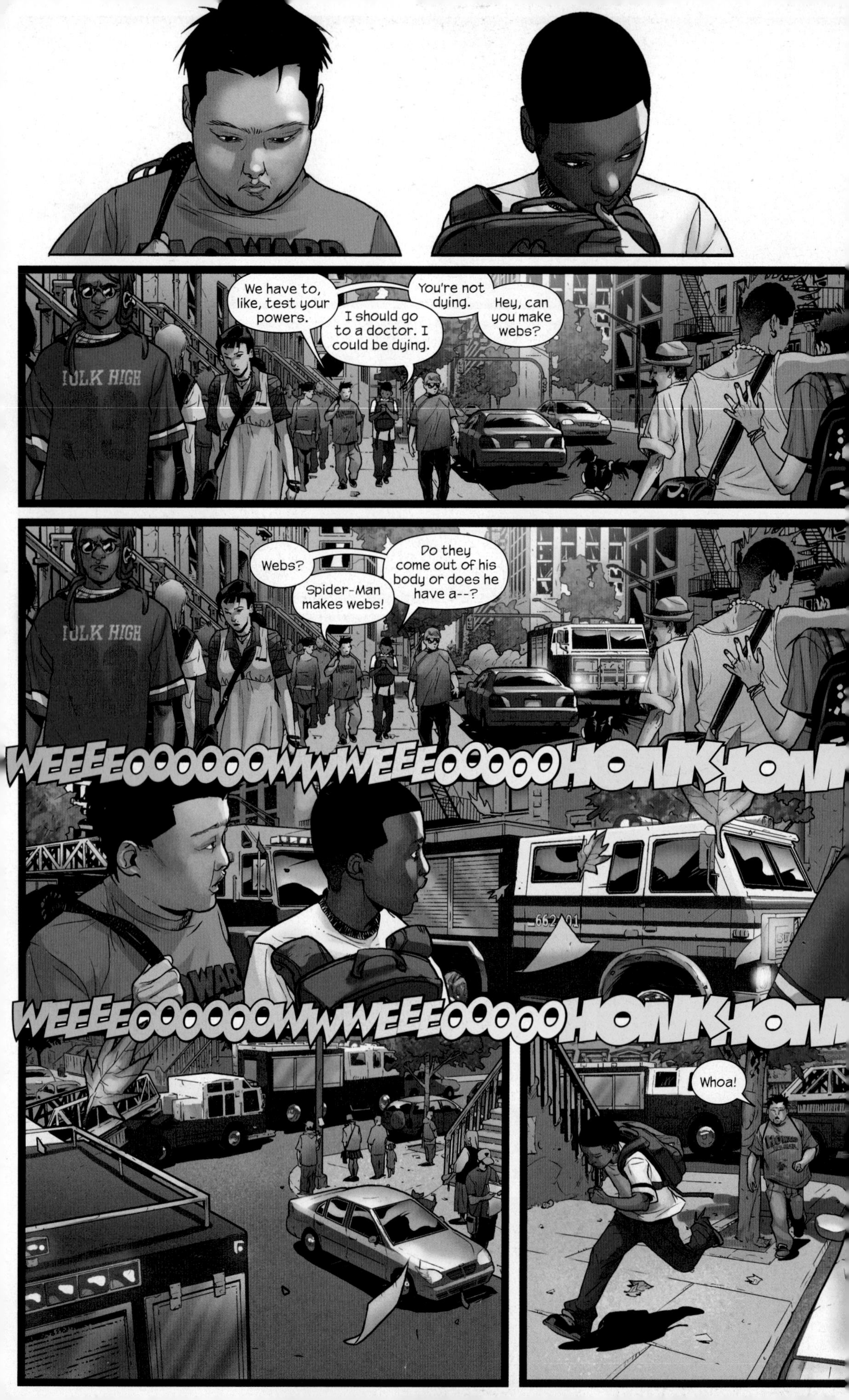
We have to, like, test your powers.
I should go to a doctor. I could be dying.
You're not dying.
Hey, can you make webs?
Webs?
Spider-Man makes webs!
Do they come out of his body or does he have a--?
WEEEEOOOOOOWWWEEEOOOOOHONKHONK
WEEEEOOOOOOWWWEEEOOOOOHONKHONK
Whoa!

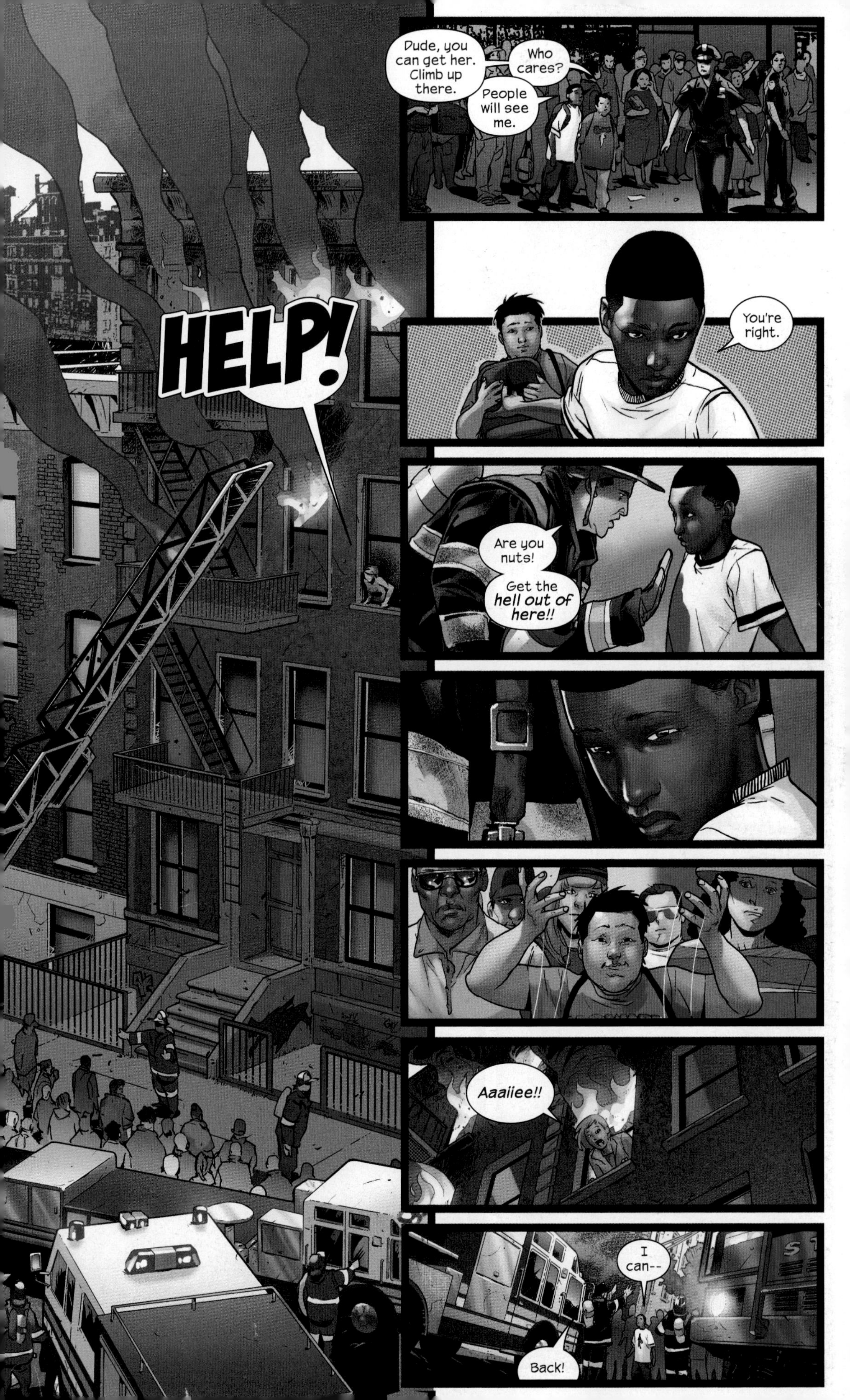
HELP!
Dude, you can get her. Climb up there.
Who cares?
People will see me.
You're right.
Are you nuts!
Get the *hell out of here!!*
Aaaiiee!!
I can--
Back!

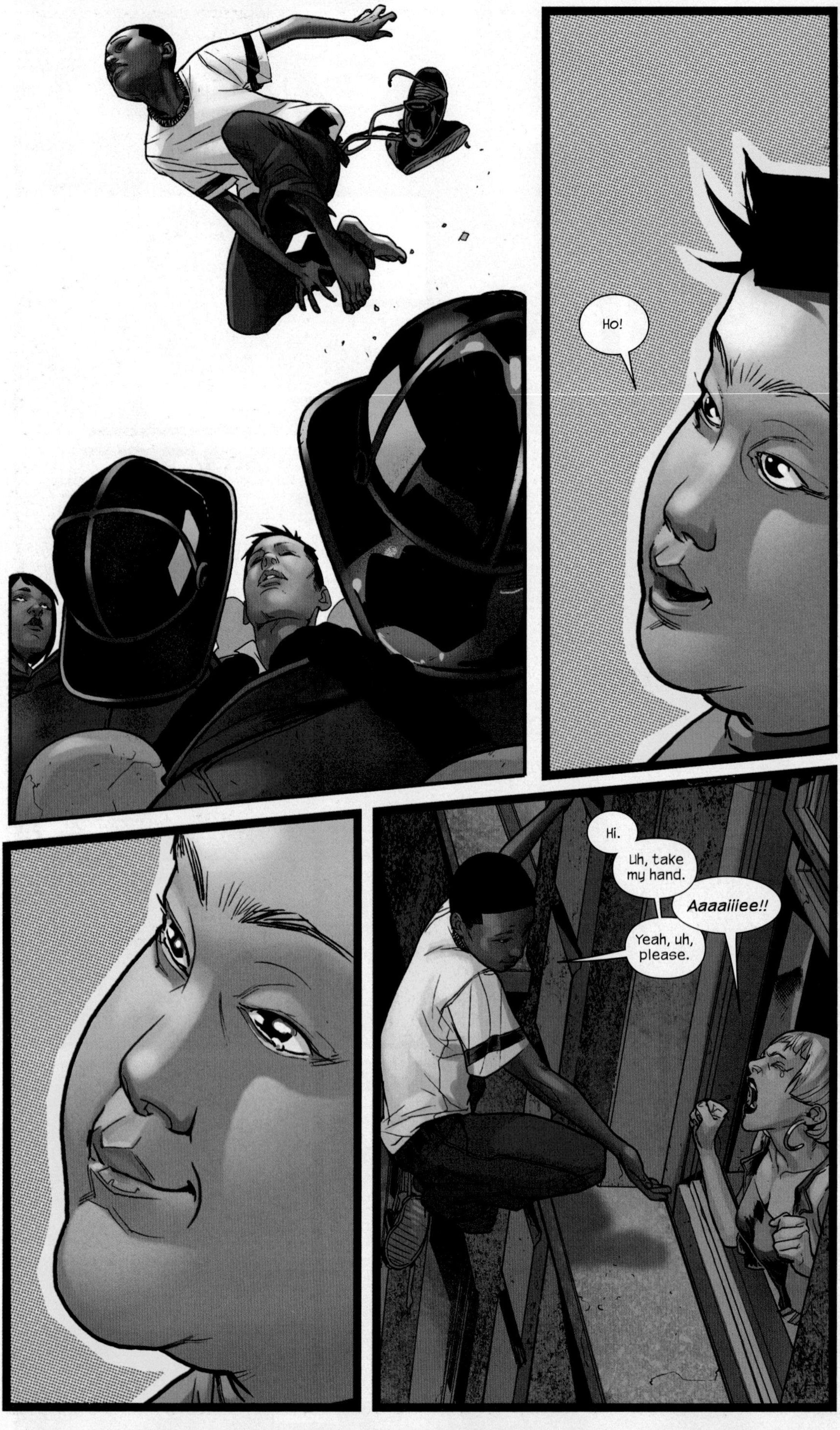
Ho!
Hi.
Uh, take my hand.
Yeah, uh, please.
Aaaaiiiee!!

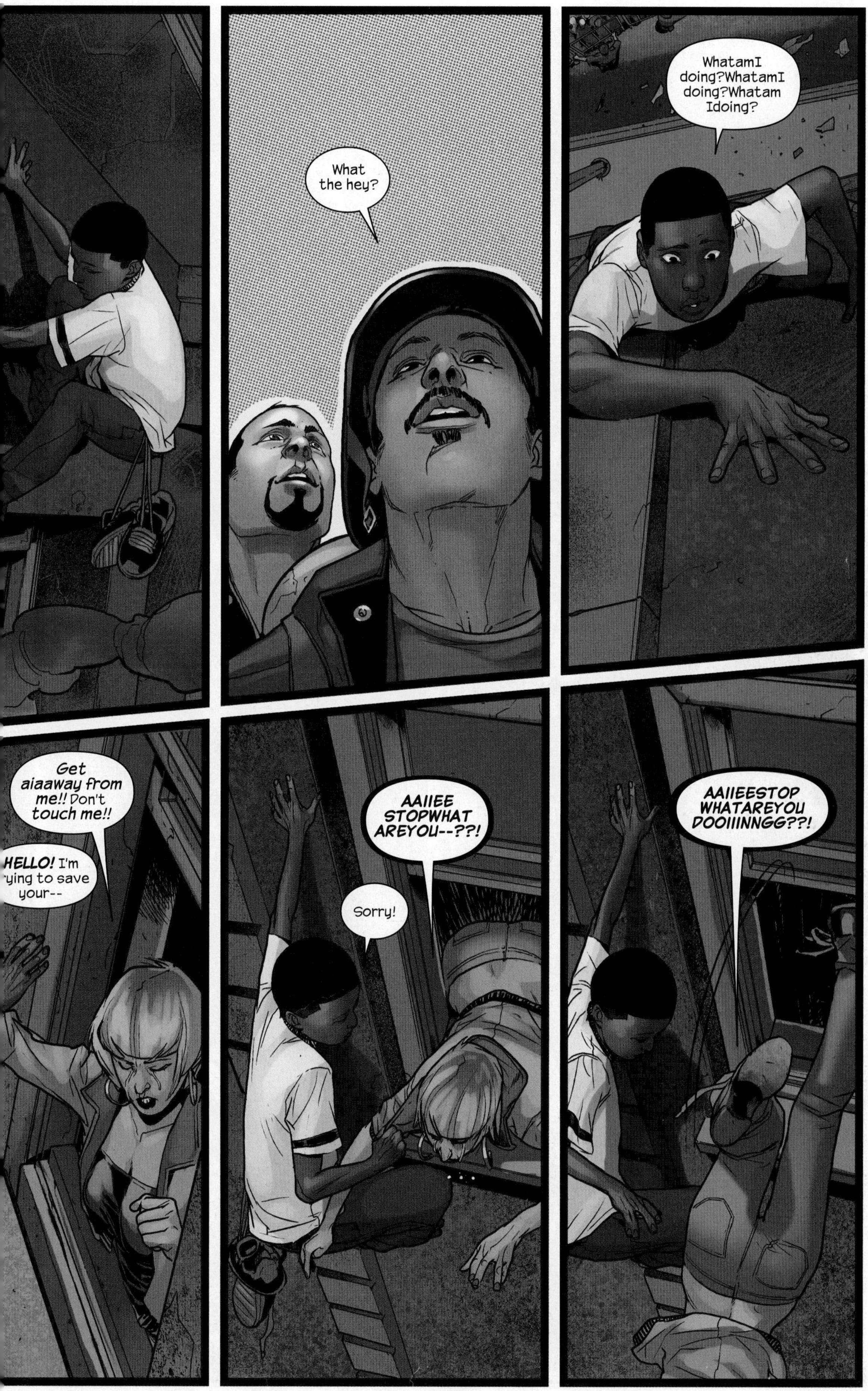
What the hey?
WhatamI doing?WhatamI doing?Whatam Idoing?
Get aiaaway from me!! Don't touch me!!
HELLO! I'm
ying to save your--
AAIIEE STOPWHAT AREYOU--??!
Sorry!
AAIIEESTOP WHATAREYOU DOOIIINNGG??!

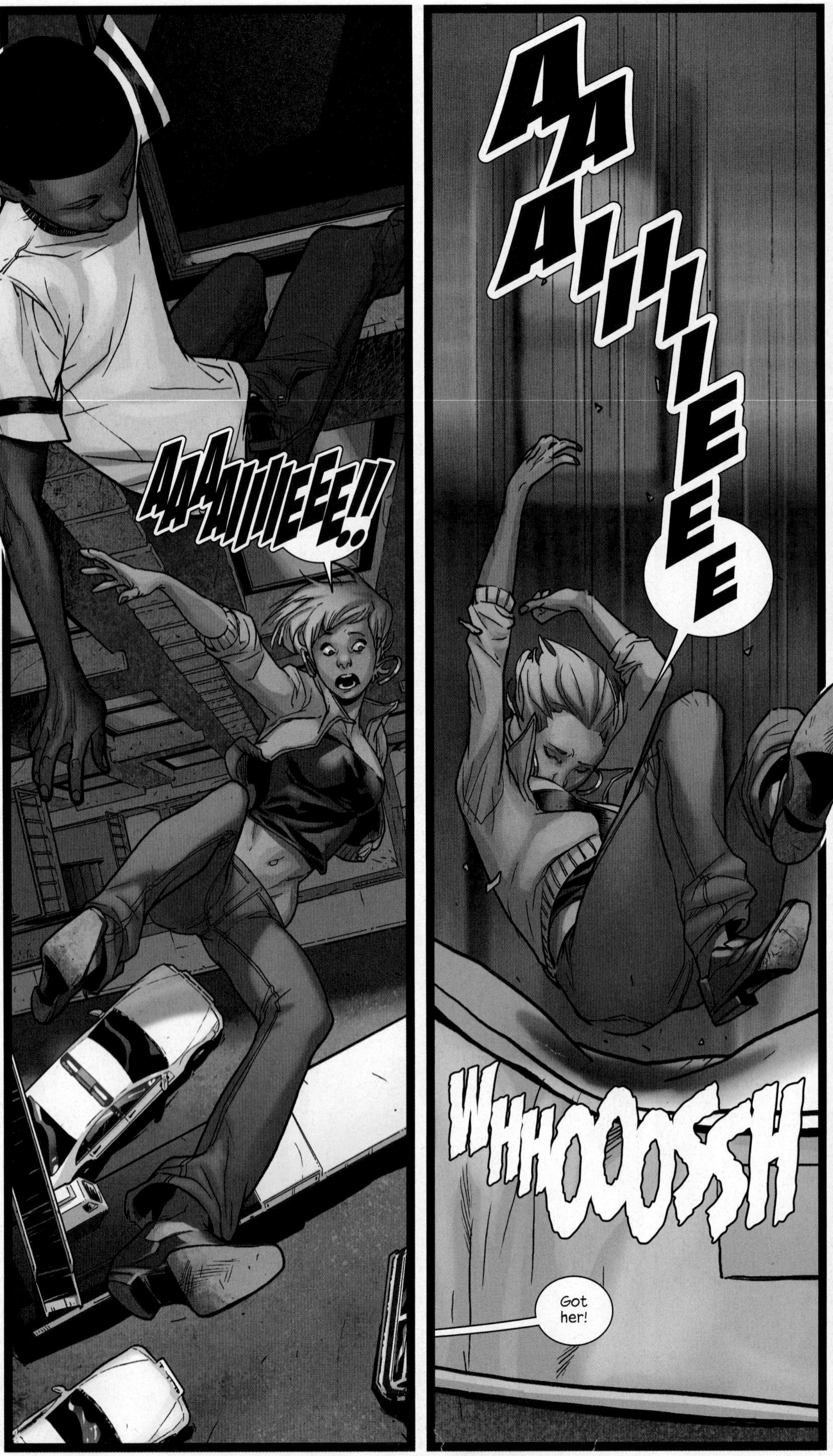

AAAAIIIIEEEE!!
AAAIIIIEEEE
WHHOOOSSH
Got her!

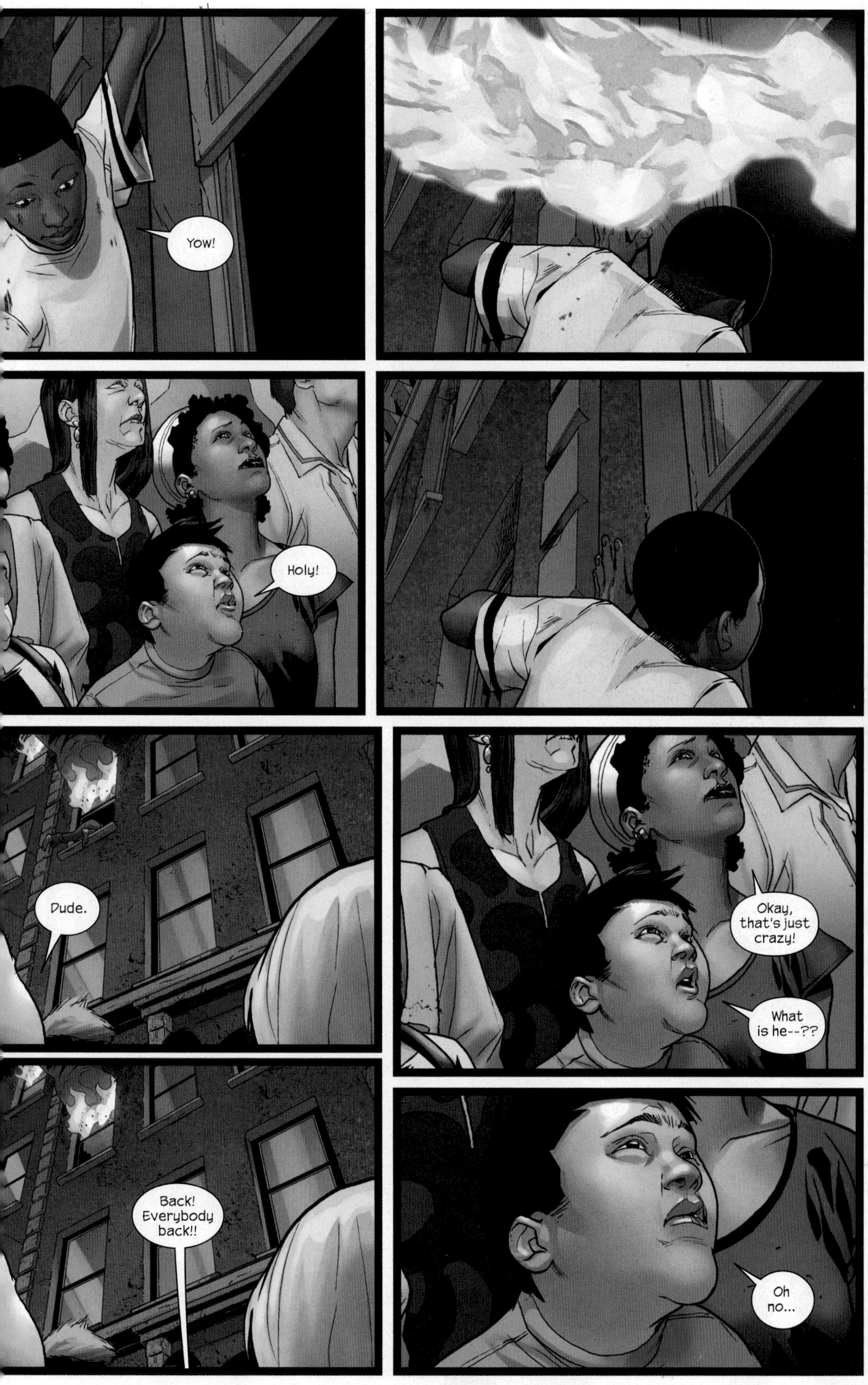
Yow!
Holy!
Dude.
Okay, that's just crazy!
What is he--??
Back! Everybody back!!
Oh no...

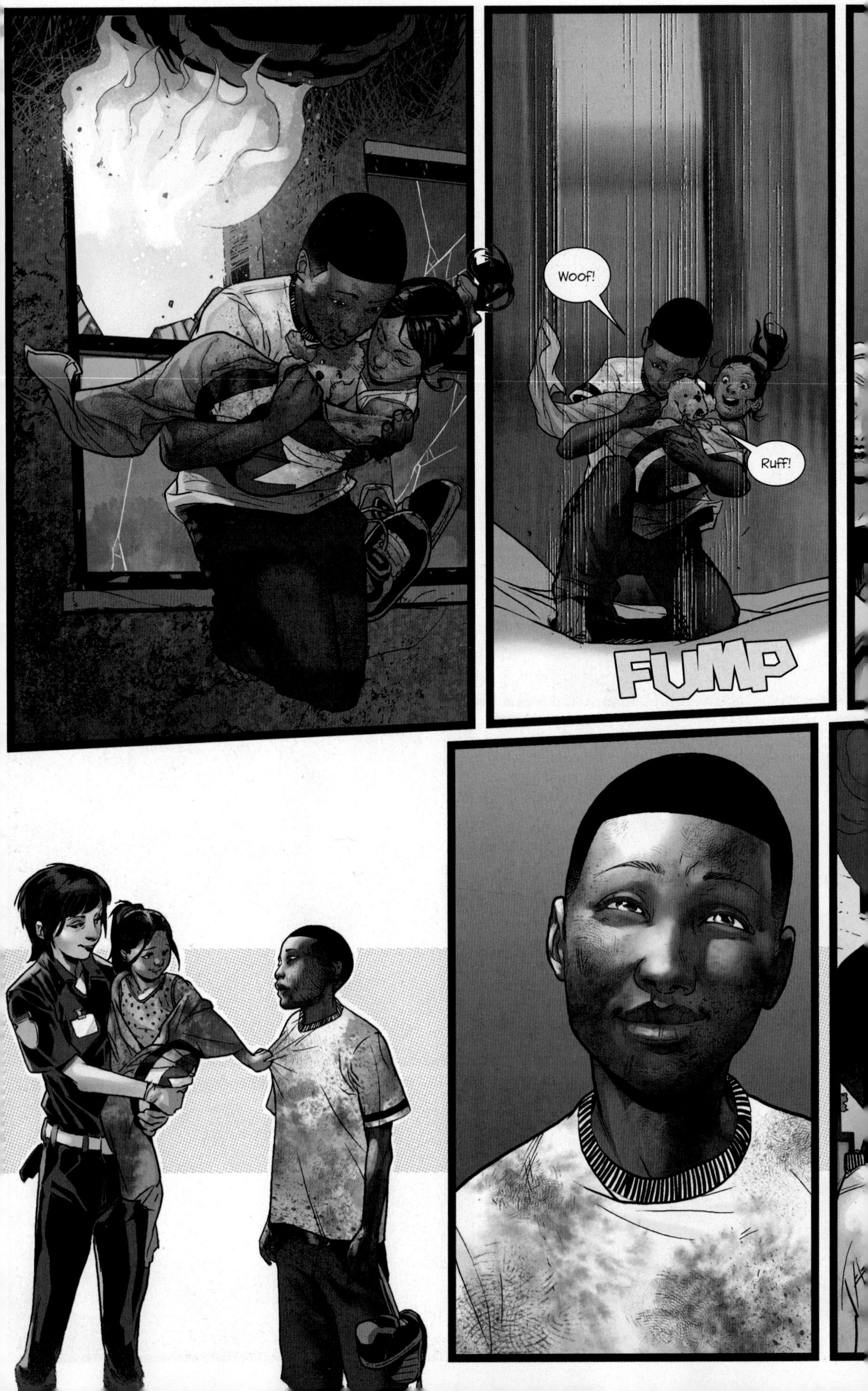
Woof!
Ruff!
FUMP

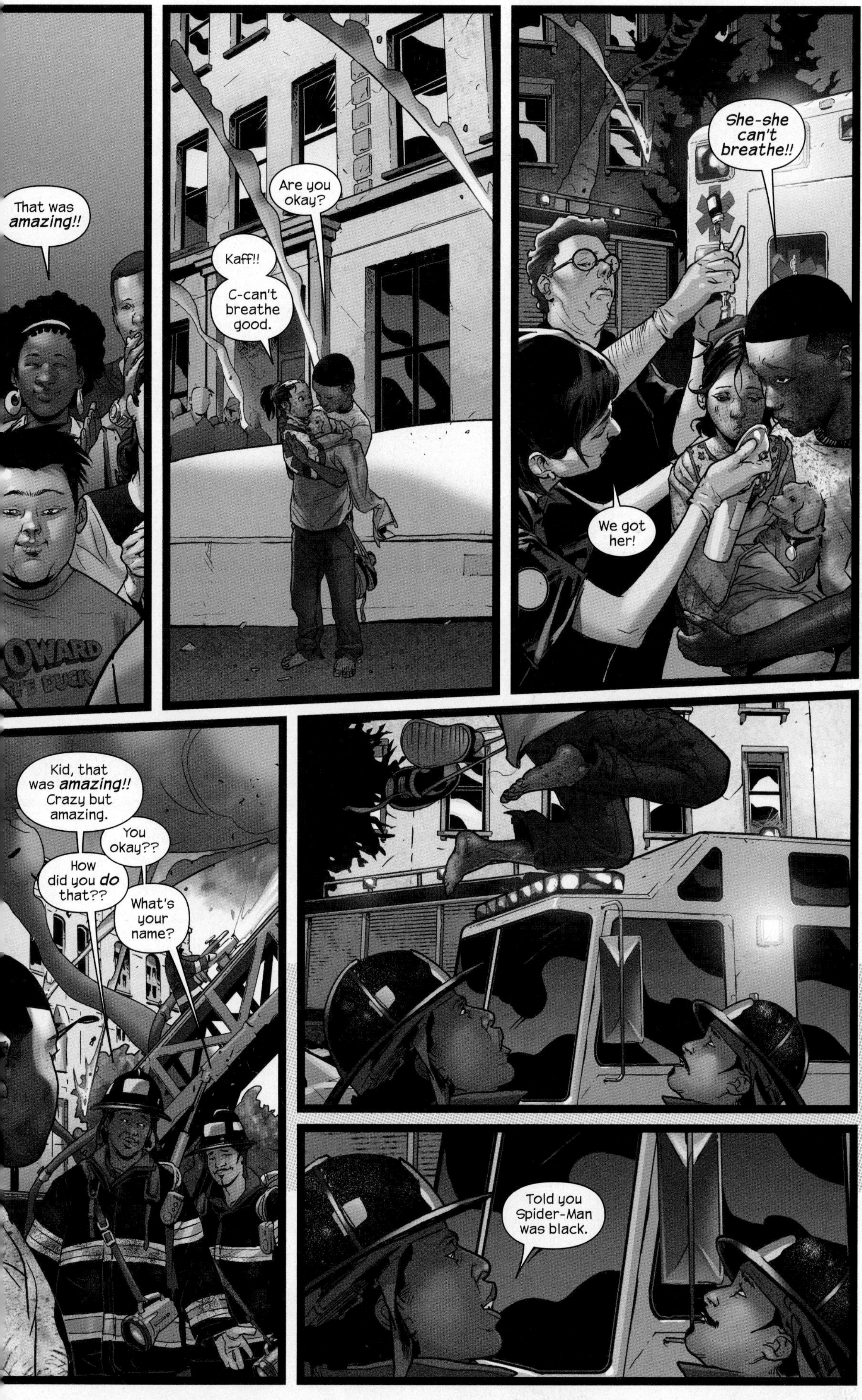
That was *amazing!!*
OWARD
THE DUCK
Are you okay?
Kaff!!
C-can't breathe good.
She-she can't breathe!!
We got her!
Kid, that was *amazing!!* Crazy but amazing.
You okay??
How did you *do* that??
What's your name?
Told you Spider-Man was black.

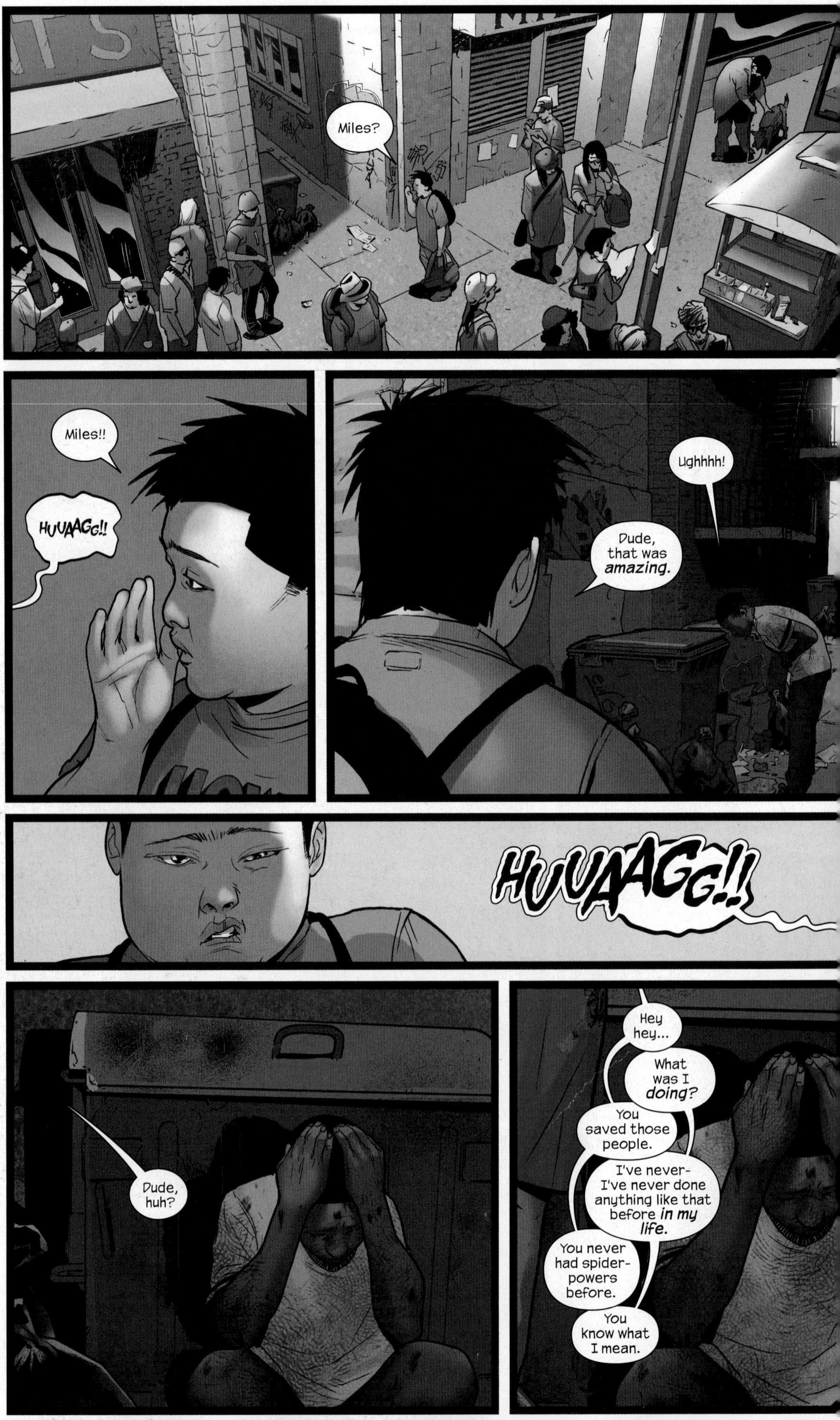
Miles?
Miles!!
HUUAAGG!!
Ughhhh!
Dude, that was *amazing.*
HUUAAGG!!
Dude, huh?
Hey hey...
What was I *doing?*
You saved those people.
I've never- I've never done anything like that before *in my life.*
You never had spider-powers before.
You know what I mean.

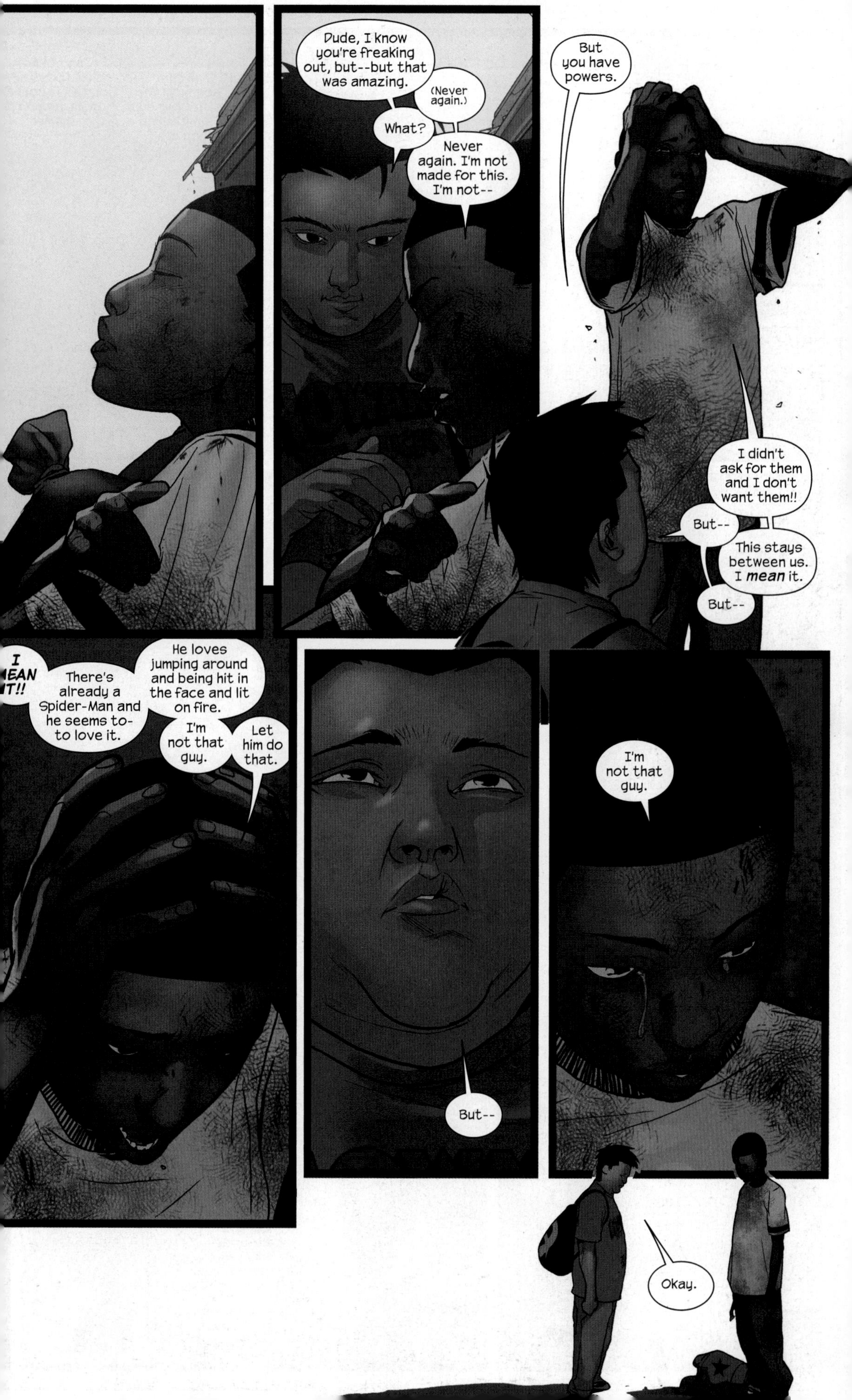

Dude, I know you're freaking out, but--but that was amazing.
(Never again.)
What?
Never again. I'm not made for this. I'm not--
But you have powers.
I didn't ask for them and I don't want them!!
But--
This stays between us. I *mean* it.
But--
I MEAN IT!!
There's already a Spider-Man and he seems to-to love it.
He loves jumping around and being hit in the face and lit on fire.
I'm not that guy.
Let him do that.
But--
I'm not that guy.
Okay.

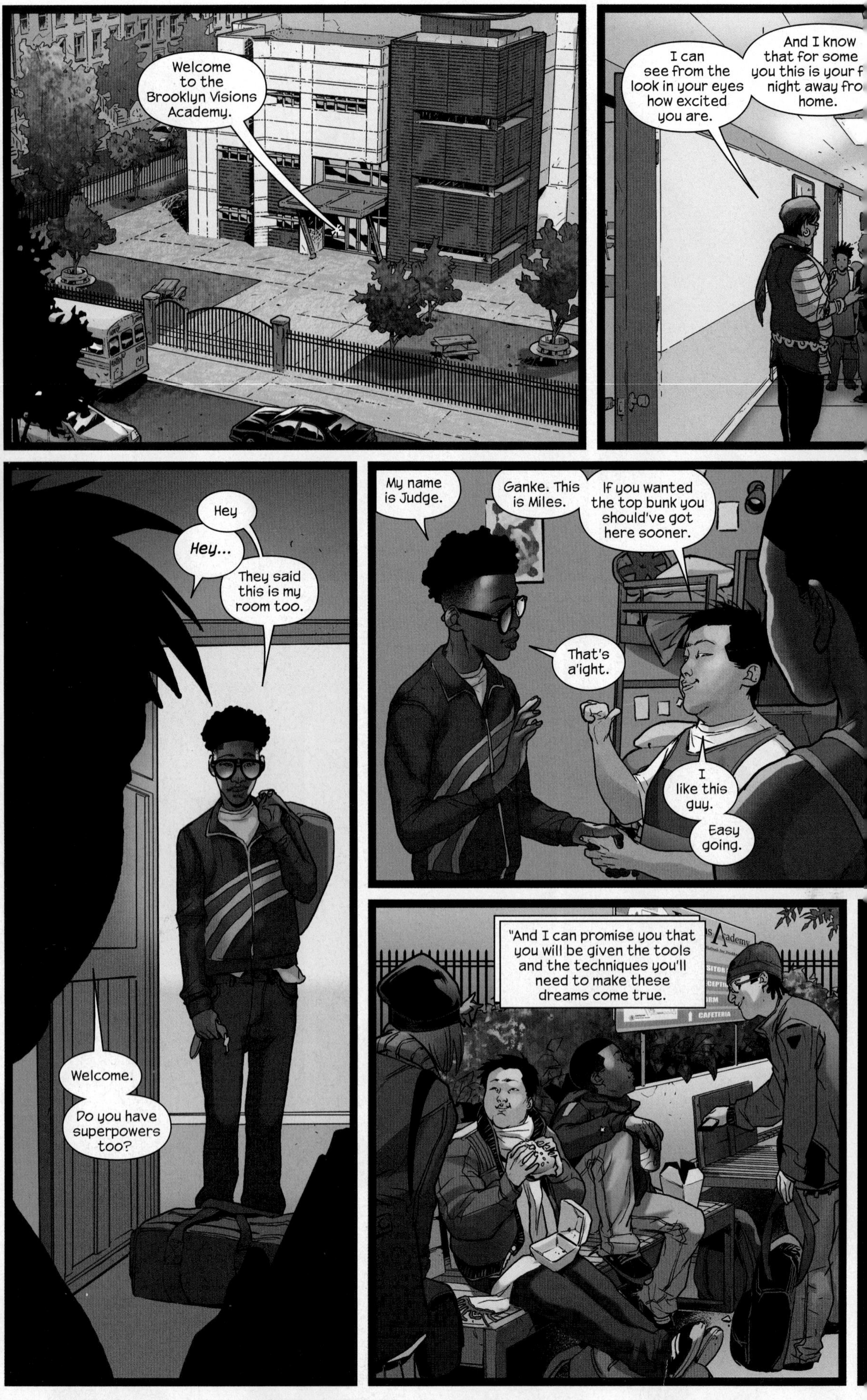

Welcome to the Brooklyn Visions Academy.
I can see from the look in your eyes how excited you are.
And I know that for some you this is your f night away fro home.
Hey
Hey...
They said this is my room too.
Welcome.
Do you have superpowers too?
My name is Judge.
Ganke. This is Miles.
If you wanted the top bunk you should've got here sooner.
That's a'ight.
I like this guy.
Easy going.
"And I can promise you that you will be given the tools and the techniques you'll need to make these dreams come true.

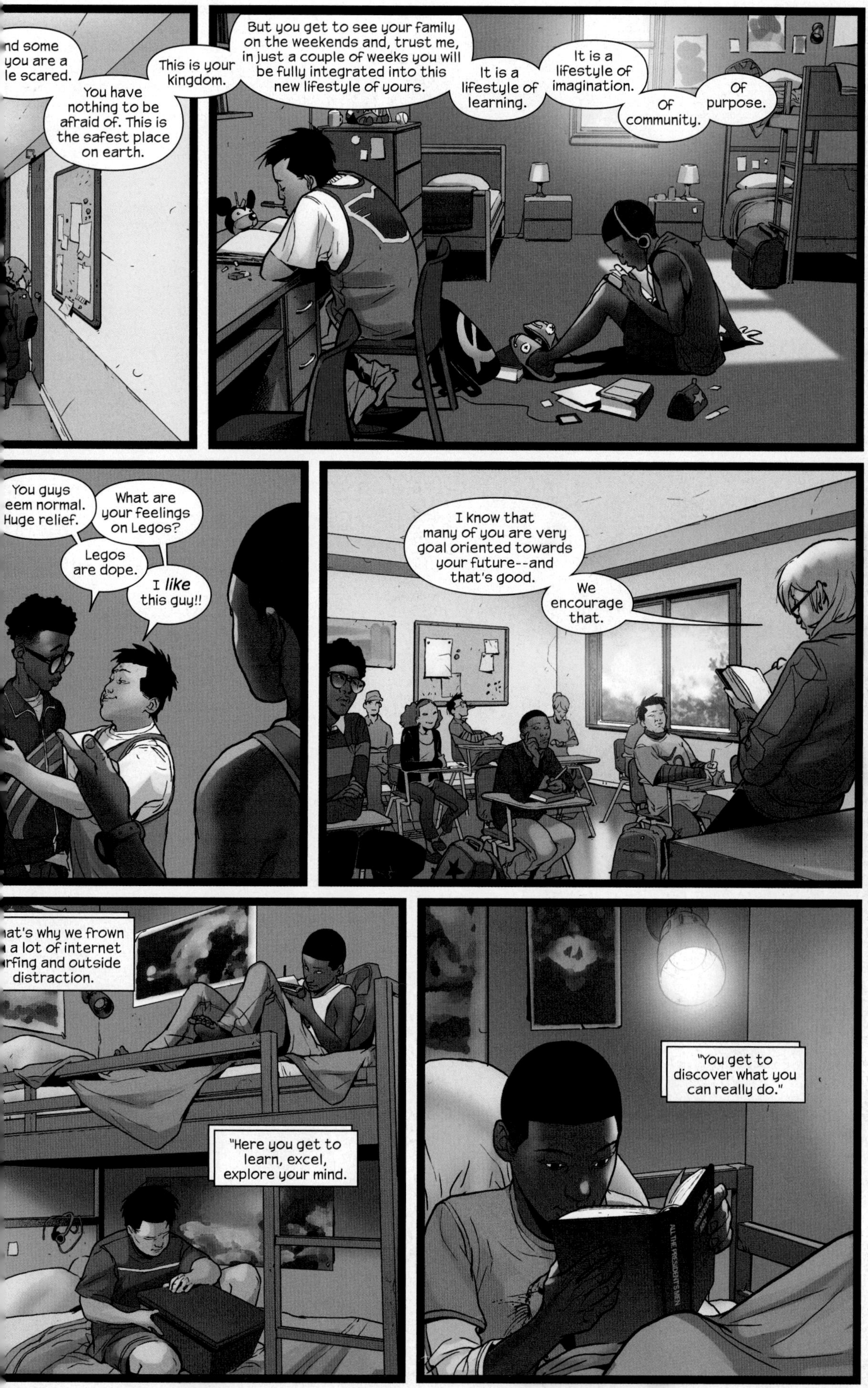
nd some
you are a
le scared.
You have nothing to be afraid of. This is the safest place on earth.
This is your kingdom.
But you get to see your family on the weekends and, trust me, in just a couple of weeks you will be fully integrated into this new lifestyle of yours.
It is a lifestyle of learning.
It is a lifestyle of imagination.
Of community.
Of purpose.
You guys
eem normal.
Huge relief.
What are your feelings on Legos?
Legos are dope.
I *like* this guy!!
I know that many of you are very goal oriented towards your future--and that's good.
We encourage that.
at's why we frown
a lot of internet
rfing and outside
distraction.
"Here you get to learn, excel, explore your mind.
"You get to discover what you can really do."
ALL THE PRESIDENT'S MEN

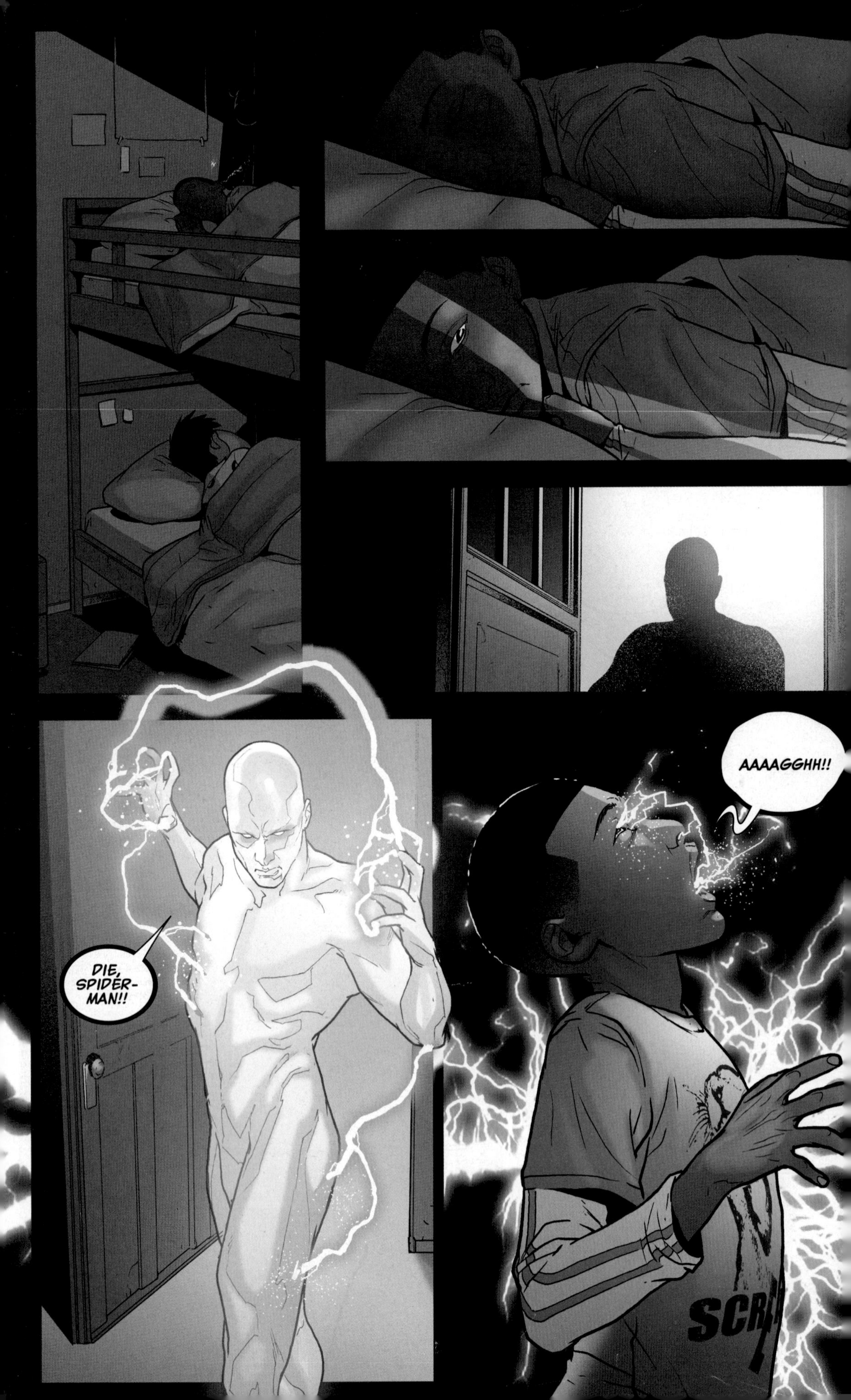
DIE, SPIDER-MAN!!
AAAAGGHH!!
SCR

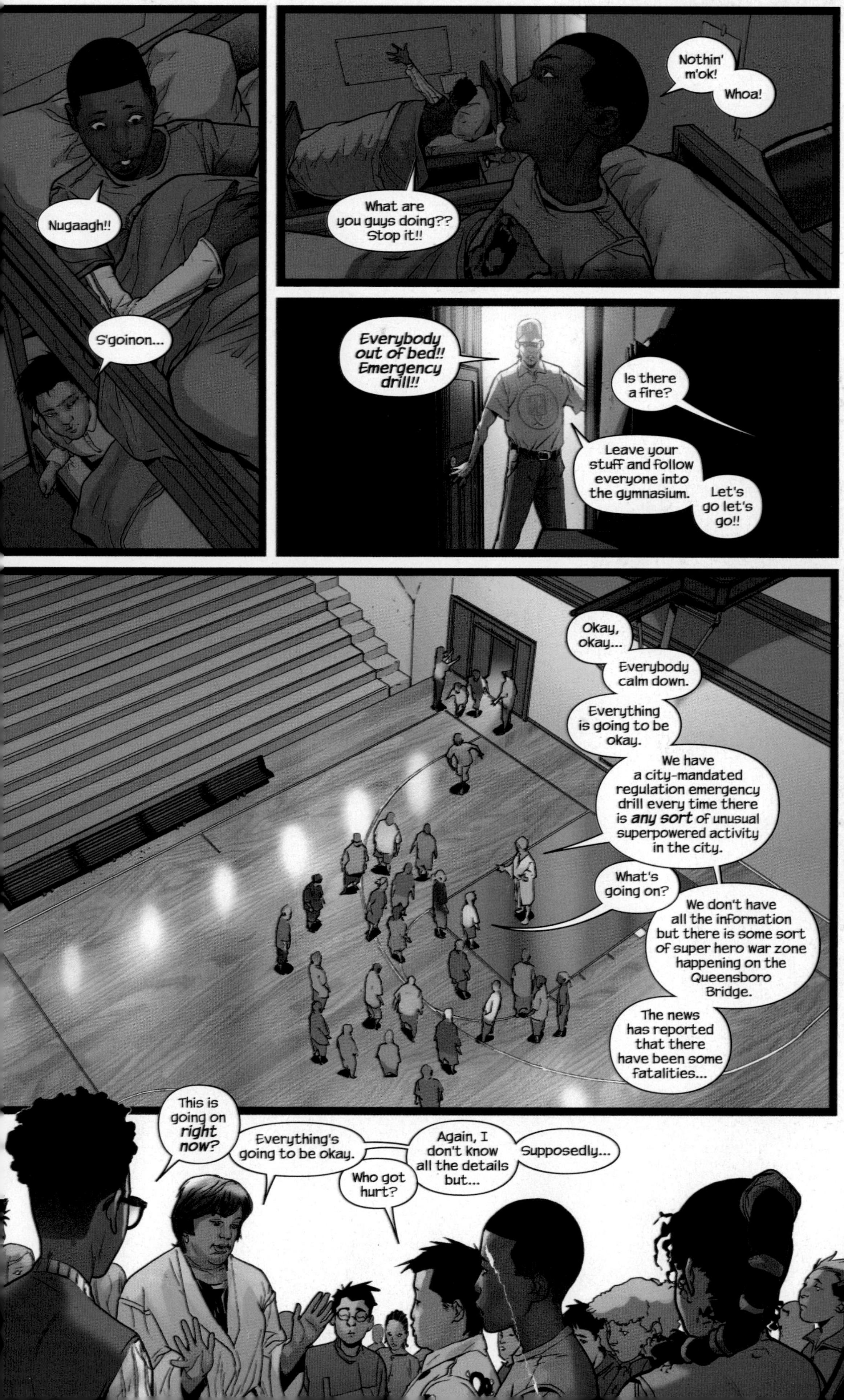
Nugaagh!!
S'goinon...
What are you guys doing?? Stop it!!
Nothin' m'ok!
Whoa!
Everybody out of bed!! Emergency drill!!
Is there a fire?
Leave your stuff and follow everyone into the gymnasium.
Let's go let's go!!
Okay, okay...
Everybody calm down.
Everything is going to be okay.
We have a city-mandated regulation emergency drill every time there is any sort of unusual superpowered activity in the city.
What's going on?
We don't have all the information but there is some sort of super hero war zone happening on the Queensboro Bridge.
The news has reported that there have been some fatalities...
This is going on right now?
Everything's going to be okay.
Who got hurt?
Again, I don't know all the details but...
Supposedly...

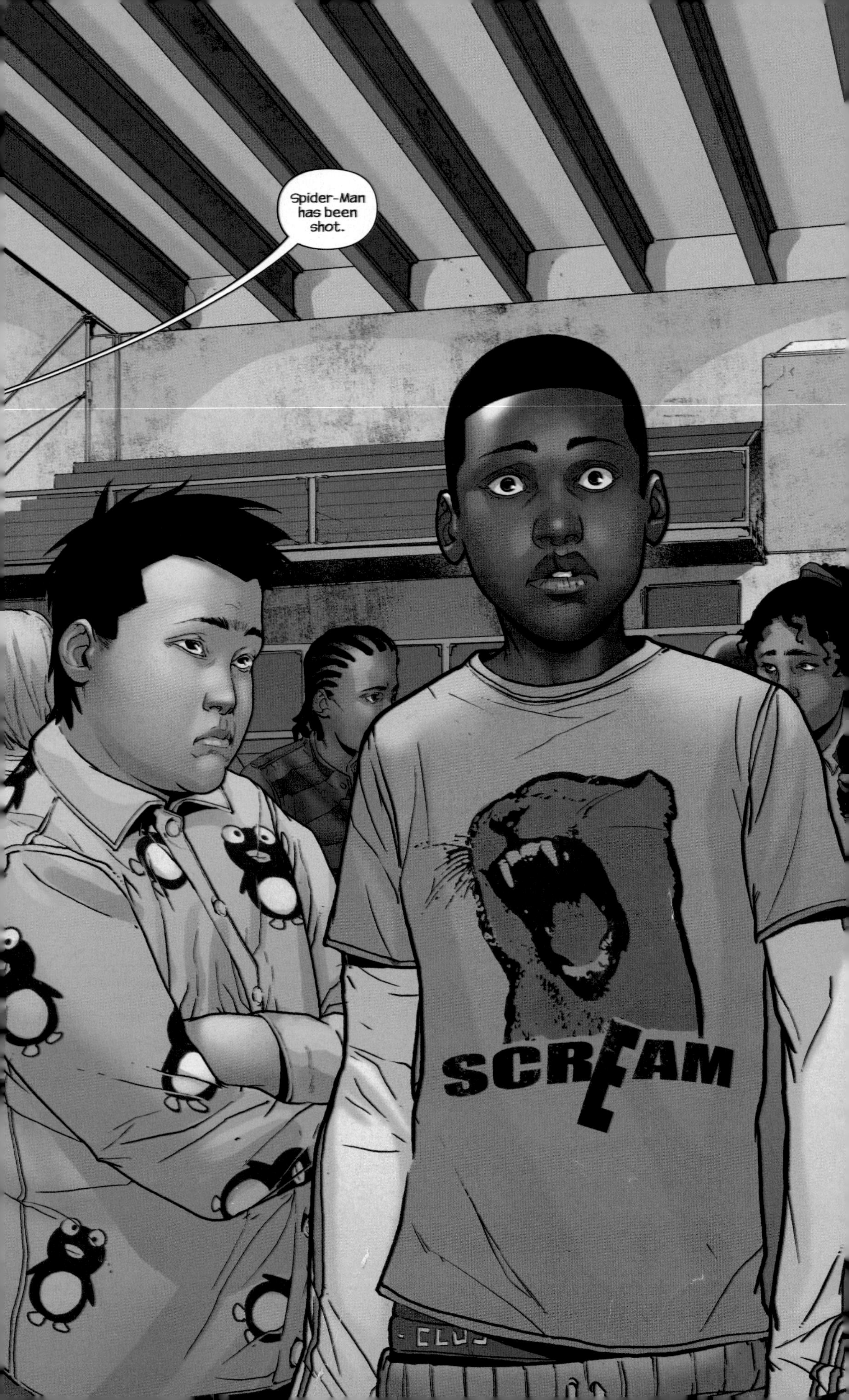
Spider-Man has been shot.
SCREAM

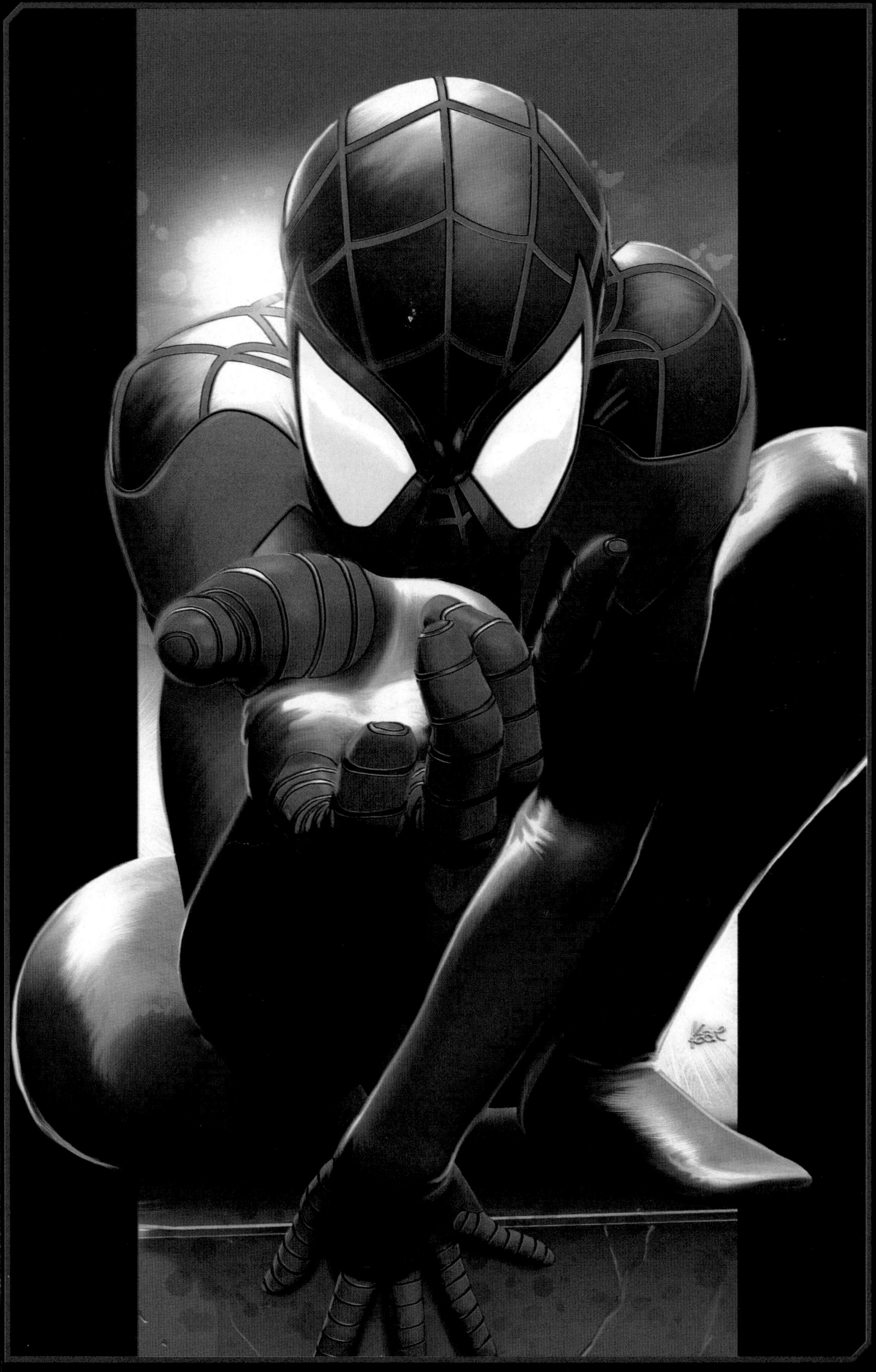

ULTIMATE COMICS SPIDER-MAN #4

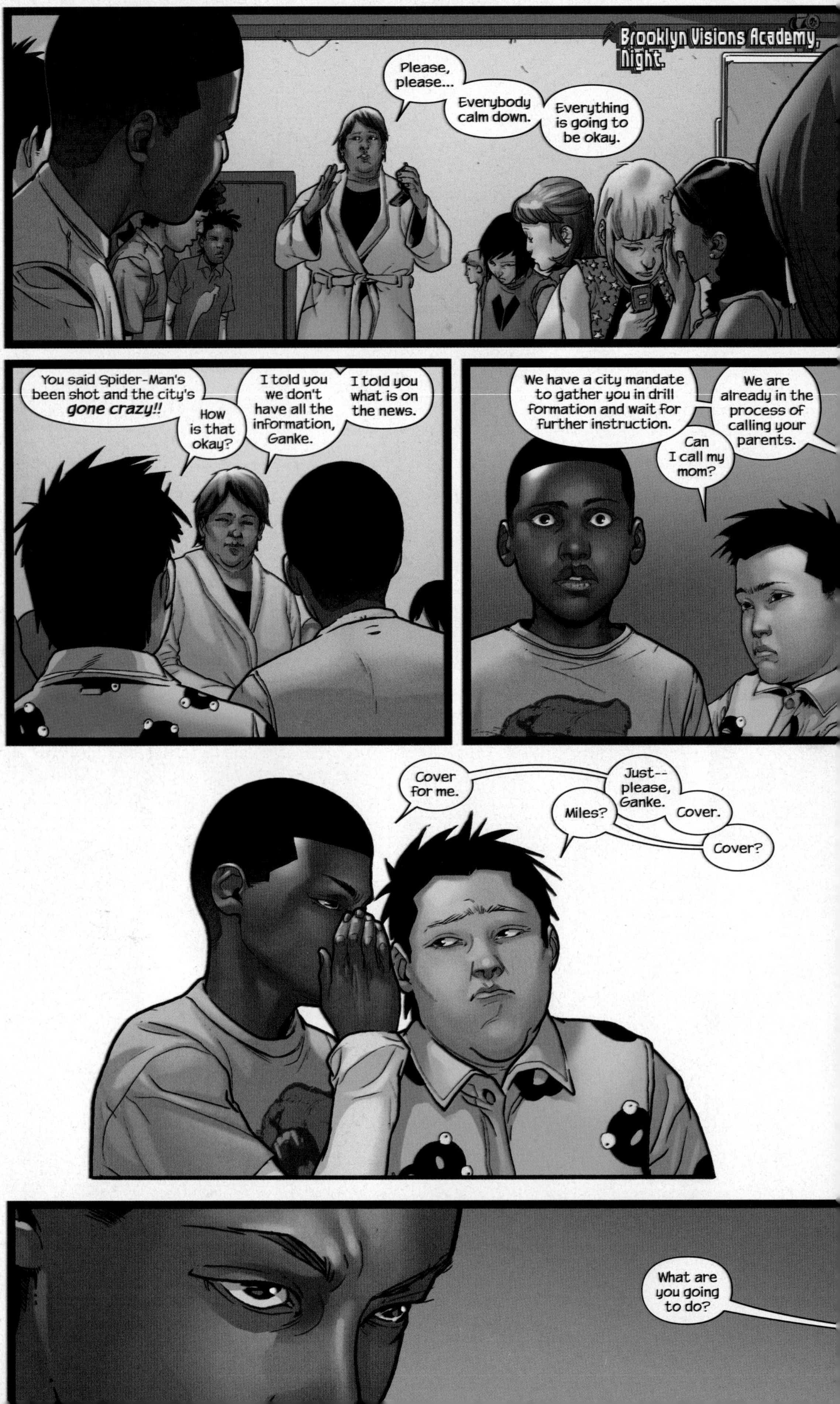
Brooklyn Visions Academy, Night.
Please, please...
Everybody calm down.
Everything is going to be okay.
You said Spider-Man's been shot and the city's gone crazy!!
How is that okay?
I told you we don't have all the information, Ganke.
I told you what is on the news.
We have a city mandate to gather you in drill formation and wait for further instruction.
We are already in the process of calling your parents.
Can I call my mom?
Cover for me.
Miles?
Just-- please, Ganke.
Cover.
Cover?
What are you going to do?

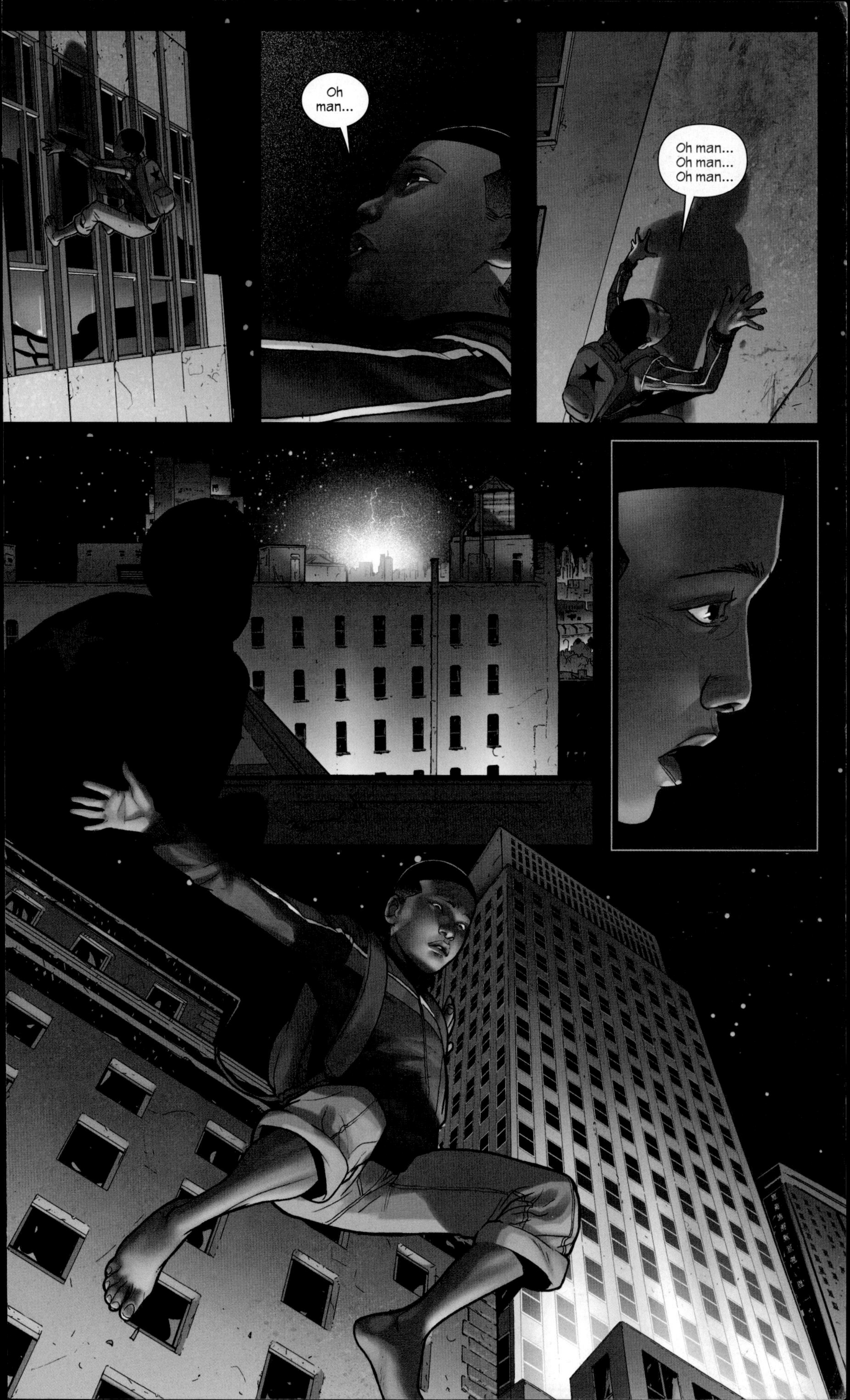
Oh man...
Oh man...
Oh man...
Oh man...

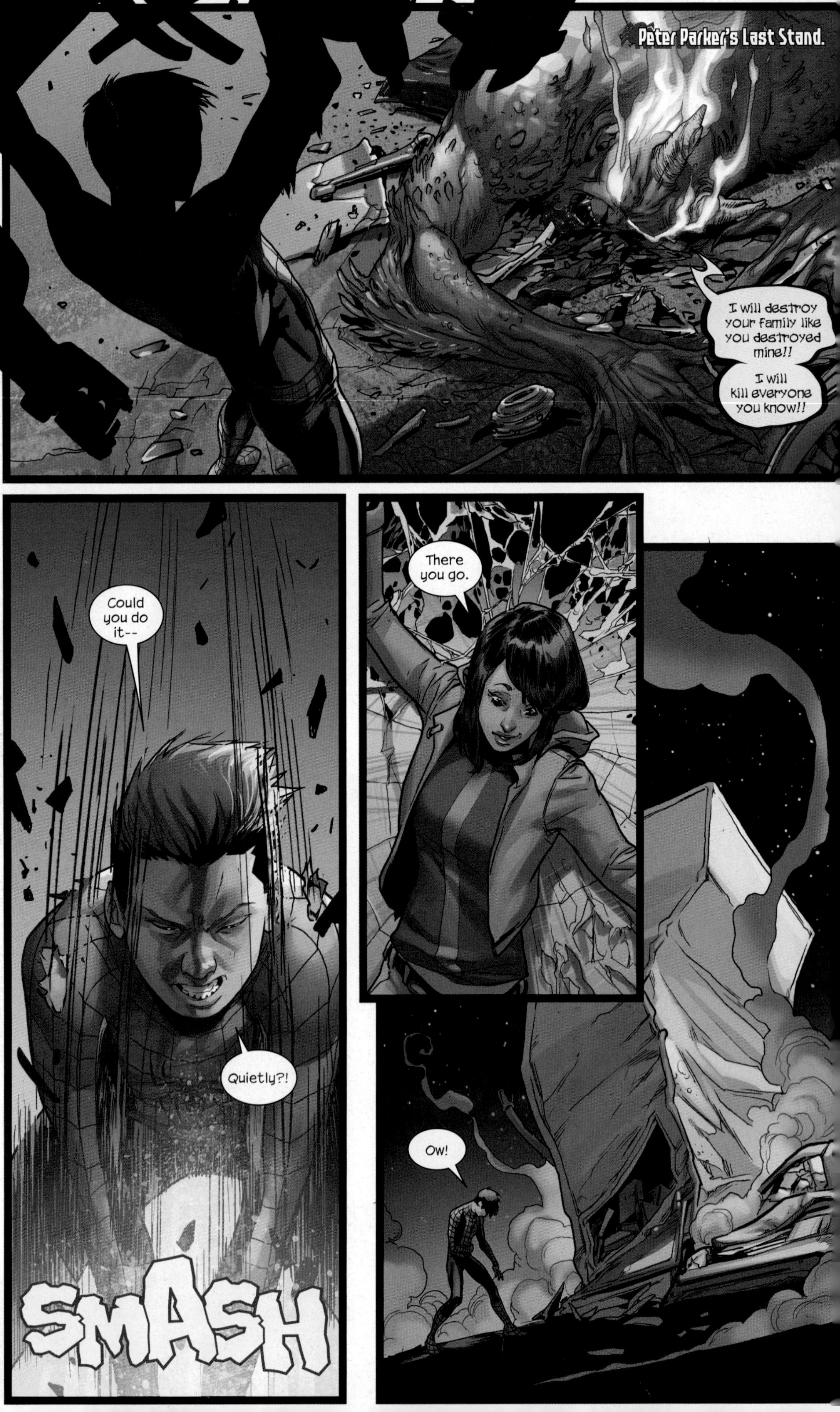
Peter Parker's Last Stand.
I will destroy your family like you destroyed mine!!
I will kill everyone you know!!
Could you do it--
Quietly?!
SMASH
There you go.
Ow!

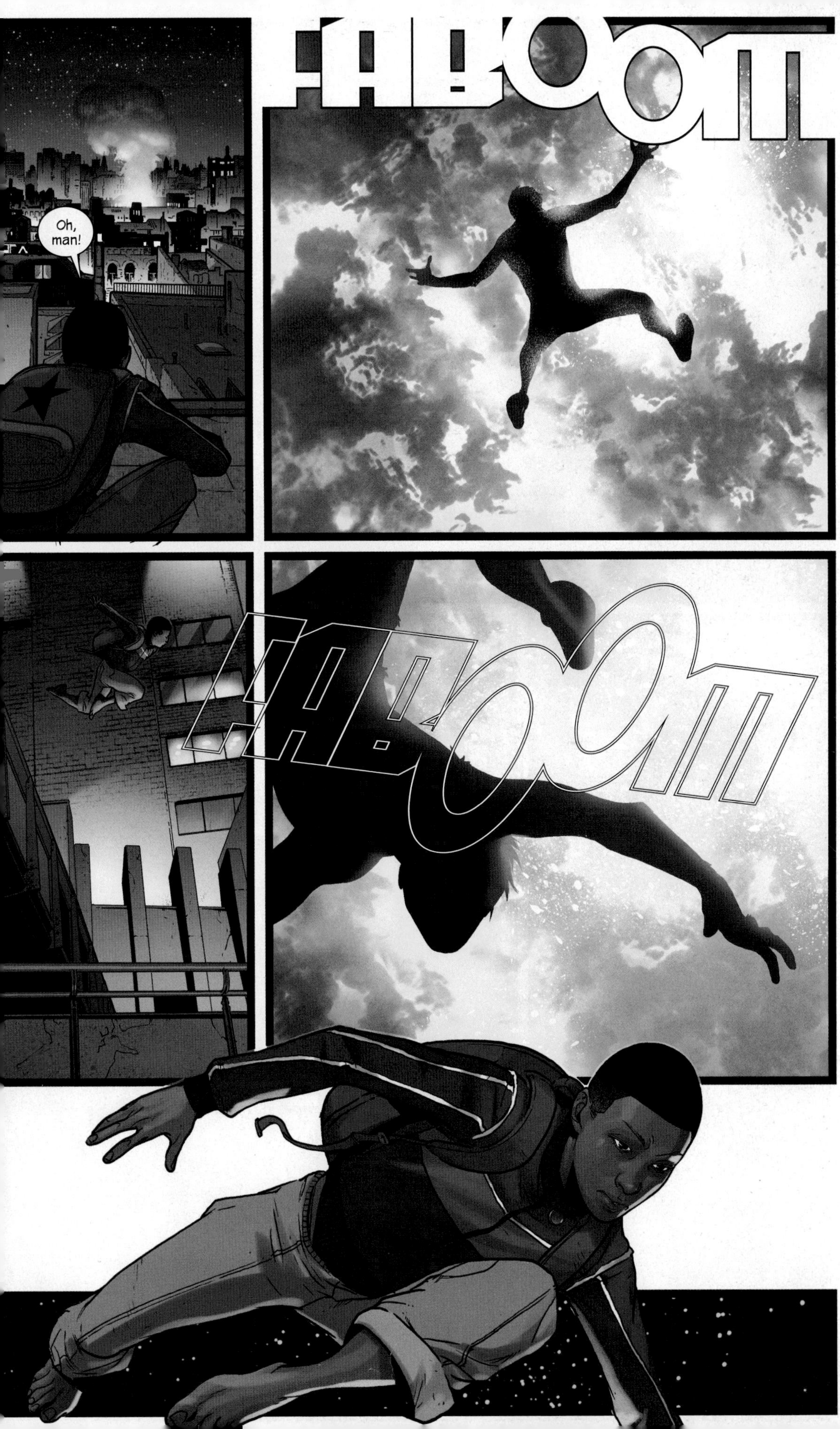
Oh, man!
KABOOM
KABOOM

It's okay.

I--I did it.

Just--just hold on. The ambulance is--

Don't you see...it's okay.

I did it.

I couldn't save him.

Uncle Ben. I couldn't save him...

No matter what I did.

But I saved you.

I did it.

I did...

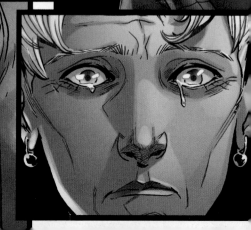

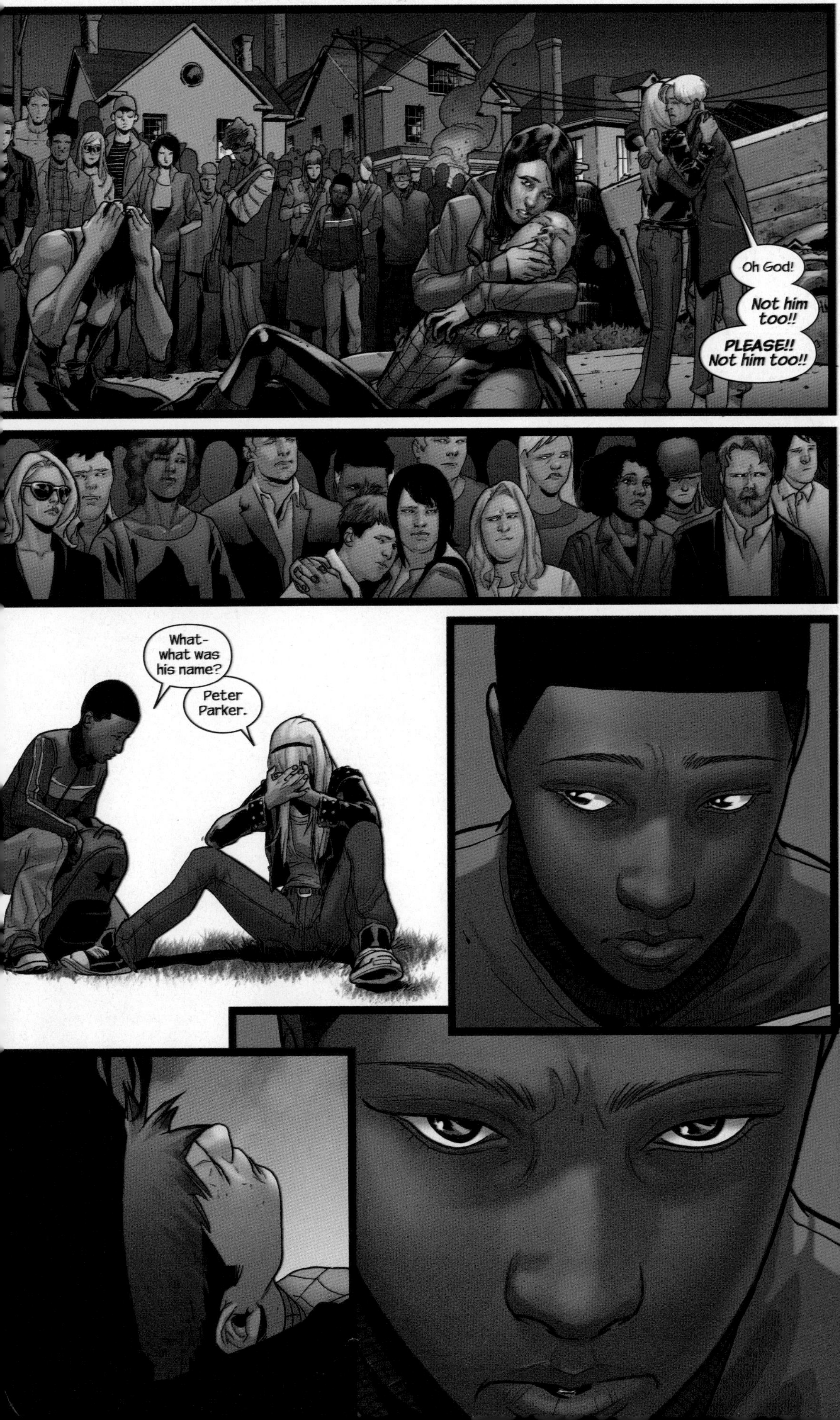
Oh God!
Not him too!!
PLEASE!! Not him too!!
What- what was his name?
Peter Parker.

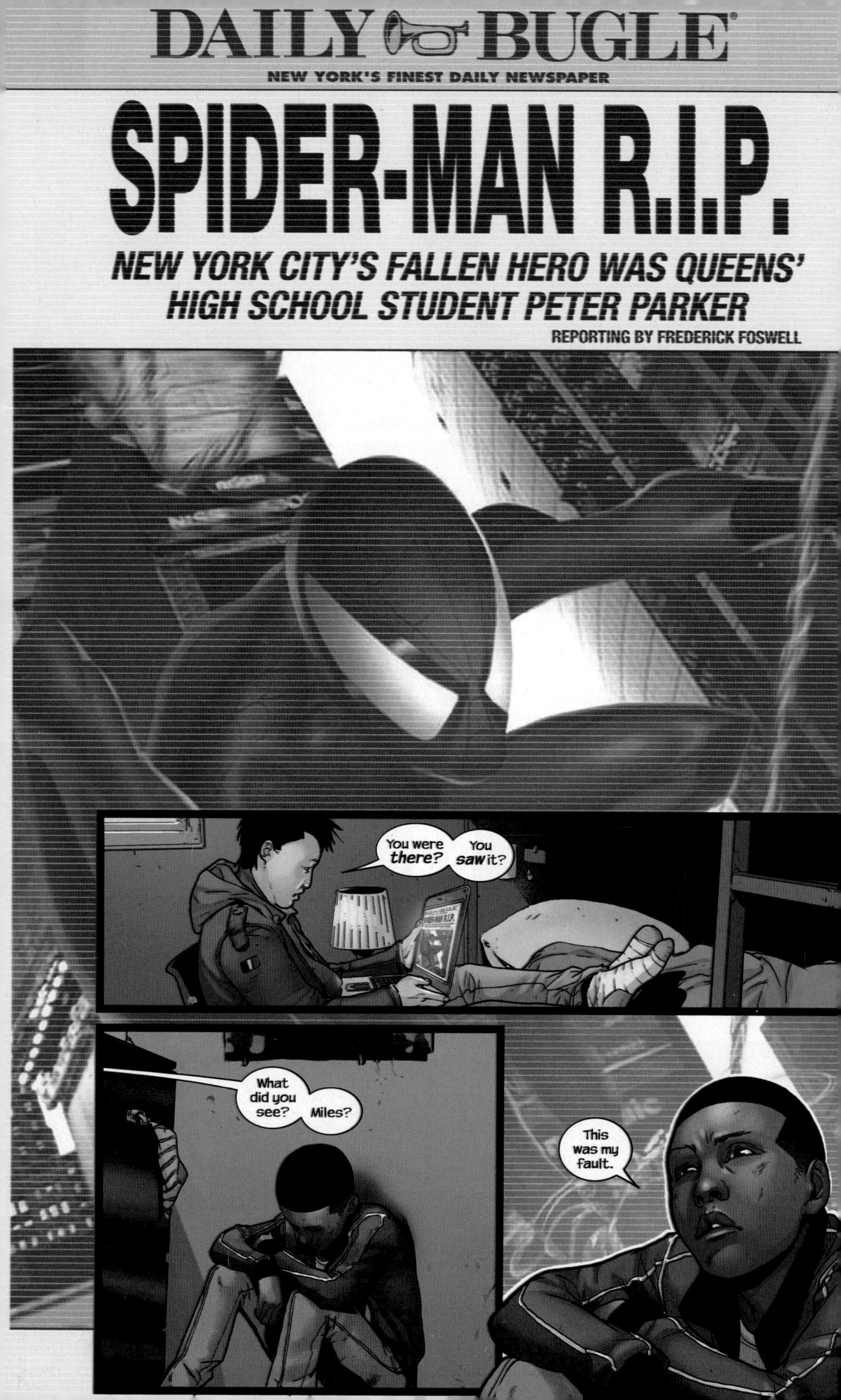

DAILY BUGLE
NEW YORK'S FINEST DAILY NEWSPAPER
SPIDER-MAN R.I.P.
NEW YORK CITY'S FALLEN HERO WAS QUEENS' HIGH SCHOOL STUDENT PETER PARKER
REPORTING BY FREDERICK FOSWELL
You were *there?*
You *saw* it?
What did you see?
Miles?
This was my fault.

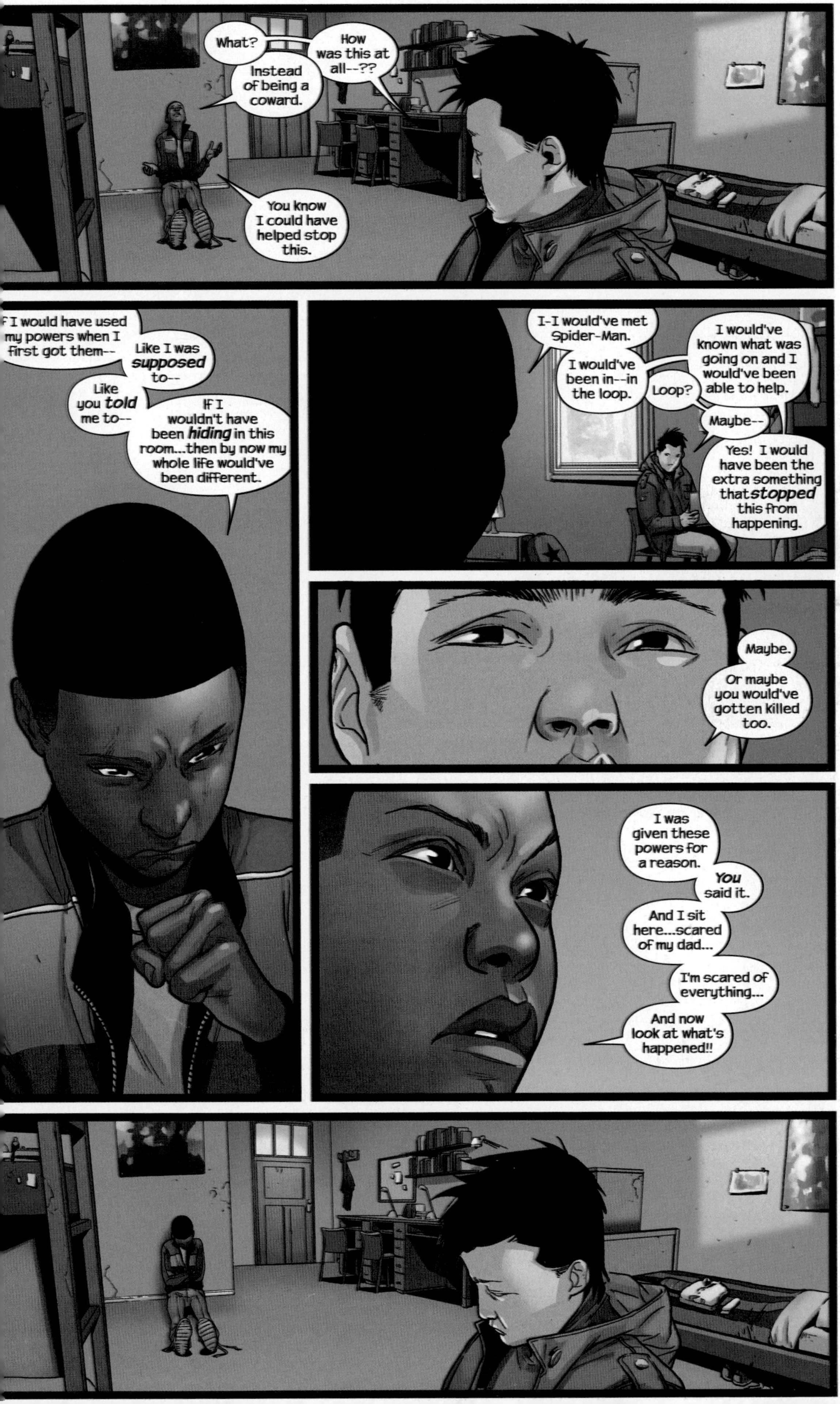

What?
How was this at all--??
Instead of being a coward.
You know I could have helped stop this.
If I would have used my powers when I first got them--
Like I was *supposed* to--
Like you *told* me to--
If I wouldn't have been *hiding* in this room...then by now my whole life would've been different.
I-I would've met Spider-Man.
I would've been in--in the loop.
I would've known what was going on and I would've been able to help.
Loop?
Maybe--
Yes! I would have been the extra something that *stopped* this from happening.
Maybe.
Or maybe you would've gotten killed too.
I was given these powers for a reason.
You said it.
And I sit here...scared of my dad...
I'm scared of everything...
And now look at what's happened!!

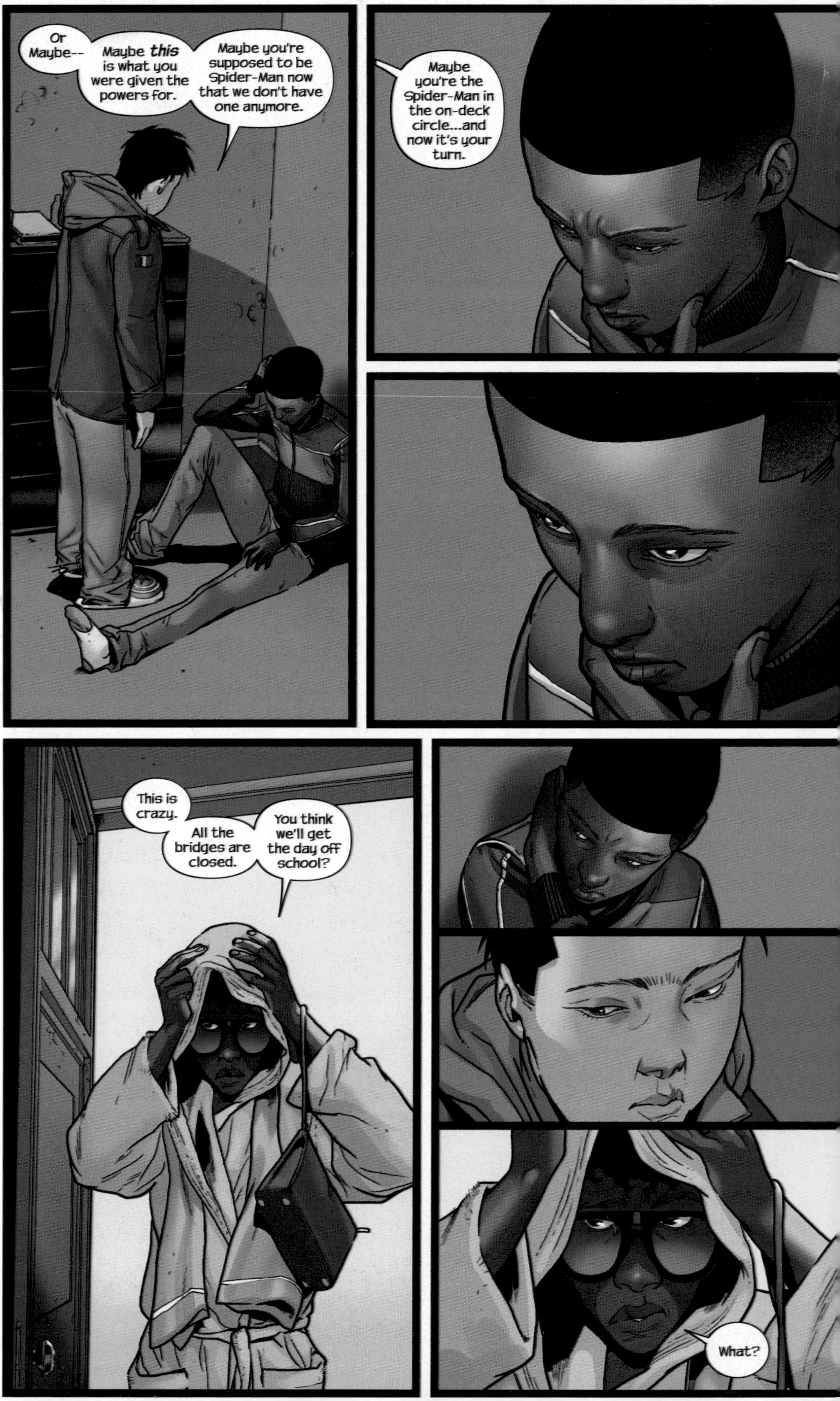
Or Maybe--
Maybe *this* is what you were given the powers for.
Maybe you're supposed to be Spider-Man now that we don't have one anymore.
Maybe you're the Spider-Man in the on-deck circle...and now it's your turn.
This is crazy.
All the bridges are closed.
You think we'll get the day off school?
What?

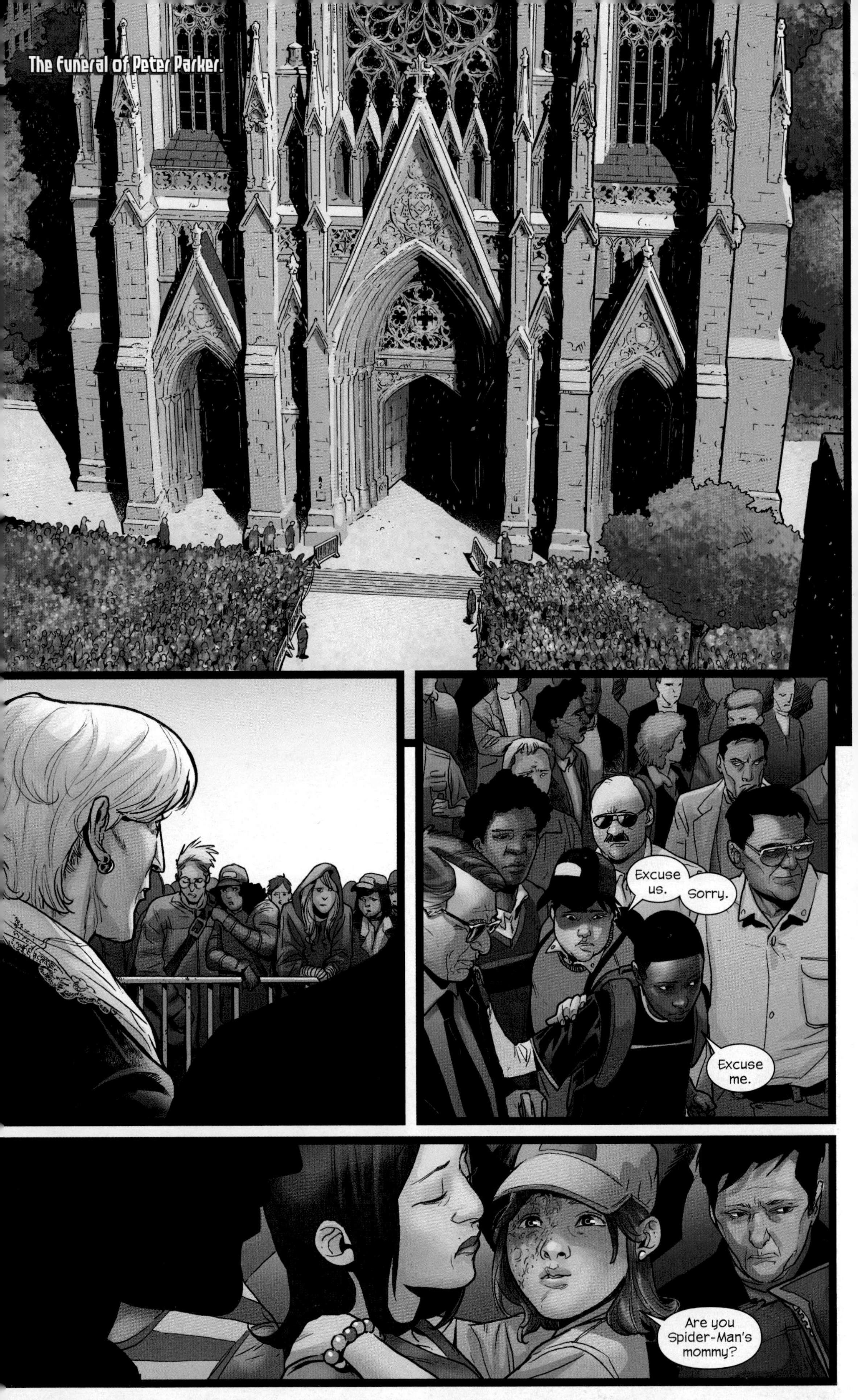
The Funeral of Peter Parker.
Excuse us.
Sorry.
Excuse me.
Are you Spider-Man's mommy?

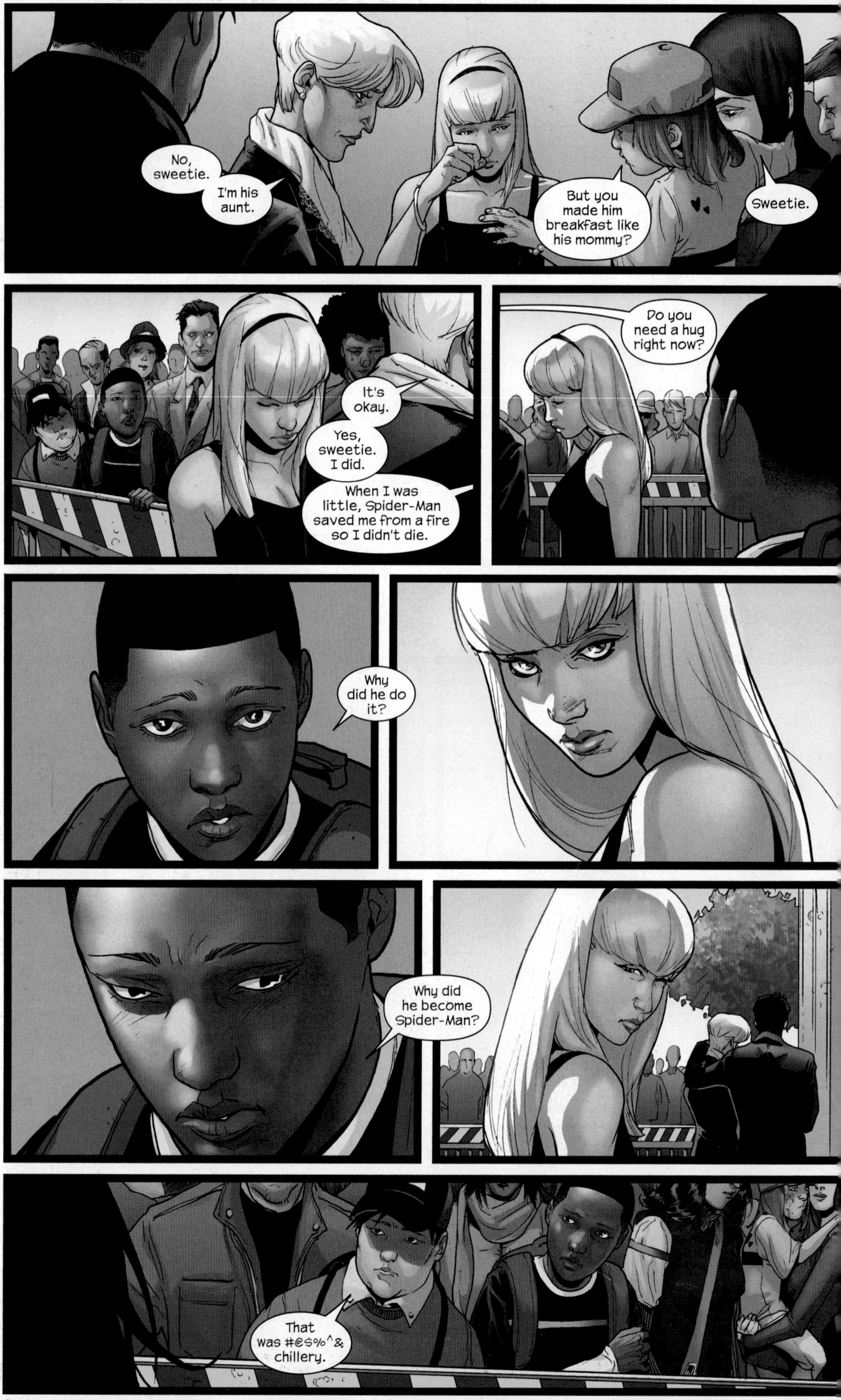
No, sweetie.
I'm his aunt.
But you made him breakfast like his mommy?
Sweetie.
It's okay.
Yes, sweetie. I did.
When I was little, Spider-Man saved me from a fire so I didn't die.
Do you need a hug right now?
Why did he do it?
Why did he become Spider-Man?
That was #@$%^& chillery.

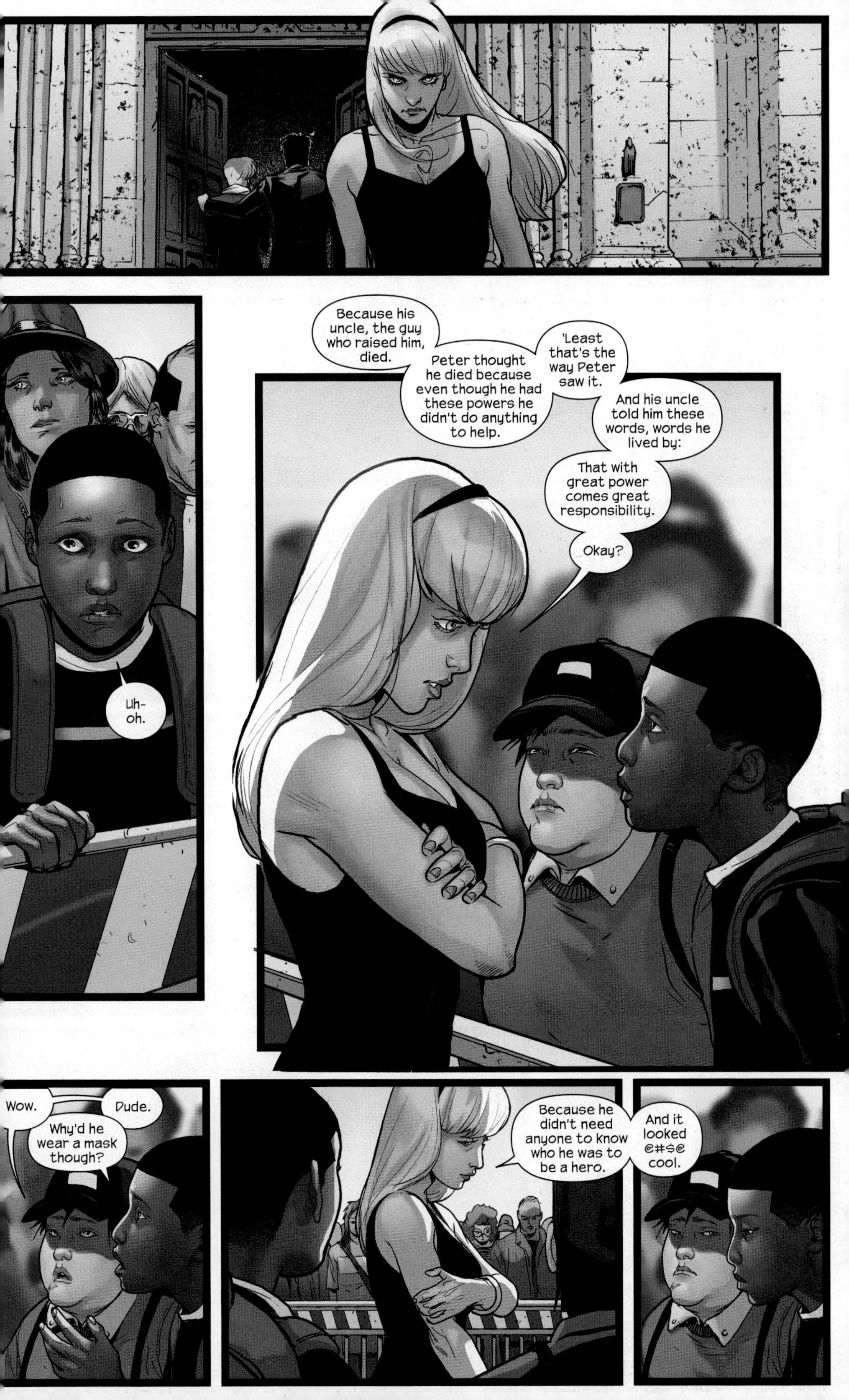

Uh-oh.
Because his uncle, the guy who raised him, died.
Peter thought he died because even though he had these powers he didn't do anything to help.
'Least that's the way Peter saw it.
And his uncle told him these words, words he lived by:
That with great power comes great responsibility.
Okay?
Wow.
Dude.
Why'd he wear a mask though?
Because he didn't need anyone to know who he was to be a hero.
And it looked @#$@ cool.

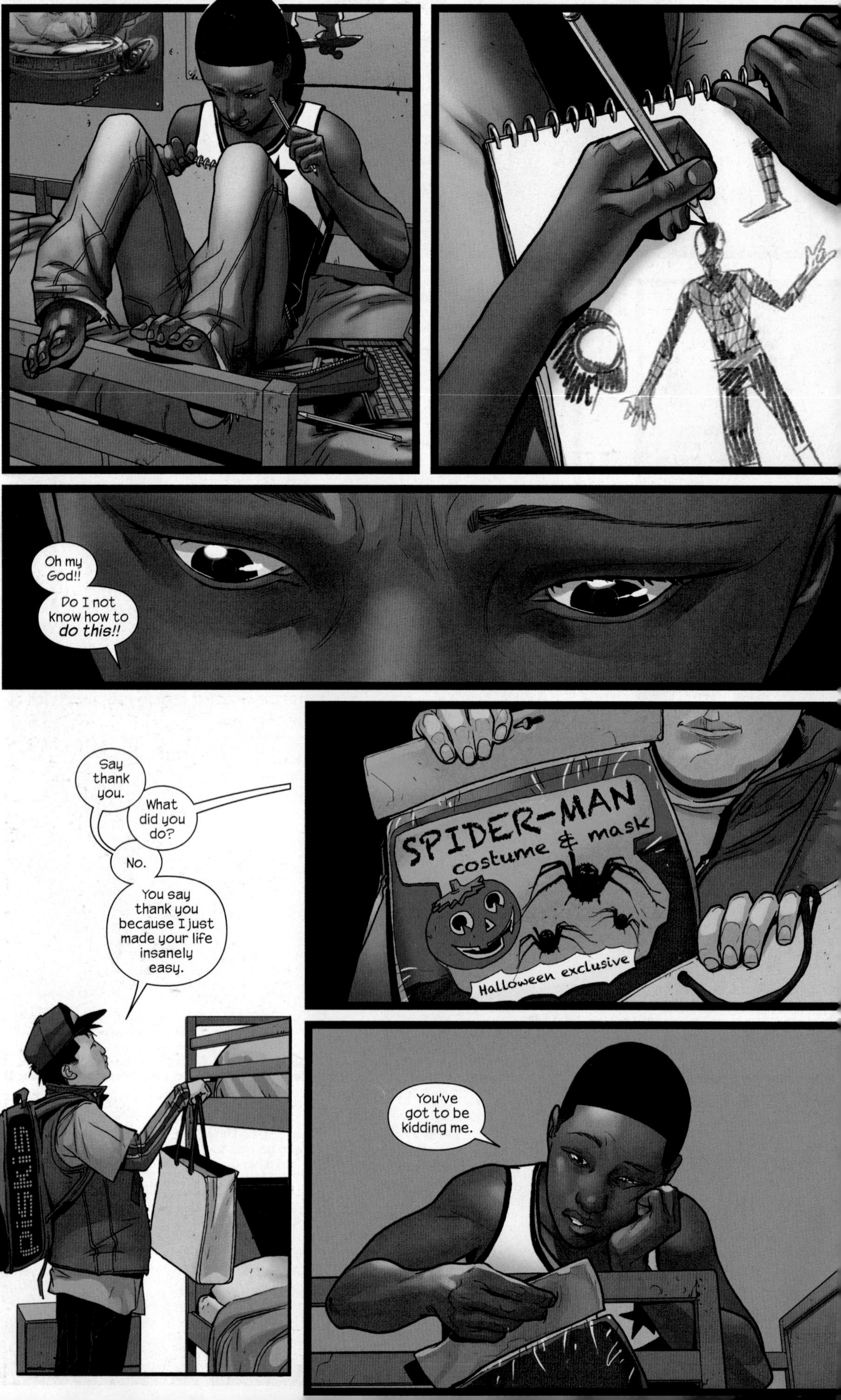
Oh my God!!
Do I not know how to do this!!
SPIDER-MAN costume & mask
Halloween exclusive
Say thank you.
What did you do?
No.
You say thank you because I just made your life insanely easy.
You've got to be kidding me.

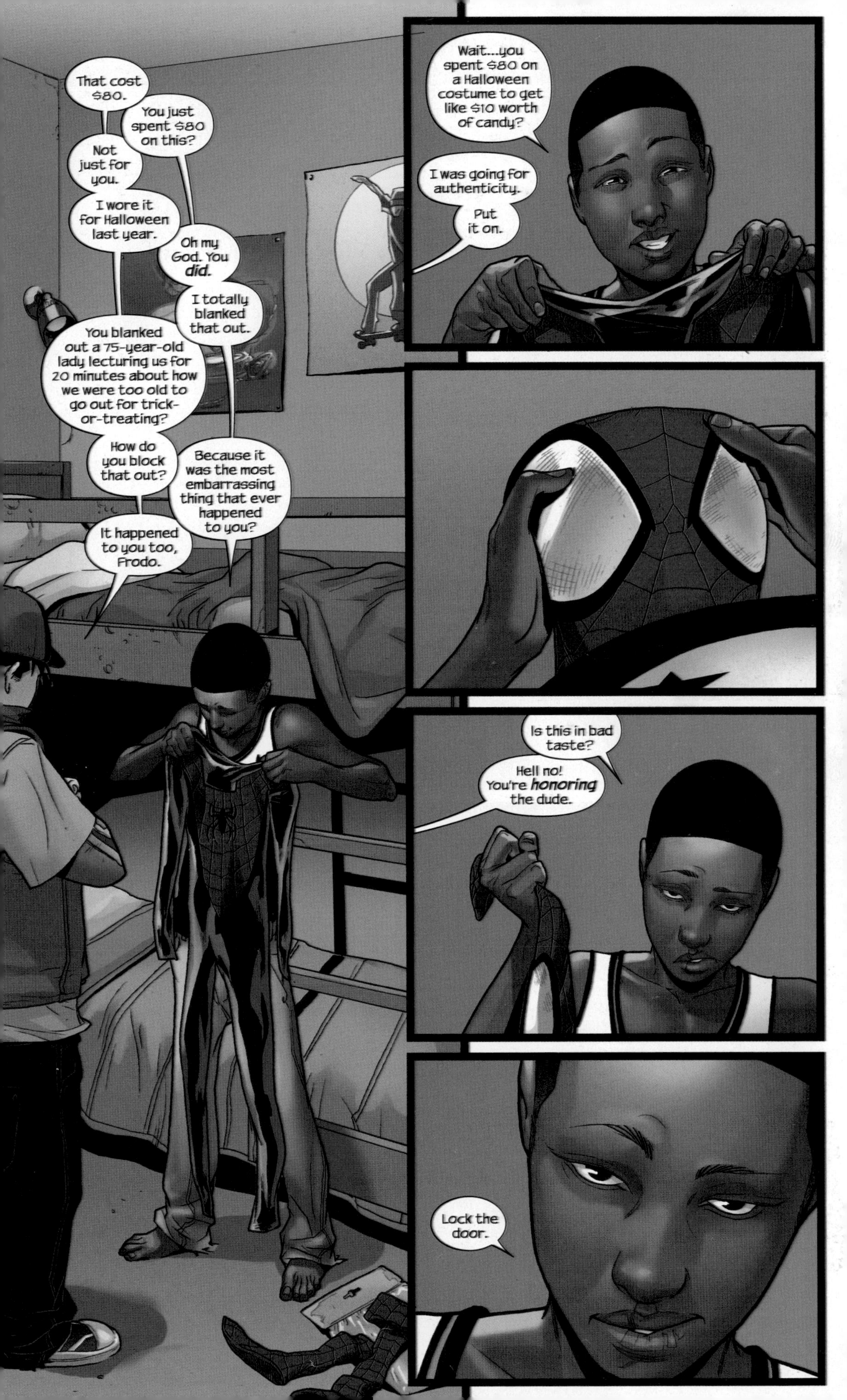
That cost $80.
You just spent $80 on this?
Not just for you.
I wore it for Halloween last year.
Oh my God. You *did*.
I totally blanked that out.
You blanked out a 75-year-old lady lecturing us for 20 minutes about how we were too old to go out for trick-or-treating?
How do you block that out?
Because it was the most embarrassing thing that ever happened to you?
It happened to you too, Frodo.
Wait...you spent $80 on a Halloween costume to get like $10 worth of candy?
I was going for authenticity.
Put it on.
Is this in bad taste?
Hell no! You're *honoring* the dude.
Lock the door.

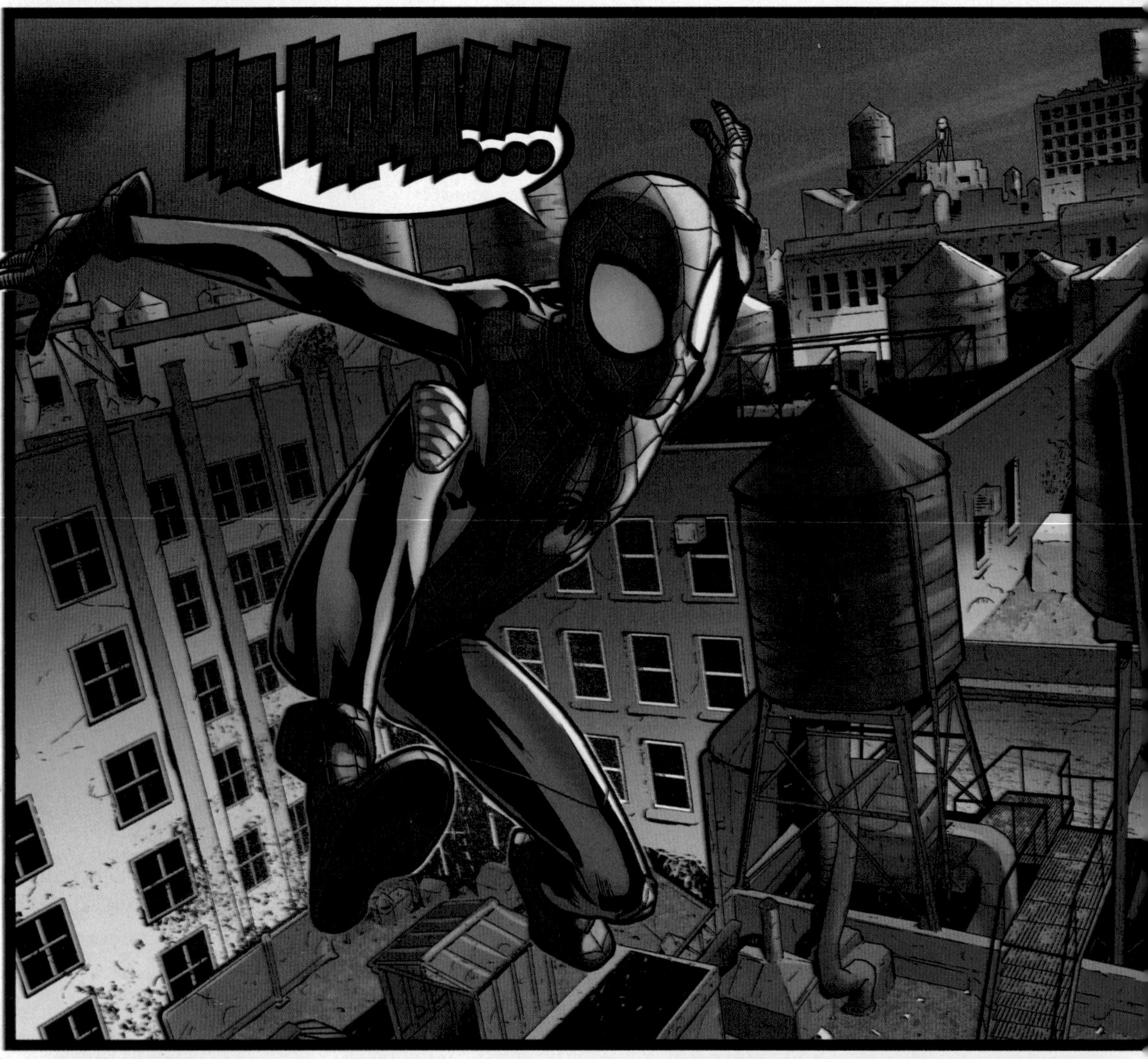
HA HA HA!!! HA...

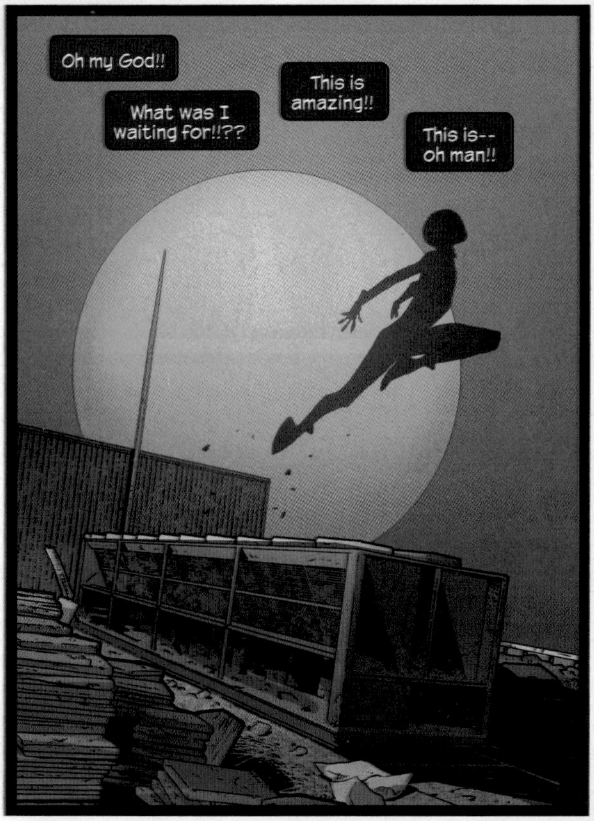
Oh my God!!
What was I waiting for!!??
This is amazing!!
This is-- oh man!!

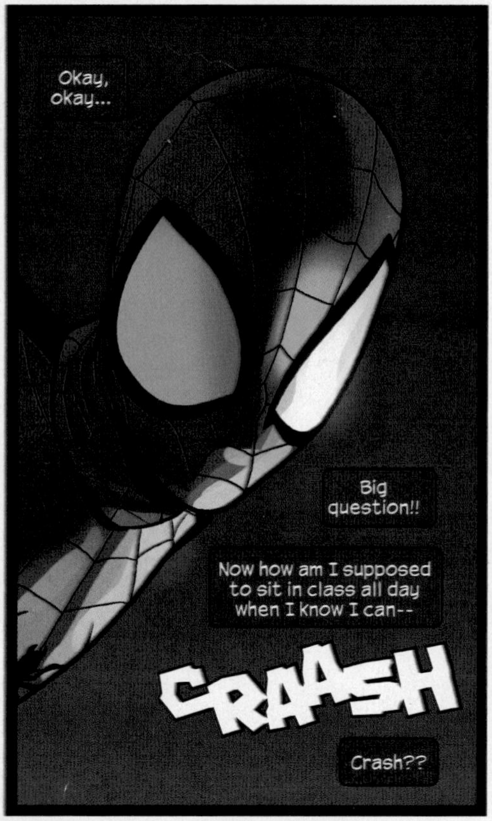
Okay, okay...
Big question!!
Now how am I supposed to sit in class all day when I know I can--
CRAASH
Crash??

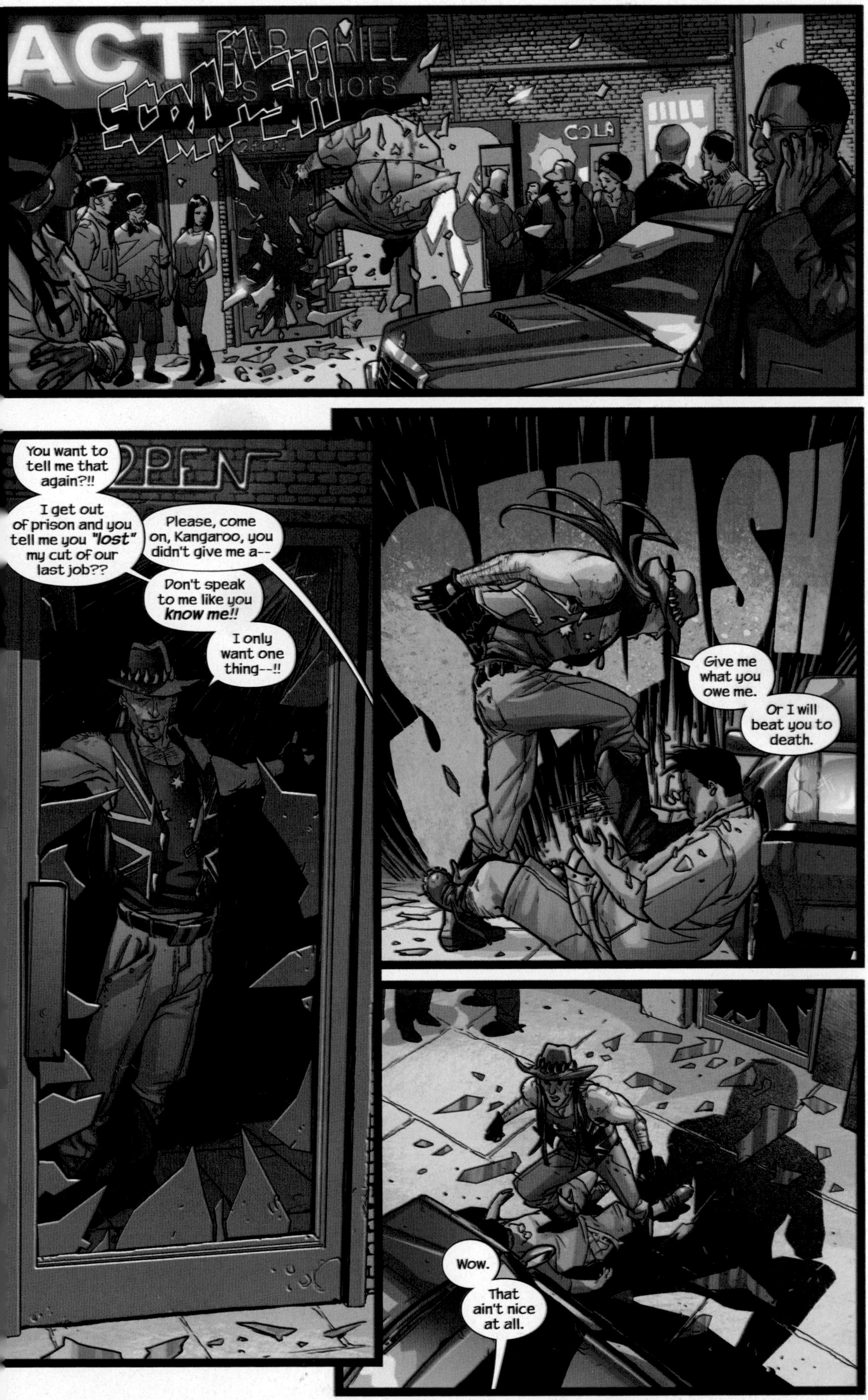
ACT
BAR GRILL
liquors
SCRASH
COLA
2PEN
You want to tell me that again?!!
I get out of prison and you tell me you "lost" my cut of our last job??
Please, come on, Kangaroo, you didn't give me a--
Don't speak to me like you know me!!
I only want one thing--!!
Give me what you owe me.
Or I will beat you to death.
Wow.
That ain't nice at all.

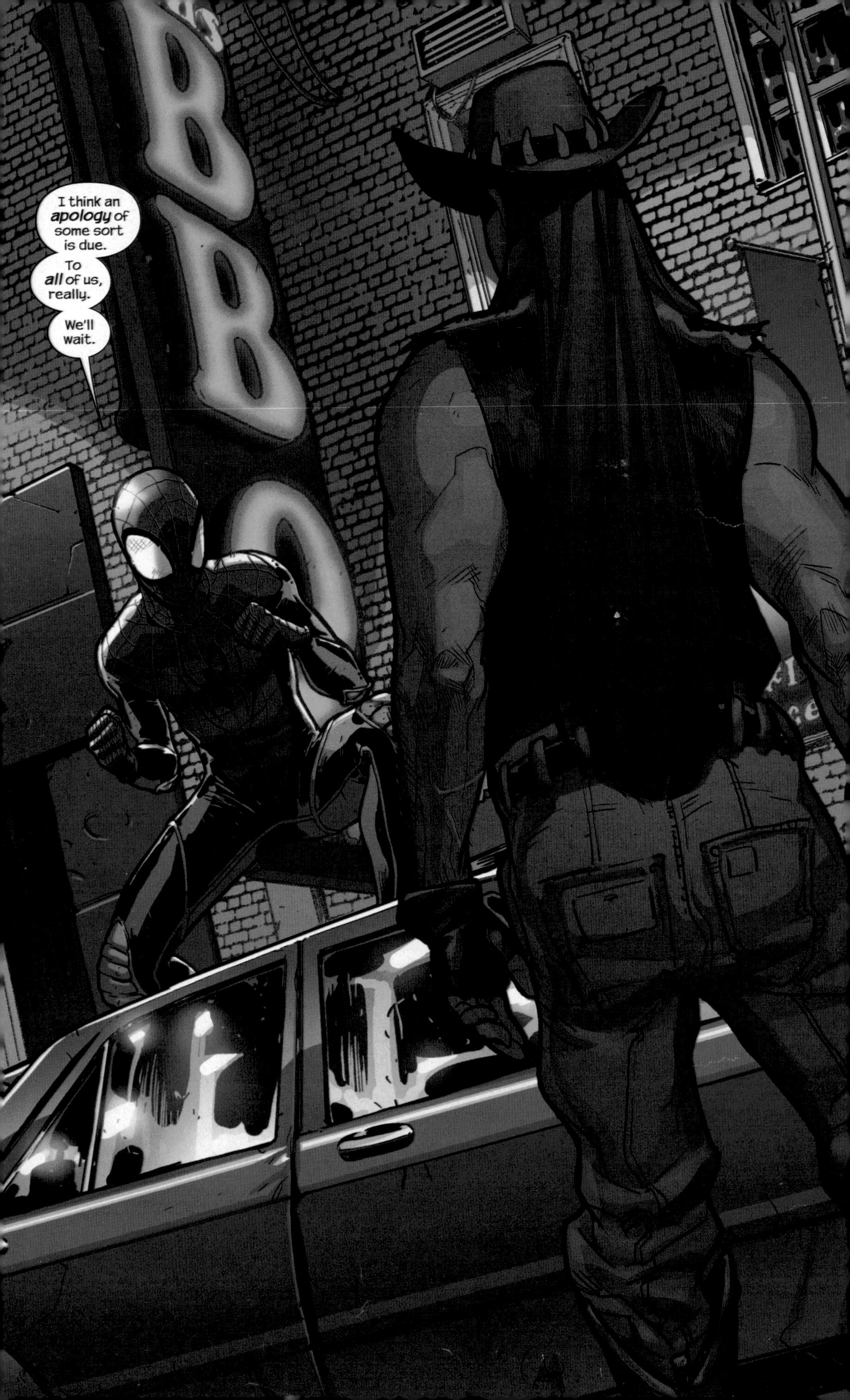
I think an *apology* of some sort is due.
To *all* of us, really.
We'll wait.

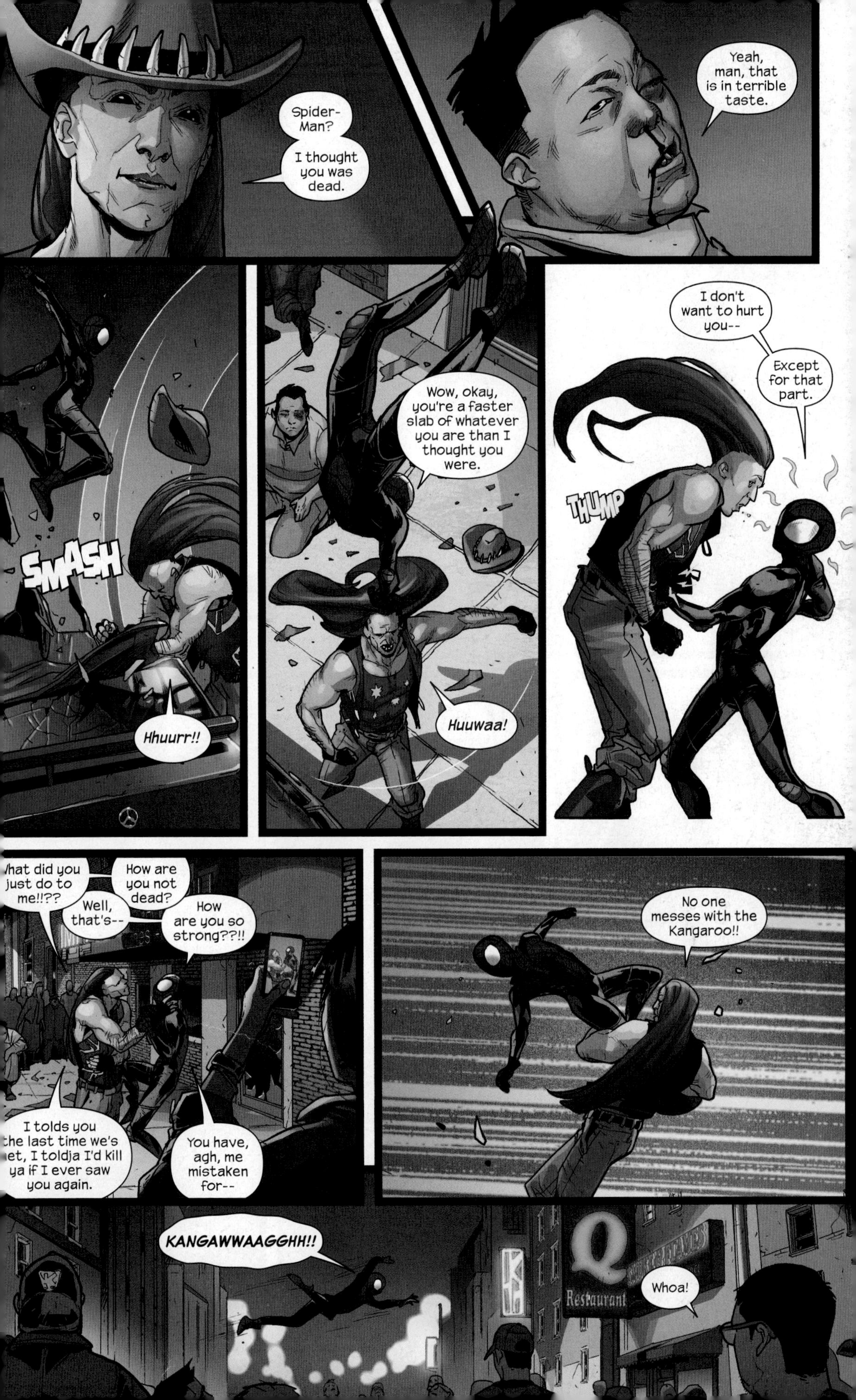
Spider-Man?
I thought you was dead.
Yeah, man, that is in terrible taste.
SMASH
Hhuurr!!
Wow, okay, you're a faster slab of whatever you are than I thought you were.
Huuwaa!
I don't want to hurt you--
Except for that part.
THUMP
hat did you just do to me!!??
How are you not dead?
Well, that's--
How are you so strong??!!
I tolds you the last time we's et, I toldja I'd kill ya if I ever saw you again.
You have, agh, me mistaken for--
No one messes with the Kangaroo!!
KANGAWWAAGGHH!!
Restaurant
Whoa!

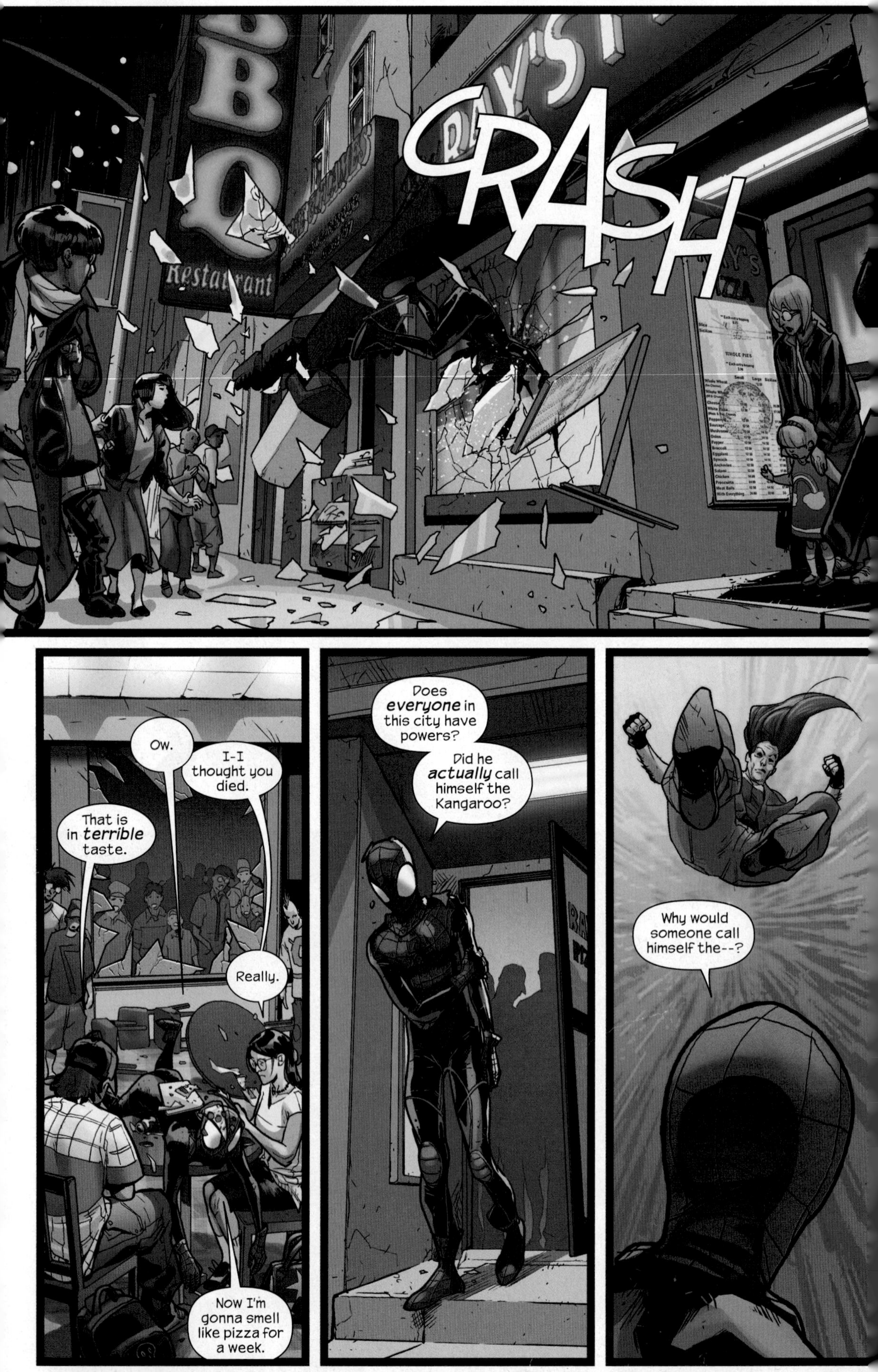

Restaurant
CRASH
Ow.
I-I thought you died.
That is in *terrible* taste.
Really.
Now I'm gonna smell like pizza for a week.
Does *everyone* in this city have powers?
Did he *actually* call himself the Kangaroo?
Why would someone call himself the--?

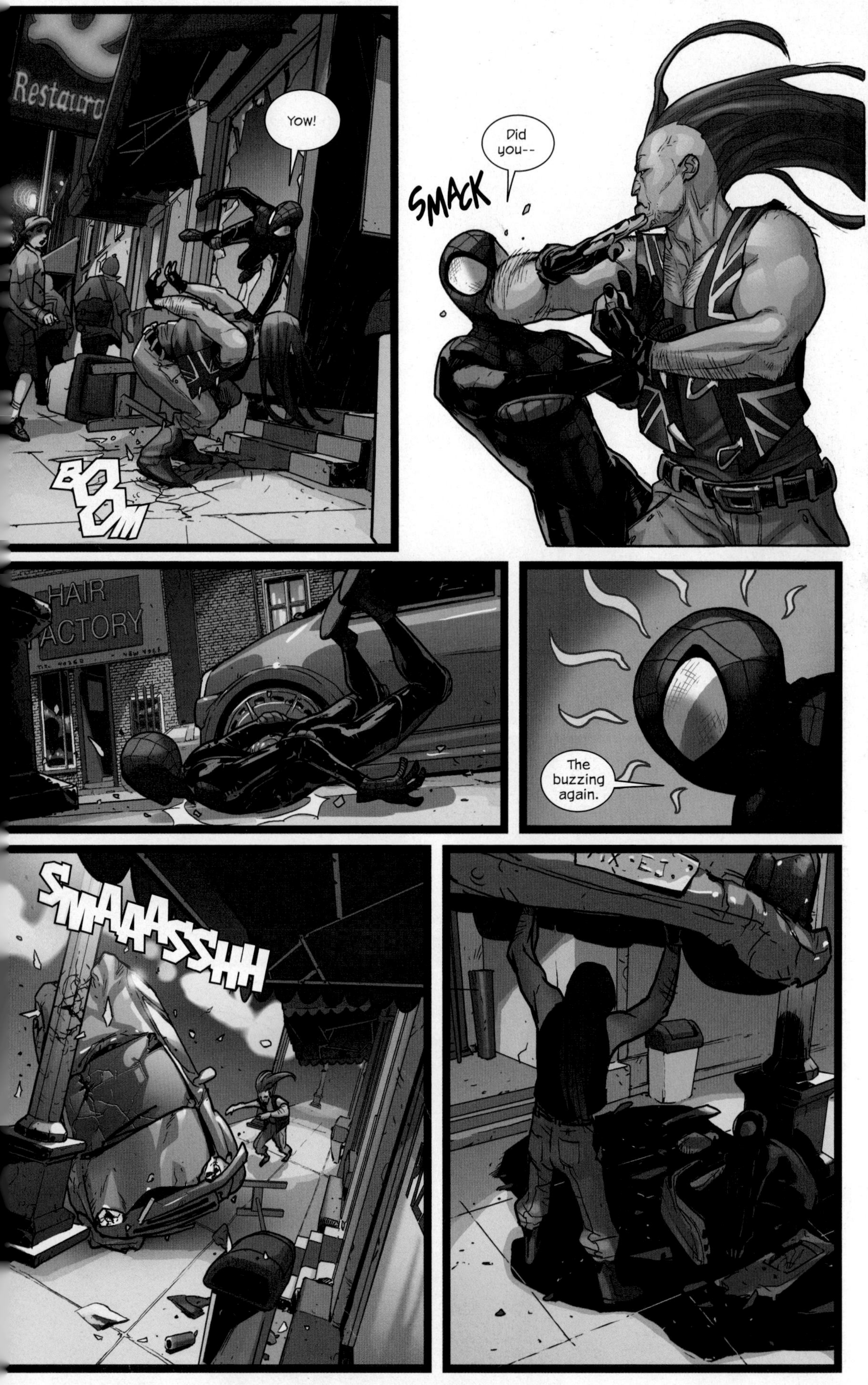
Restaura
YOW!
BOOM
Did you--
SMACK
HAIR
ACTORY
The buzzing again.
SMAAASSHH

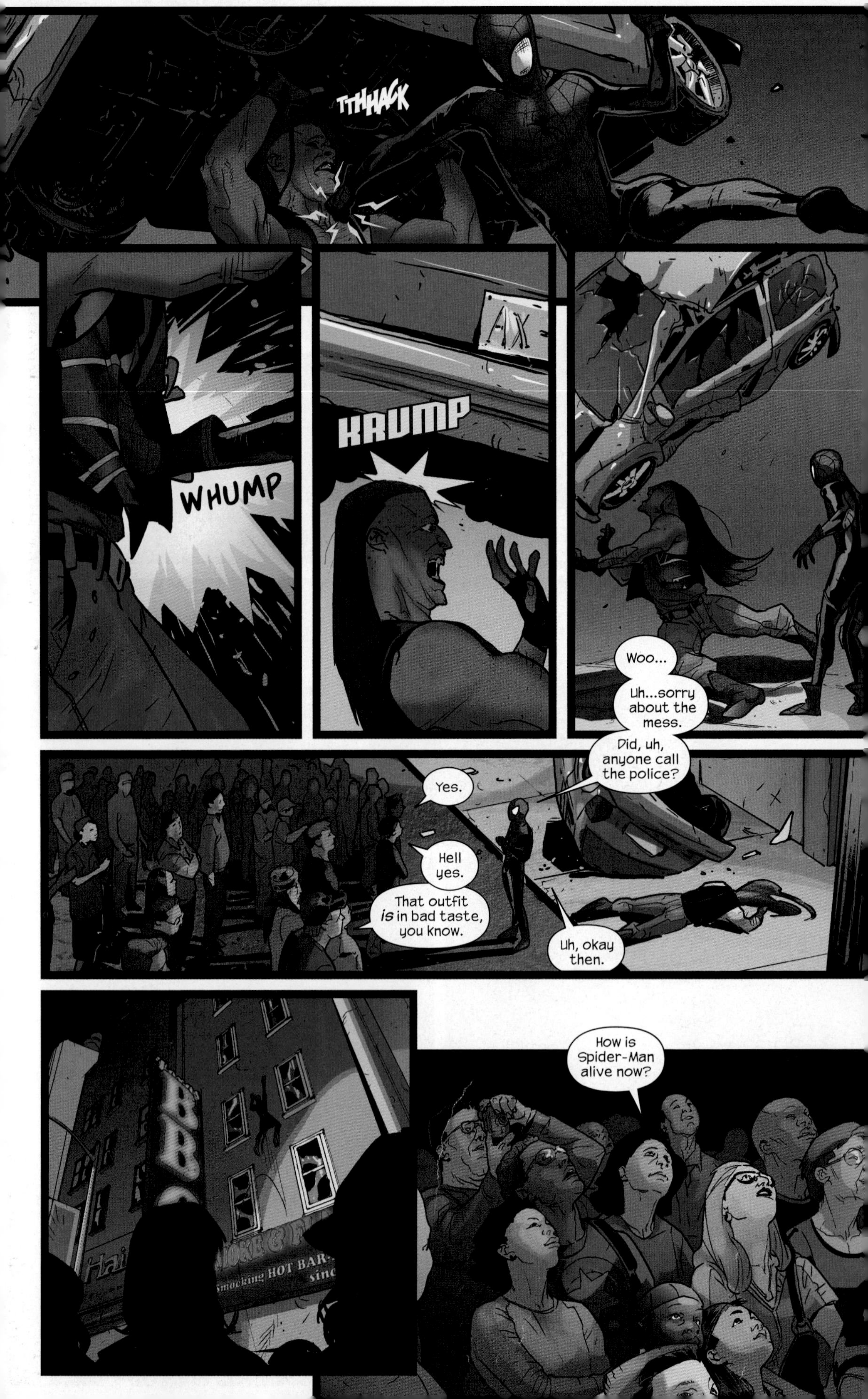
TTHHACK
WHUMP
KRUMP
Woo...
Uh...sorry about the mess.
Did, uh, anyone call the police?
Yes.
Hell yes.
That outfit *is* in bad taste, you know.
Uh, okay then.
How is Spider-Man alive now?
BBQ
SMOKE & F
Smoking HOT BAR-

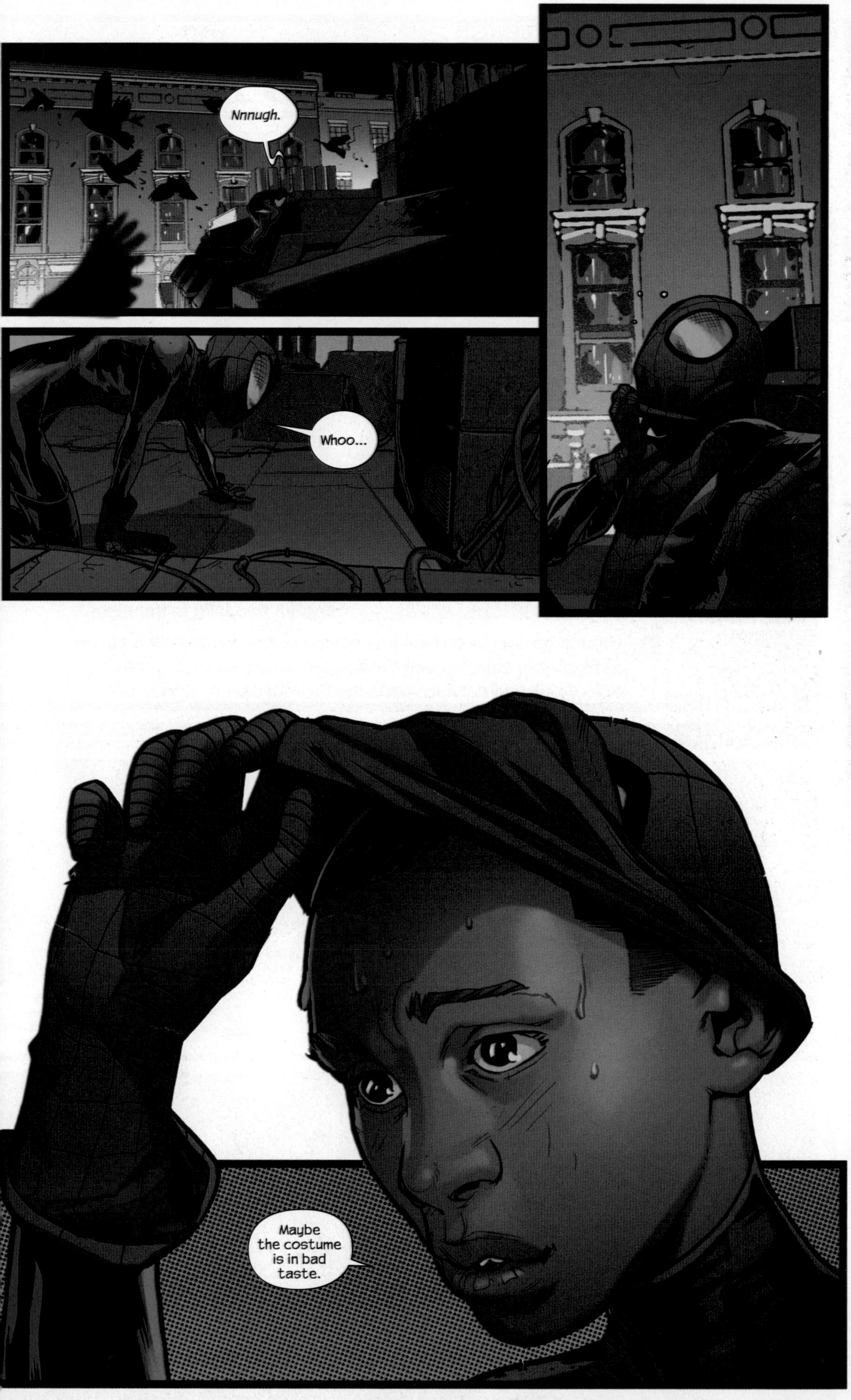
Nnnugh.
Whoo...
Maybe the costume is in bad taste.

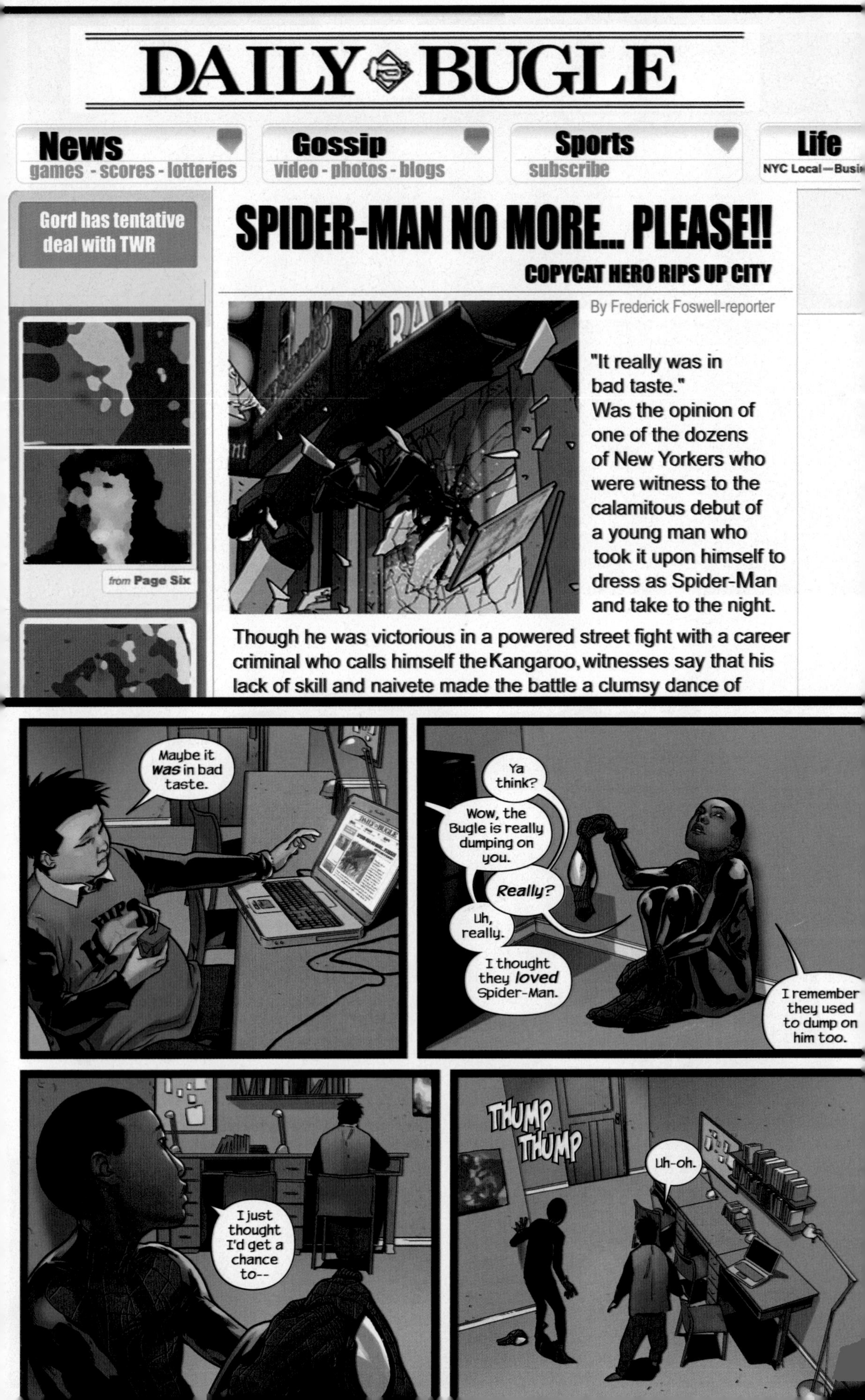
DAILY BUGLE
News
games - scores - lotteries
Gossip
video - photos - blogs
Sports
subscribe
Life
NYC Local—Busi
Gord has tentative deal with TWR
from Page Six
SPIDER-MAN NO MORE... PLEASE!!
COPYCAT HERO RIPS UP CITY
By Frederick Foswell-reporter
"It really was in bad taste."
Was the opinion of one of the dozens of New Yorkers who were witness to the calamitous debut of a young man who took it upon himself to dress as Spider-Man and take to the night.
Though he was victorious in a powered street fight with a career criminal who calls himself the Kangaroo, witnesses say that his lack of skill and naivete made the battle a clumsy dance of
Maybe it *was* in bad taste.
Ya think?
Wow, the Bugle is really dumping on you.
Really?
Uh, really.
I thought they *loved* Spider-Man.
I remember they used to dump on him too.
I just thought I'd get a chance to--
THUMP THUMP
Uh-oh.

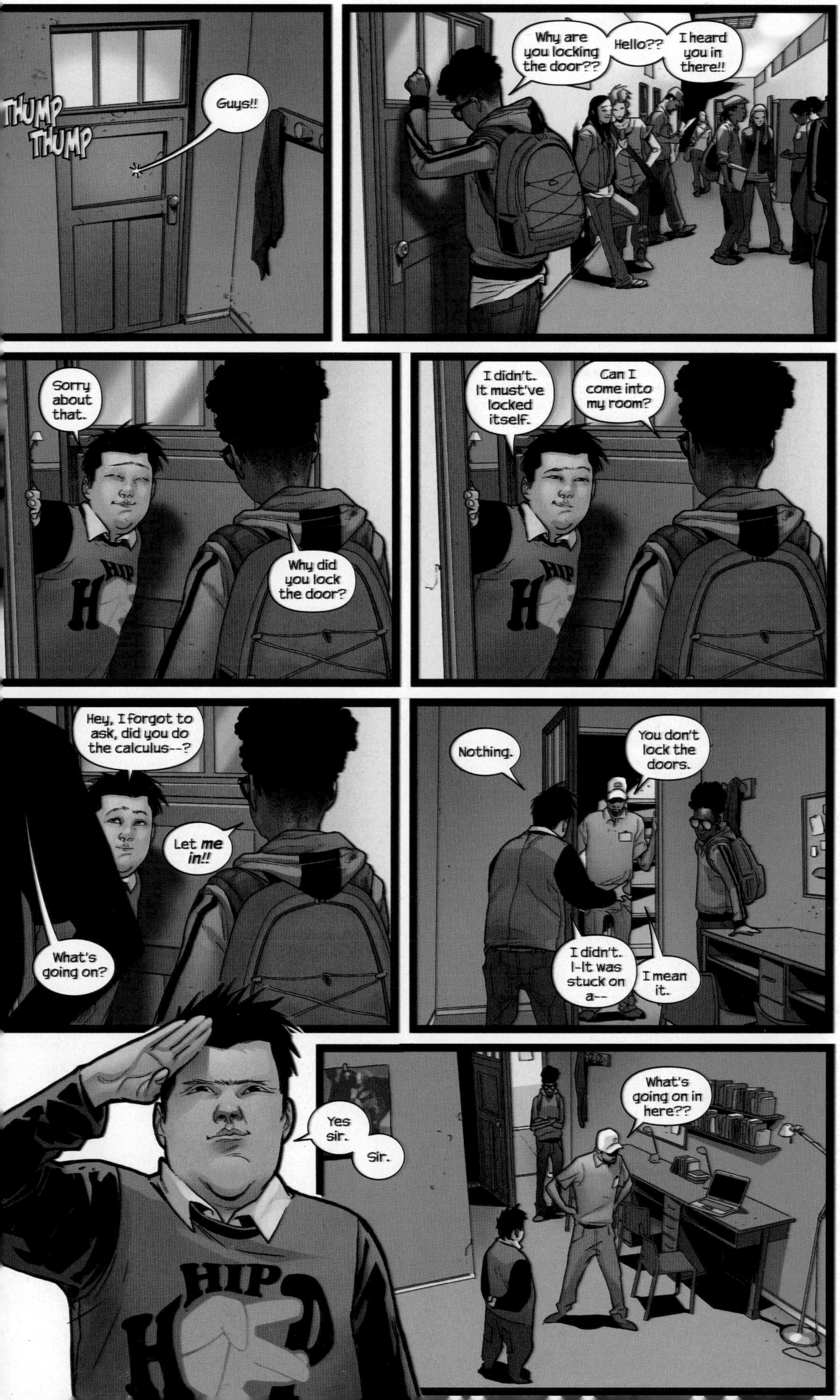
THUMP
THUMP
Guys!!
Why are you locking the door??
Hello??
I heard you in there!!
Sorry about that.
Why did you lock the door?
I didn't. It must've locked itself.
Can I come into my room?
Hey, I forgot to ask, did you do the calculus--?
Let me in!!
What's going on?
Nothing.
You don't lock the doors.
I didn't. I-It was stuck on a--
I mean it.
Yes sir.
Sir.
What's going on in here??

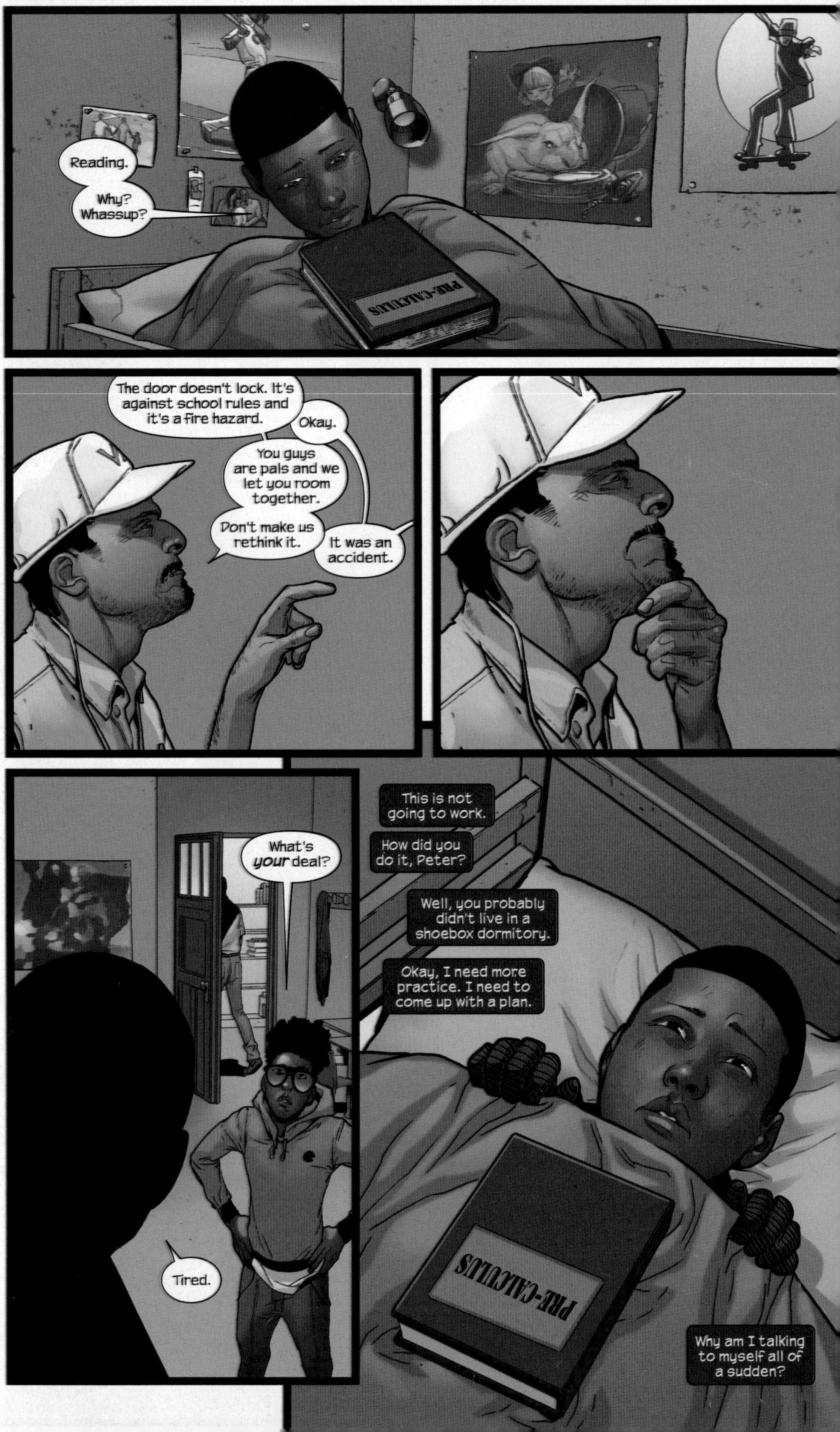
Reading.
Why? Whassup?
The door doesn't lock. It's against school rules and it's a fire hazard.
Okay.
You guys are pals and we let you room together.
Don't make us rethink it.
It was an accident.
What's *your* deal?
Tired.
This is not going to work.
How did you do it, Peter?
Well, you probably didn't live in a shoebox dormitory.
Okay, I need more practice. I need to come up with a plan.
Why am I talking to myself all of a sudden?
PRE-CALCULUS

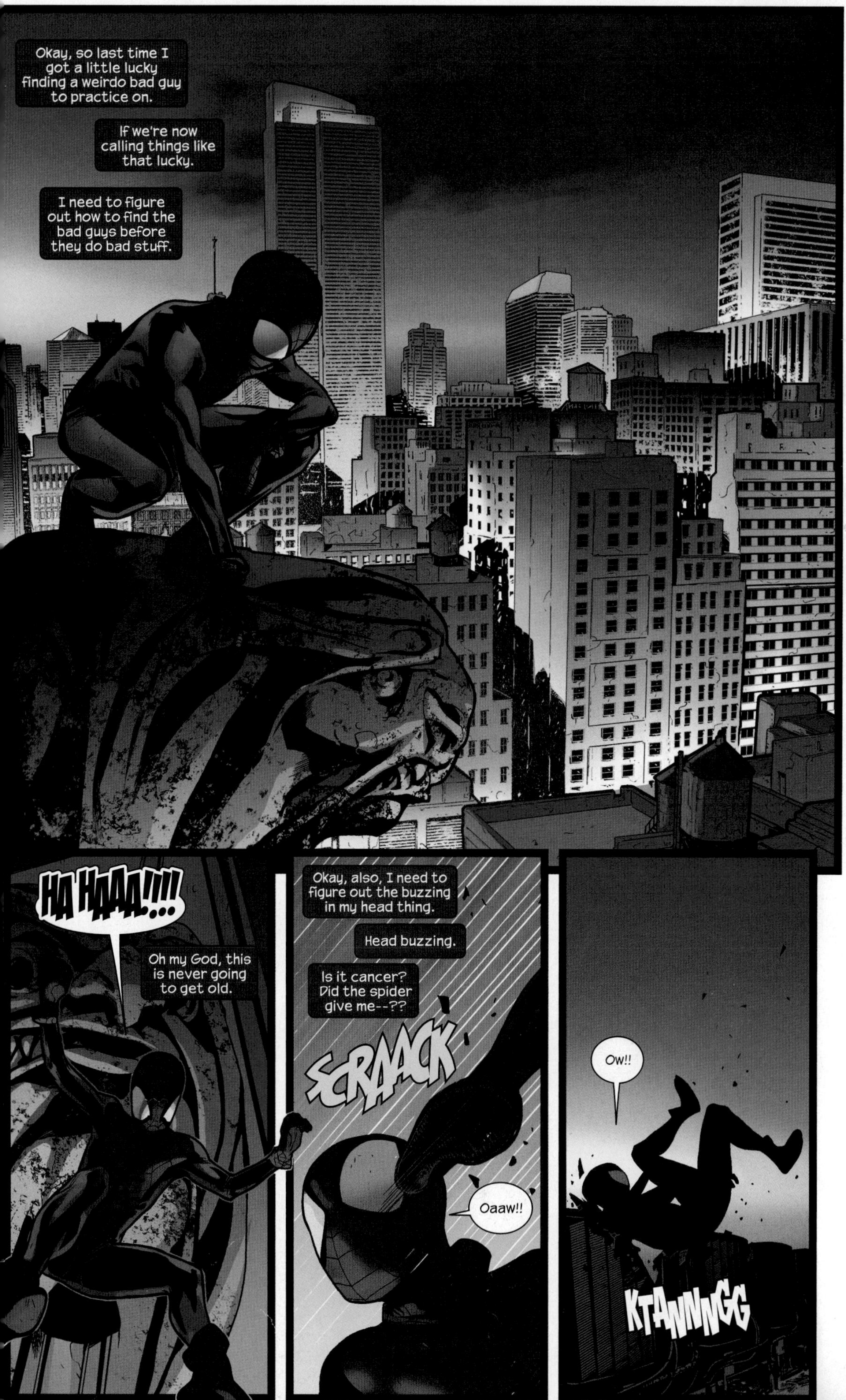
Okay, so last time I got a little lucky finding a weirdo bad guy to practice on.
If we're now calling things like that lucky.
I need to figure out how to find the bad guys before they do bad stuff.
HA HAAA!!!!...
Oh my God, this is never going to get old.
Okay, also, I need to figure out the buzzing in my head thing.
Head buzzing.
Is it cancer? Did the spider give me--??
SCRAACK
Oaaw!!
Ow!!
KTANNNGG

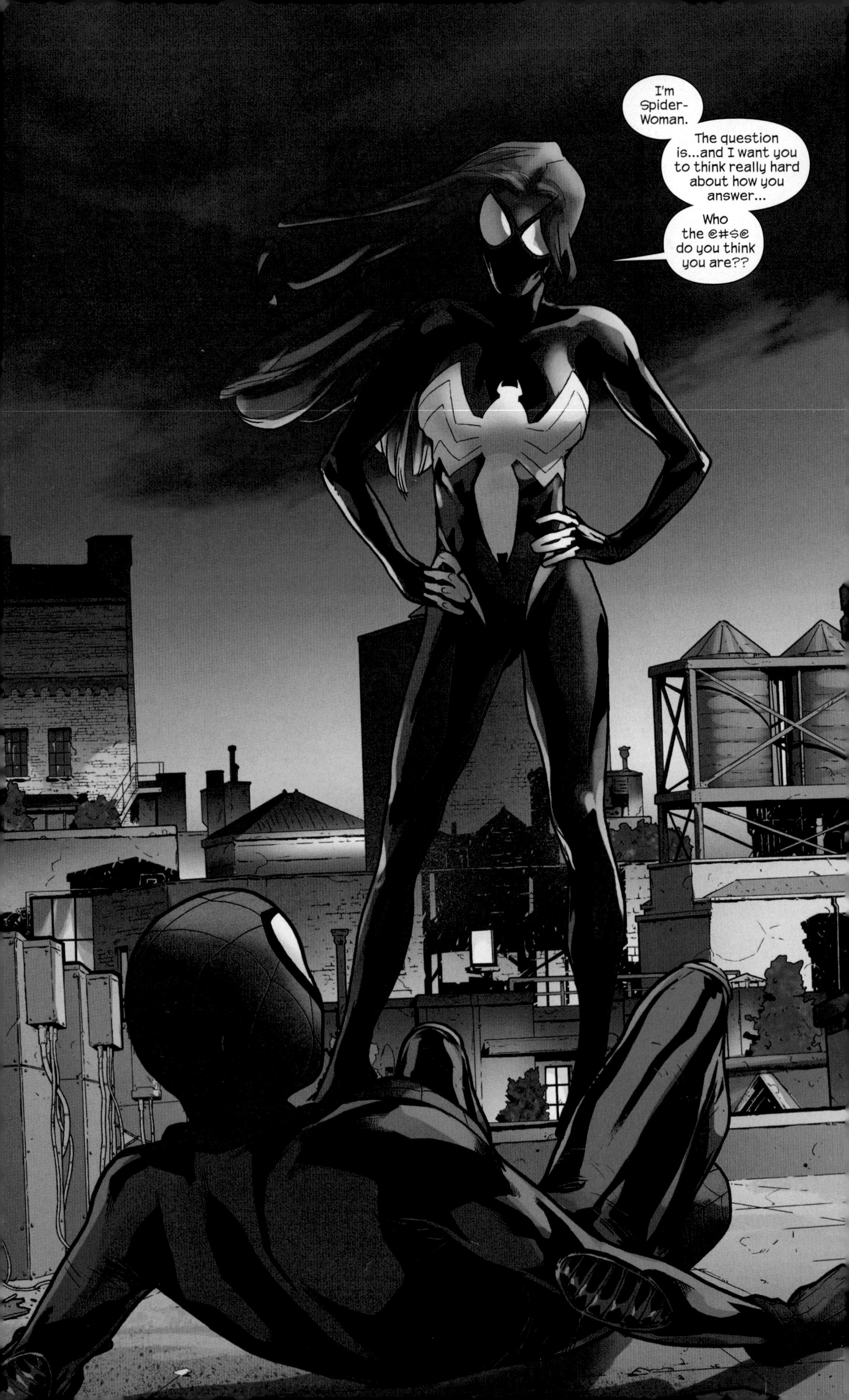
I'm Spider-Woman.
The question is...and I want you to think really hard about how you answer...
Who the @#$@ do you think you are??

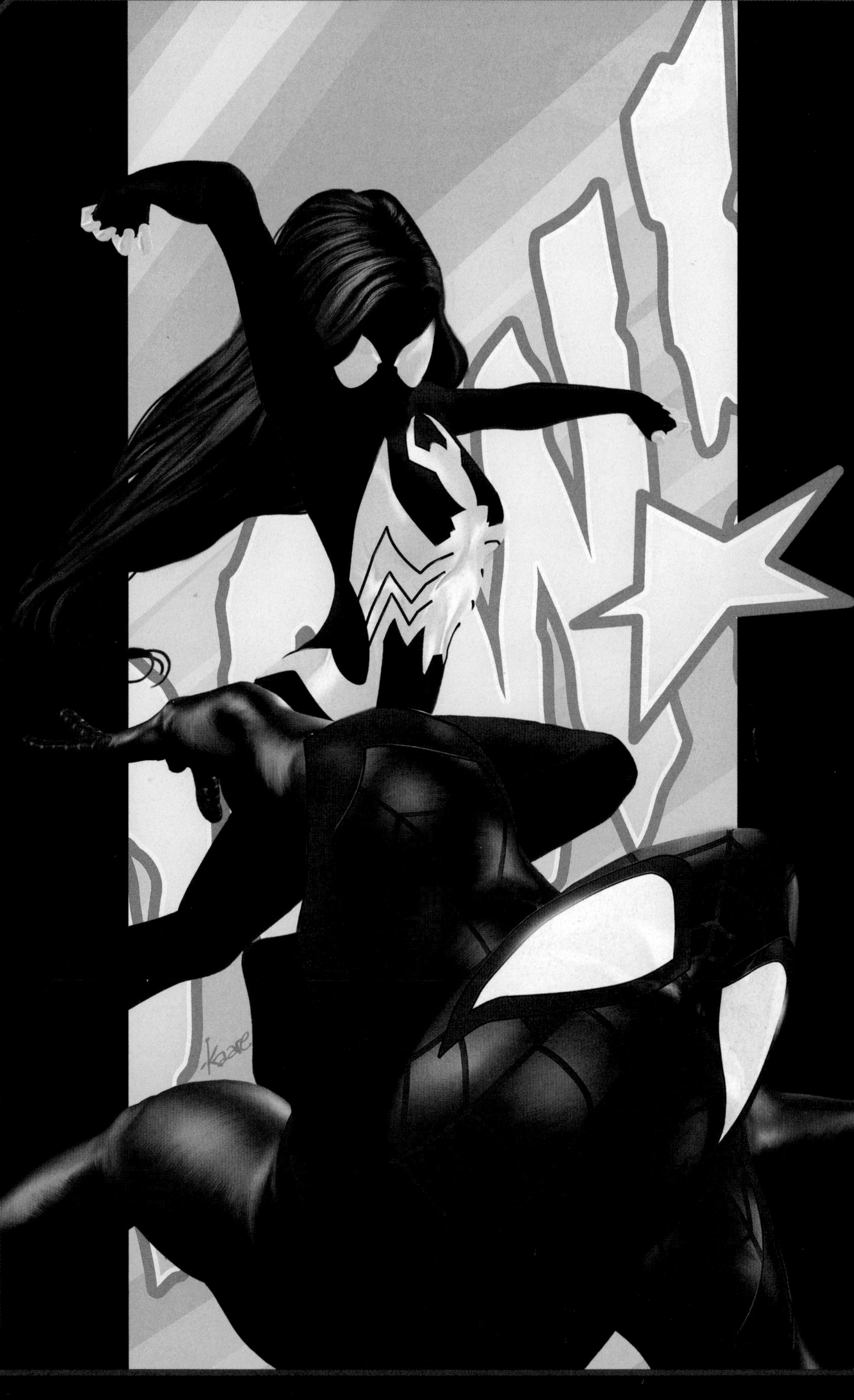

ULTIMATE COMICS SPIDER-MAN #5

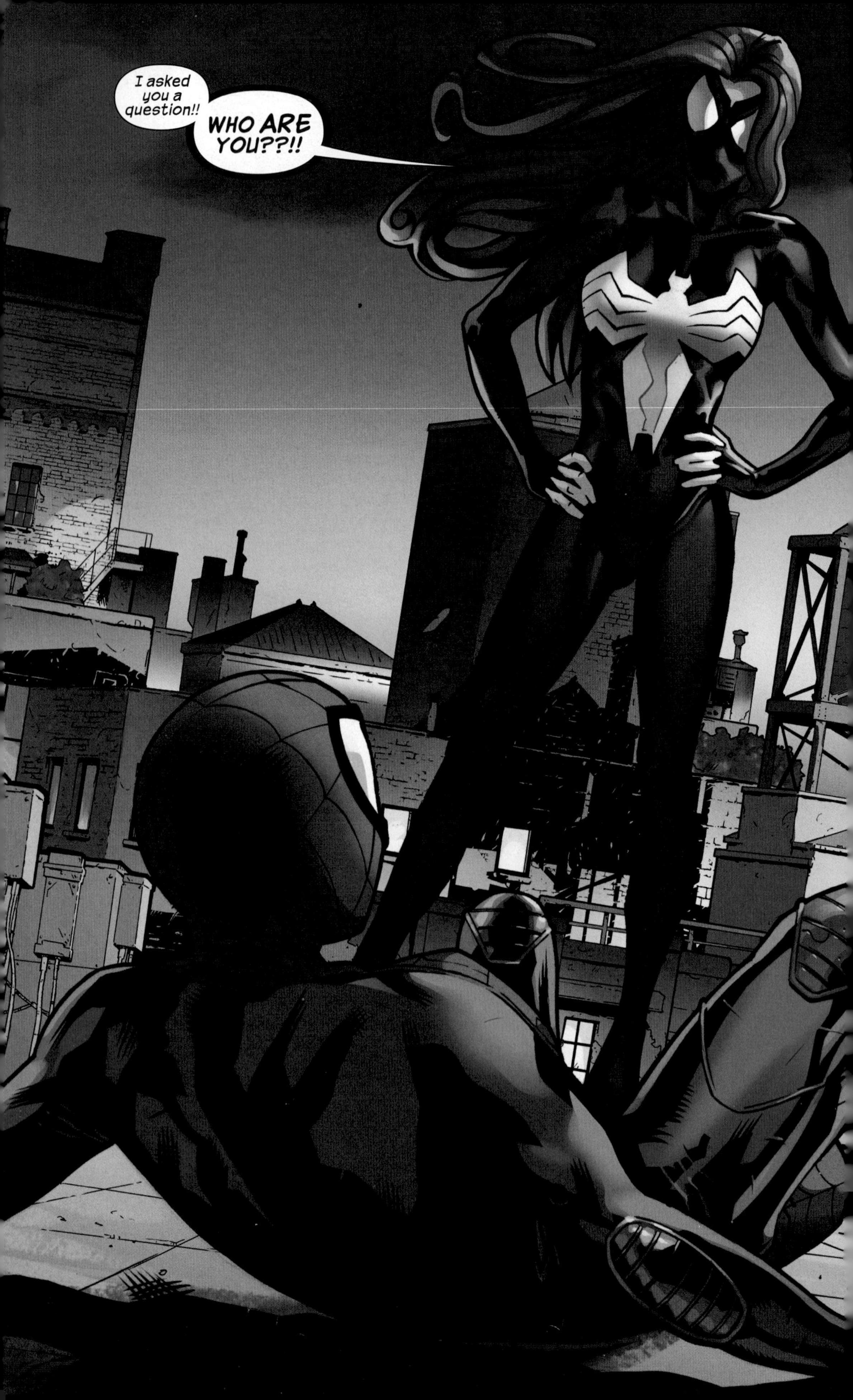
I asked you a question!!
WHO ARE YOU??!!

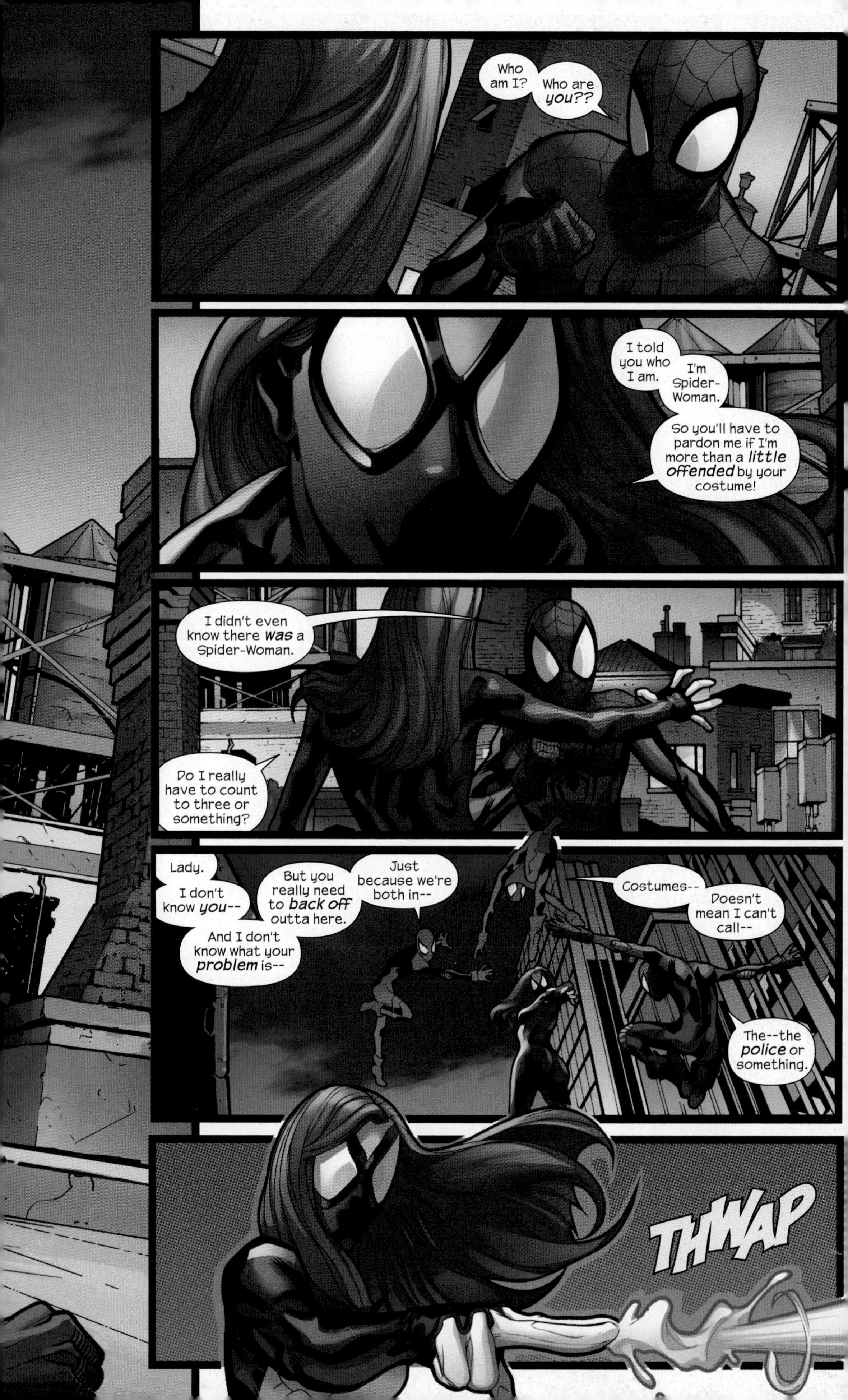
Who am I?
Who are you??
I told you who I am.
I'm Spider-Woman.
So you'll have to pardon me if I'm more than a little offended by your costume!
I didn't even know there was a Spider-Woman.
Do I really have to count to three or something?
Lady.
I don't know you--
And I don't know what your problem is--
But you really need to back off outta here.
Just because we're both in--
Costumes--
Doesn't mean I can't call--
The--the police or something.
THWAP

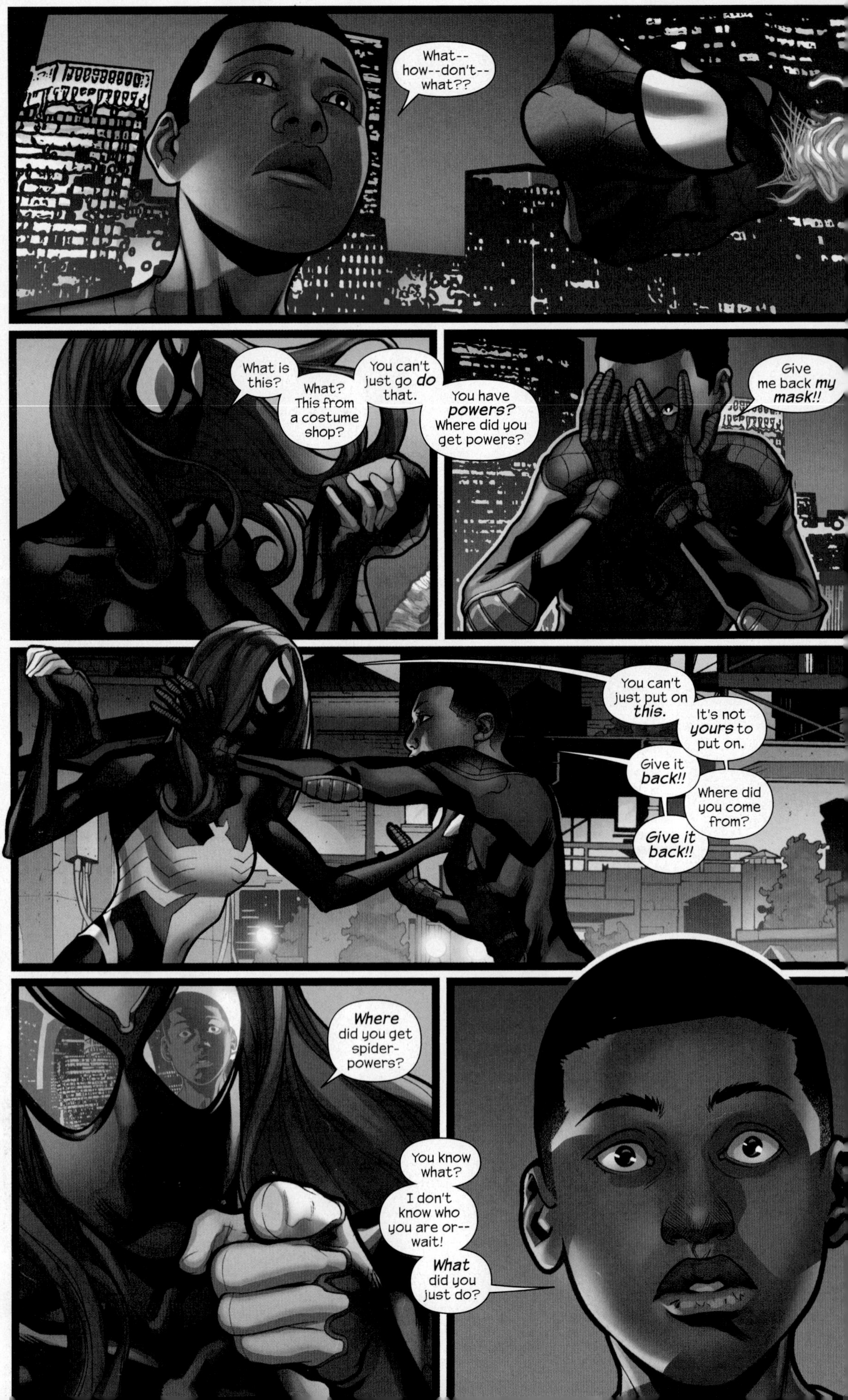

What--
how--don't--
what??
What is
this?
What?
This from
a costume
shop?
You can't
just go *do*
that.
You have
powers?
Where did you
get powers?
Give
me back *my*
mask!!
You can't
just put on
this.
It's not
yours to
put on.
Give it
back!!
Where did
you come
from?
Give it
back!!
Where
did you get
spider-
powers?
You know
what?
I don't
know who
you are or--
wait!
What
did you
just do?

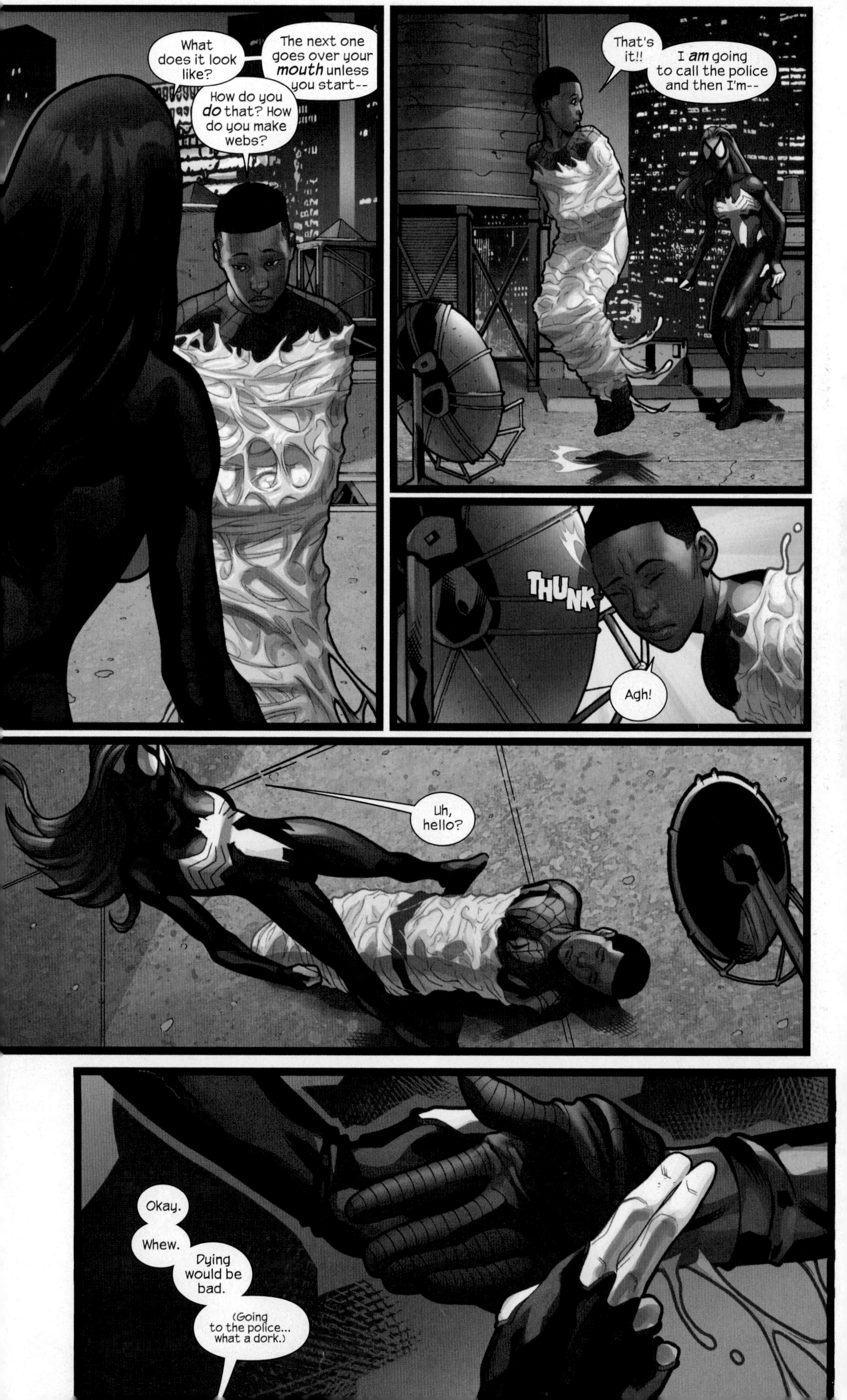

What does it look like?
The next one goes over your mouth unless you start--
How do you do that? How do you make webs?
That's it!!
I am going to call the police and then I'm--
THUNK
Agh!
Uh, hello?
Okay.
Whew.
Dying would be bad.
(Going to the police... what a dork.)

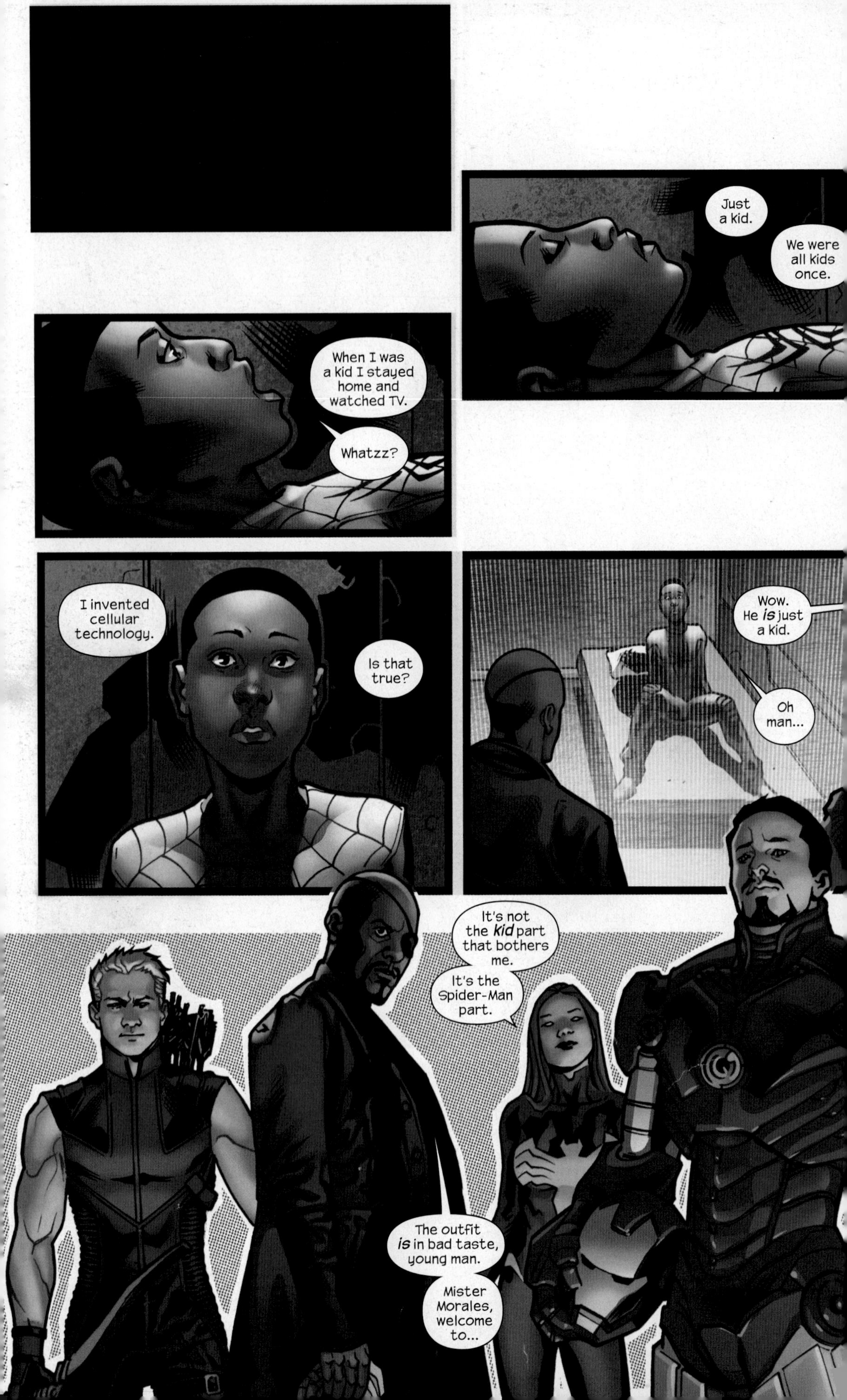
Just a kid.
We were all kids once.
When I was a kid I stayed home and watched TV.
Whatzz?
I invented cellular technology.
Is that true?
Wow. He *is* just a kid.
Oh man...
It's not the *kid* part that bothers me.
It's the Spider-Man part.
The outfit *is* in bad taste, young man.
Mister Morales, welcome to...

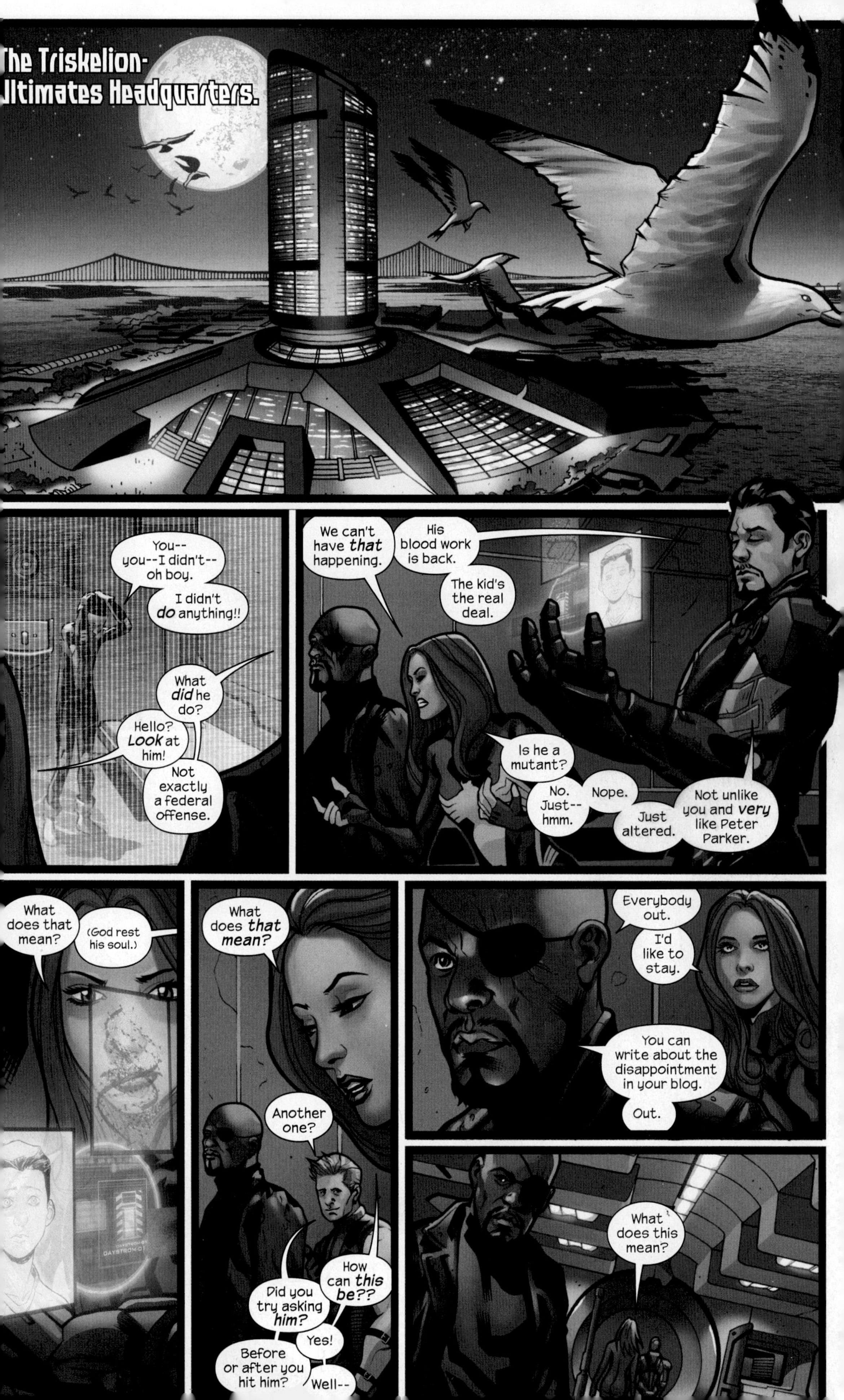
The Triskelion-
Ultimates Headquarters.
You--
you--I didn't--
oh boy.
I didn't
do anything!!
What
did he
do?
Hello?
Look at
him!
Not
exactly
a federal
offense.
We can't
have that
happening.
His
blood work
is back.
The kid's
the real
deal.
Is he a
mutant?
No.
Just--
hmm.
Nope.
Just
altered.
Not unlike
you and very
like Peter
Parker.
What
does that
mean?
(God rest
his soul.)
What
does that
mean?
Another
one?
How
can this
be??
Did you
try asking
him?
Yes!
Before
or after you
hit him?
Well--
Everybody
out.
I'd
like to
stay.
You can
write about the
disappointment
in your blog.
Out.
What
does this
mean?

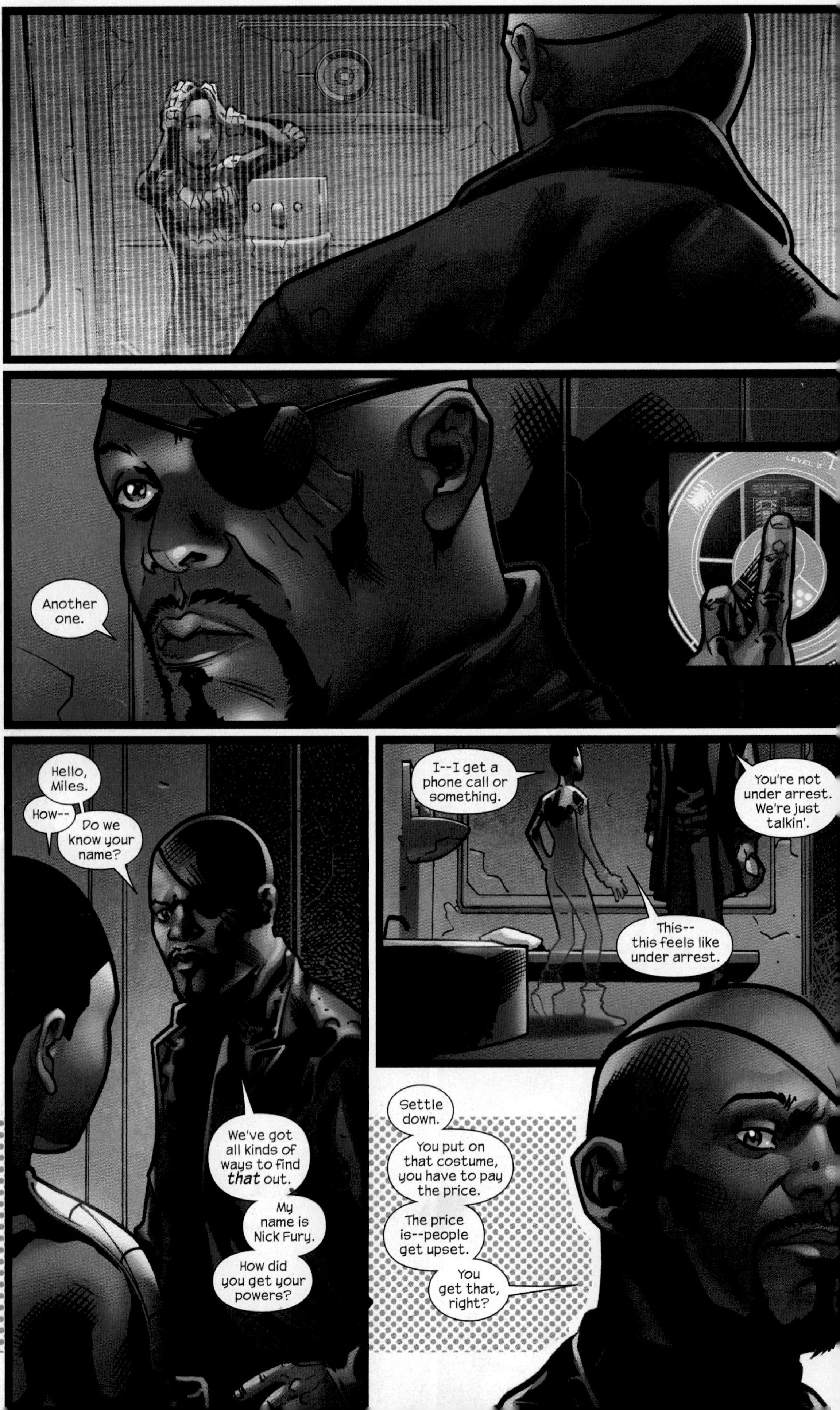
LEVEL 3
Another one.
Hello, Miles.
How--
Do we know your name?
We've got all kinds of ways to find *that* out.
My name is Nick Fury.
How did you get your powers?
I--I get a phone call or something.
You're not under arrest. We're just talkin'.
This--this feels like under arrest.
Settle down.
You put on that costume, you have to pay the price.
The price is--people get upset.
You get that, right?

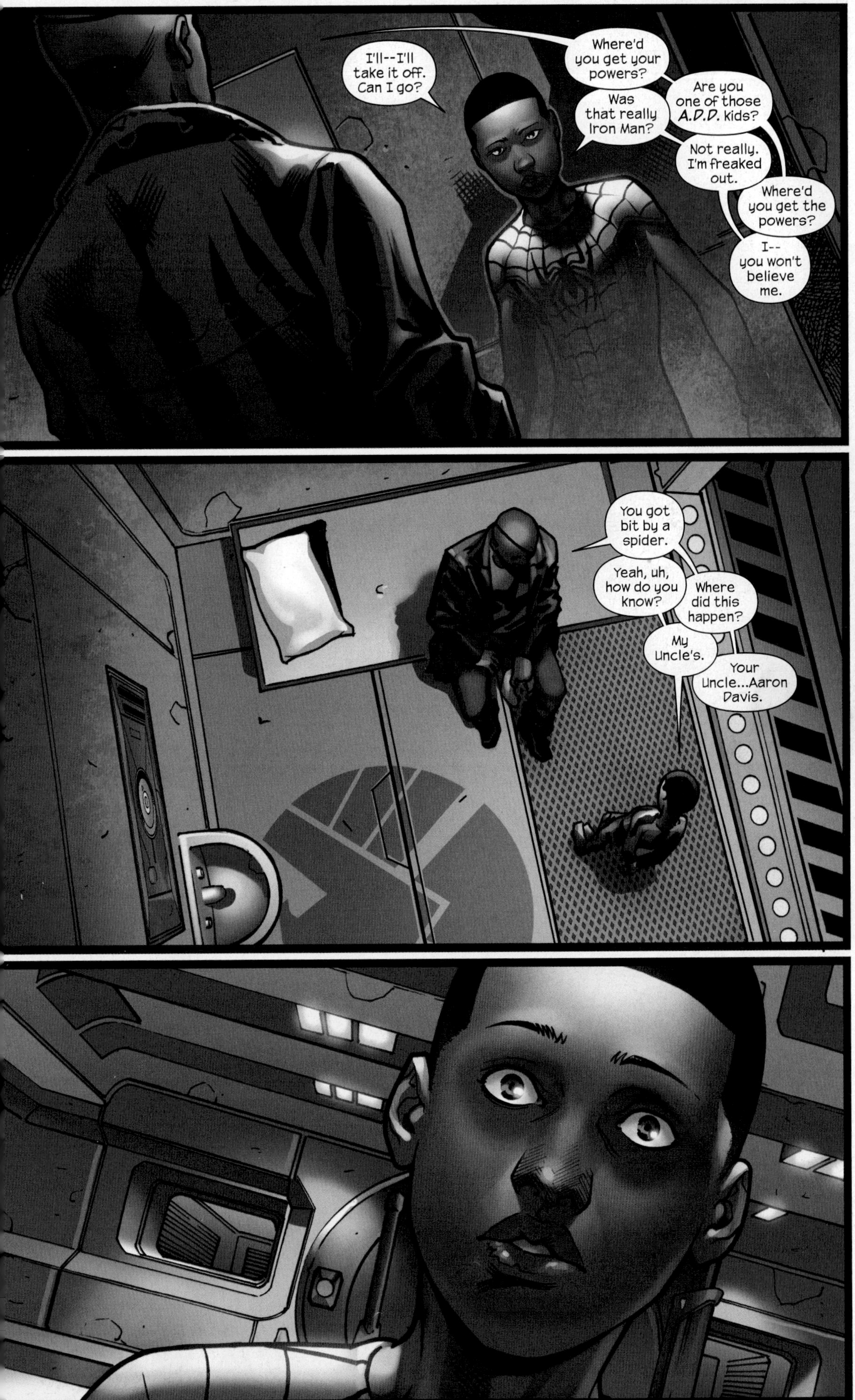
Where'd you get your powers?
I'll--I'll take it off. Can I go?
Was that really Iron Man?
Are you one of those *A.D.D.* kids?
Not really. I'm freaked out.
Where'd you get the powers?
I-- you won't believe me.
You got bit by a spider.
Yeah, uh, how do you know?
Where did this happen?
My Uncle's.
Your Uncle...Aaron Davis.

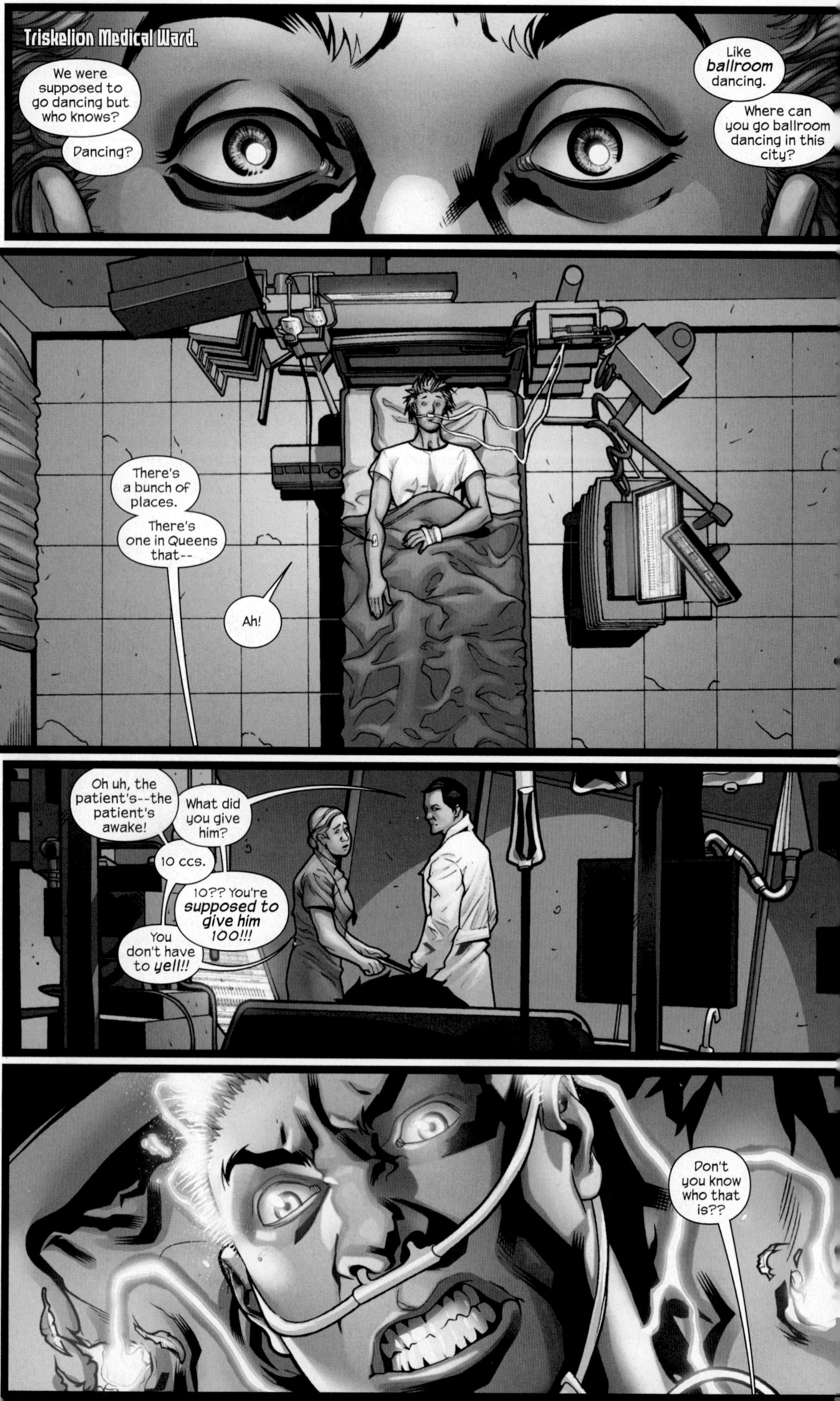
Triskelion Medical Ward.
We were supposed to go dancing but who knows?
Dancing?
Like ballroom dancing.
Where can you go ballroom dancing in this city?
There's a bunch of places.
There's one in Queens that--
Ah!
Oh uh, the patient's--the patient's awake!
What did you give him?
10 ccs.
10?? You're supposed to give him 100!!!
You don't have to yell!!
Don't you know who that is??

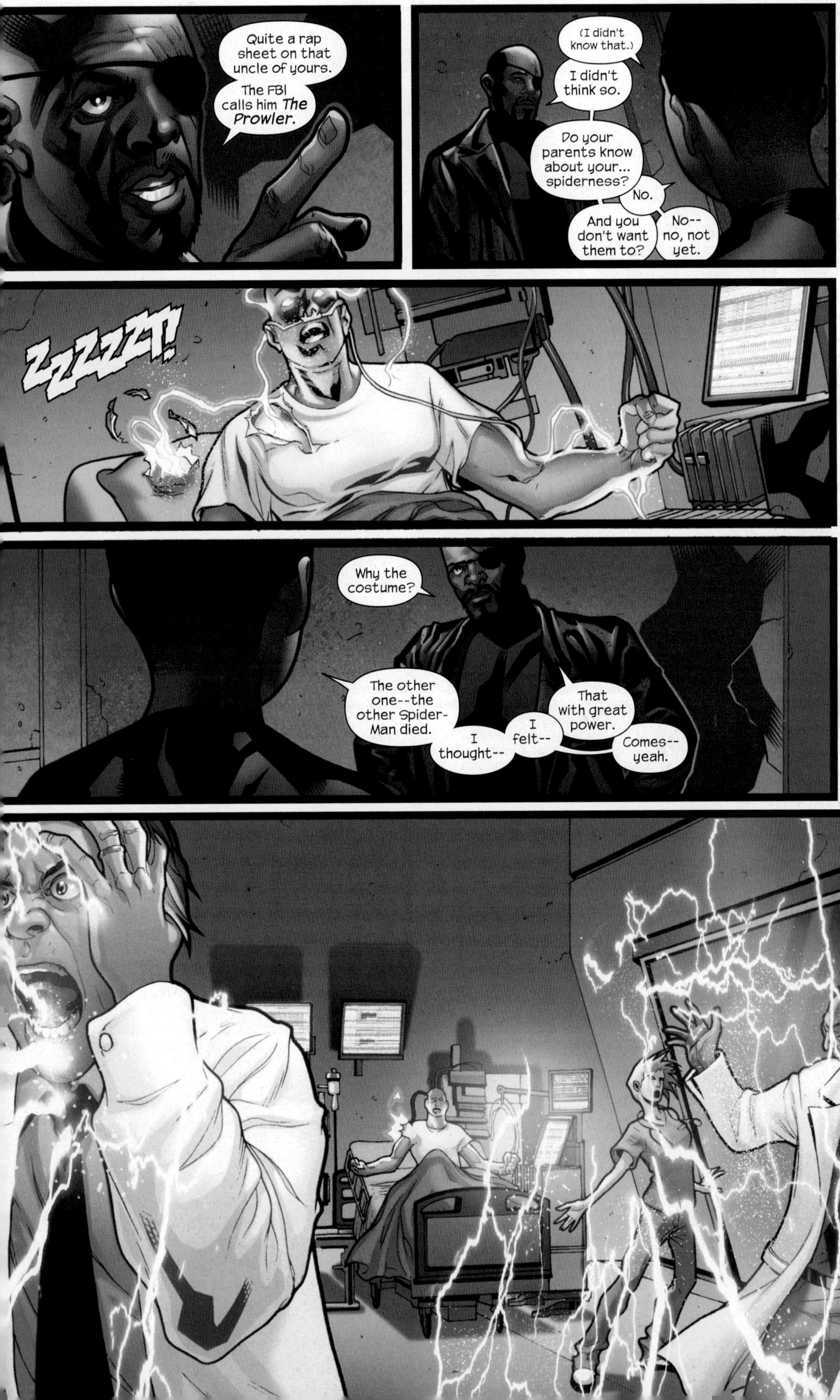
Quite a rap sheet on that uncle of yours.
The FBI calls him *The Prowler.*
(I didn't know that.)
I didn't think so.
Do your parents know about your... spiderness?
No.
And you don't want them to?
No-- no, not yet.
ZZZZZT!
Why the costume?
The other one--the other Spider-Man died.
I thought--
I felt--
That with great power.
Comes-- yeah.

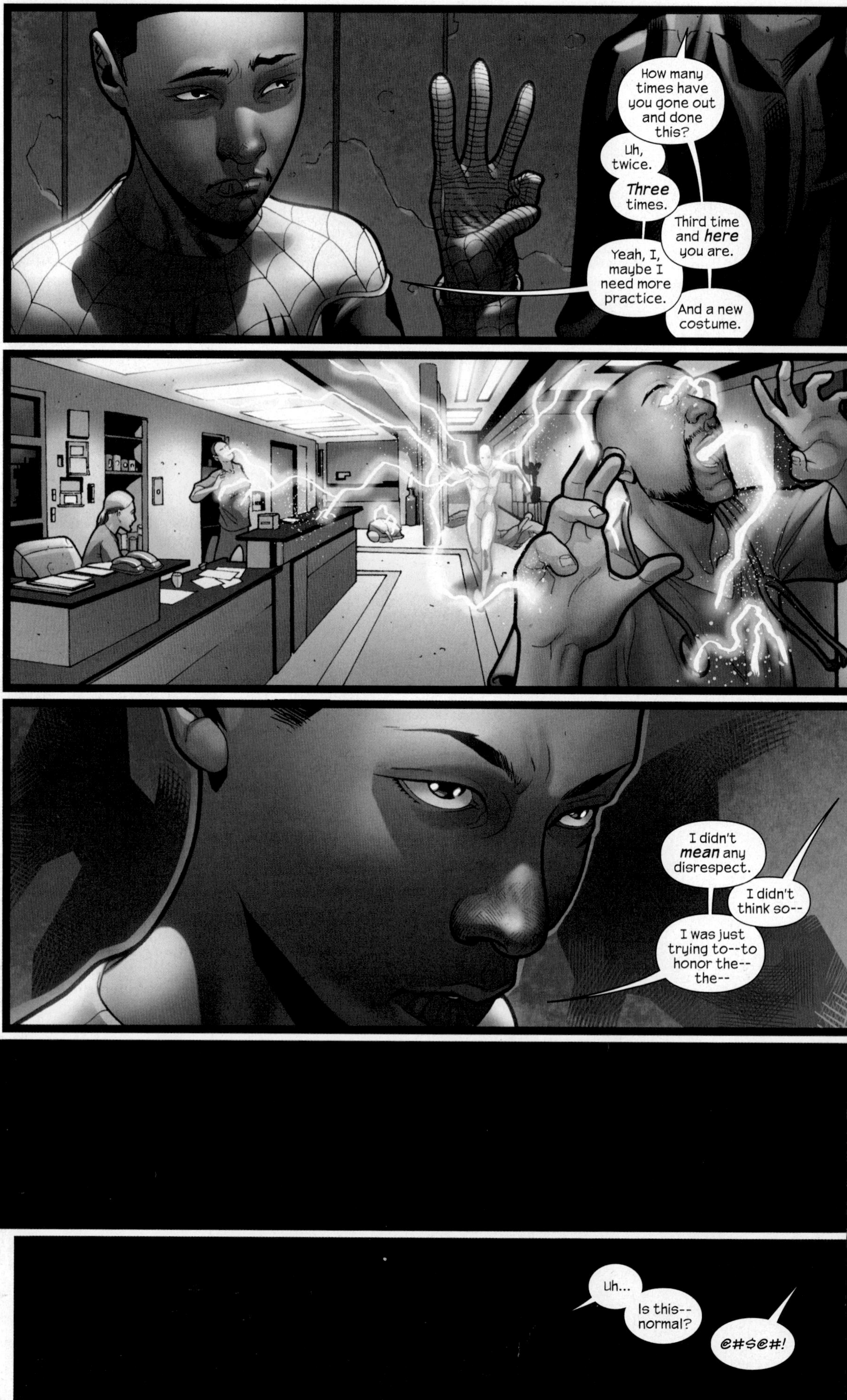
How many times have you gone out and done this?
Uh, twice.
Three times.
Third time and here you are.
Yeah, I, maybe I need more practice.
And a new costume.
I didn't mean any disrespect.
I didn't think so--
I was just trying to--to honor the--the--
Uh...
Is this--normal?
@#$@#!

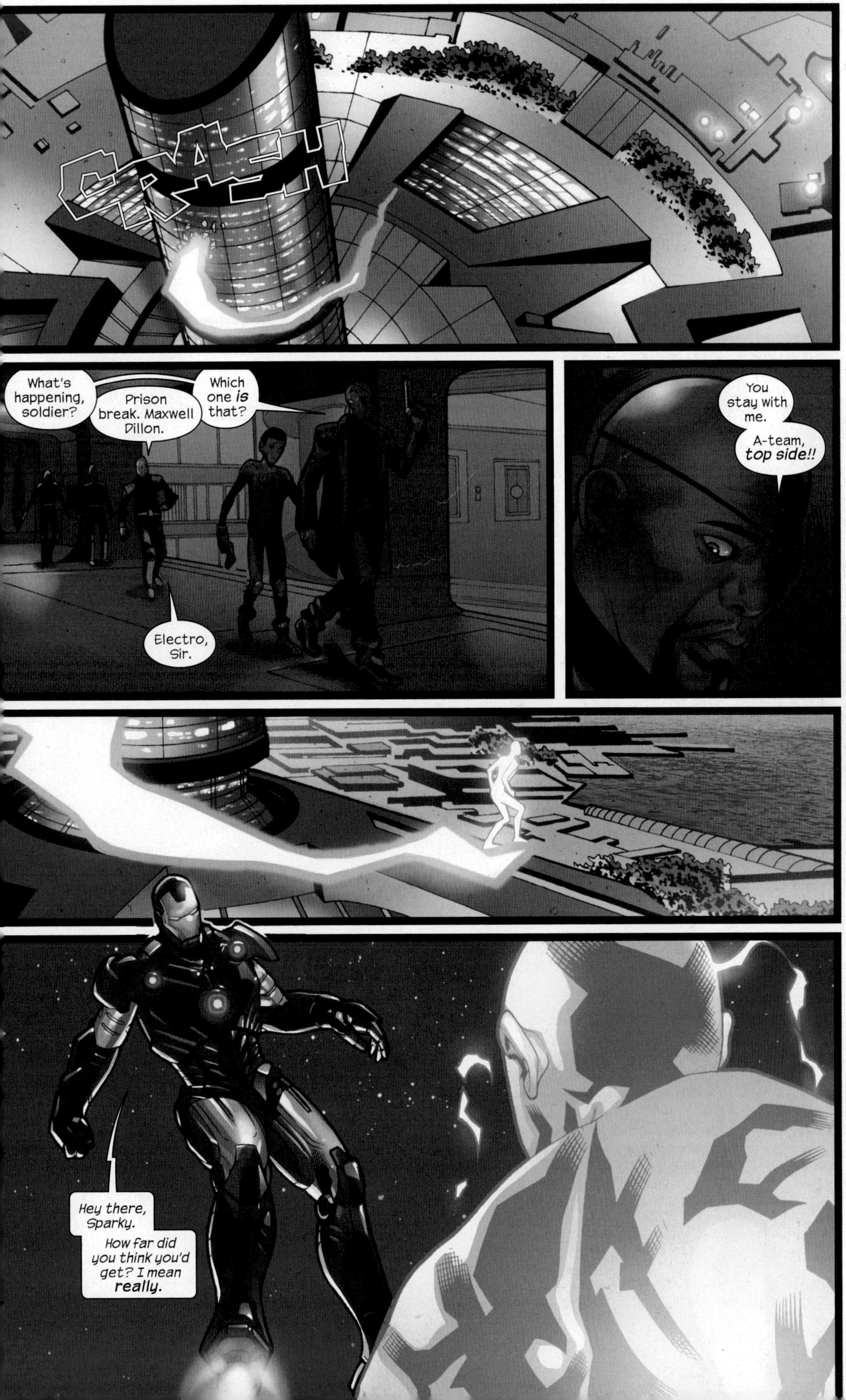
CRASH
What's happening, soldier?
Prison break. Maxwell Dillon.
Which one *is* that?
Electro, Sir.
You stay with me.
A-team, *top side!!*
Hey there, Sparky.
How far did you think you'd get? I mean **really.**

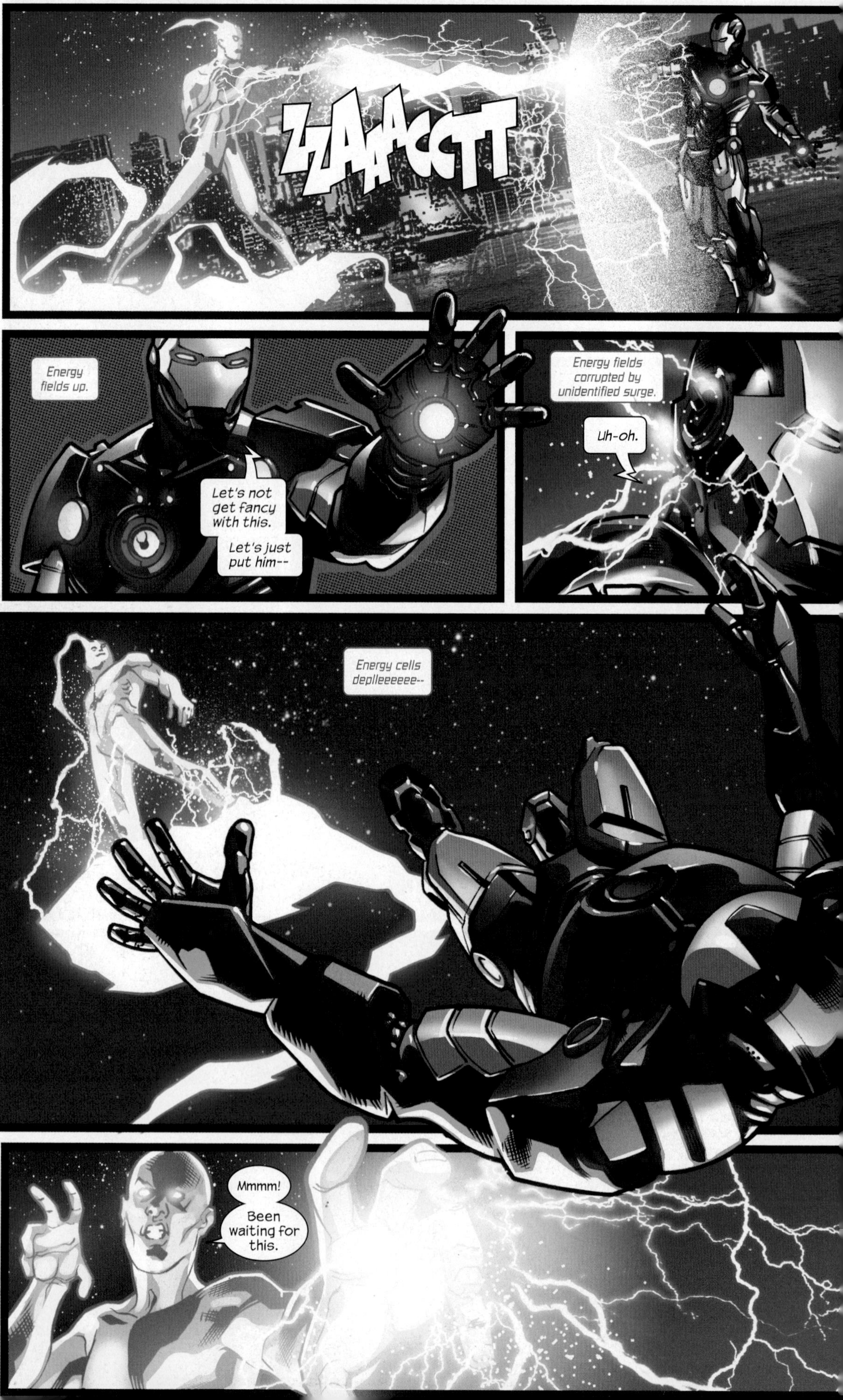
ZZAAACCTT
Energy fields up.
Let's not get fancy with this.
Let's just put him--
Energy fields corrupted by unidentified surge.
Uh-oh.
Energy cells deplleeeeee--
Mmmm!
Been waiting for this.

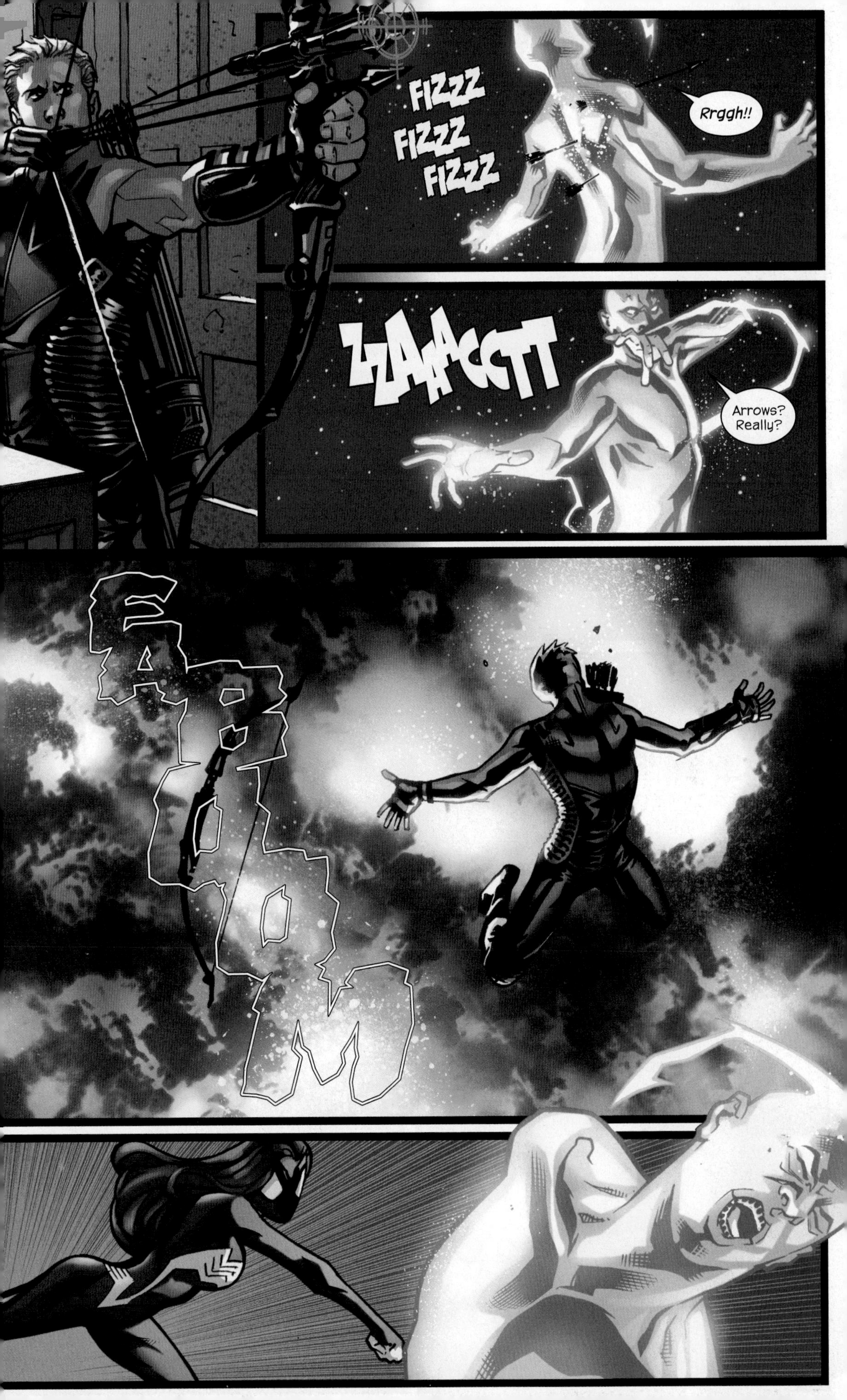
FIZZZ
FIZZZ
FIZZZ
Rrggh!!
ZZZAAACCTT
Arrows? Really?
FABOOM

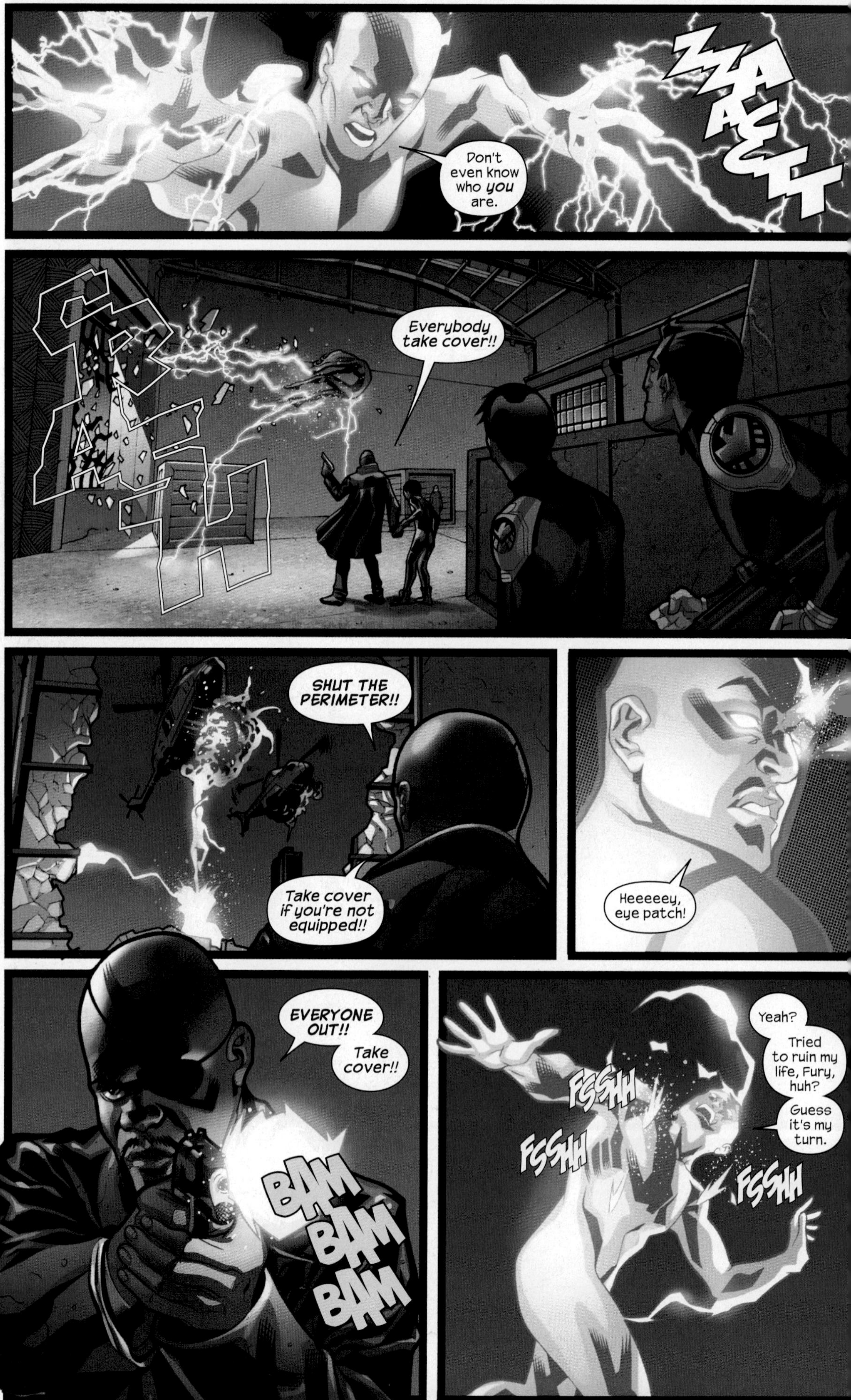
Don't even know who you are.
ZZAAKT
Everybody take cover!!
SHUT THE PERIMETER!!
Take cover if you're not equipped!!
Heeeeey, eye patch!
EVERYONE OUT!!
Take cover!!
BAM BAM BAM
Yeah?
Tried to ruin my life, Fury, huh?
Guess it's my turn.
FSSHH
FSSHH
FSSHH

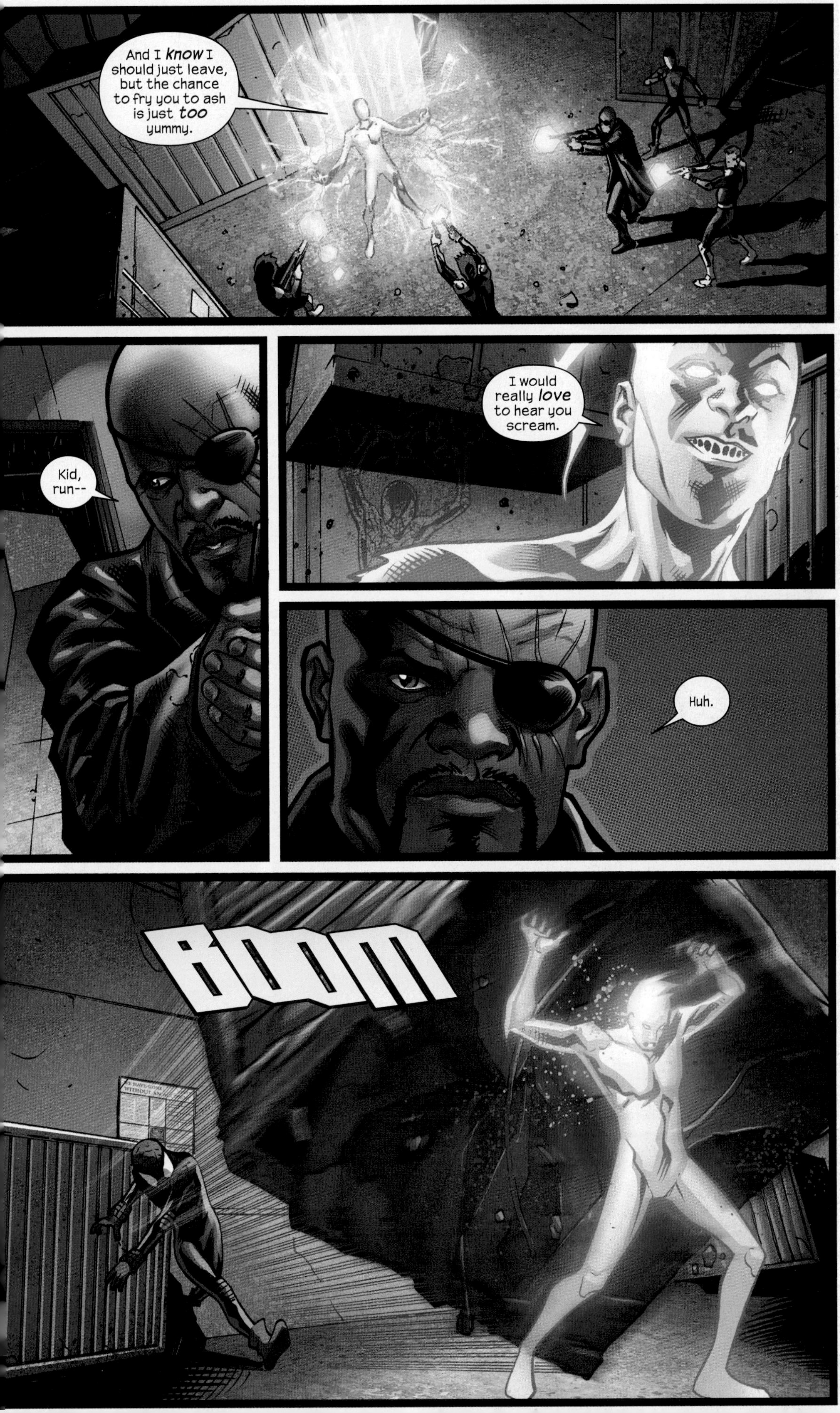
And I *know* I should just leave, but the chance to fry you to ash is just *too* yummy.
Kid, run--
I would really *love* to hear you scream.
Huh.
BOOM

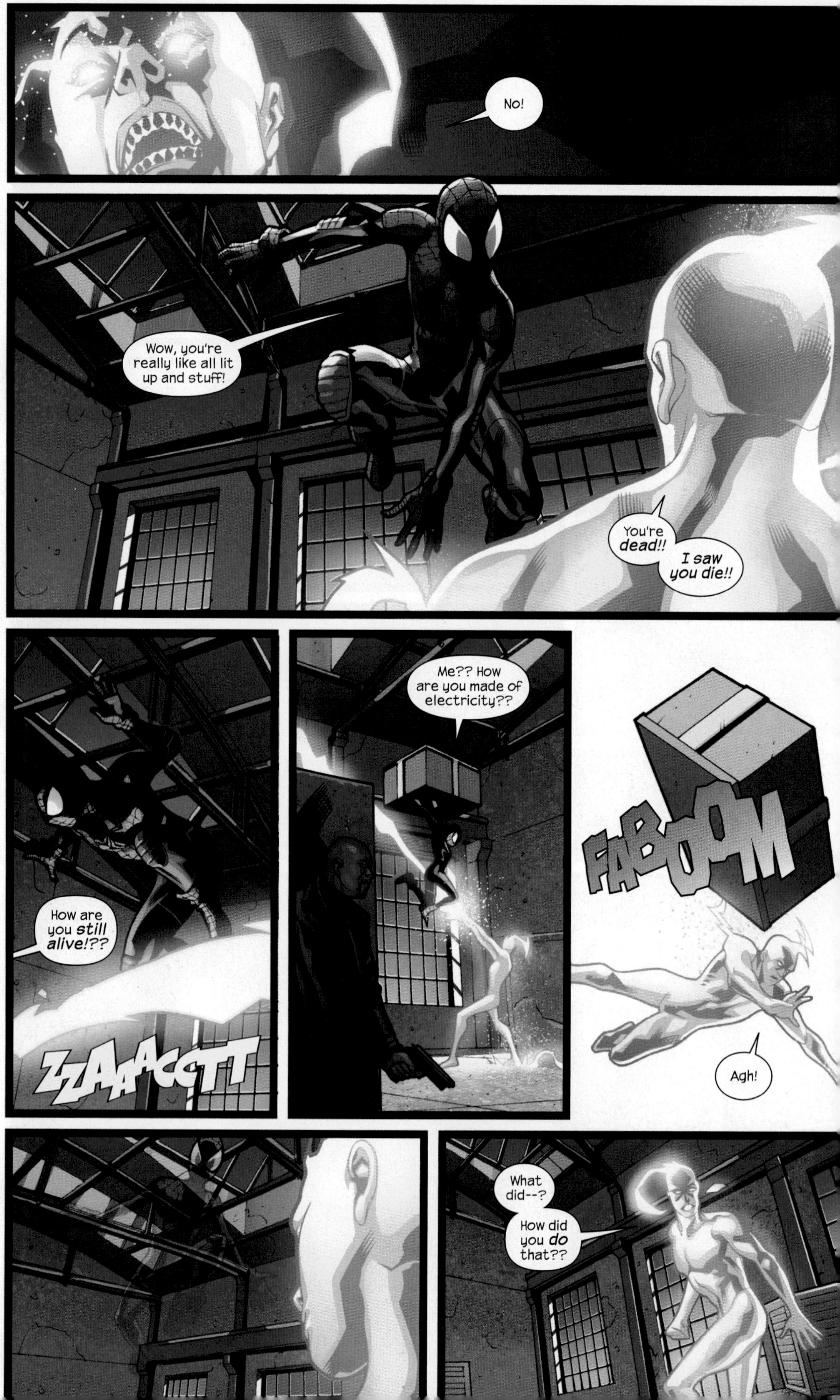
No!
Wow, you're really like all lit up and stuff!
You're dead!!
I saw you die!!
How are you still alive!??
ZZAAACCTT
Me?? How are you made of electricity??
FABOOM
Agh!
What did--?
How did you do that??

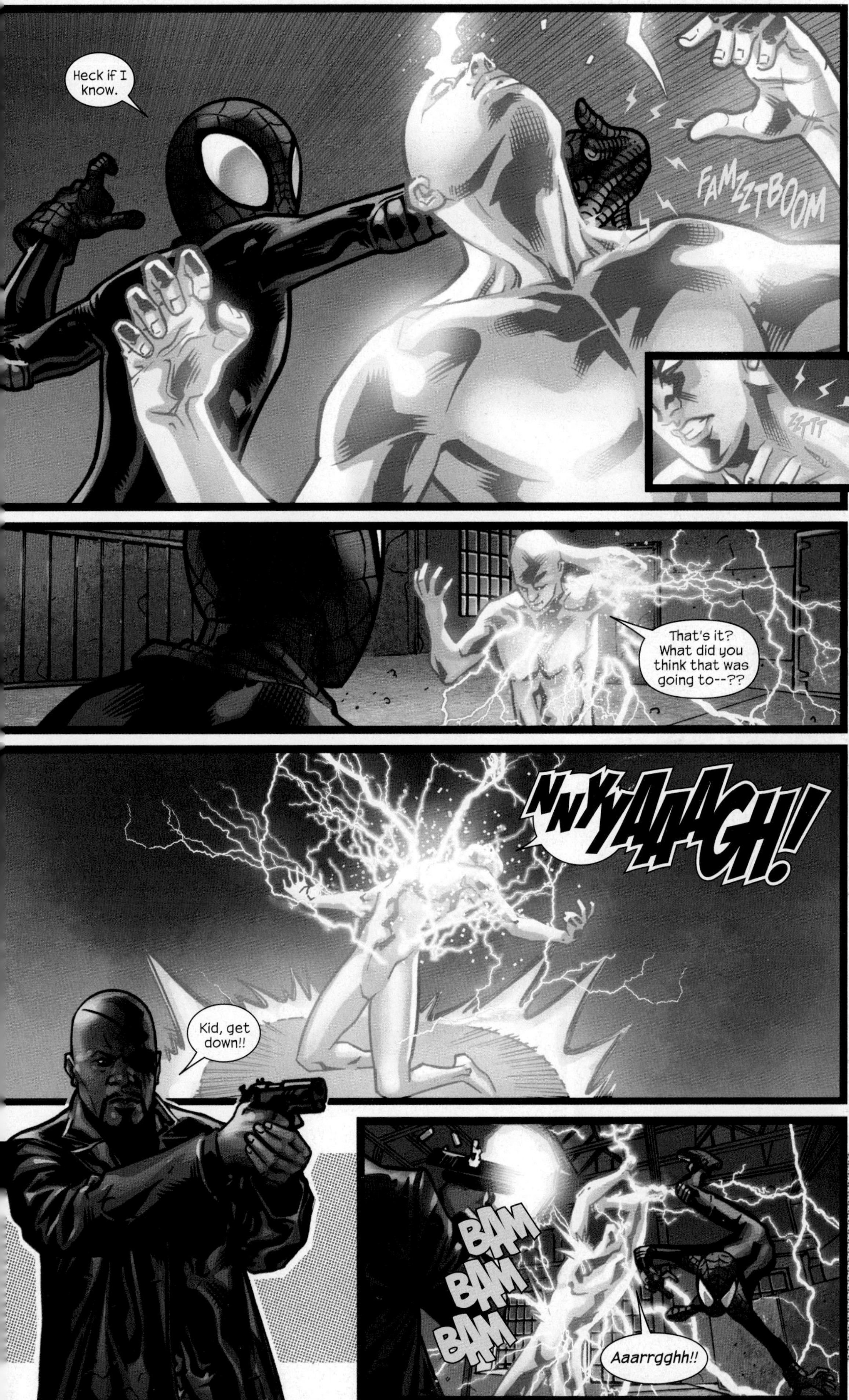
Heck if I know.
FAMZZTBOOM
ZZTTT
That's it? What did you think that was going to--??
NNYYAAAAGH!
Kid, get down!!
BAM
BAM
BAM
Aaarrgghh!!

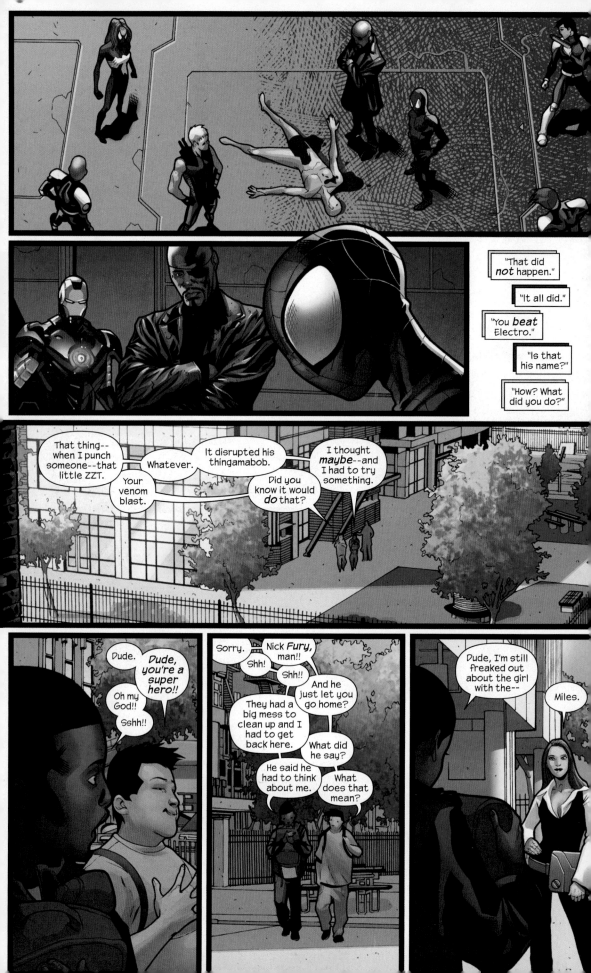

"That did **not** happen."

"It all did."

"You **beat** Electro."

"Is that his name?"

"How? What did you do?"

That thing-- when I punch someone--that little ZZT.

Whatever.

Your venom blast.

It disrupted his thingamabob.

Did you know it would **do** that?

I thought **maybe**--and I had to try something.

Dude.

Oh my God!!

Sshh!!

Dude, you're a super hero!!

Sorry.

Shh!

Nick **Fury**, man!!

Shh!!

And he just let you go home?

They had a big mess to clean up and I had to get back here.

What did he say?

He said he had to think about me.

What does that mean?

Dude, I'm still freaked out about the girl with the--

Miles.

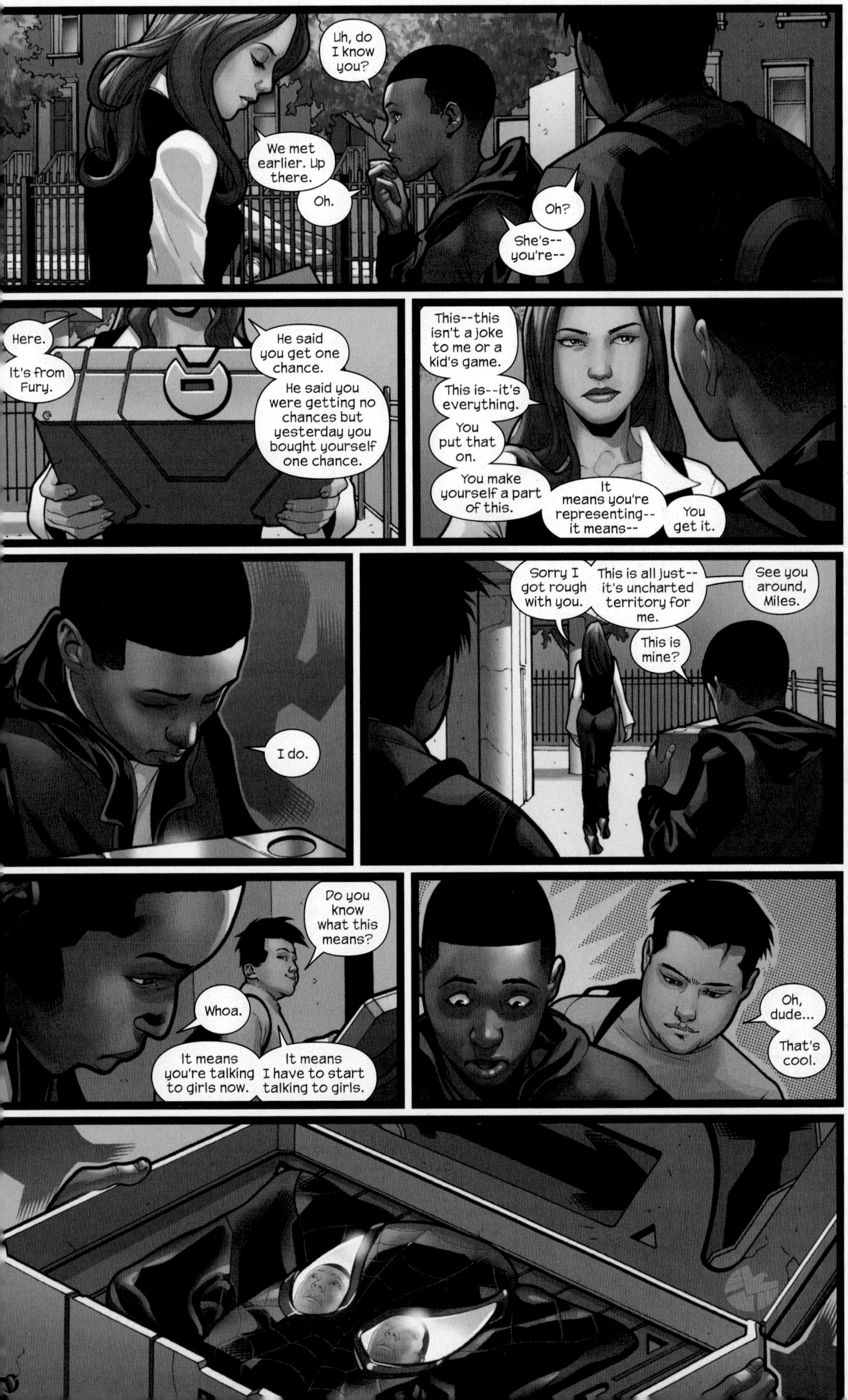
Uh, do I know you?
We met earlier. Up there.
Oh.
Oh?
She's-- you're--
Here.
It's from Fury.
He said you get one chance.
He said you were getting no chances but yesterday you bought yourself one chance.
This--this isn't a joke to me or a kid's game.
This is--it's everything.
You put that on.
You make yourself a part of this.
It means you're representing-- it means--
You get it.
I do.
Sorry I got rough with you.
This is all just-- it's uncharted territory for me.
See you around, Miles.
This is mine?
Do you know what this means?
Whoa.
It means you're talking to girls now.
It means I have to start talking to girls.
Oh, dude...
That's cool.

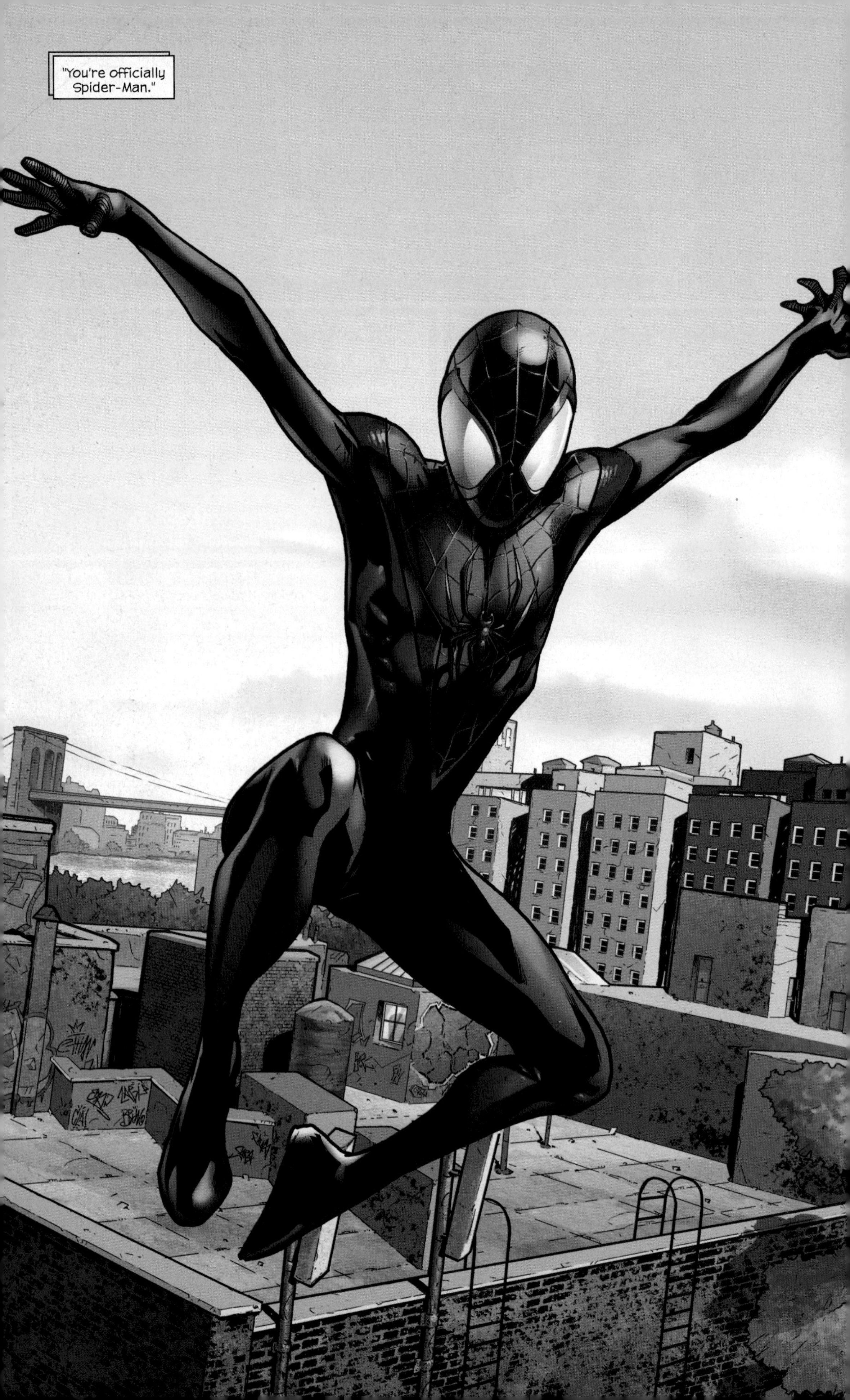
"You're officially Spider-Man."

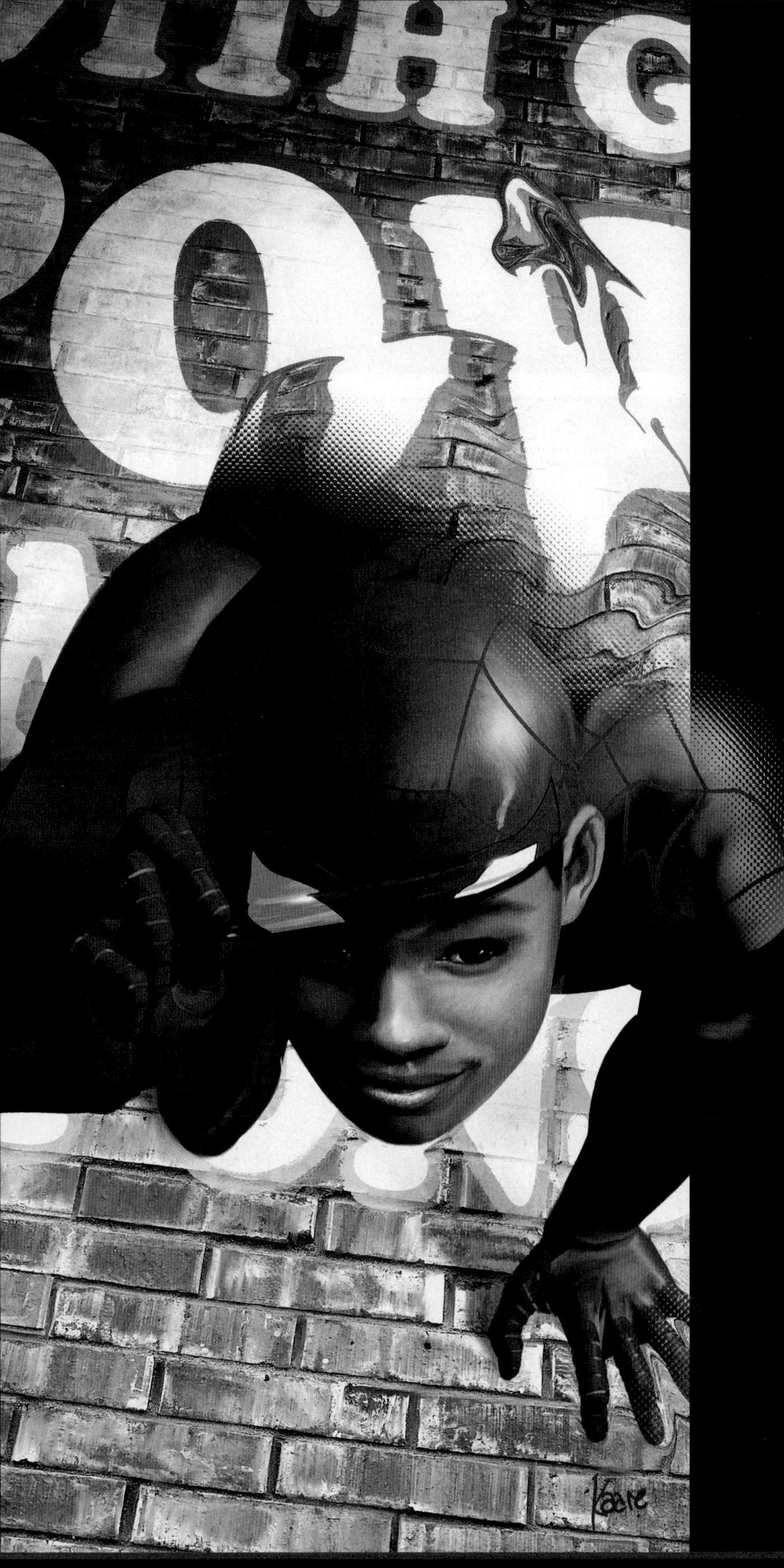
Kaare

ULTIMATE COMICS SPIDER-MAN #6

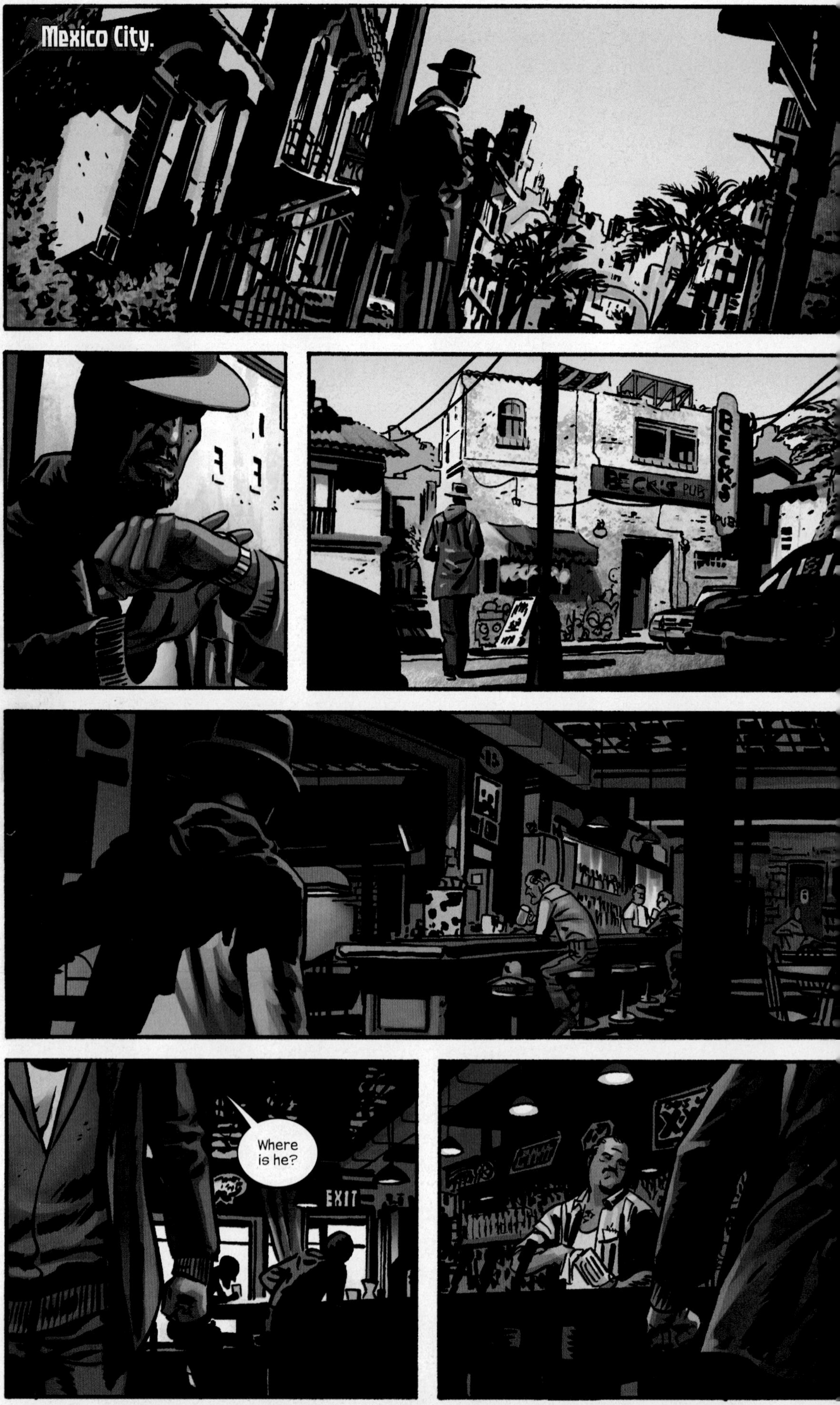
Mexico City.
BECK'S PUB
BECK'S PUB
Where is he?
EXIT

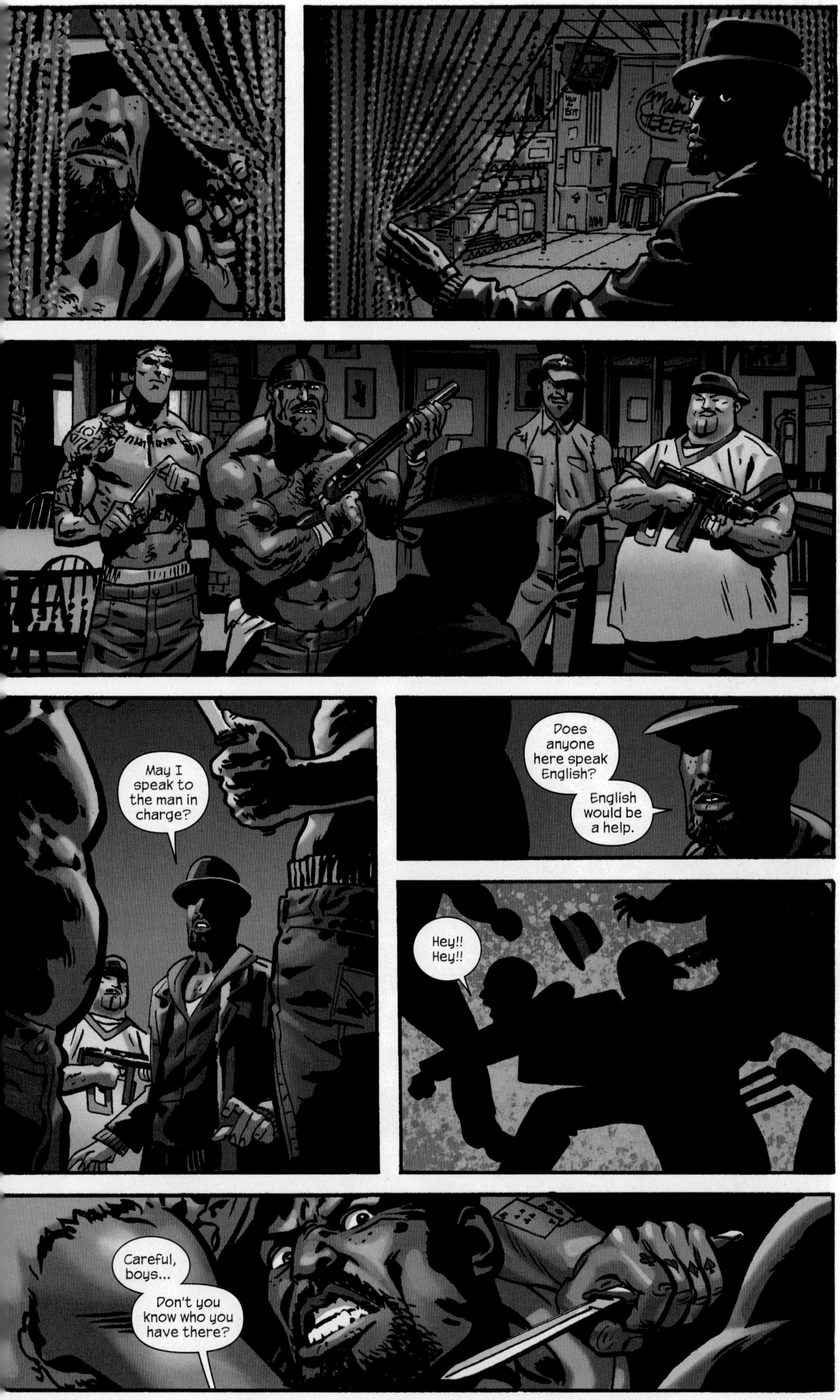
May I speak to the man in charge?
Does anyone here speak English?
English would be a help.
Hey!! Hey!!
Careful, boys...
Don't you know who you have there?

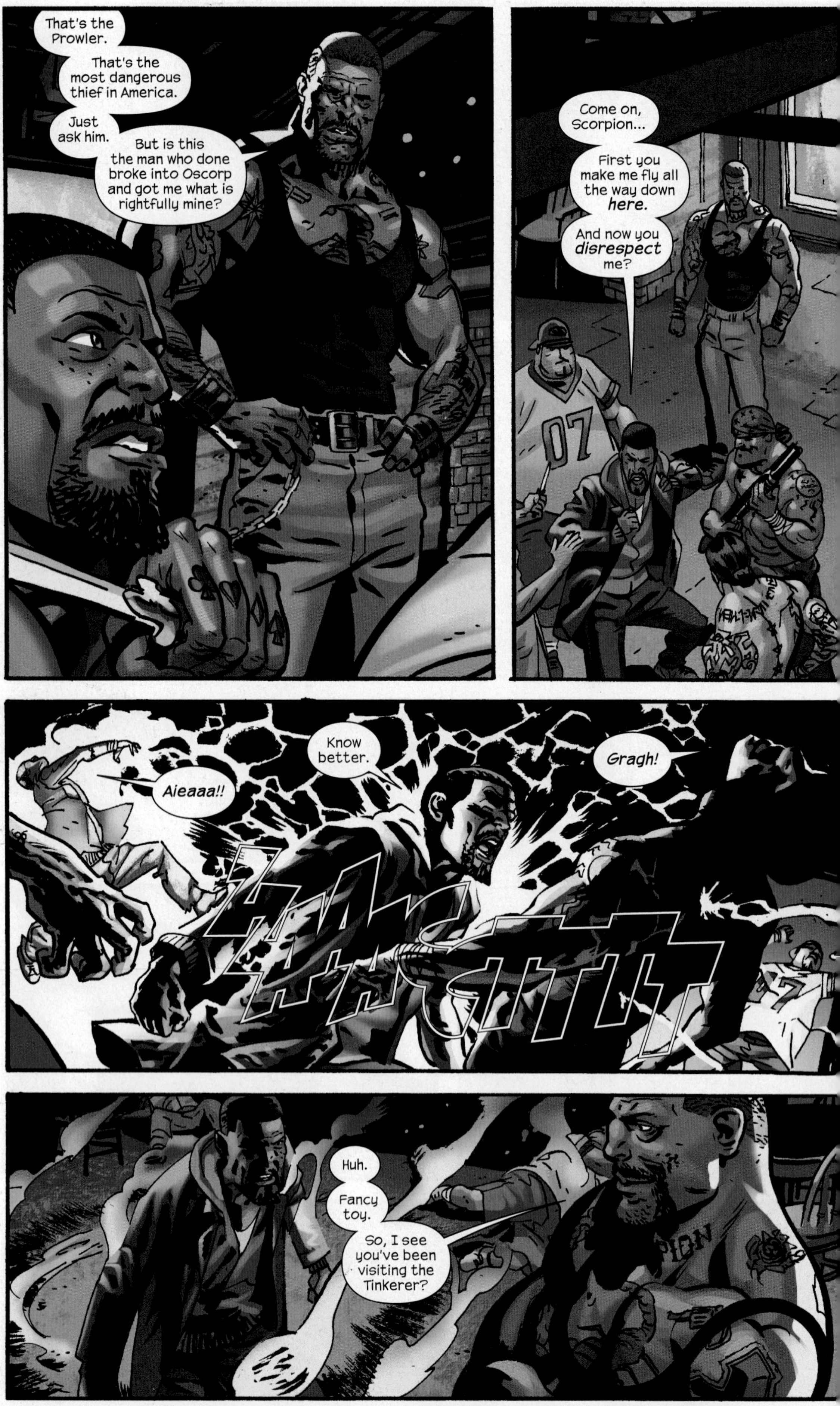
That's the Prowler.
That's the most dangerous thief in America.
Just ask him.
But is this the man who done broke into Oscorp and got me what is rightfully mine?
Come on, Scorpion...
First you make me fly all the way down *here.*
And now you *disrespect* me?
Aieaaa!!
Know better.
Gragh!
Huh.
Fancy toy.
So, I see you've been visiting the Tinkerer?

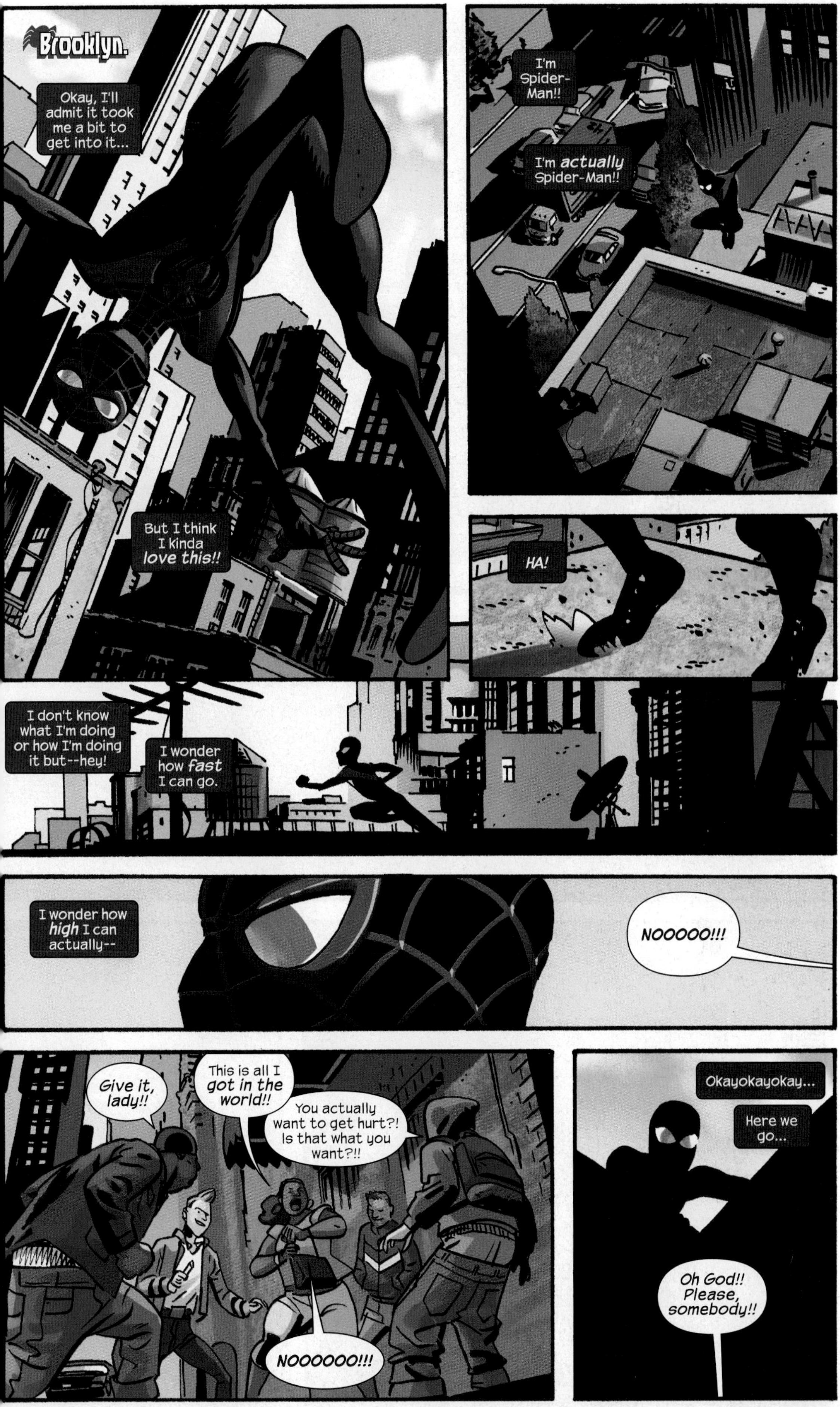
Brooklyn.
Okay, I'll admit it took me a bit to get into it...
But I think I kinda love this!!
I'm Spider-Man!!
I'm actually Spider-Man!!
HA!
I don't know what I'm doing or how I'm doing it but--hey!
I wonder how fast I can go.
I wonder how high I can actually--
NOOOOO!!!
Give it, lady!!
This is all I got in the world!!
You actually want to get hurt?! Is that what you want?!!
NOOOOOO!!!
Okayokayokay...
Here we go...
Oh God!! Please, somebody!!

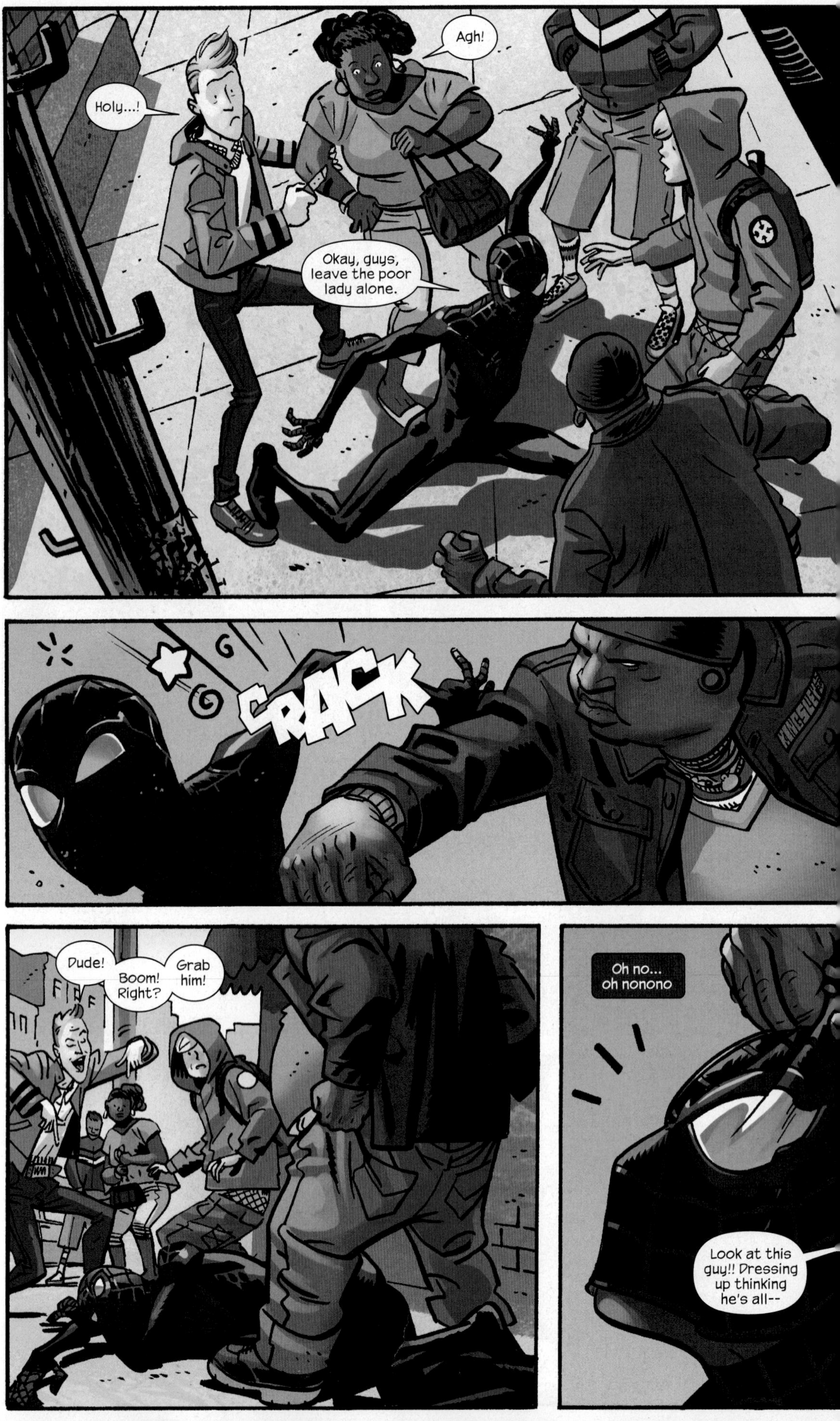
Holy...!
Agh!
Okay, guys, leave the poor lady alone.
CRACK
Dude!
Boom! Right?
Grab him!
Oh no... oh nonono
Look at this guy!! Dressing up thinking he's all--

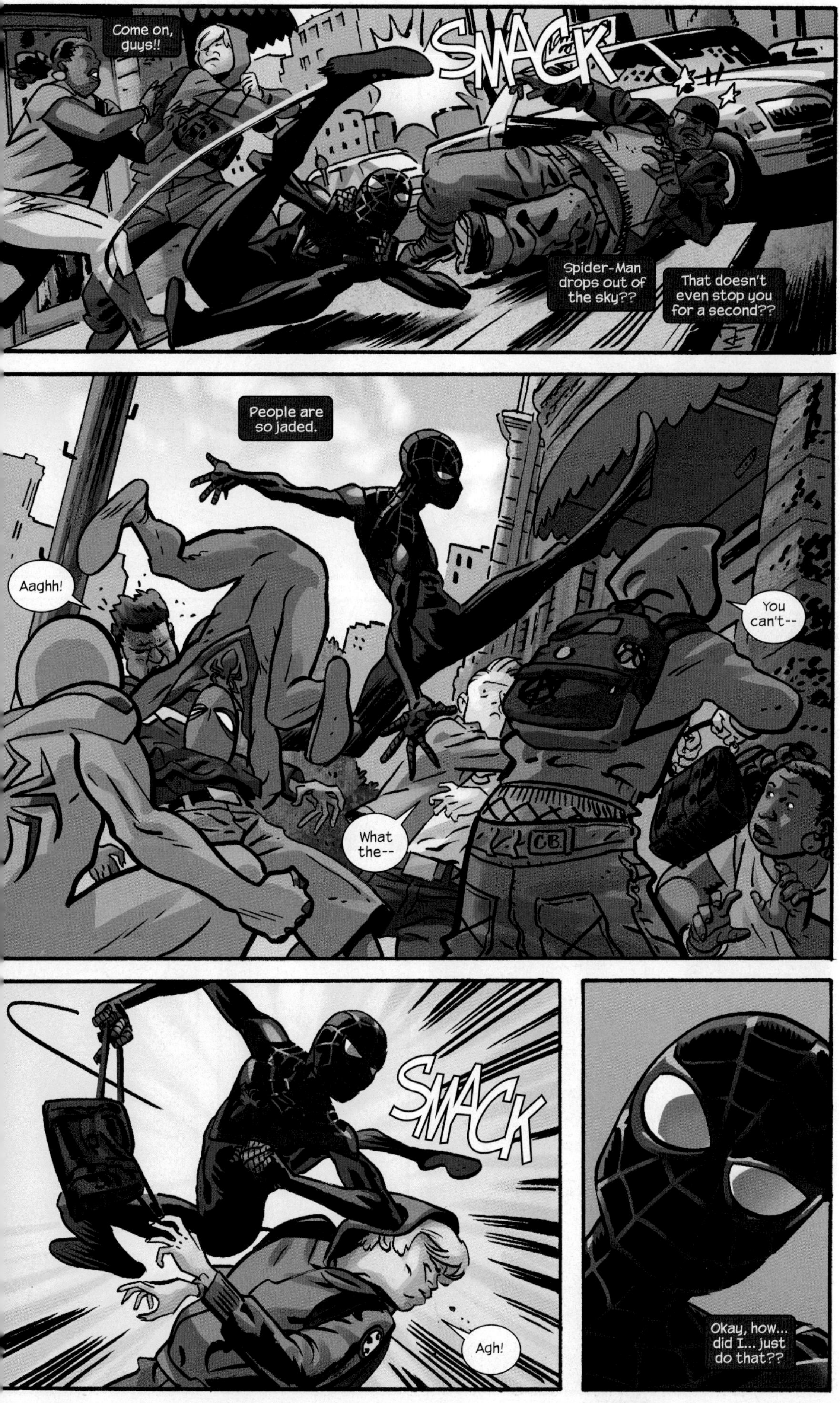
Come on, guys!!
SMACK
Spider-Man drops out of the sky??
That doesn't even stop you for a second??
People are so jaded.
Aaghh!
You can't--
What the--
SMACK
Agh!
Okay, how... did I... just do that??

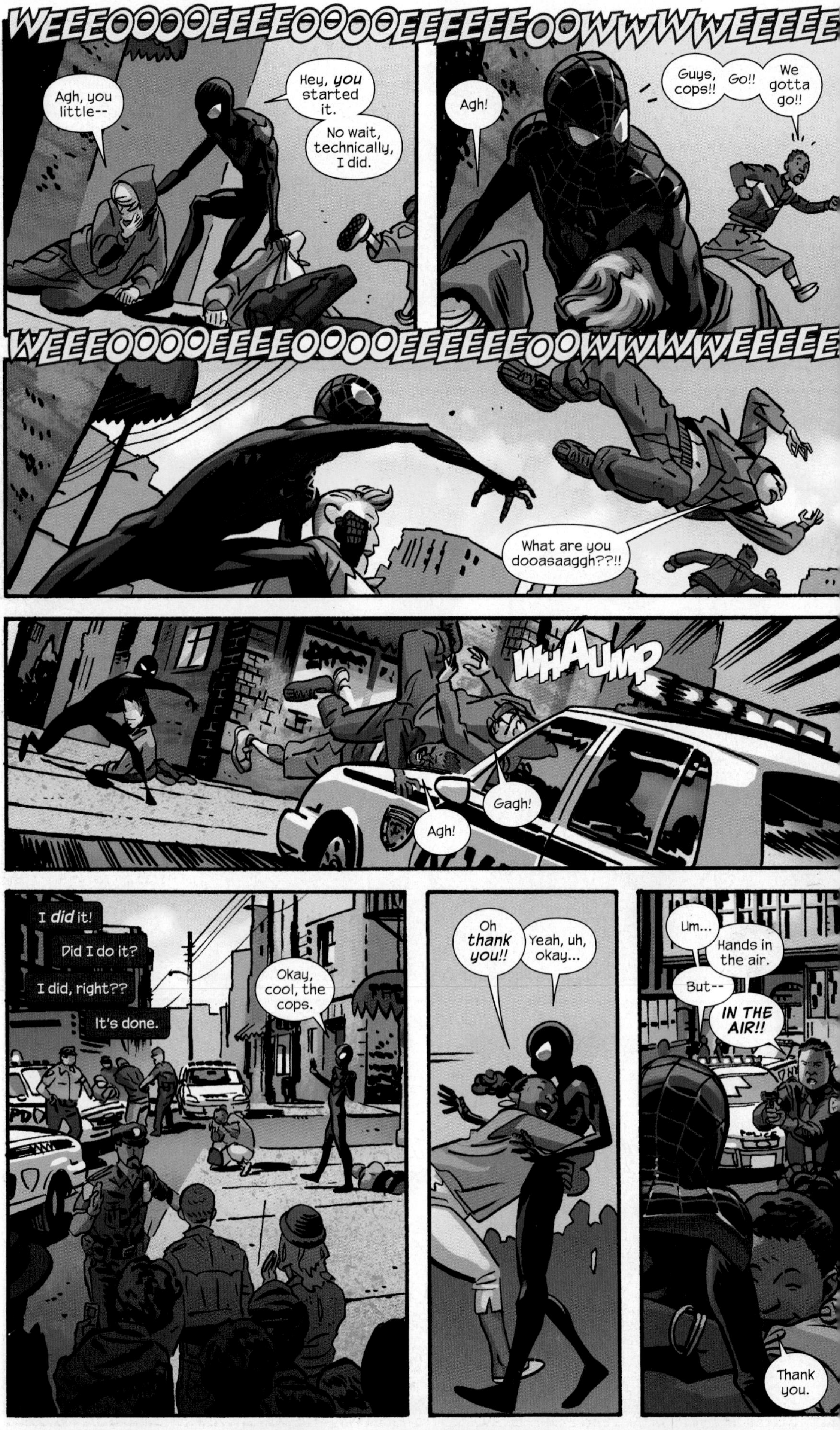
WEEEOOOOEEEEOOOOEEEEEEOOWWWWEEEEE
Agh, you little--
Hey, you started it.
No wait, technically, I did.
Agh!
Guys, cops!!
Go!!
We gotta go!!
WEEEOOOOEEEEOOOOEEEEEEOOWWWWWEEEEE
What are you dooasaaggh??!!
WHAUMP
Gagh!
Agh!
I did it!
Did I do it?
I did, right??
It's done.
Okay, cool, the cops.
Oh thank you!!
Yeah, uh, okay...
Um...
Hands in the air.
But--
IN THE AIR!!
Thank you.

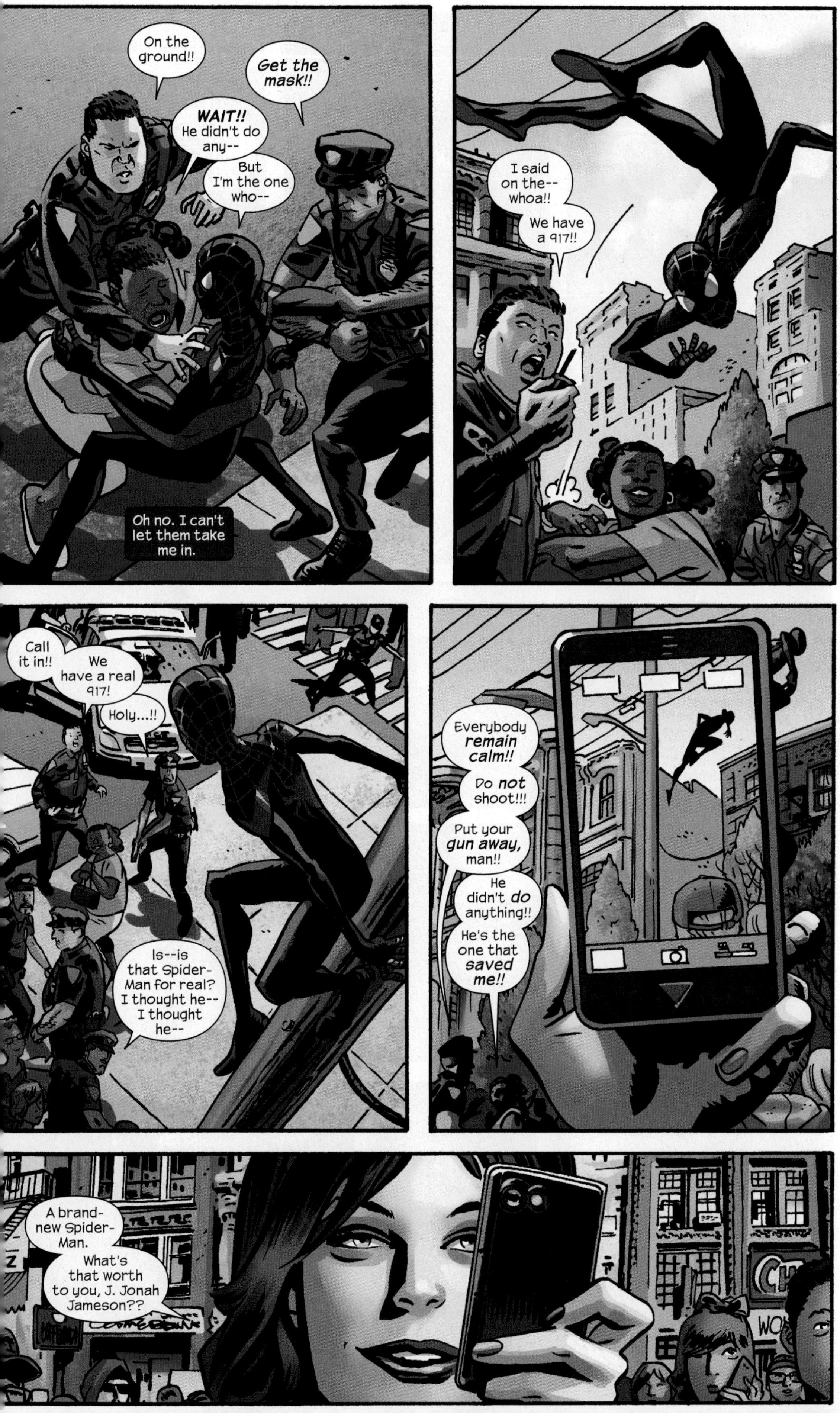
On the ground!!
Get the mask!!
WAIT!! He didn't do any--
But I'm the one who--
Oh no. I can't let them take me in.
I said on the-- whoa!!
We have a 917!!
Call it in!!
We have a real 917!
Holy...!!
Is--is that Spider-Man for real? I thought he-- I thought he--
Everybody remain calm!!
Do not shoot!!!
Put your gun away, man!!
He didn't do anything!!
He's the one that saved me!!
A brand-new Spider-Man.
What's that worth to you, J. Jonah Jameson??

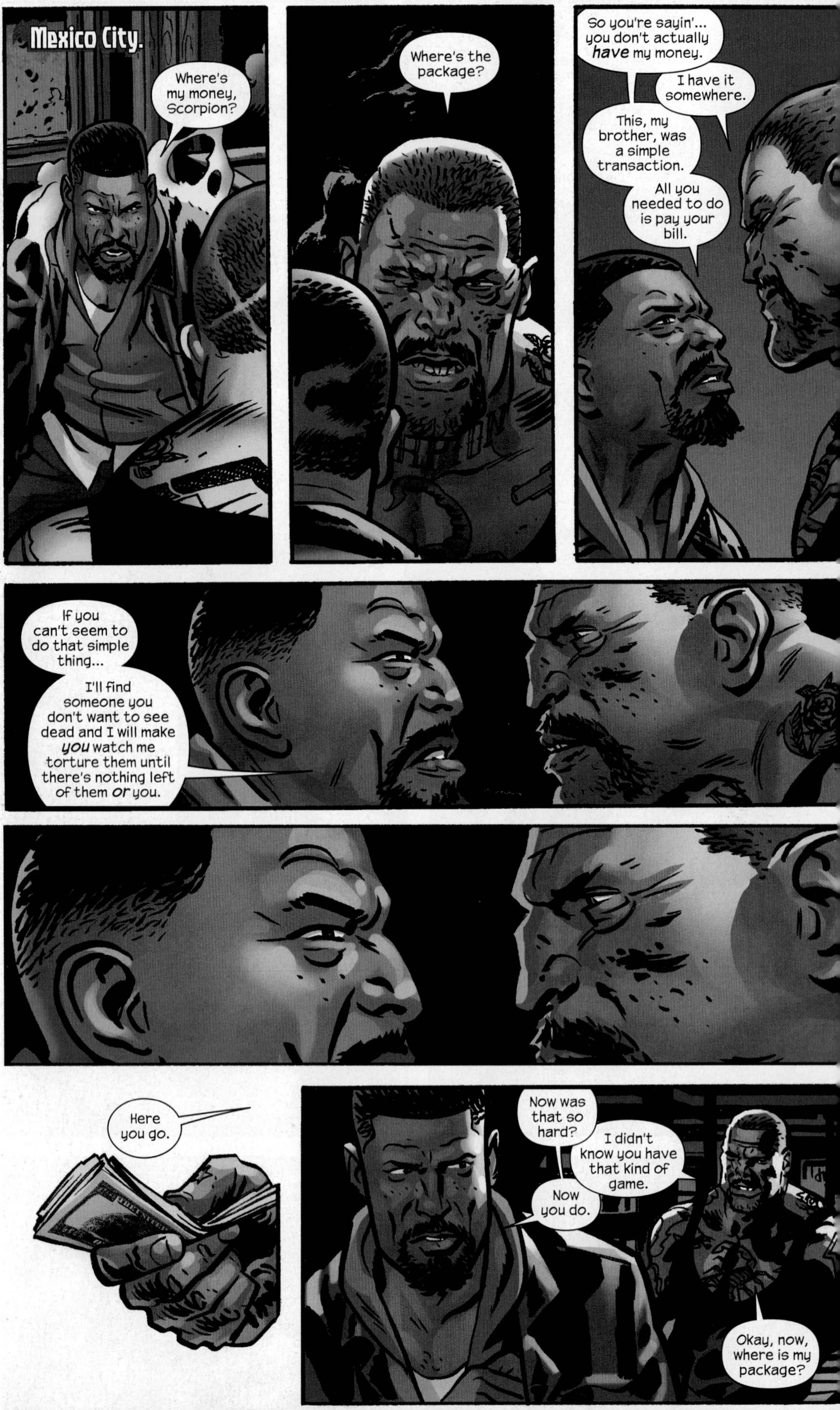
Mexico City.
Where's my money, Scorpion?
Where's the package?
So you're sayin'... you don't actually have my money.
I have it somewhere.
This, my brother, was a simple transaction.
All you needed to do is pay your bill.
If you can't seem to do that simple thing...
I'll find someone you don't want to see dead and I will make you watch me torture them until there's nothing left of them or you.
Here you go.
Now was that so hard?
I didn't know you have that kind of game.
Now you do.
Okay, now, where is my package?

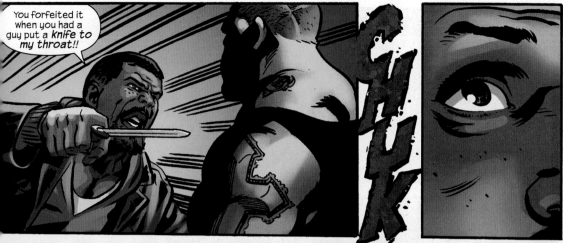

You forfeited it when you had a guy put a *knife to my throat!!*

CHUK

You're regretting that almost immediately, right?

ZZAAACCCTTT

How much did the Tinkerer charge you for that clunker?

Curious. Just talking shop.

CHUK

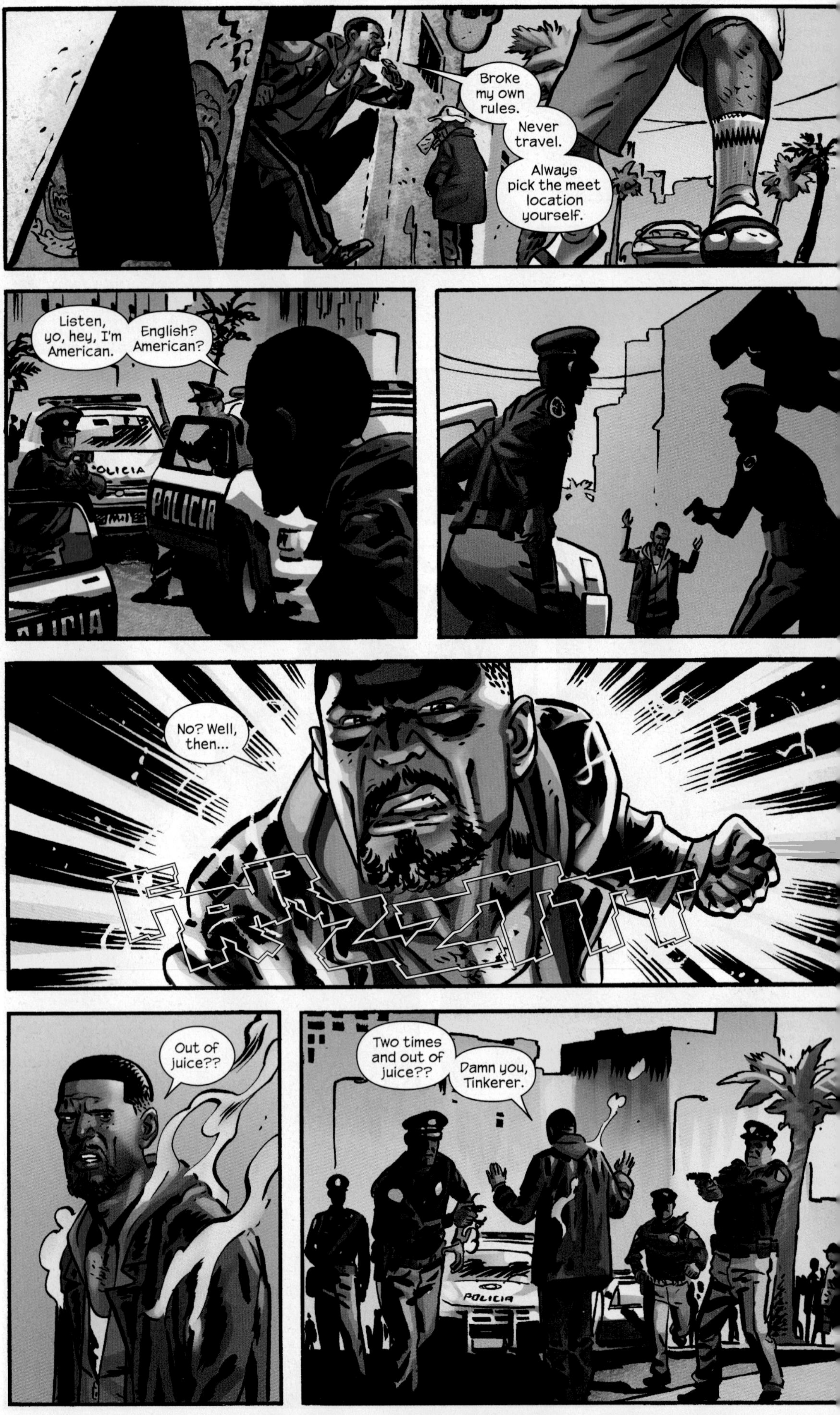
Broke my own rules.
Never travel.
Always pick the meet location yourself.
Listen, yo, hey, I'm American.
English? American?
POLICIA
POLICIA
No? Well, then...
Out of juice??
Two times and out of juice??
Damn you, Tinkerer.
POLICIA

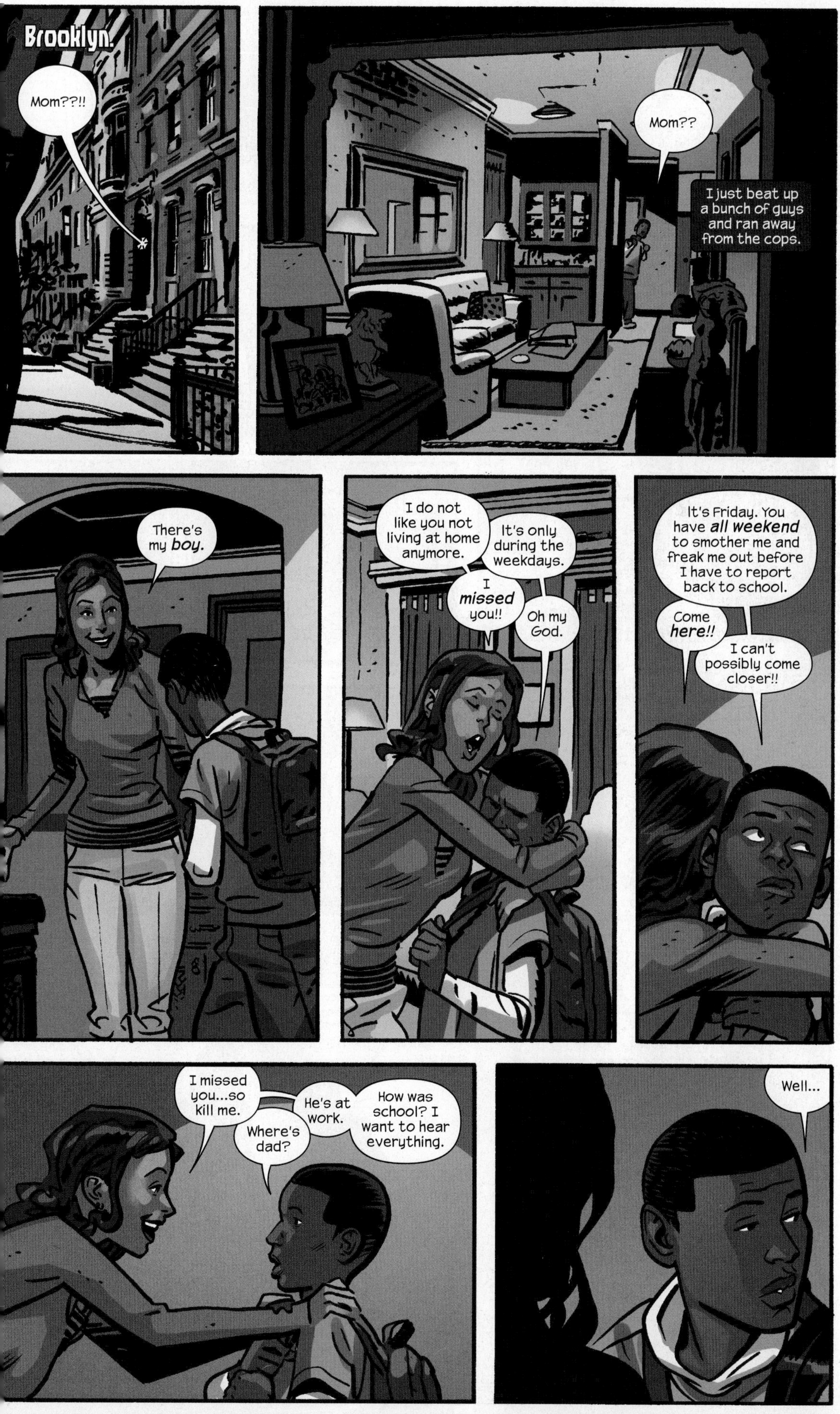
Brooklyn.
Mom??!!
Mom??
I just beat up a bunch of guys and ran away from the cops.
There's my boy.
I do not like you not living at home anymore.
It's only during the weekdays.
I missed you!!
Oh my God.
It's Friday. You have all weekend to smother me and freak me out before I have to report back to school.
Come here!!
I can't possibly come closer!!
I missed you...so kill me.
Where's dad?
He's at work.
How was school? I want to hear everything.
Well...

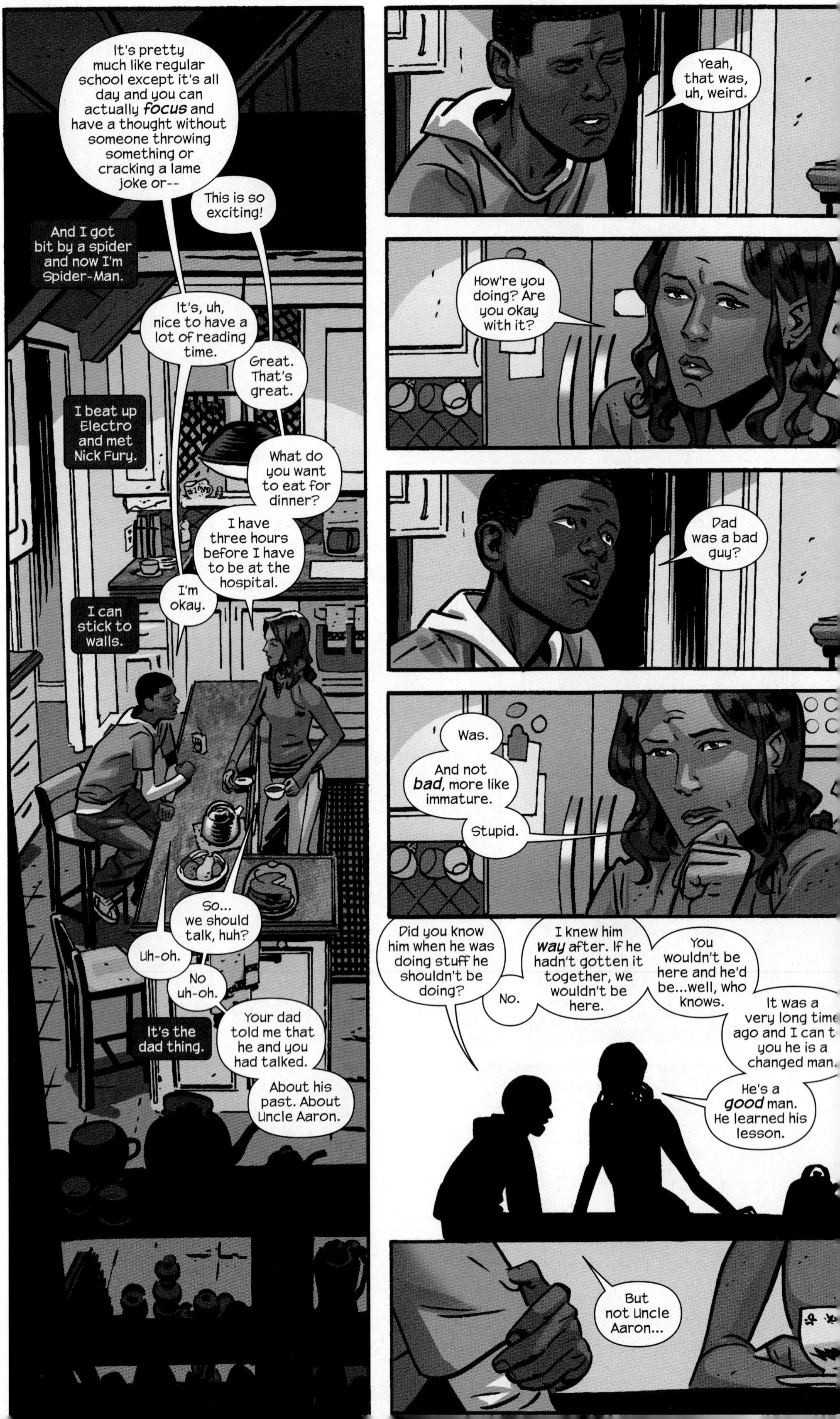

It's pretty much like regular school except it's all day and you can actually focus and have a thought without someone throwing something or cracking a lame joke or--
This is so exciting!
And I got bit by a spider and now I'm Spider-Man.
It's, uh, nice to have a lot of reading time.
Great. That's great.
I beat up Electro and met Nick Fury.
What do you want to eat for dinner?
I have three hours before I have to be at the hospital.
I'm okay.
I can stick to walls.
So... we should talk, huh?
Uh-oh.
No uh-oh.
It's the dad thing.
Your dad told me that he and you had talked.
About his past. About Uncle Aaron.
Yeah, that was, uh, weird.
How're you doing? Are you okay with it?
Dad was a bad guy?
Was.
And not bad, more like immature.
Stupid.
Did you know him when he was doing stuff he shouldn't be doing?
No.
I knew him way after. If he hadn't gotten it together, we wouldn't be here.
You wouldn't be here and he'd be...well, who knows.
He's a good man. He learned his lesson.
But not Uncle Aaron...

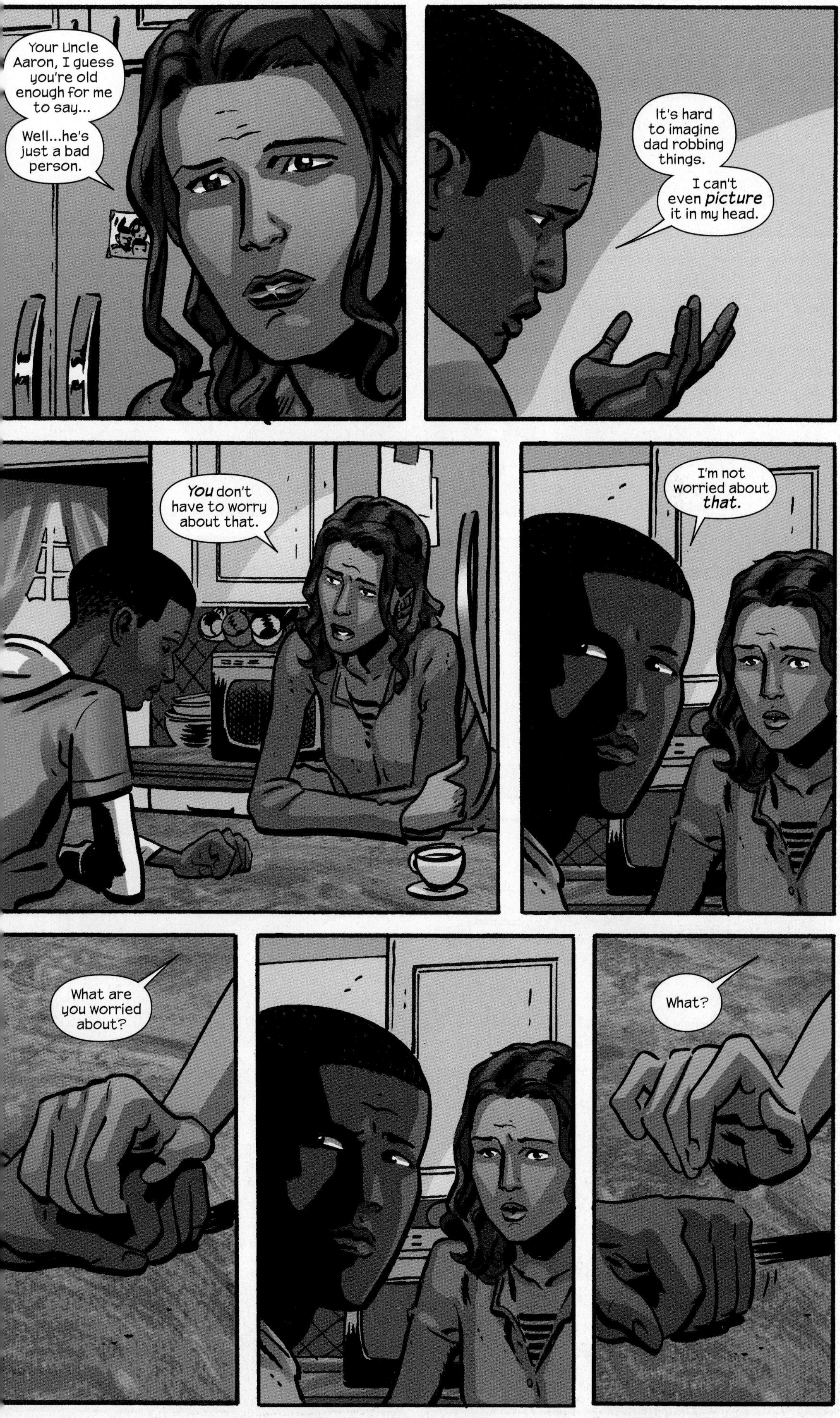
Your Uncle Aaron, I guess you're old enough for me to say...
Well...he's just a bad person.
It's hard to imagine dad robbing things.
I can't even *picture* it in my head.
You don't have to worry about that.
I'm not worried about *that.*
What are you worried about?
What?

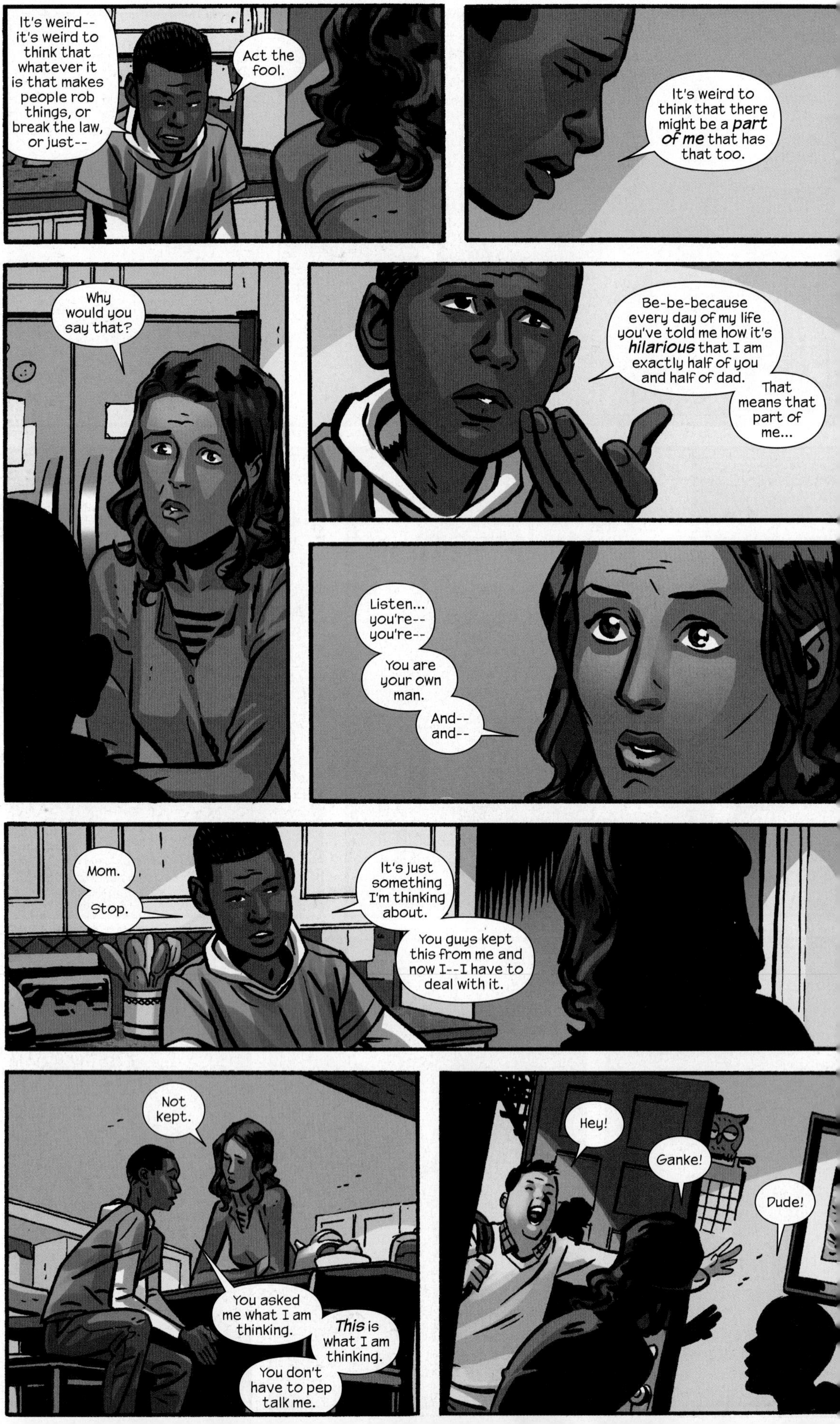

It's weird-- it's weird to think that whatever it is that makes people rob things, or break the law, or just--
Act the fool.
It's weird to think that there might be a *part of me* that has that too.
Why would you say that?
Be-be-because every day of my life you've told me how it's *hilarious* that I am exactly half of you and half of dad.
That means that part of me...
Listen... you're-- you're--
You are your own man.
And-- and--
Mom.
Stop.
It's just something I'm thinking about.
You guys kept this from me and now I--I have to deal with it.
Not kept.
You asked me what I am thinking.
This is what I am thinking.
You don't have to pep talk me.
Hey!
Ganke!
Dude!

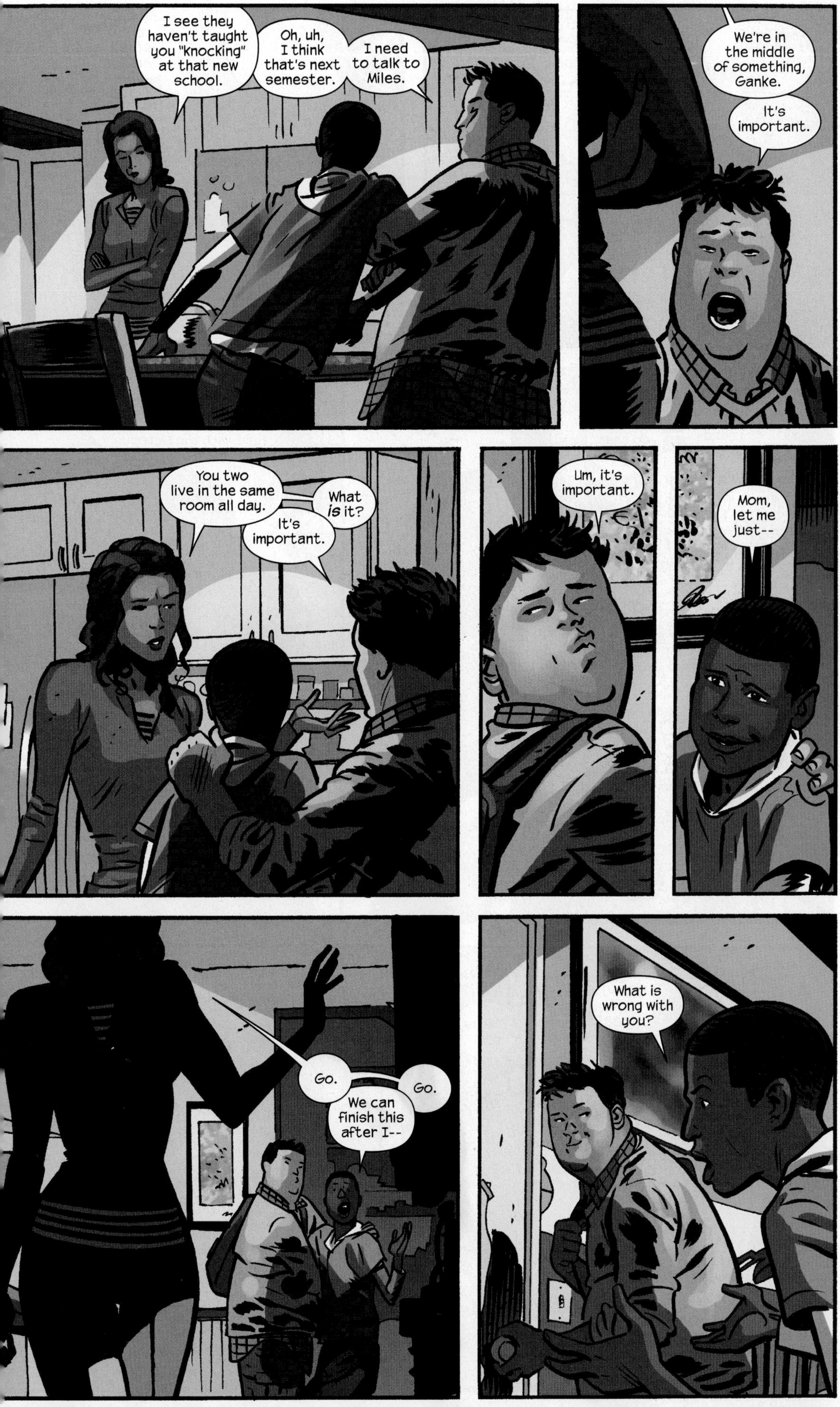
I see they haven't taught you "knocking" at that new school.
Oh, uh, I think that's next semester.
I need to talk to Miles.
We're in the middle of something, Ganke.
It's important.
You two live in the same room all day.
What *is* it?
It's important.
Um, it's important.
Mom, let me just--
Go.
Go.
We can finish this after I--
What is wrong with you?

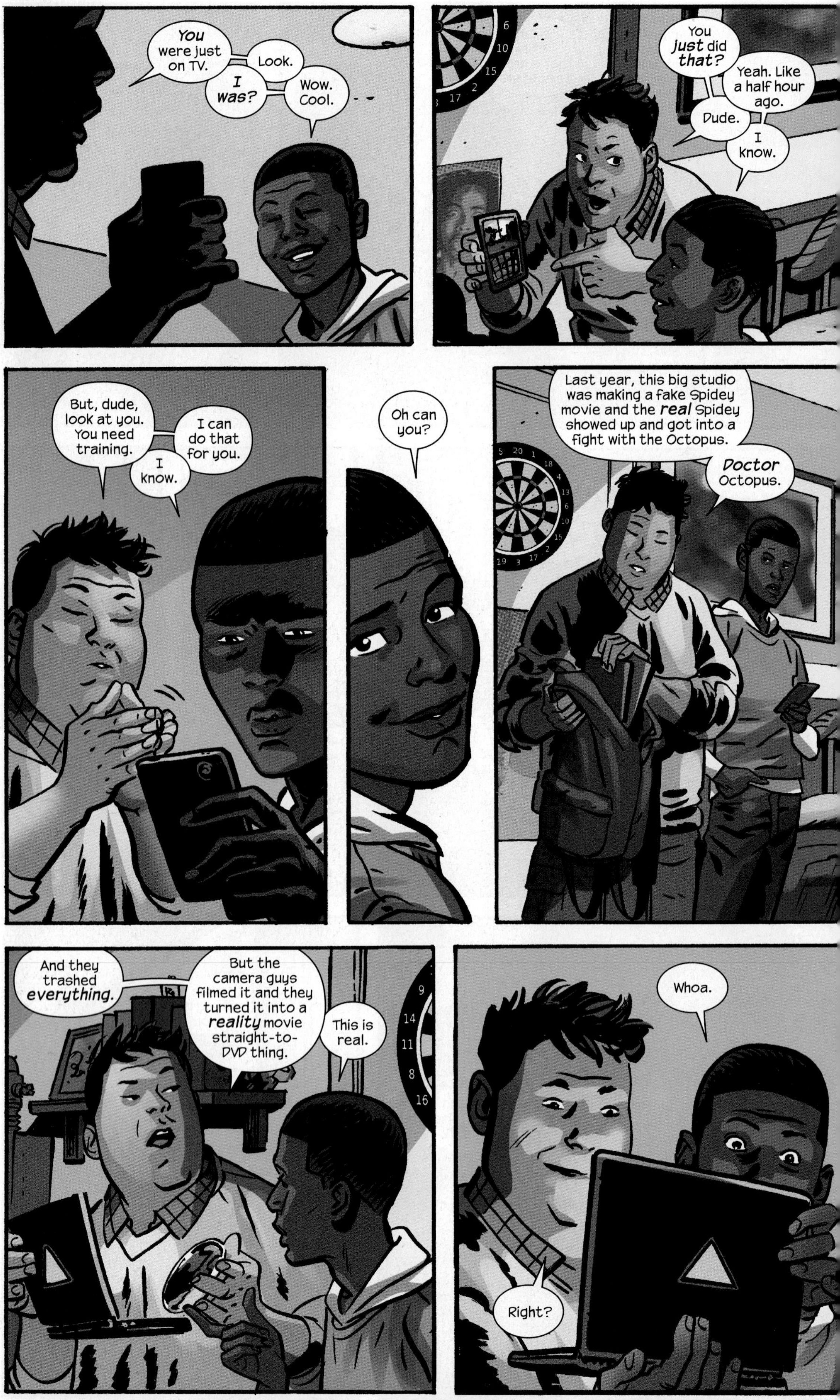
You were just on TV.
Look.
I was?
Wow. Cool.
You just did that?
Yeah. Like a half hour ago.
Dude.
I know.
But, dude, look at you. You need training.
I can do that for you.
I know.
Oh can you?
Last year, this big studio was making a fake Spidey movie and the real Spidey showed up and got into a fight with the Octopus.
Doctor Octopus.
And they trashed everything.
But the camera guys filmed it and they turned it into a reality movie straight-to-DVD thing.
This is real.
Whoa.
Right?

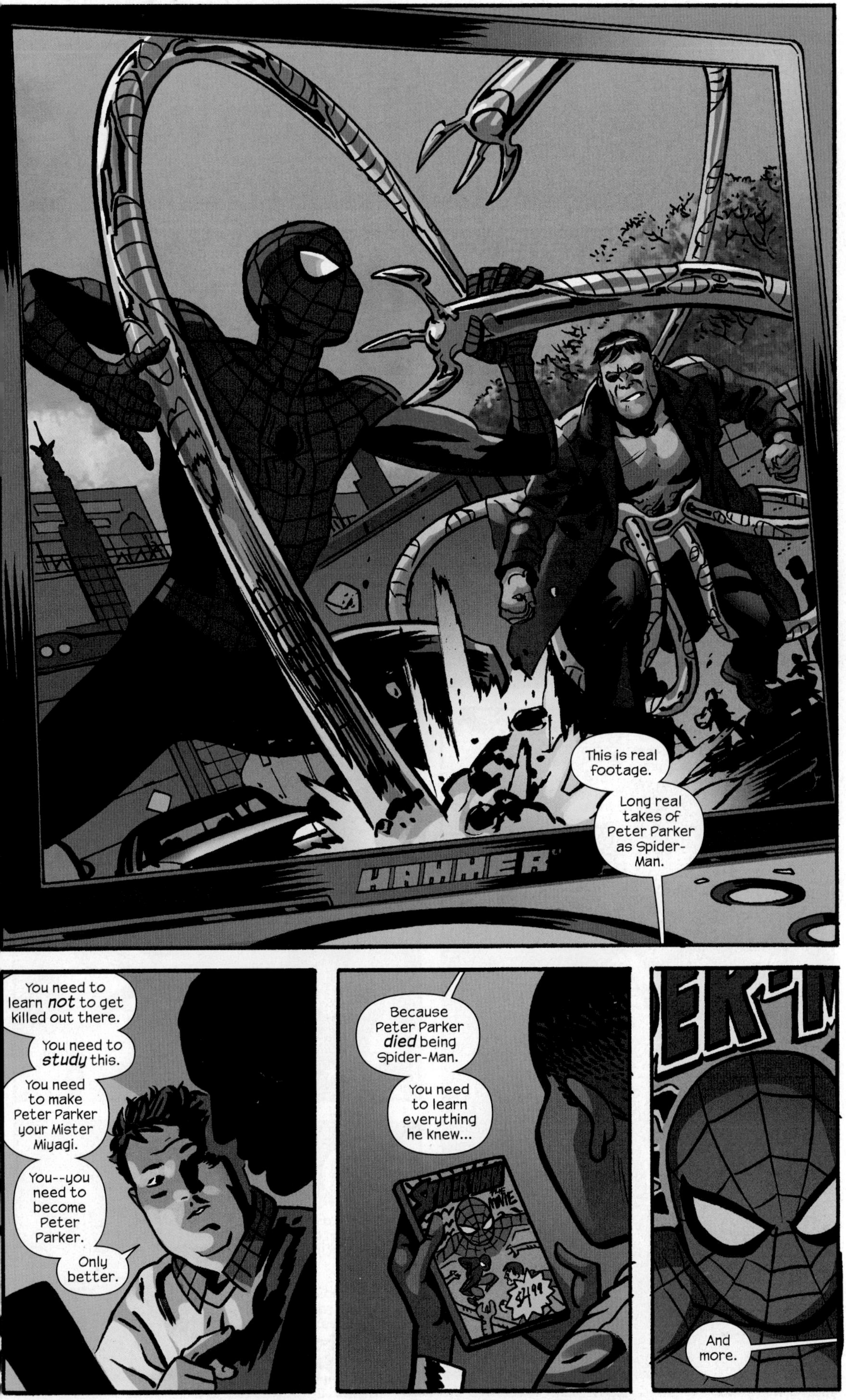
HAMMER
This is real footage.
Long real takes of Peter Parker as Spider-Man.
You need to learn *not* to get killed out there.
You need to *study* this.
You need to make Peter Parker your Mister Miyagi.
You--you need to become Peter Parker.
Only better.
Because Peter Parker *died* being Spider-Man.
You need to learn everything he knew...
$4.99
And more.

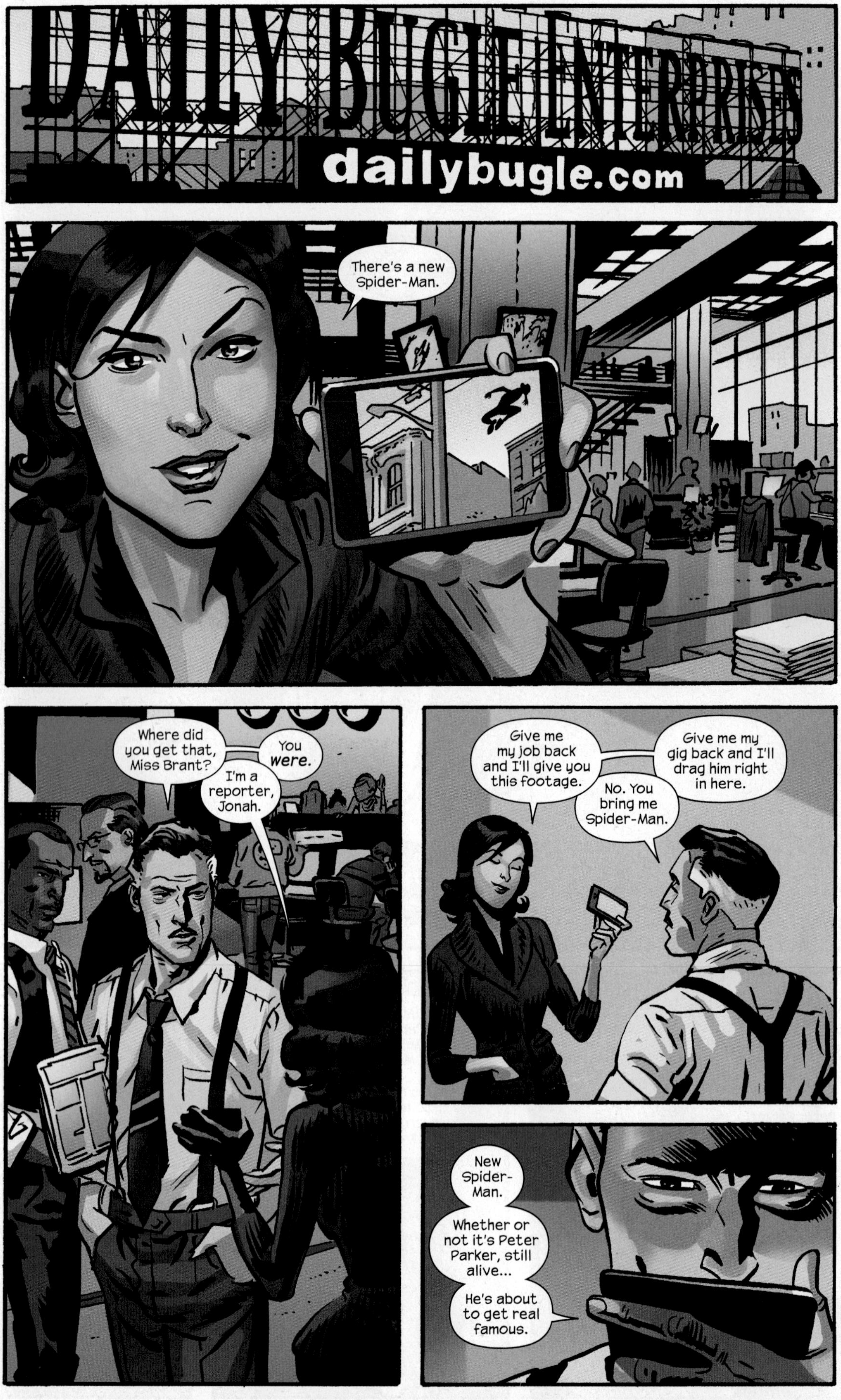
DAILY BUGLE ENTERPRISES
dailybugle.com
There's a new Spider-Man.
Where did you get that, Miss Brant?
You were.
I'm a reporter, Jonah.
Give me my job back and I'll give you this footage.
Give me my gig back and I'll drag him right in here.
No. You bring me Spider-Man.
New Spider-Man.
Whether or not it's Peter Parker, still alive...
He's about to get real famous.

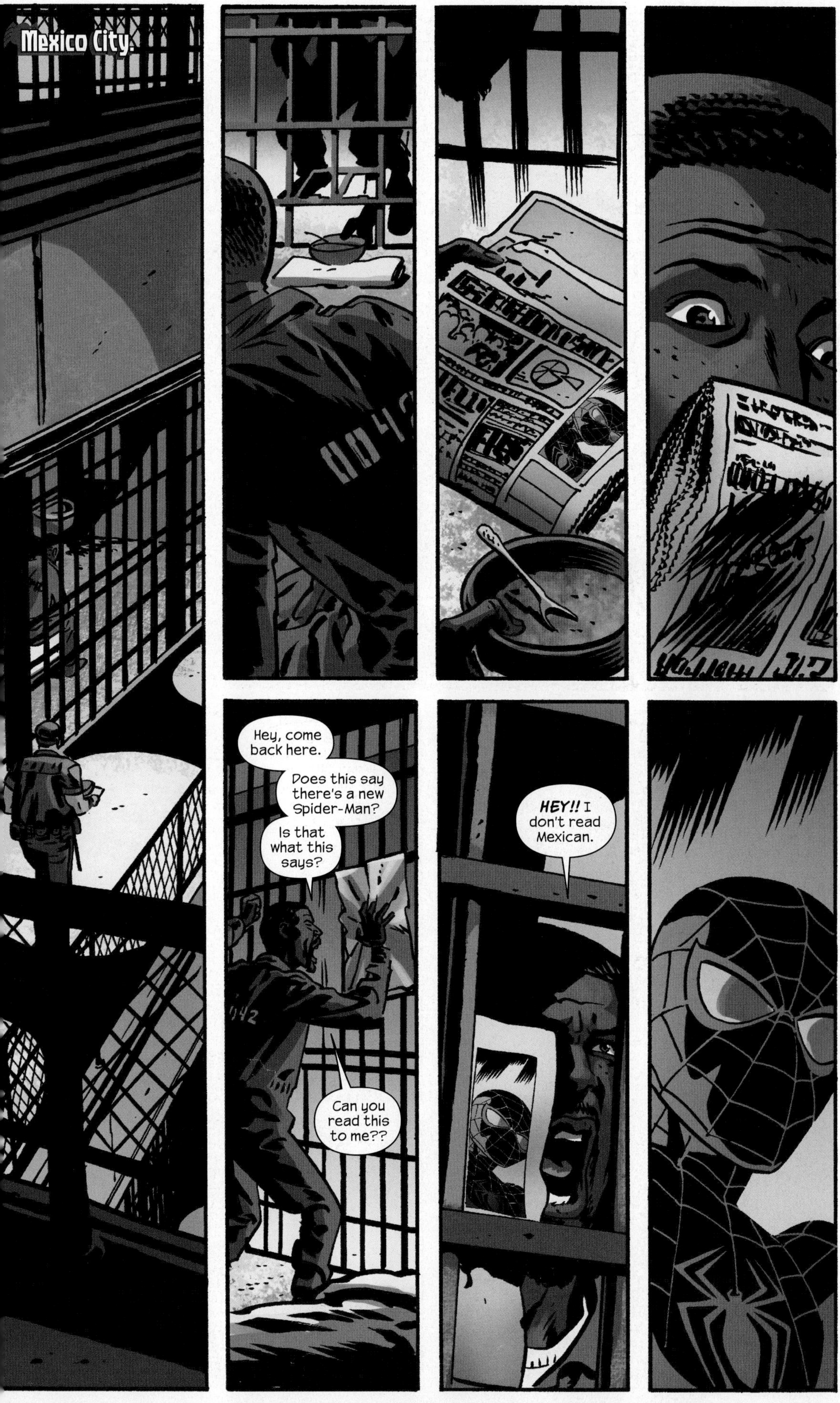
Mexico City.
Hey, come back here.
Does this say there's a new Spider-Man?
Is that what this says?
Can you read this to me??
HEY!! I don't read Mexican.

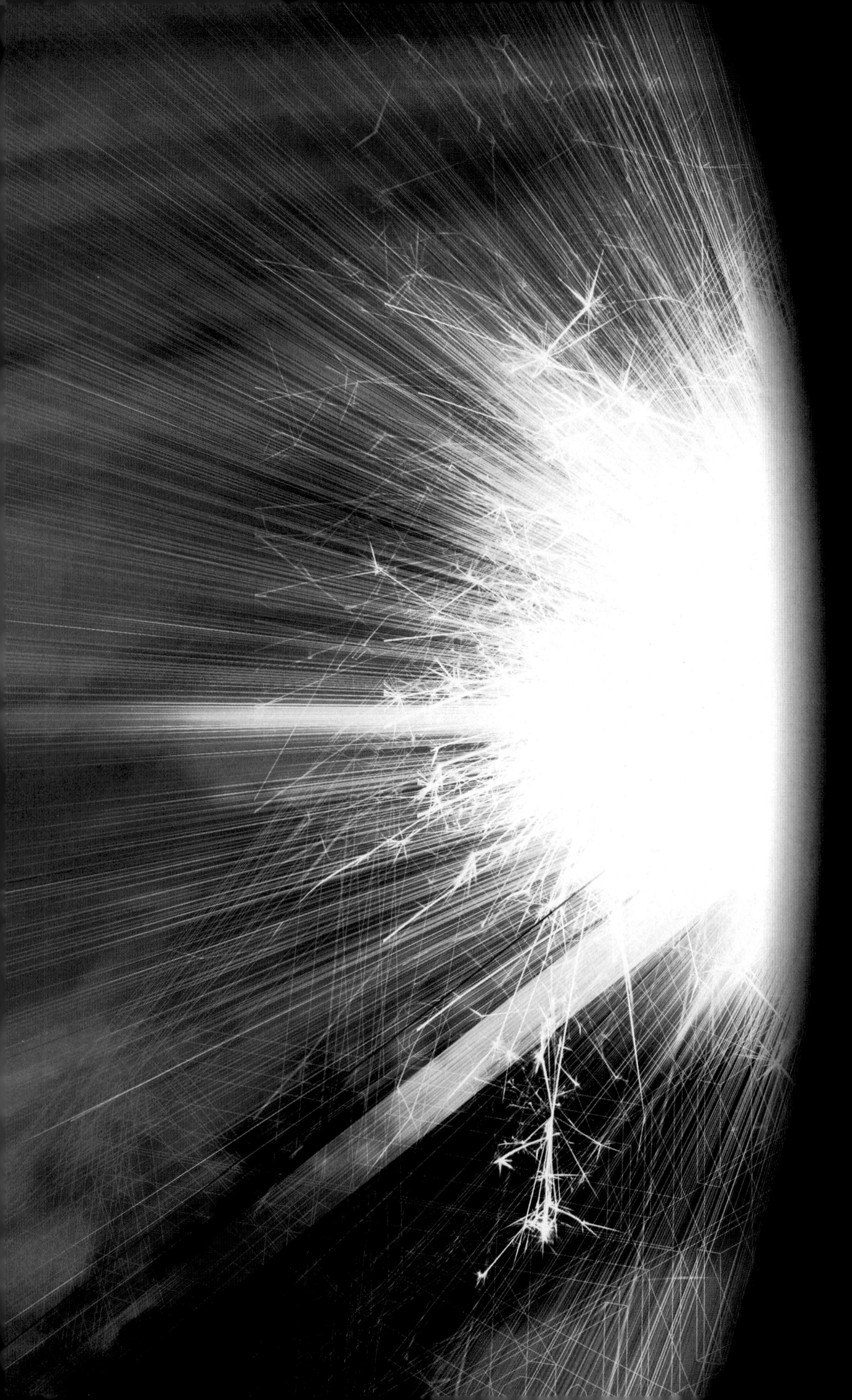

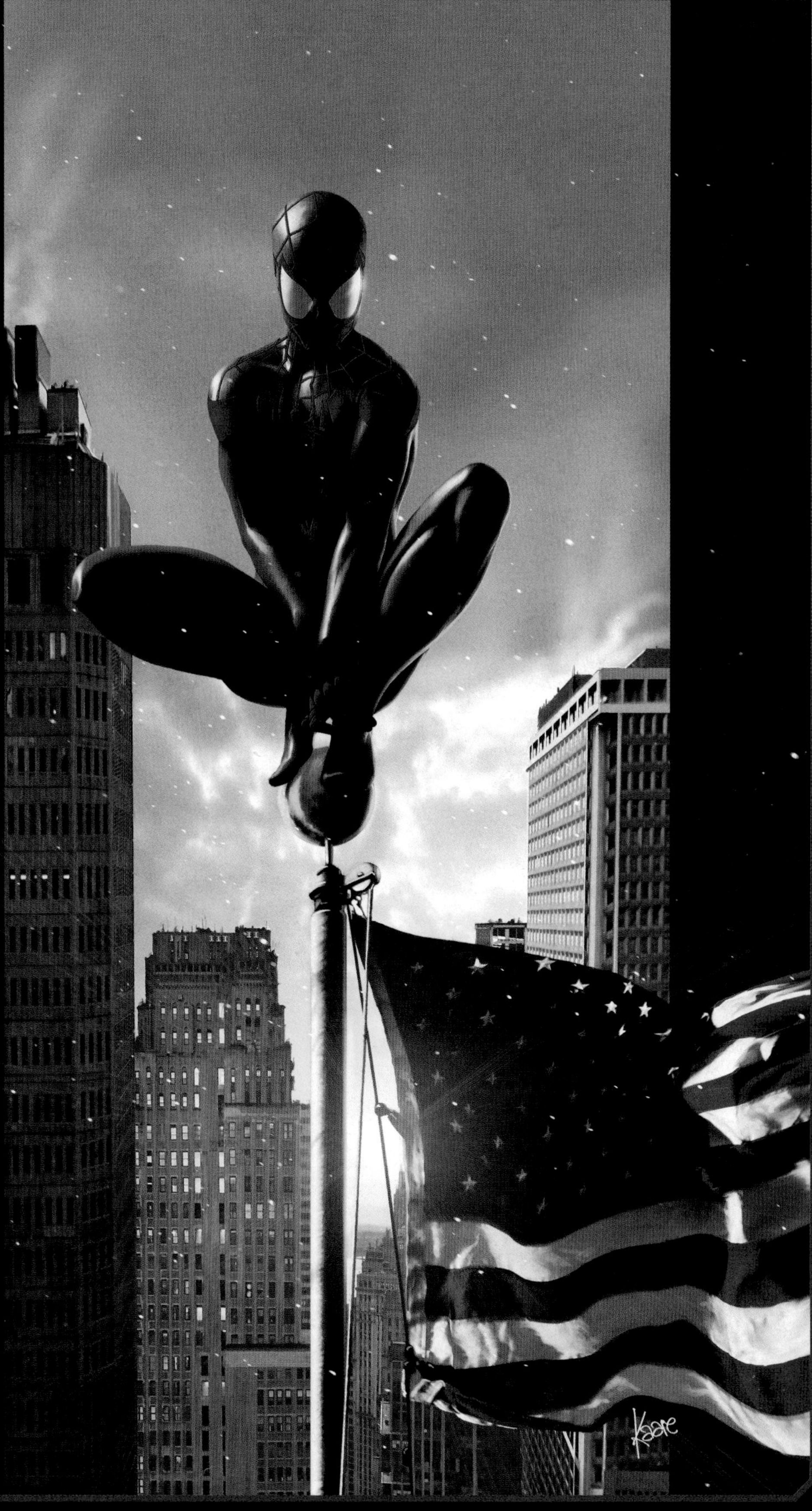
Kaare

ULTIMATE COMICS SPIDER-MAN #7

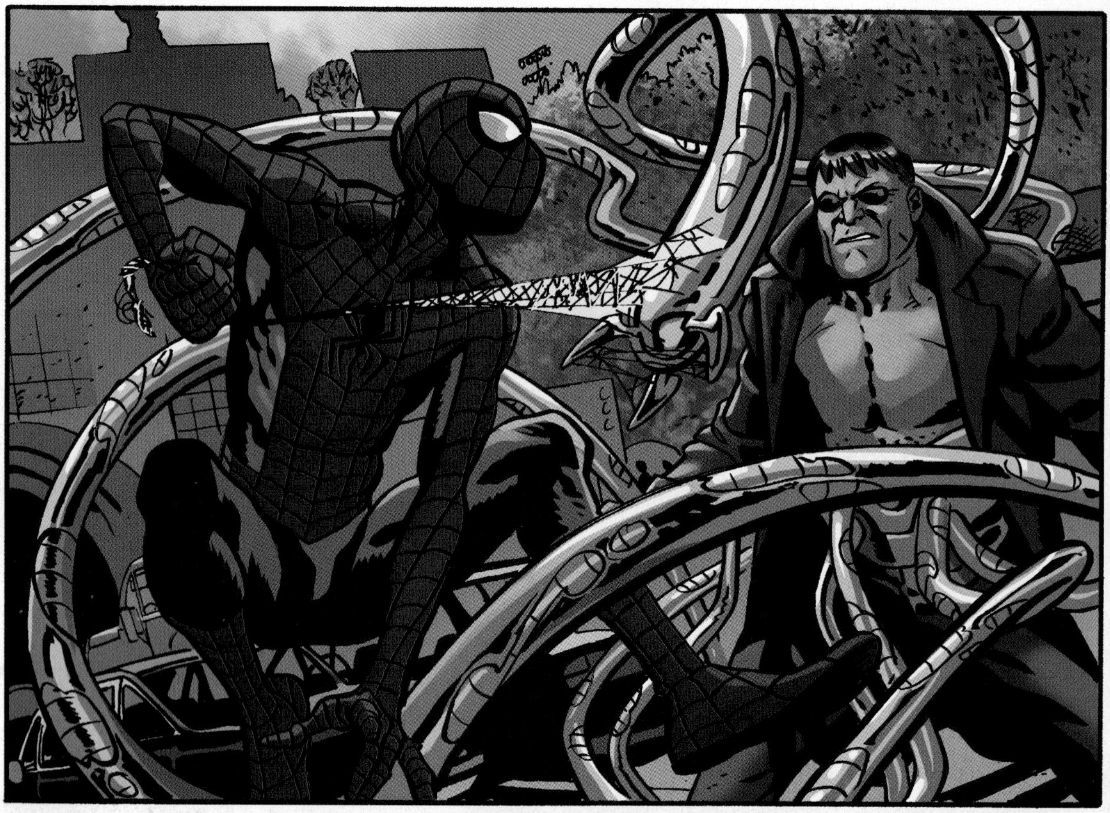

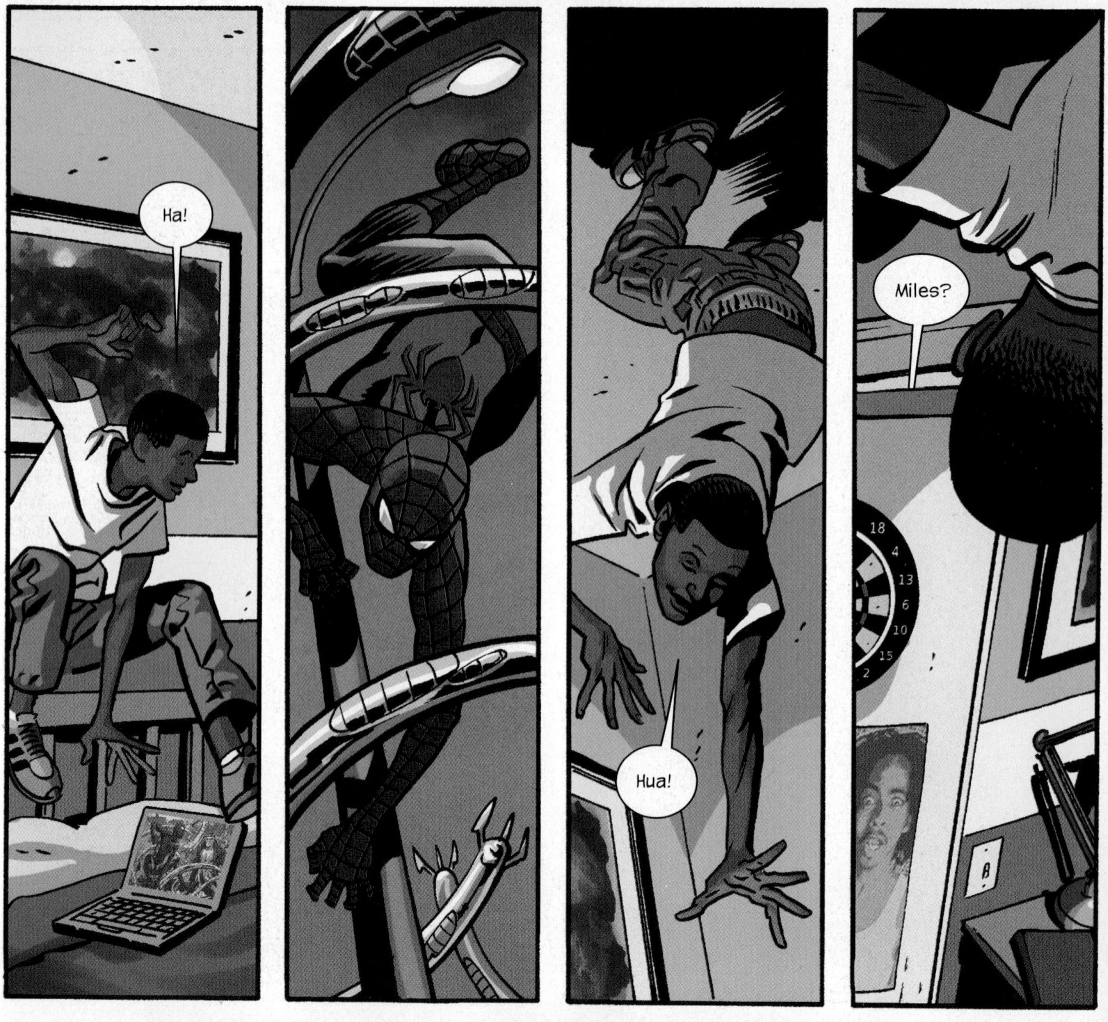
Ha!
Hua!
Miles?
18
4
13
6
10
15
2

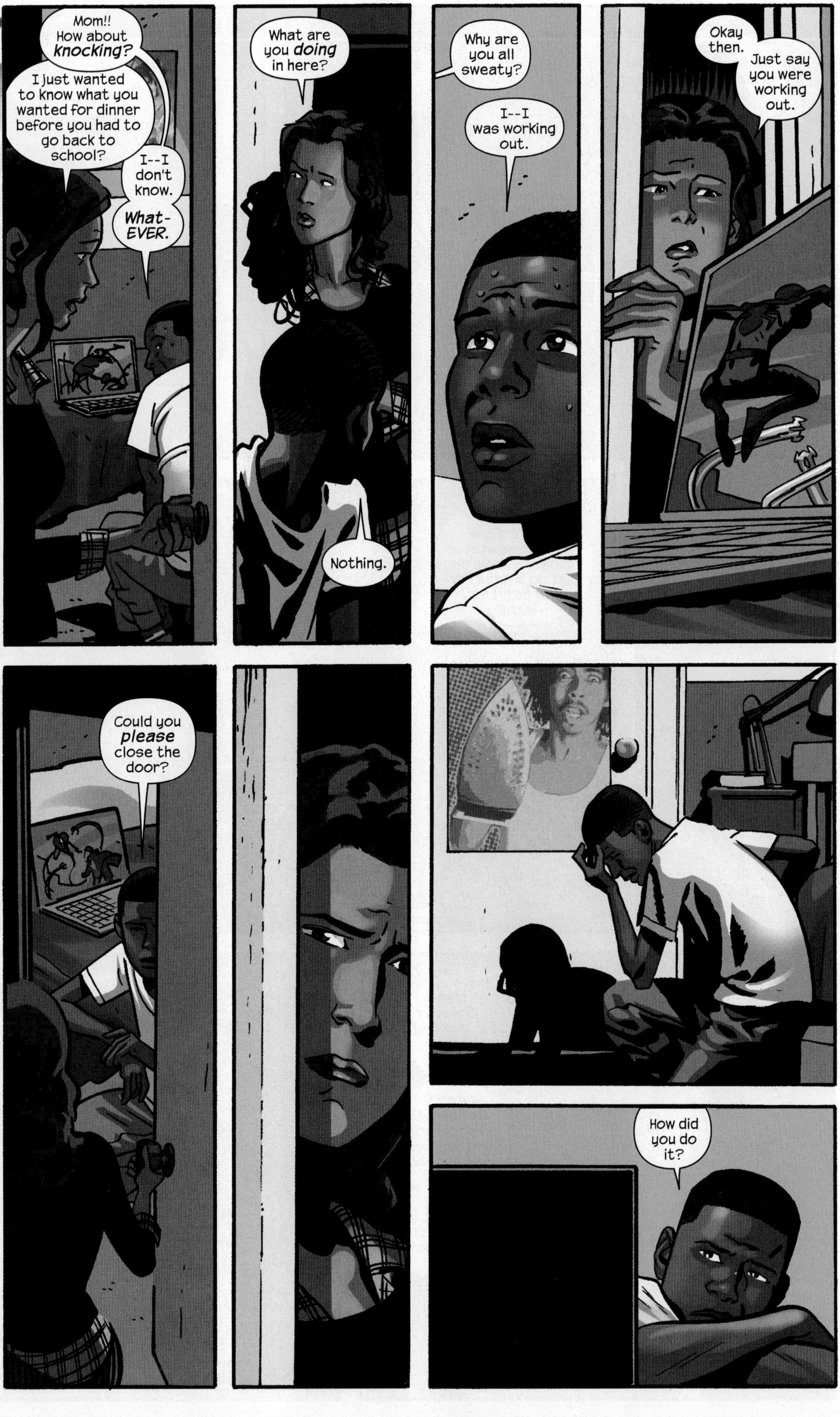
Mom!! How about *knocking?*
I just wanted to know what you wanted for dinner before you had to go back to school?
I--I don't know.
What-EVER.
What are you *doing* in here?
Nothing.
Why are you all sweaty?
I--I was working out.
Okay then.
Just say you were working out.
Could you *please* close the door?
How did you do it?

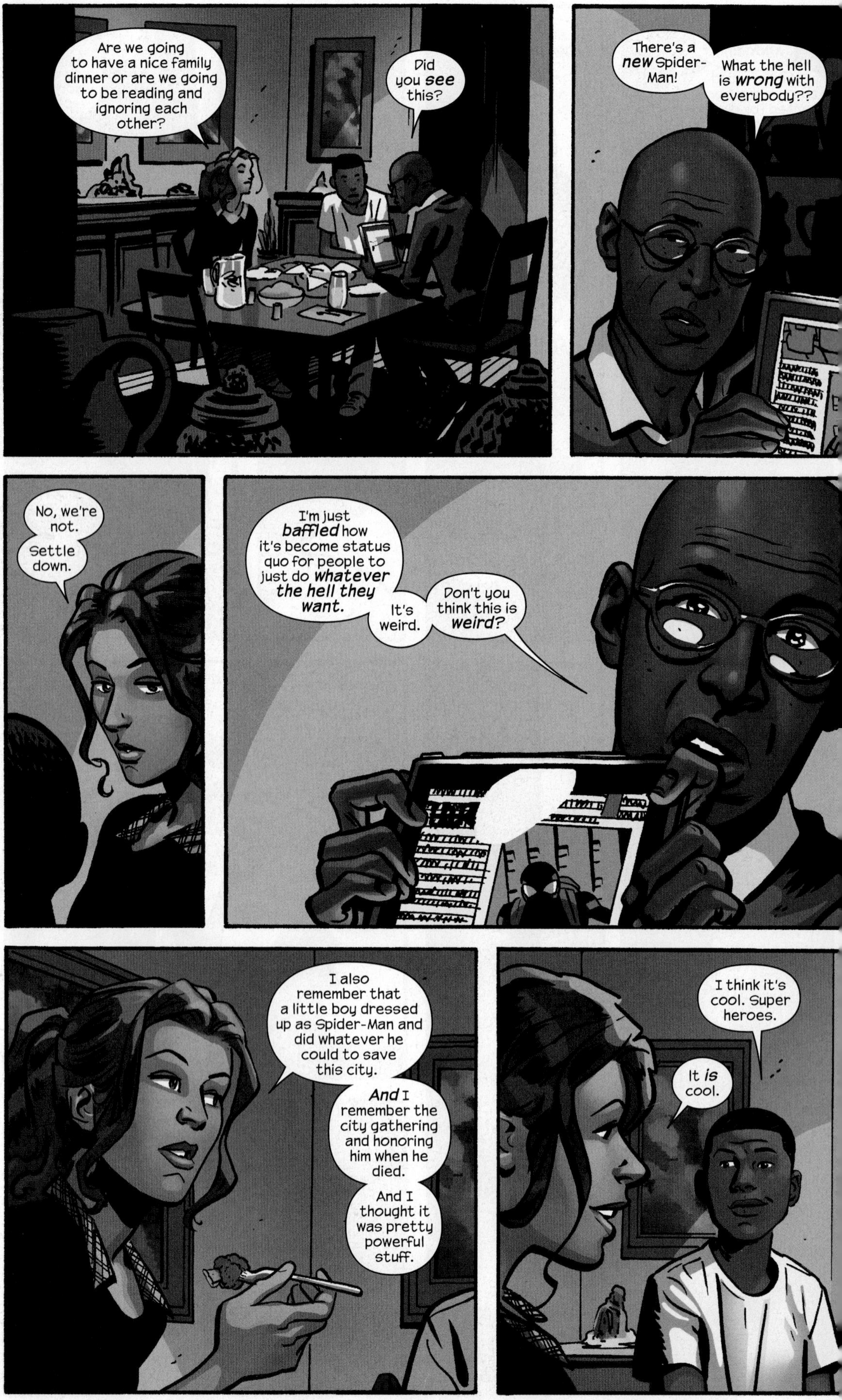

Are we going to have a nice family dinner or are we going to be reading and ignoring each other?
Did you *see* this?
There's a *new* Spider-Man!
What the hell is *wrong* with everybody??
No, we're not.
Settle down.
I'm just *baffled* how it's become status quo for people to just do *whatever the hell they want.*
It's weird.
Don't you think this is *weird?*
I also remember that a little boy dressed up as Spider-Man and did whatever he could to save this city.
And I remember the city gathering and honoring him when he died.
And I thought it was pretty powerful stuff.
I think it's cool. Super heroes.
It *is* cool.

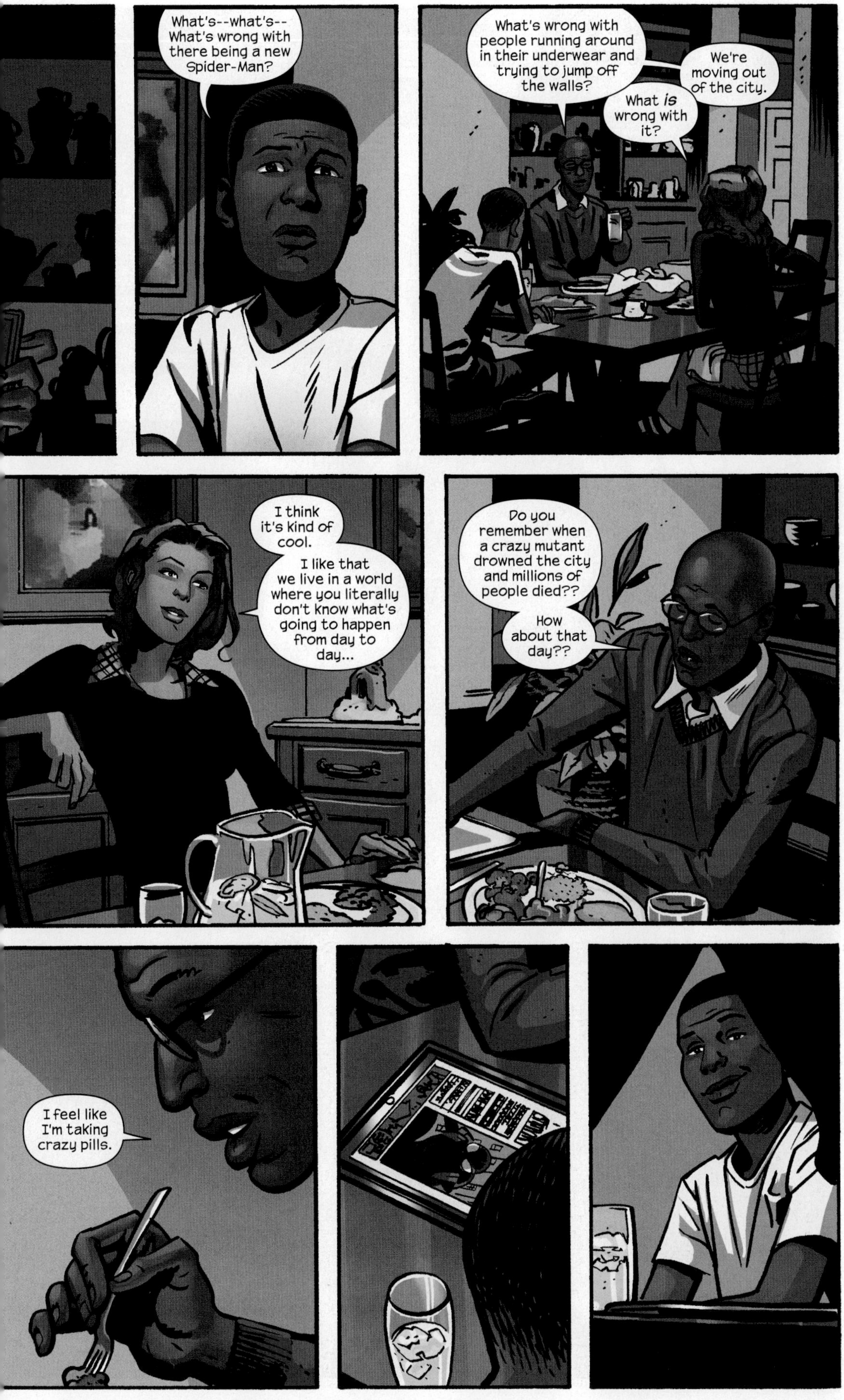
What's--what's--
What's wrong with there being a new Spider-Man?
What's wrong with people running around in their underwear and trying to jump off the walls?
What *is* wrong with it?
We're moving out of the city.
I think it's kind of cool.
I like that we live in a world where you literally don't know what's going to happen from day to day...
Do you remember when a crazy mutant drowned the city and millions of people died??
How about that day??
I feel like I'm taking crazy pills.

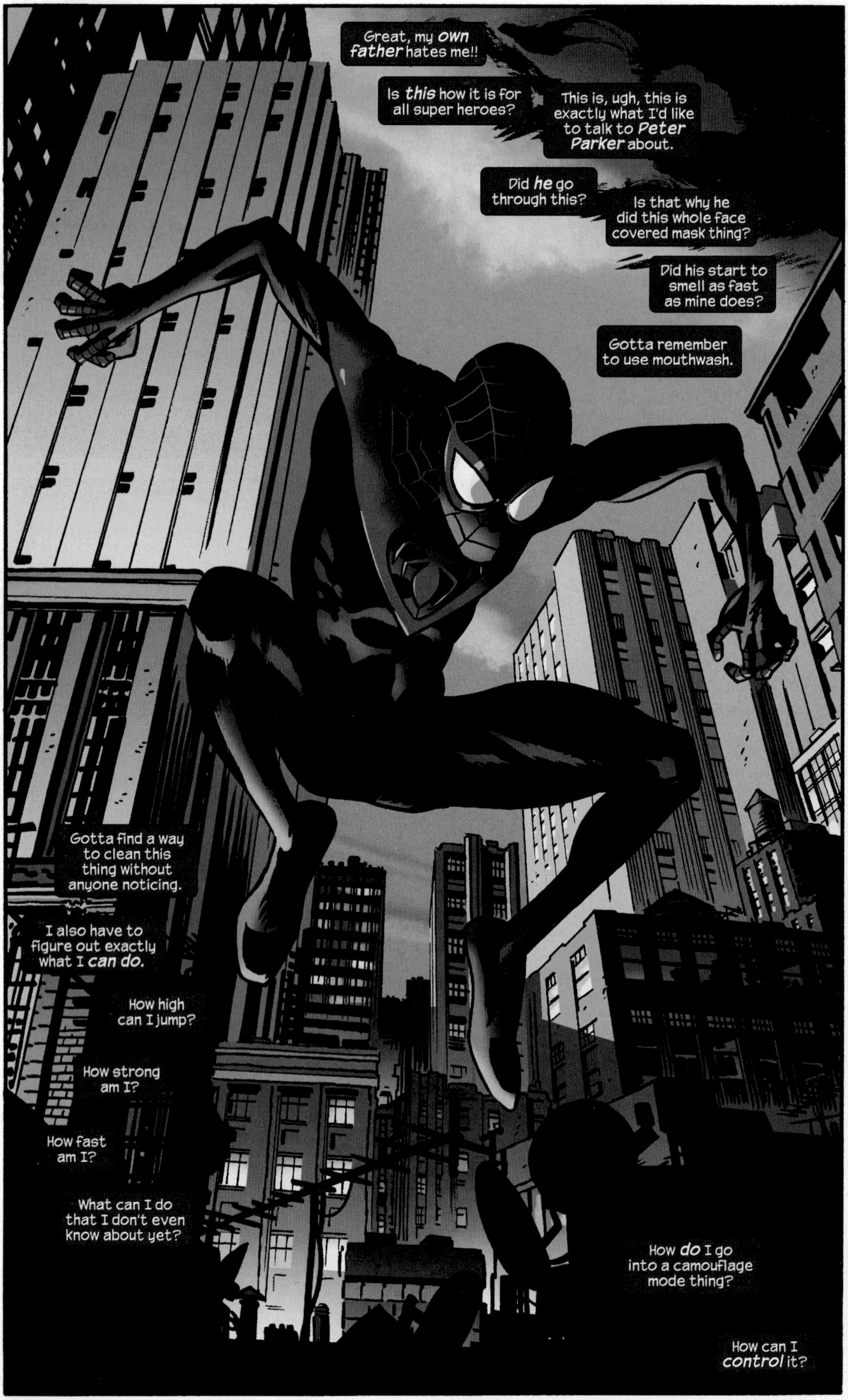
Great, my *own father* hates me!!
Is *this* how it is for all super heroes?
This is, ugh, this is exactly what I'd like to talk to *Peter Parker* about.
Did *he* go through this?
Is that why he did this whole face covered mask thing?
Did his start to smell as fast as mine does?
Gotta remember to use mouthwash.
Gotta find a way to clean this thing without anyone noticing.
I also have to figure out exactly what I *can do.*
How high can I jump?
How strong am I?
How fast am I?
What can I do that I don't even know about yet?
How *do* I go into a camouflage mode thing?
How can I *control* it?

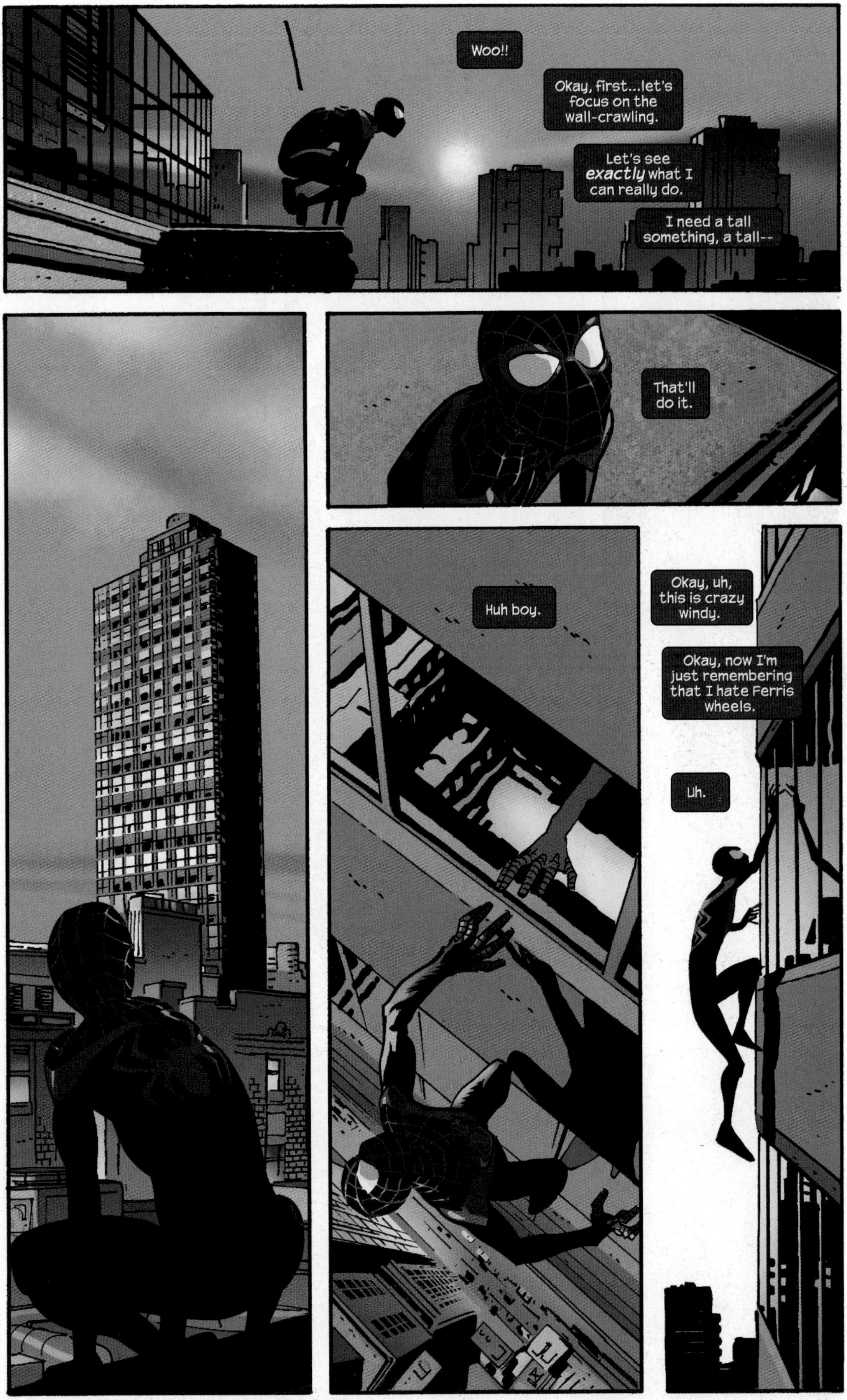
Woo!!
Okay, first...let's focus on the wall-crawling.
Let's see *exactly* what I can really do.
I need a tall something, a tall--
That'll do it.
Huh boy.
Okay, uh, this is crazy windy.
Okay, now I'm just remembering that I hate Ferris wheels.
Uh.

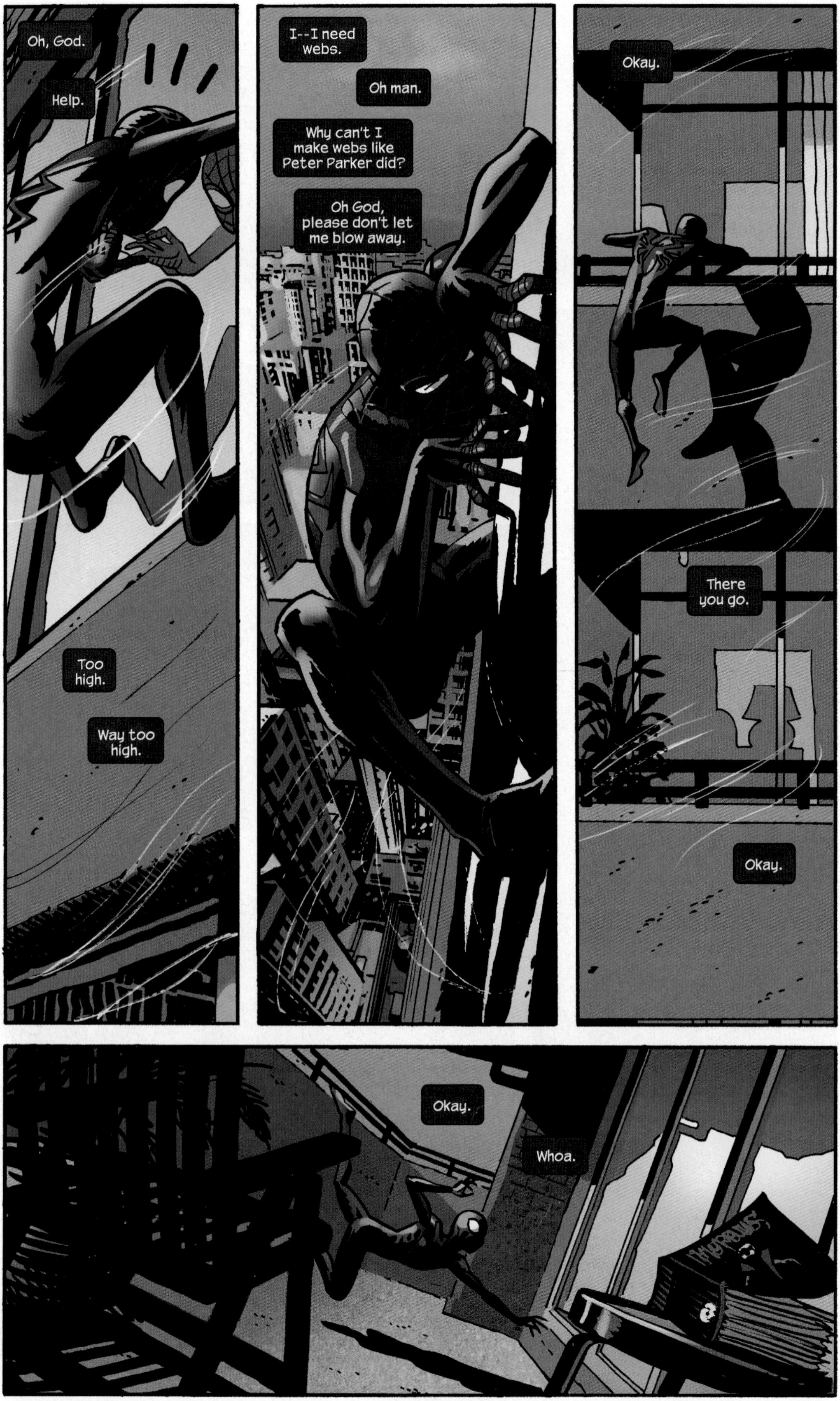
Oh, God.
Help.
Too high.
Way too high.
I--I need webs.
Oh man.
Why can't I make webs like Peter Parker did?
Oh God, please don't let me blow away.
Okay.
There you go.
Okay.
Okay.
Whoa.

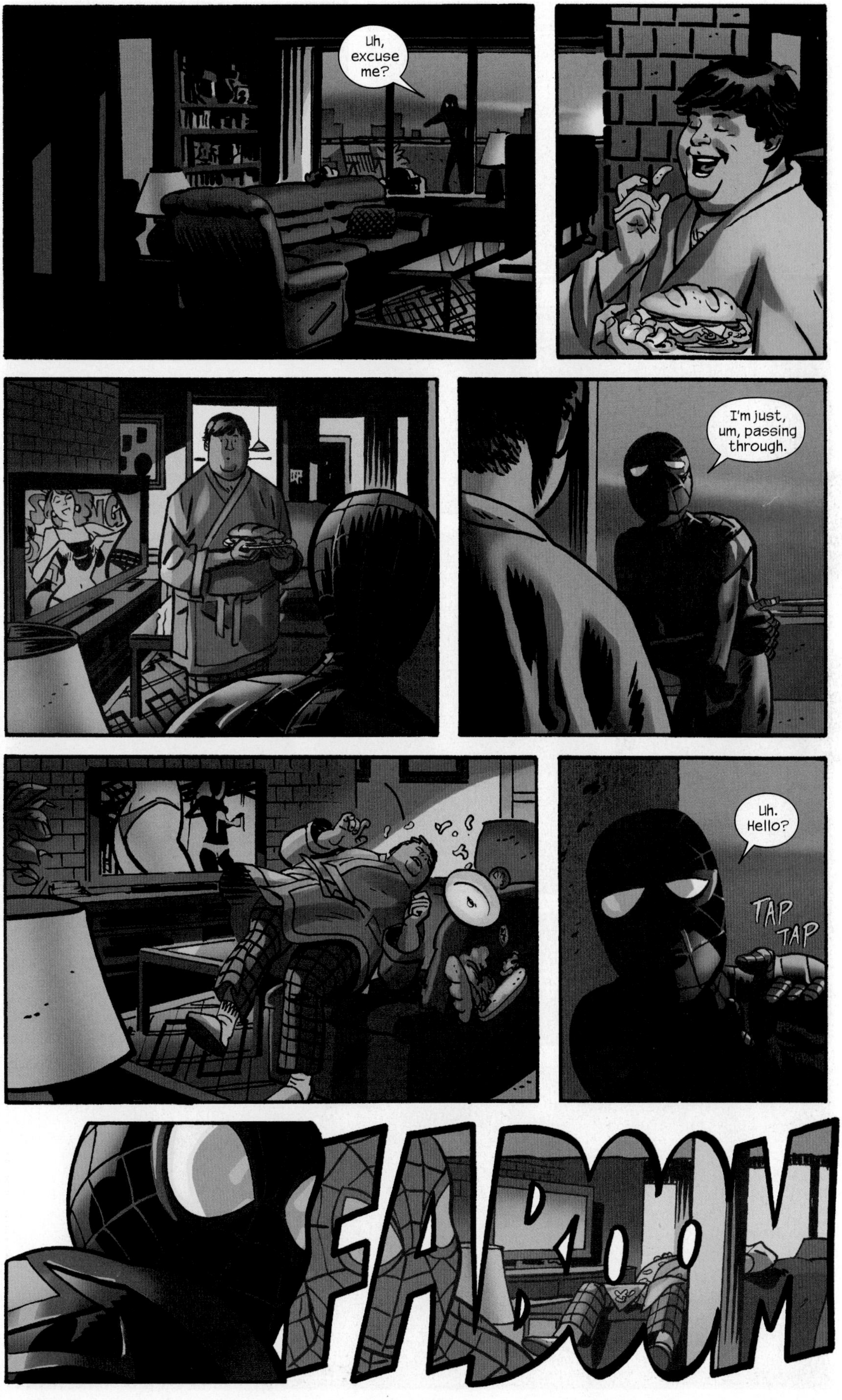
Uh, excuse me?
I'm just, um, passing through.
Uh. Hello?
TAP TAP
FADOOM

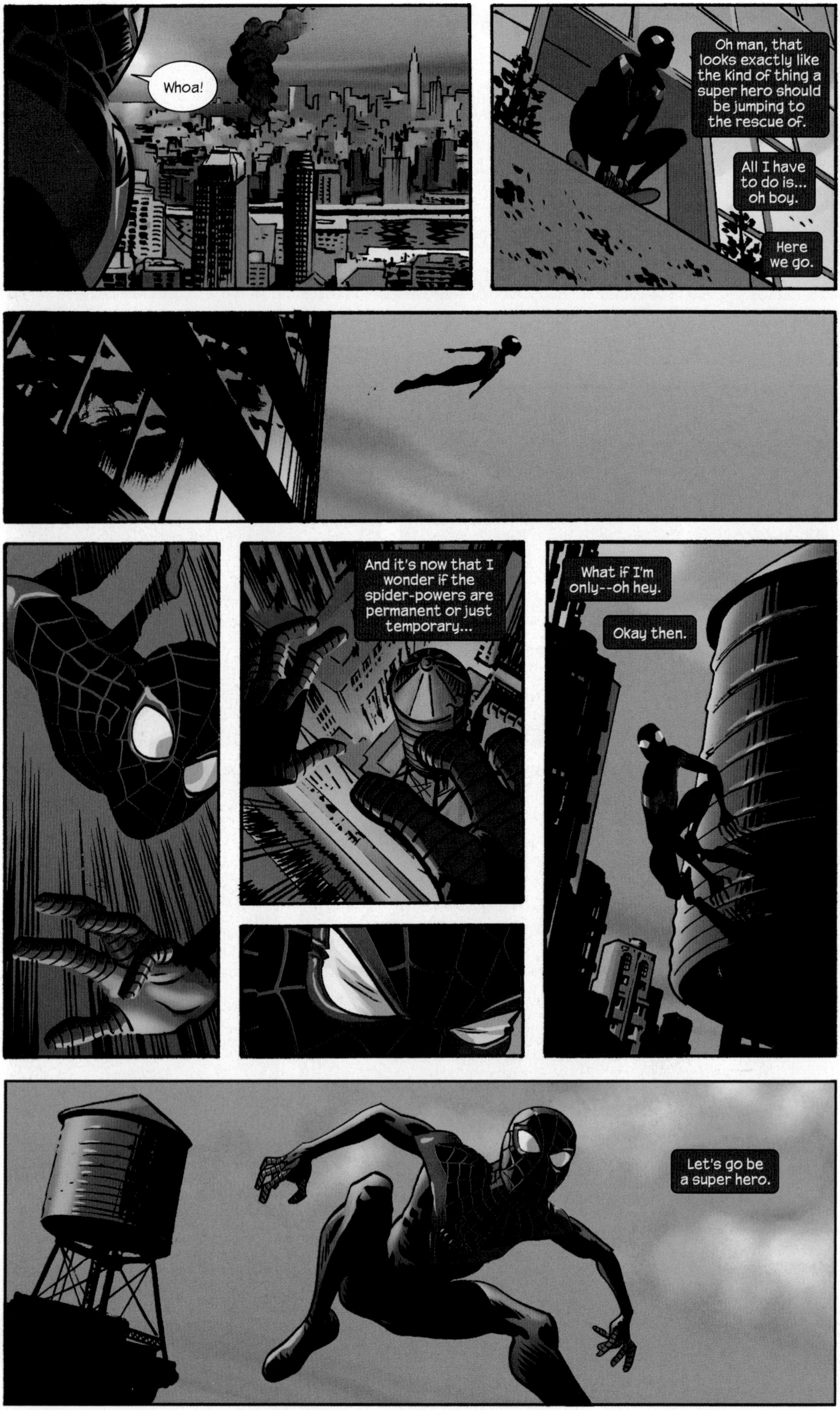

Whoa!
Oh man, that looks exactly like the kind of thing a super hero should be jumping to the rescue of.
All I have to do is... oh boy.
Here we go.
And it's now that I wonder if the spider-powers are permanent or just temporary...
What if I'm only--oh hey.
Okay then.
Let's go be a super hero.

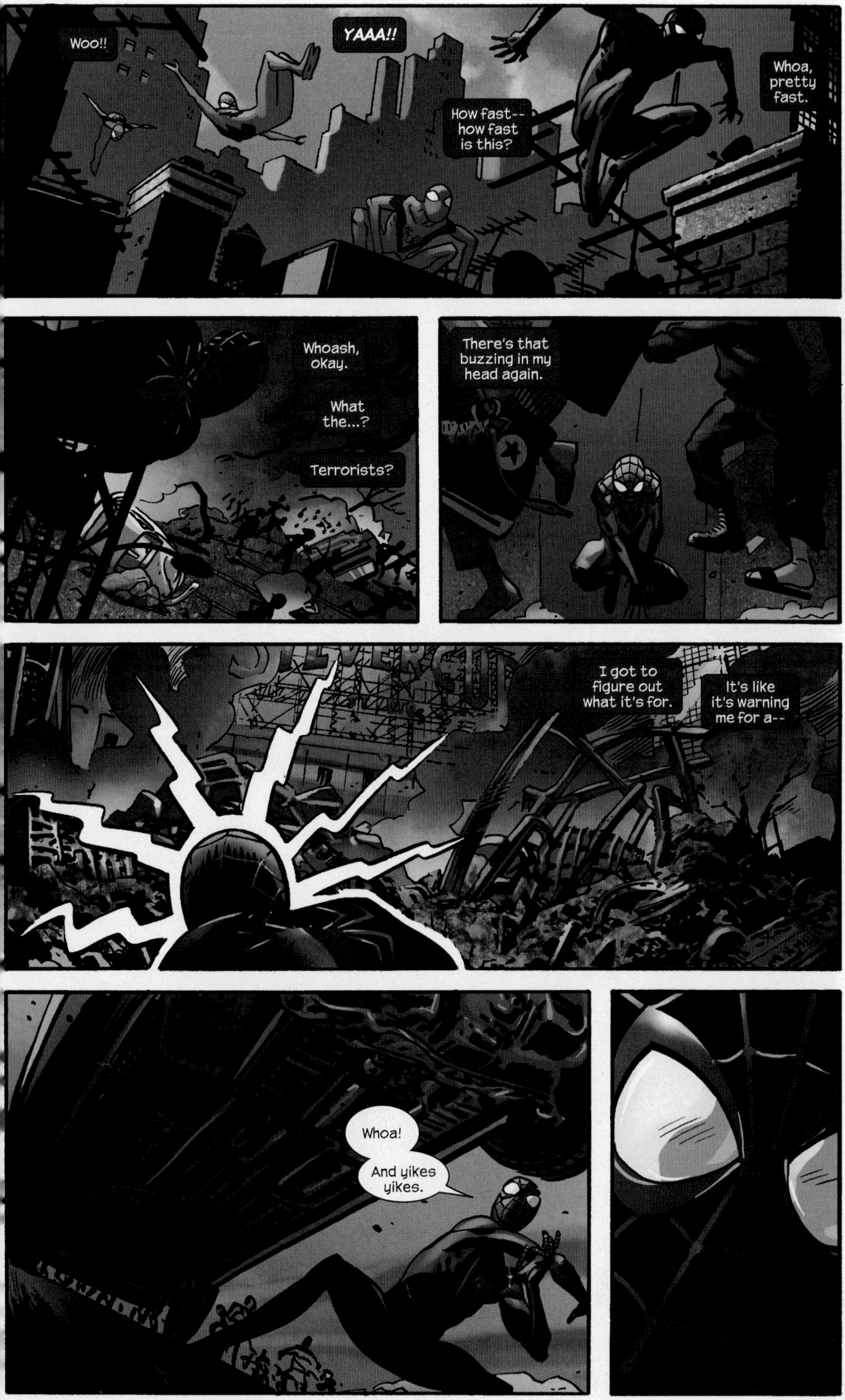
Woo!!
YAAA!!
How fast--how fast is this?
Whoa, pretty fast.
Whoash, okay.
What the...?
Terrorists?
There's that buzzing in my head again.
I got to figure out what it's for.
It's like it's warning me for a--
Whoa!
And yikes yikes.

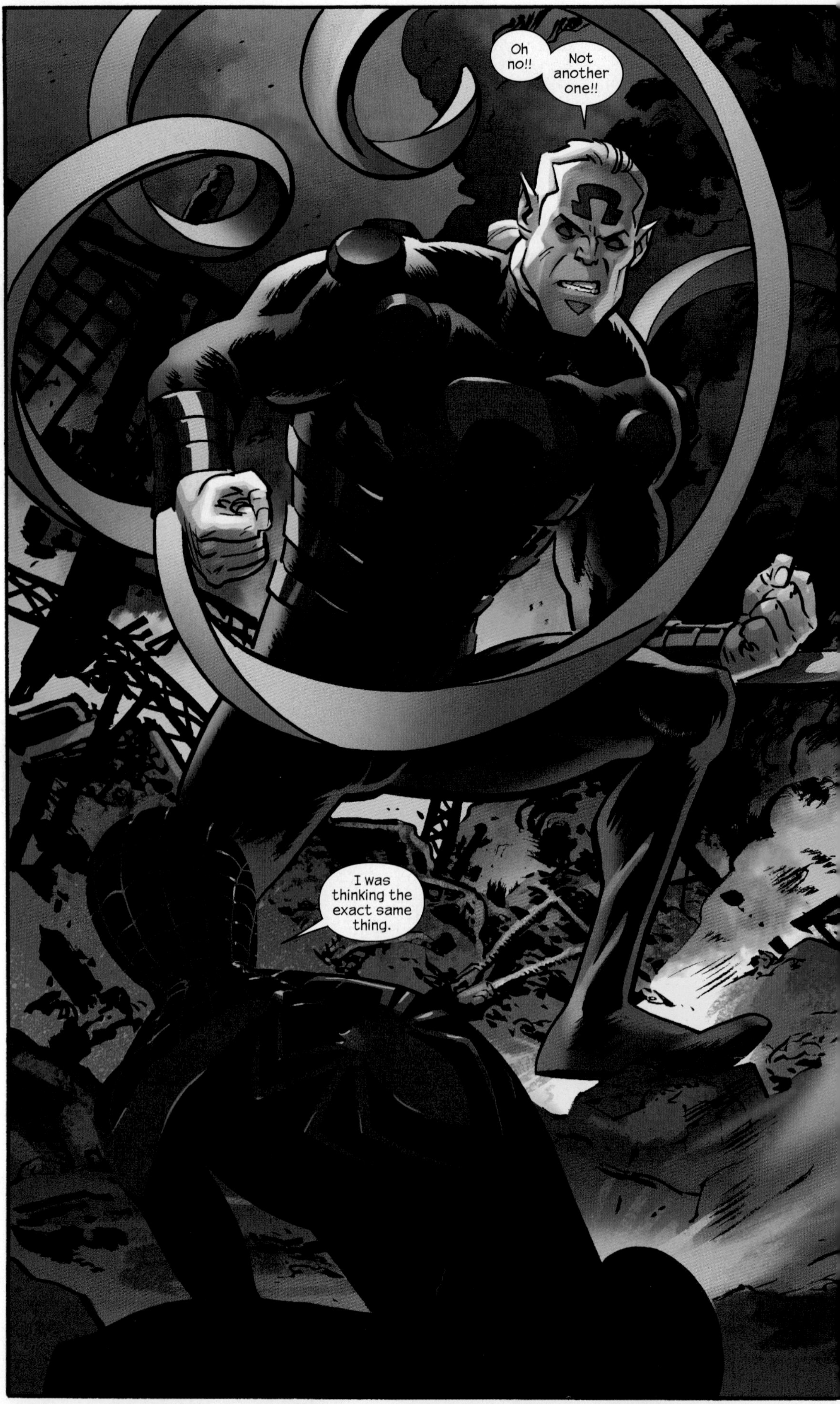
Oh no!!
Not another one!!
I was thinking the exact same thing.

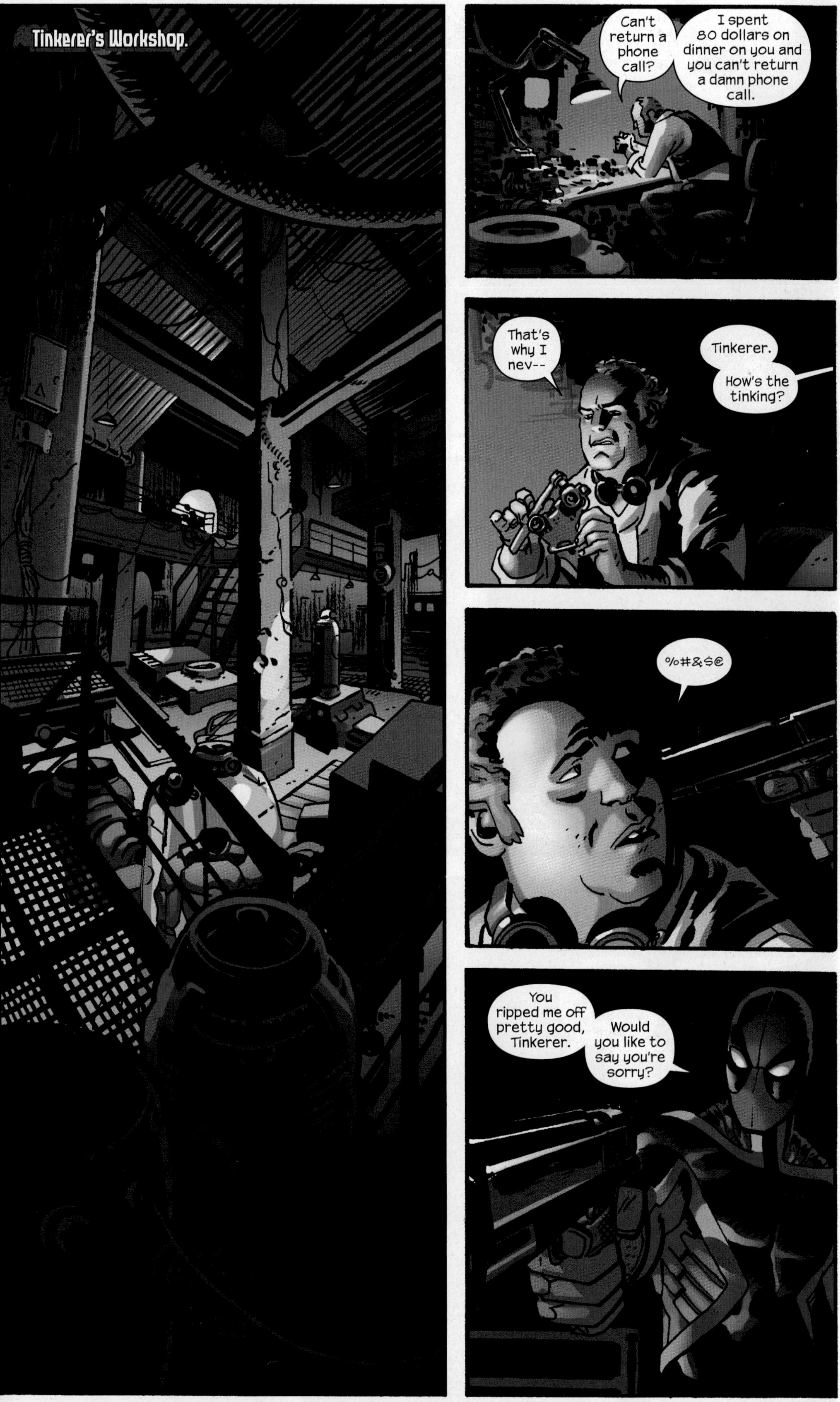
Tinkerer's Workshop.
Can't return a phone call?
I spent 80 dollars on dinner on you and you can't return a damn phone call.
That's why I nev--
Tinkerer.
How's the tinking?
%#&$@
You ripped me off pretty good, Tinkerer.
Would you like to say you're sorry?

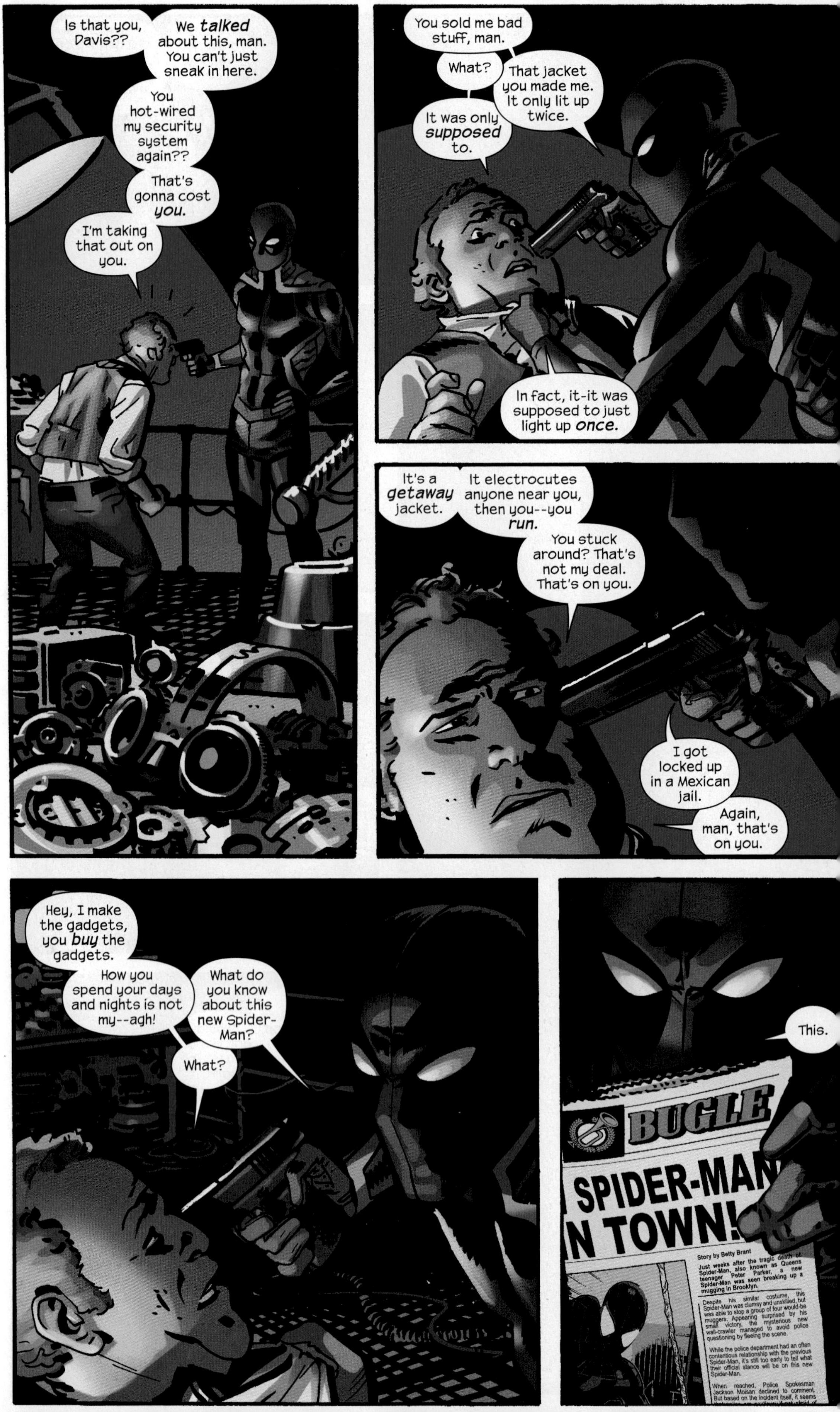
Is that you, Davis??
We *talked* about this, man. You can't just sneak in here.
You hot-wired my security system again??
That's gonna cost *you.*
I'm taking that out on you.
You sold me bad stuff, man.
What?
That jacket you made me. It only lit up twice.
It was only *supposed* to.
In fact, it-it was supposed to just light up *once.*
It's a *getaway* jacket.
It electrocutes anyone near you, then you--you *run.*
You stuck around? That's not my deal. That's on you.
I got locked up in a Mexican jail.
Again, man, that's on you.
Hey, I make the gadgets, you *buy* the gadgets.
How you spend your days and nights is not my--agh!
What do you know about this new Spider-Man?
What?
This.
BUGLE
SPIDER-MAN
N TOWN!
Story by Betty Brant
Just weeks after the tragic death of Spider-Man, also known as Queens teenager Peter Parker, a new Spider-Man was seen breaking up a mugging in Brooklyn.
Despite his similar costume, this Spider-Man was clumsy and unskilled, but was able to stop a group of four would-be muggers. Appearing surprised by his small victory, the mysterious new wall-crawler managed to avoid police questioning by fleeing the scene.
While the police department had an often contentious relationship with the previous Spider-Man, it's still too early to tell what their official stance will be on this new Spider-Man.
When reached, Police Spokesman Jackson Moisan declined to comment. But based on the incident itself, it seems

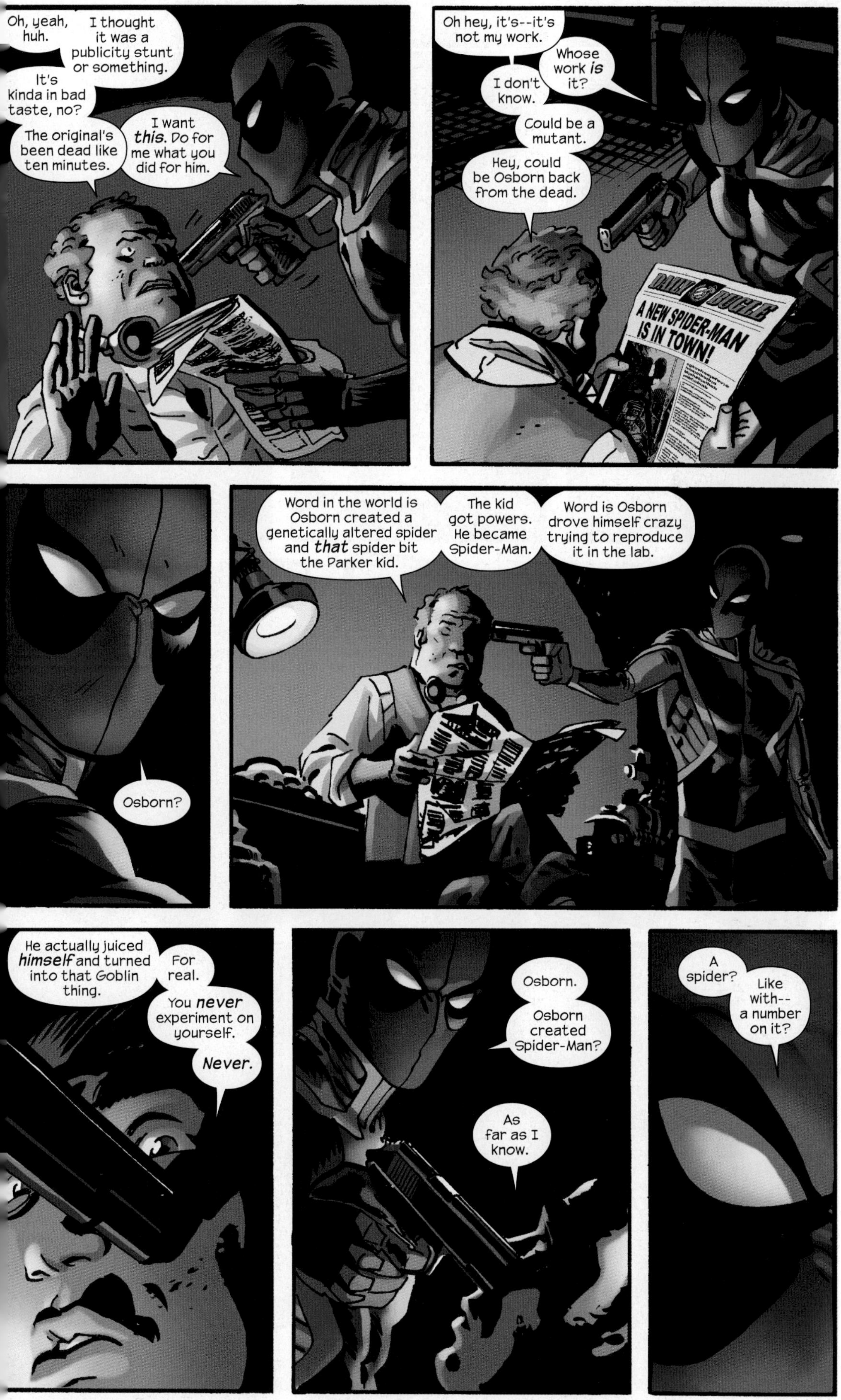

Oh, yeah, huh.
I thought it was a publicity stunt or something.
It's kinda in bad taste, no?
The original's been dead like ten minutes.
I want *this*. Do for me what you did for him.
Oh hey, it's--it's not my work.
Whose work *is* it?
I don't know.
Could be a mutant.
Hey, could be Osborn back from the dead.
DAILY BUGLE
A NEW SPIDER-MAN IS IN TOWN!
Osborn?
Word in the world is Osborn created a genetically altered spider and *that* spider bit the Parker kid.
The kid got powers. He became Spider-Man.
Word is Osborn drove himself crazy trying to reproduce it in the lab.
He actually juiced *himself* and turned into that Goblin thing.
For real.
You *never* experiment on yourself.
Never.
Osborn.
Osborn created Spider-Man?
As far as I know.
A spider?
Like with-- a number on it?

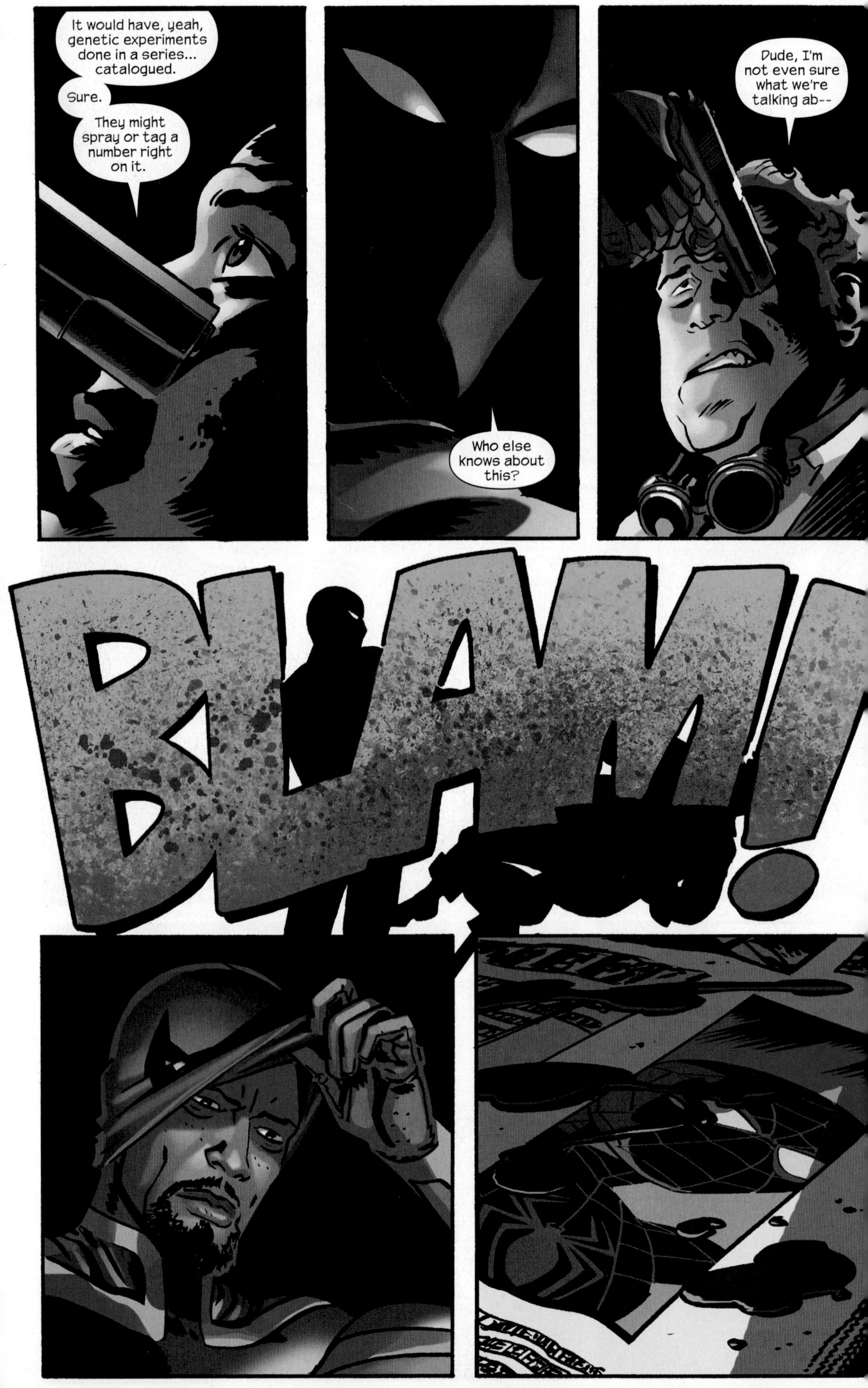

It would have, yeah, genetic experiments done in a series... catalogued.
Sure.
They might spray or tag a number right on it.
Who else knows about this?
Dude, I'm not even sure what we're talking ab--
BLAM!

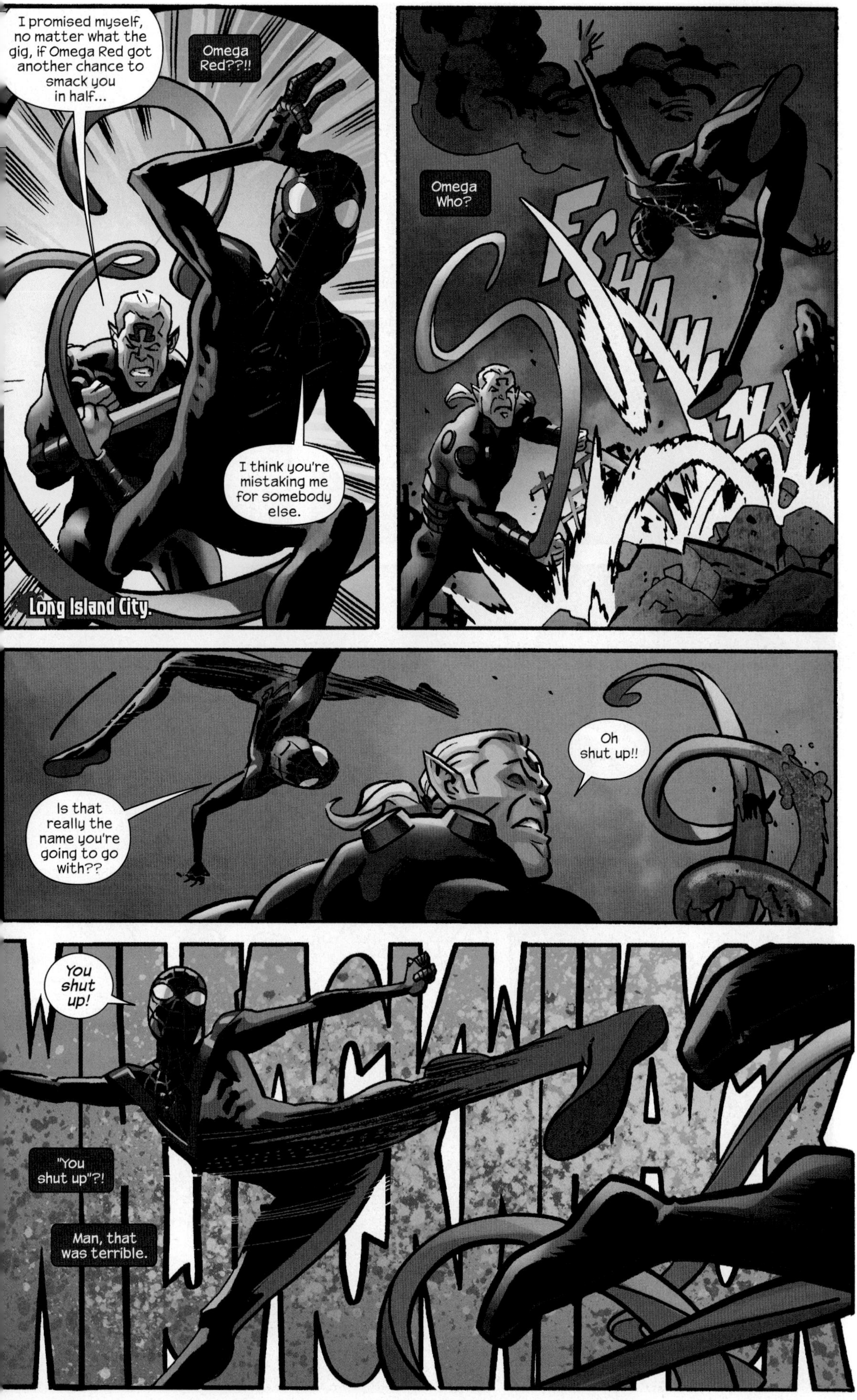

I promised myself, no matter what the gig, if Omega Red got another chance to smack you in half...
Omega Red??!!
I think you're mistaking me for somebody else.
Long Island City.
Omega Who?
FSHAMM
Is that really the name you're going to go with??
Oh shut up!!
You shut up!
"You shut up"?!
Man, that was terrible.

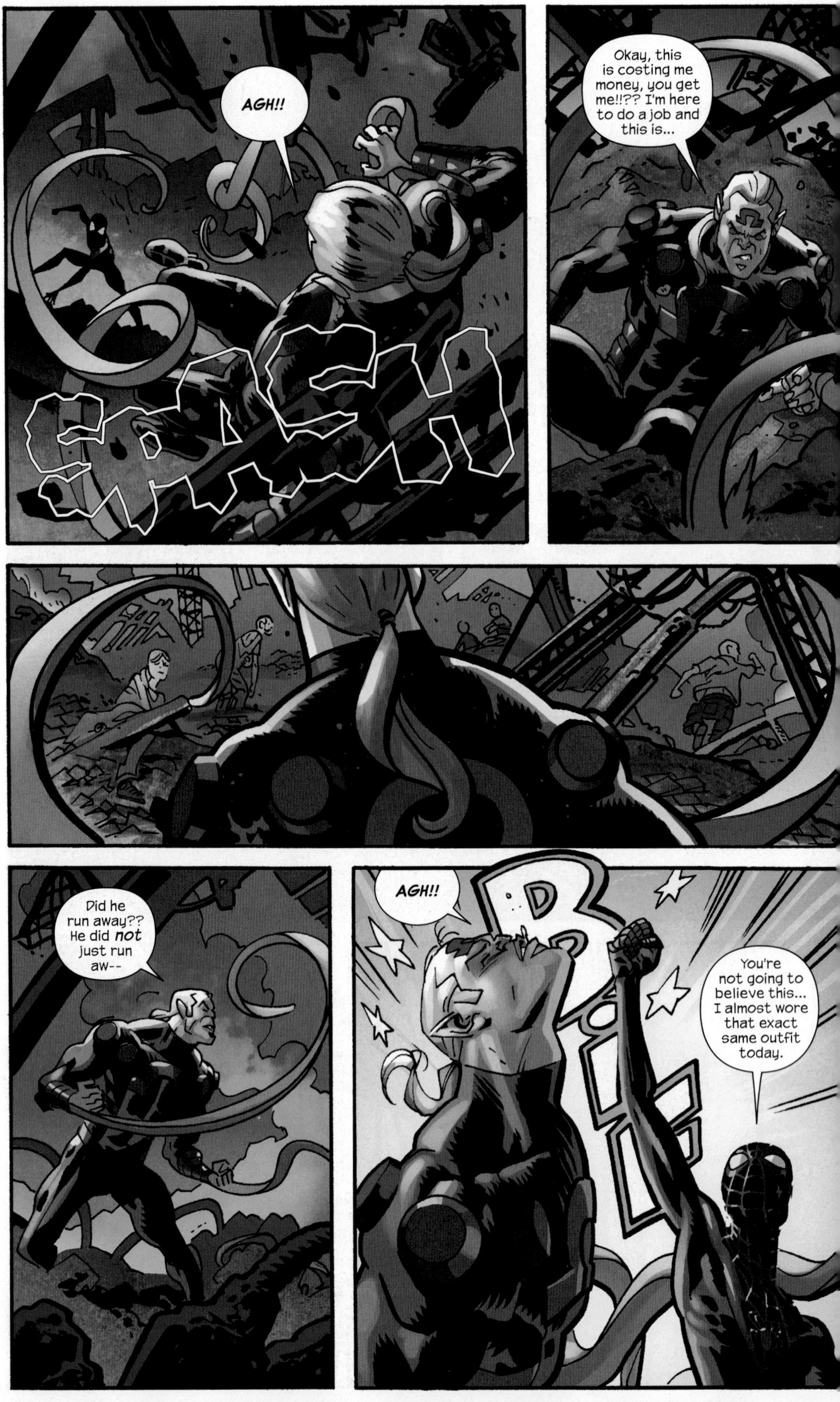
AGH!!
Okay, this is costing me money, you get me!!?? I'm here to do a job and this is...
Did he run away?? He did *not* just run aw--
AGH!!
You're not going to believe this... I almost wore that exact same outfit today.

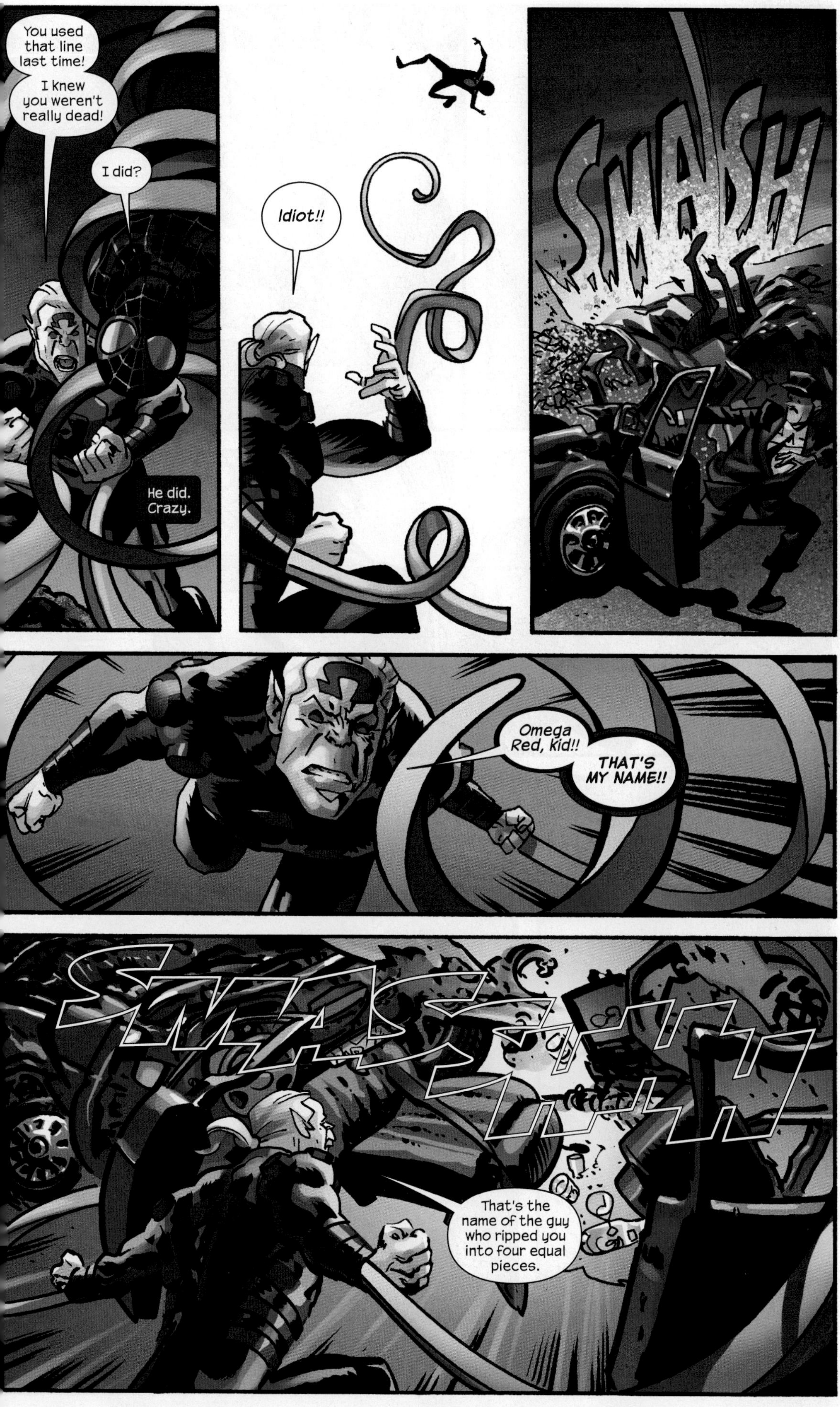
You used that line last time!
I knew you weren't really dead!
I did?
He did. Crazy.
Idiot!!
SMASH
Omega Red, kid!!
THAT'S MY NAME!!
SMASSHH
That's the name of the guy who ripped you into four equal pieces.

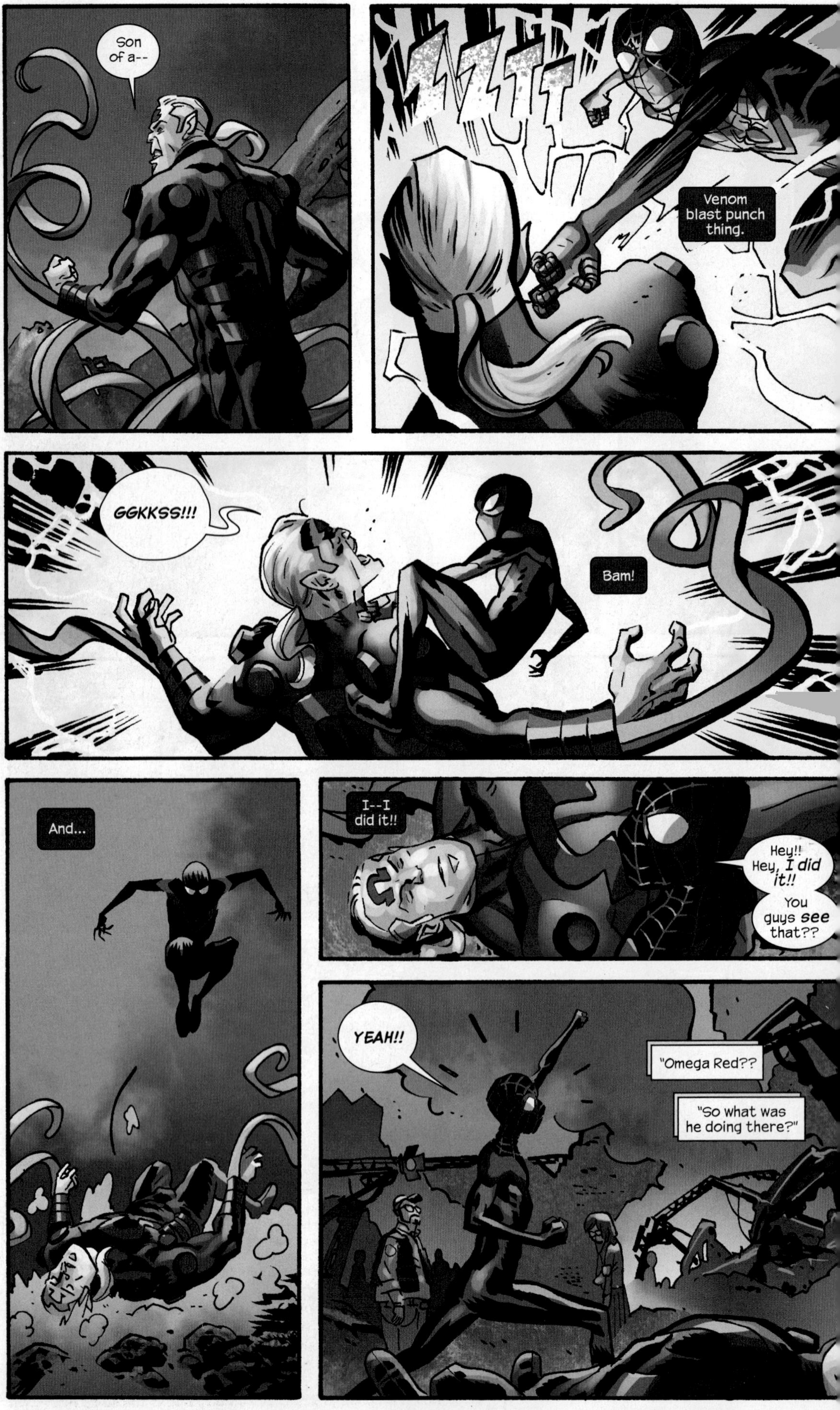
Son of a--
Venom blast punch thing.
GGKKSS!!!
Bam!
And...
I--I did it!!
Hey!! Hey, I did it!!
You guys see that??
YEAH!!
"Omega Red??
"So what was he doing there?"

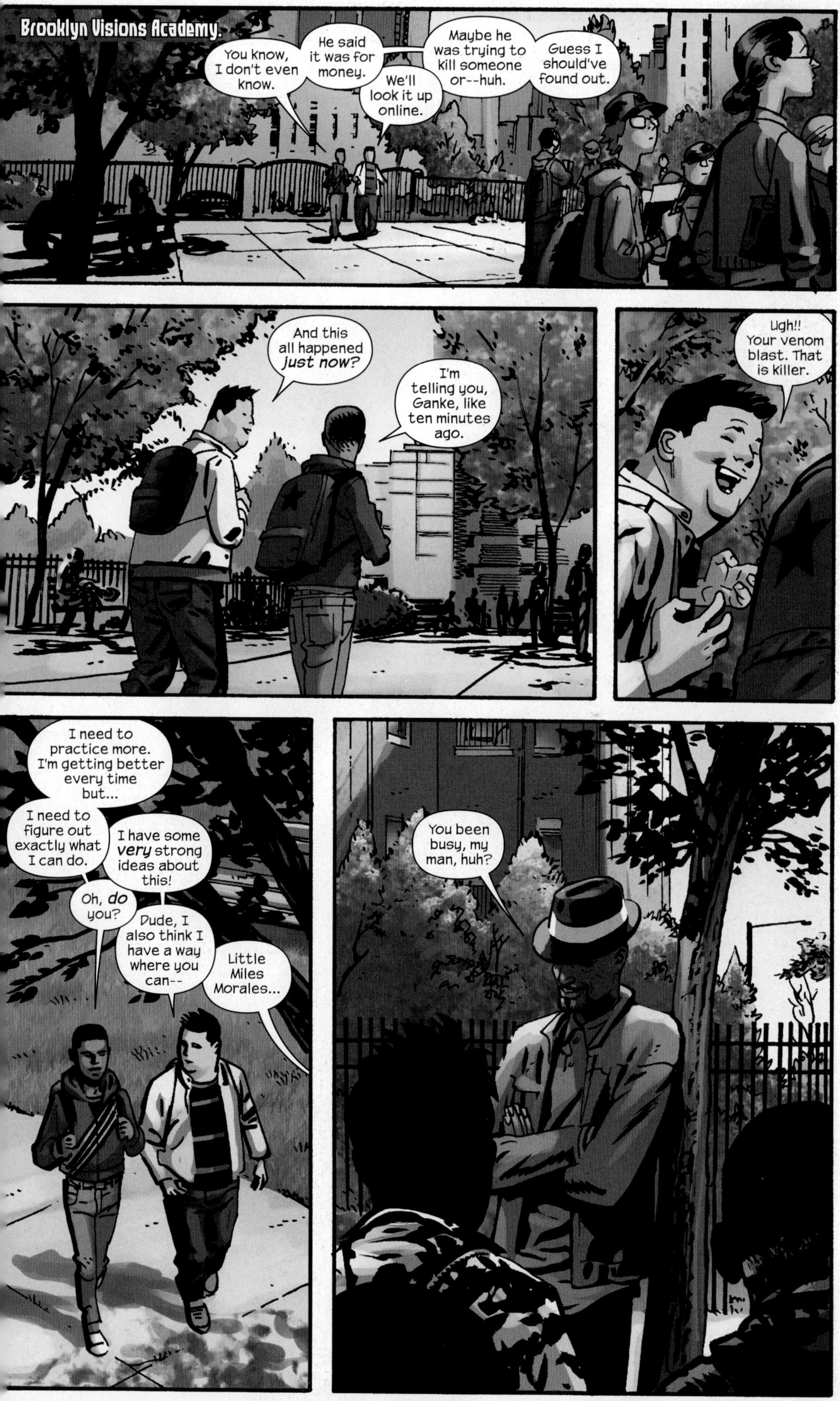
Brooklyn Visions Academy.
You know, I don't even know.
He said it was for money.
We'll look it up online.
Maybe he was trying to kill someone or--huh.
Guess I should've found out.
And this all happened *just now?*
I'm telling you, Ganke, like ten minutes ago.
Ugh!! Your venom blast. That is killer.
I need to practice more. I'm getting better every time but...
I need to figure out exactly what I can do.
I have some *very* strong ideas about this!
Oh, *do* you?
Dude, I also think I have a way where you can--
Little Miles Morales...
You been busy, my man, huh?

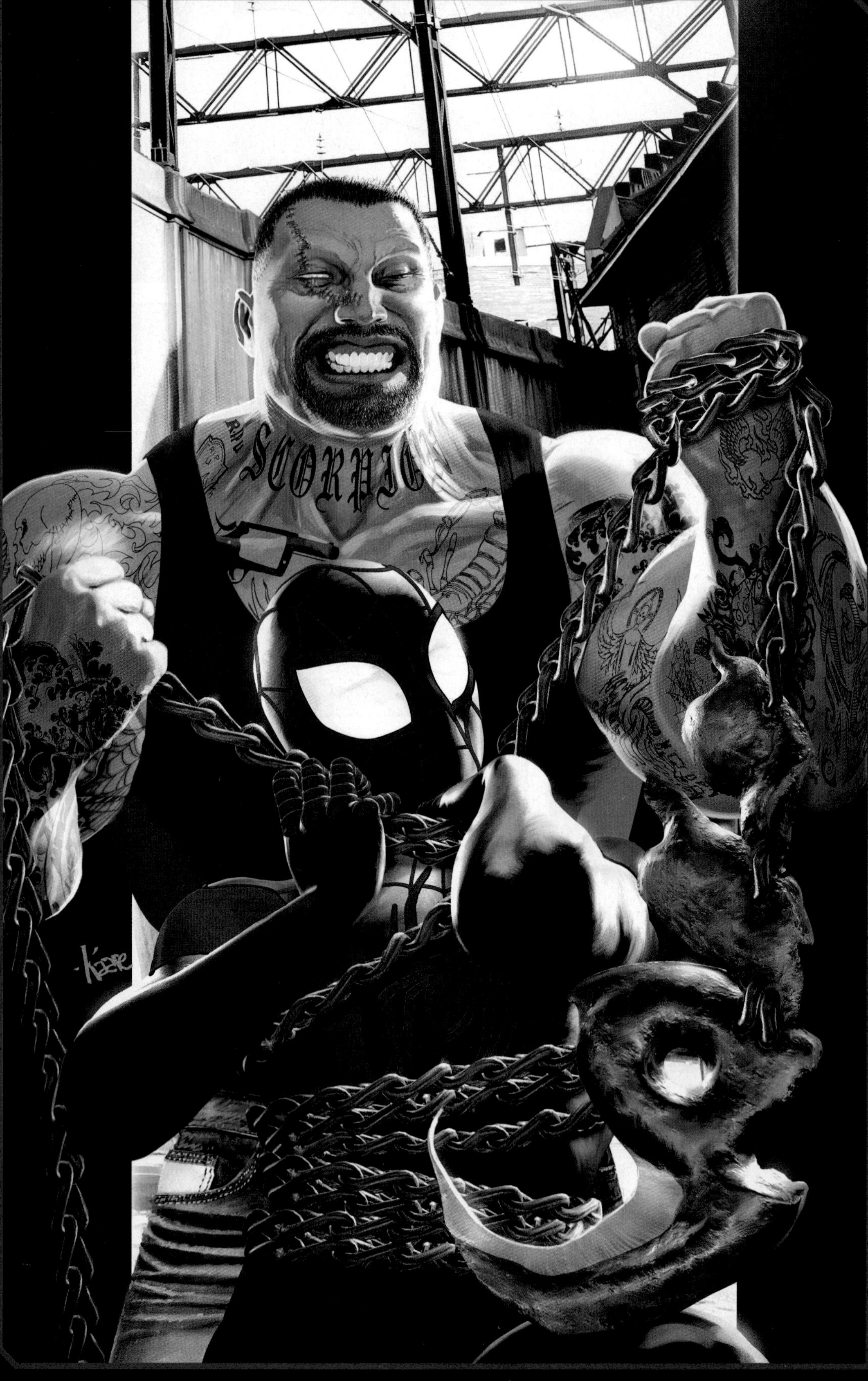
SCORPION

ULTIMATE COMICS SPIDER-MAN #8

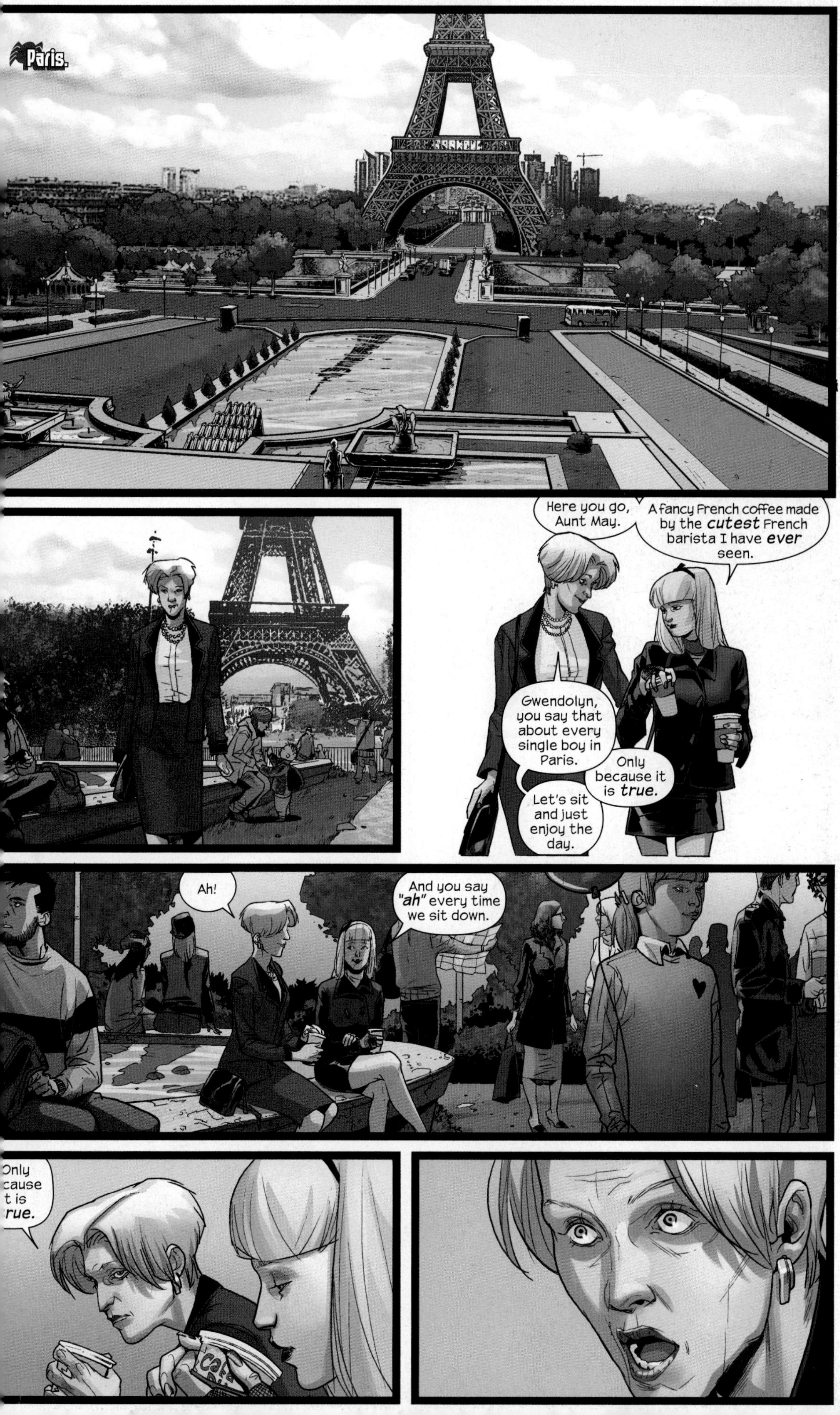
Paris.
Here you go, Aunt May.
A fancy French coffee made by the cutest French barista I have ever seen.
Gwendolyn, you say that about every single boy in Paris.
Only because it is true.
Let's sit and just enjoy the day.
Ah!
And you say "ah" every time we sit down.
Only
cause
t is
rue.

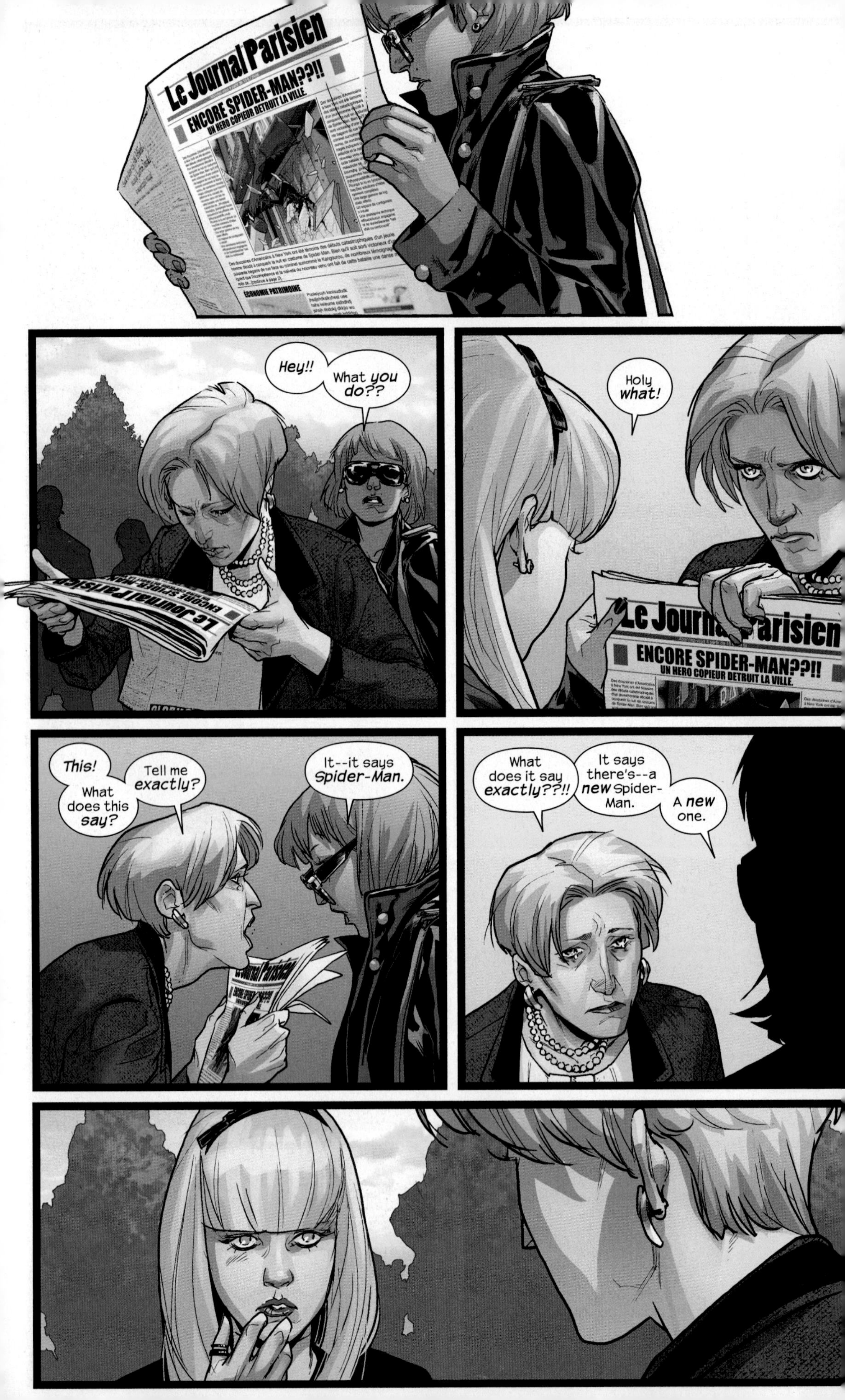
Le Journal Parisien
ENCORE SPIDER-MAN??!!
UN HERO COPIEUR DETRUIT LA VILLE.
Hey!!
What you do??
Holy what!
This!
What does this say?
Tell me exactly?
It--it says Spider-Man.
What does it say exactly??!!
It says there's--a new Spider-Man.
A new one.

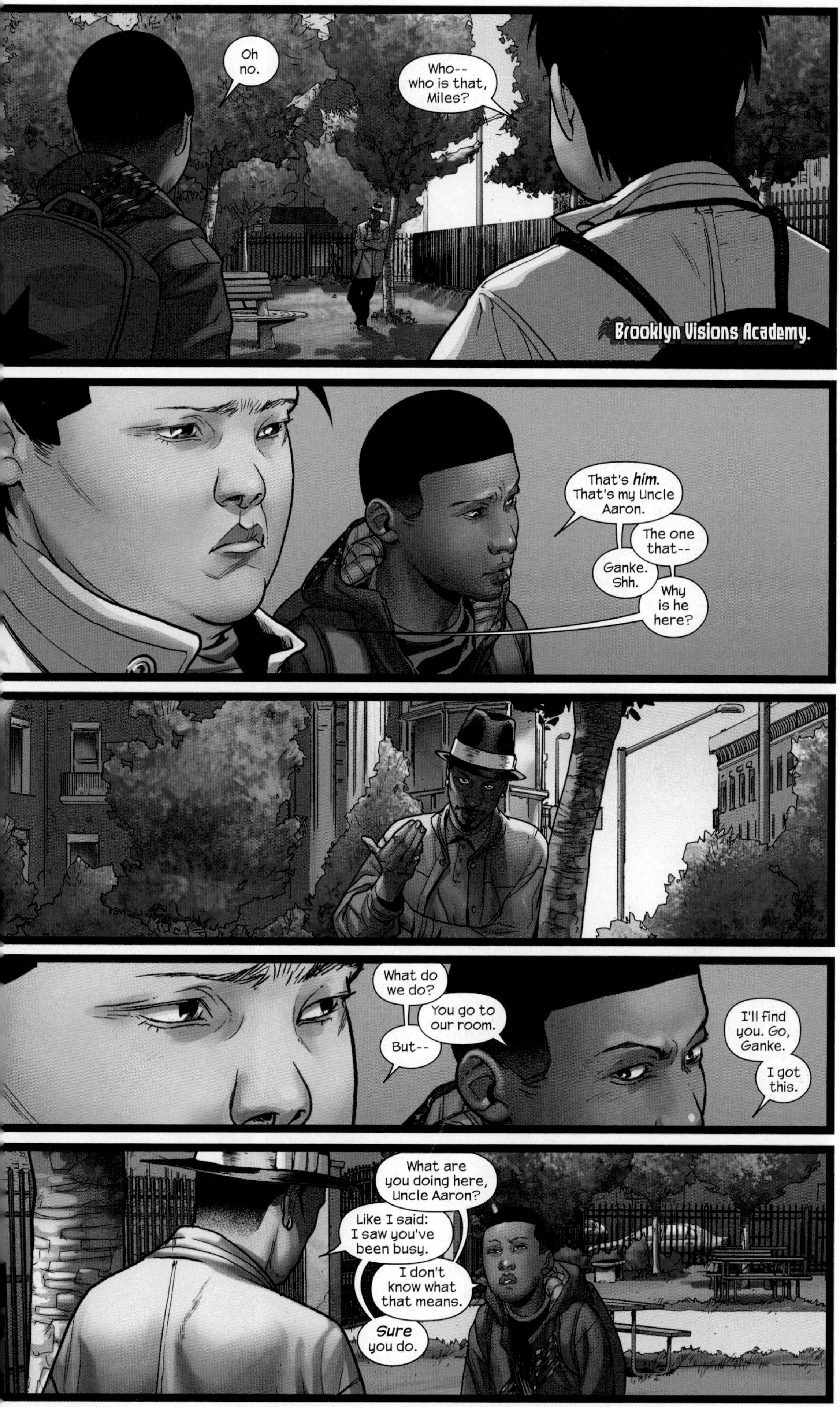
Oh no.
Who-- who is that, Miles?
Brooklyn Visions Academy.
That's *him.* That's my Uncle Aaron.
The one that--
Ganke. Shh.
Why is he here?
What do we do?
You go to our room.
But--
I'll find you. Go, Ganke.
I got this.
What are you doing here, Uncle Aaron?
Like I said: I saw you've been busy.
I don't know what that means.
Sure you do.

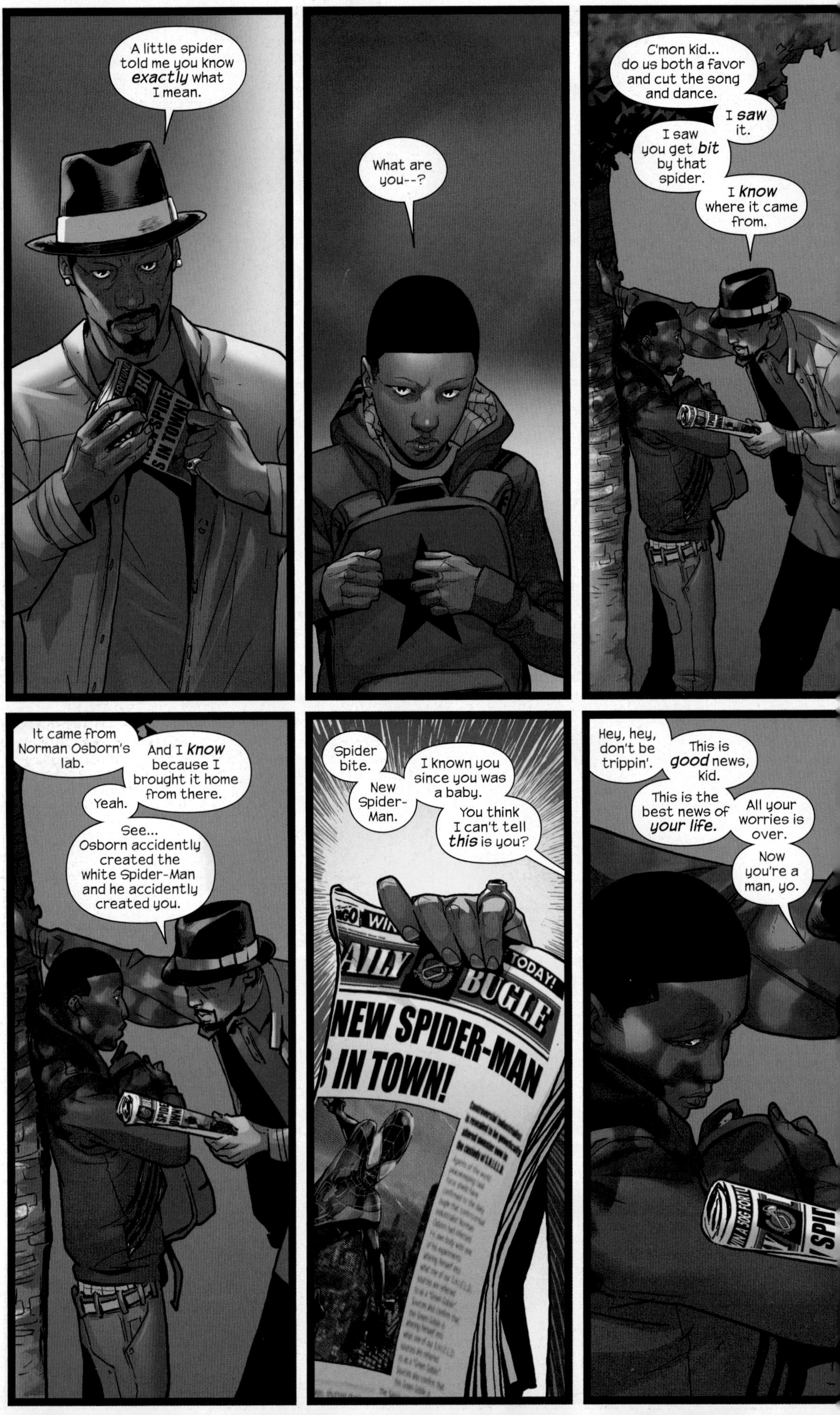
A little spider told me you know *exactly* what I mean.
What are you--?
C'mon kid... do us both a favor and cut the song and dance.
I *saw* it.
I saw you get *bit* by that spider.
I *know* where it came from.
It came from Norman Osborn's lab.
And I *know* because I brought it home from there.
Yeah.
See... Osborn accidently created the white Spider-Man and he accidently created you.
Spider bite.
New Spider-Man.
I known you since you was a baby.
You think I can't tell *this* is you?
DAILY BUGLE
TODAY!
NEW SPIDER-MAN IS IN TOWN!
Hey, hey, don't be trippin'.
This is *good* news, kid.
This is the best news of *your life.*
All your worries is over.
Now you're a man, yo.

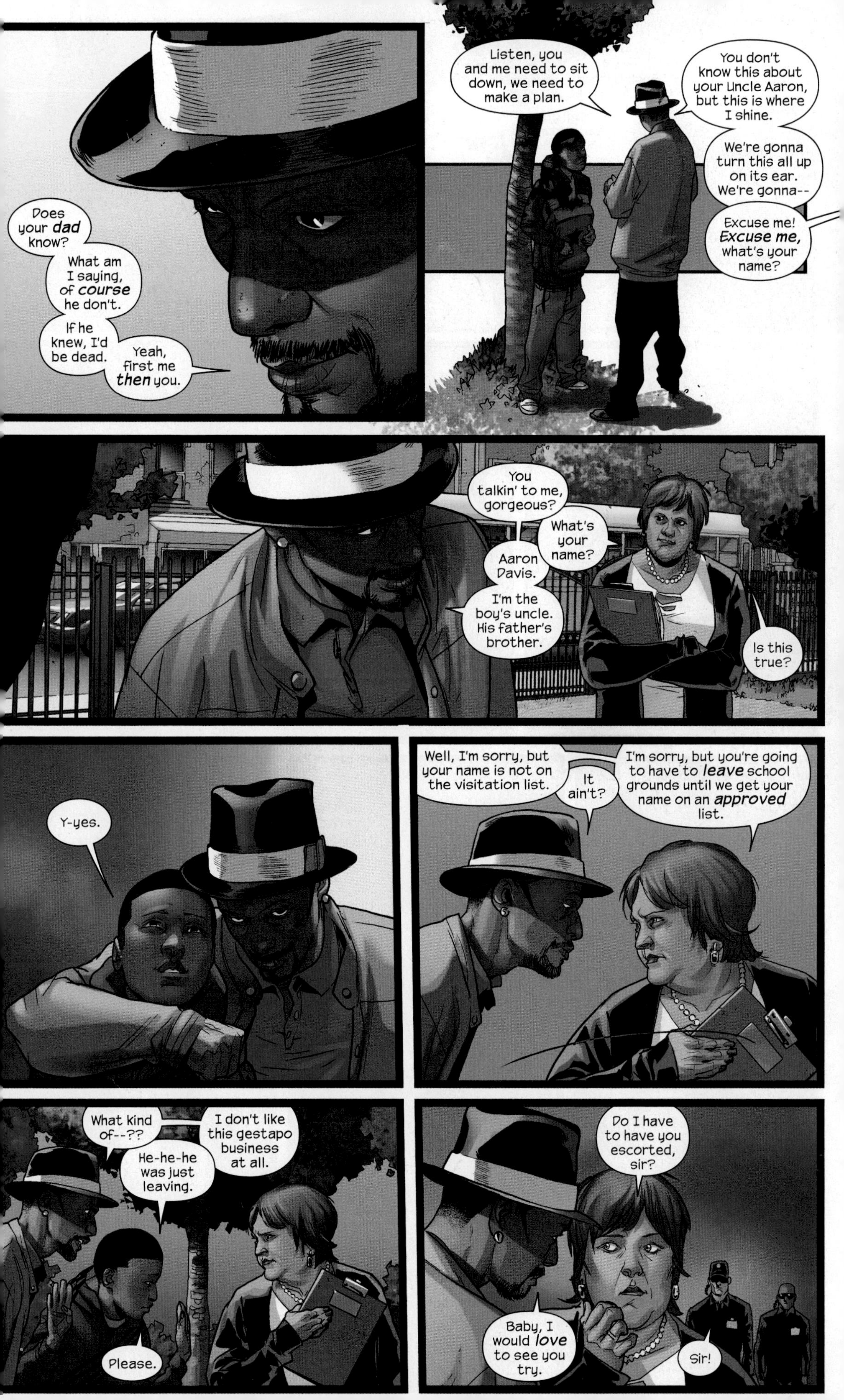
Does your *dad* know?
What am I saying, of *course* he don't.
If he knew, I'd be dead.
Yeah, first me *then* you.
Listen, you and me need to sit down, we need to make a plan.
You don't know this about your Uncle Aaron, but this is where I shine.
We're gonna turn this all up on its ear. We're gonna--
Excuse me! *Excuse me,* what's your name?
You talkin' to me, gorgeous?
What's your name?
Aaron Davis.
I'm the boy's uncle. His father's brother.
Is this true?
Y-yes.
Well, I'm sorry, but your name is not on the visitation list.
It ain't?
I'm sorry, but you're going to have to *leave* school grounds until we get your name on an *approved* list.
What kind of--??
I don't like this gestapo business at all.
He-he-he was just leaving.
Please.
Do I have to have you escorted, sir?
Baby, I would *love* to see you try.
Sir!

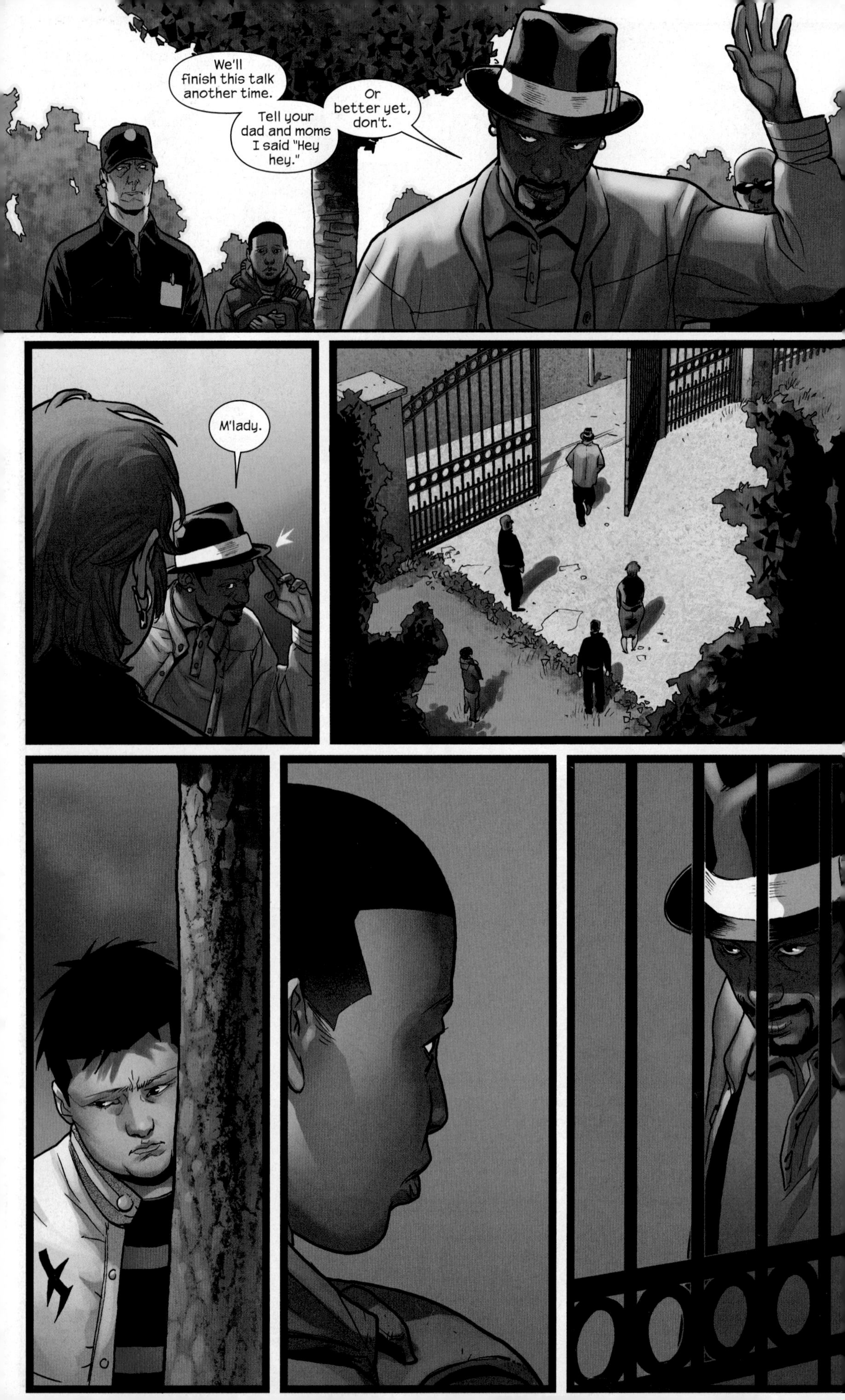
We'll finish this talk another time.
Tell your dad and moms I said "Hey hey."
Or better yet, don't.
M'lady.

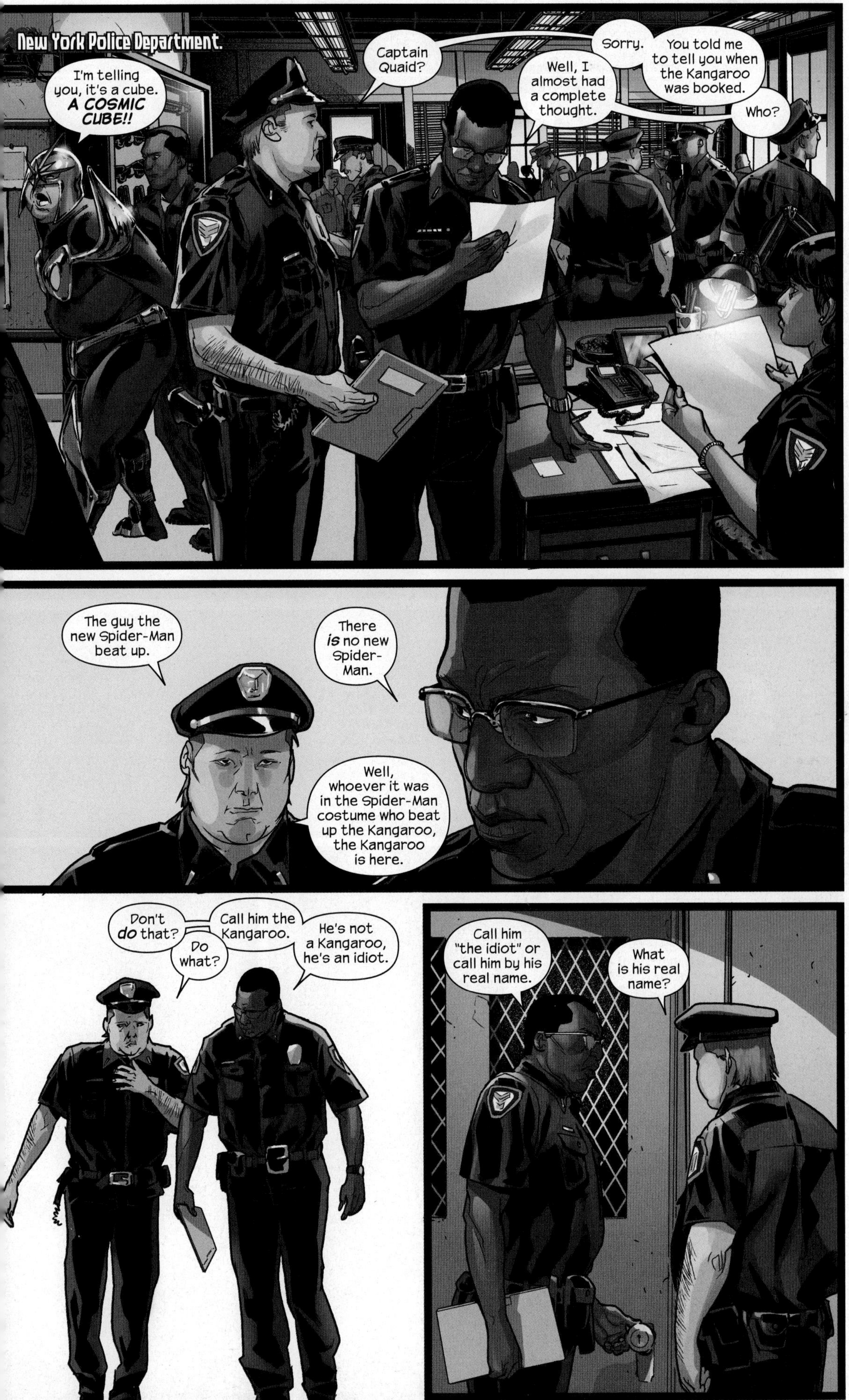

New York Police Department.
I'm telling you, it's a cube. A COSMIC CUBE!!
Captain Quaid?
Well, I almost had a complete thought.
Sorry.
You told me to tell you when the Kangaroo was booked.
Who?
The guy the new Spider-Man beat up.
There is no new Spider-Man.
Well, whoever it was in the Spider-Man costume who beat up the Kangaroo, the Kangaroo is here.
Don't do that?
Do what?
Call him the Kangaroo.
He's not a Kangaroo, he's an idiot.
Call him "the idiot" or call him by his real name.
What is his real name?

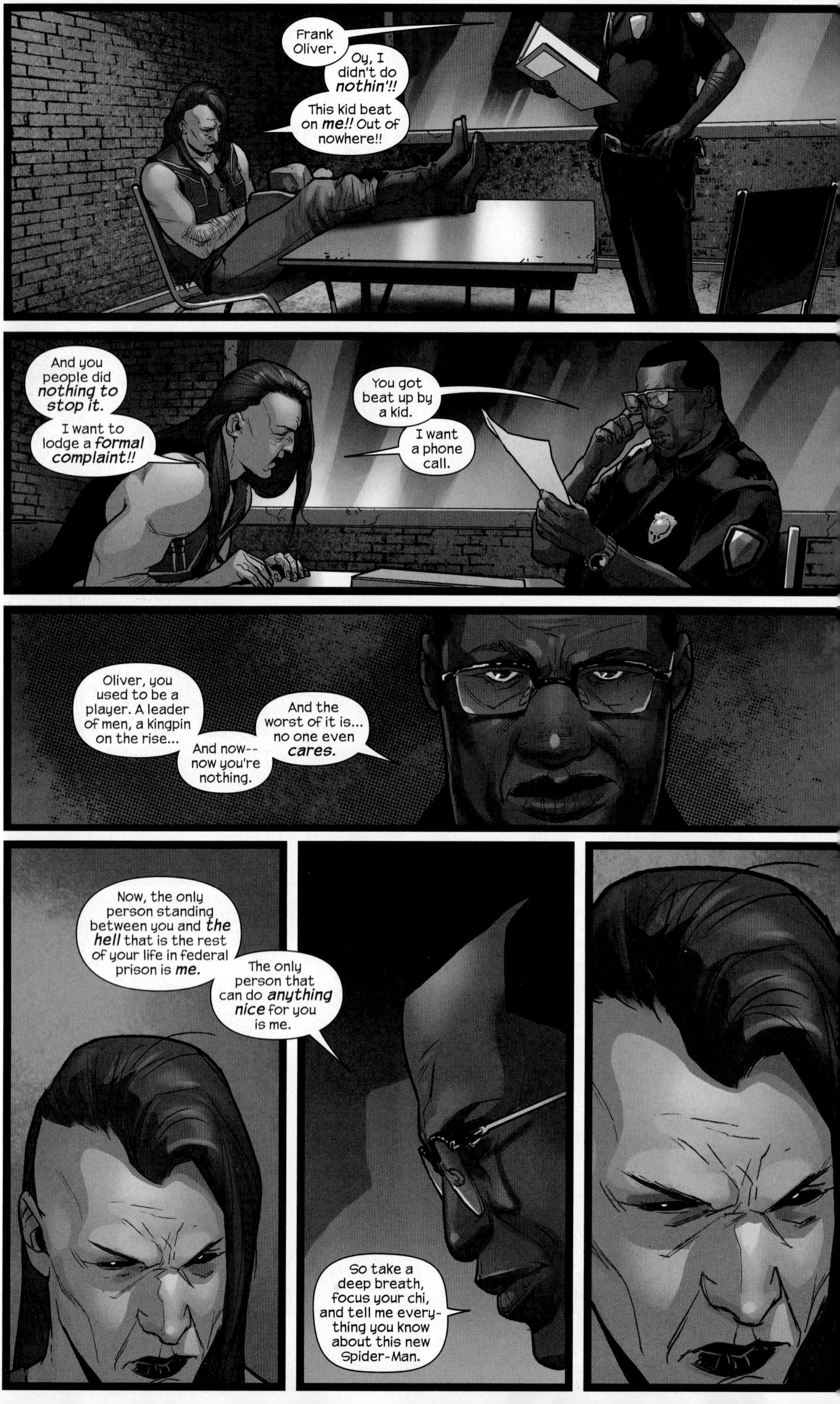
Frank Oliver.
Oy, I didn't do *nothin'!!*
This kid beat on *me!!* Out of nowhere!!
And you people did *nothing to stop it.*
I want to lodge a *formal complaint!!*
You got beat up by a kid.
I want a phone call.
Oliver, you used to be a player. A leader of men, a kingpin on the rise...
And now-- now you're nothing.
And the worst of it is... no one even *cares.*
Now, the only person standing between you and *the hell* that is the rest of your life in federal prison is *me.*
The only person that can do *anything nice* for you is me.
So take a deep breath, focus your chi, and tell me every-thing you know about this new Spider-Man.

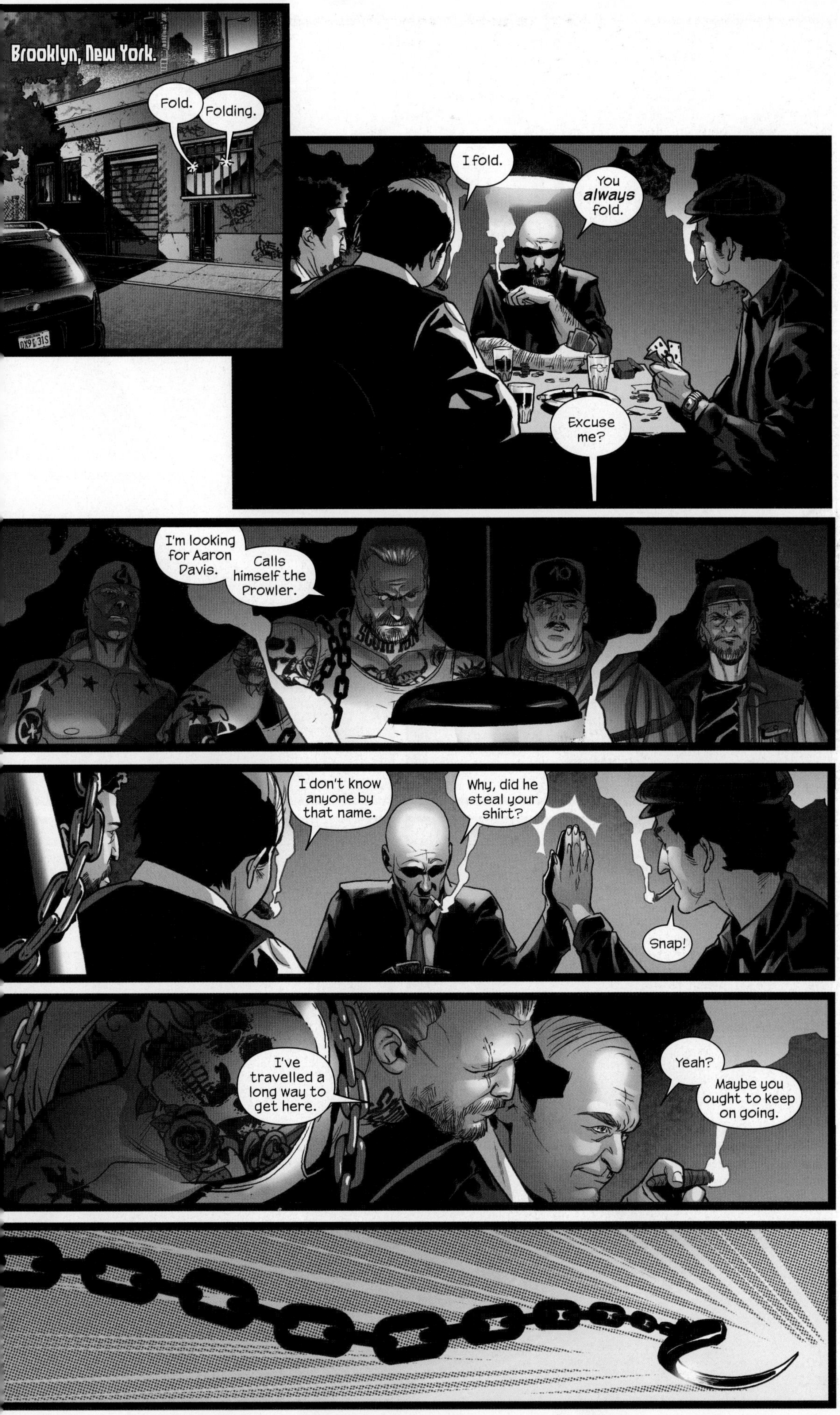
Brooklyn, New York.
Fold.
Folding.
I fold.
You always fold.
Excuse me?
I'm looking for Aaron Davis.
Calls himself the Prowler.
I don't know anyone by that name.
Why, did he steal your shirt?
Snap!
I've travelled a long way to get here.
Yeah?
Maybe you ought to keep on going.

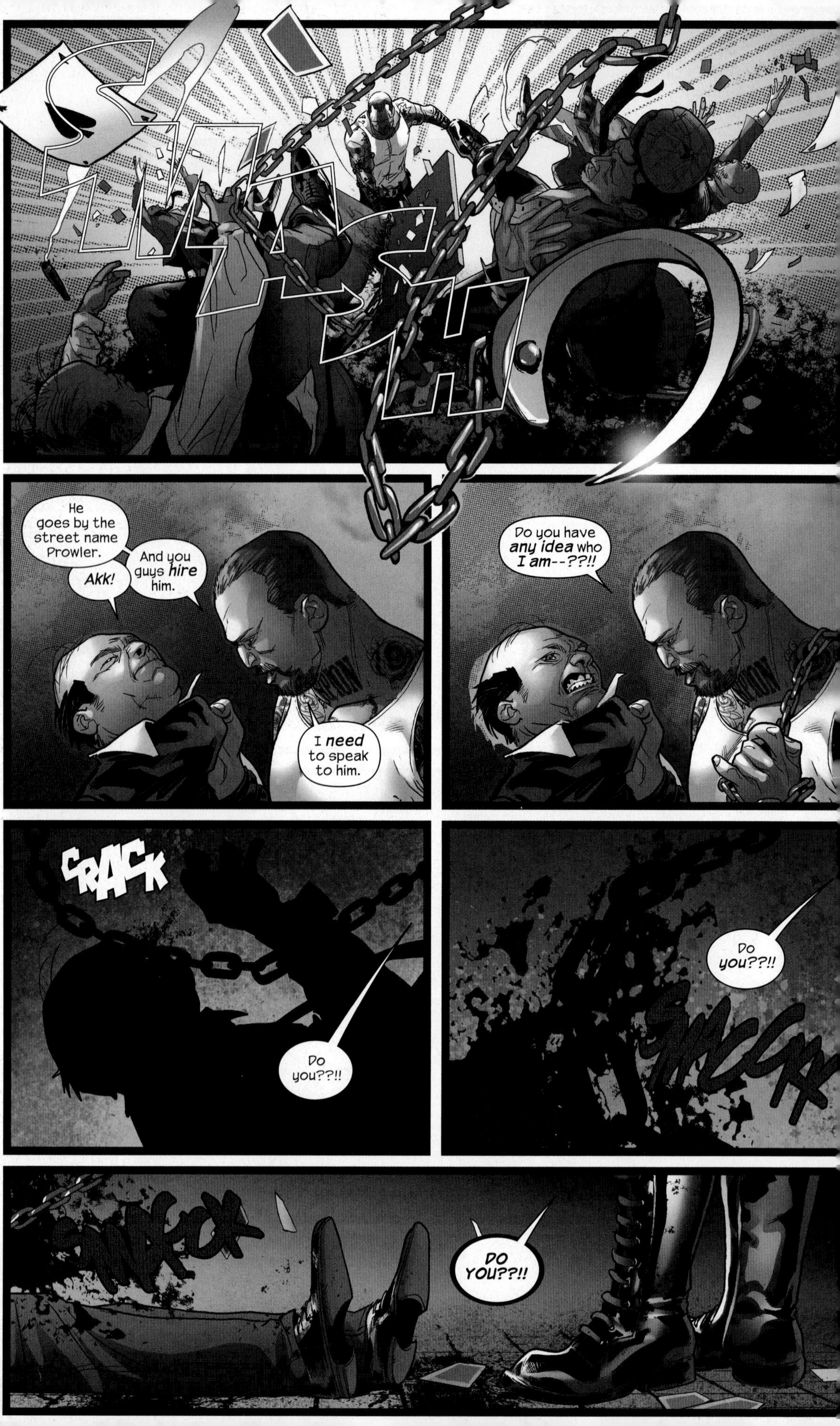
He goes by the street name Prowler.
Akk!
And you guys hire him.
I need to speak to him.
Do you have any idea who I am--??!!
CRACK
Do you??!!
Do you??!!
DO YOU??!!

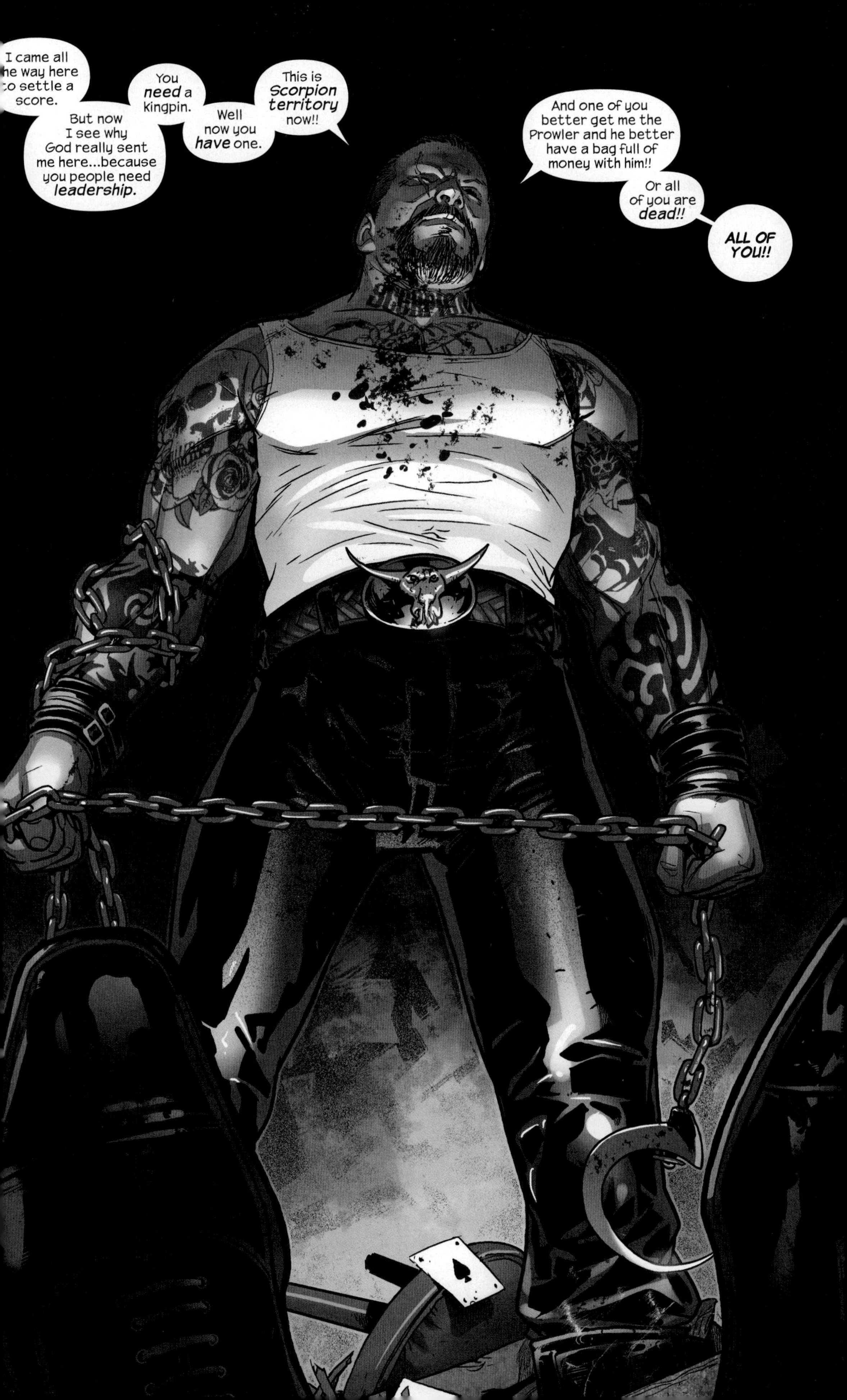
I came all
he way here
to settle a
score.
But now
I see why
God really sent
me here...because
you people need
leadership.
You
need a
kingpin.
Well
now you
have one.
This is
*Scorpion
territory*
now!!
And one of you
better get me the
Prowler and he better
have a bag full of
money with him!!
Or all
of you are
dead!!
ALL OF
YOU!!

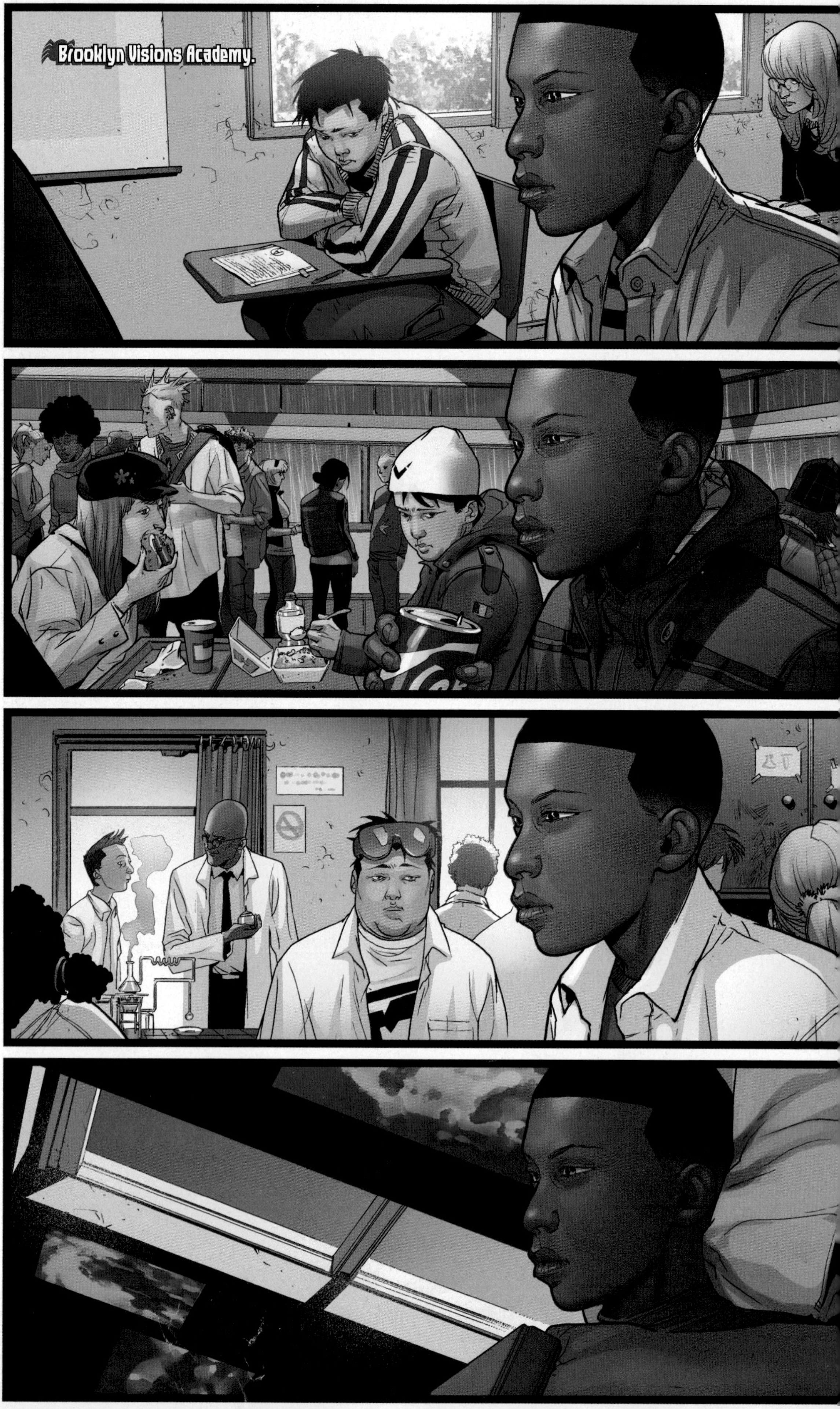
Brooklyn Visions Academy.

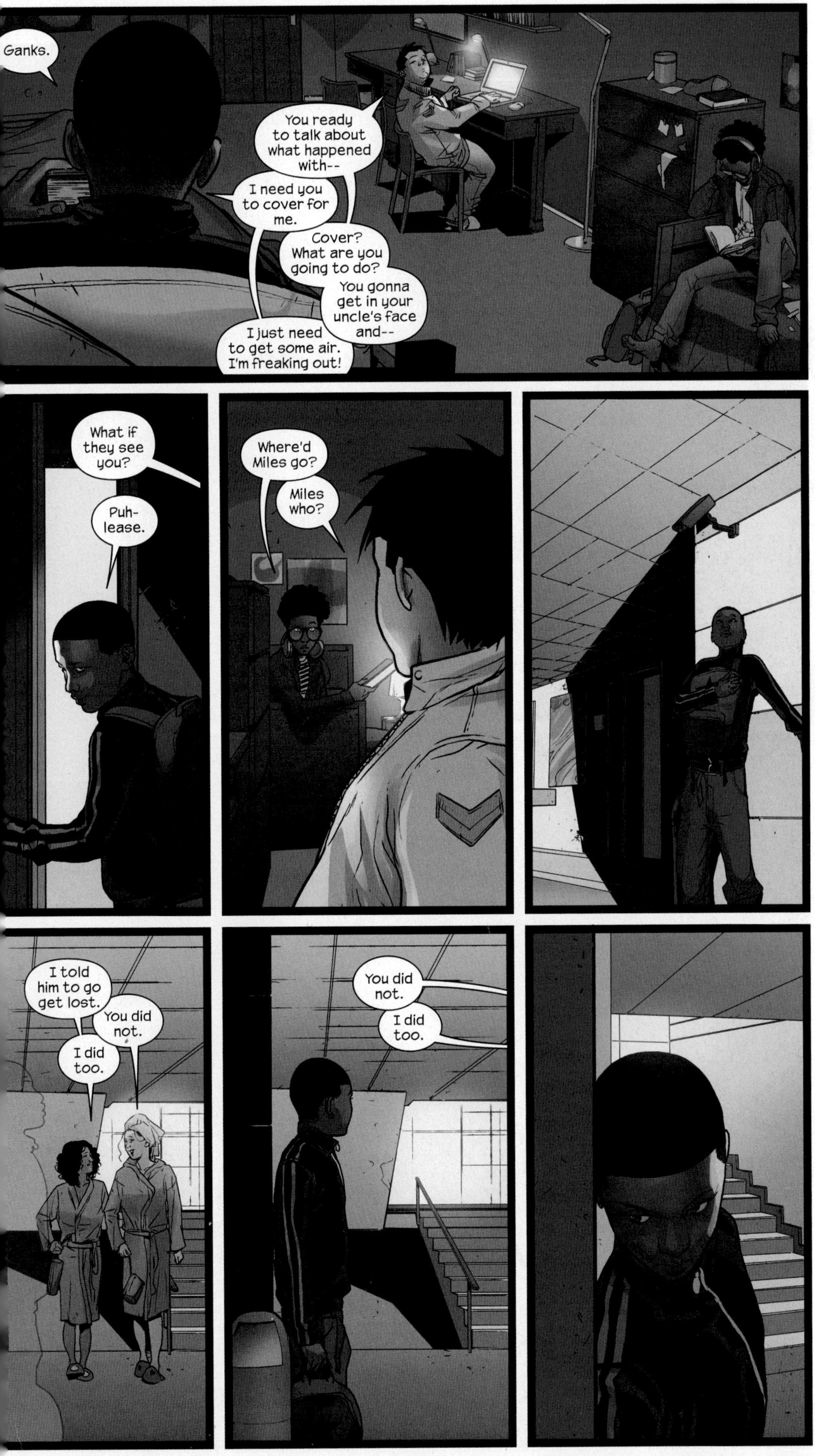
Ganks.
You ready to talk about what happened with--
I need you to cover for me.
Cover? What are you going to do?
You gonna get in your uncle's face and--
I just need to get some air. I'm freaking out!
What if they see you?
Puh-lease.
Where'd Miles go?
Miles who?
I told him to go get lost.
You did not.
I did too.
You did not.
I did too.

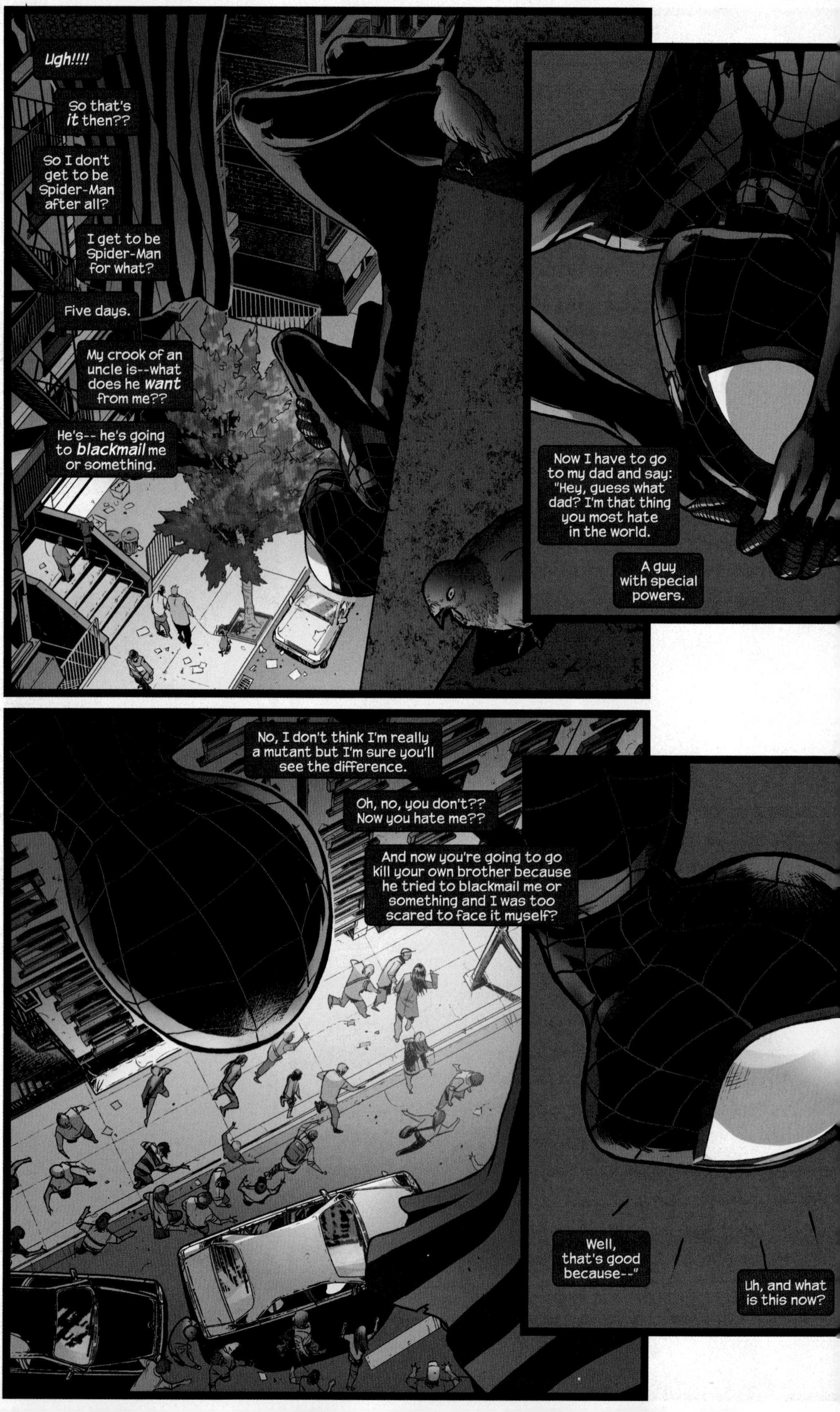
Ugh!!!!
So that's it then??
So I don't get to be Spider-Man after all?
I get to be Spider-Man for what?
Five days.
My crook of an uncle is--what does he want from me??
He's-- he's going to blackmail me or something.
Now I have to go to my dad and say: "Hey, guess what dad? I'm that thing you most hate in the world.
A guy with special powers.
No, I don't think I'm really a mutant but I'm sure you'll see the difference.
Oh, no, you don't?? Now you hate me??
And now you're going to go kill your own brother because he tried to blackmail me or something and I was too scared to face it myself?
Well, that's good because--"
Uh, and what is this now?

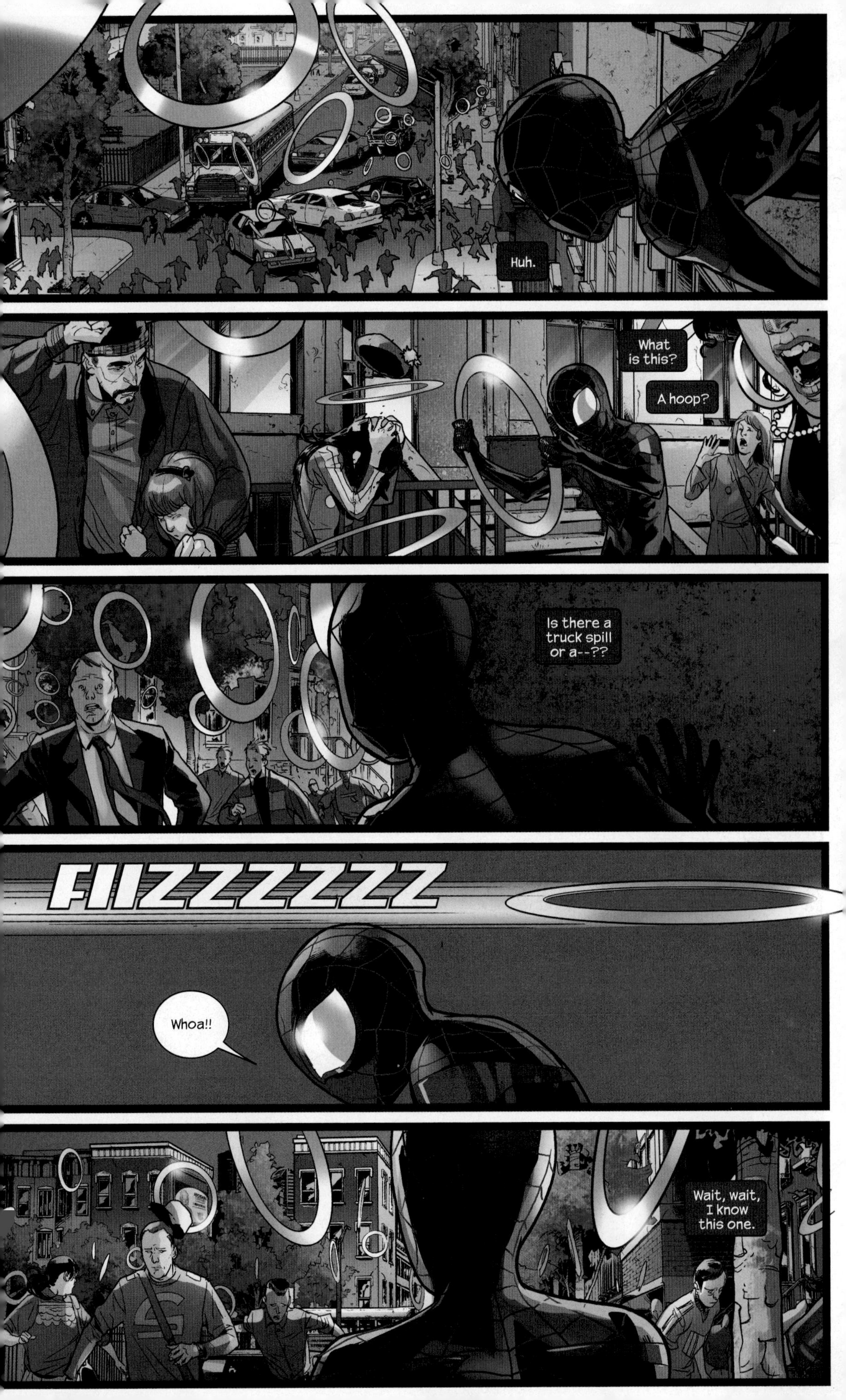
Huh.
What is this?
A hoop?
Is there a truck spill or a--??
FIIZZZZZZ
Whoa!!
Wait, wait, I know this one.

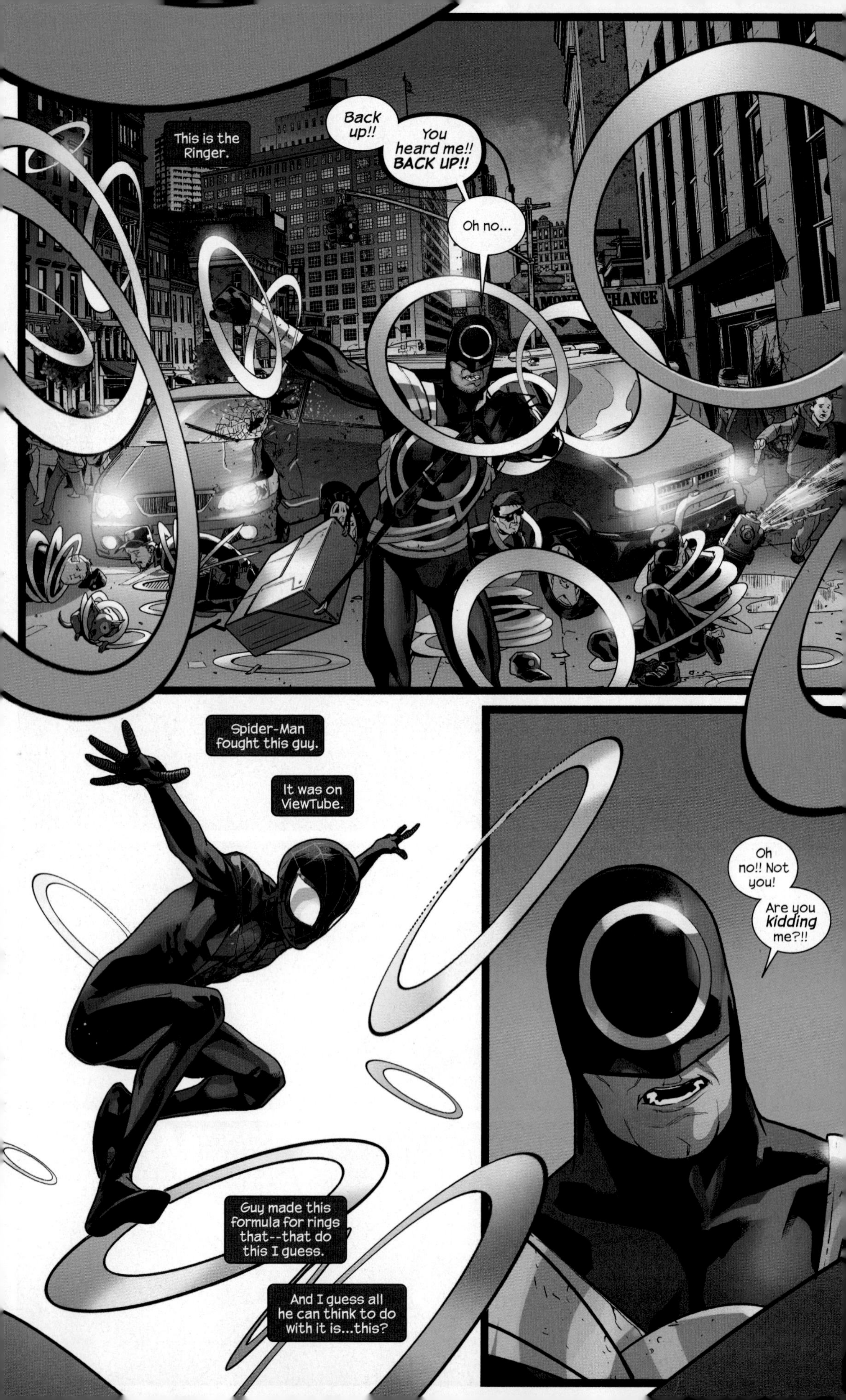
This is the Ringer.
Back up!!
You heard me!! BACK UP!!
Oh no...
CHANGE
Spider-Man fought this guy.
It was on ViewTube.
Guy made this formula for rings that--that do this I guess.
And I guess all he can think to do with it is...this?
Oh no!! Not you!
Are you *kidding* me?!!

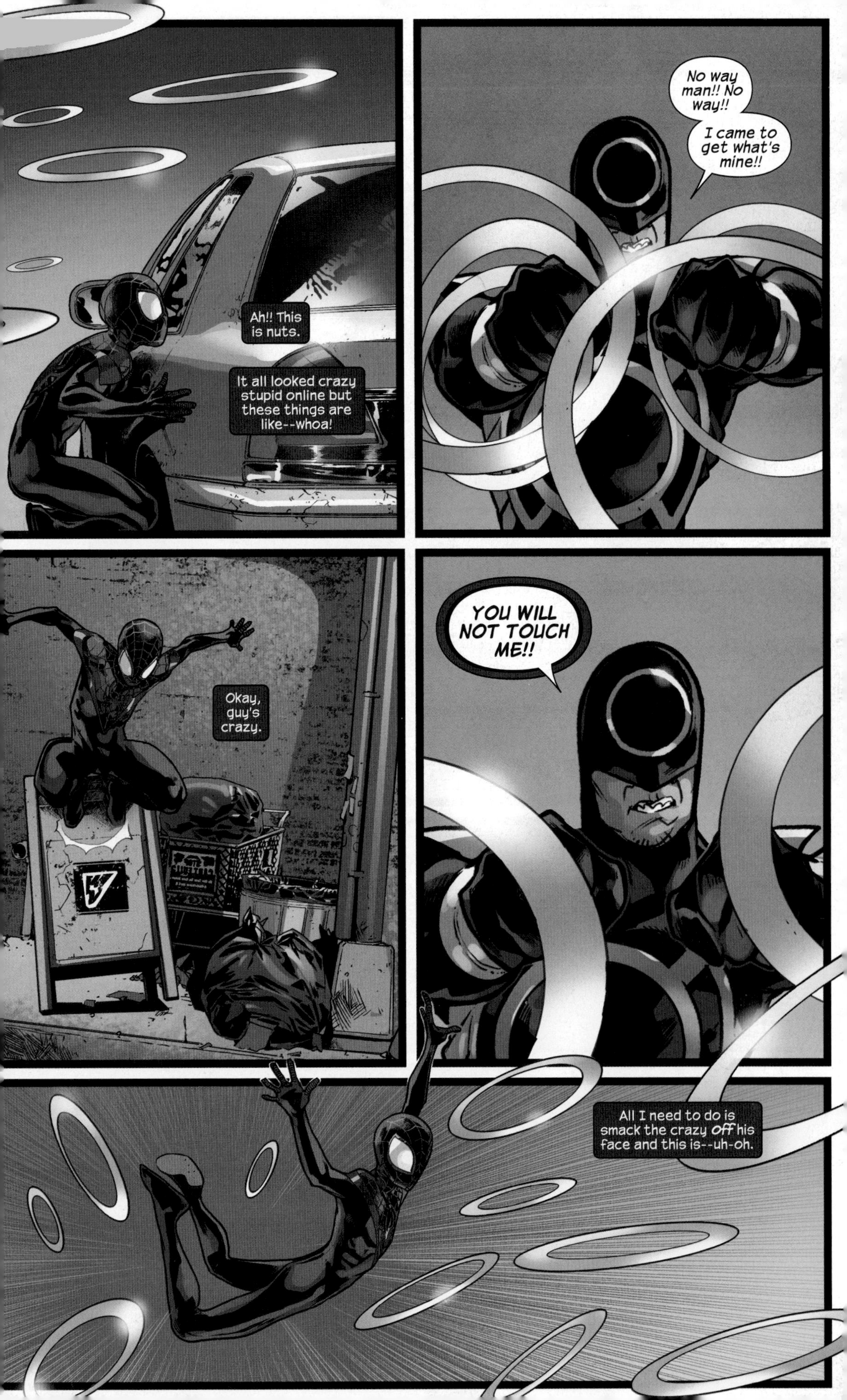
Ah!! This is nuts.
It all looked crazy stupid online but these things are like--whoa!
No way man!! No way!!
I came to get what's mine!!
Okay, guy's crazy.
YOU WILL NOT TOUCH ME!!
All I need to do is smack the crazy *off* his face and this is--uh-oh.

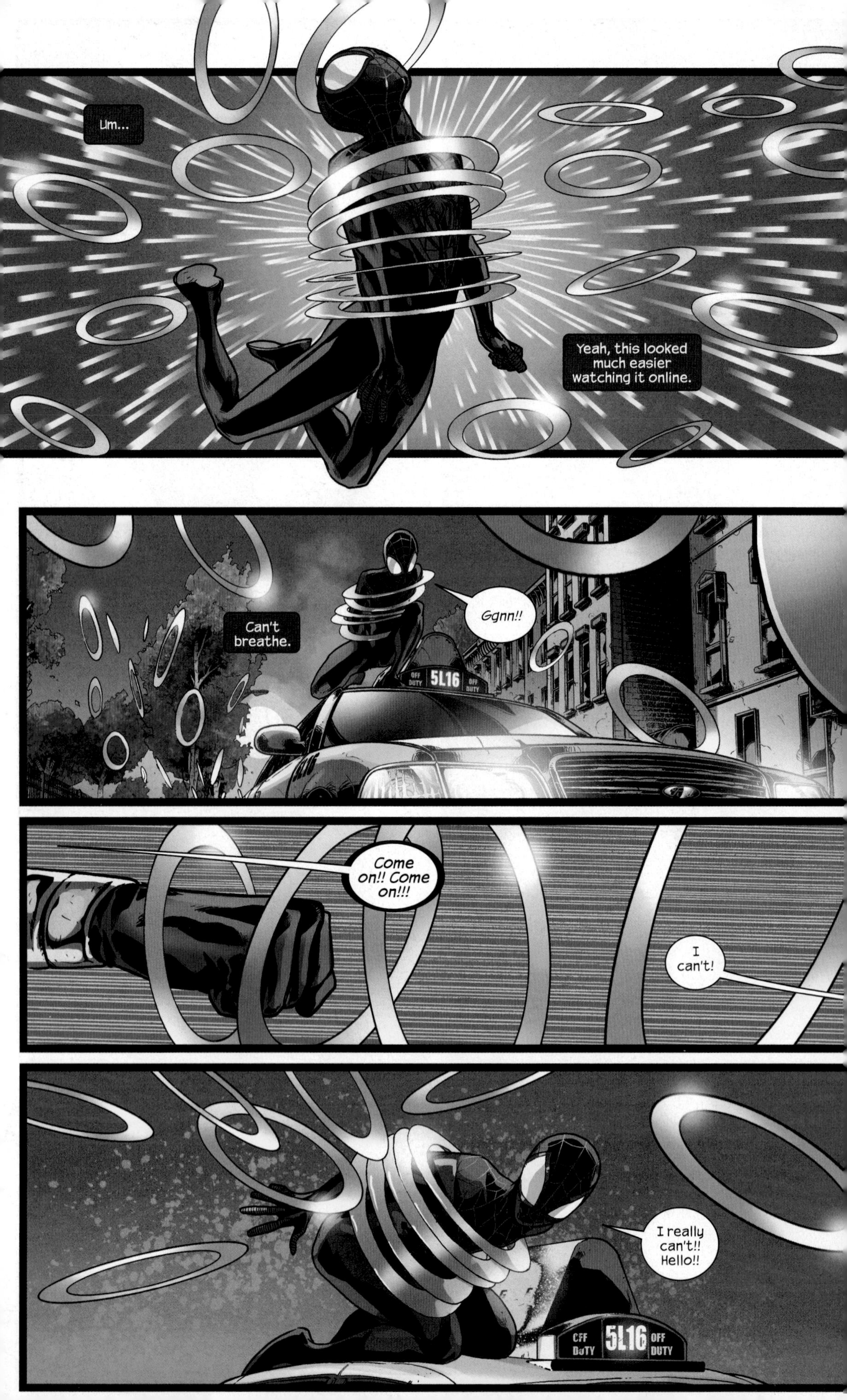
Um...
Yeah, this looked much easier watching it online.
Can't breathe.
Ggnn!!
OFF DUTY 5L16 OFF DUTY
Come on!! Come on!!!
I can't!
I really can't!! Hello!!
OFF DUTY 5L16 OFF DUTY

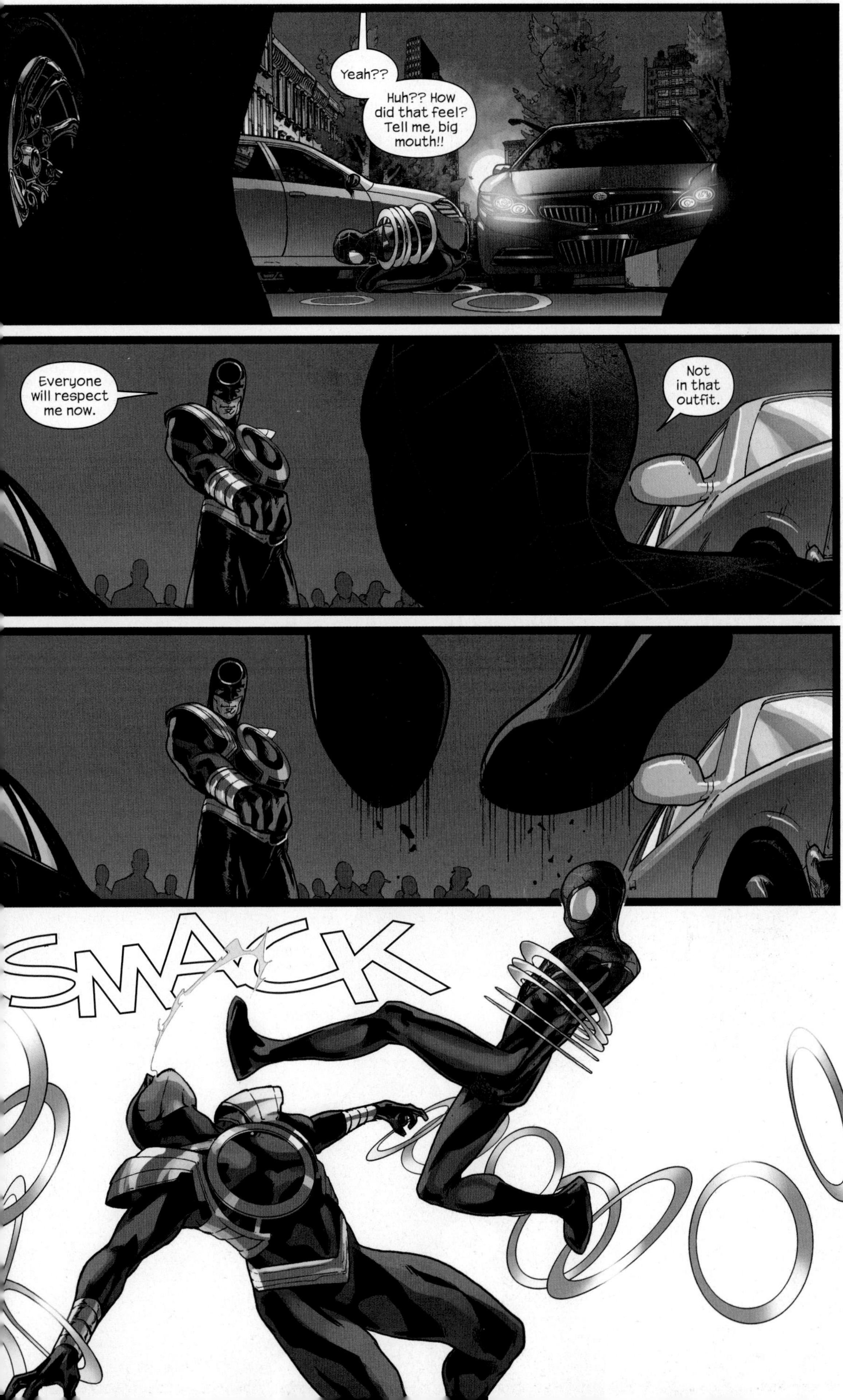
Yeah??
Huh?? How did that feel? Tell me, big mouth!!
Everyone will respect me now.
Not in that outfit.
SMACK

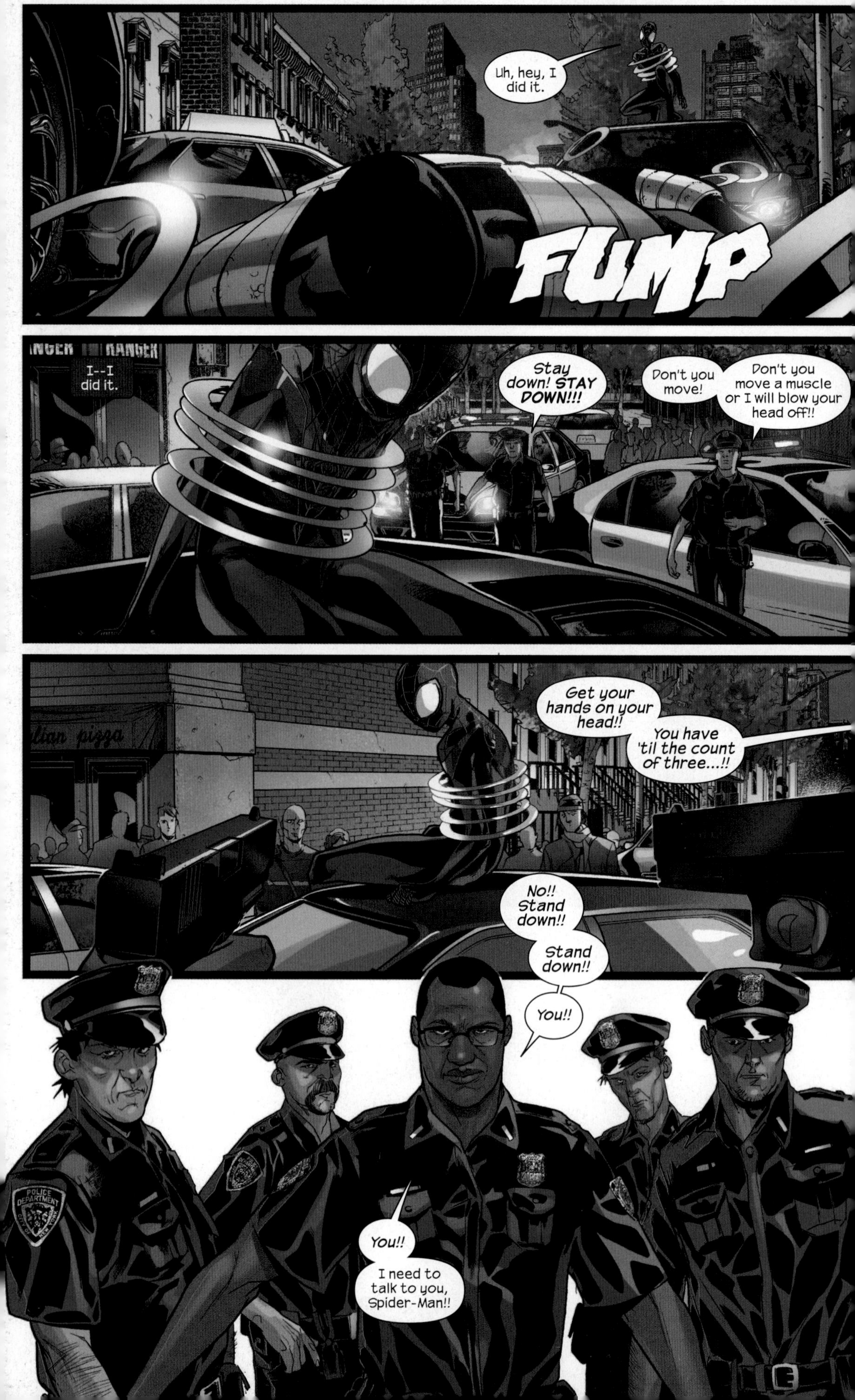
Uh, hey, I did it.
FUMP
I--I did it.
Stay down! STAY DOWN!!!
Don't you move!
Don't you move a muscle or I will blow your head off!!
Get your hands on your head!!
You have 'til the count of three...!!
No!! Stand down!!
Stand down!!
You!!
You!!
I need to talk to you, Spider-Man!!

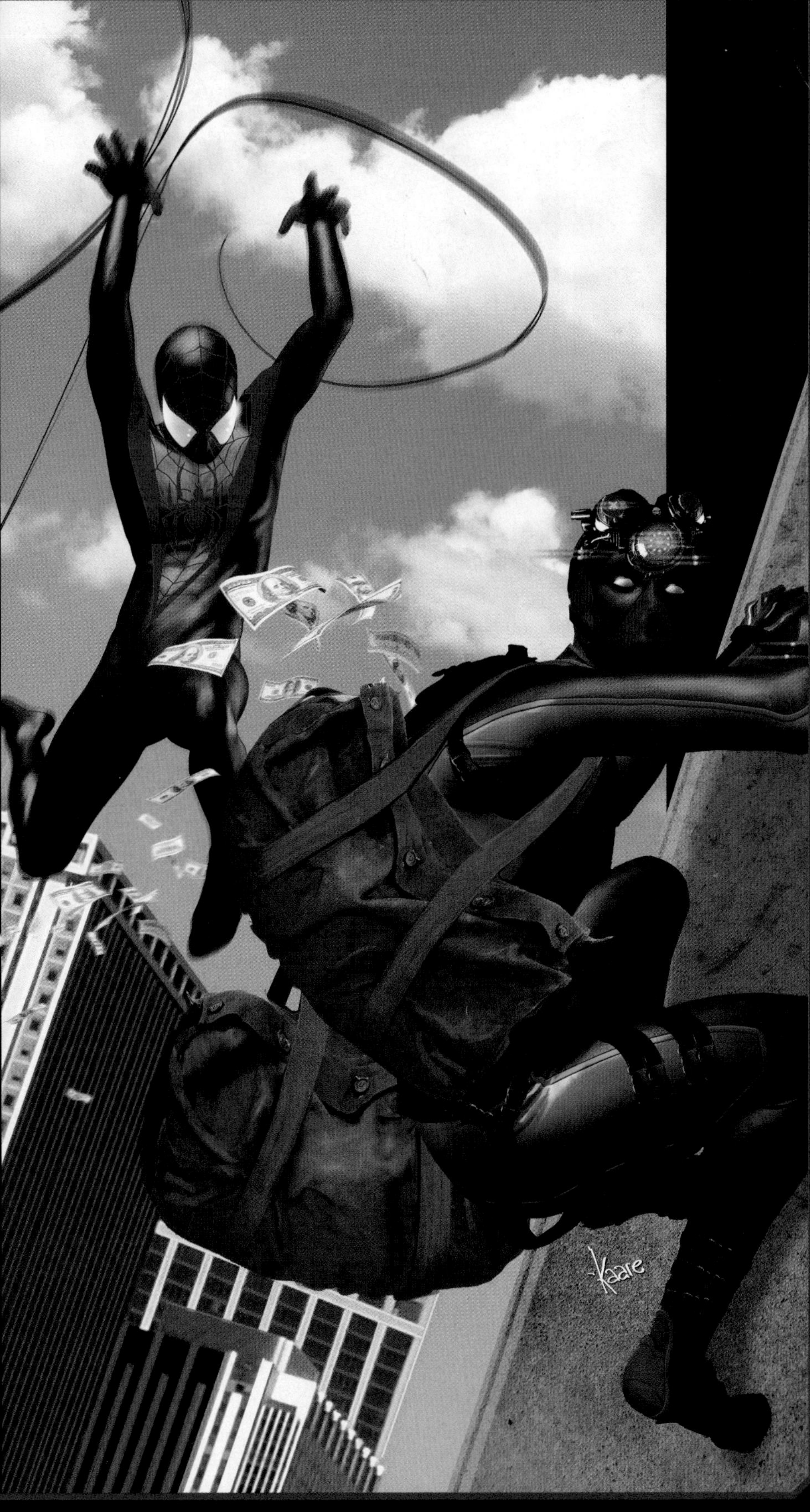
Kaare

ULTIMATE COMICS SPIDER-MAN #9

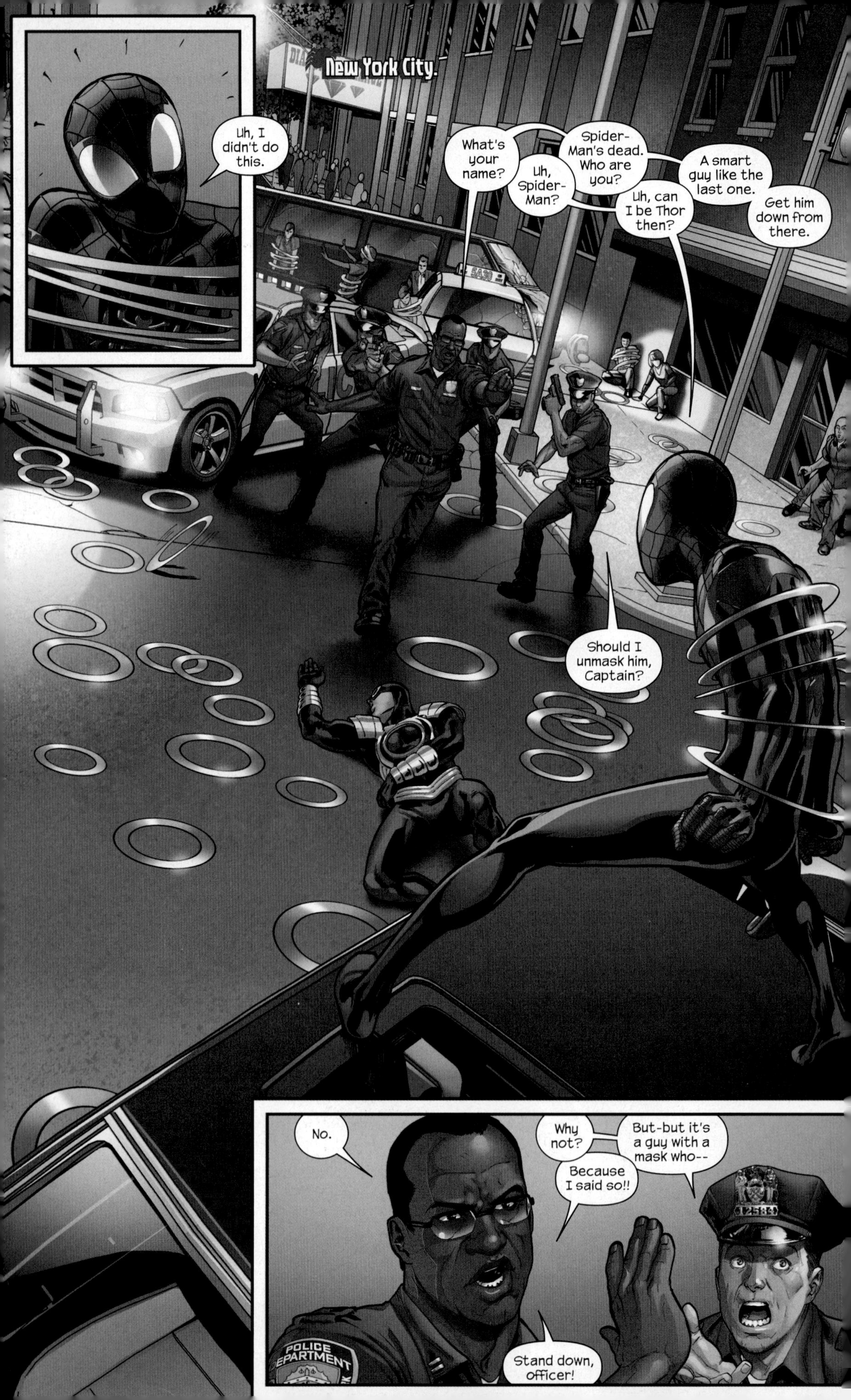

Uh, I didn't do this.
New York City.
What's your name?
Uh, Spider-Man?
Spider-Man's dead. Who are you?
Uh, can I be Thor then?
A smart guy like the last one.
Get him down from there.
Should I unmask him, Captain?
No.
Why not?
But-but it's a guy with a mask who--
Because I said so!!
Stand down, officer!
POLICE DEPARTMENT

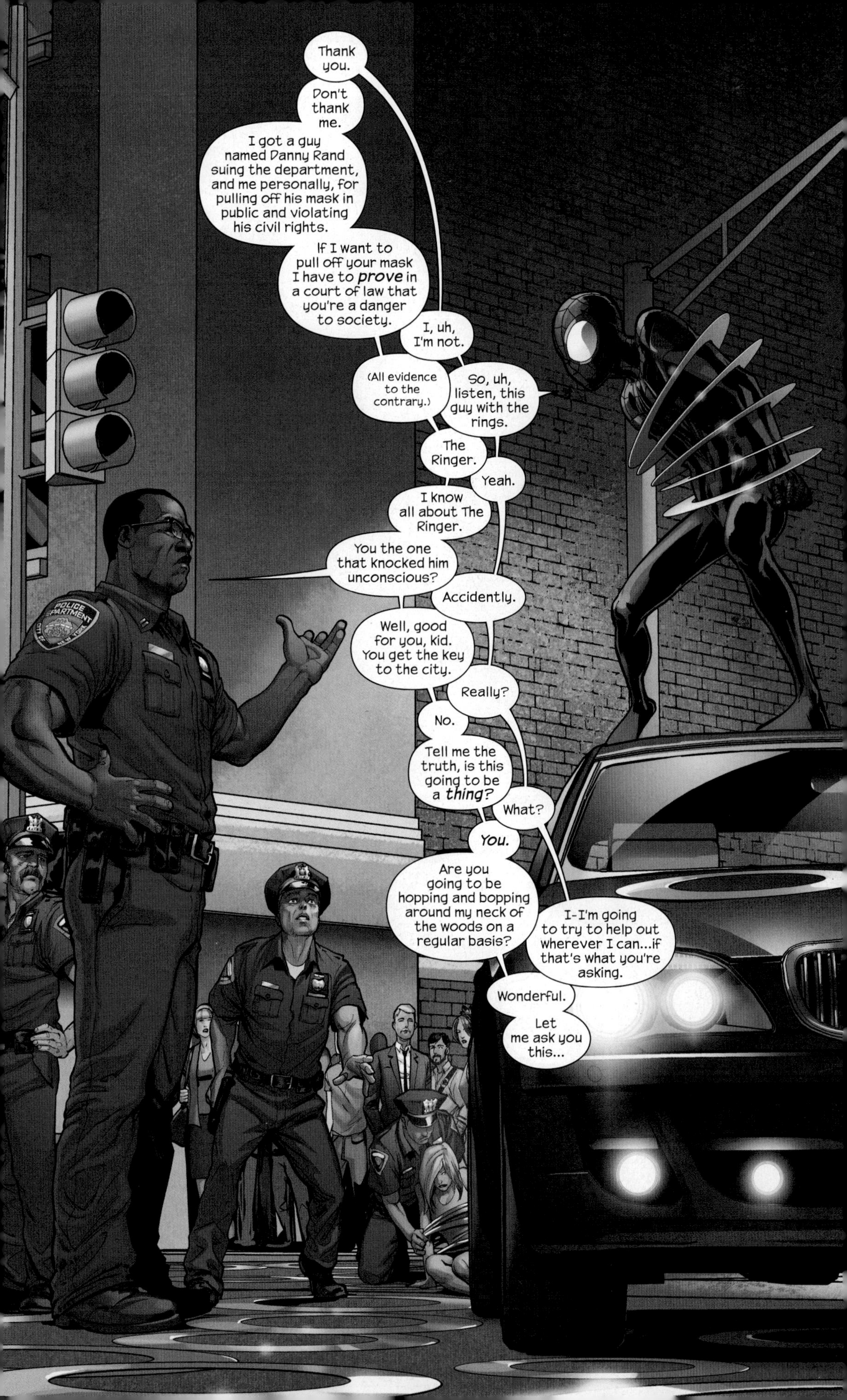
Thank you.
Don't thank me.
I got a guy named Danny Rand suing the department, and me personally, for pulling off his mask in public and violating his civil rights.
If I want to pull off your mask I have to *prove* in a court of law that you're a danger to society.
I, uh, I'm not.
(All evidence to the contrary.)
So, uh, listen, this guy with the rings.
The Ringer.
Yeah.
I know all about The Ringer.
You the one that knocked him unconscious?
Accidently.
Well, good for you, kid. You get the key to the city.
Really?
No.
Tell me the truth, is this going to be a *thing*?
What?
You.
Are you going to be hopping and bopping around my neck of the woods on a regular basis?
I-I'm going to try to help out wherever I can...if that's what you're asking.
Wonderful.
Let me ask you this...

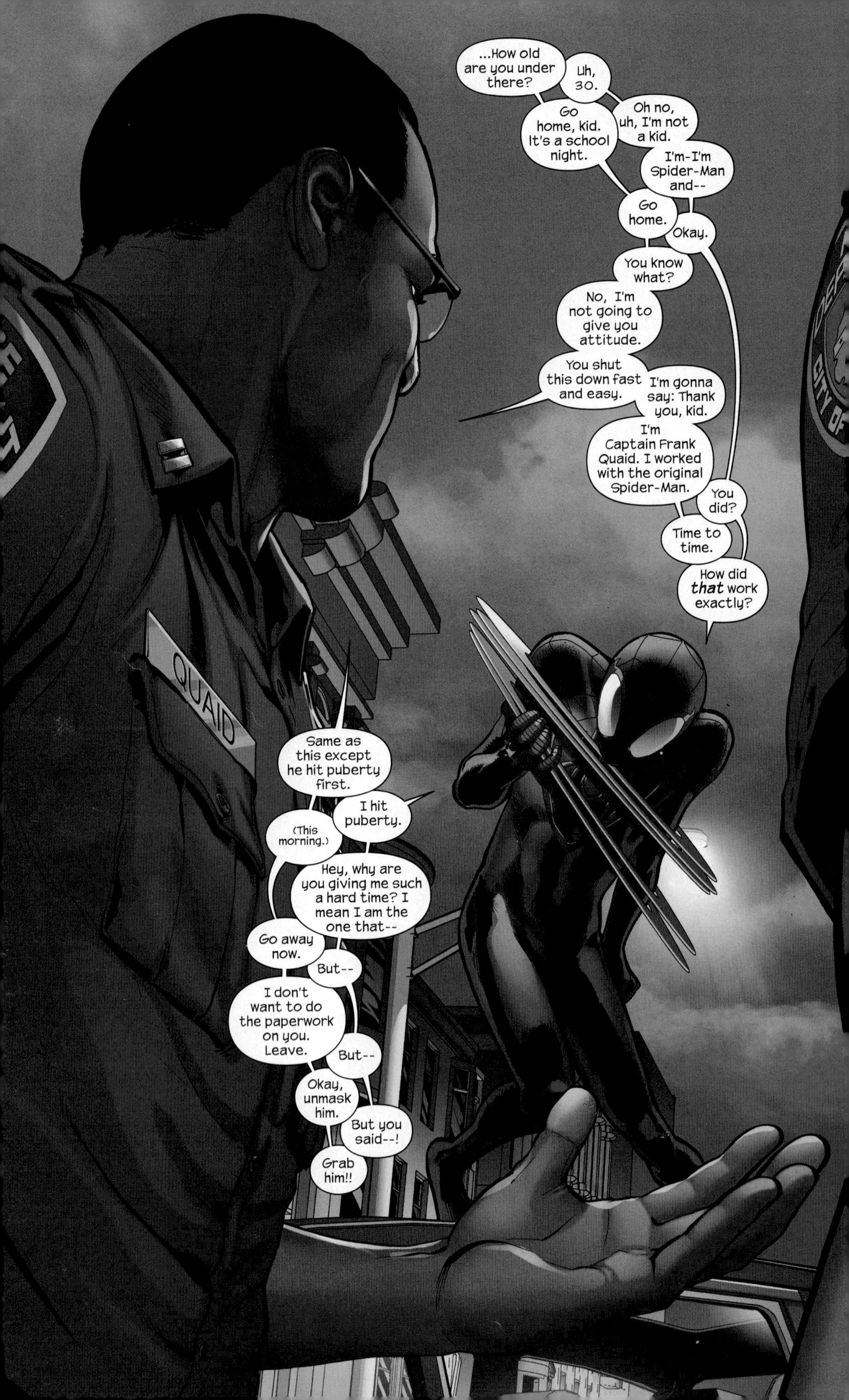
...How old are you under there?
Uh, 30.
Go home, kid. It's a school night.
Oh no, uh, I'm not a kid.
I'm-I'm Spider-Man and--
Go home.
Okay.
You know what?
No, I'm not going to give you attitude.
You shut this down fast and easy.
I'm gonna say: Thank you, kid.
I'm Captain Frank Quaid. I worked with the original Spider-Man.
You did?
Time to time.
How did *that* work exactly?
QUAID
Same as this except he hit puberty first.
I hit puberty.
(This morning.)
Hey, why are you giving me such a hard time? I mean I am the one that--
Go away now.
But--
I don't want to do the paperwork on you. Leave.
But--
Okay, unmask him.
But you said--!
Grab him!!

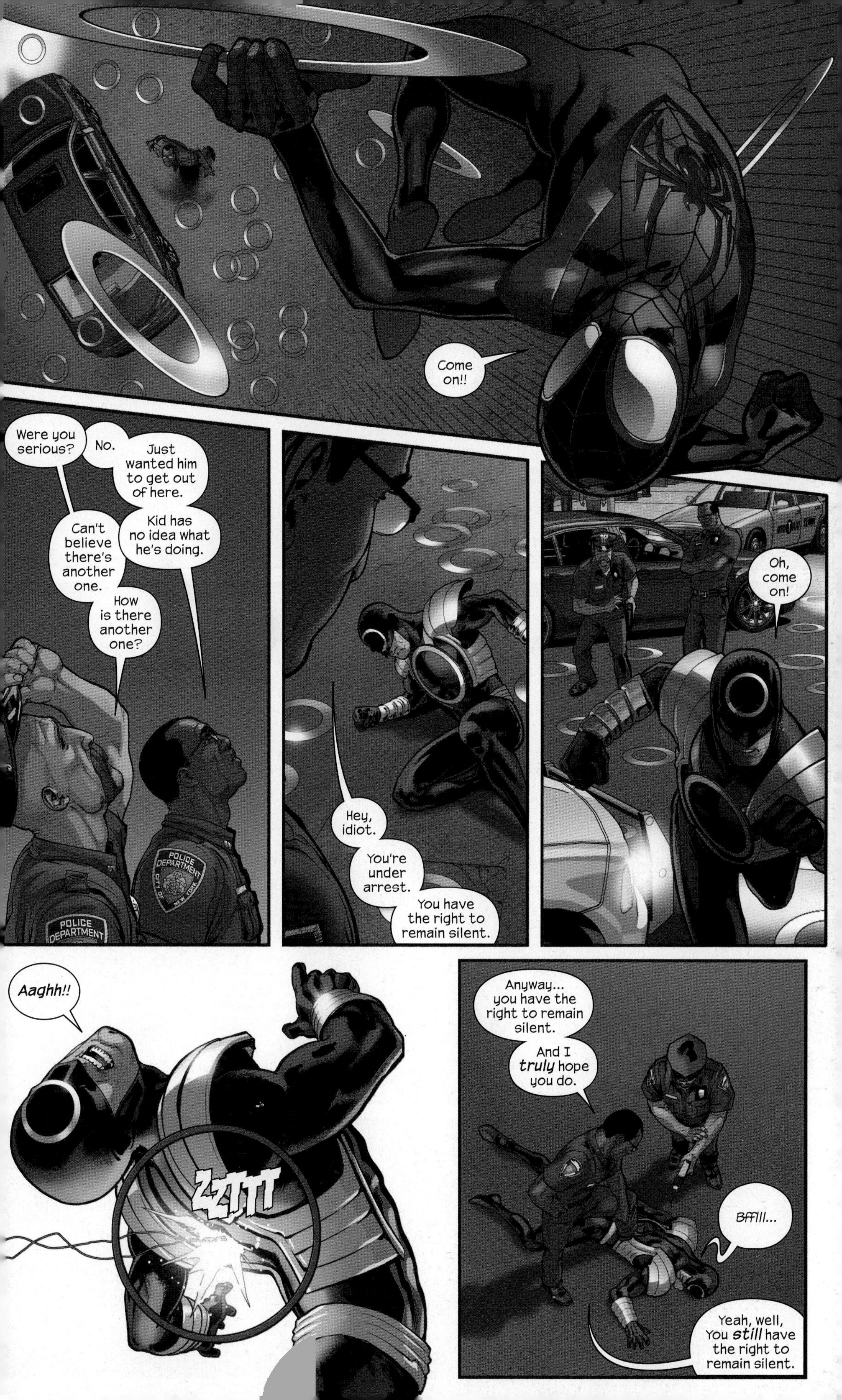
Come on!!
Were you serious?
No.
Just wanted him to get out of here.
Can't believe there's another one.
Kid has no idea what he's doing.
How is there another one?
POLICE DEPARTMENT
POLICE DEPARTMENT CITY OF NEW YORK
Hey, idiot.
You're under arrest.
You have the right to remain silent.
Oh, come on!
Aaghh!!
ZZTTT
Anyway... you have the right to remain silent.
And I *truly* hope you do.
Bfflll...
Yeah, well, You *still* have the right to remain silent.

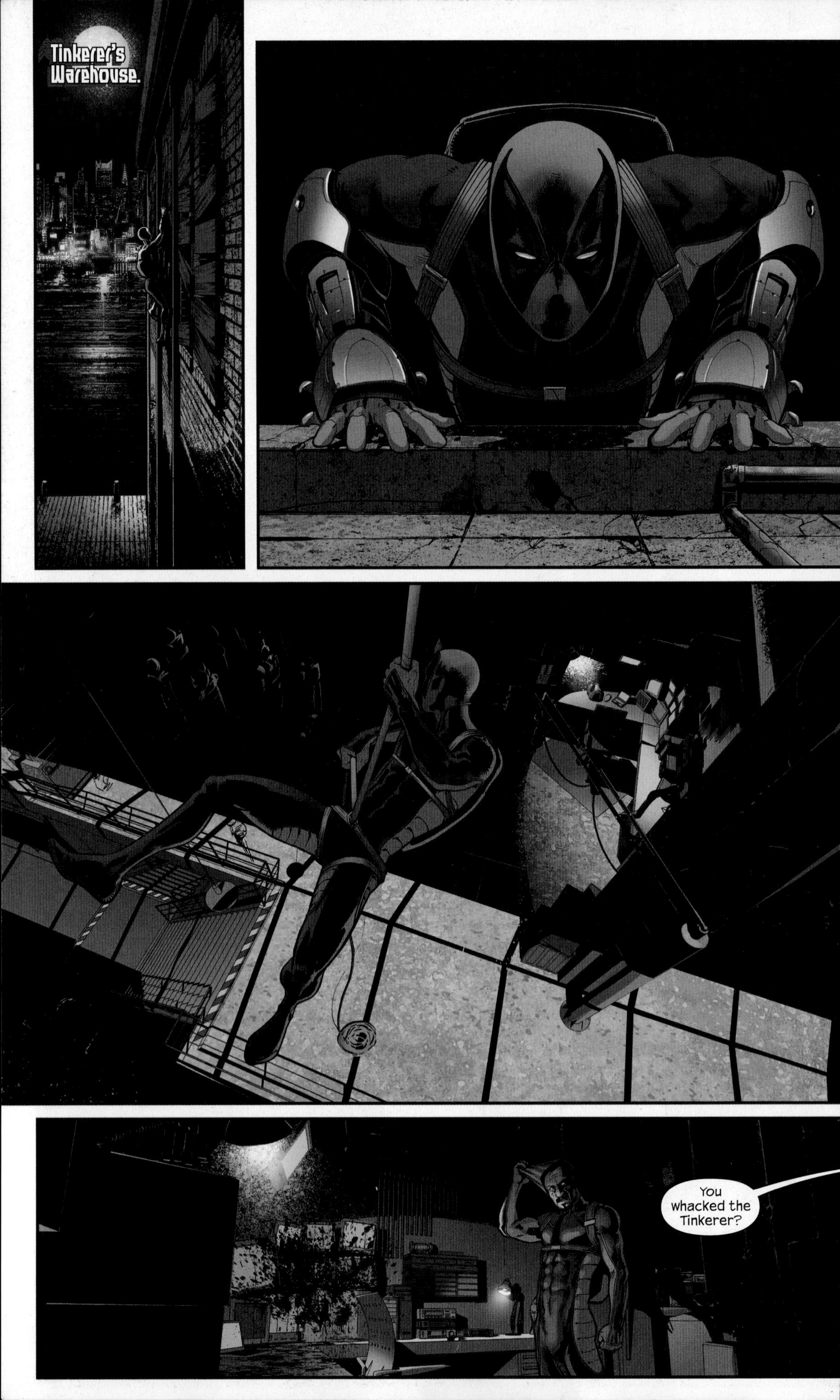
Tinkerer's Warehouse.
You whacked the Tinkerer?

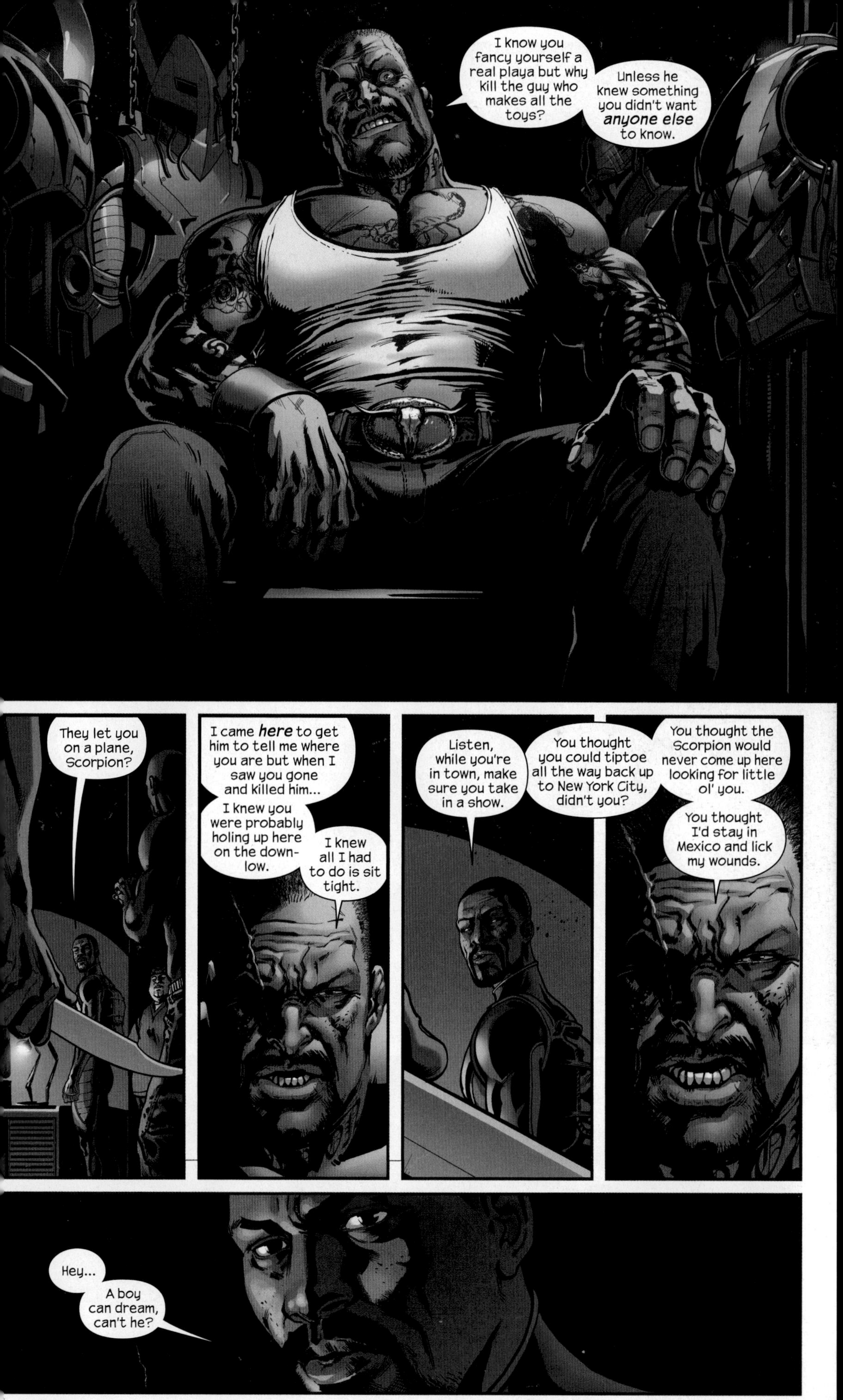
I know you fancy yourself a real playa but why kill the guy who makes all the toys?
Unless he knew something you didn't want *anyone else* to know.
They let you on a plane, Scorpion?
I came *here* to get him to tell me where you are but when I saw you gone and killed him...
I knew you were probably holing up here on the down-low.
I knew all I had to do is sit tight.
Listen, while you're in town, make sure you take in a show.
You thought you could tiptoe all the way back up to New York City, didn't you?
You thought the Scorpion would never come up here looking for little ol' you.
You thought I'd stay in Mexico and lick my wounds.
Hey...
A boy can dream, can't he?

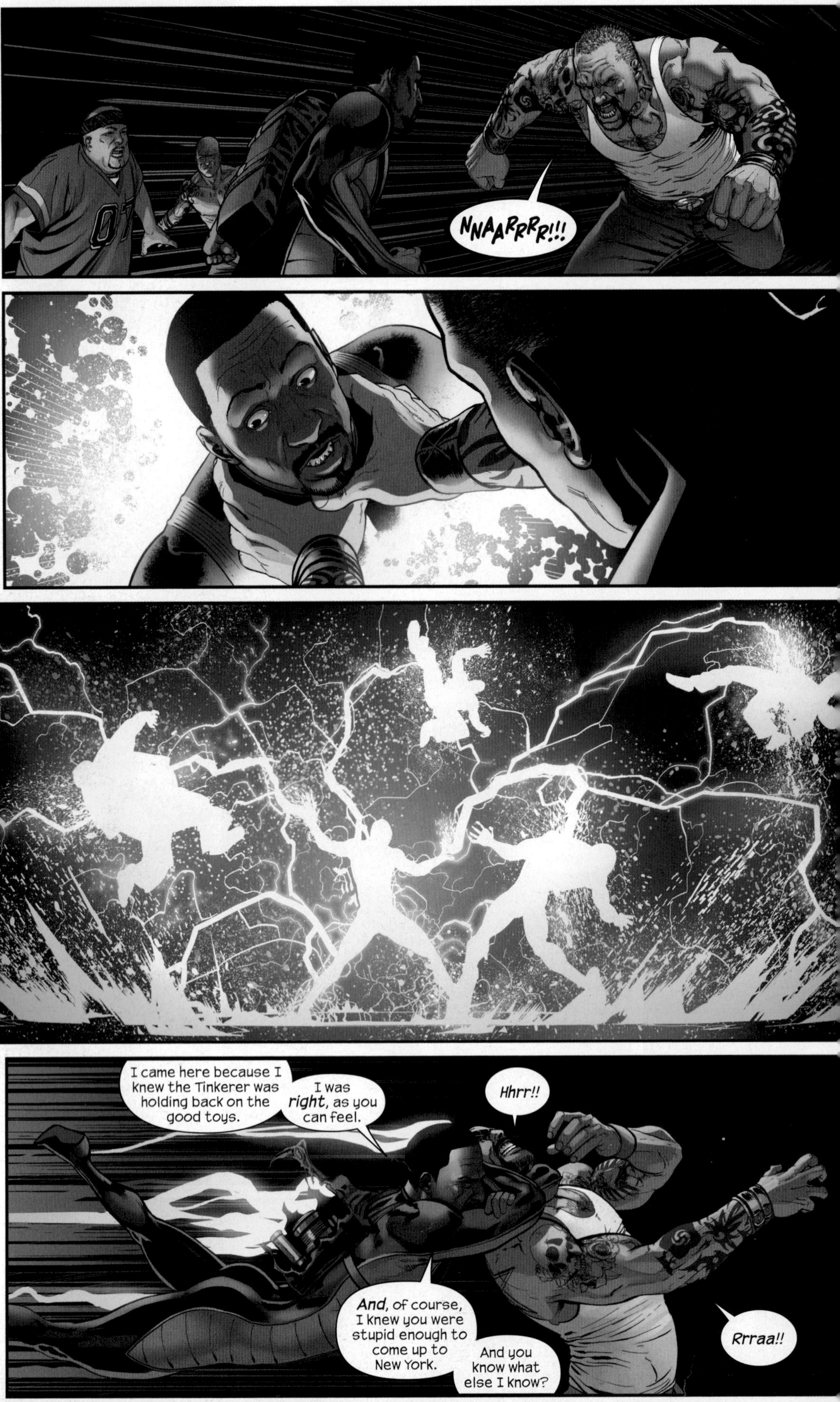
NNAARRRR!!!
I came here because I knew the Tinkerer was holding back on the good toys.
I was right, as you can feel.
Hhrr!!
And, of course, I knew you were stupid enough to come up to New York.
And you know what else I know?
Rrraa!!

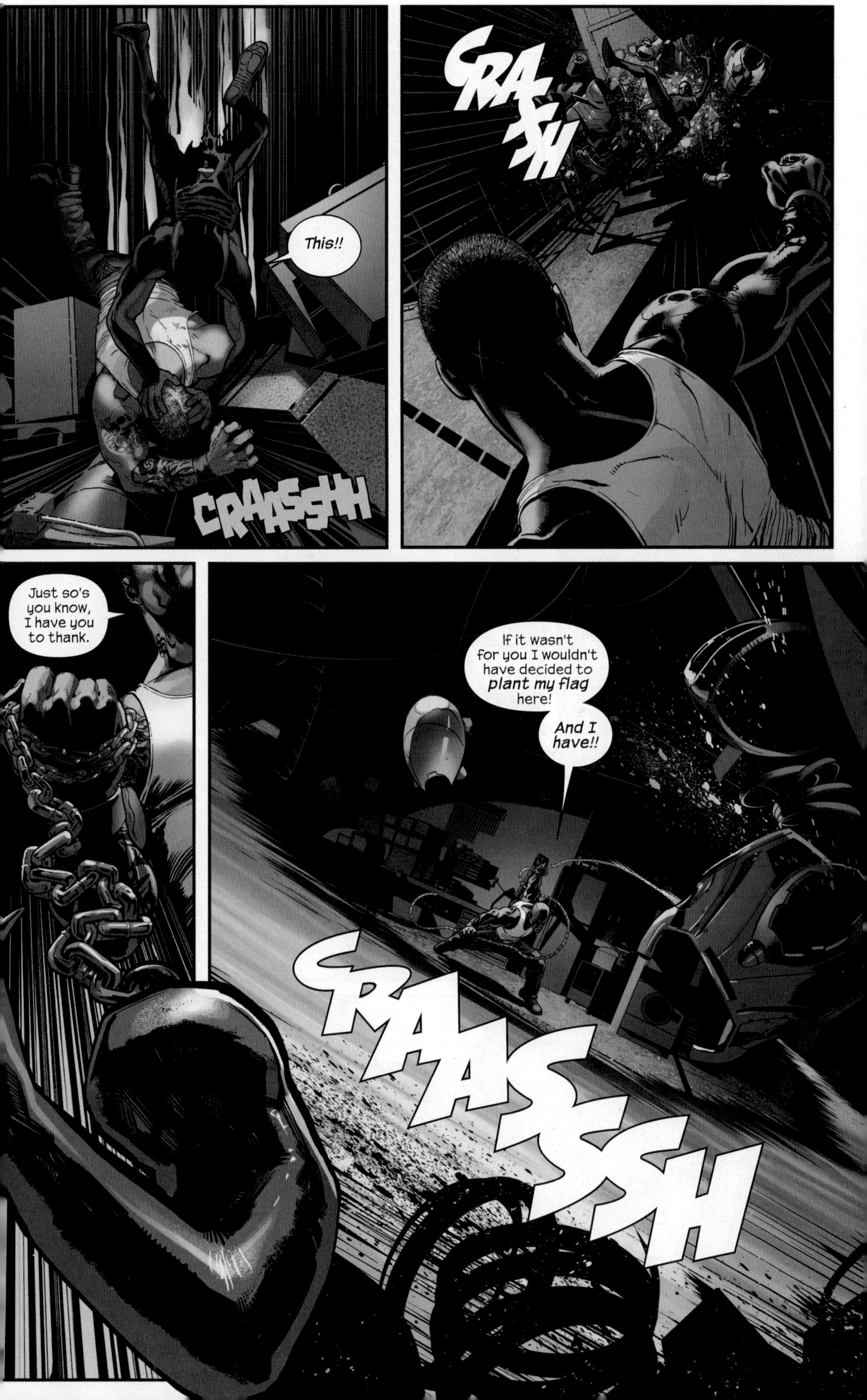
This!!
CRAASSHH
CRASSH
Just so's you know, I have you to thank.
If it wasn't for you I wouldn't have decided to *plant my flag* here!
And I have!!
CRAASSSH

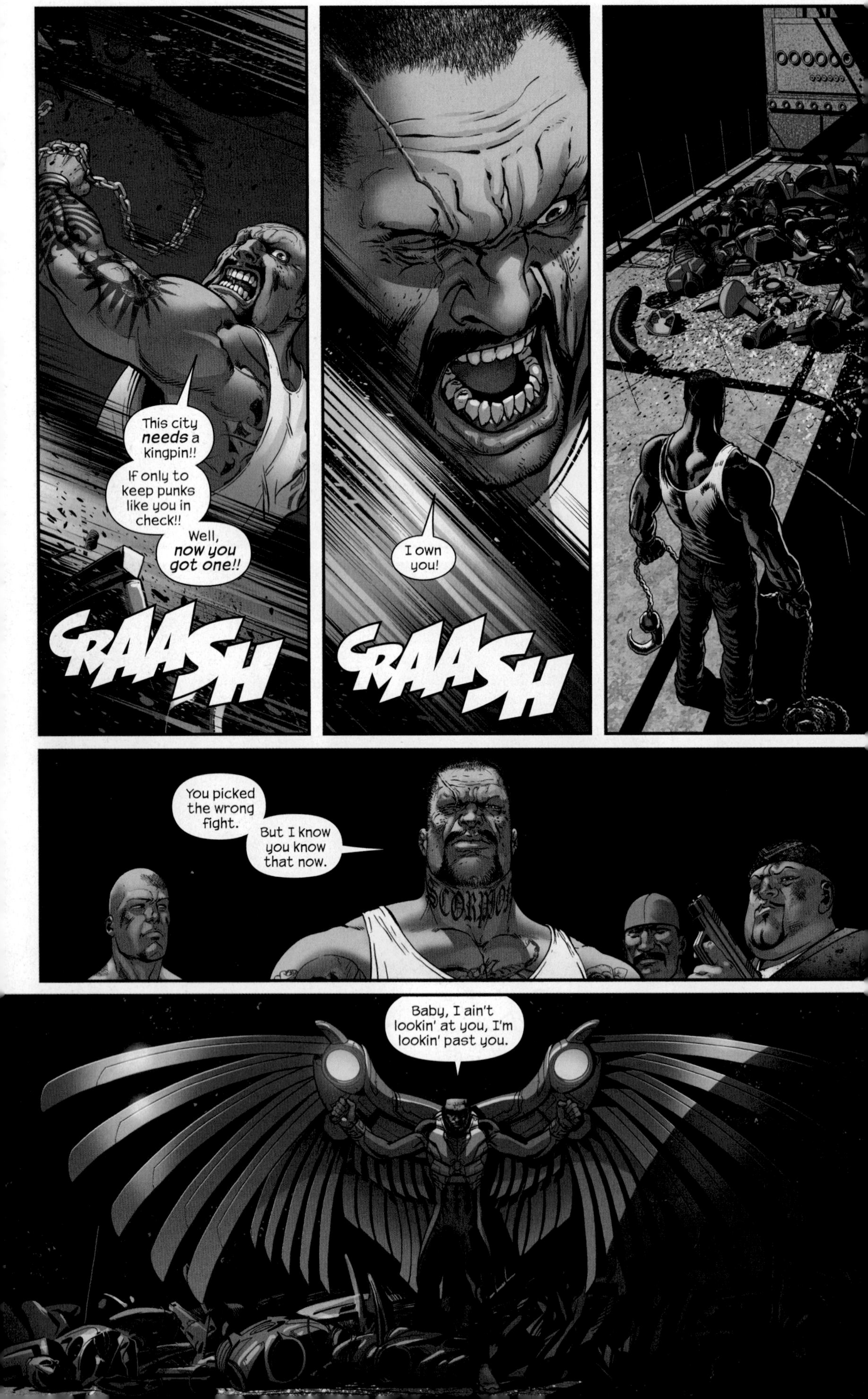

This city needs a kingpin!!
If only to keep punks like you in check!!
Well, now you got one!!
CRAASH
I own you!
CRAASH
You picked the wrong fight.
But I know you know that now.
Baby, I ain't lookin' at you, I'm lookin' past you.

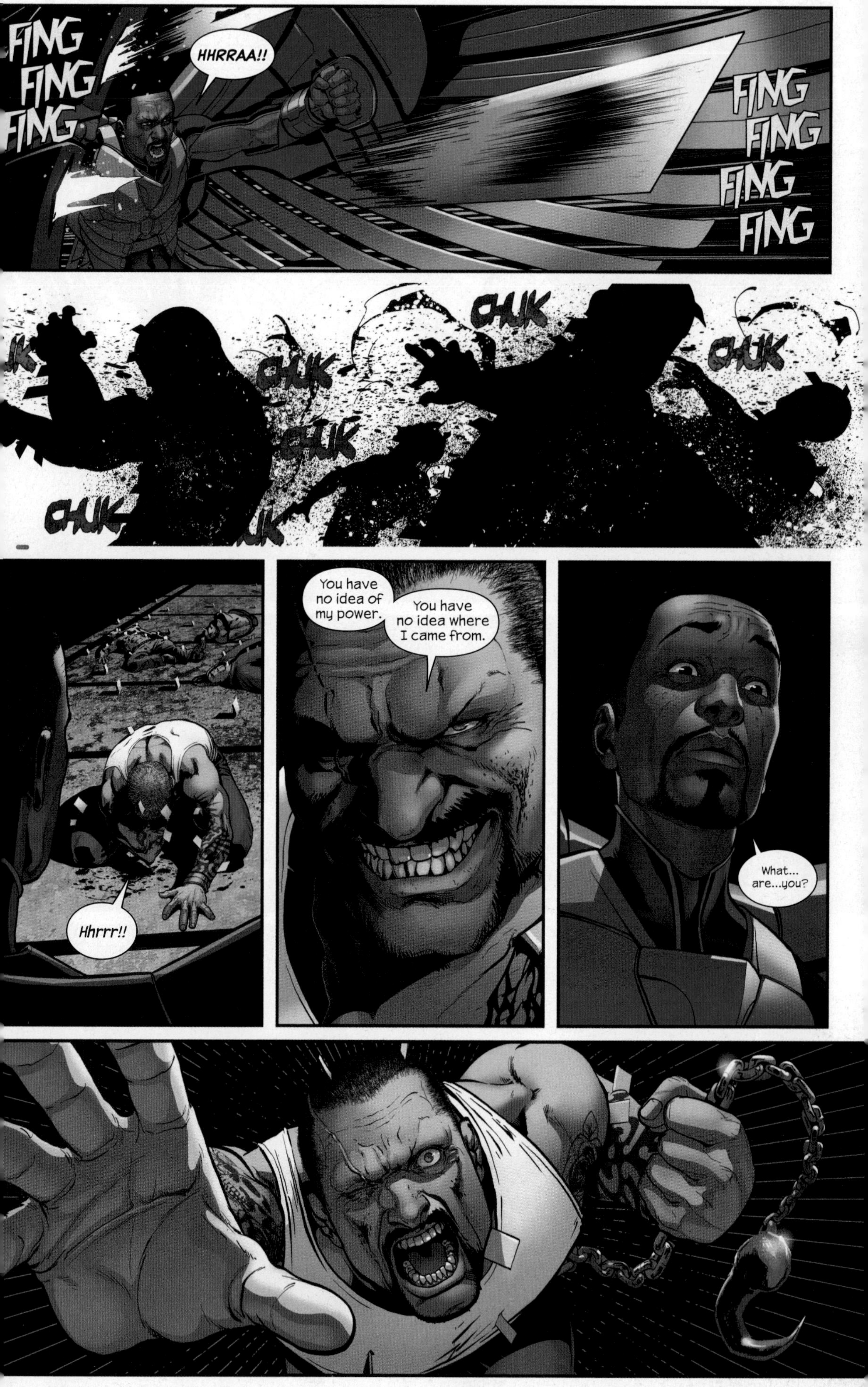
FING
FING
FING
HHRRAA!!
FING
FING
FING
FING
CHUK
CHUK
CHUK
CHUK
CHUK
You have no idea of my power.
You have no idea where I came from.
Hhrrr!!
What... are...you?

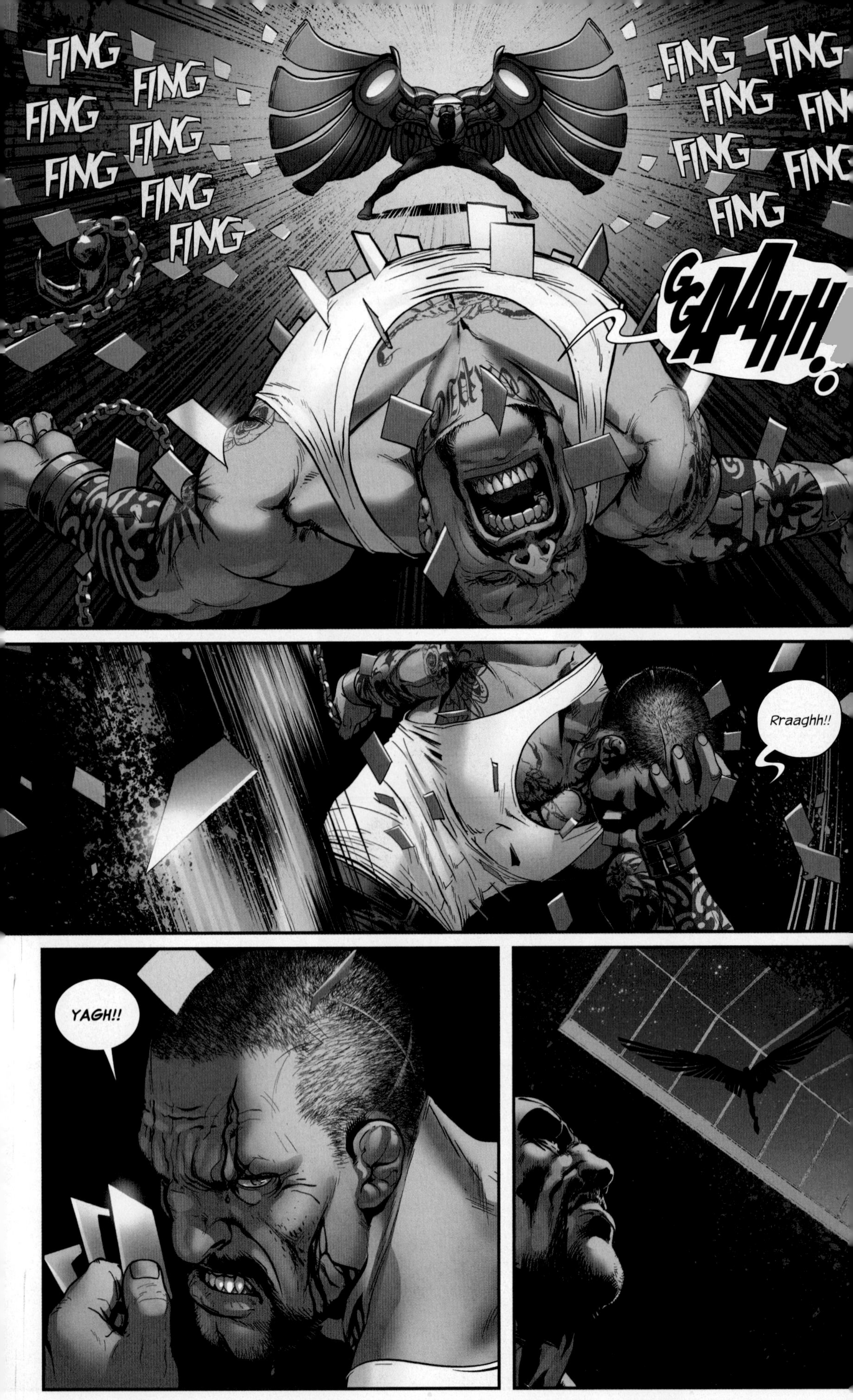
FING
FING
FING
FING
FING
FING
FING
FING
FING
FING
FING
FING
GGAAHH
Rraaghh!!
YAGH!!

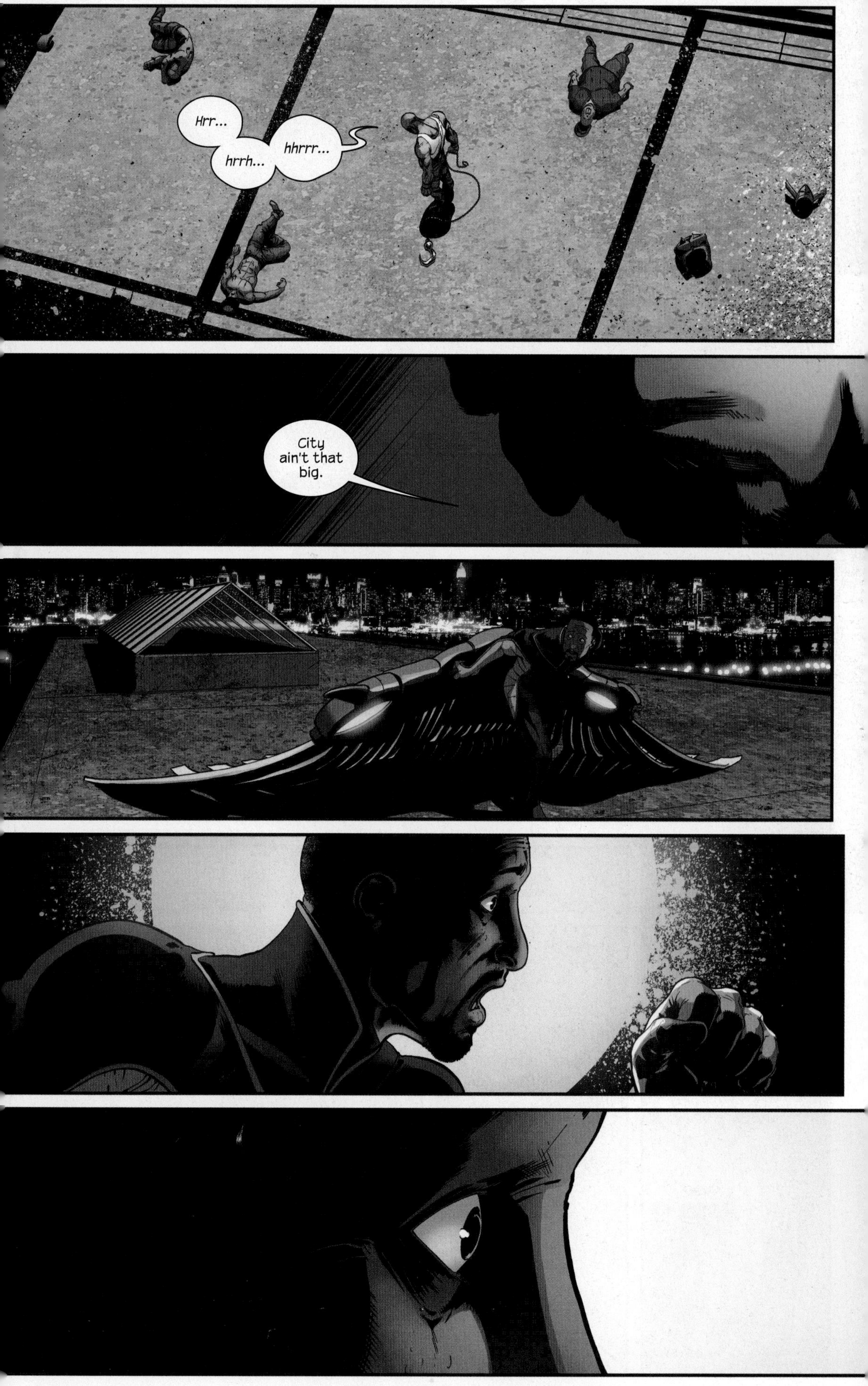
Hrr...
hrrh...
hhrrr...
City ain't that big.

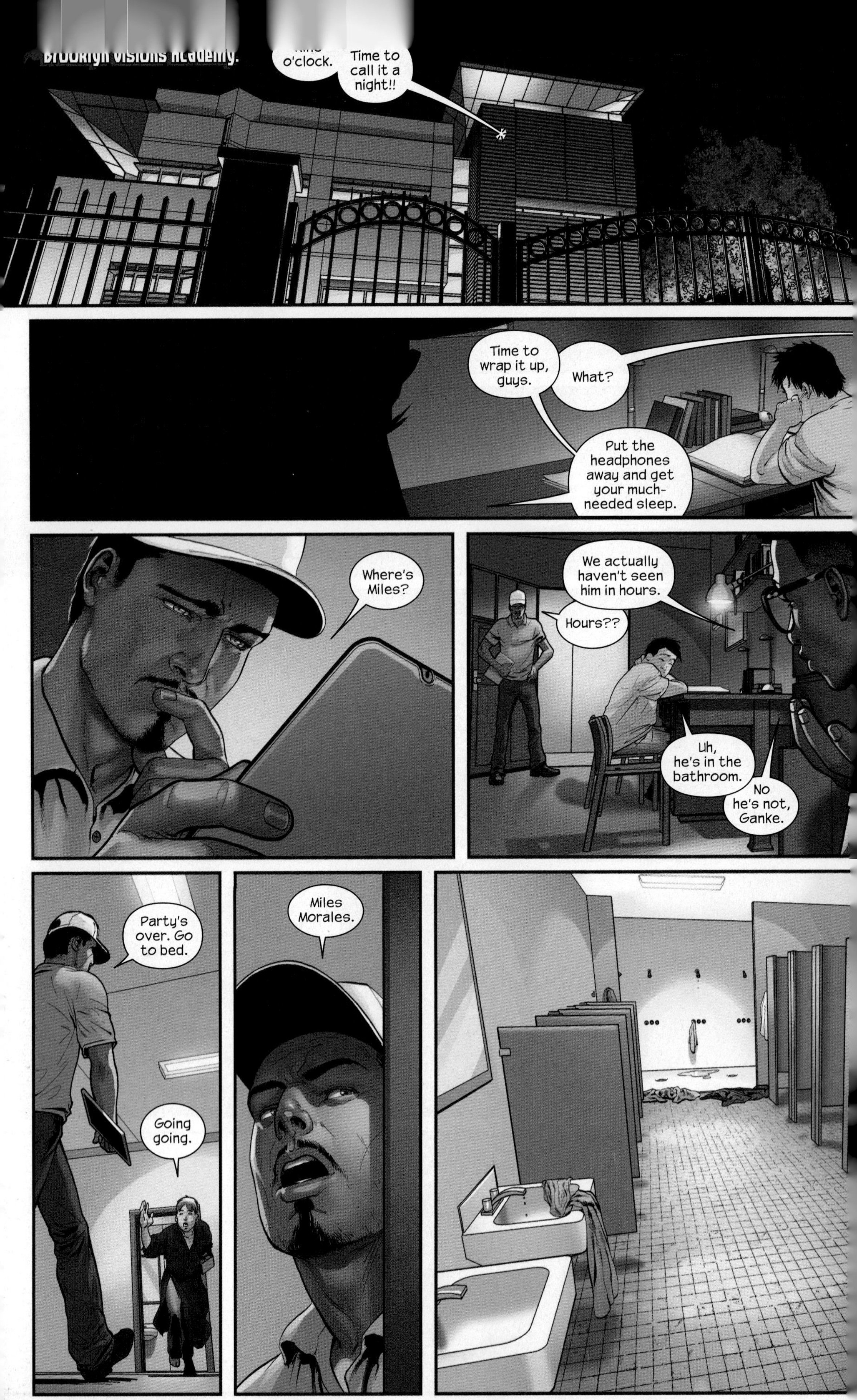
o'clock.
Time to call it a night!!
Time to wrap it up, guys.
What?
Put the headphones away and get your much-needed sleep.
Where's Miles?
We actually haven't seen him in hours.
Hours??
Uh, he's in the bathroom.
No he's not, Ganke.
Party's over. Go to bed.
Going going.
Miles Morales.

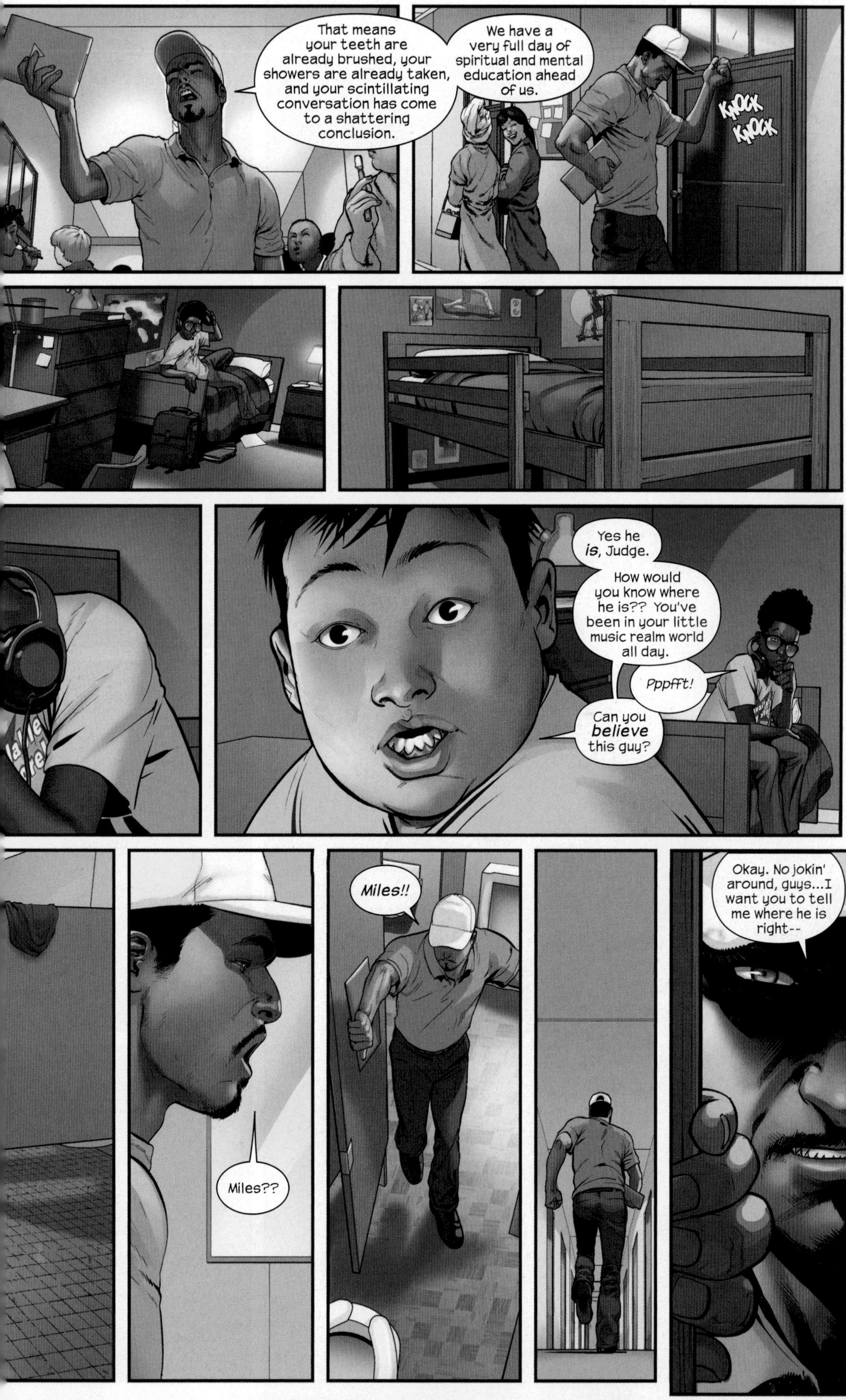
That means your teeth are already brushed, your showers are already taken, and your scintillating conversation has come to a shattering conclusion.
We have a very full day of spiritual and mental education ahead of us.
KNOCK KNOCK
Yes he is, Judge.
How would you know where he is?? You've been in your little music realm world all day.
Pppfft!
Can you believe this guy?
Miles??
Miles!!
Okay. No jokin' around, guys...I want you to tell me where he is right--

S'up?

Where **were** you, Miles?

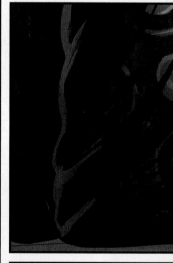

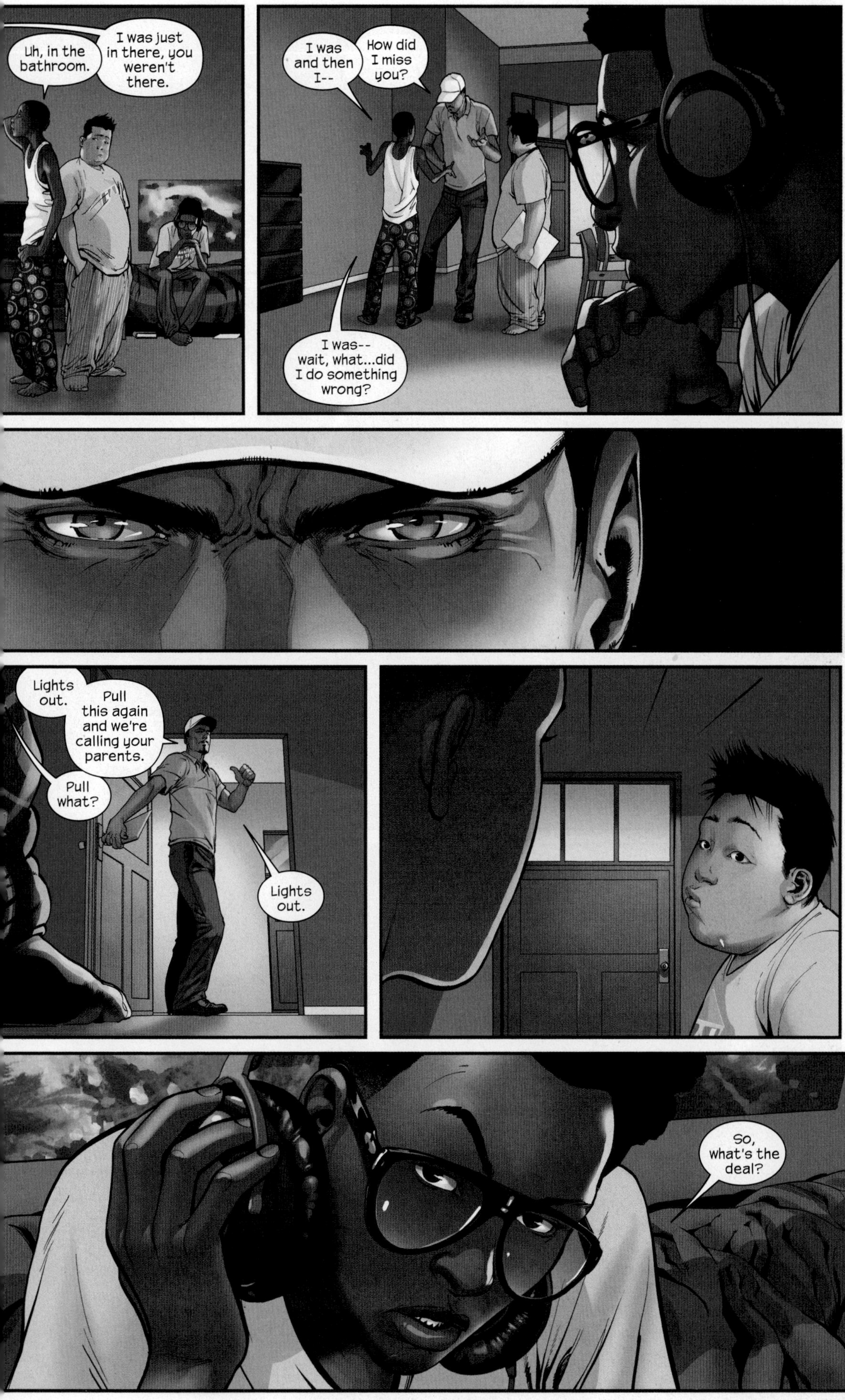

Uh, in the bathroom.
I was just in there, you weren't there.
I was and then I--
How did I miss you?
I was-- wait, what...did I do something wrong?
Lights out.
Pull this again and we're calling your parents.
Pull what?
Lights out.
So, what's the deal?

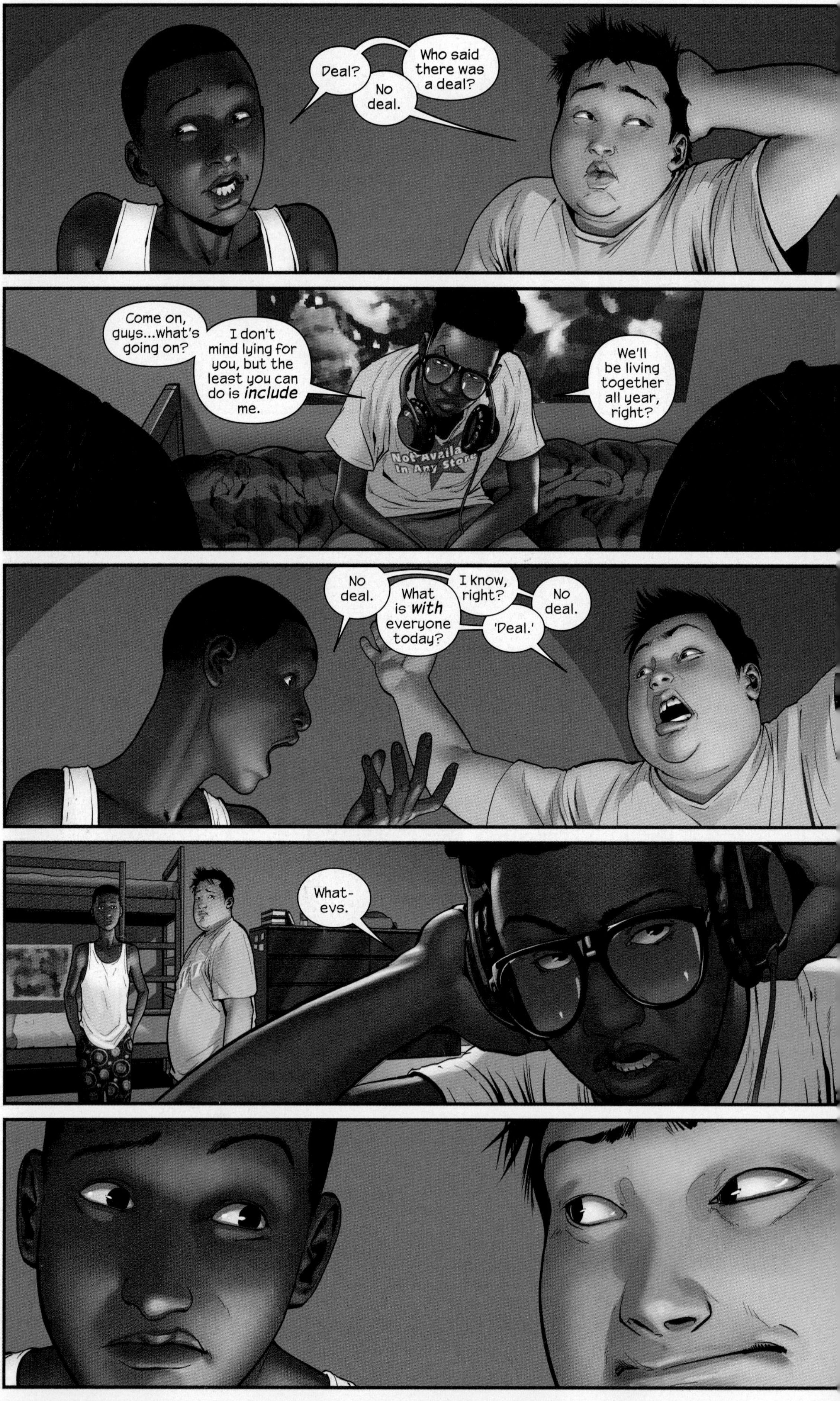
Deal?
No deal.
Who said there was a deal?
Come on, guys...what's going on?
I don't mind lying for you, but the least you can do is *include* me.
We'll be living together all year, right?
Not Available In Any Store
No deal.
What is *with* everyone today?
I know, right?
'Deal.'
No deal.
What-evs.

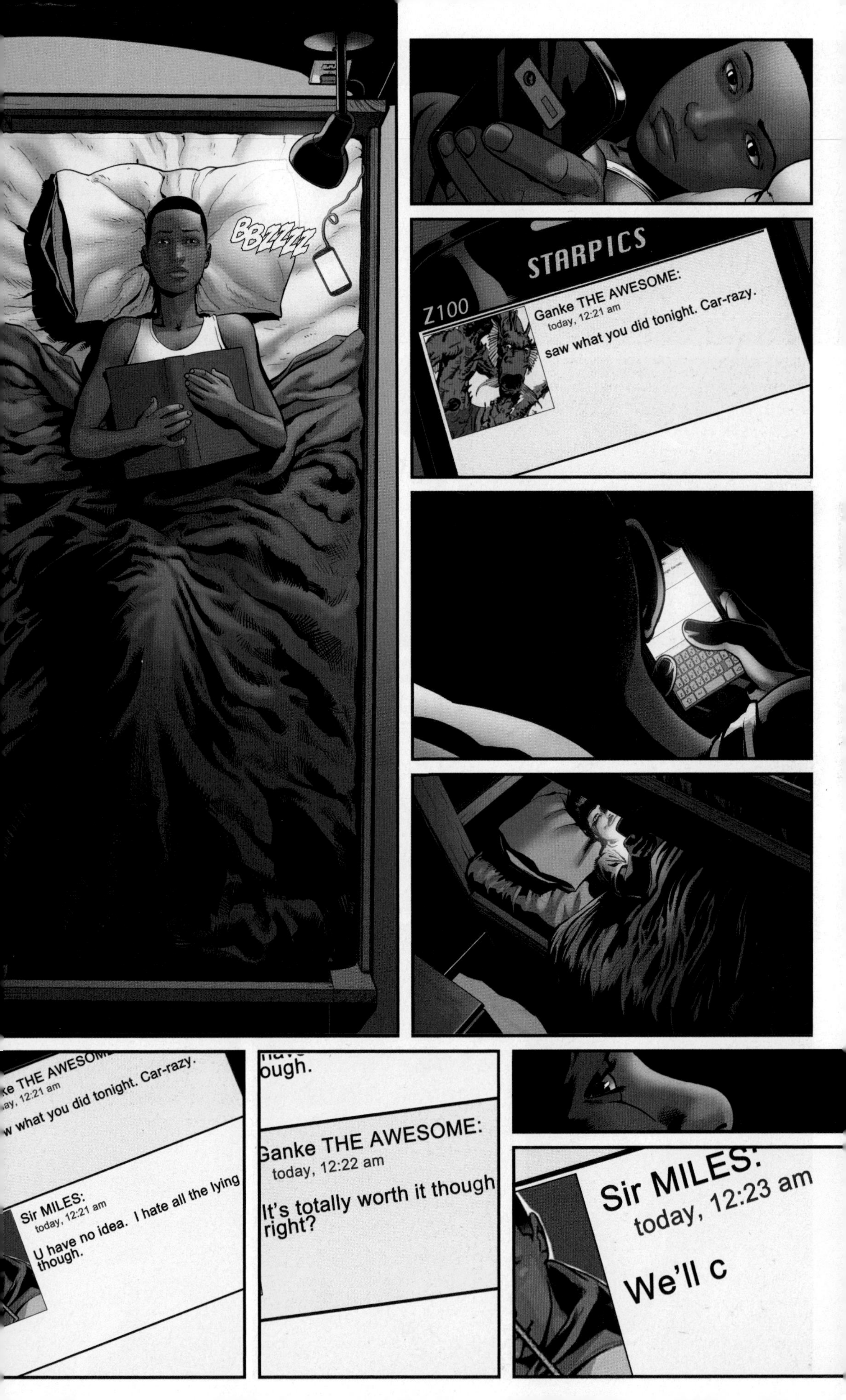

BBZZZZ
STARPICS
Z100
Ganke THE AWESOME:
today, 12:21 am
saw what you did tonight. Car-razy.
Sir MILES:
today, 12:21 am
U have no idea. I hate all the lying though.
Ganke THE AWESOME:
today, 12:22 am
It's totally worth it though right?
Sir MILES:
today, 12:23 am
We'll c

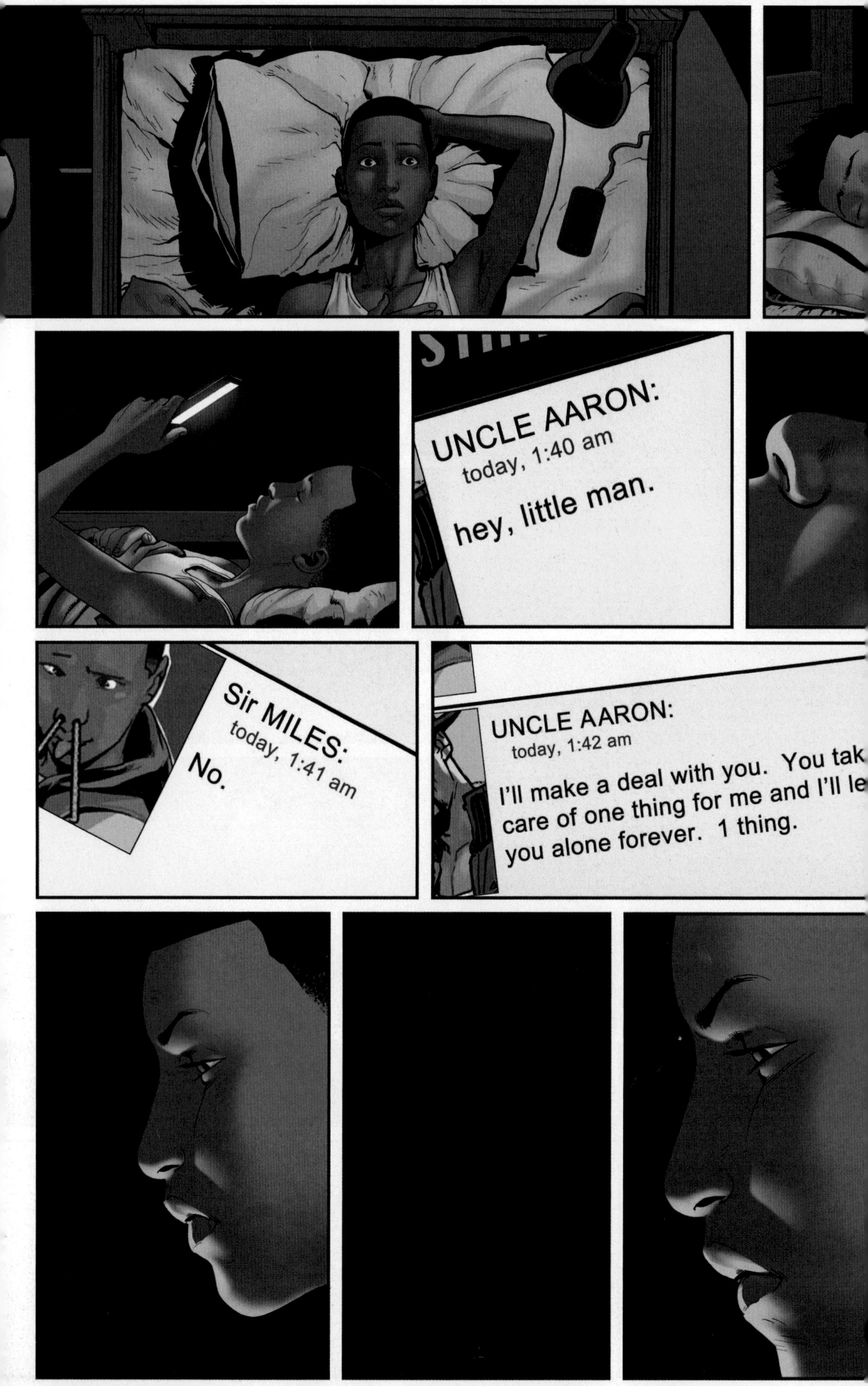
UNCLE AARON:
today, 1:40 am
hey, little man.
Sir MILES:
today, 1:41 am
No.
UNCLE AARON:
today, 1:42 am
I'll make a deal with you. You tak
care of one thing for me and I'll le
you alone forever. 1 thing.

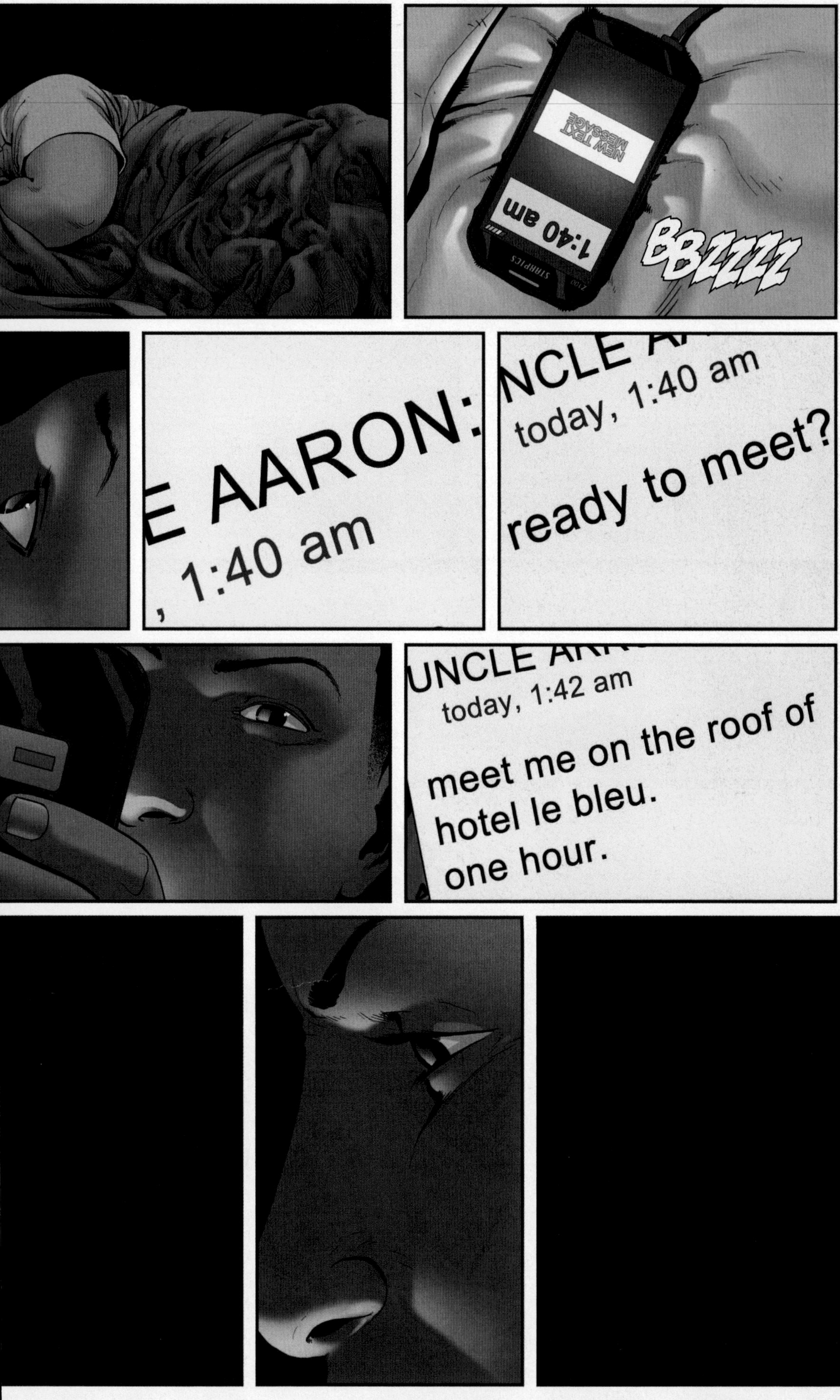
NEW TEXT MESSAGE
1:40 am
BBZZZZ
E AARON:
, 1:40 am
NCLE
today, 1:40 am
ready to meet?
UNCLE
today, 1:42 am
meet me on the roof of
hotel le bleu.
one hour.

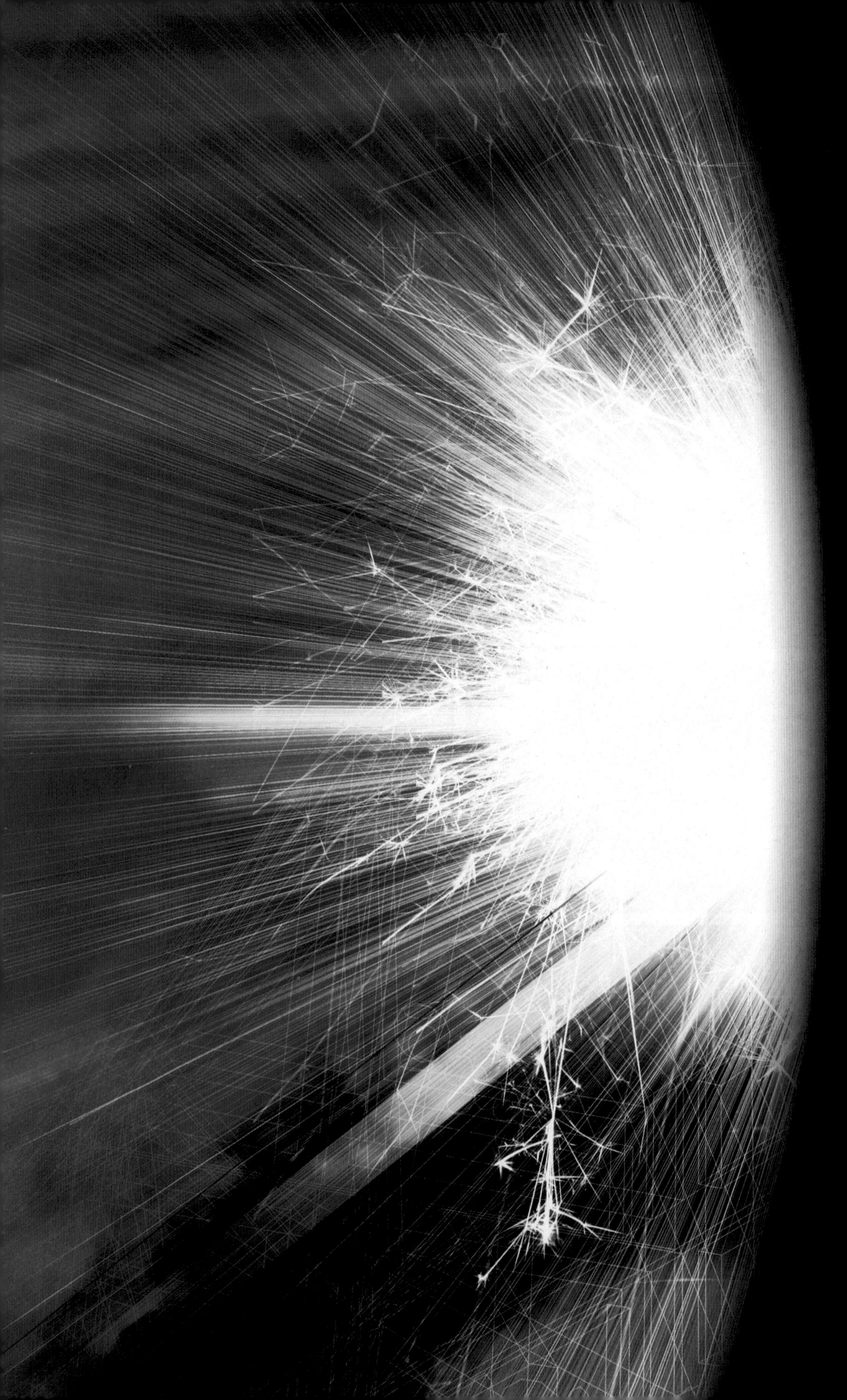

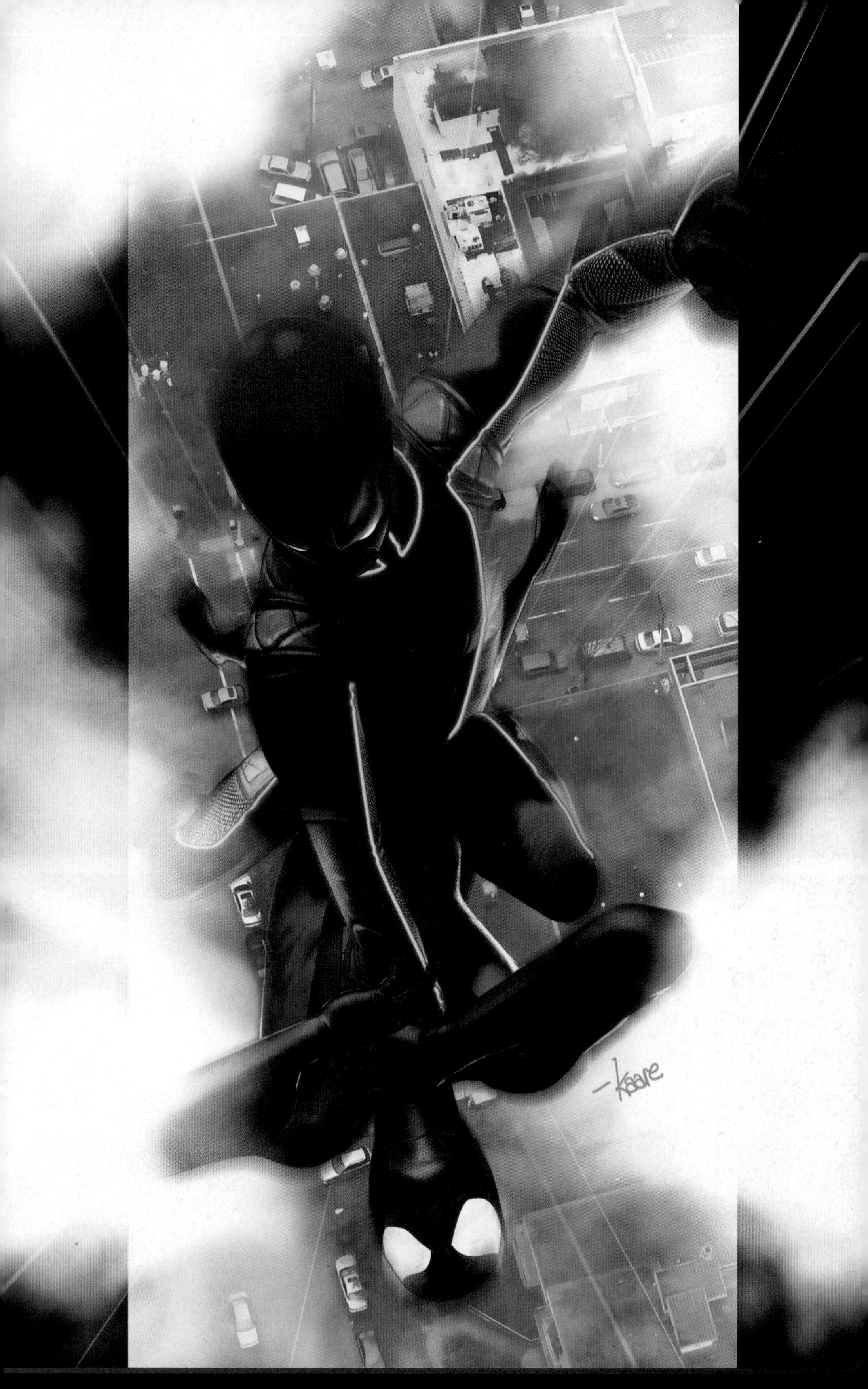
-kaare

ULTIMATE COMICS SPIDER MAN #10

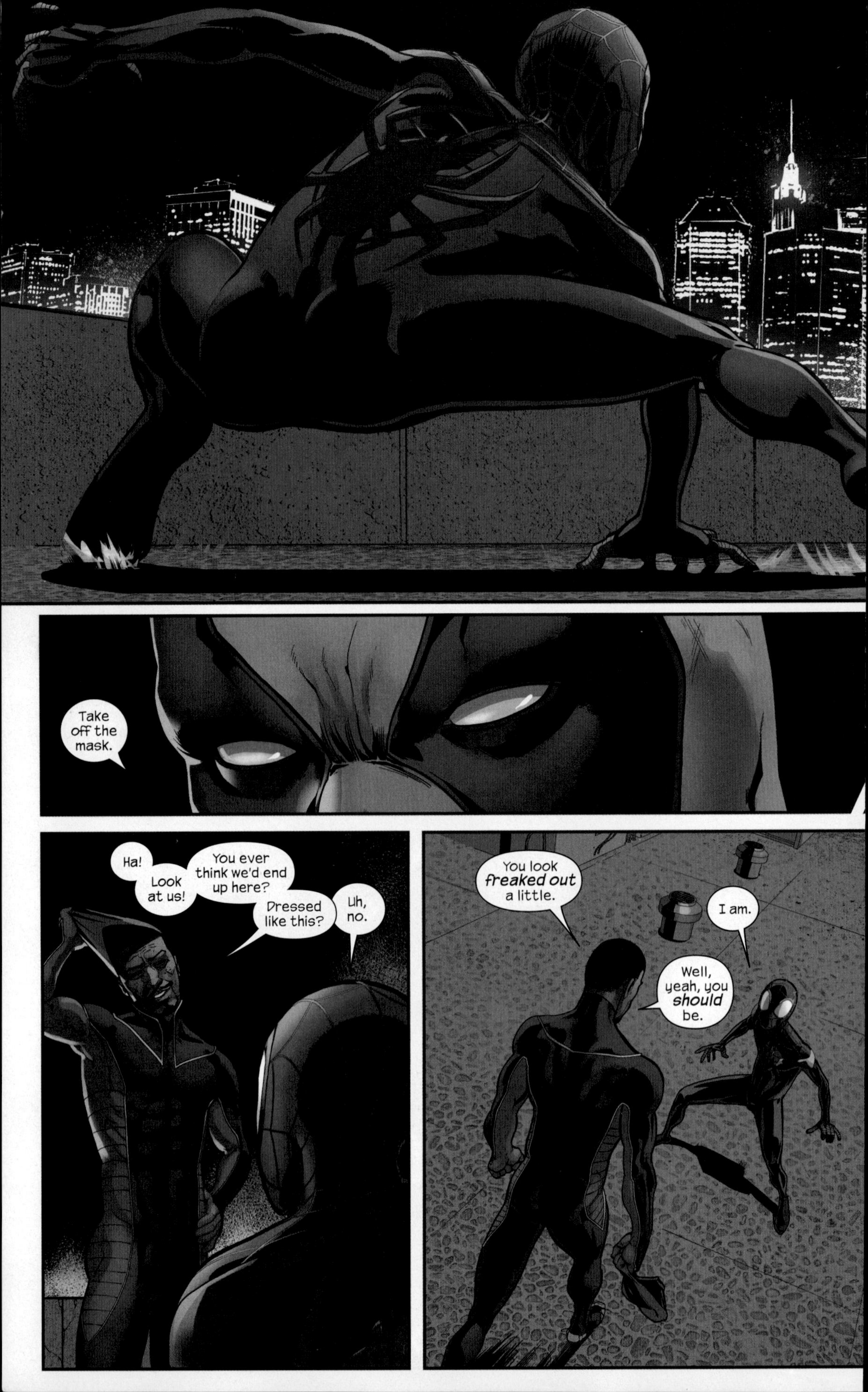
Take off the mask.
Ha!
Look at us!
You ever think we'd end up here?
Dressed like this?
Uh, no.
You look *freaked out* a little.
I am.
Well, yeah, you *should* be.

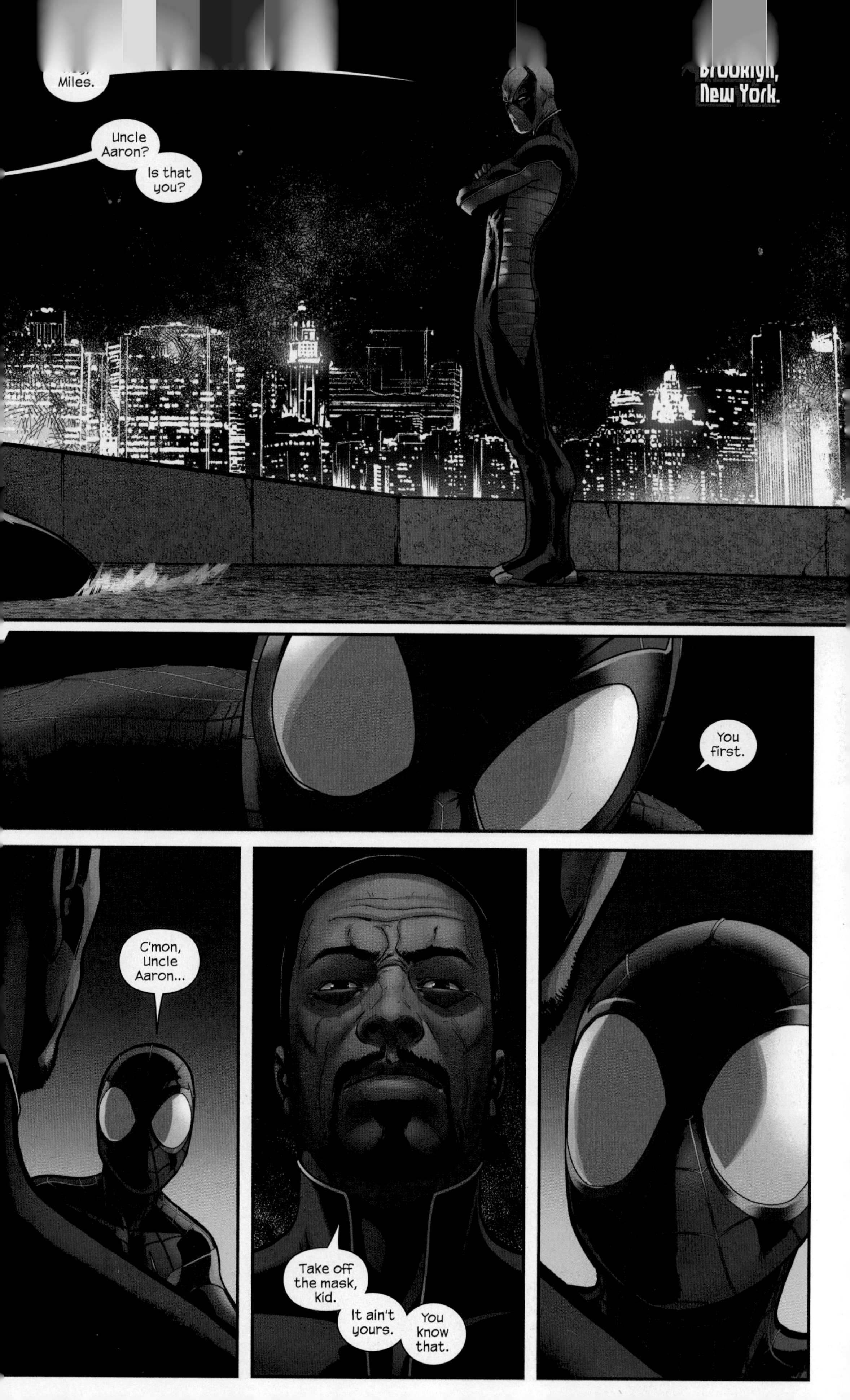

Miles.
New York.
Uncle Aaron?
Is that you?
You first.
C'mon, Uncle Aaron...
Take off the mask, kid.
It ain't yours.
You know that.

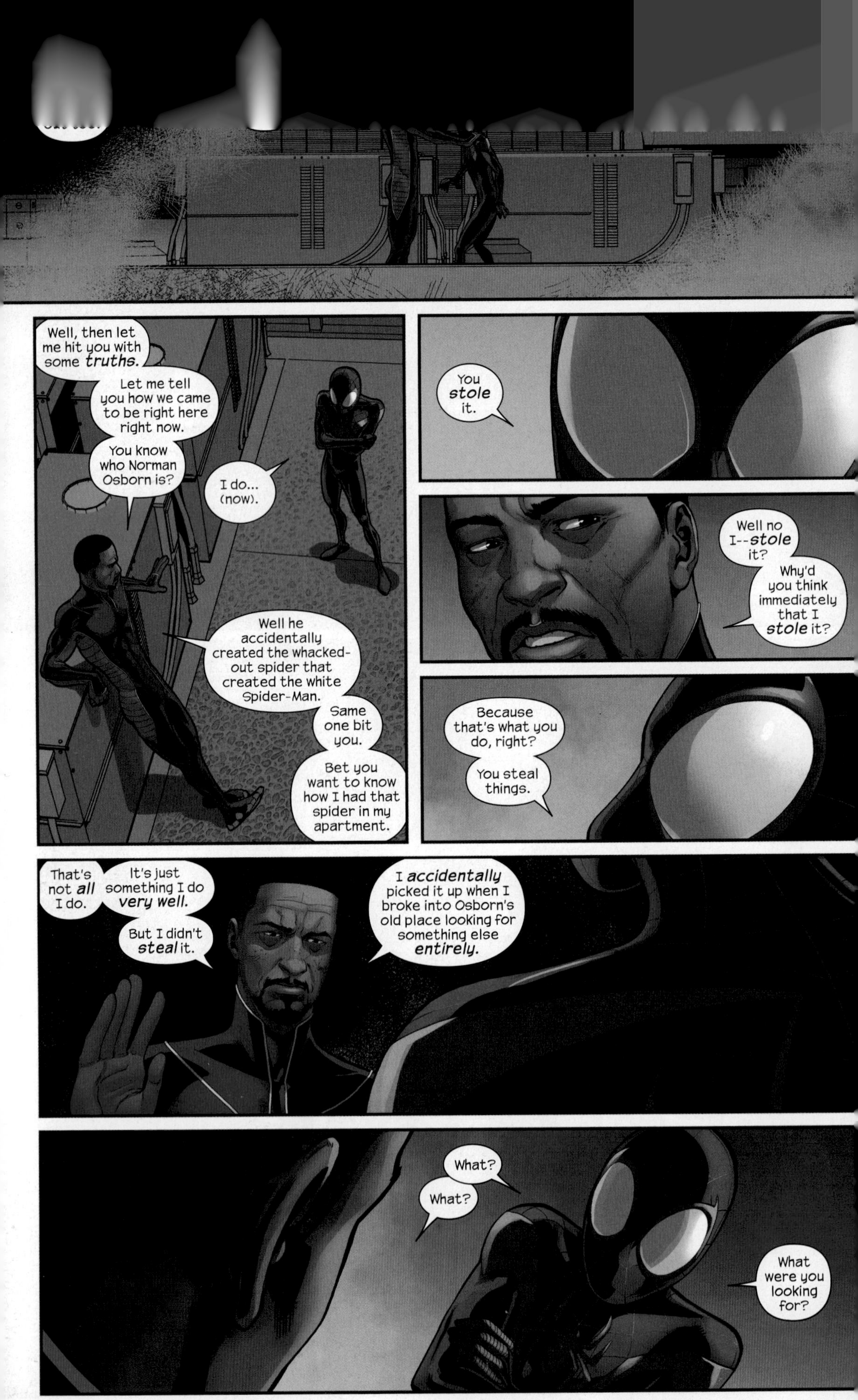

Well, then let me hit you with some *truths.*
Let me tell you how we came to be right here right now.
You know who Norman Osborn is?
I do... (now).
Well he accidentally created the whacked-out spider that created the white Spider-Man.
Same one bit you.
Bet you want to know how I had that spider in my apartment.
You *stole* it.
Well no I--*stole* it?
Why'd you think immediately that I *stole* it?
Because that's what you do, right?
You steal things.
That's not *all* I do.
It's just something I do *very well.*
But I didn't *steal* it.
I *accidentally* picked it up when I broke into Osborn's old place looking for something else *entirely.*
What?
What?
What were you looking for?

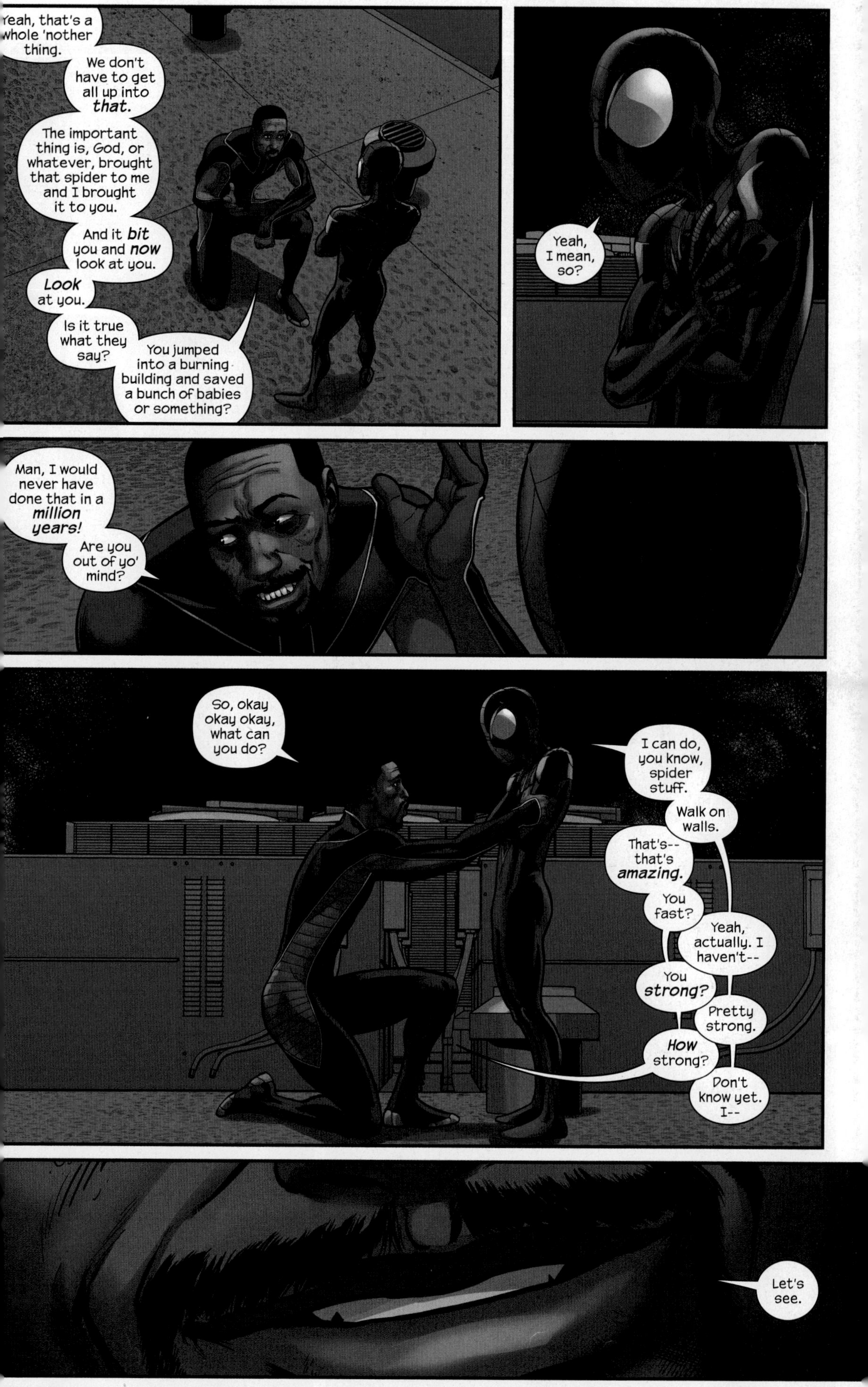

Yeah, that's a whole 'nother thing.
We don't have to get all up into *that.*
The important thing is, God, or whatever, brought that spider to me and I brought it to you.
And it *bit* you and *now* look at you.
Look at you.
Is it true what they say?
You jumped into a burning building and saved a bunch of babies or something?
Yeah, I mean, so?
Man, I would never have done that in a *million years!*
Are you out of yo' mind?
So, okay okay okay, what can you do?
I can do, you know, spider stuff.
Walk on walls.
That's-- that's *amazing.*
You fast?
Yeah, actually. I haven't--
You *strong?*
Pretty strong.
How strong?
Don't know yet. I--
Let's see.

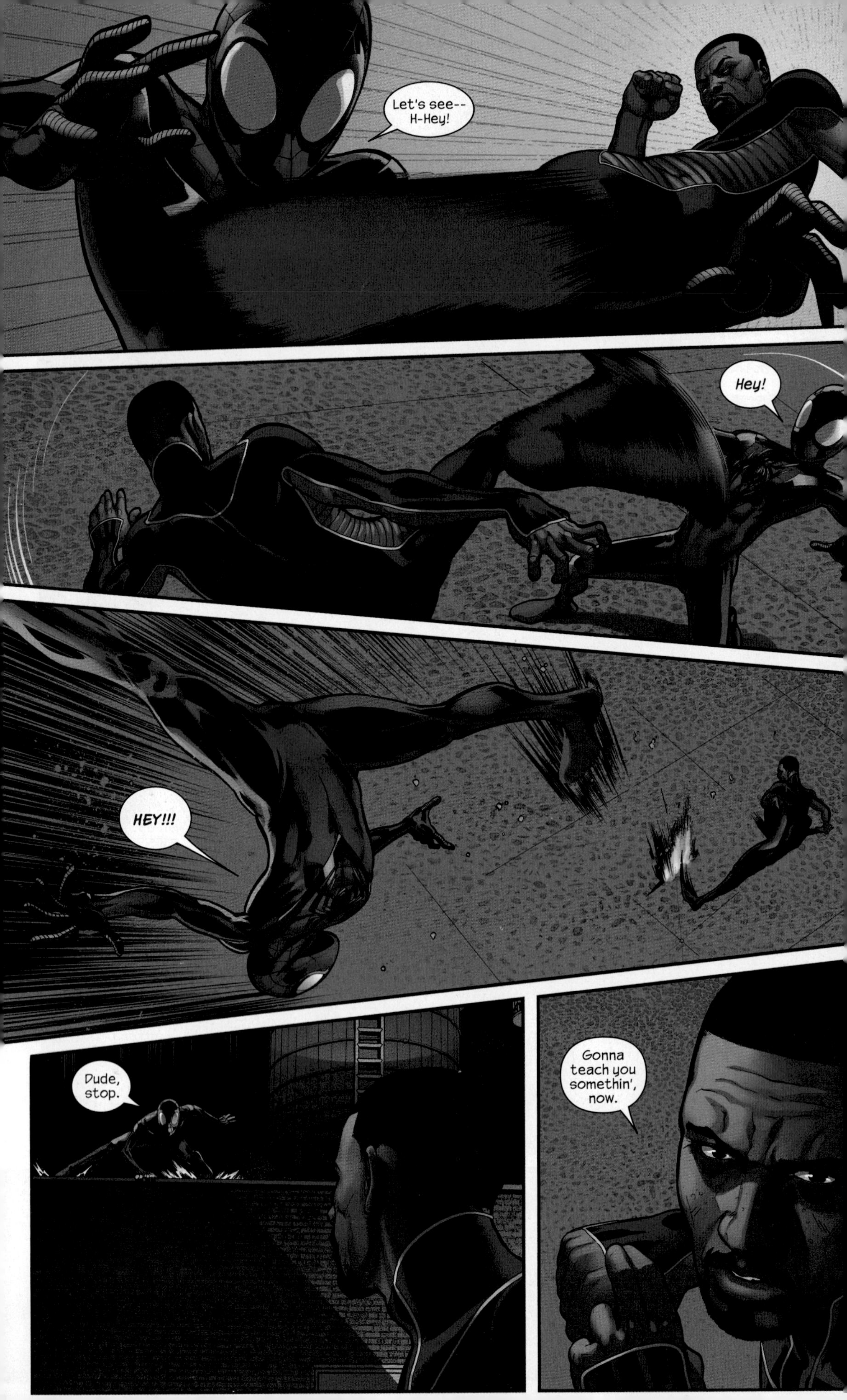
Let's see--
H-Hey!
Hey!
HEY!!!
Dude,
stop.
Gonna
teach you
somethin',
now.

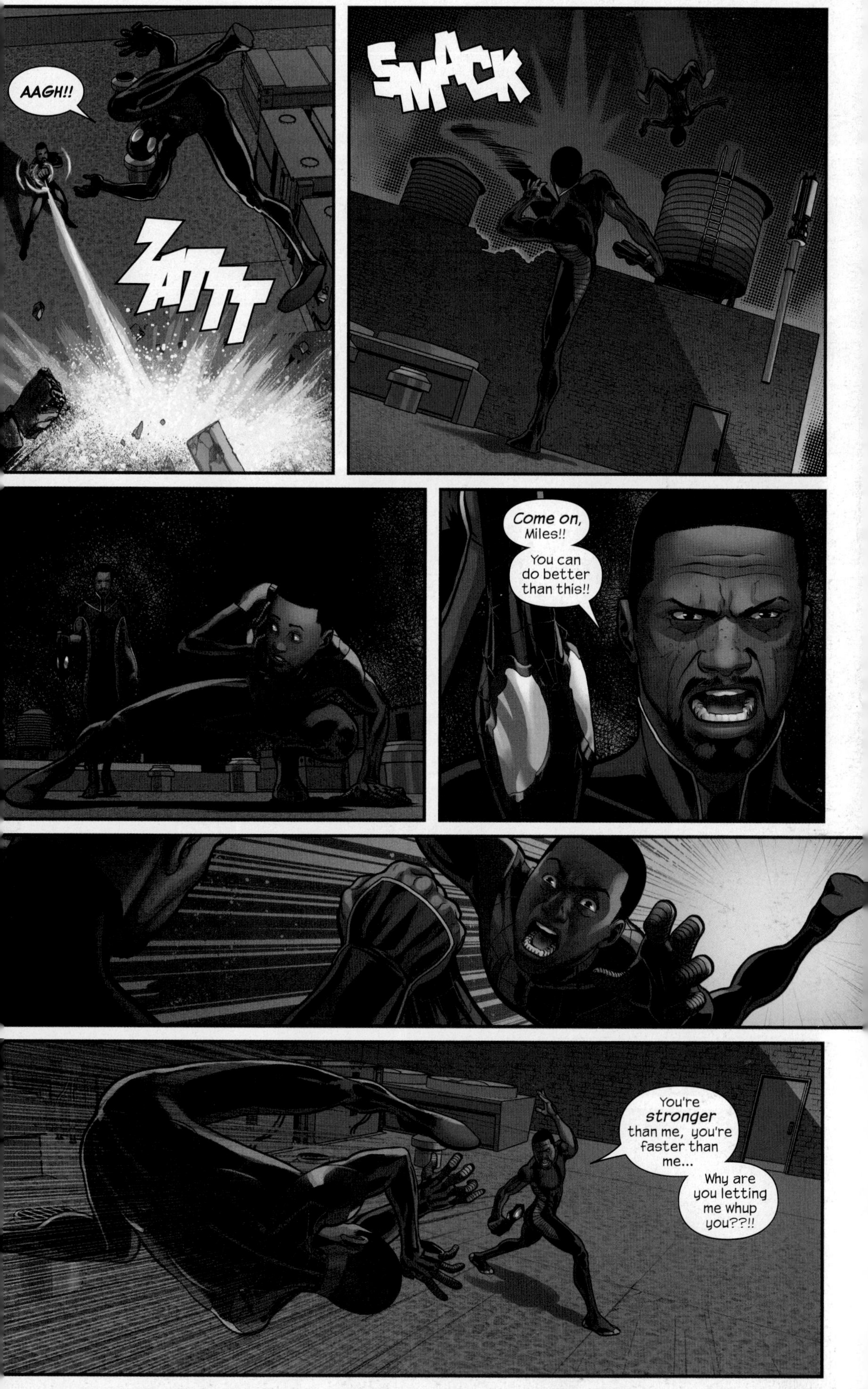
AAGH!!
ZATTT
SMACK
Come on, Miles!!
You can do better than this!!
You're *stronger* than me, you're faster than me...
Why are you letting me whup you??!!

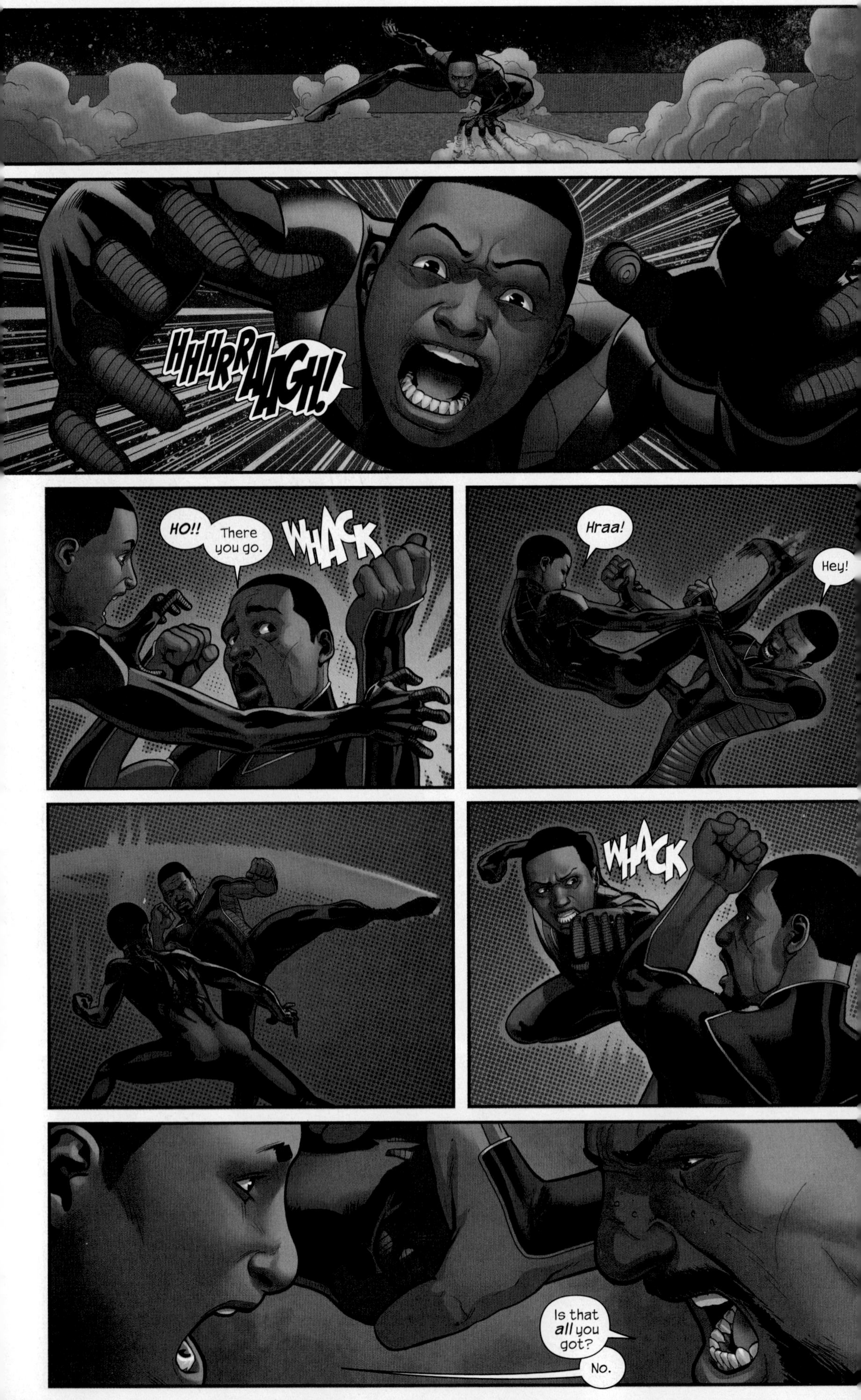
HHHRRAAGH!
HO!!
There you go.
WHACK
Hraa!
Hey!
WHACK
Is that all you got?
No.

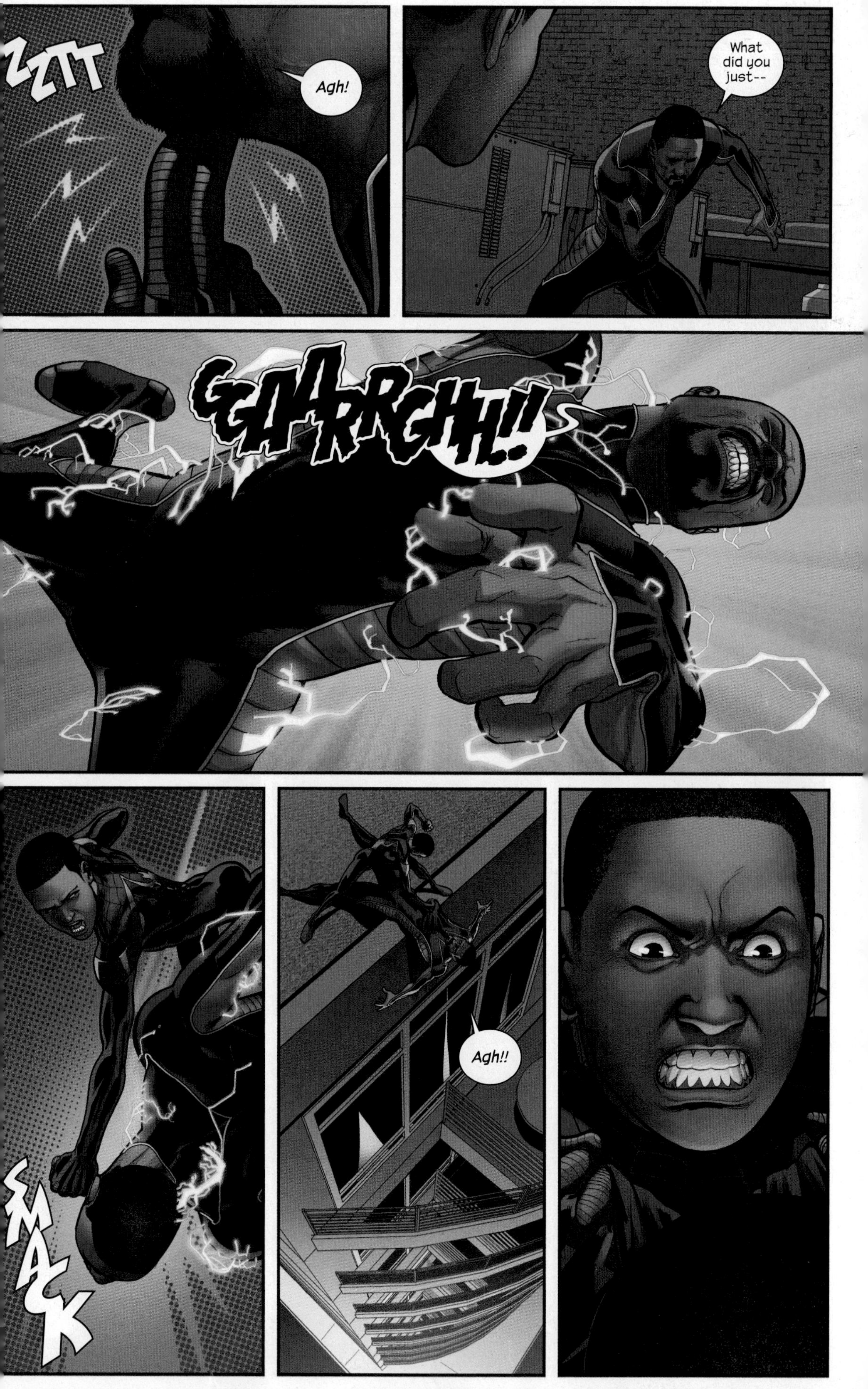
ZZTT
Agh!
What did you just--
GGAARGHH!!
SMACK
Agh!!

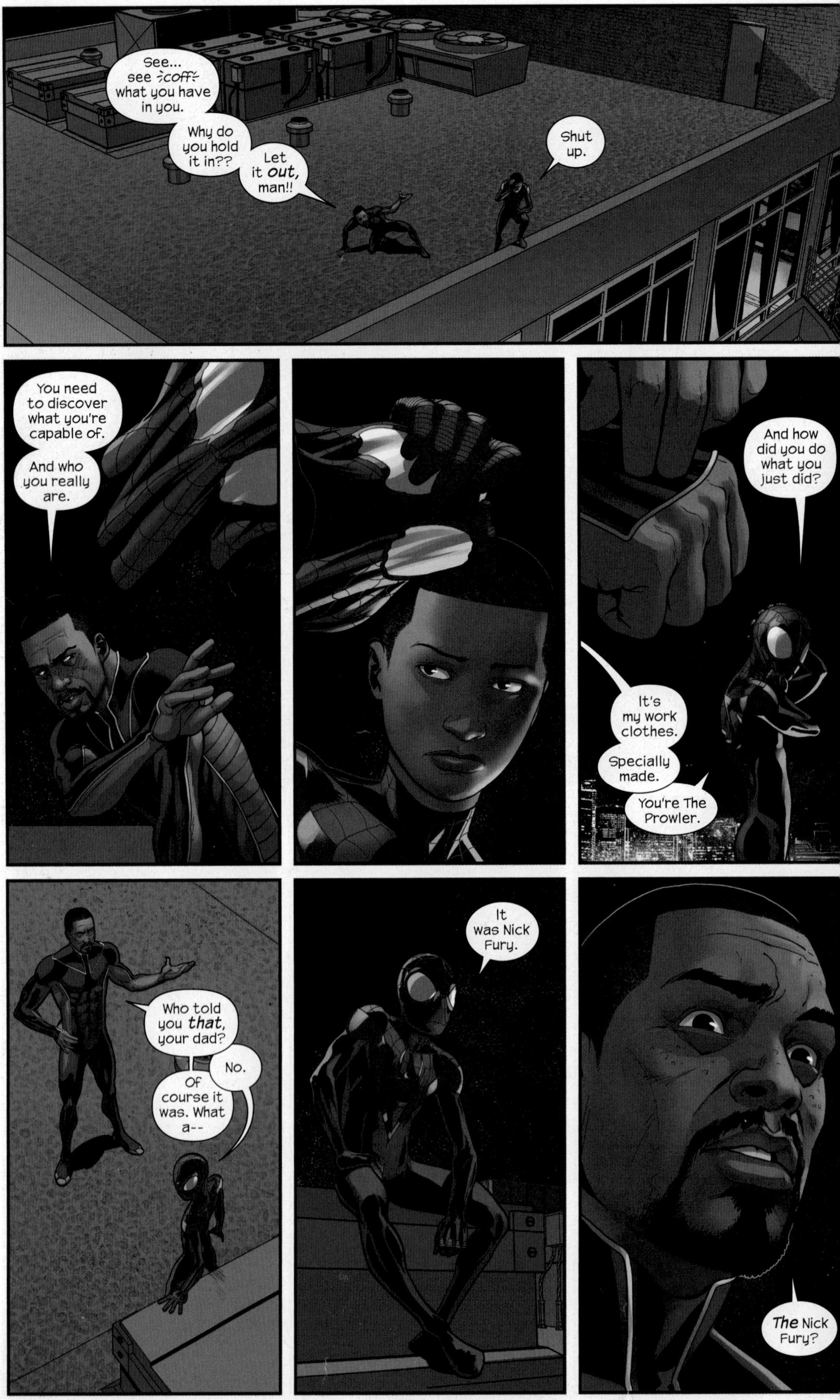
See... see ⸗coff⸗ what you have in you.
Why do you hold it in??
Let it *out,* man!!
Shut up.
You need to discover what you're capable of.
And who you really are.
And how did you do what you just did?
It's my work clothes.
Specially made.
You're The Prowler.
Who told you *that,* your dad?
No.
Of course it was. What a--
It was Nick Fury.
The Nick Fury?

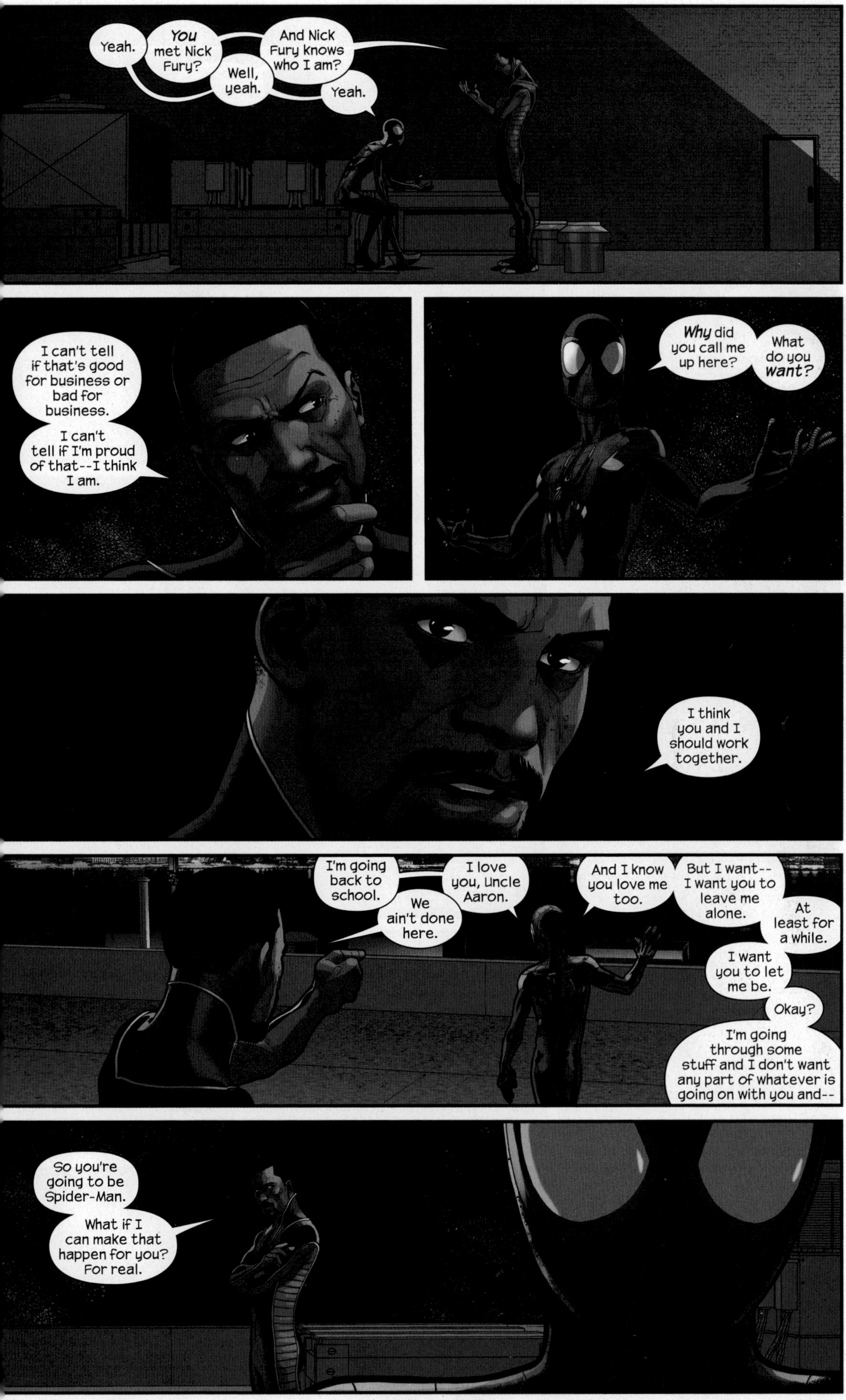
Yeah.
You met Nick Fury?
And Nick Fury knows who I am?
Well, yeah.
Yeah.
I can't tell if that's good for business or bad for business.
I can't tell if I'm proud of that--I think I am.
Why did you call me up here?
What do you want?
I think you and I should work together.
I'm going back to school.
I love you, Uncle Aaron.
We ain't done here.
And I know you love me too.
But I want--I want you to leave me alone.
At least for a while.
I want you to let me be.
Okay?
I'm going through some stuff and I don't want any part of whatever is going on with you and--
So you're going to be Spider-Man.
What if I can make that happen for you? For real.

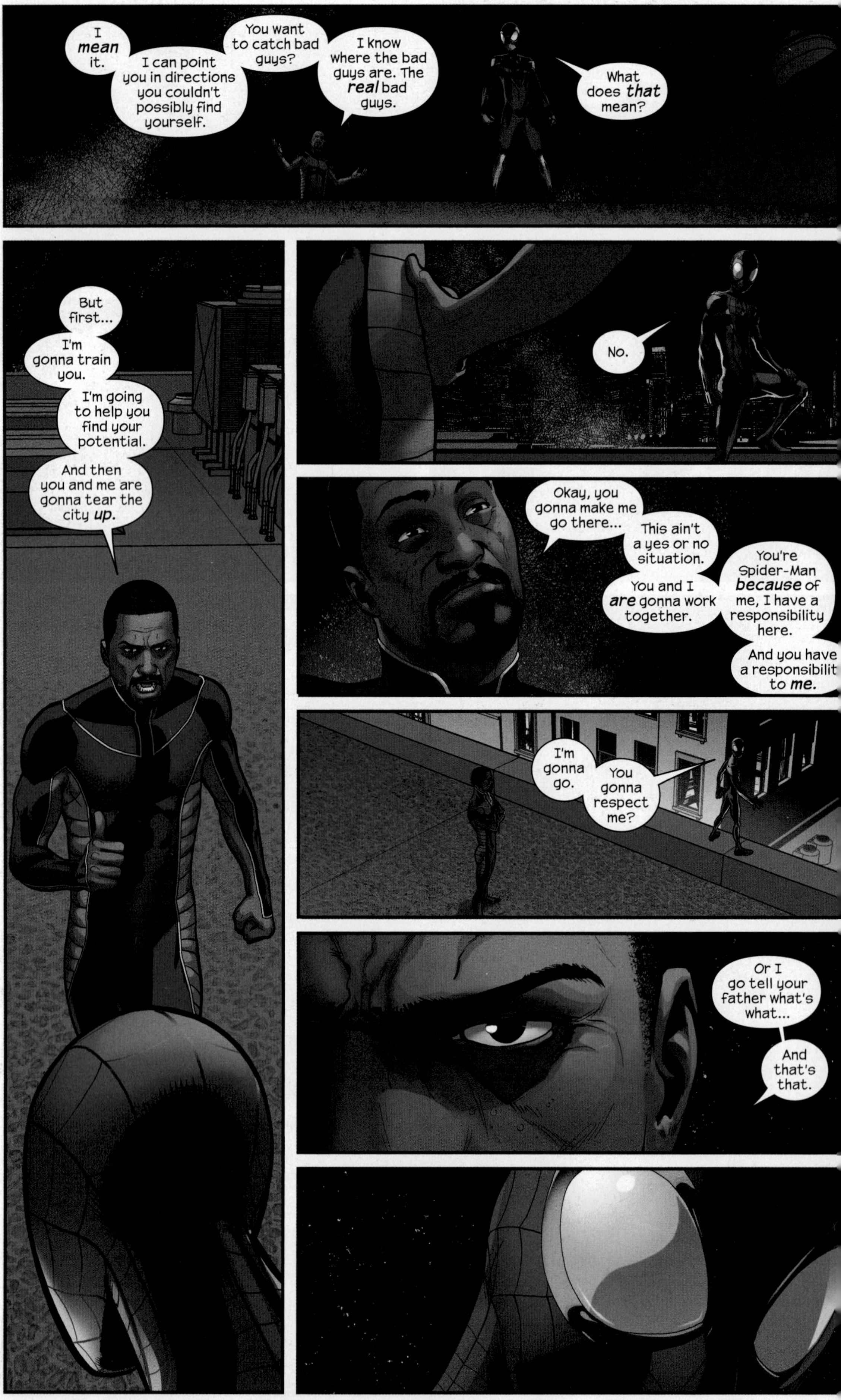

I *mean* it.
I can point you in directions you couldn't possibly find yourself.
You want to catch bad guys?
I know where the bad guys are. The *real* bad guys.
What does *that* mean?
But first...
I'm gonna train you.
I'm going to help you find your potential.
And then you and me are gonna tear the city *up*.
No.
Okay, you gonna make me go there...
This ain't a yes or no situation.
You and I *are* gonna work together.
You're Spider-Man *because* of me, I have a responsibility here.
And you have a responsibilit to *me*.
I'm gonna go.
You gonna respect me?
Or I go tell your father what's what...
And that's that.

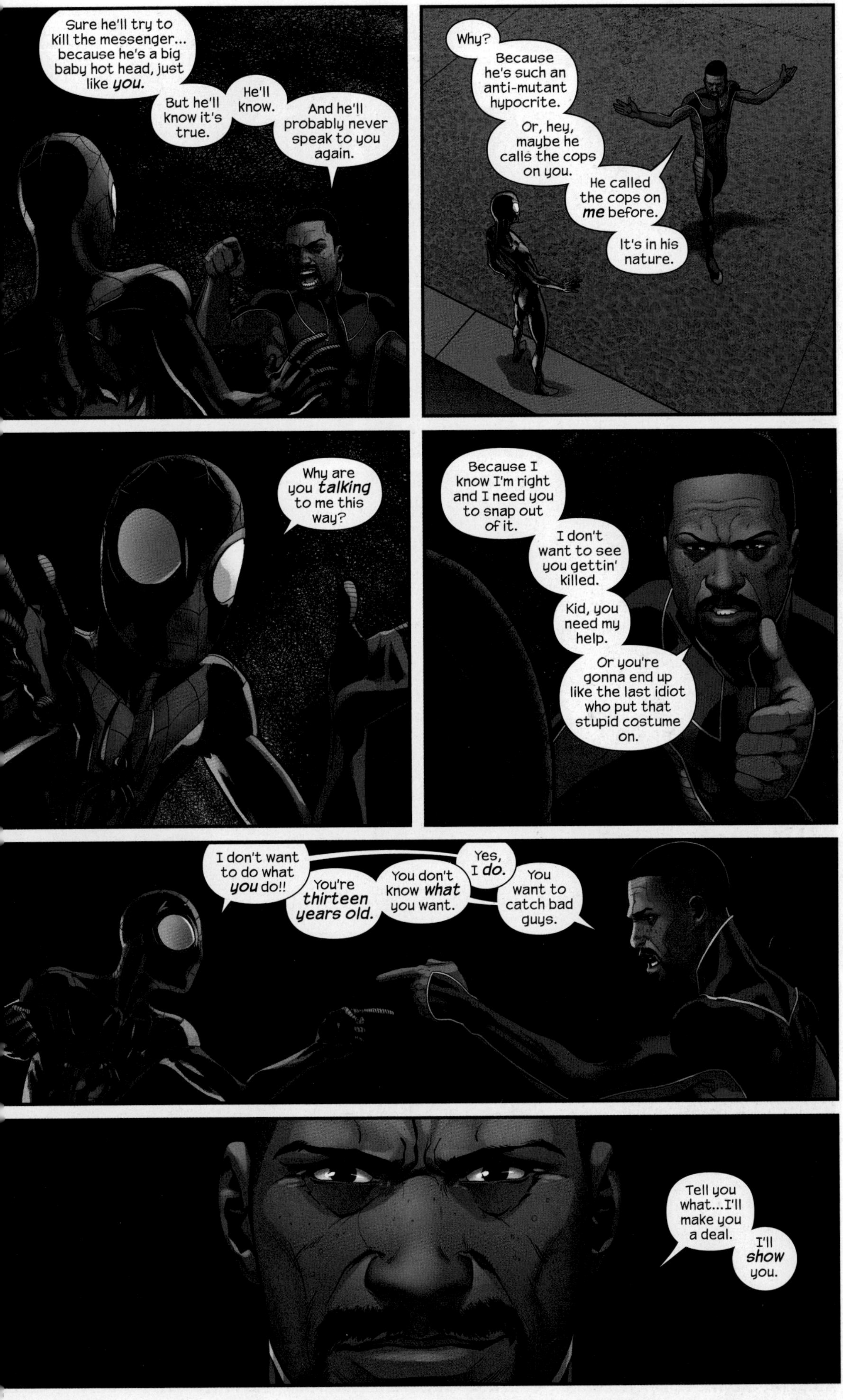
Sure he'll try to kill the messenger... because he's a big baby hot head, just like *you.*
But he'll know it's true.
He'll know.
And he'll probably never speak to you again.
Why?
Because he's such an anti-mutant hypocrite.
Or, hey, maybe he calls the cops on you.
He called the cops on *me* before.
It's in his nature.
Why are you *talking* to me this way?
Because I know I'm right and I need you to snap out of it.
I don't want to see you gettin' killed.
Kid, you need my help.
Or you're gonna end up like the last idiot who put that stupid costume on.
I don't want to do what *you* do!!
You're *thirteen years old.*
You don't know *what* you want.
Yes, I *do.*
You want to catch bad guys.
Tell you what...I'll make you a deal.
I'll *show* you.

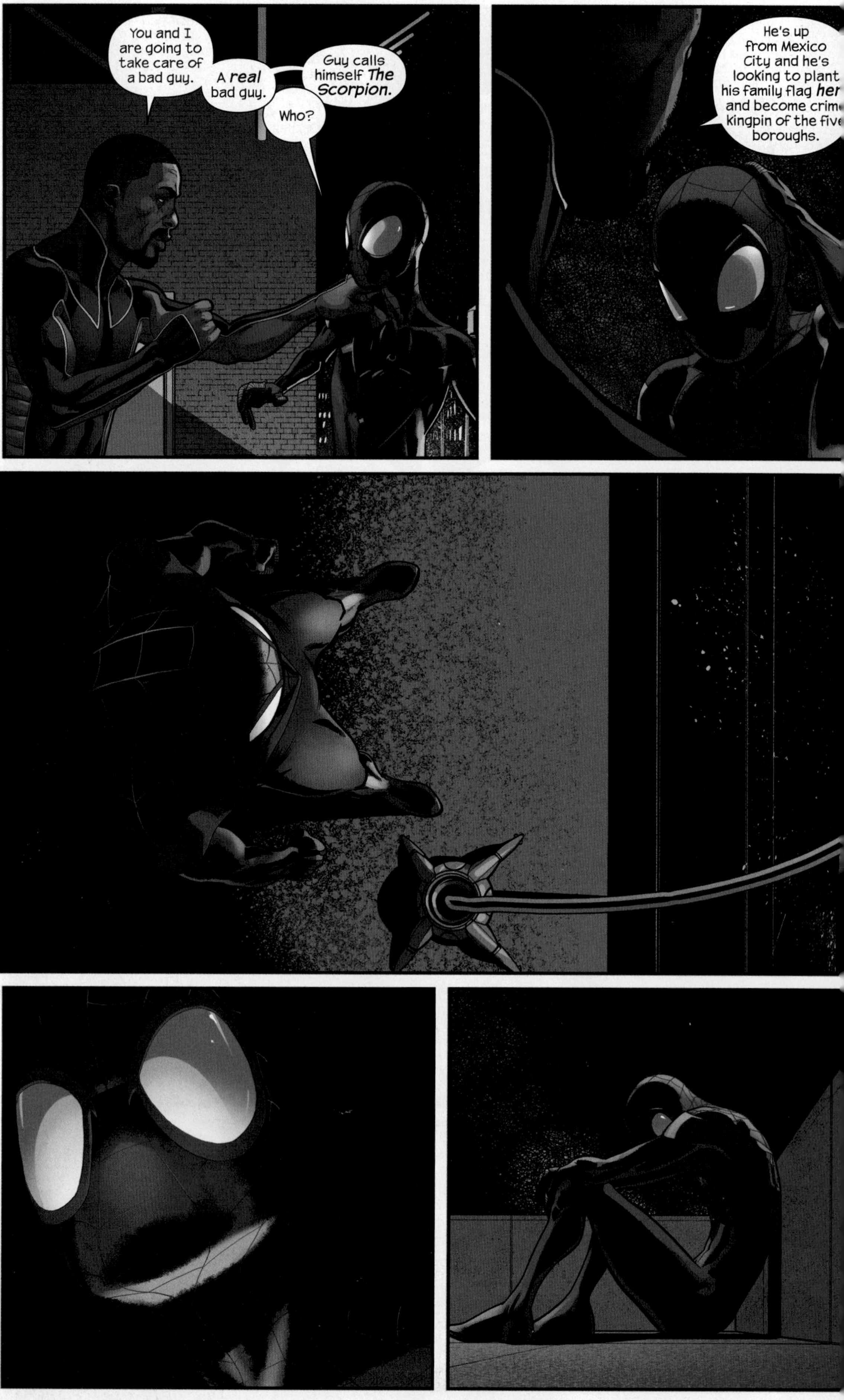
You and I are going to take care of a bad guy.
A *real* bad guy.
Guy calls himself *The Scorpion.*
Who?
He's up from Mexico City and he's looking to plant his family flag *her*
and become crim
kingpin of the fiv
boroughs.

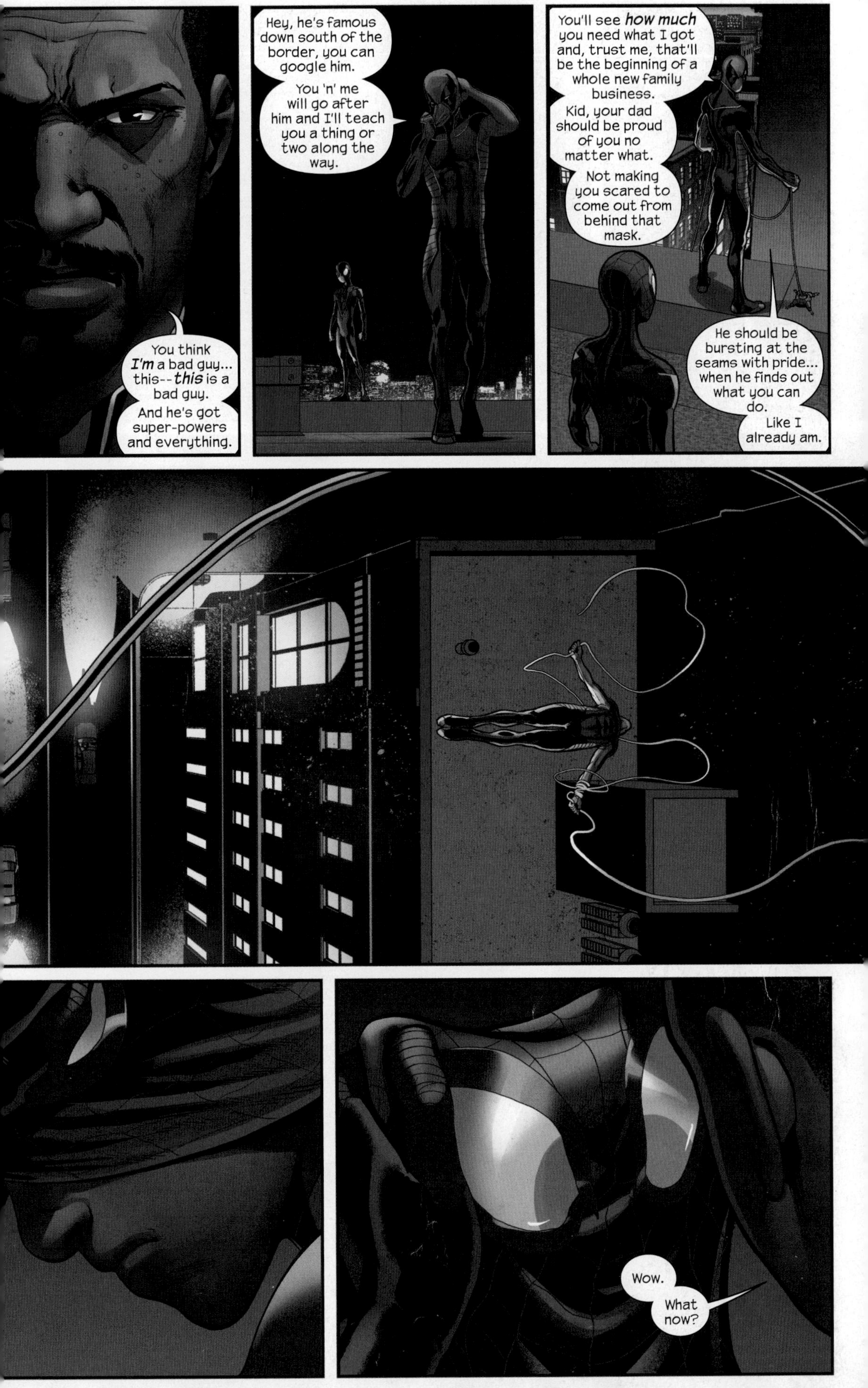

You think I'm a bad guy... this--this is a bad guy.
And he's got super-powers and everything.
Hey, he's famous down south of the border, you can google him.
You 'n' me will go after him and I'll teach you a thing or two along the way.
You'll see how much you need what I got and, trust me, that'll be the beginning of a whole new family business.
Kid, your dad should be proud of you no matter what.
Not making you scared to come out from behind that mask.
He should be bursting at the seams with pride... when he finds out what you can do.
Like I already am.
Wow.
What now?

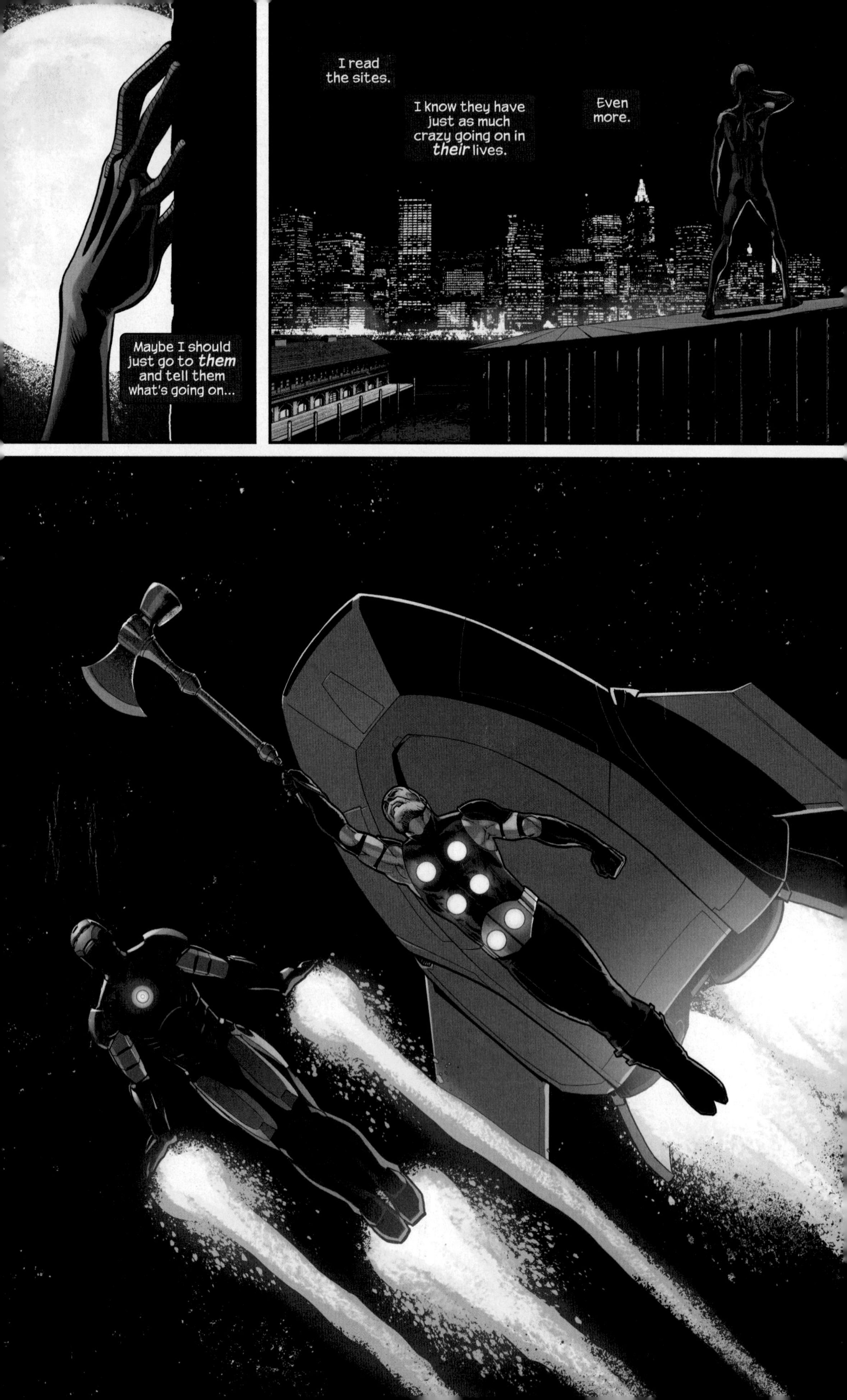
Maybe I should just go to *them* and tell them what's going on...
I read the sites.
I know they have just as much crazy going on in *their* lives.
Even more.

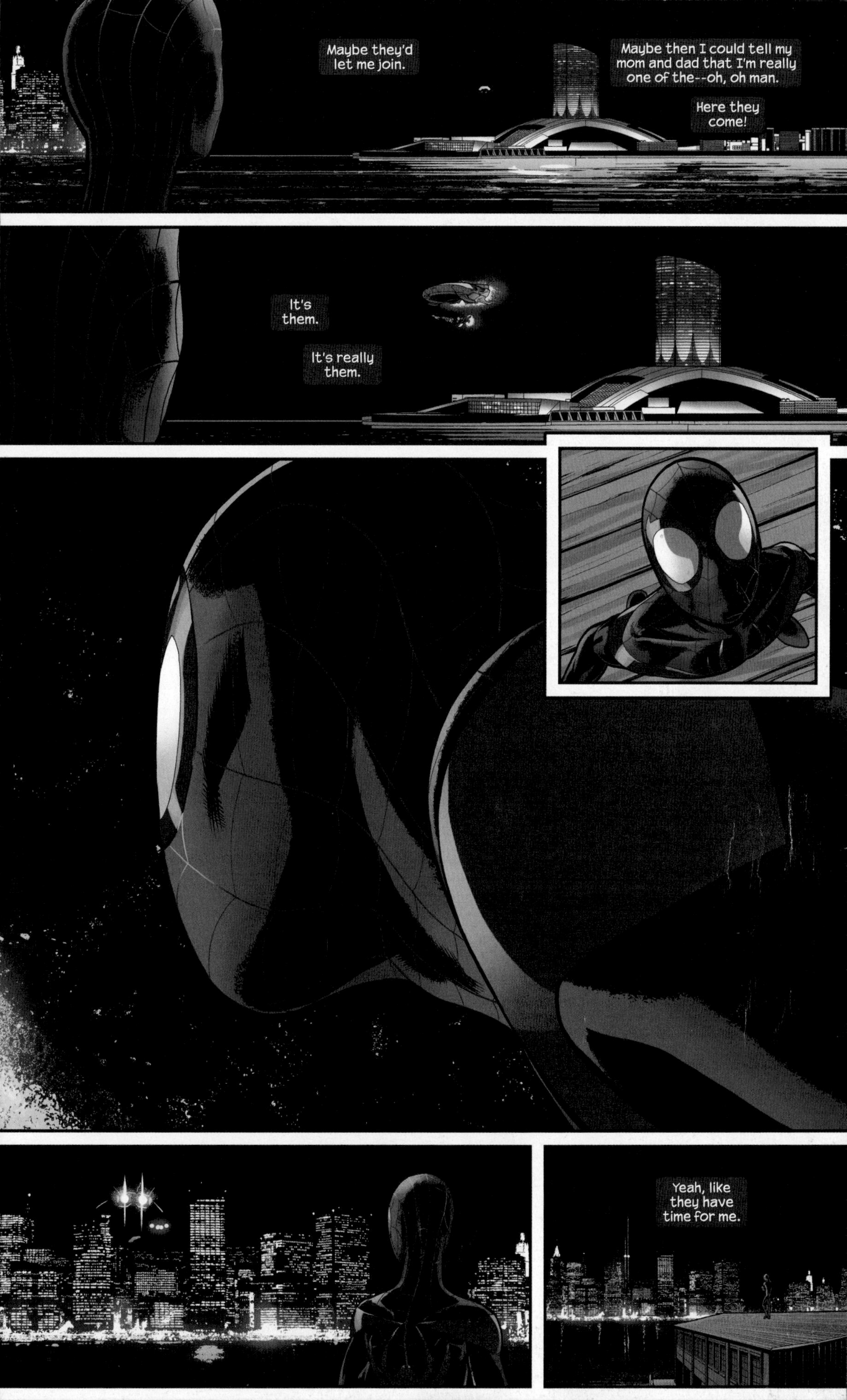

Maybe they'd let me join.
Maybe then I could tell my mom and dad that I'm really one of the--oh, oh man.
Here they come!
It's them.
It's really them.
Yeah, like they have time for me.

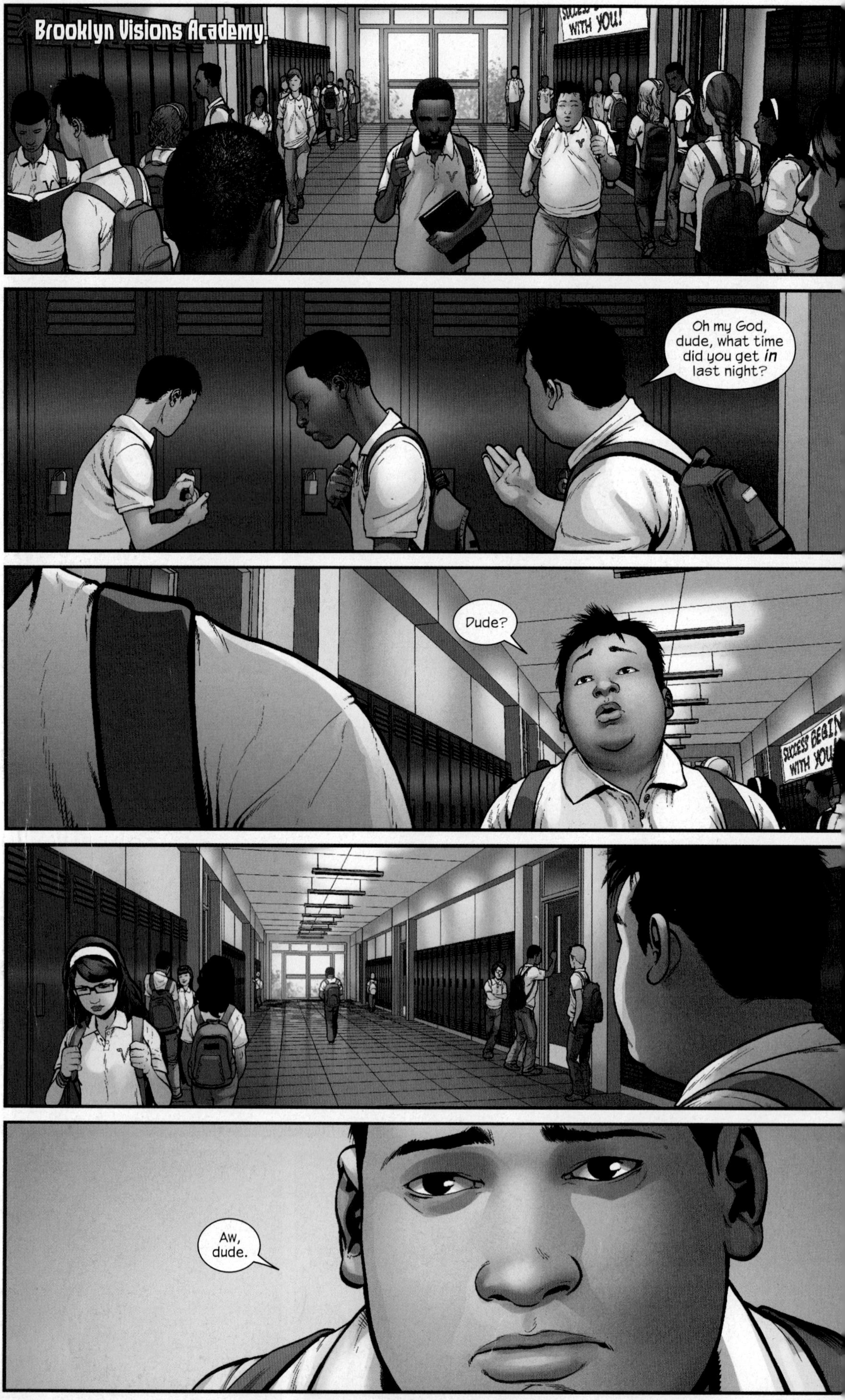
Brooklyn Visions Academy.
SUCCESS BEGINS WITH YOU!
Oh my God, dude, what time did you get *in* last night?
Dude?
SUCCESS BEGINS WITH YOU!
Aw, dude.

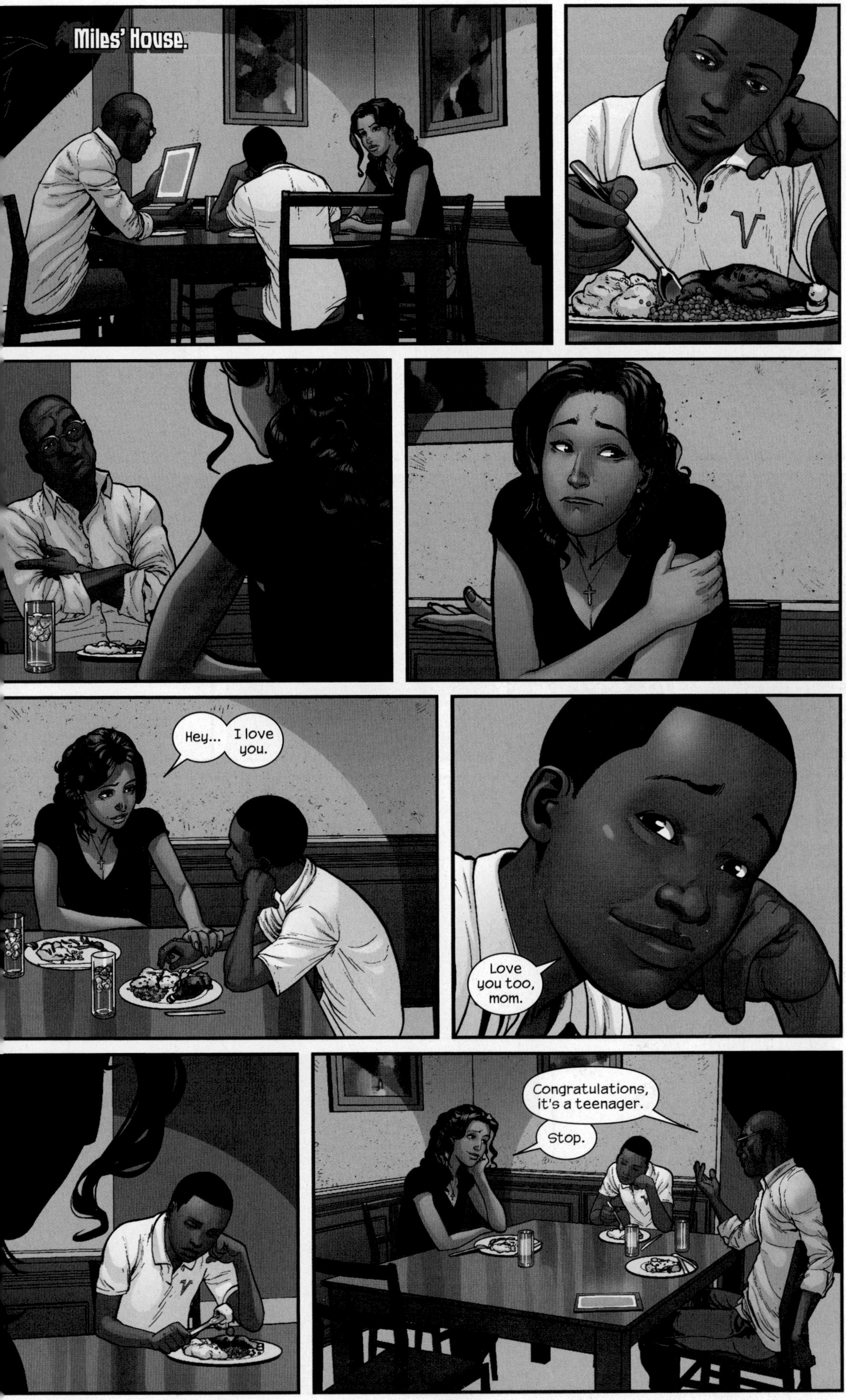
Miles' House.
Hey...
I love you.
Love you too, mom.
Congratulations, it's a teenager.
Stop.

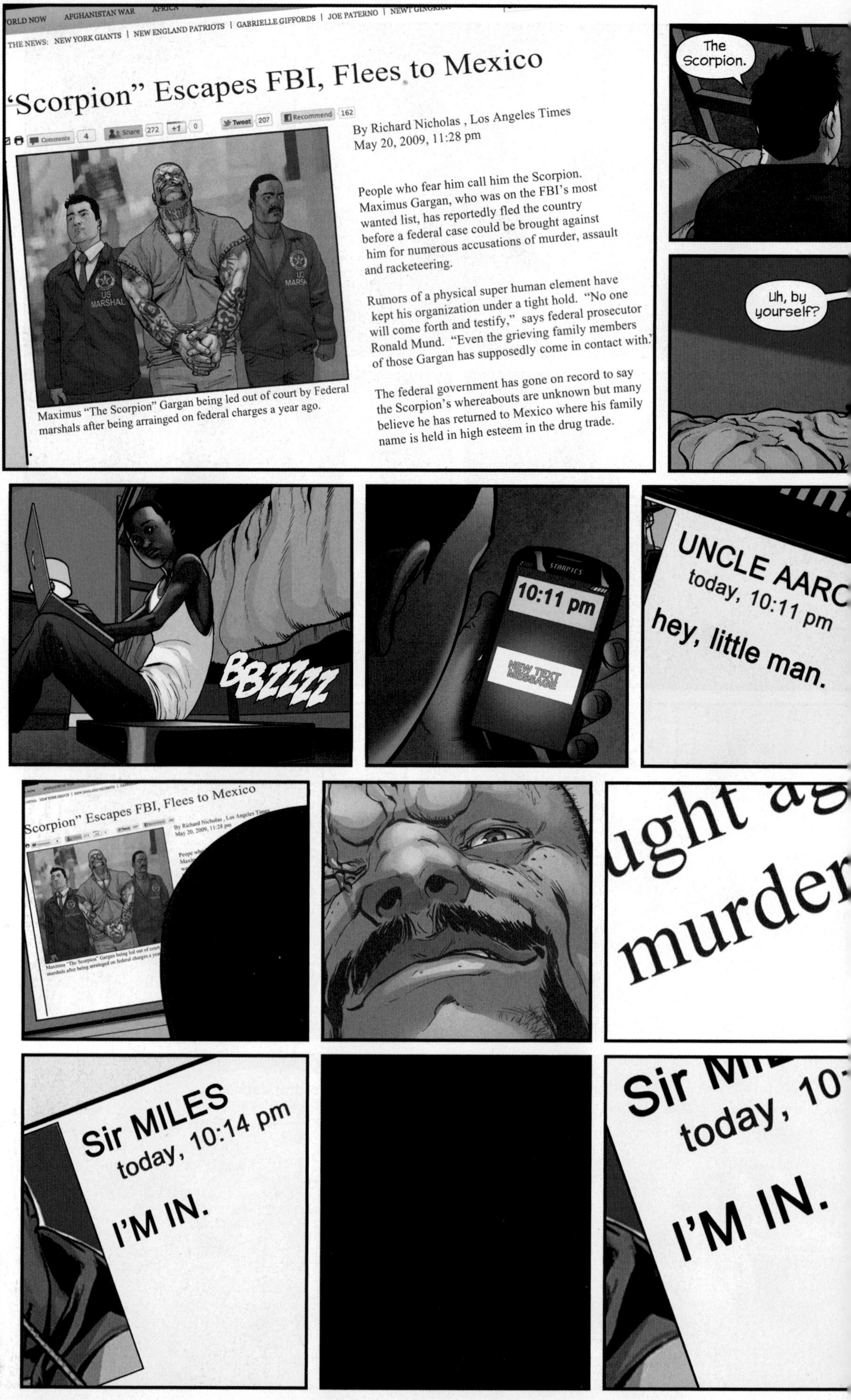

ORLD NOW AFGHANISTAN WAR AFRICA
THE NEWS: NEW YORK GIANTS | NEW ENGLAND PATRIOTS | GABRIELLE GIFFORDS | JOE PATERNO | NEWT GINGRICH
'Scorpion" Escapes FBI, Flees to Mexico
Comments 4 Share 272 +1 0 Tweet 207 Recommend 162
By Richard Nicholas , Los Angeles Times
May 20, 2009, 11:28 pm
People who fear him call him the Scorpion. Maximus Gargan, who was on the FBI's most wanted list, has reportedly fled the country before a federal case could be brought against him for numerous accusations of murder, assault and racketeering.
Rumors of a physical super human element have kept his organization under a tight hold. "No one will come forth and testify," says federal prosecutor Ronald Mund. "Even the grieving family members of those Gargan has supposedly come in contact with."
The federal government has gone on record to say the Scorpion's whereabouts are unknown but many believe he has returned to Mexico where his family name is held in high esteem in the drug trade.
US MARSHAL
Maximus "The Scorpion" Gargan being led out of court by Federal marshals after being arraigned on federal charges a year ago.
The Scorpion.
Uh, by yourself?
BBZZZZZ
STARPICS
10:11 pm
NEW TEXT MESSAGE
UNCLE AARC
today, 10:11 pm
hey, little man.
Scorpion" Escapes FBI, Flees to Mexico
ught ag
murder
Sir MILES
today, 10:14 pm
I'M IN.
Sir MI
today, 10
I'M IN.

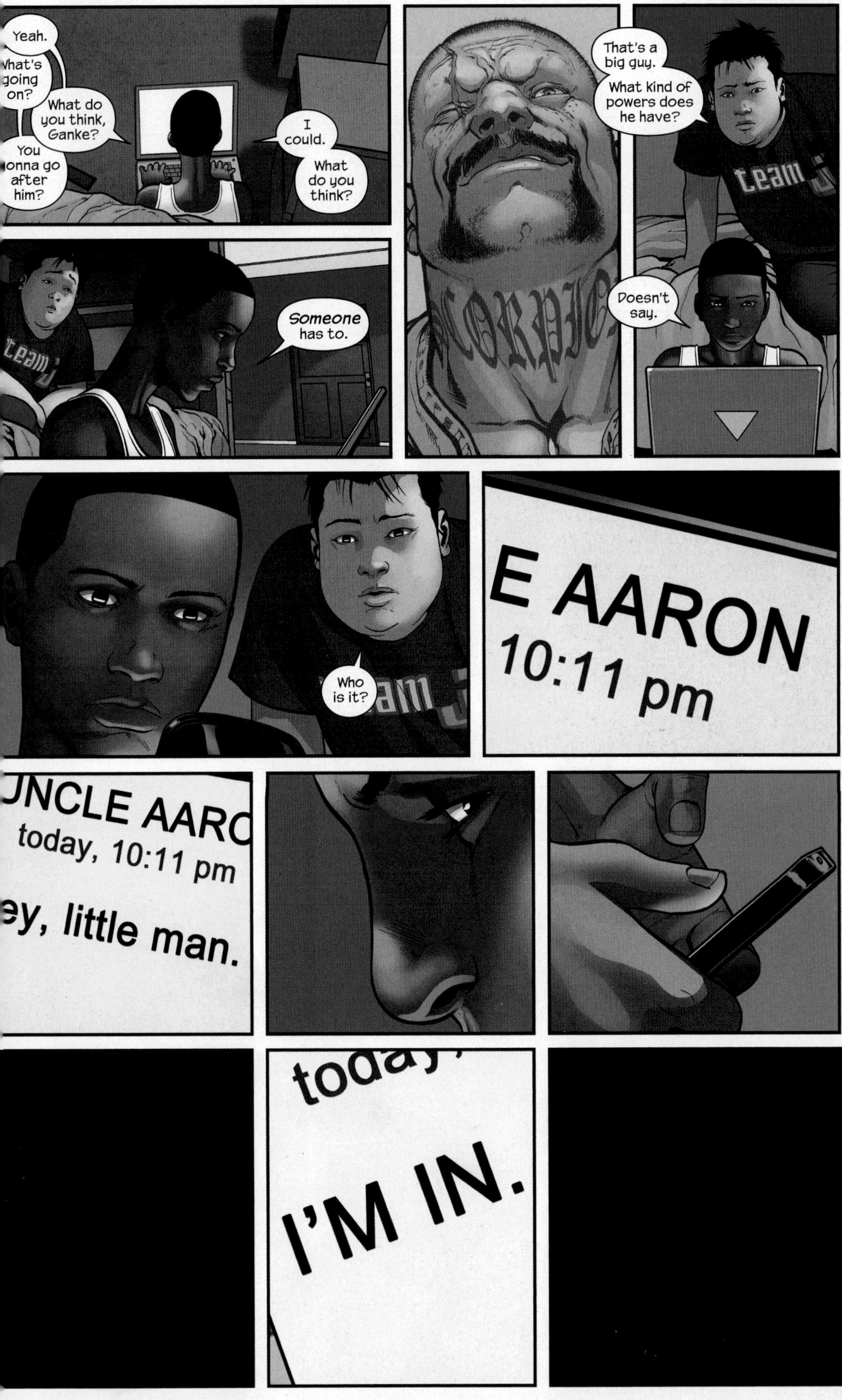

Yeah.
What's going on?
What do you think, Ganke?
You gonna go after him?
I could.
What do you think?
That's a big guy.
What kind of powers does he have?
Someone has to.
Doesn't say.
Who is it?
E AARON
10:11 pm
UNCLE AARO
today, 10:11 pm
ey, little man.
today,
I'M IN.

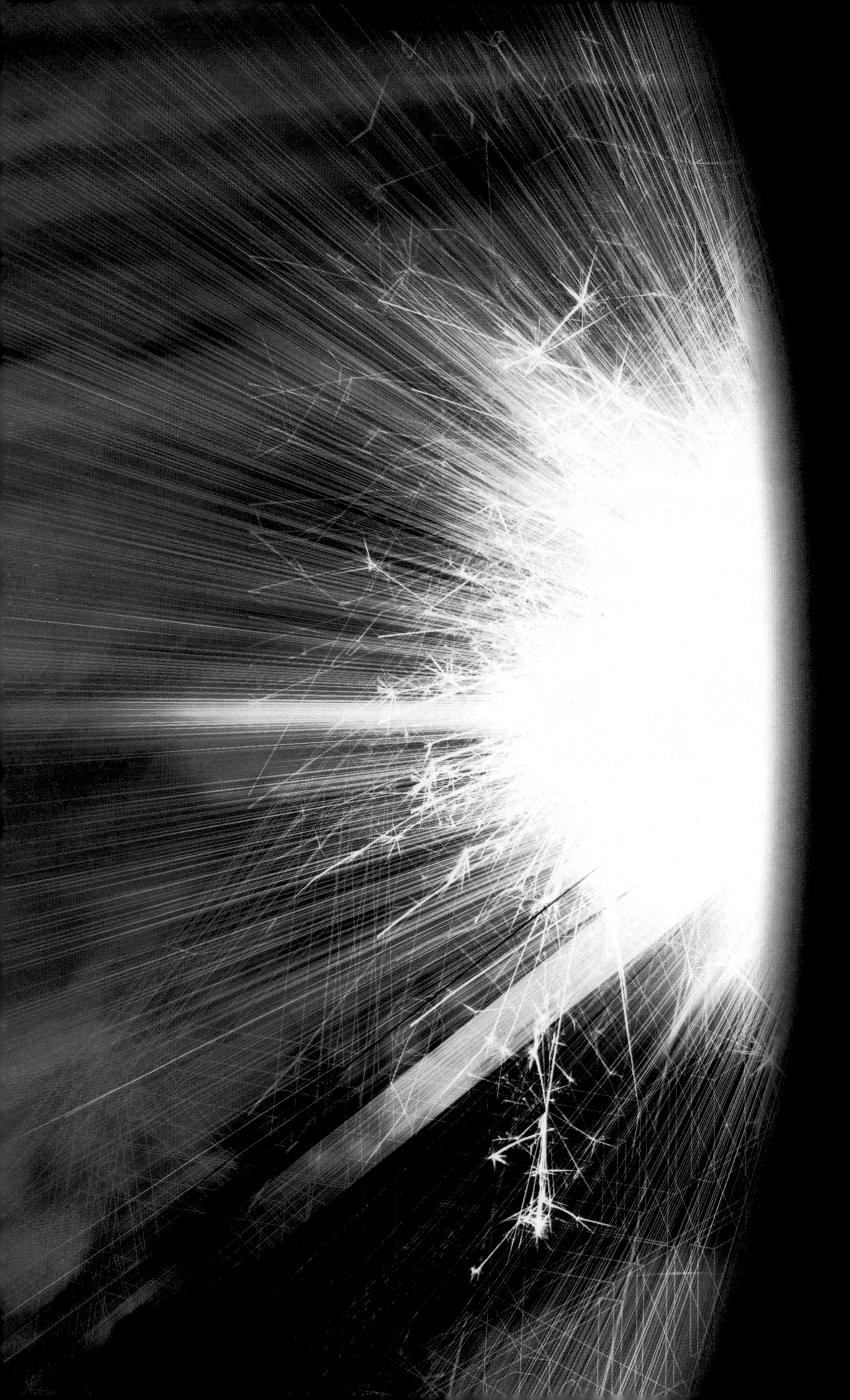

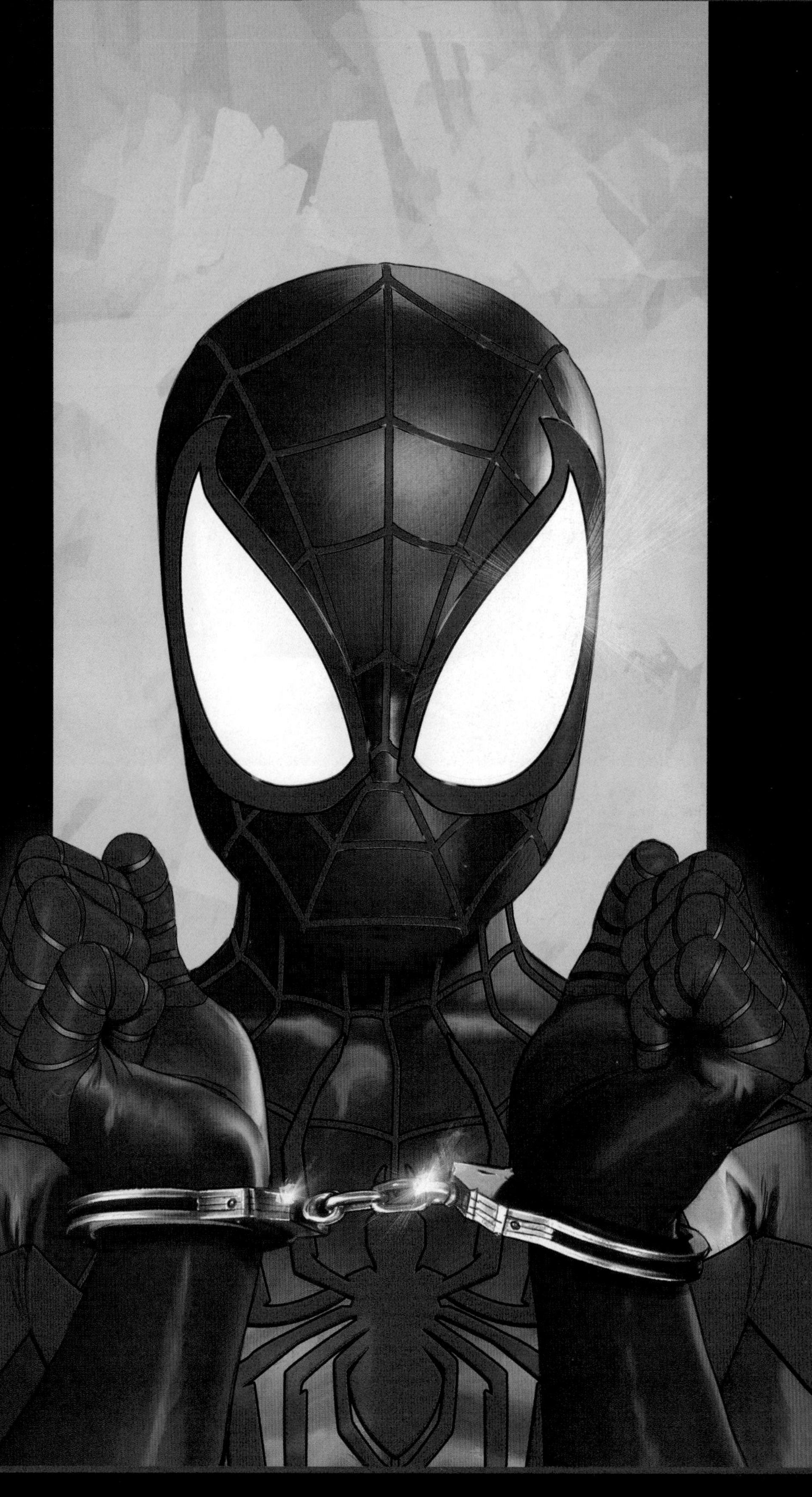

ULTIMATE COMICS SPIDER-MAN #11

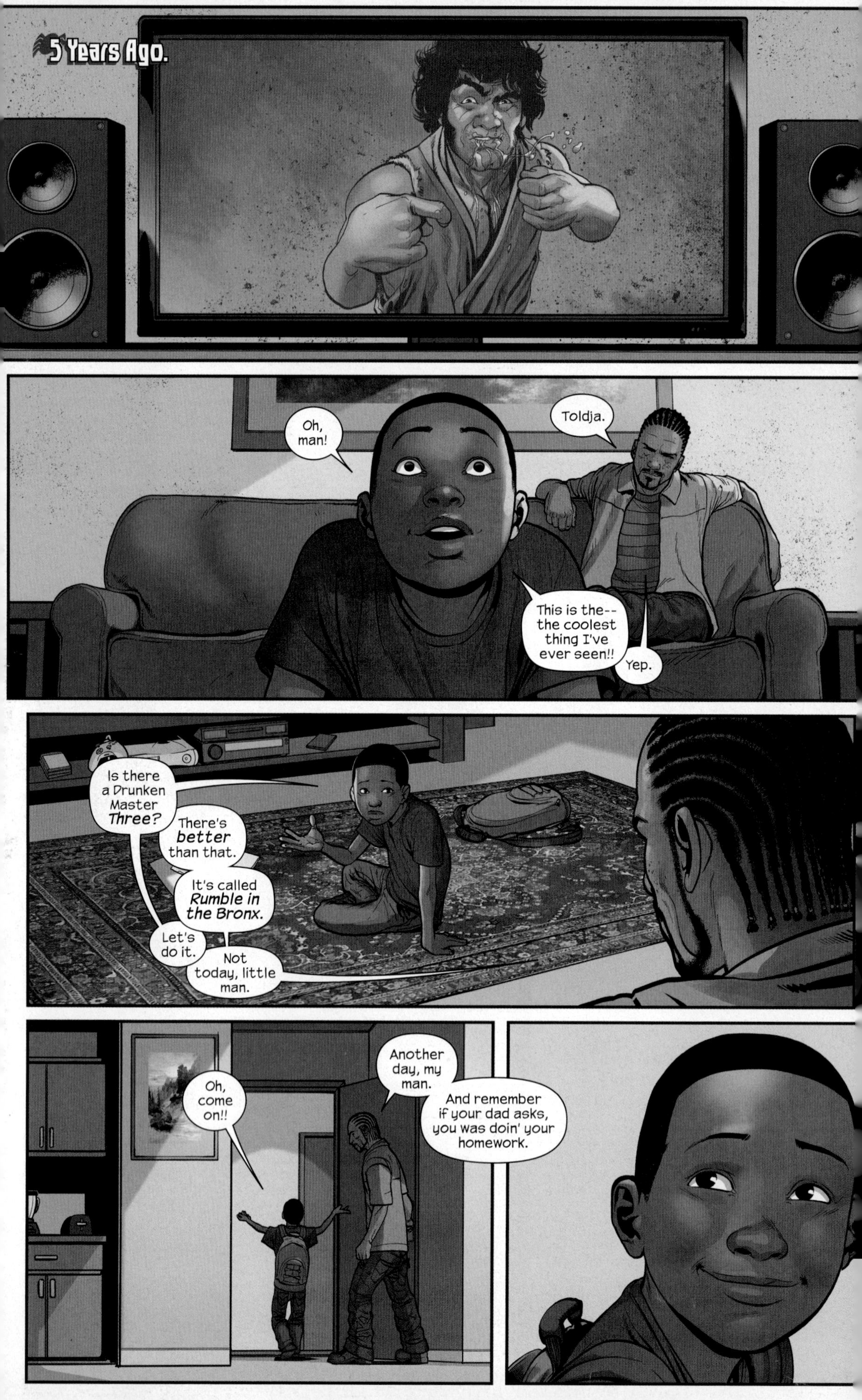
5 Years Ago.
Oh, man!
Toldja.
This is the-- the coolest thing I've ever seen!!
Yep.
Is there a Drunken Master *Three?*
There's *better* than that.
It's called *Rumble in the Bronx.*
Let's do it.
Not today, little man.
Oh, come on!!
Another day, my man.
And remember if your dad asks, you was doin' your homework.

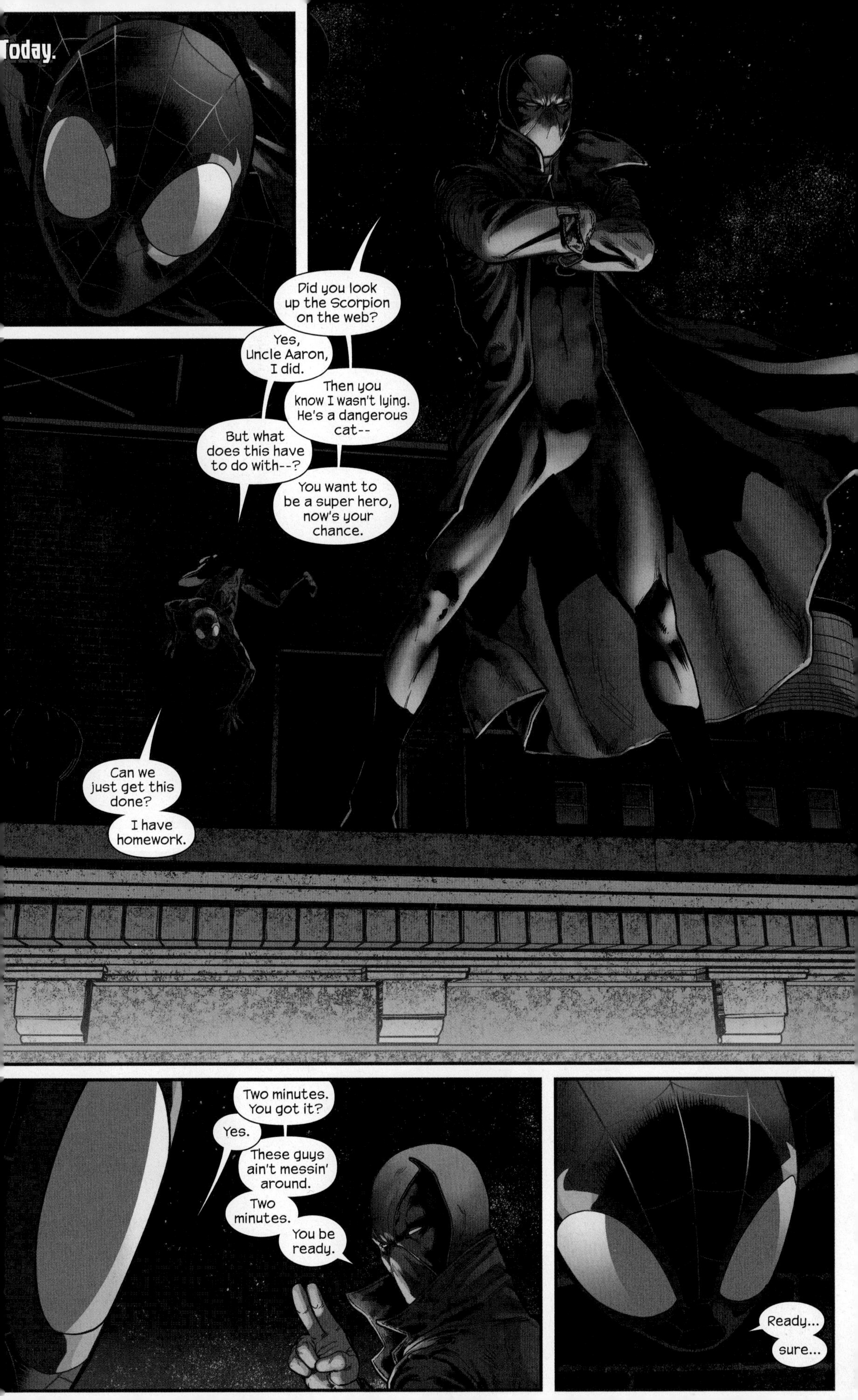

Today.
Did you look up the Scorpion on the web?
Yes, Uncle Aaron, I did.
Then you know I wasn't lying. He's a dangerous cat--
But what does this have to do with--?
You want to be a super hero, now's your chance.
Can we just get this done?
I have homework.
Two minutes. You got it?
Yes.
These guys ain't messin' around.
Two minutes.
You be ready.
Ready...
sure...

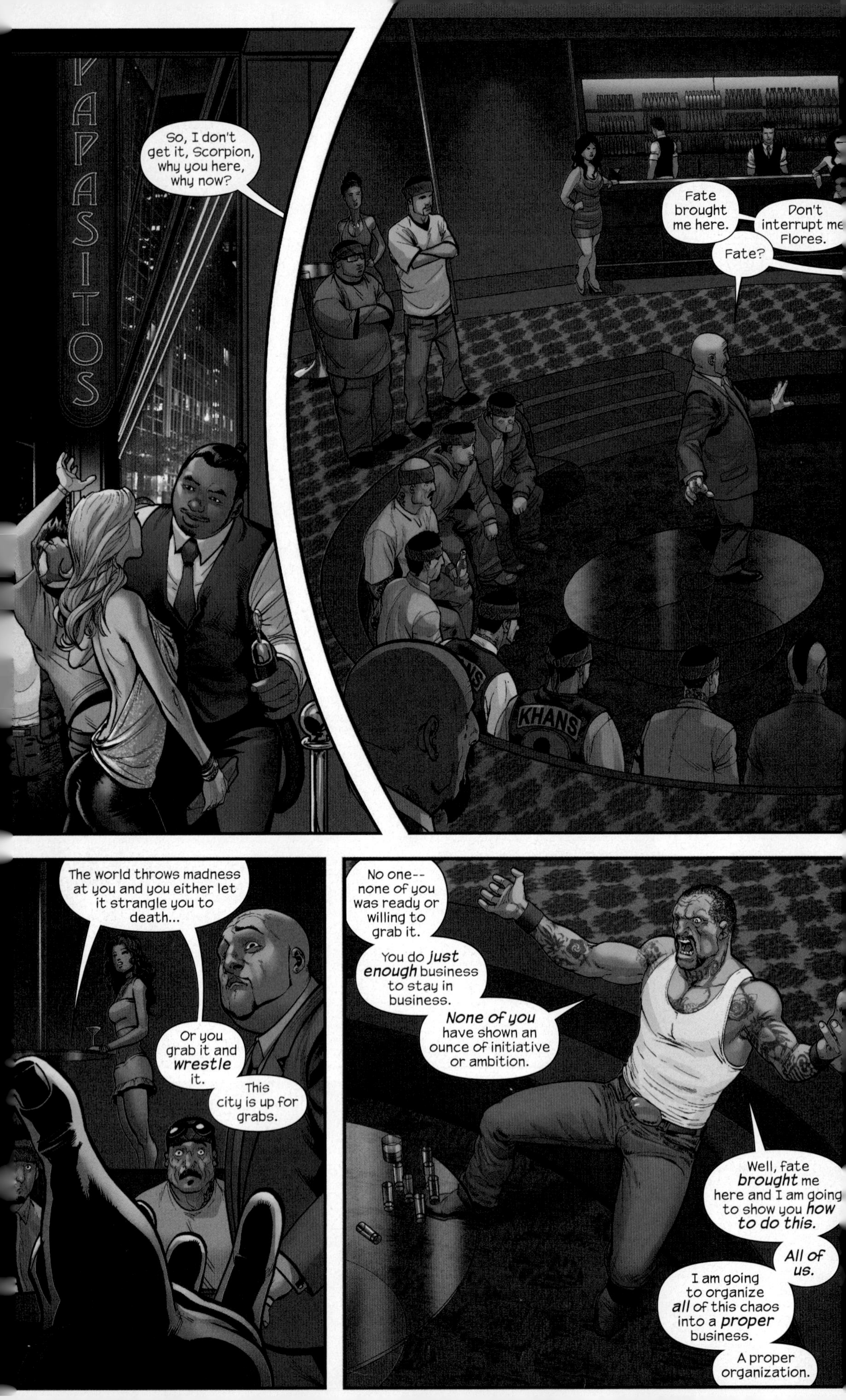
PAPASITOS
So, I don't get it, Scorpion, why you here, why now?
Fate brought me here.
Don't interrupt me Flores.
Fate?
KHANS
The world throws madness at you and you either let it strangle you to death...
Or you grab it and *wrestle* it.
This city is up for grabs.
No one-- none of you was ready or willing to grab it.
You do *just enough* business to stay in business.
None of you have shown an ounce of initiative or ambition.
Well, fate *brought* me here and I am going to show you *how to do this.*
All of us.
I am going to organize *all* of this chaos into a *proper* business.
A proper organization.

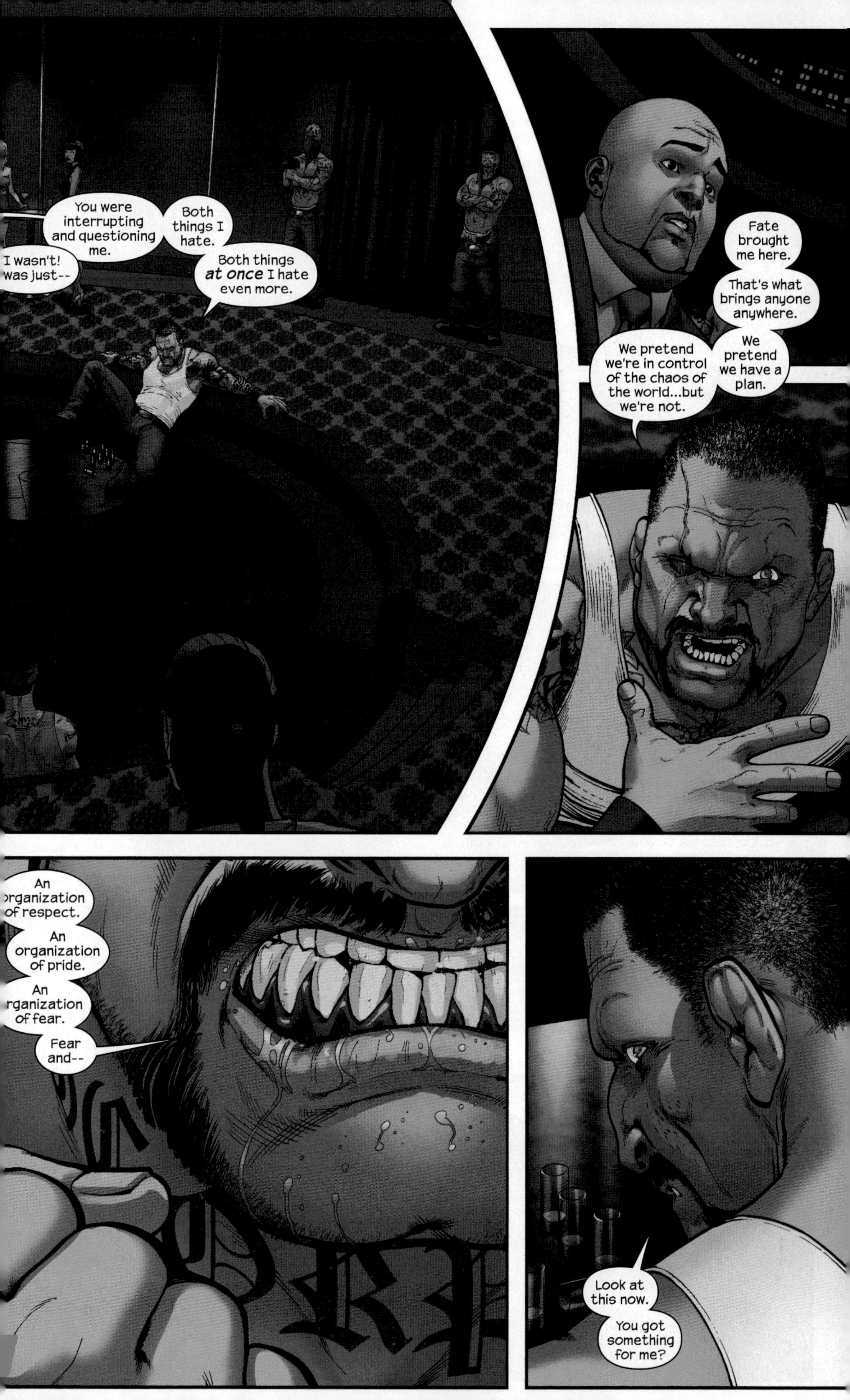
You were interrupting and questioning me.
I wasn't! was just--
Both things I hate.
Both things *at once* I hate even more.
Fate brought me here.
That's what brings anyone anywhere.
We pretend we have a plan.
We pretend we're in control of the chaos of the world...but we're not.
An rganization of respect.
An organization of pride.
An rganization of fear.
Fear and--
Look at this now.
You got something for me?

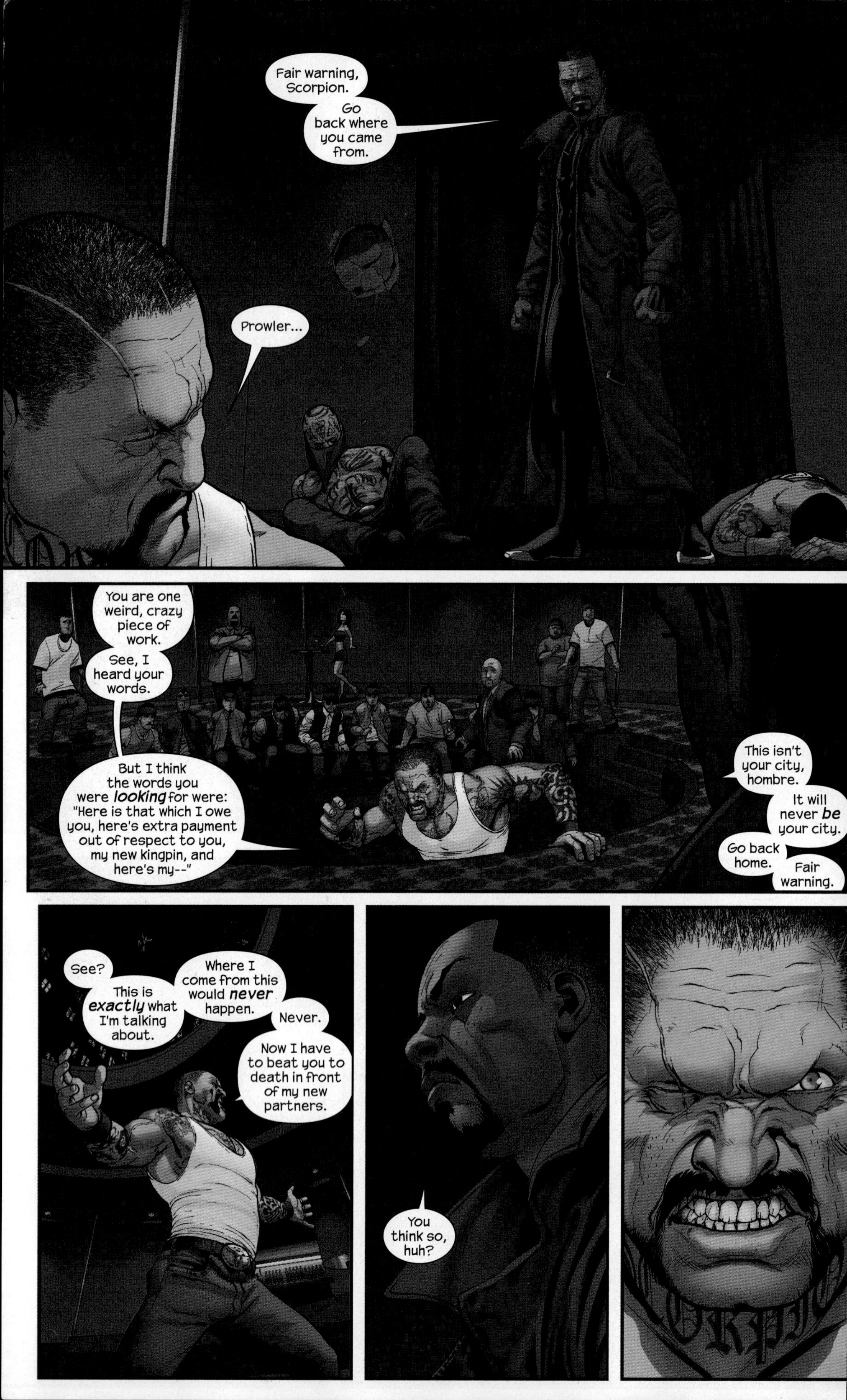
Fair warning, Scorpion.
Go back where you came from.
Prowler...
You are one weird, crazy piece of work.
See, I heard your words.
But I think the words you were *looking* for were: "Here is that which I owe you, here's extra payment out of respect to you, my new kingpin, and here's my--"
This isn't your city, hombre.
It will never *be* your city.
Go back home.
Fair warning.
See?
This is *exactly* what I'm talking about.
Where I come from this would *never* happen.
Never.
Now I have to beat you to death in front of my new partners.
You think so, huh?

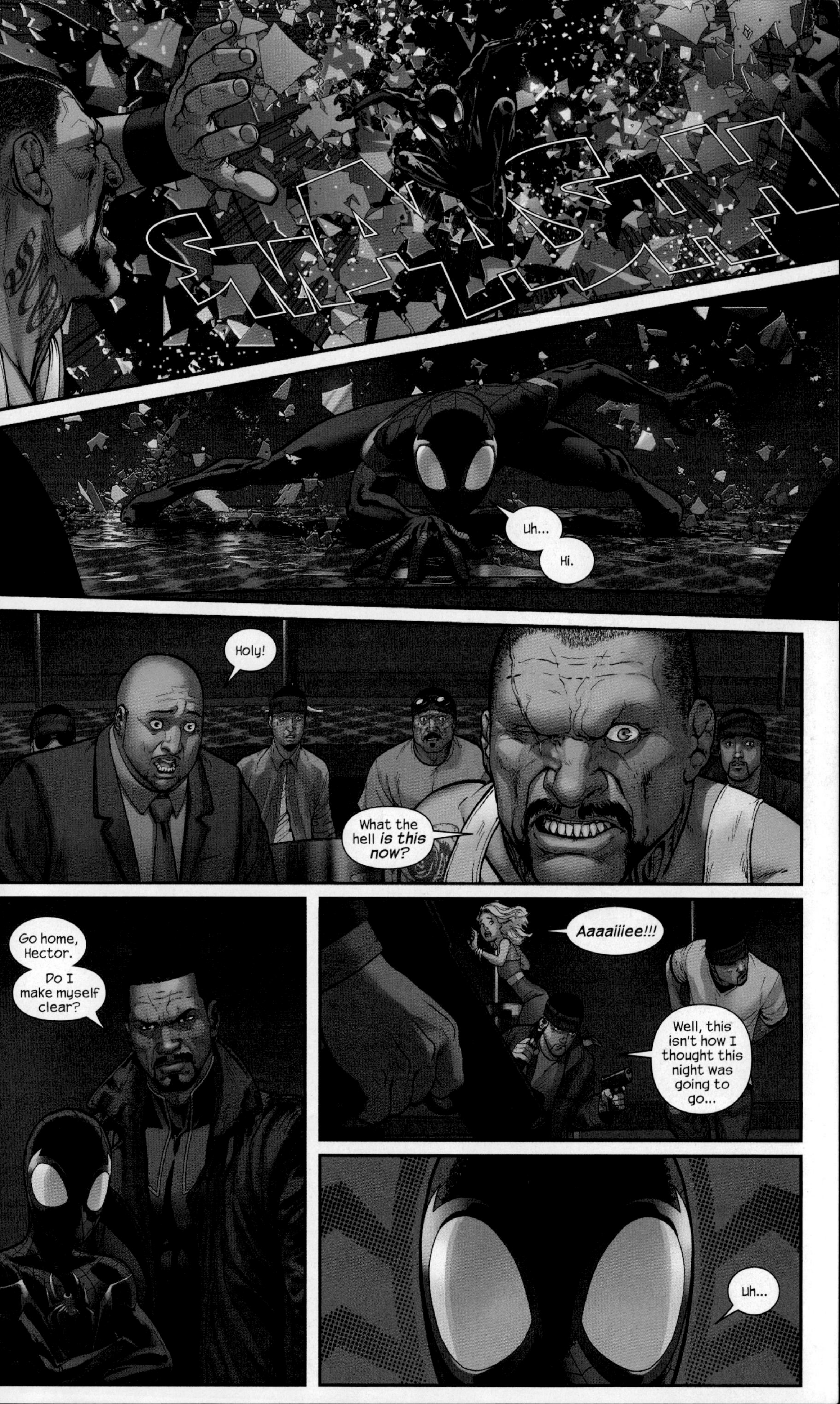
SMASH
Uh...
Hi.
Holy!
What the hell is this now?
Go home, Hector.
Do I make myself clear?
Aaaaiiiee!!!
Well, this isn't how I thought this night was going to go...
Uh...

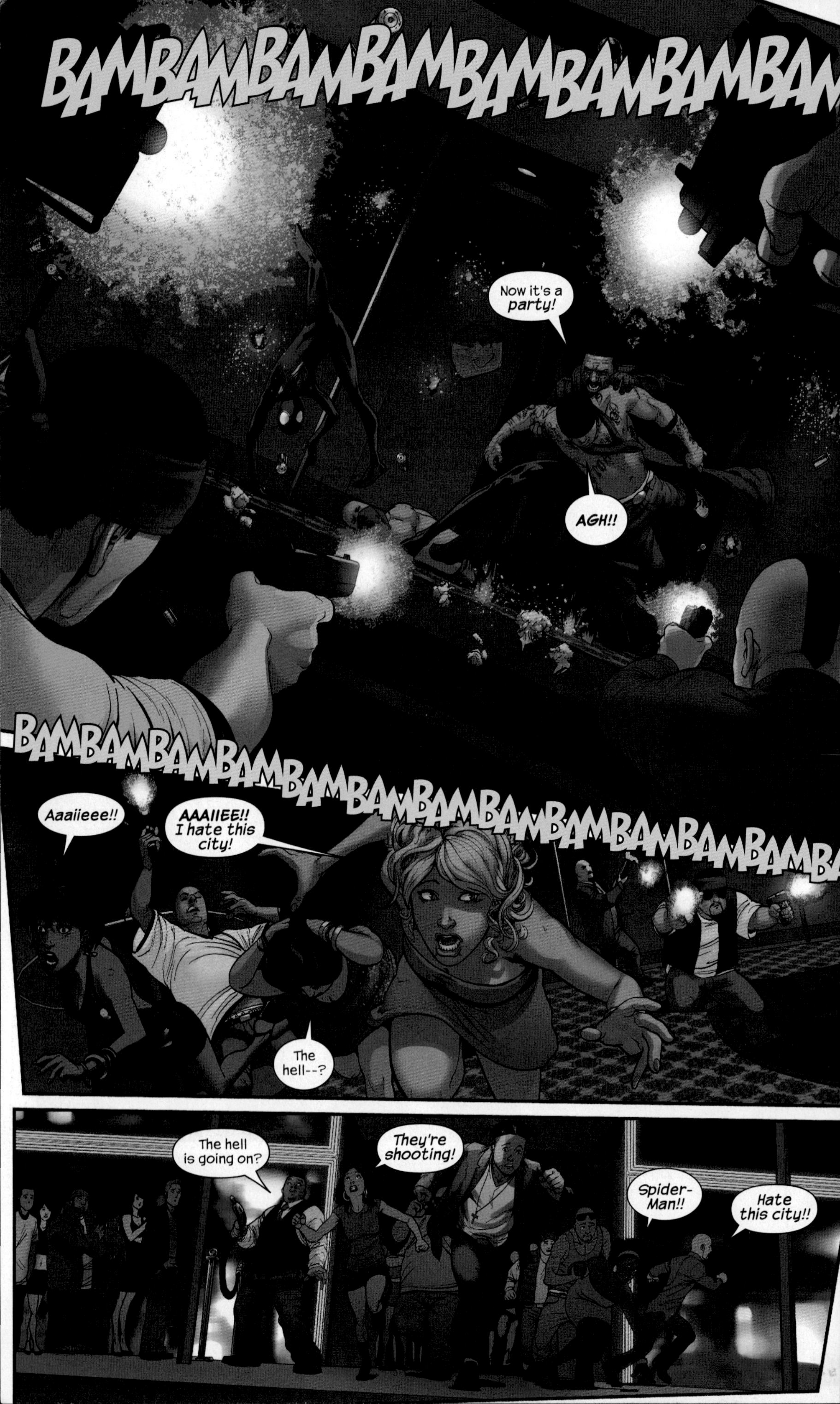

BAMBAMBAMBAMBAMBAMBAMBAM
Now it's a party!
AGH!!
BAMBAMBAMBAMBAMBAMBAMBAMBAMBAMBAMBAMBAMBA
Aaaiieee!!
AAAIIEE!! I hate this city!
The hell--?
The hell is going on?
They're shooting!
Spider-Man!!
Hate this city!!

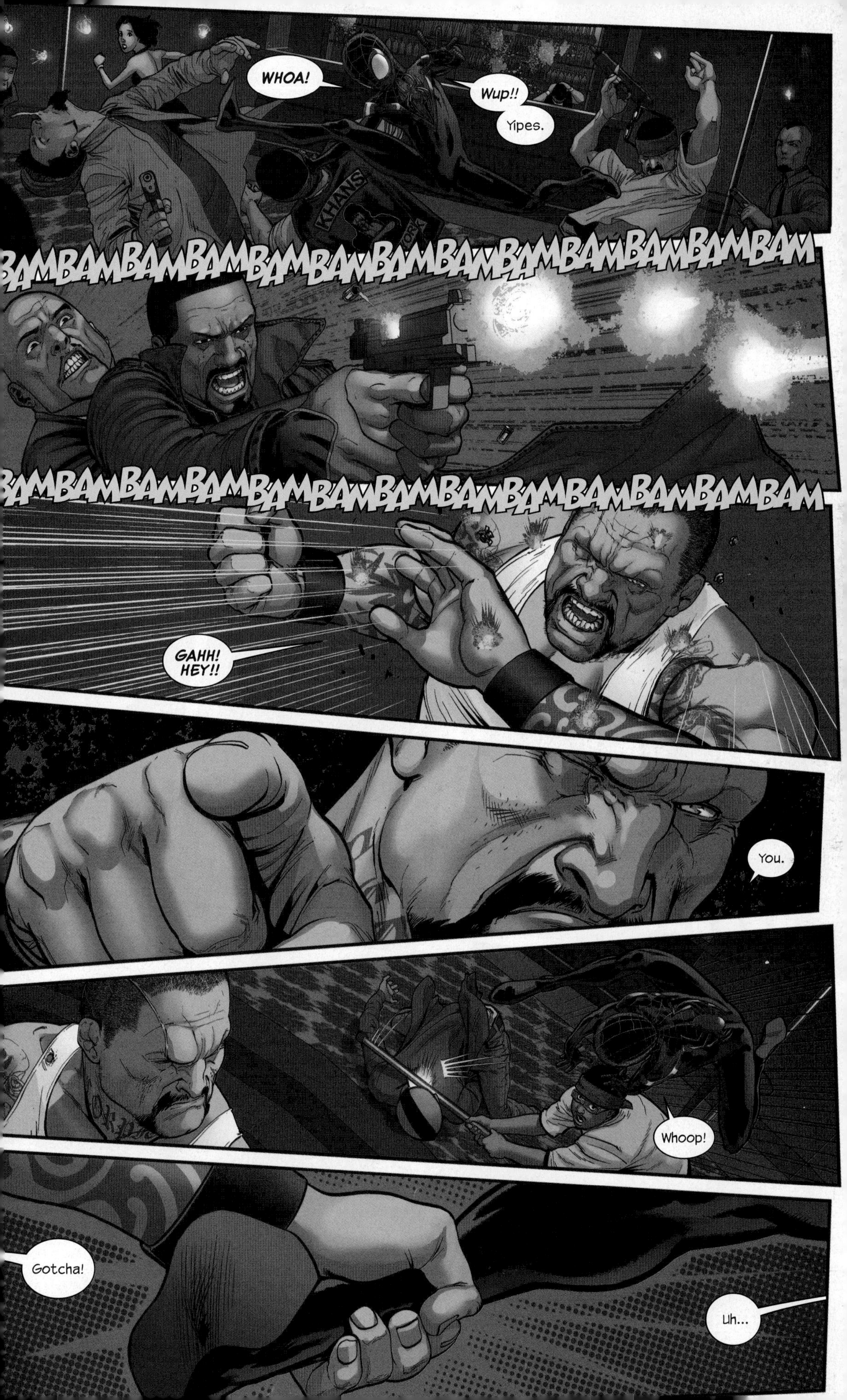
WHOA!
Wup!!
Yipes.
KHANS
BAMBAMBAMBAMBAMBAMBAMBAMBAMBAMBAMBAMBAM
BAMBAMBAMBAMBAMBAMBAMBAMBAMBAMBAMBAMBAM
GAHH! HEY!!
You.
Whoop!
Gotcha!
Uh...

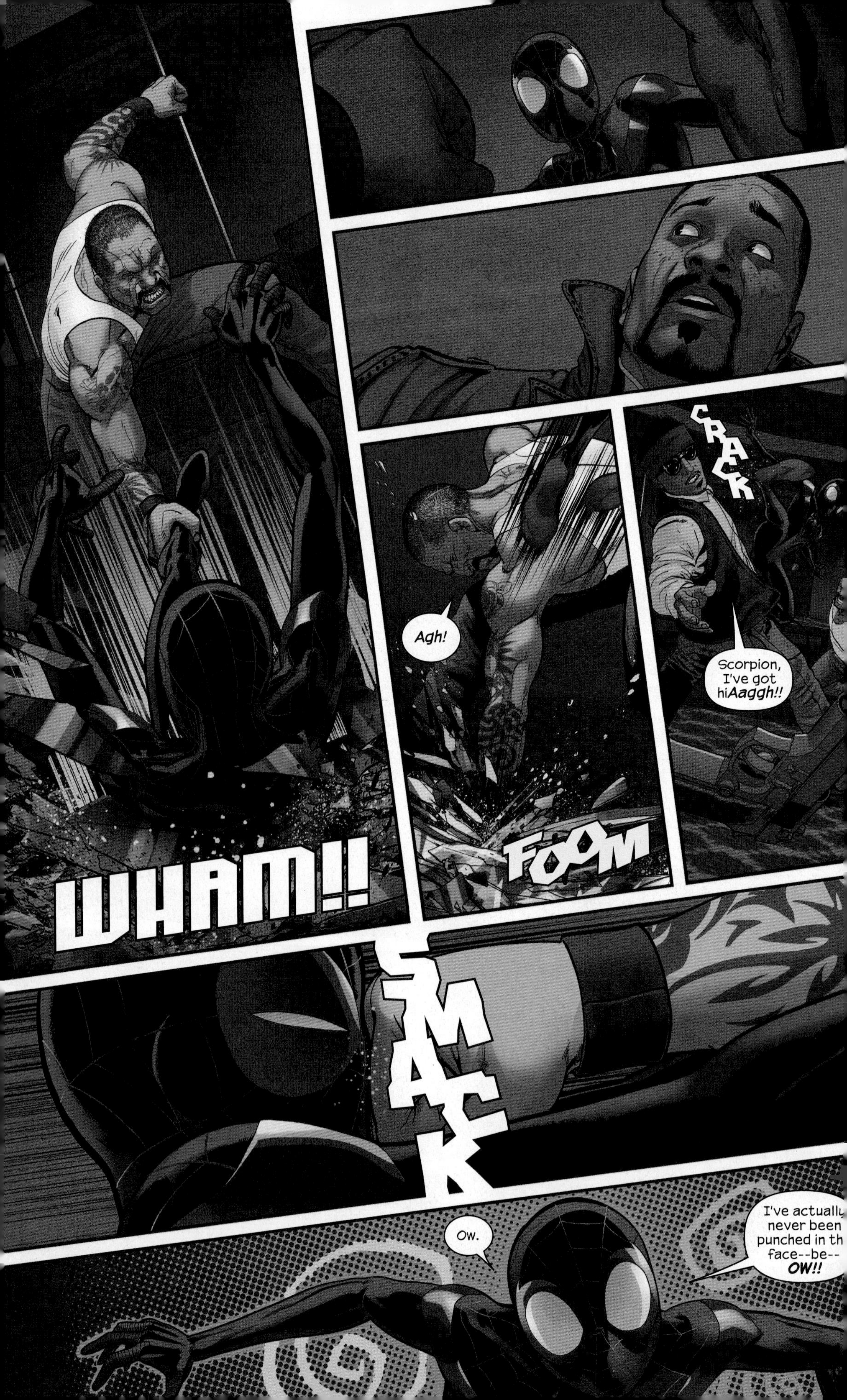
CRACK
Agh!
Scorpion,
I've got
hiAaggh!!
WHAM!!
FOOM
SMACK
Ow.
I've actually
never been
punched in th
face--be--
OW!!

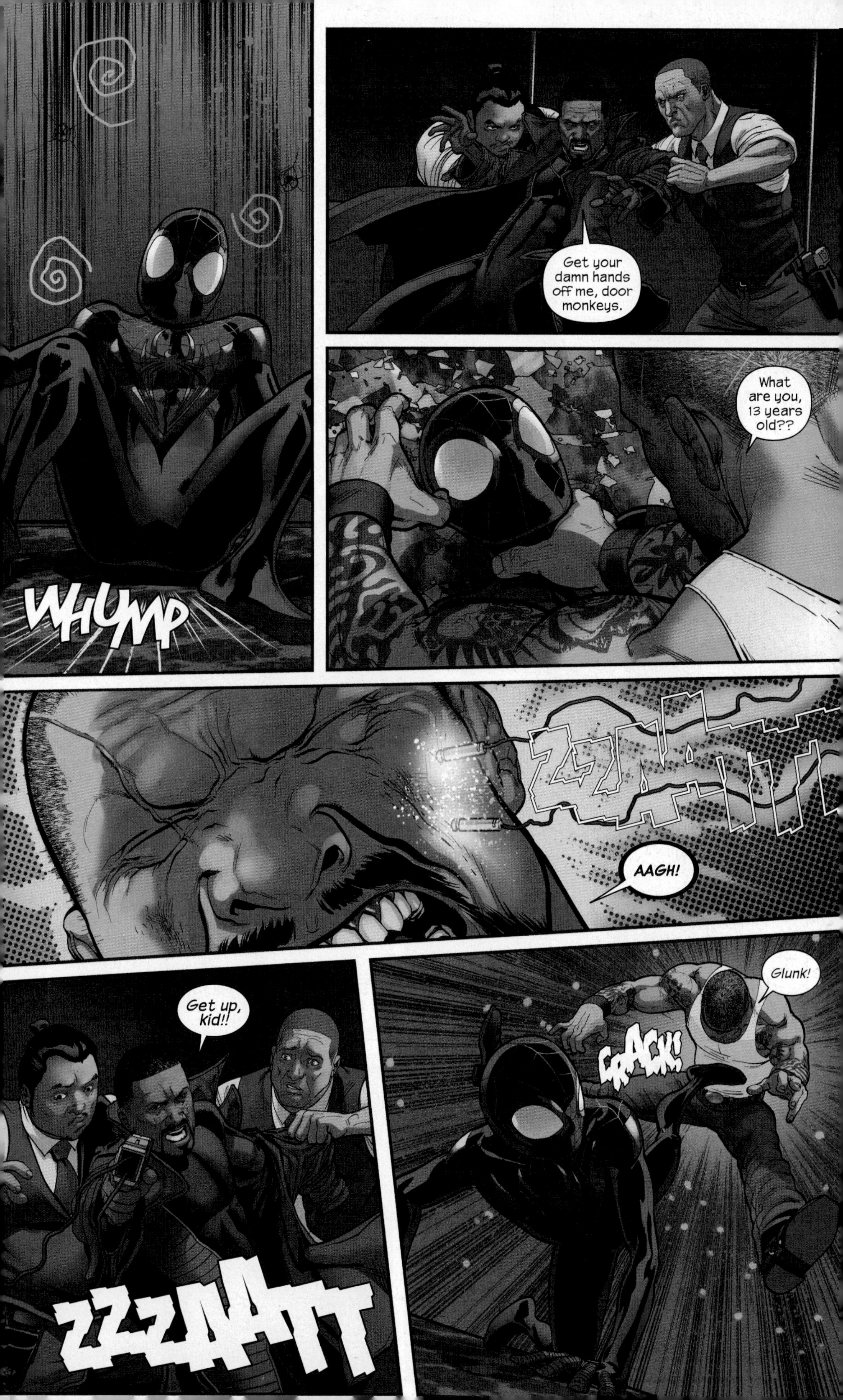
WHUMP
Get your damn hands off me, door monkeys.
What are you, 13 years old??
ZZZAATT
AAGH!
Get up, kid!!
ZZZAATT
CRACK!
Glunk!

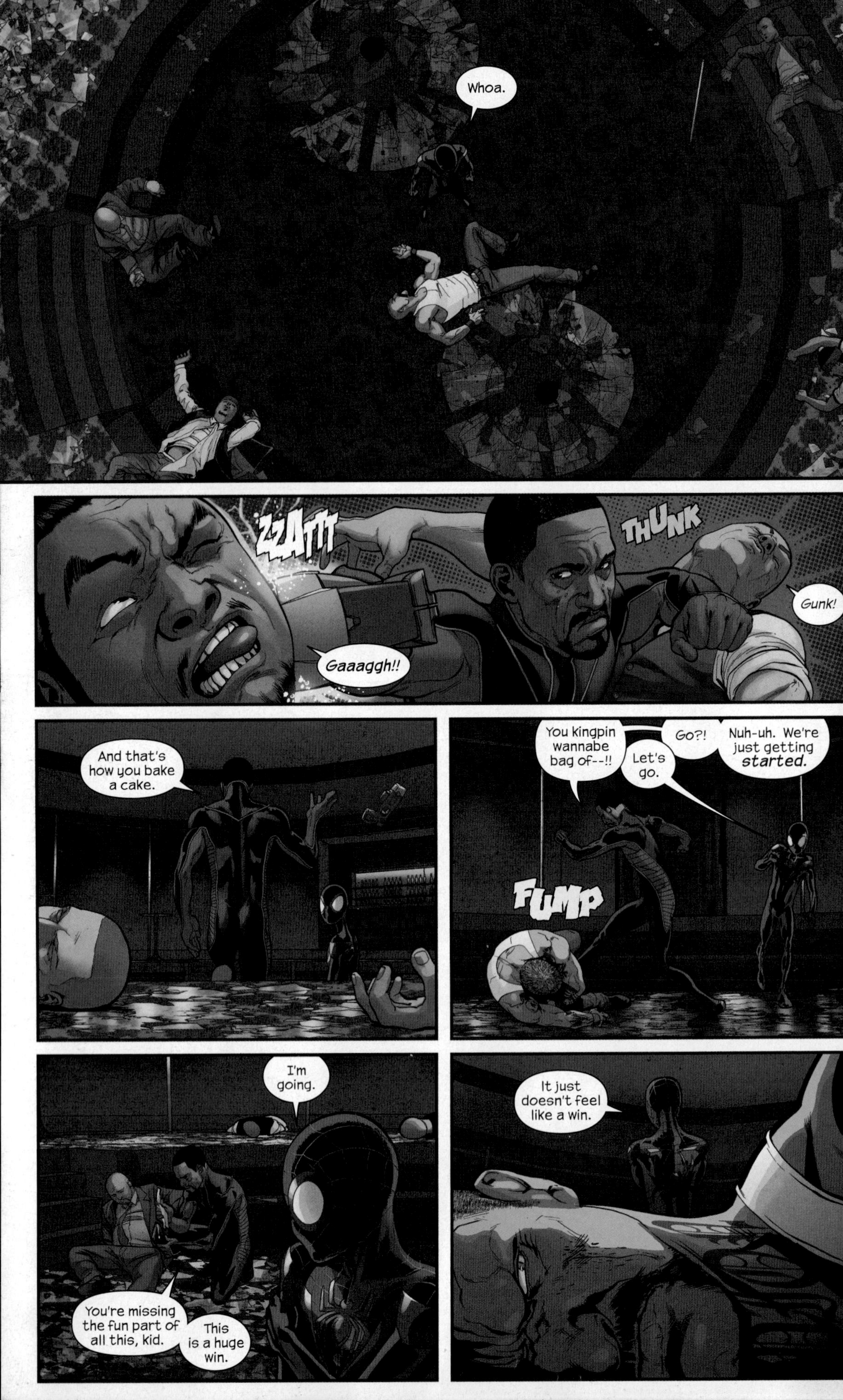

Whoa.
ZZATTT
Gaaaggh!!
THUNK
Gunk!
And that's how you bake a cake.
You kingpin wannabe bag of--!!
Go?!
Nuh-uh. We're just getting started.
Let's go.
FUMP
I'm going.
You're missing the fun part of all this, kid.
This is a huge win.
It just doesn't feel like a win.

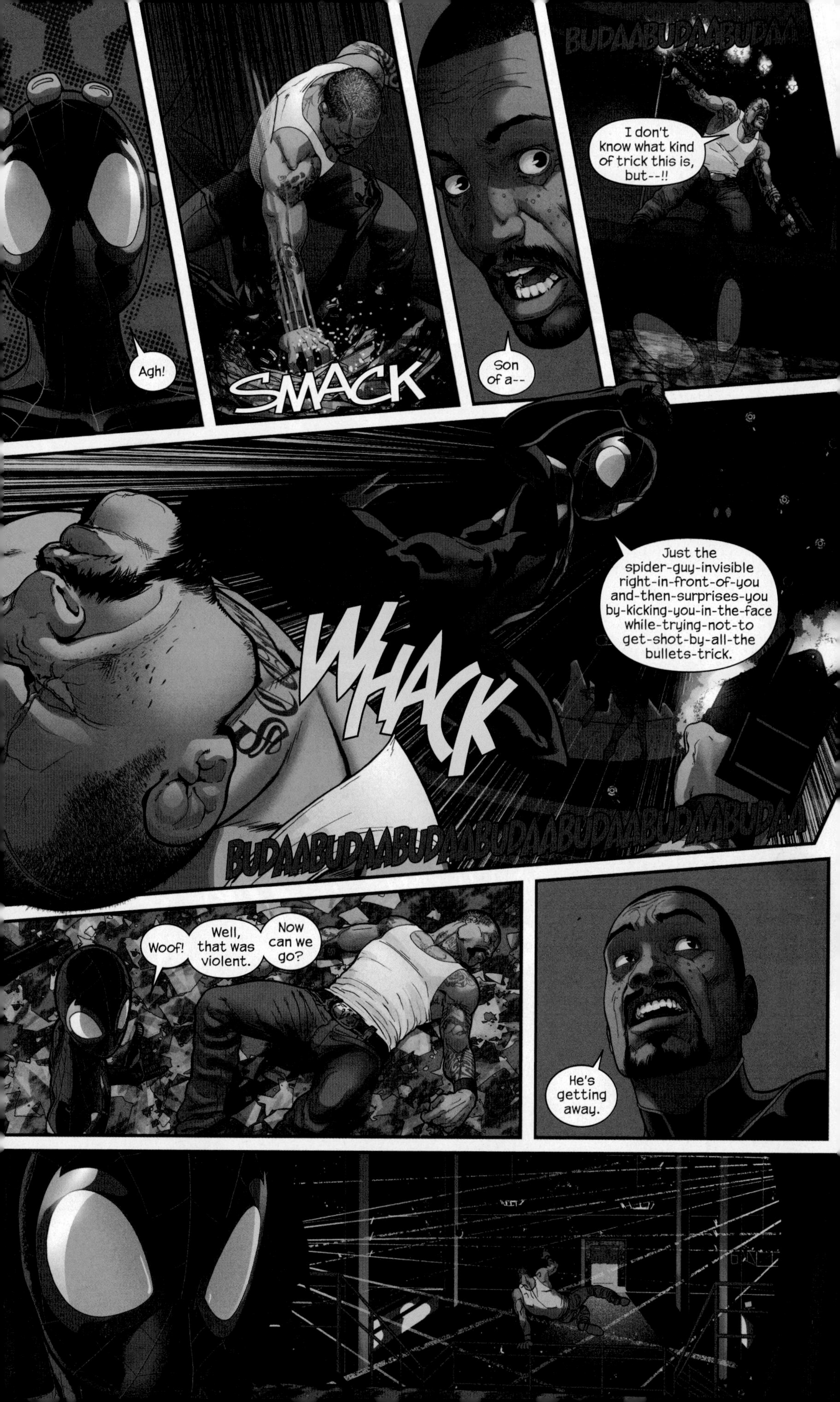
Agh!
SMACK
Son of a--
BUDAABUDAABUDAA
I don't know what kind of trick this is, but--!!
Just the spider-guy-invisible right-in-front-of-you and-then-surprises-you by-kicking-you-in-the-face while-trying-not-to get-shot-by-all-the bullets-trick.
WHACK
BUDAABUDAABUDAABUDAABUDAABUDAA
Woof!
Well, that was violent.
Now can we go?
He's getting away.

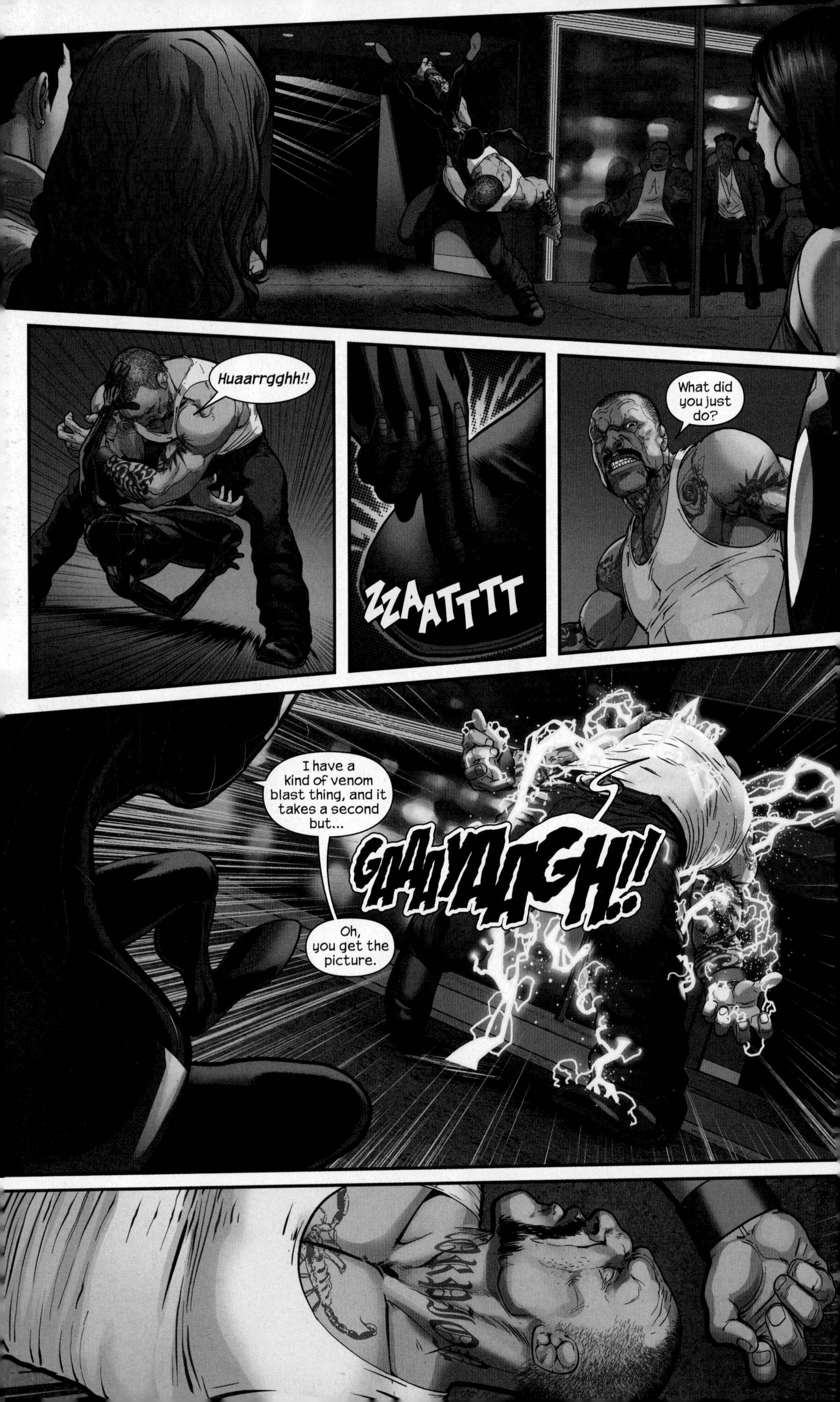
Huaarrgghh!!
ZZAATTTT
What did you just do?
I have a kind of venom blast thing, and it takes a second but...
GZZAAAYAAAGH!!
Oh, you get the picture.

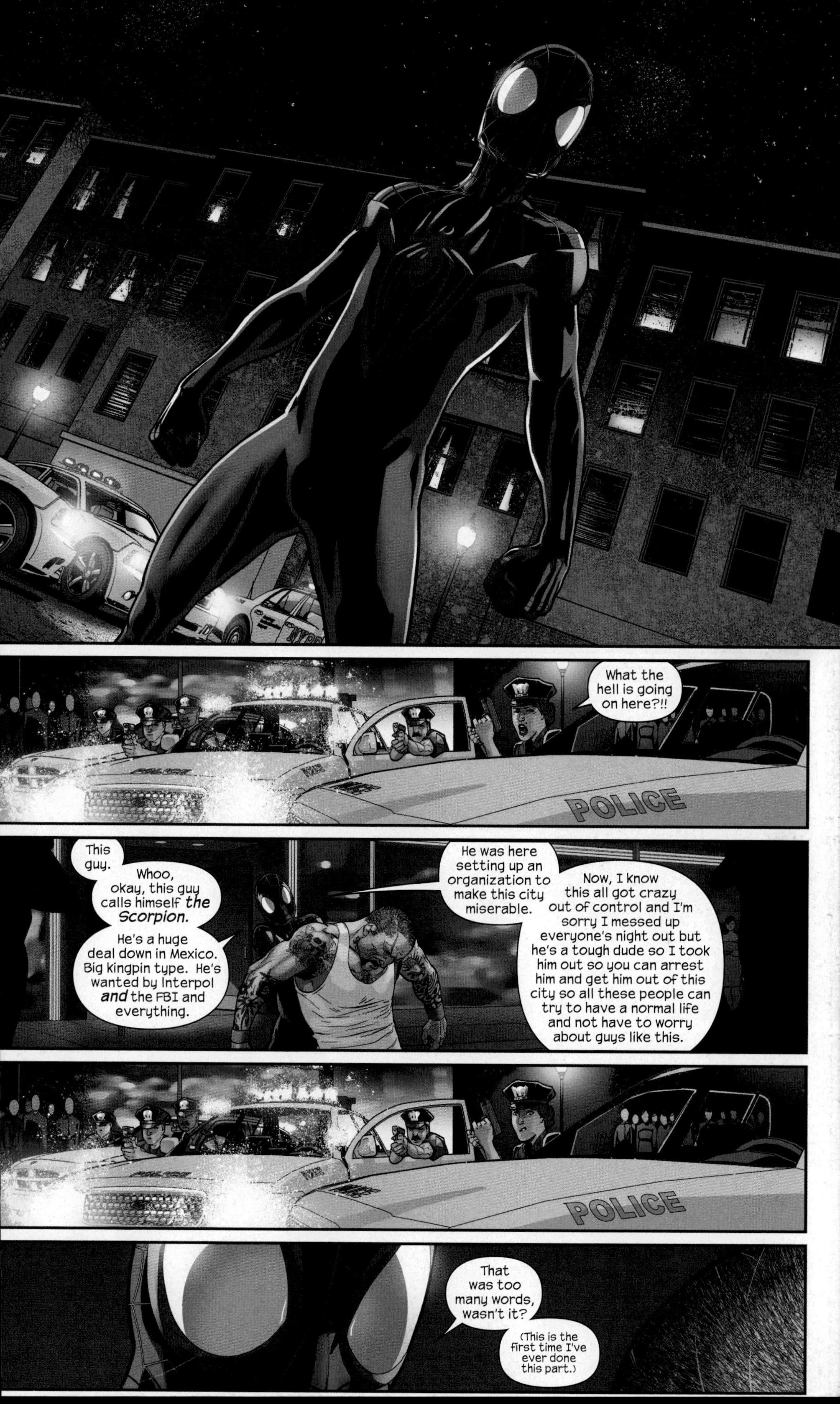

NYPD
What the hell is going on here?!!
POLICE
This guy.
Whoo, okay, this guy calls himself *the Scorpion.*
He's a huge deal down in Mexico. Big kingpin type. He's wanted by Interpol *and* the FBI and everything.
He was here setting up an organization to make this city miserable.
Now, I know this all got crazy out of control and I'm sorry I messed up everyone's night out but he's a tough dude so I took him out so you can arrest him and get him out of this city so all these people can try to have a normal life and not have to worry about guys like this.
POLICE
That was too many words, wasn't it?
(This is the first time I've ever done this part.)

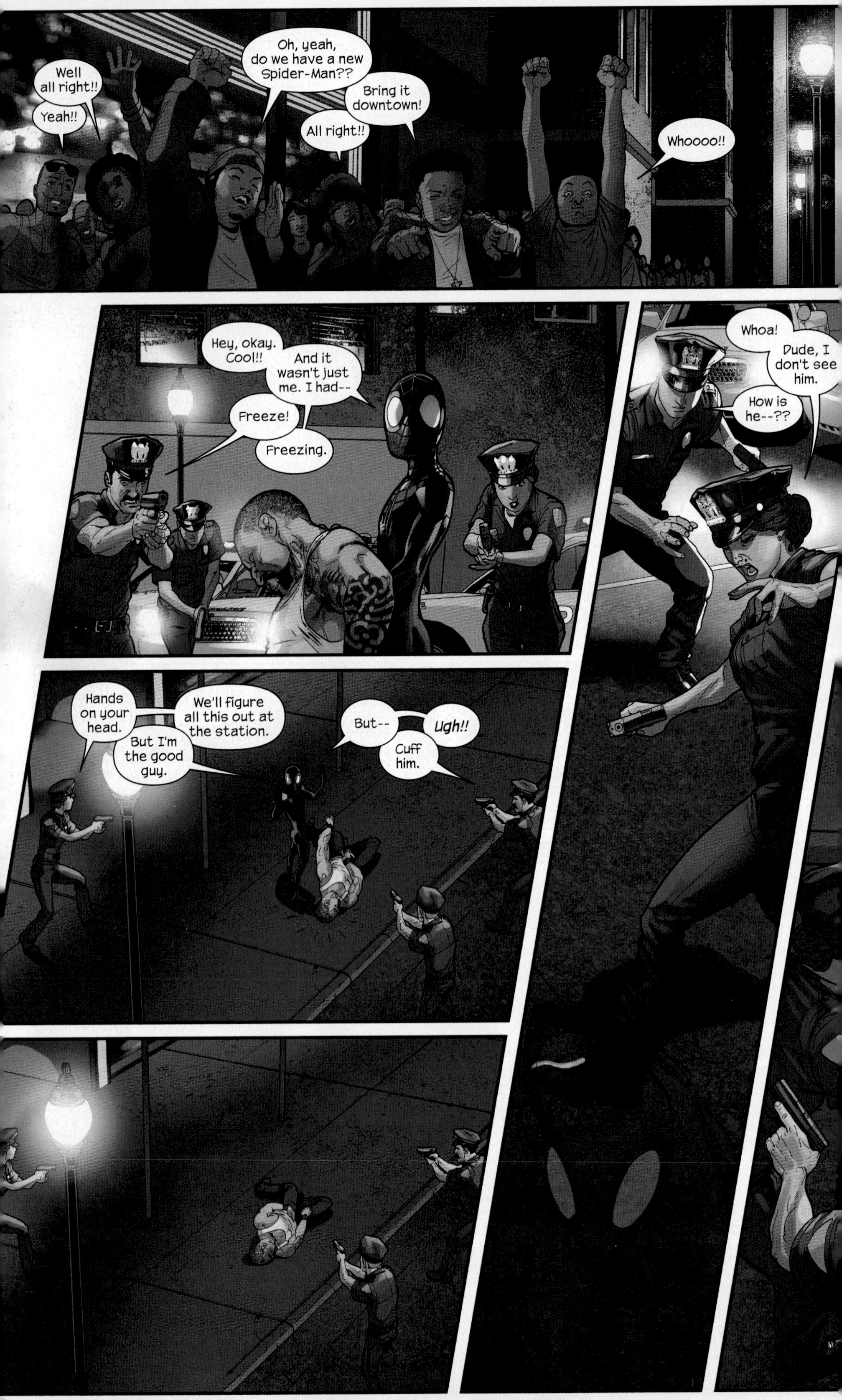
Well all right!!
Yeah!!
Oh, yeah, do we have a new Spider-Man??
Bring it downtown!
All right!!
Whoooo!!
Hey, okay. Cool!!
And it wasn't just me. I had--
Freeze!
Freezing.
Whoa!
Dude, I don't see him.
How is he--??
Hands on your head.
We'll figure all this out at the station.
But I'm the good guy.
But--
Ugh!!
Cuff him.

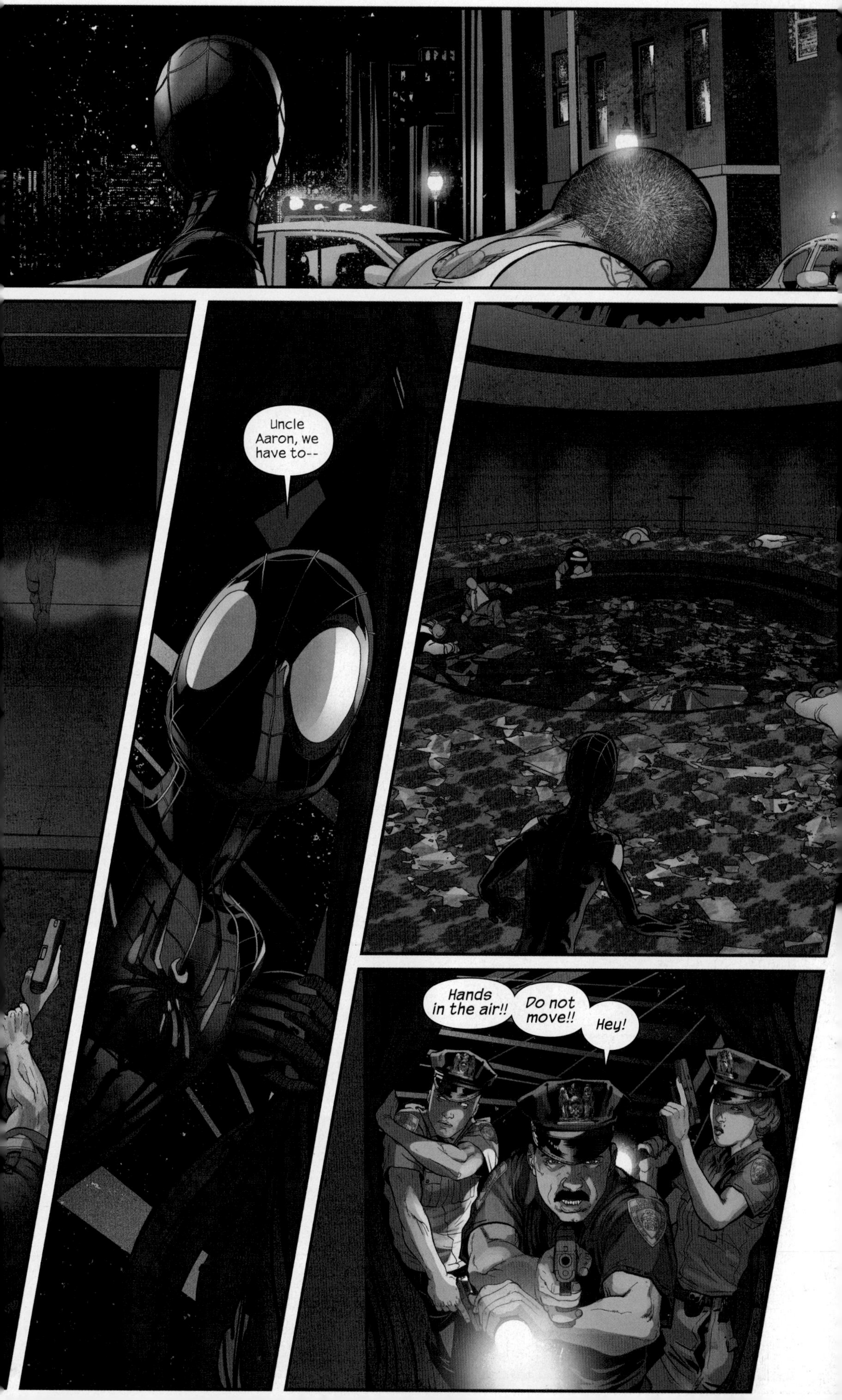
Uncle Aaron, we have to--
Hands in the air!!
Do not move!!
Hey!

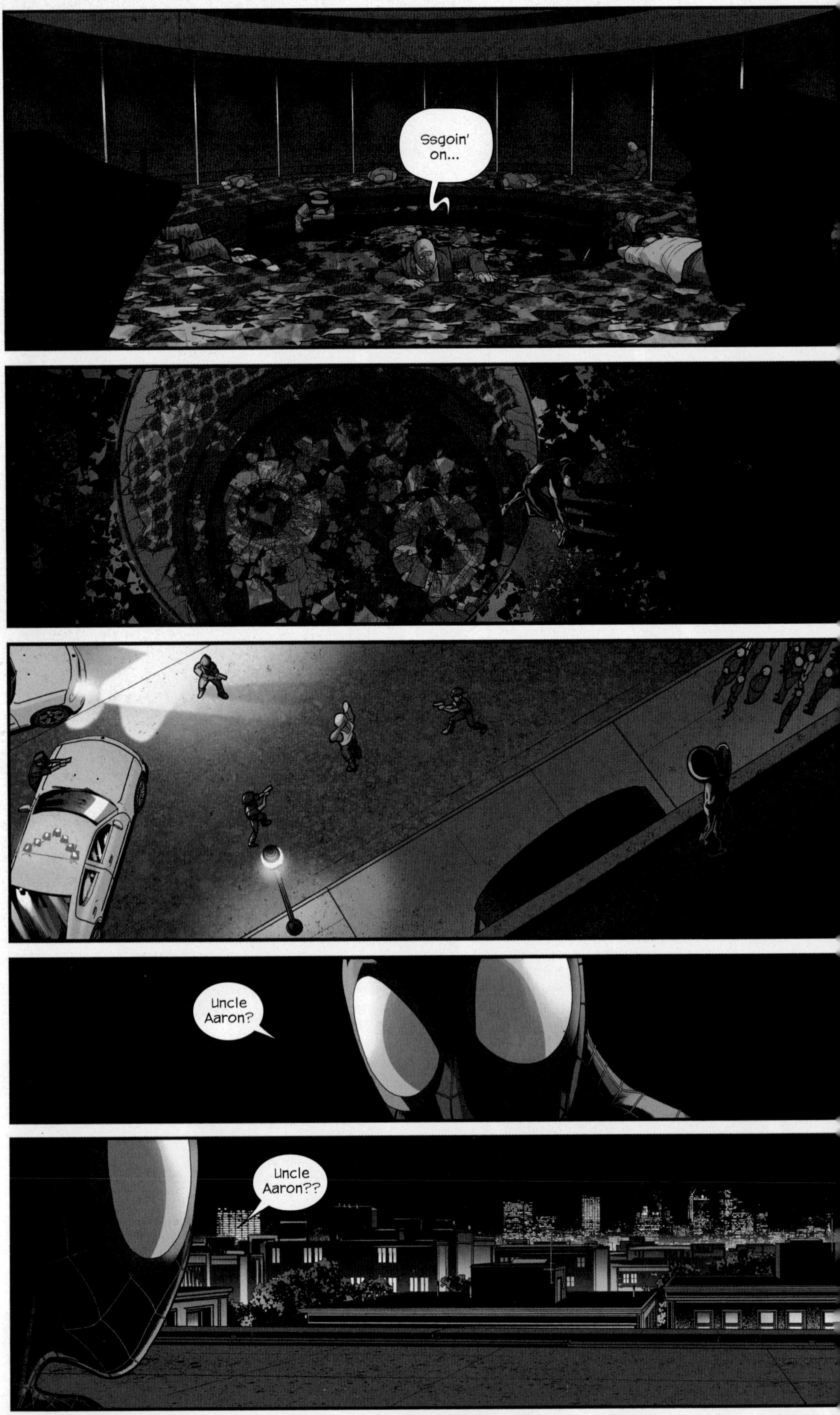
Ssgoin' on...
Uncle Aaron?
Uncle Aaron??

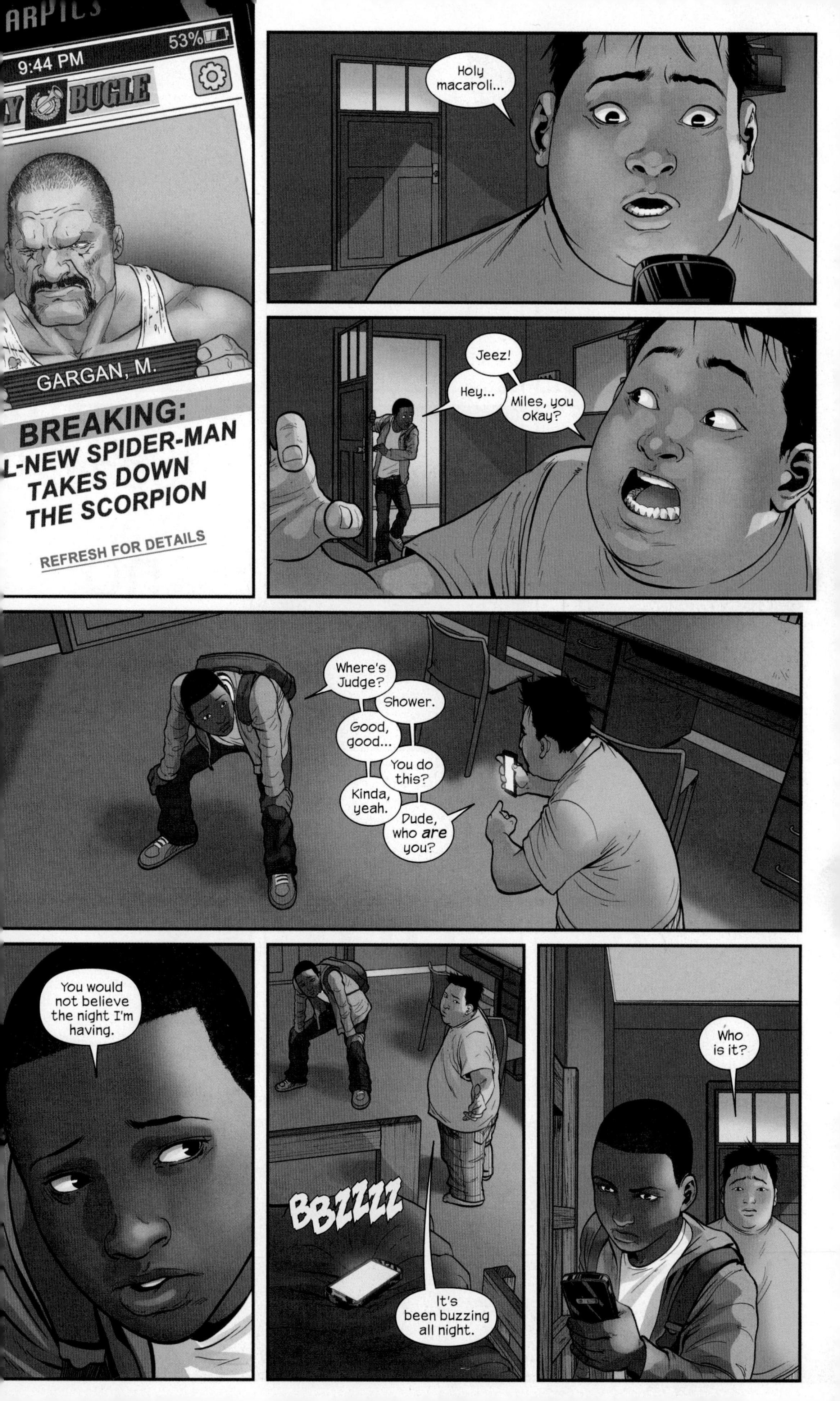
9:44 PM
53%
BUGLE
GARGAN, M.
BREAKING:
L-NEW SPIDER-MAN TAKES DOWN THE SCORPION
REFRESH FOR DETAILS
Holy macaroli...
Hey...
Jeez!
Miles, you okay?
Where's Judge?
Shower.
Good, good...
You do this?
Kinda, yeah.
Dude, who *are* you?
You would not believe the night I'm having.
BBZZZZ
It's been buzzing all night.
Who is it?

STARPICS
UNCLE AARON
today, 8:15 pm
hey, little man. you in one piece?
piece?
SIR MILES
today, 9:47 pm
Where'd you go?
UNCLE AARON
today, 9:48 pm
Get some rest. We're just getting started.
today, 9
no.
today, 9:49
no?
today,
no.
UNCLE AARON
today, 9:50 pm
Then maybe I should call your dad?

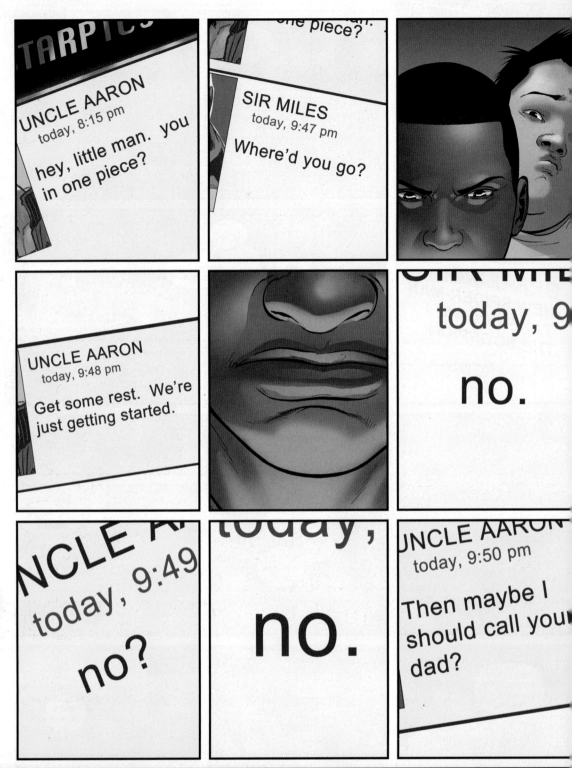

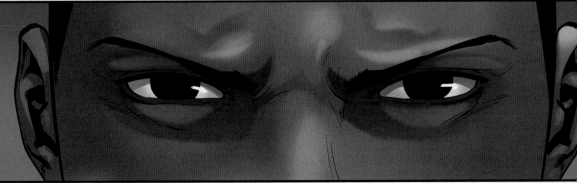

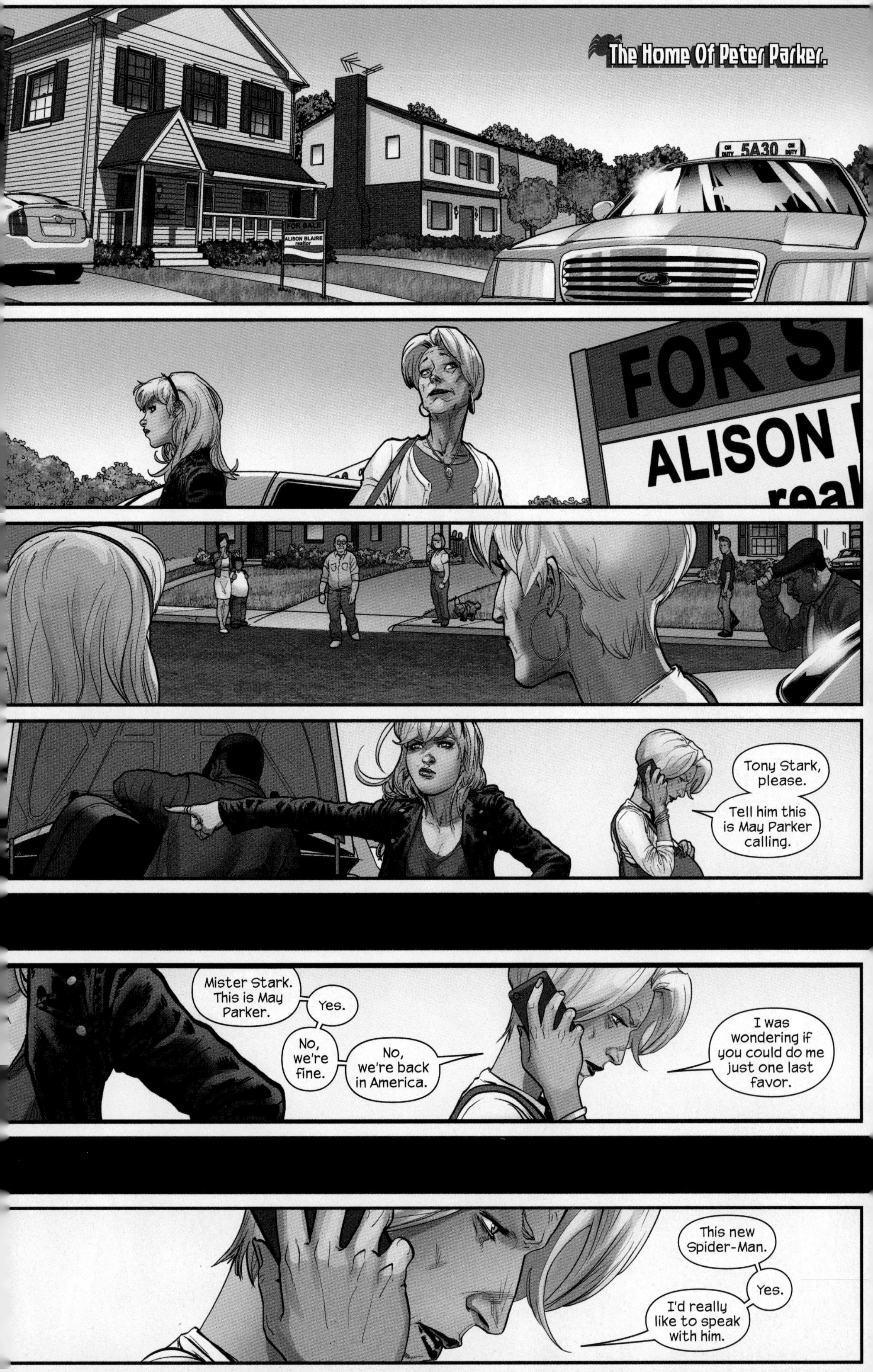
The Home Of Peter Parker.
FOR SALE
ALISON BLAIRE realtor
5A30
FOR S
ALISON
rea
Tony Stark, please.
Tell him this is May Parker calling.
Mister Stark. This is May Parker.
Yes.
No, we're fine.
No, we're back in America.
I was wondering if you could do me just one last favor.
This new Spider-Man.
Yes.
I'd really like to speak with him.

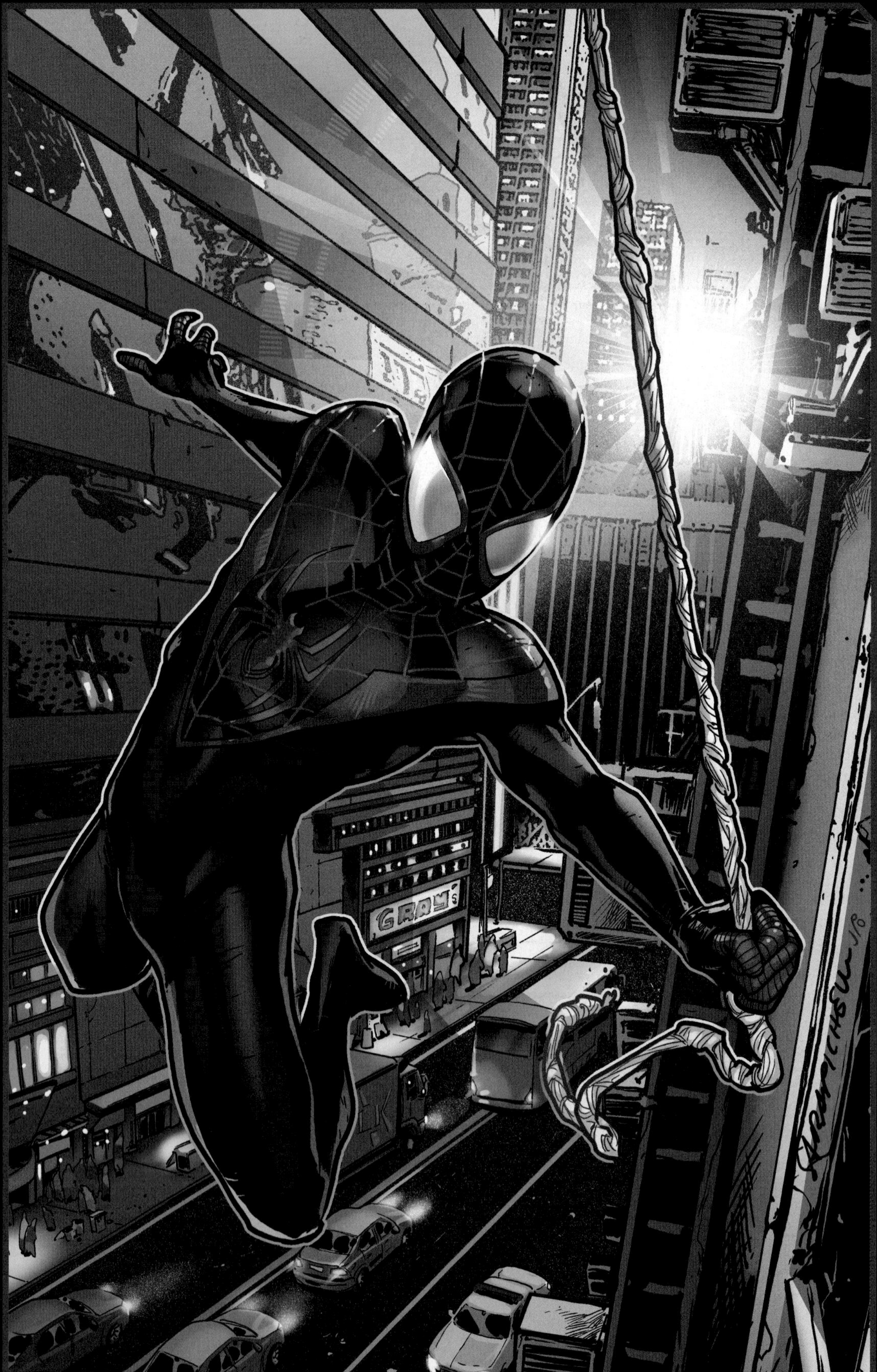
GRAY'S

ULTIMATE COMICS SPIDER-MAN #1 VARIANT BY SARA PICHELLI & JUSTIN PONSOR

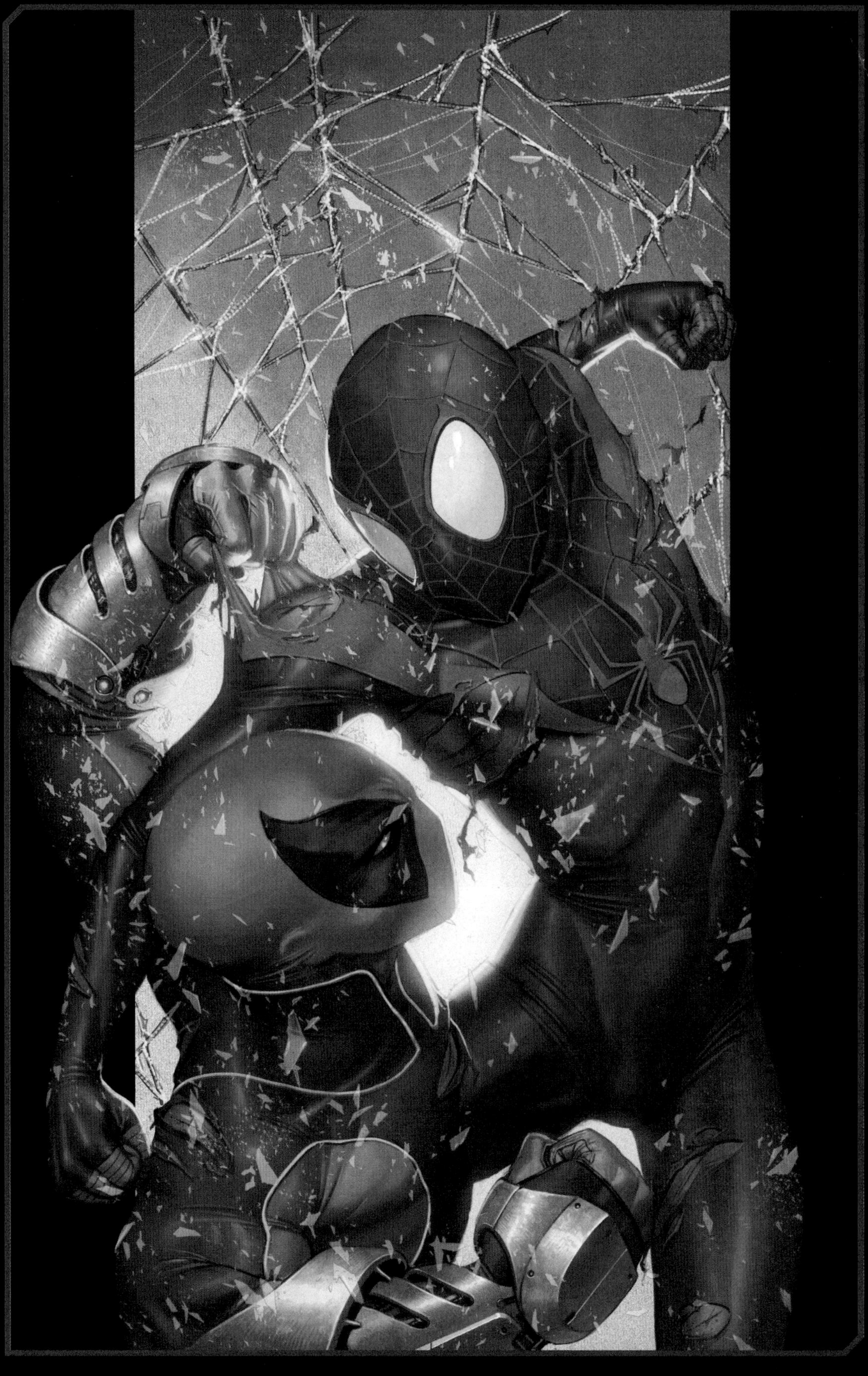

ULTIMATE COMICS SPIDER-MAN #12

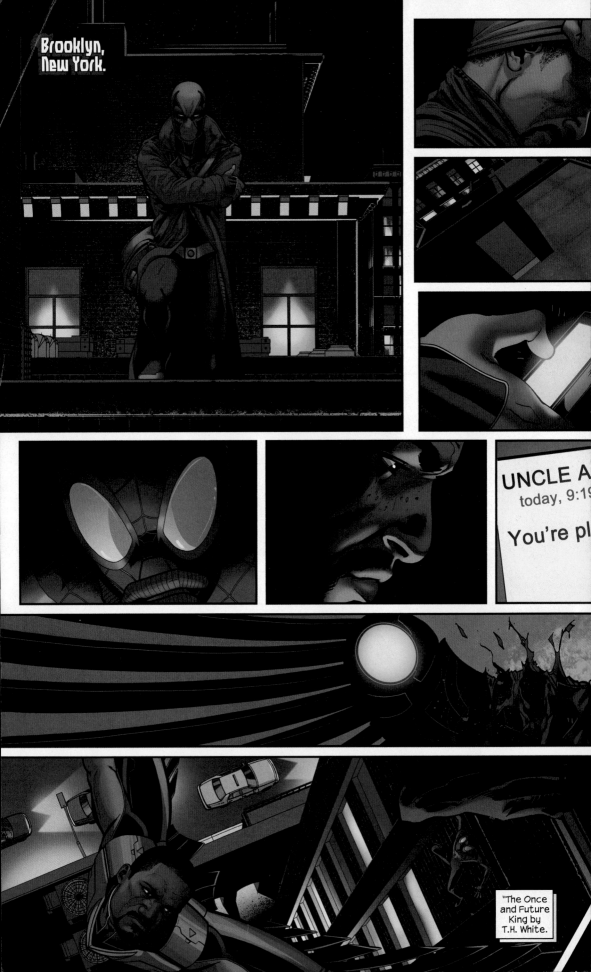

Brooklyn,
New York.

UNCLE A
today, 9:19

You're pl

"The Once and Future King by T.H. White.

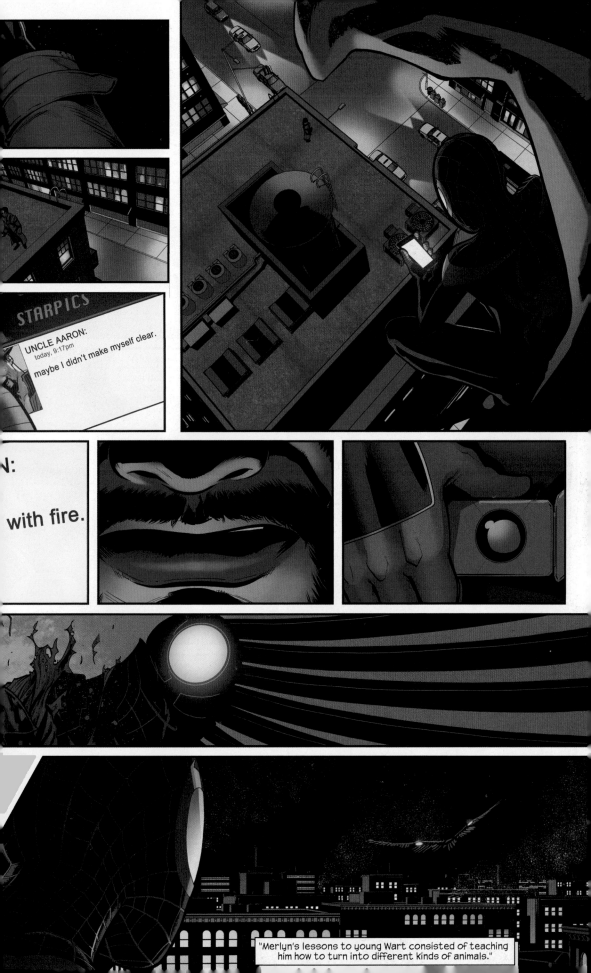

STARPICS

UNCLE AARON:
today, 9:17pm

maybe I didn't make myself clear.

N:

with fire.

"Merlyn's lessons to young Wart consisted of teaching him how to turn into different kinds of animals."

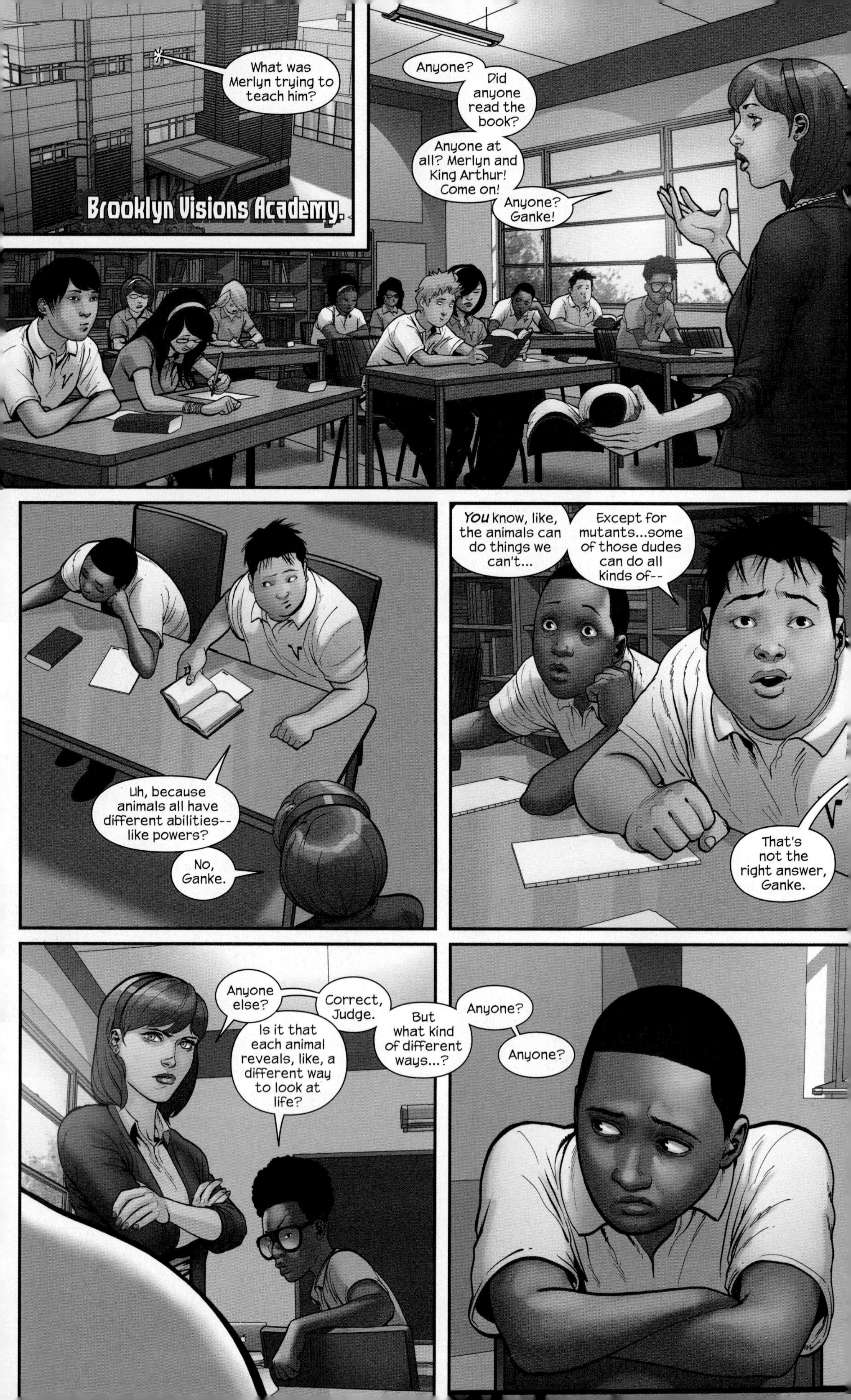
What was Merlyn trying to teach him?
Brooklyn Visions Academy.
Anyone?
Did anyone read the book?
Anyone at all? Merlyn and King Arthur! Come on!
Anyone? Ganke!
Uh, because animals all have different abilities--like powers?
No, Ganke.
YOU know, like, the animals can do things we can't...
Except for mutants...some of those dudes can do all kinds of--
That's not the right answer, Ganke.
Anyone else?
Is it that each animal reveals, like, a different way to look at life?
Correct, Judge.
But what kind of different ways...?
Anyone?
Anyone?

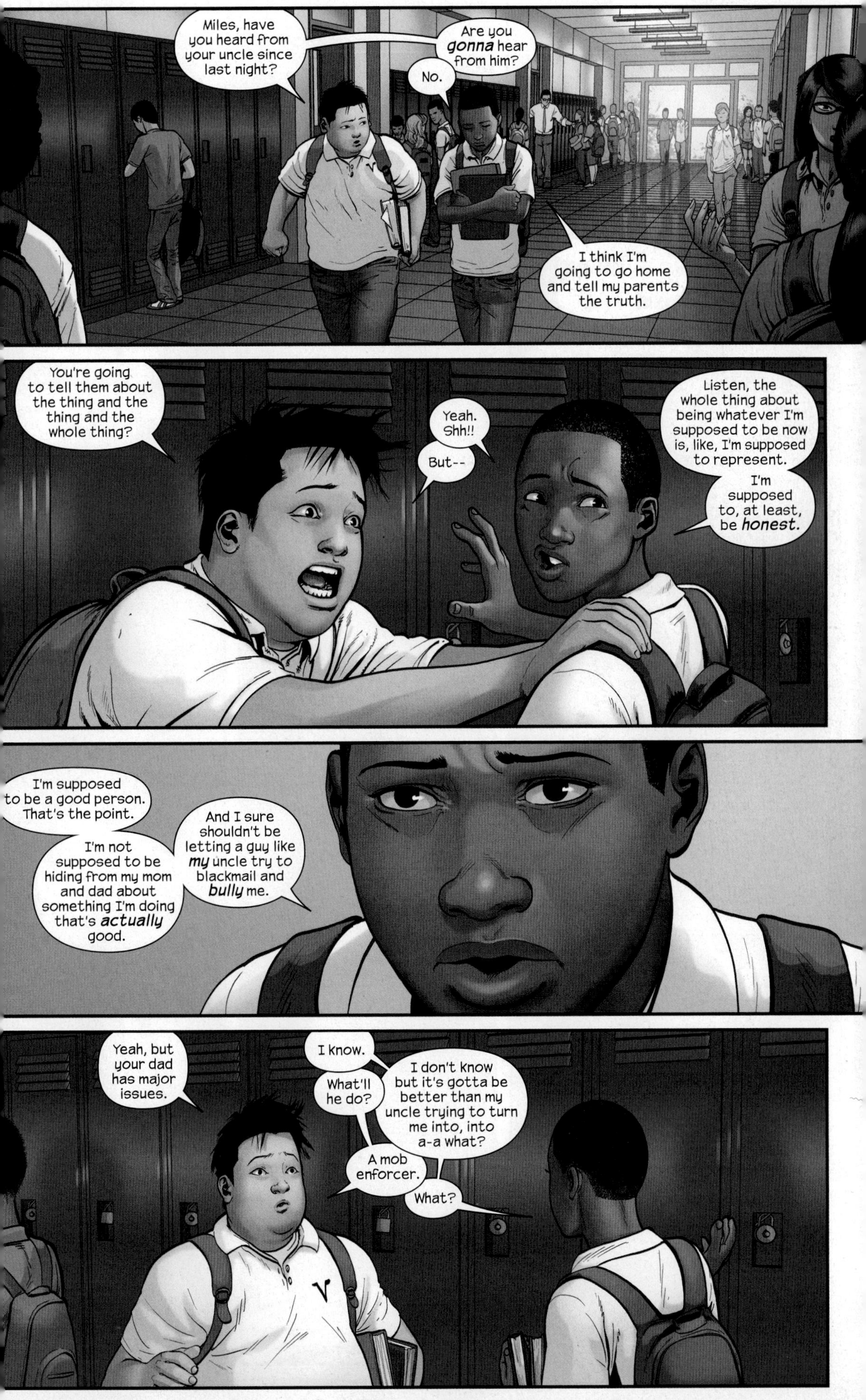

Miles, have you heard from your uncle since last night?
Are you *gonna* hear from him?
No.
I think I'm going to go home and tell my parents the truth.
You're going to tell them about the thing and the thing and the whole thing?
Yeah. Shh!!
But--
Listen, the whole thing about being whatever I'm supposed to be now is, like, I'm supposed to represent.
I'm supposed to, at least, be *honest.*
I'm supposed to be a good person. That's the point.
I'm not supposed to be hiding from my mom and dad about something I'm doing that's *actually* good.
And I sure shouldn't be letting a guy like *my* uncle try to blackmail and *bully* me.
Yeah, but your dad has major issues.
I know.
What'll he do?
I don't know but it's gotta be better than my uncle trying to turn me into, into a-a what?
A mob enforcer.
What?

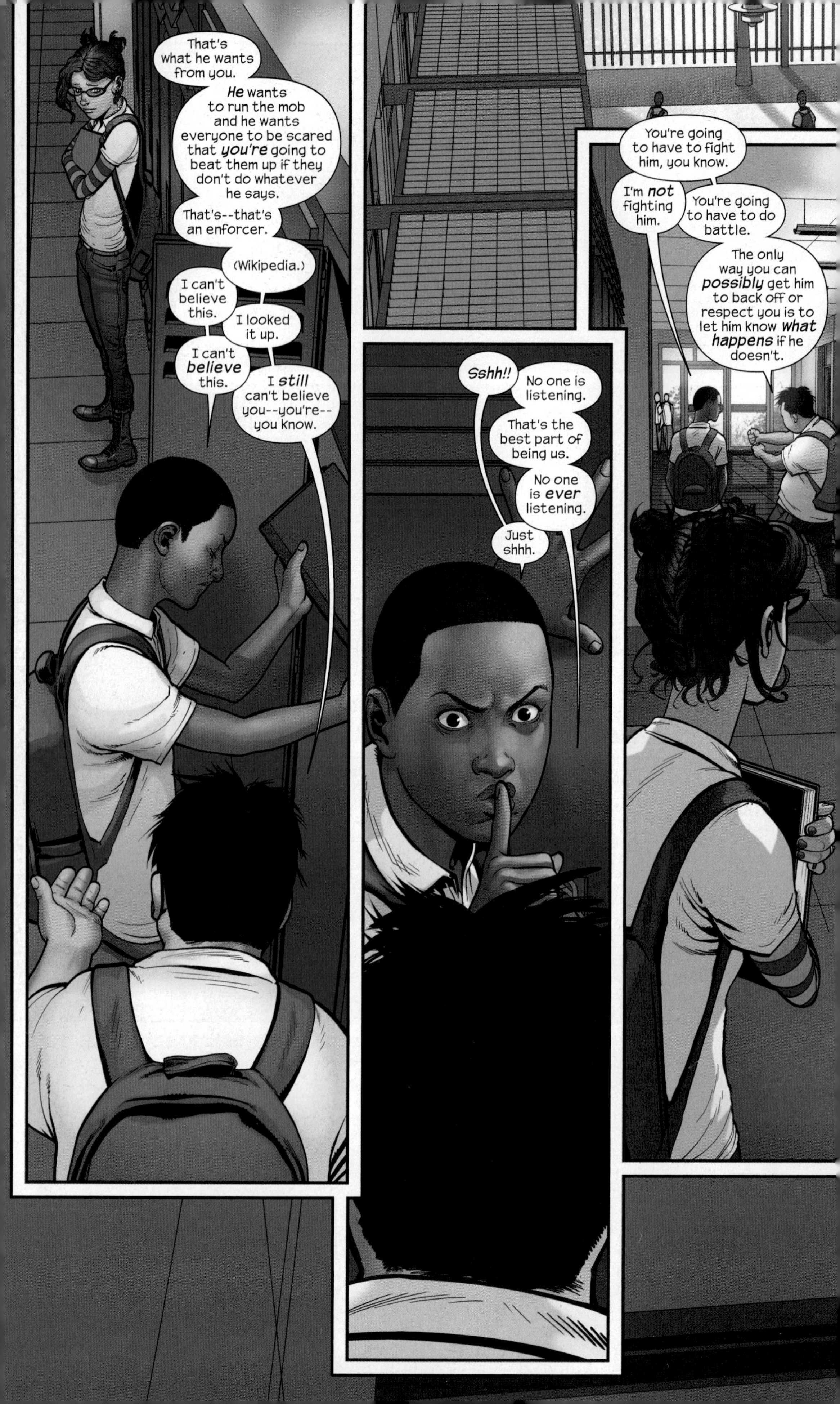
That's what he wants from you.
He wants to run the mob and he wants everyone to be scared that you're going to beat them up if they don't do whatever he says.
That's--that's an enforcer.
(Wikipedia.)
I can't believe this.
I looked it up.
I can't believe this.
I still can't believe you--you're--you know.
You're going to have to fight him, you know.
I'm not fighting him.
You're going to have to do battle.
The only way you can possibly get him to back off or respect you is to let him know what happens if he doesn't.
Sshh!!
No one is listening.
That's the best part of being us.
No one is ever listening.
Just shhh.

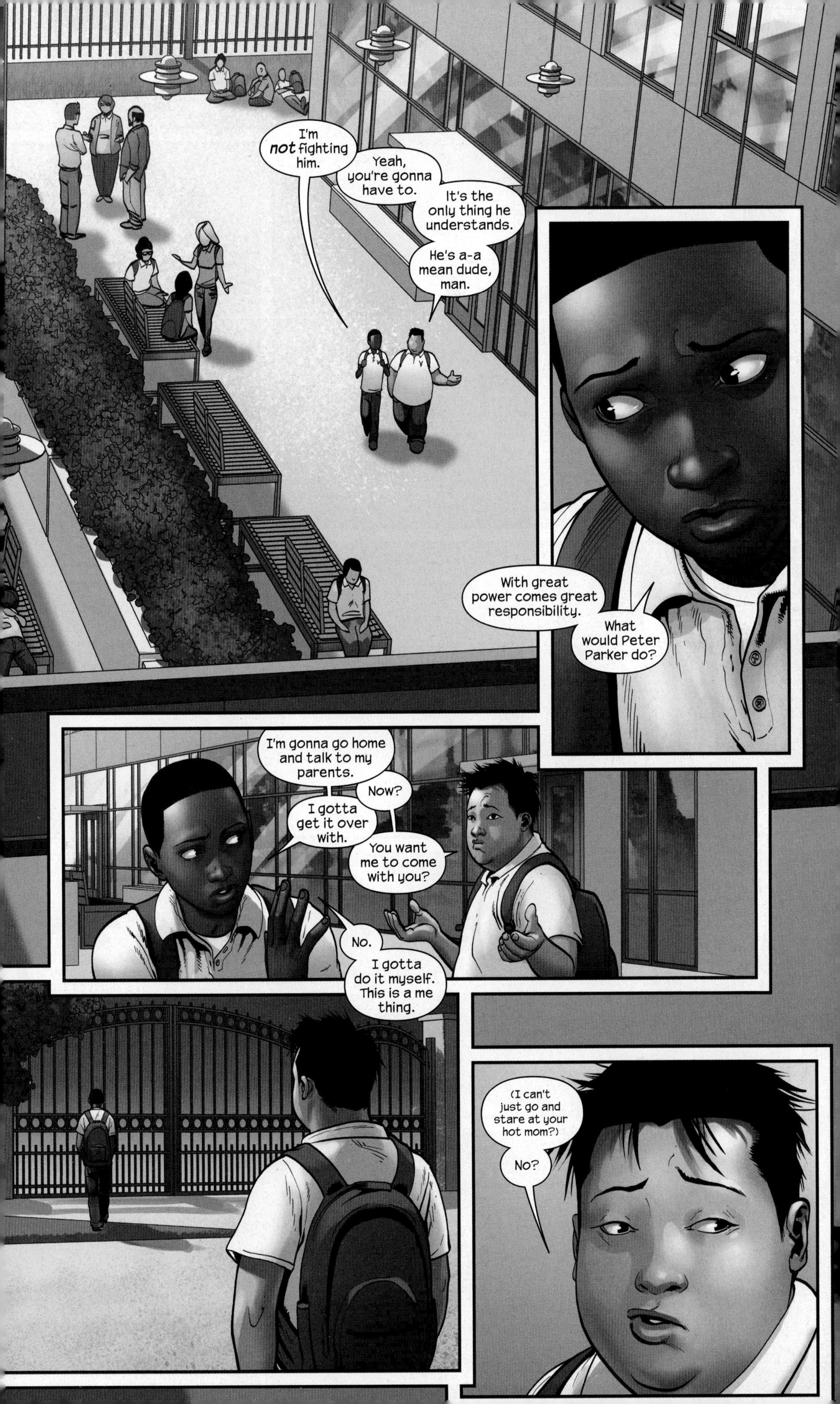
I'm not fighting him.
Yeah, you're gonna have to.
It's the only thing he understands.
He's a-a mean dude, man.
With great power comes great responsibility.
What would Peter Parker do?
I'm gonna go home and talk to my parents.
Now?
I gotta get it over with.
You want me to come with you?
No.
I gotta do it myself. This is a me thing.
(I can't just go and stare at your hot mom?)
No?

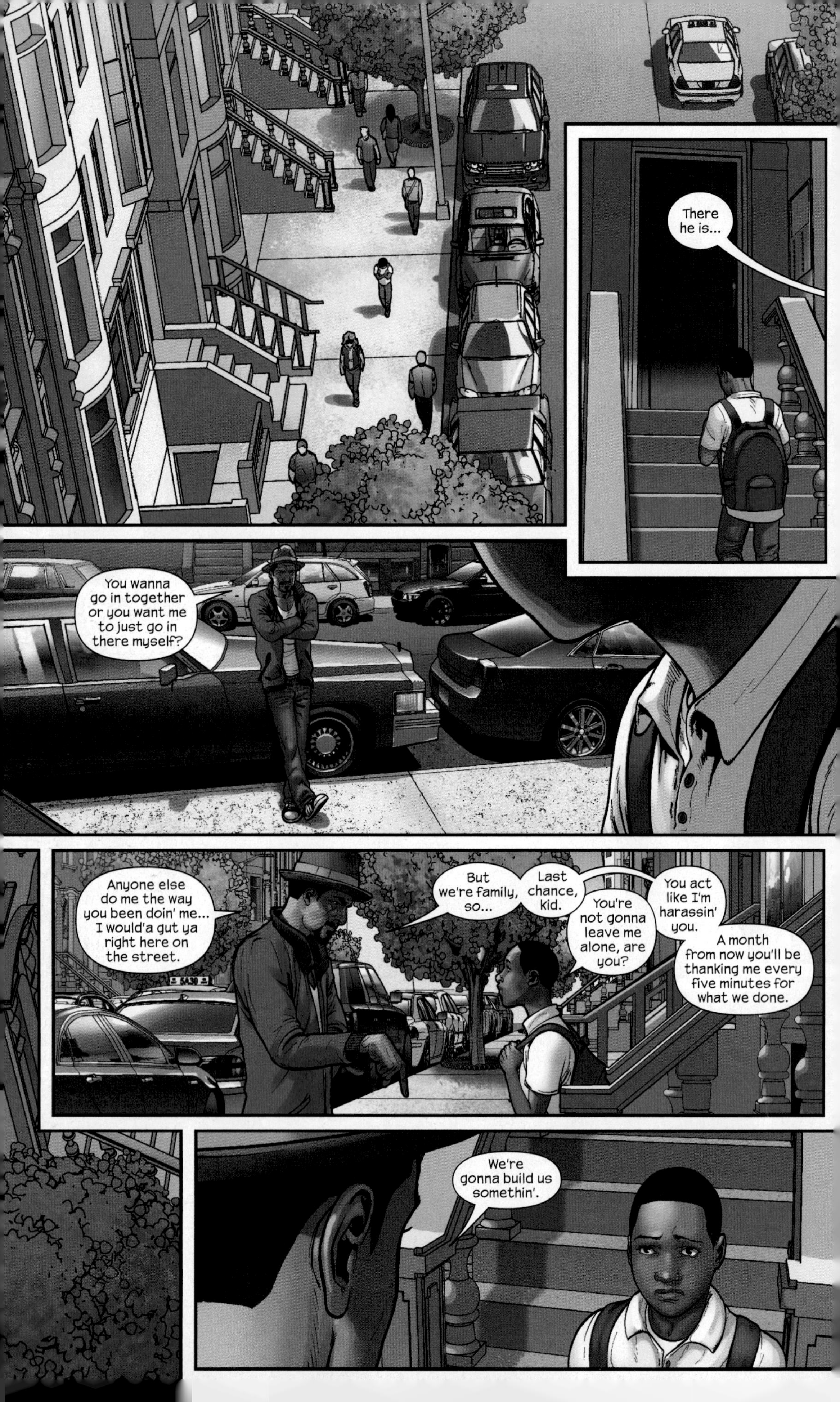

There he is...
You wanna go in together or you want me to just go in there myself?
Anyone else do me the way you been doin' me... I would'a gut ya right here on the street.
But we're family, so...
Last chance, kid.
You're not gonna leave me alone, are you?
You act like I'm harassin' you.
A month from now you'll be thanking me every five minutes for what we done.
We're gonna build us somethin'.

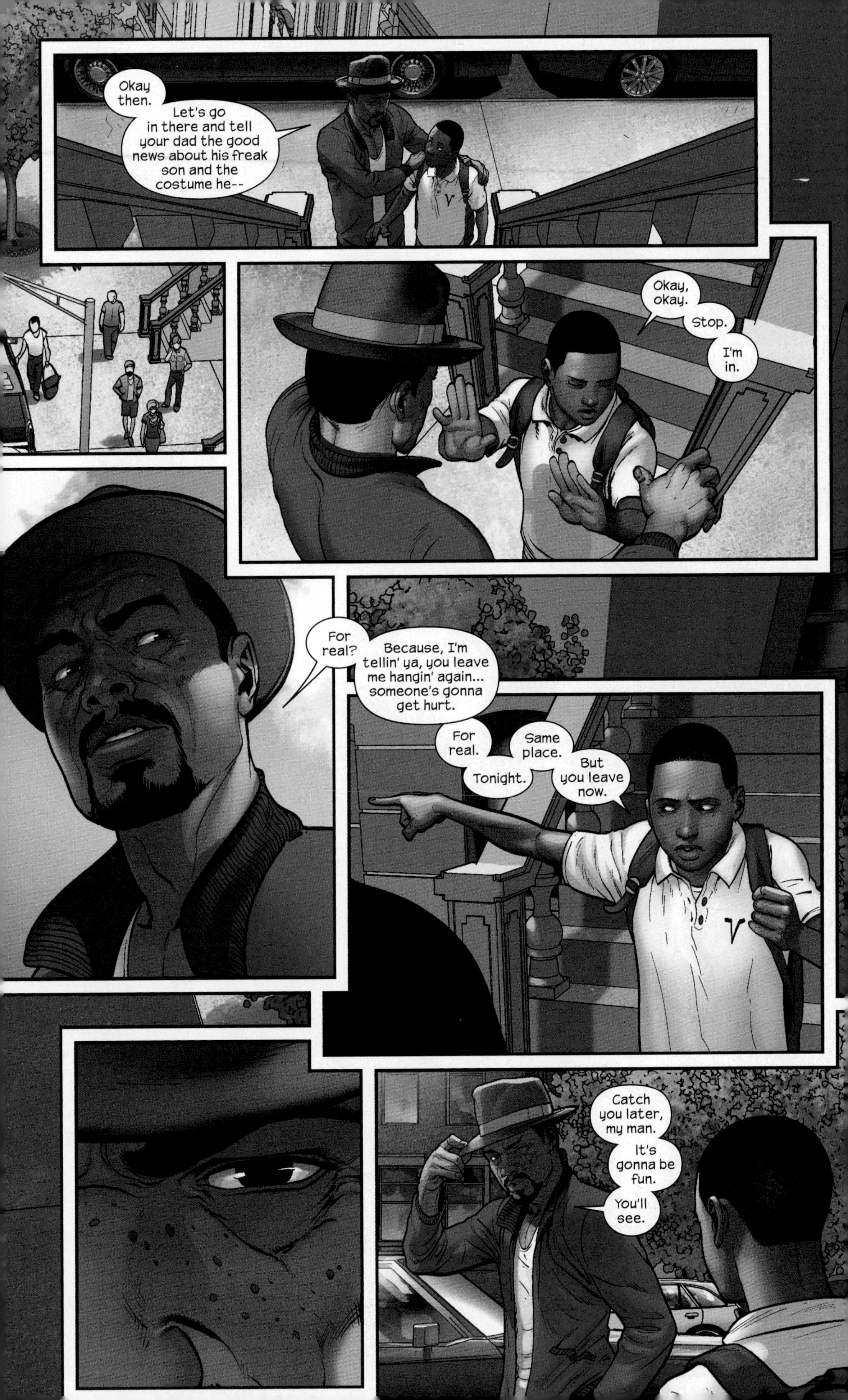

Okay then.
Let's go in there and tell your dad the good news about his freak son and the costume he--
Okay, okay.
Stop.
I'm in.
For real?
Because, I'm tellin' ya, you leave me hangin' again... someone's gonna get hurt.
For real.
Tonight.
Same place.
But you leave now.
Catch you later, my man.
It's gonna be fun.
You'll see.

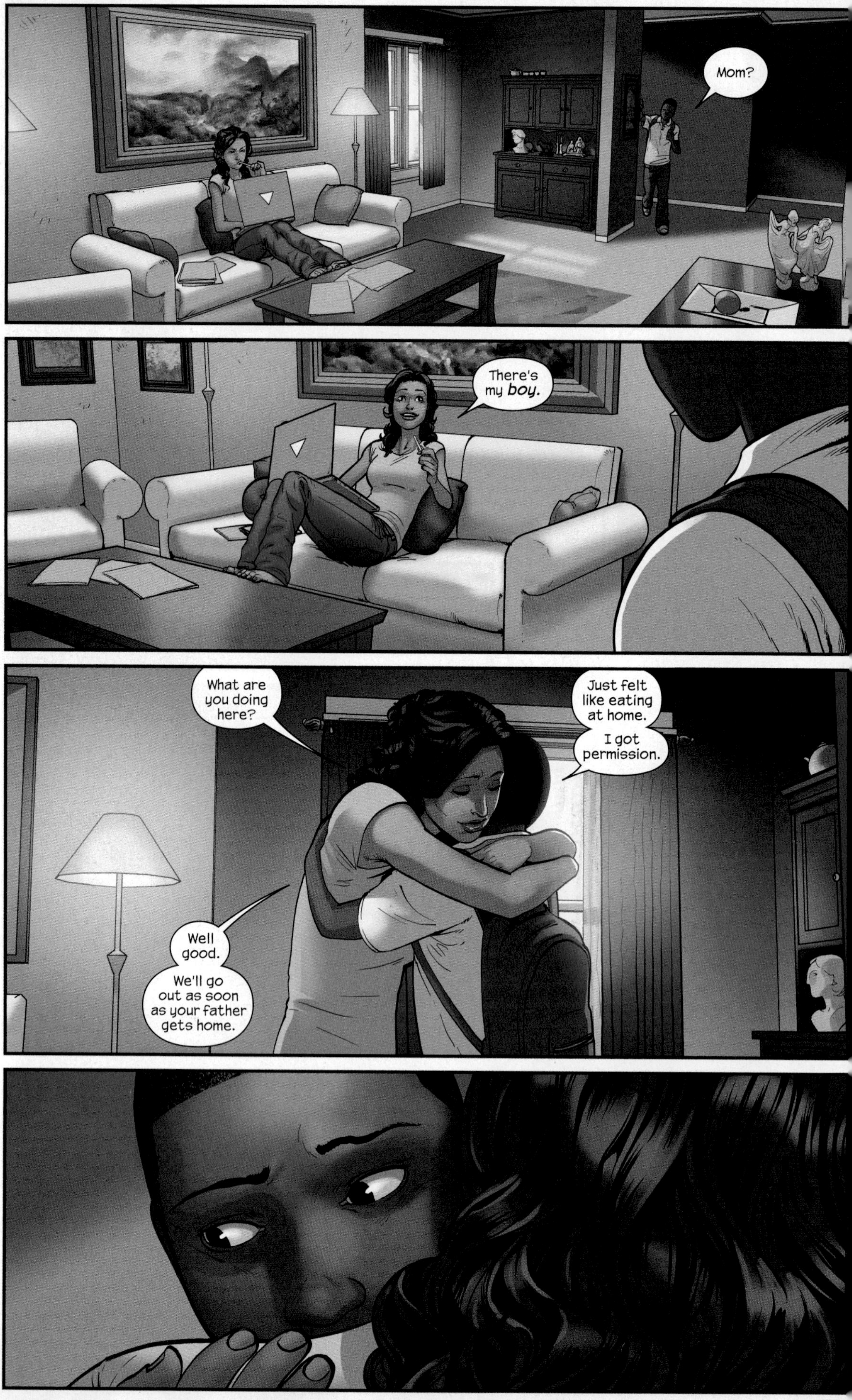
Mom?
There's my *boy.*
What are you doing here?
Just felt like eating at home.
I got permission.
Well good.
We'll go out as soon as your father gets home.

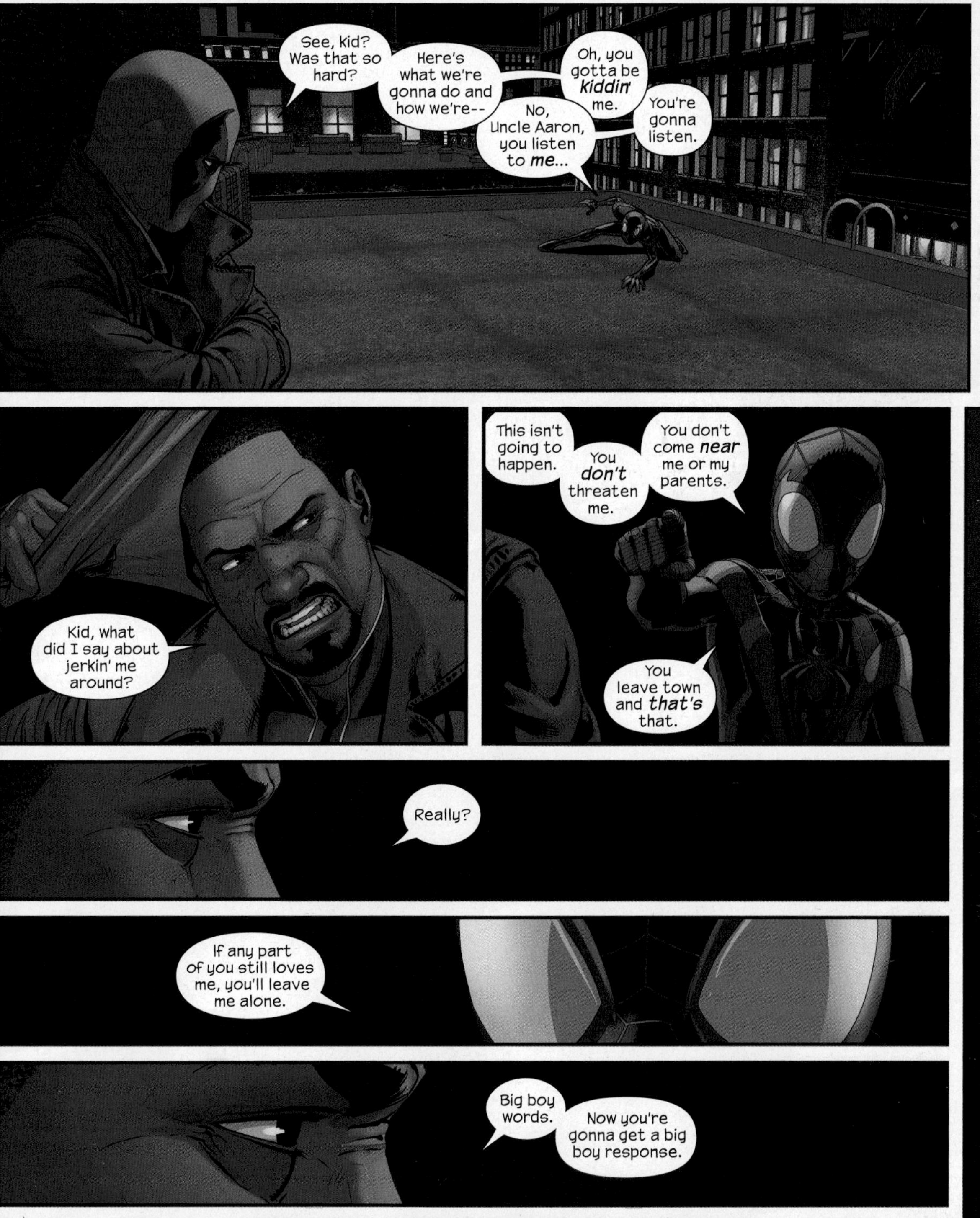
See, kid? Was that so hard?
Here's what we're gonna do and how we're--
Oh, you gotta be *kiddin'* me.
You're gonna listen.
No, Uncle Aaron, you listen to *me*...
Kid, what did I say about jerkin' me around?
This isn't going to happen.
You *don't* threaten me.
You don't come *near* me or my parents.
You leave town and *that's* that.
Really?
If any part of you still loves me, you'll leave me alone.
Big boy words.
Now you're gonna get a big boy response.

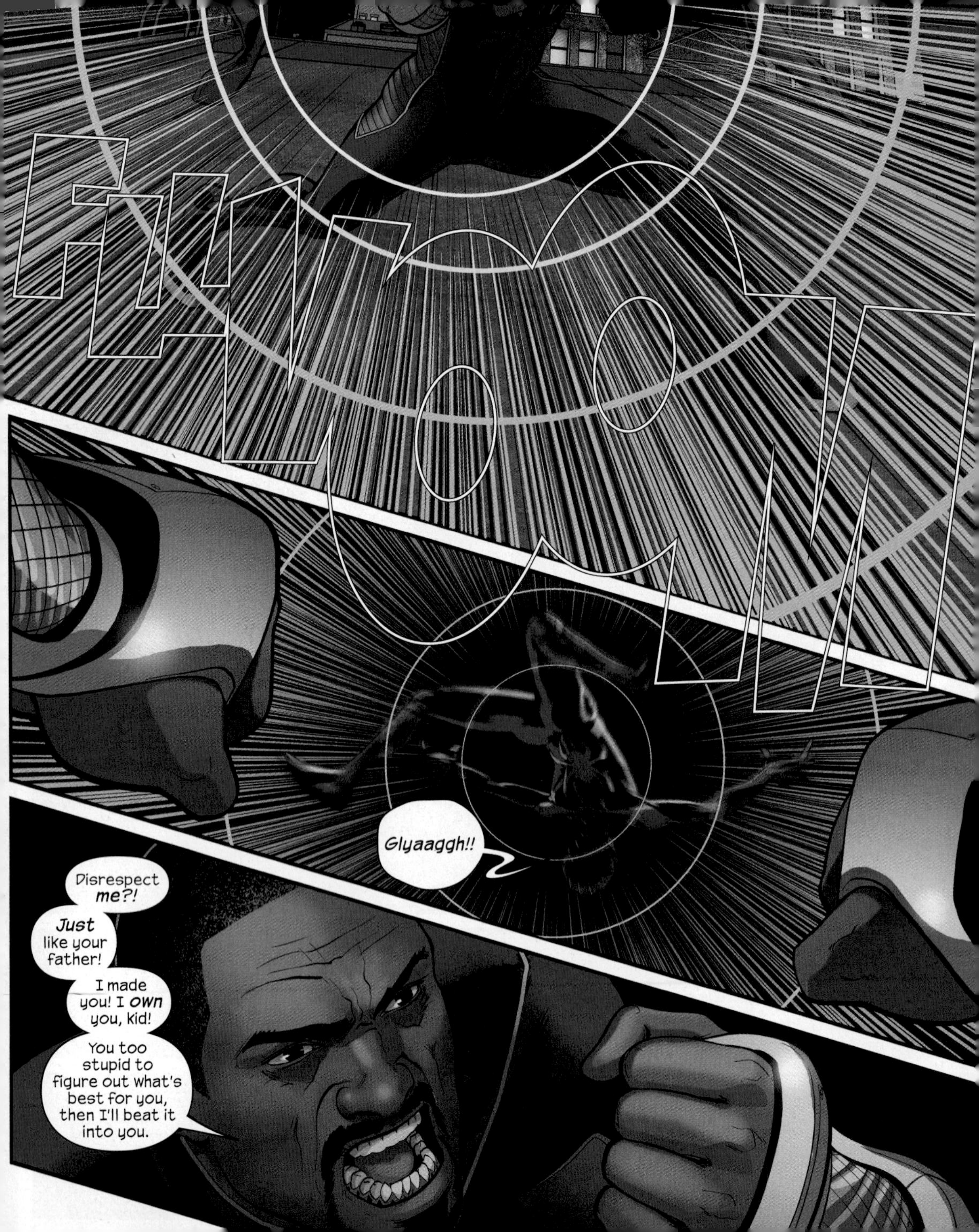
Glyaaggh!!
Disrespect *me?!*
Just like your father!
I made you! I *own* you, kid!
You too stupid to figure out what's best for you, then I'll beat it into you.

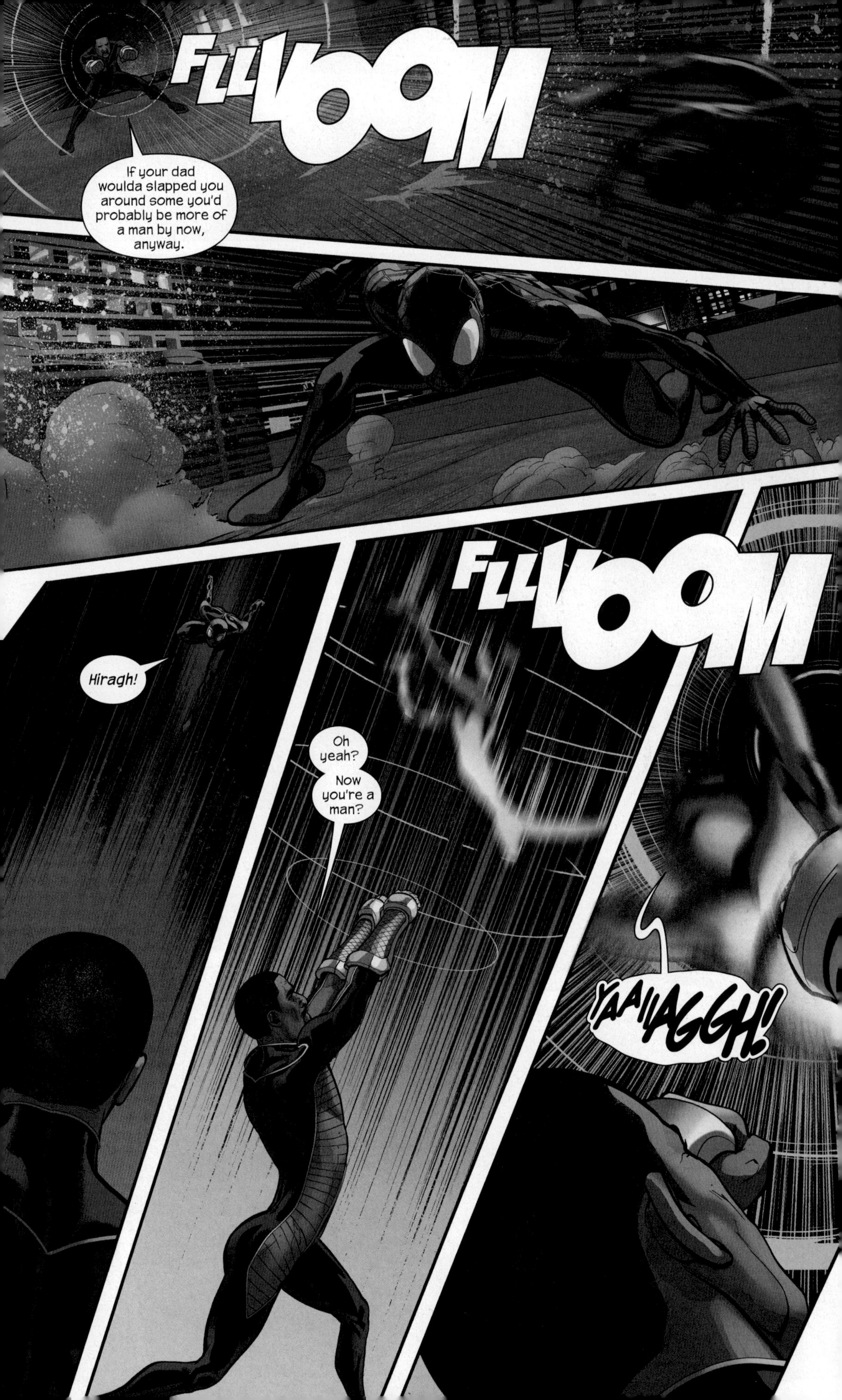
FLLVOOM
If your dad woulda slapped you around some you'd probably be more of a man by now, anyway.
Hiragh!
FLLVOOM
Oh yeah?
Now you're a man?
YAAIIAGGH!

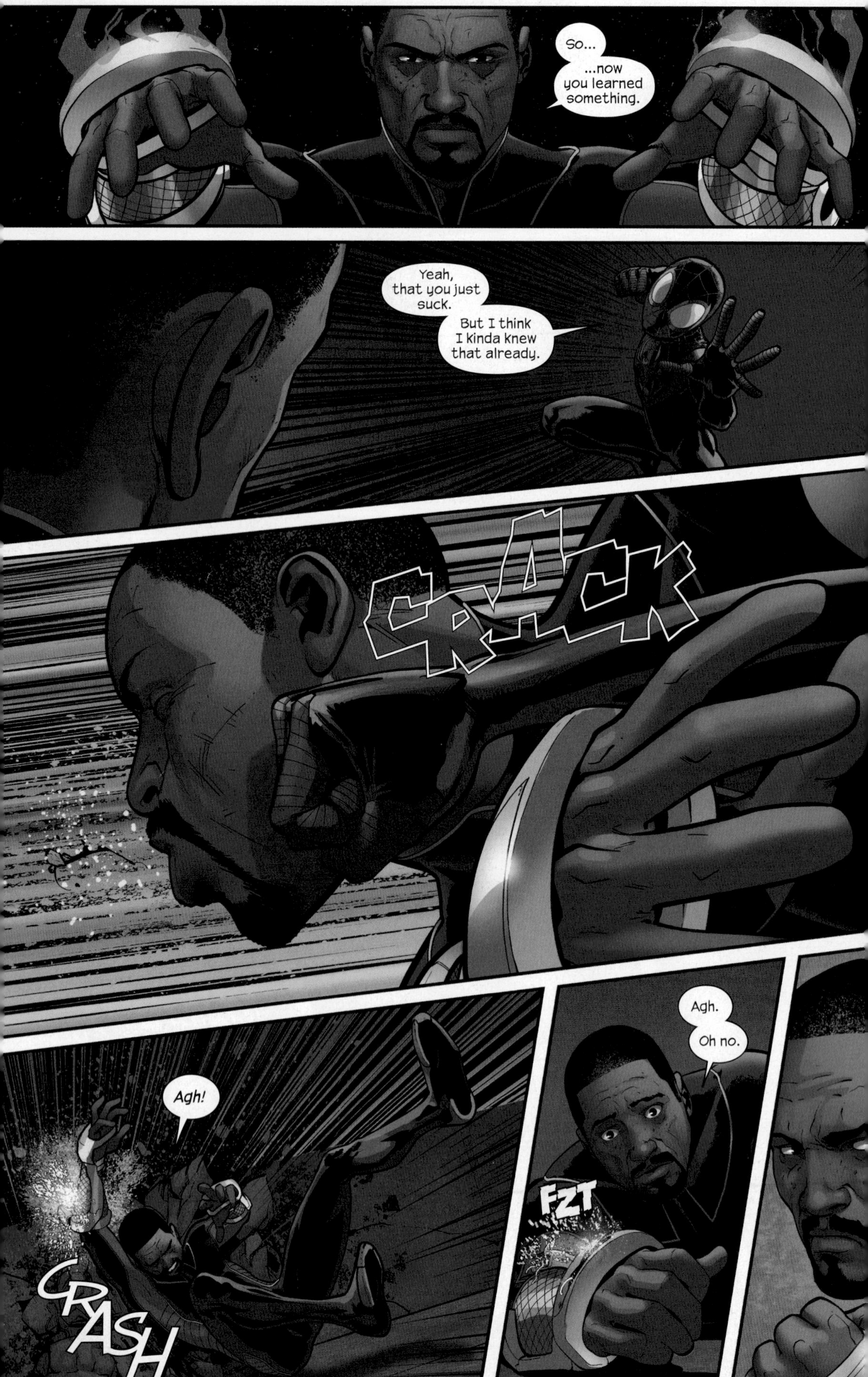

So...
...now you learned something.
Yeah, that you just suck.
But I think I kinda knew that already.
CRACK
Agh!
CRASH
Agh.
Oh no.
FZT

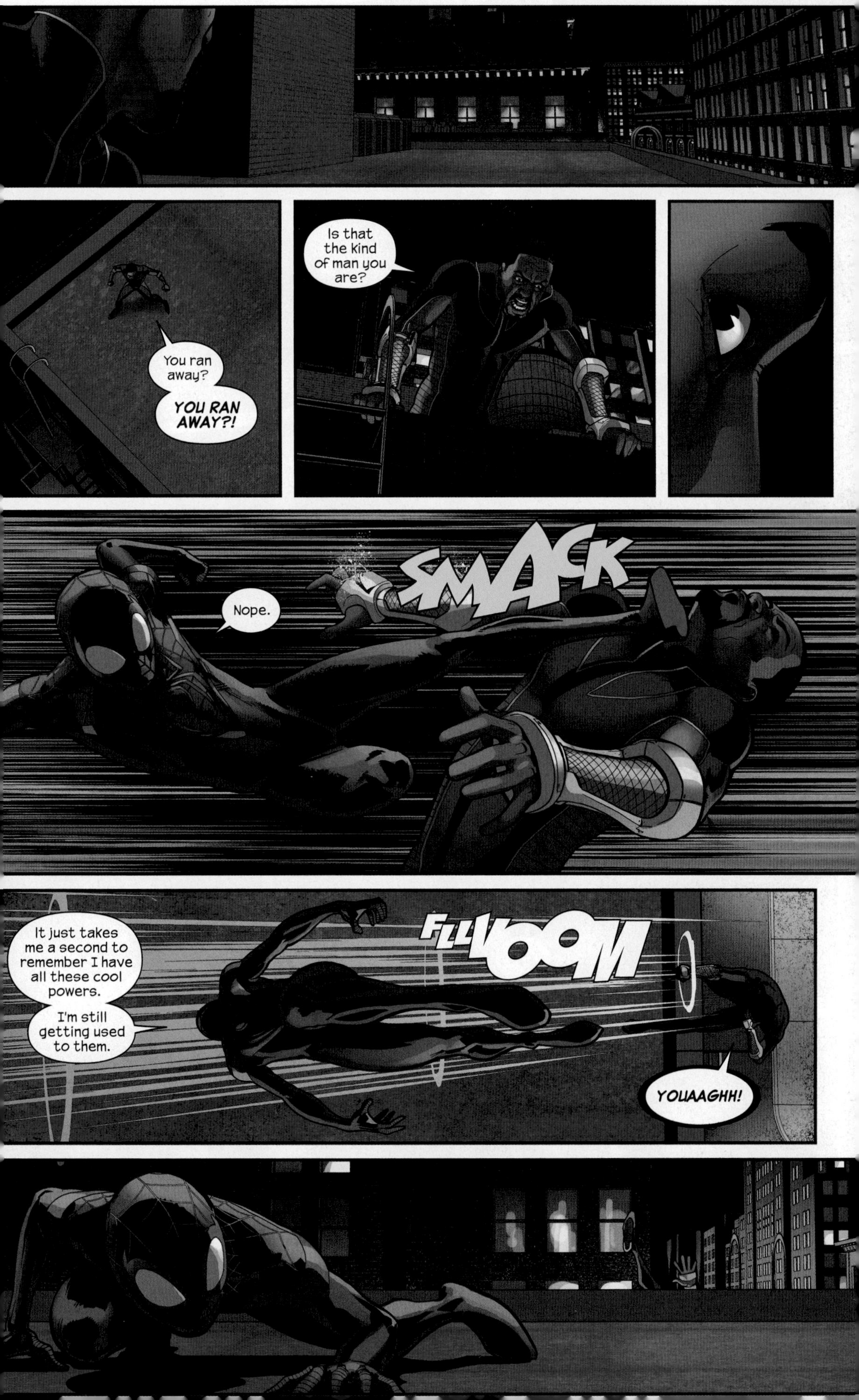
You ran away?
YOU RAN AWAY?!
Is that the kind of man you are?
Nope.
SMACK
It just takes me a second to remember I have all these cool powers.
I'm still getting used to them.
FLLLVOOM
YOUAAGHH!

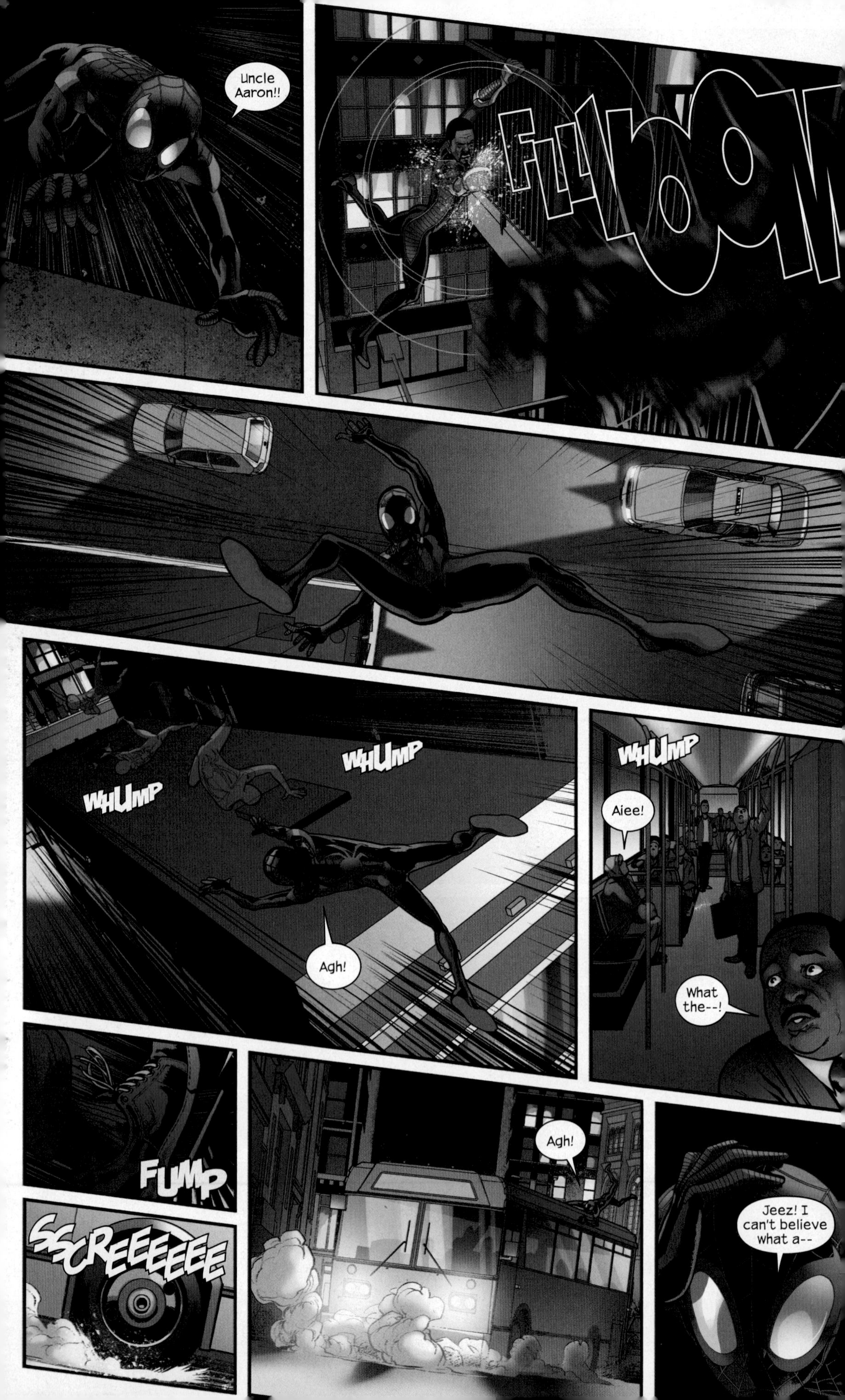
Uncle Aaron!!
FZZWOOM
WHUMP
WHUMP
Agh!
WHUMP
Aiee!
What the--!
FUMP
SSCREEEEEEE
Agh!
Jeez! I can't believe what a--

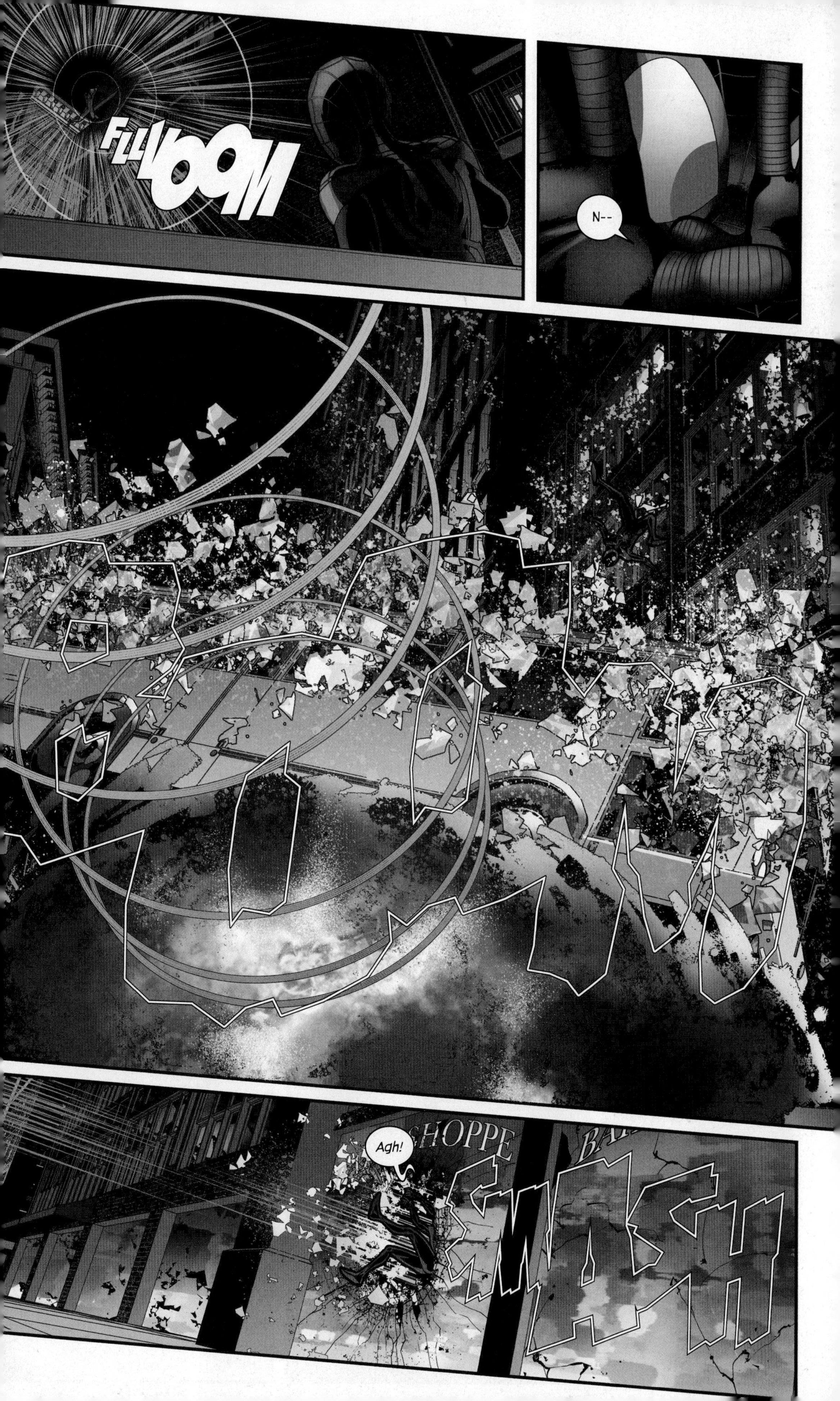
FLLVOOM
N--
Agh!
SHOPPE
SMASH

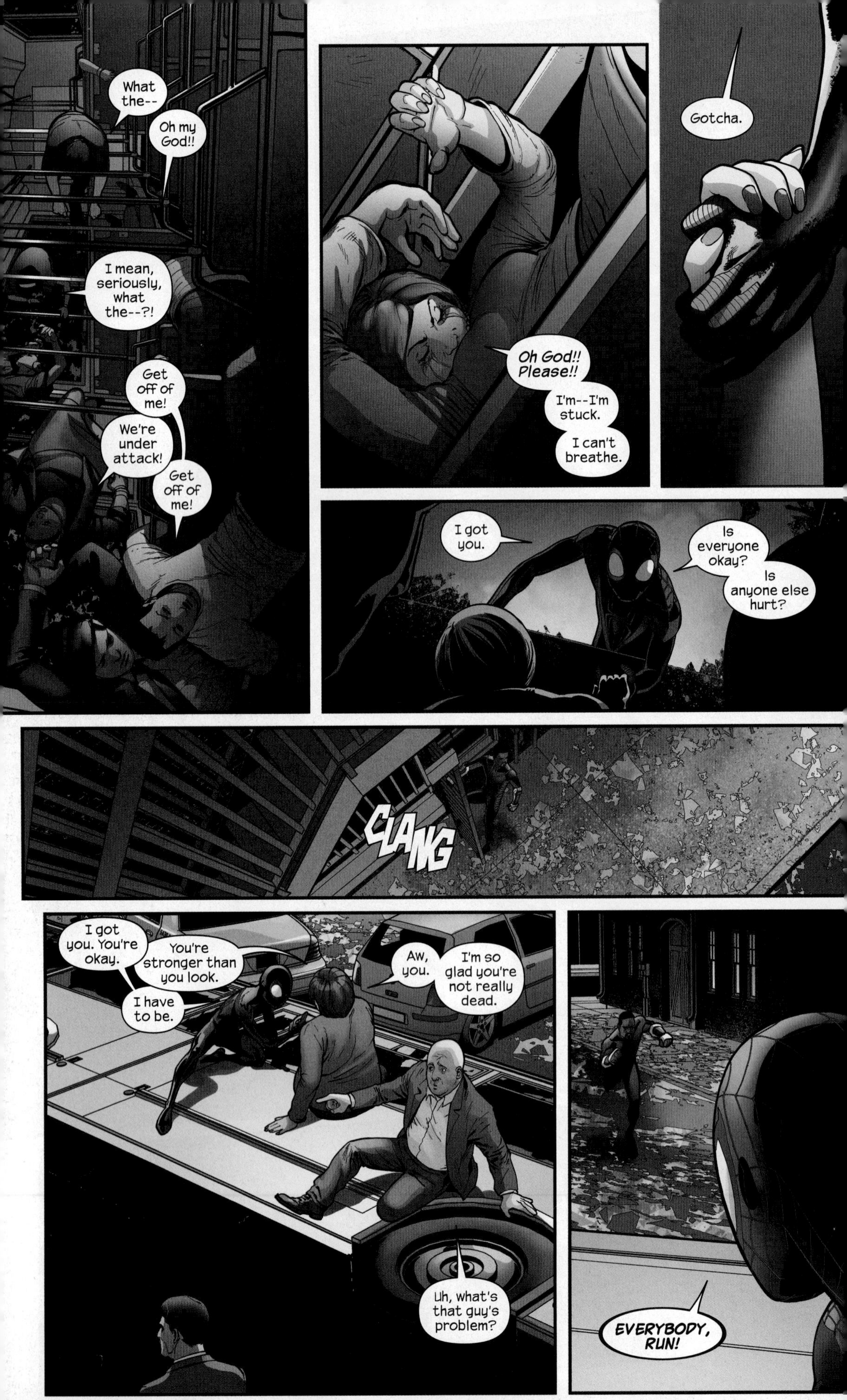

What the--
Oh my God!!
I mean, seriously, what the--?!
Get off of me!
We're under attack!
Get off of me!
Oh God!! Please!!
I'm--I'm stuck.
I can't breathe.
Gotcha.
I got you.
Is everyone okay?
Is anyone else hurt?
CLANG
I got you. You're okay.
You're stronger than you look.
I have to be.
Aw, you.
I'm so glad you're not really dead.
Uh, what's that guy's problem?
EVERYBODY, RUN!

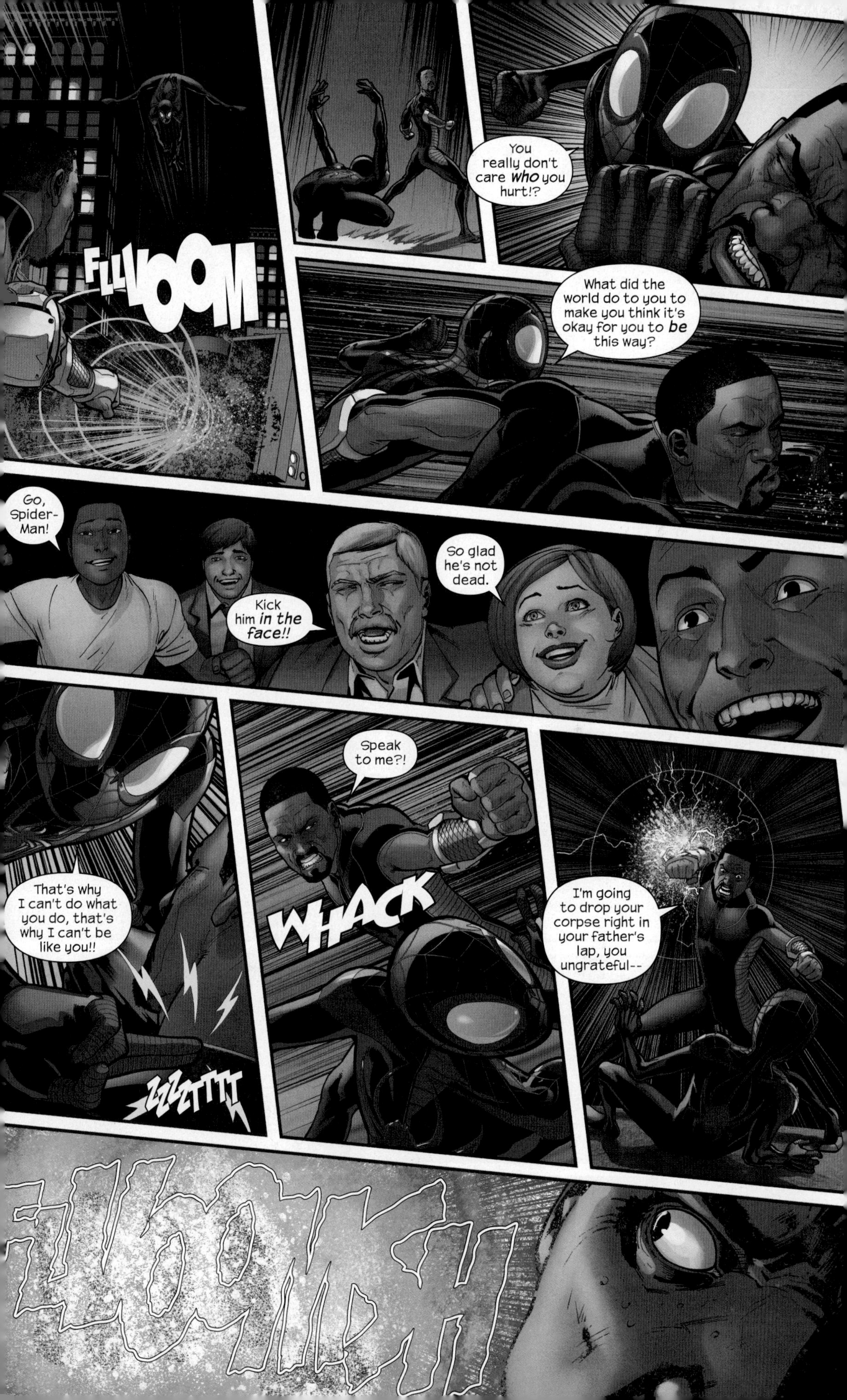
FLLLVOOM
You really don't care *who* you hurt!?
What did the world do to you to make you think it's okay for you to *be* this way?
Go, Spider-Man!
Kick him *in the face!!*
So glad he's not dead.
That's why I can't do what you do, that's why I can't be like you!!
ZZZZTTTTT
Speak to me?!
WHACK
I'm going to drop your corpse right in your father's lap, you ungrateful--

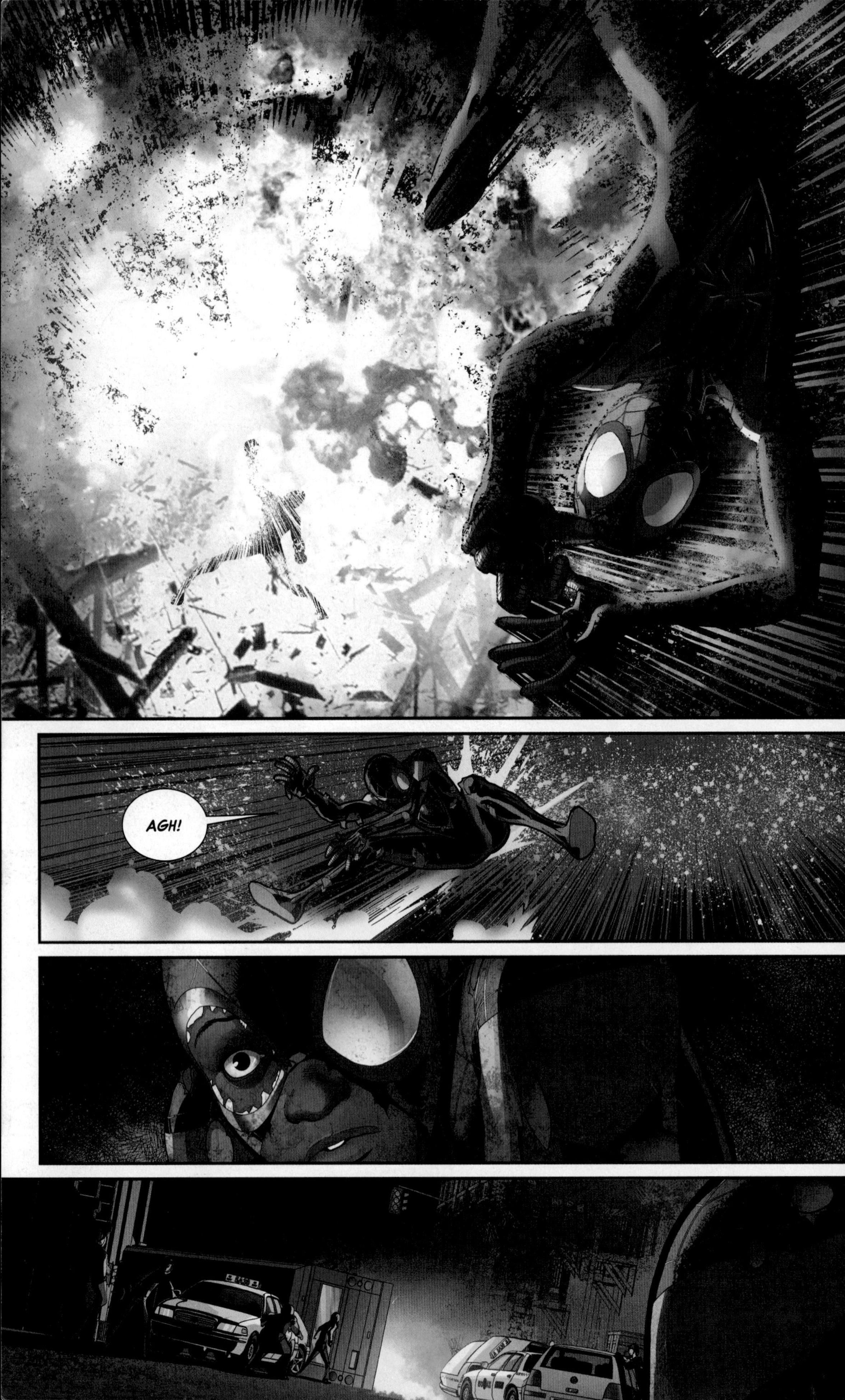
AGH!

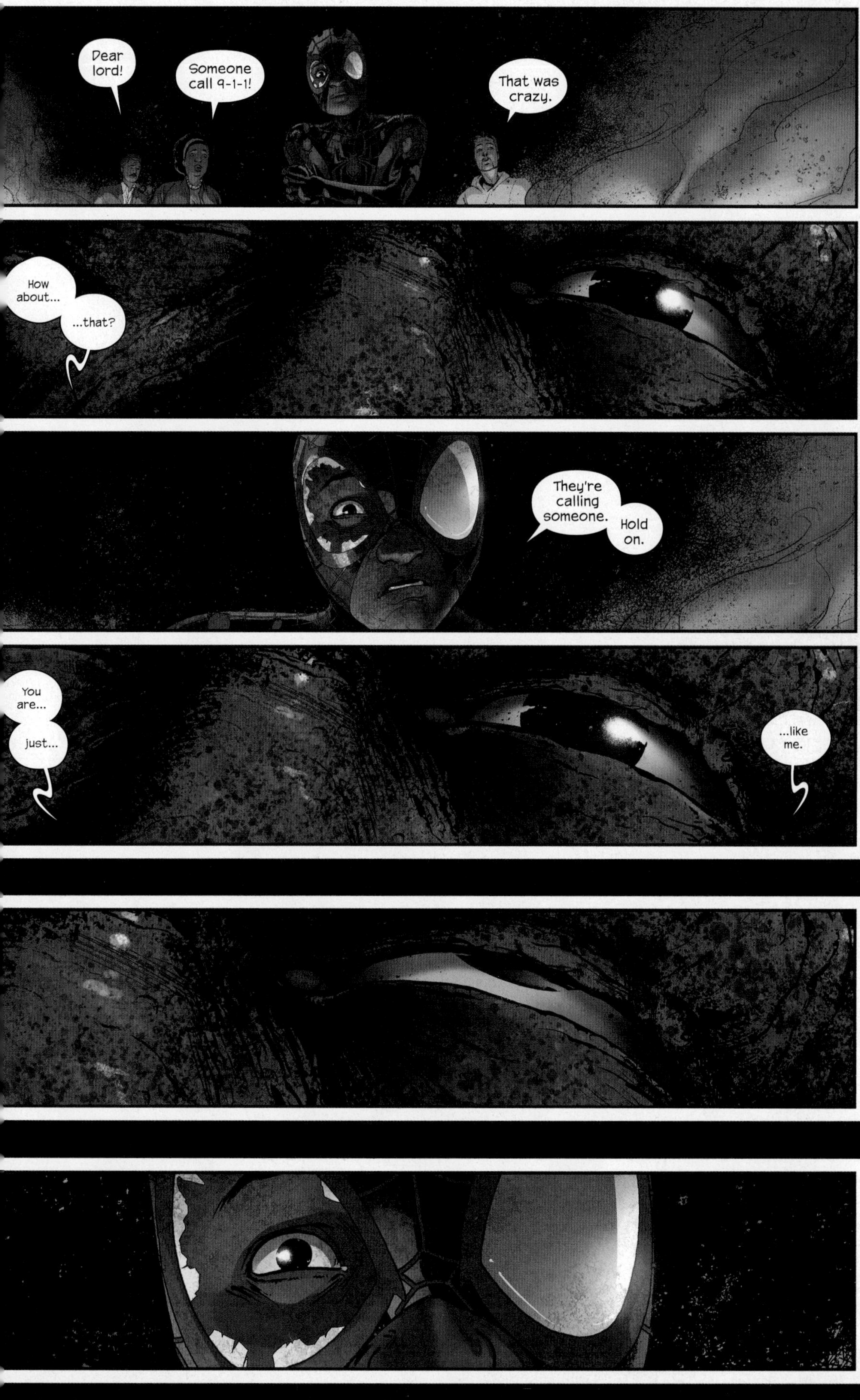
Dear lord!
Someone call 9-1-1!
That was crazy.
How about...
...that?
They're calling someone.
Hold on.
You are...
just...
...like me.

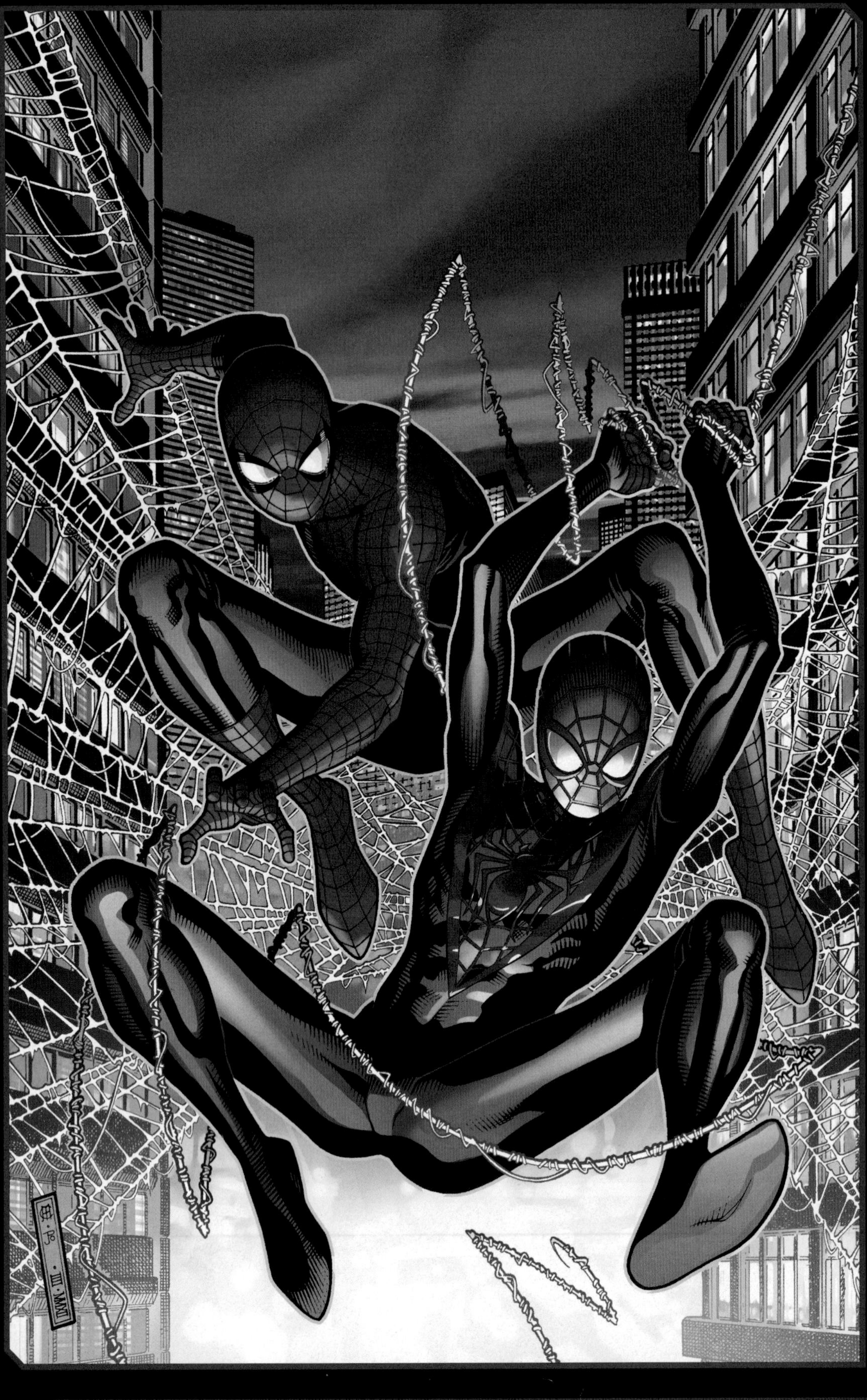

SPIDER-MEN #1

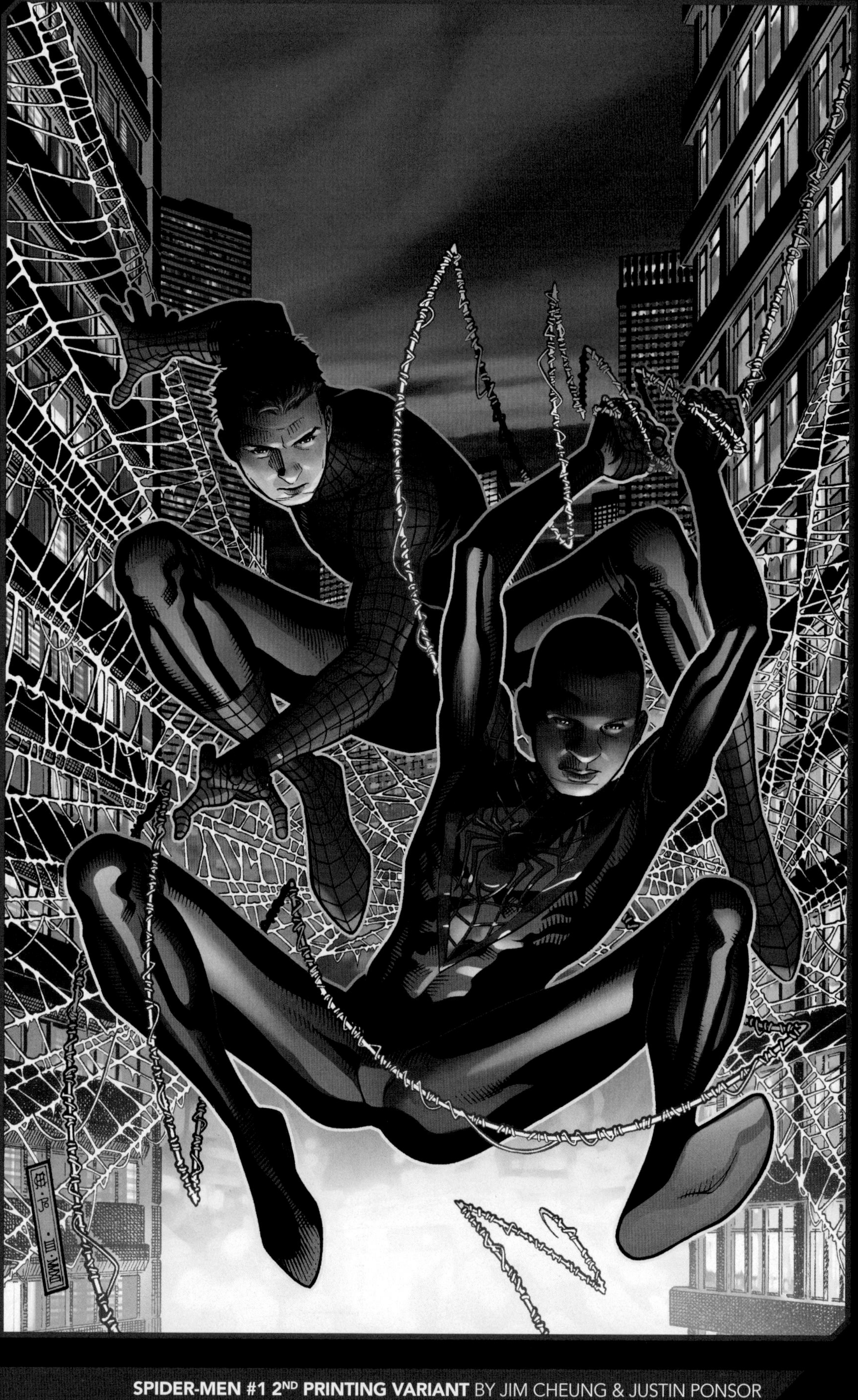

SPIDER-MEN #1 2ND PRINTING VARIANT BY JIM CHEUNG & JUSTIN PONSOR

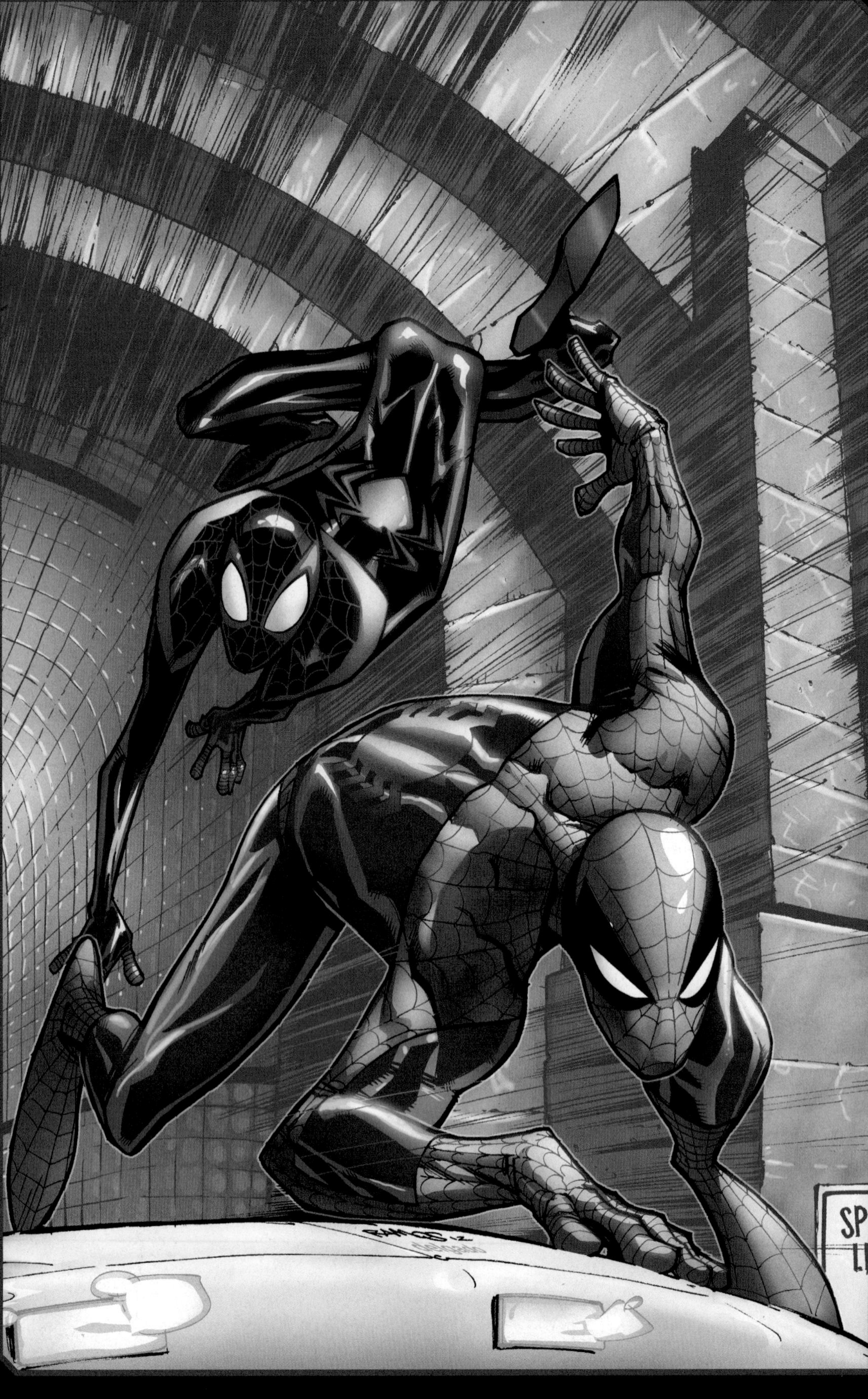

SPIDER-MEN #1 VARIANT BY HUMBERTO RAMOS & EDGAR DELGADO

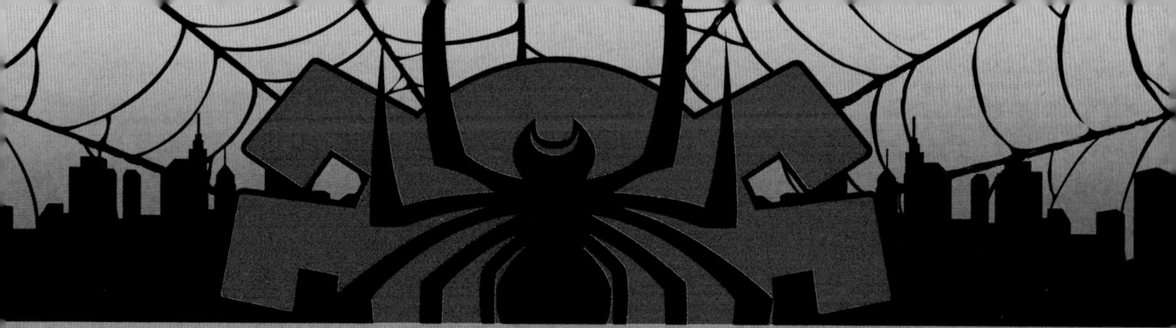

hile attending a demonstration in radiology, high school student Peter Parker was bitten by a ider which had accidentally been exposed to radioactive rays. Through a miracle of science, eter soon found that he gained the spider's powers and had, in effect, become a human spider! om that day and he was

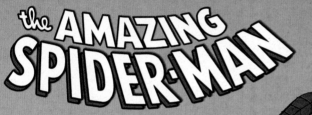

the AMAZING SPIDER-MAN

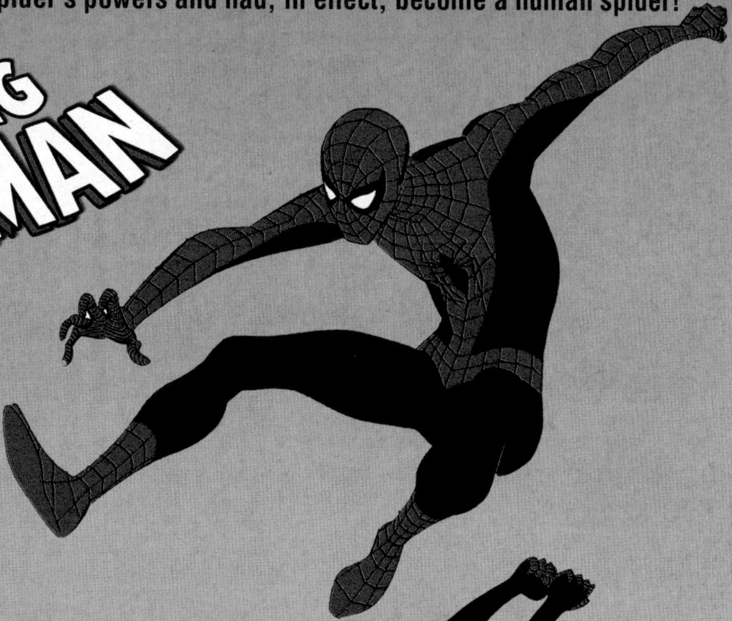

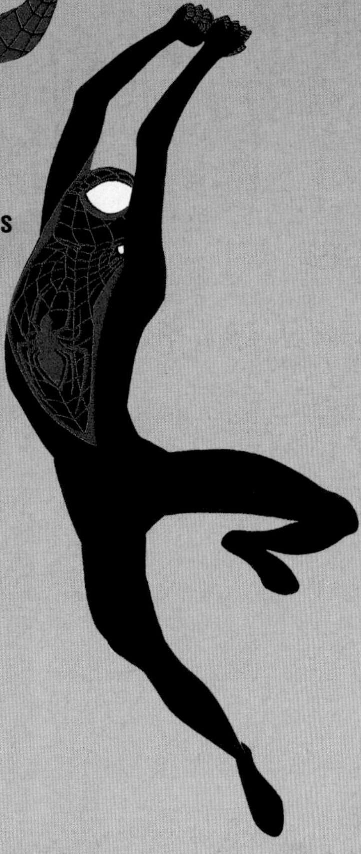

a world where Peter Parker was shot and killed, grade schooler iles Morales is bitten by a stolen, genetically altered Spider that ants him incredible arachnid-like powers.

e has chosen to dedicate his life to the legacy of Spider-Man. He is

ULTIMATE SPIDER-MAN

When you see this: AR, open up the MARVEL AR APP (available on applicable Apple ® iOS or Android TM devices) and use your camera-enabled device to unlock extra-special exclusive features!

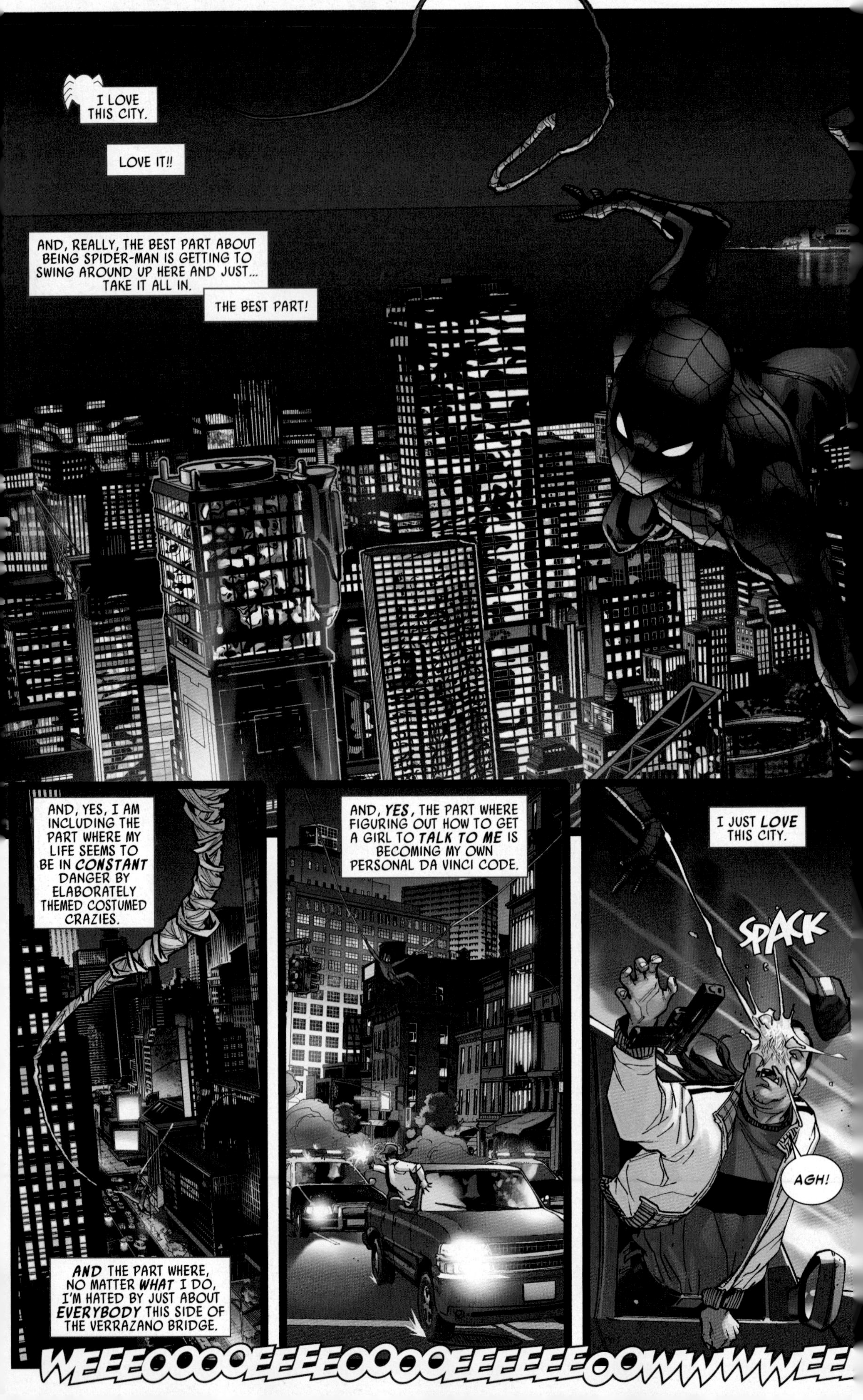
I LOVE THIS CITY.
LOVE IT!!
AND, REALLY, THE BEST PART ABOUT BEING SPIDER-MAN IS GETTING TO SWING AROUND UP HERE AND JUST... TAKE IT ALL IN.
THE BEST PART!
AND, YES, I AM INCLUDING THE PART WHERE MY LIFE SEEMS TO BE IN CONSTANT DANGER BY ELABORATELY THEMED COSTUMED CRAZIES.
AND THE PART WHERE, NO MATTER WHAT I DO, I'M HATED BY JUST ABOUT EVERYBODY THIS SIDE OF THE VERRAZANO BRIDGE.
AND, YES, THE PART WHERE FIGURING OUT HOW TO GET A GIRL TO TALK TO ME IS BECOMING MY OWN PERSONAL DA VINCI CODE.
I JUST LOVE THIS CITY.
SPACK
AGH!
WEEEOOOOEEEEOOOOEEEEEEOOWWWWEE

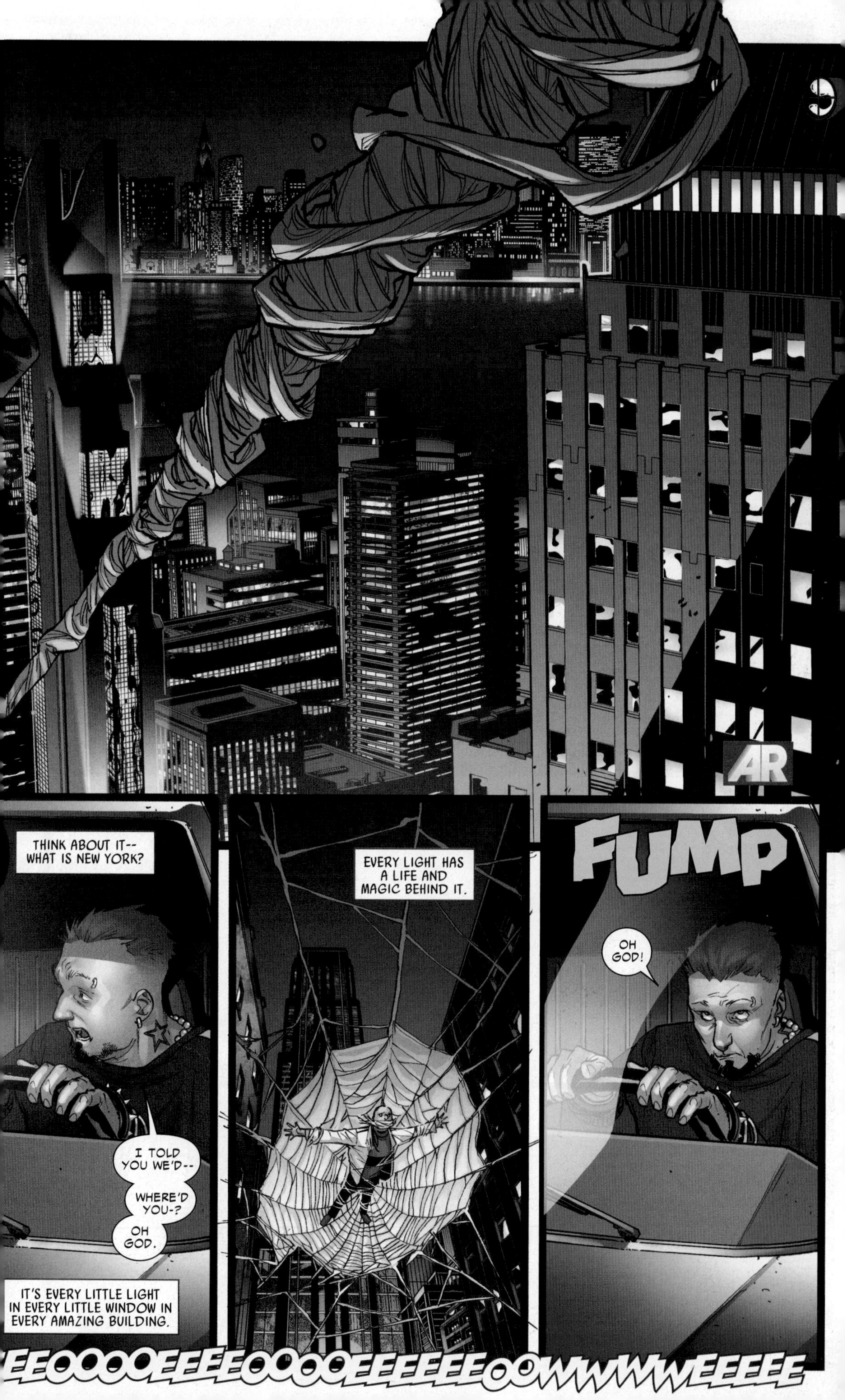
THINK ABOUT IT-- WHAT IS NEW YORK?
I TOLD YOU WE'D--
WHERE'D YOU-?
OH GOD.
IT'S EVERY LITTLE LIGHT IN EVERY LITTLE WINDOW IN EVERY AMAZING BUILDING.
EVERY LIGHT HAS A LIFE AND MAGIC BEHIND IT.
FUMP
OH GOD!
EEOOOOEEEEOOOOEEEEEEEOOWWWWEEEEE

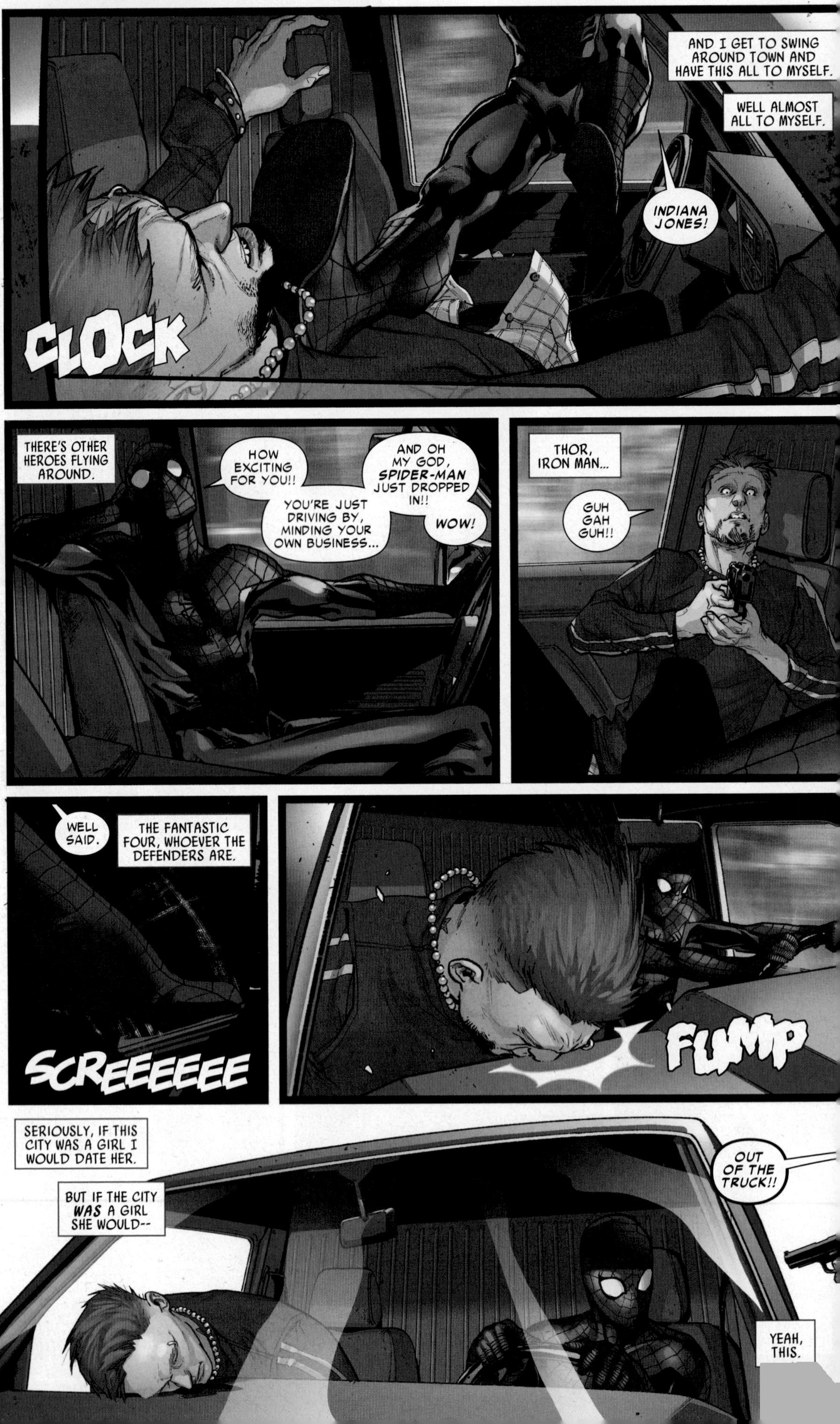
AND I GET TO SWING AROUND TOWN AND HAVE THIS ALL TO MYSELF.
WELL ALMOST ALL TO MYSELF.
INDIANA JONES!
CLOCK
THERE'S OTHER HEROES FLYING AROUND.
HOW EXCITING FOR YOU!!
YOU'RE JUST DRIVING BY, MINDING YOUR OWN BUSINESS...
AND OH MY GOD, SPIDER-MAN JUST DROPPED IN!!
WOW!
THOR, IRON MAN...
GUH GAH GUH!!
WELL SAID.
THE FANTASTIC FOUR, WHOEVER THE DEFENDERS ARE.
SCREEEEEEE
FUMP
SERIOUSLY, IF THIS CITY WAS A GIRL I WOULD DATE HER.
BUT IF THE CITY WAS A GIRL SHE WOULD--
OUT OF THE TRUCK!!
YEAH, THIS.

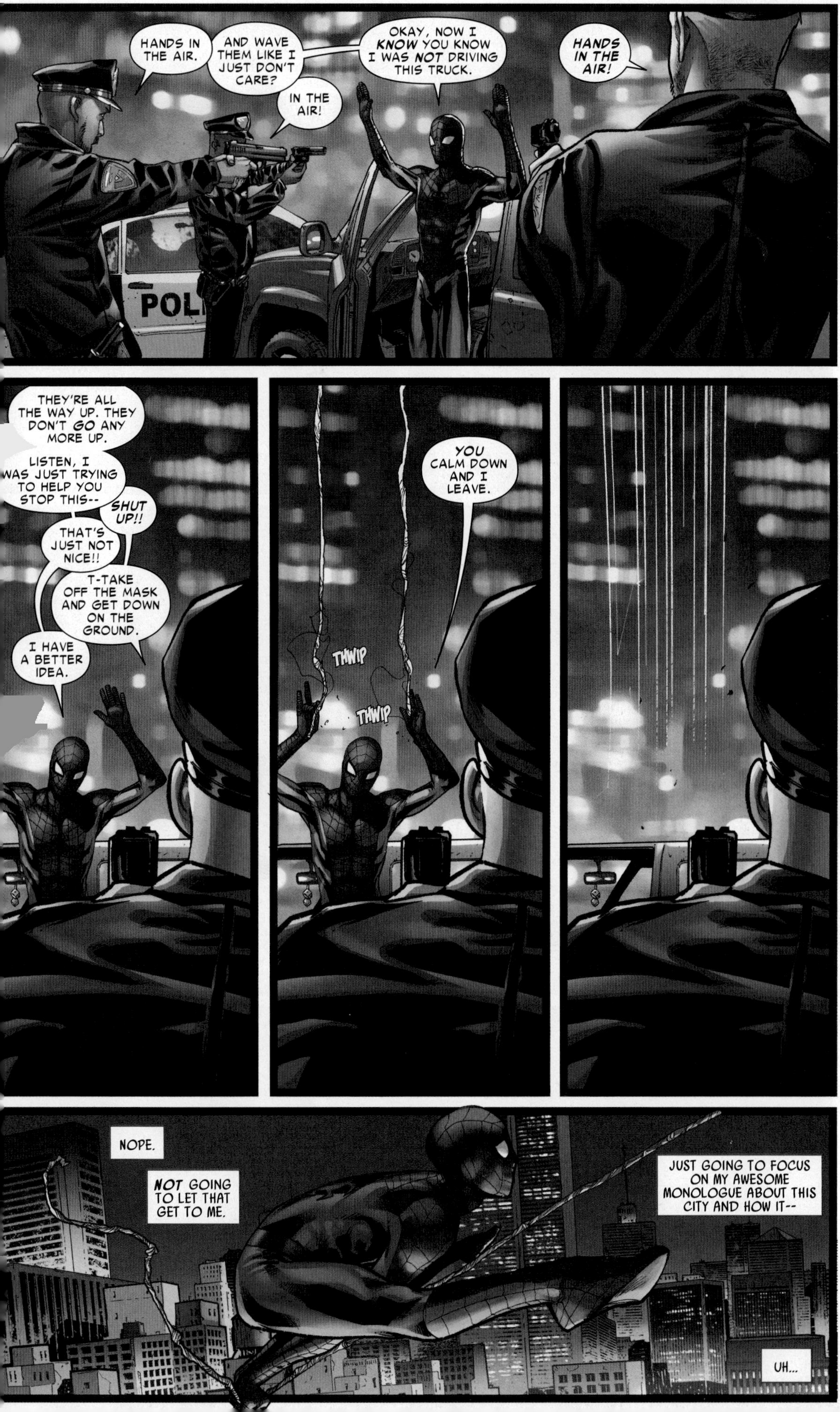
HANDS IN THE AIR.
AND WAVE THEM LIKE I JUST DON'T CARE?
IN THE AIR!
OKAY, NOW I KNOW YOU KNOW I WAS NOT DRIVING THIS TRUCK.
HANDS IN THE AIR!
POLI
THEY'RE ALL THE WAY UP. THEY DON'T GO ANY MORE UP.
LISTEN, I WAS JUST TRYING TO HELP YOU STOP THIS--
SHUT UP!!
THAT'S JUST NOT NICE!!
T-TAKE OFF THE MASK AND GET DOWN ON THE GROUND.
I HAVE A BETTER IDEA.
YOU CALM DOWN AND I LEAVE.
THWIP
THWIP
NOPE.
NOT GOING TO LET THAT GET TO ME.
JUST GOING TO FOCUS ON MY AWESOME MONOLOGUE ABOUT THIS CITY AND HOW IT--
UH...

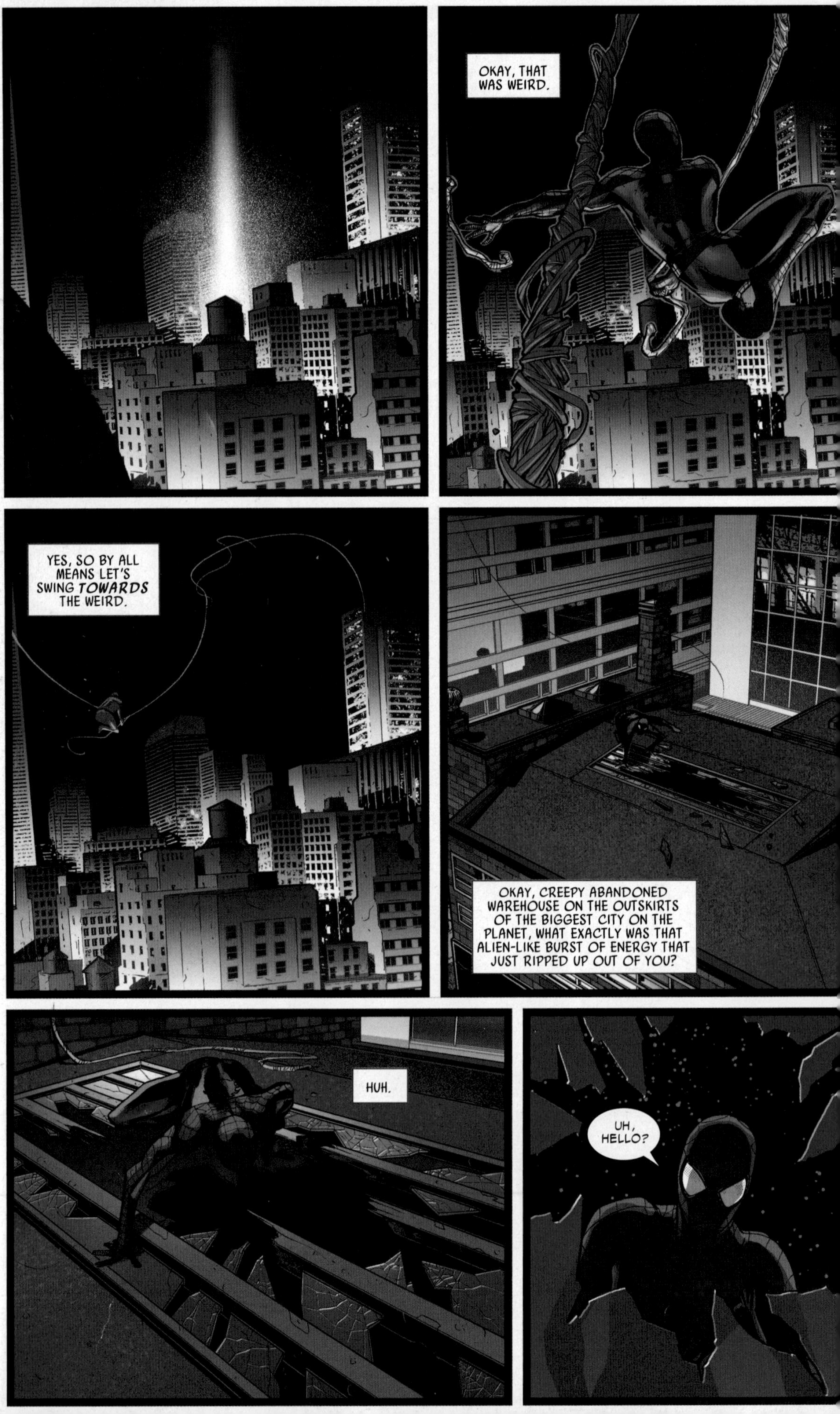
OKAY, THAT WAS WEIRD.
YES, SO BY ALL MEANS LET'S SWING TOWARDS THE WEIRD.
OKAY, CREEPY ABANDONED WAREHOUSE ON THE OUTSKIRTS OF THE BIGGEST CITY ON THE PLANET, WHAT EXACTLY WAS THAT ALIEN-LIKE BURST OF ENERGY THAT JUST RIPPED UP OUT OF YOU?
HUH.
UH, HELLO?

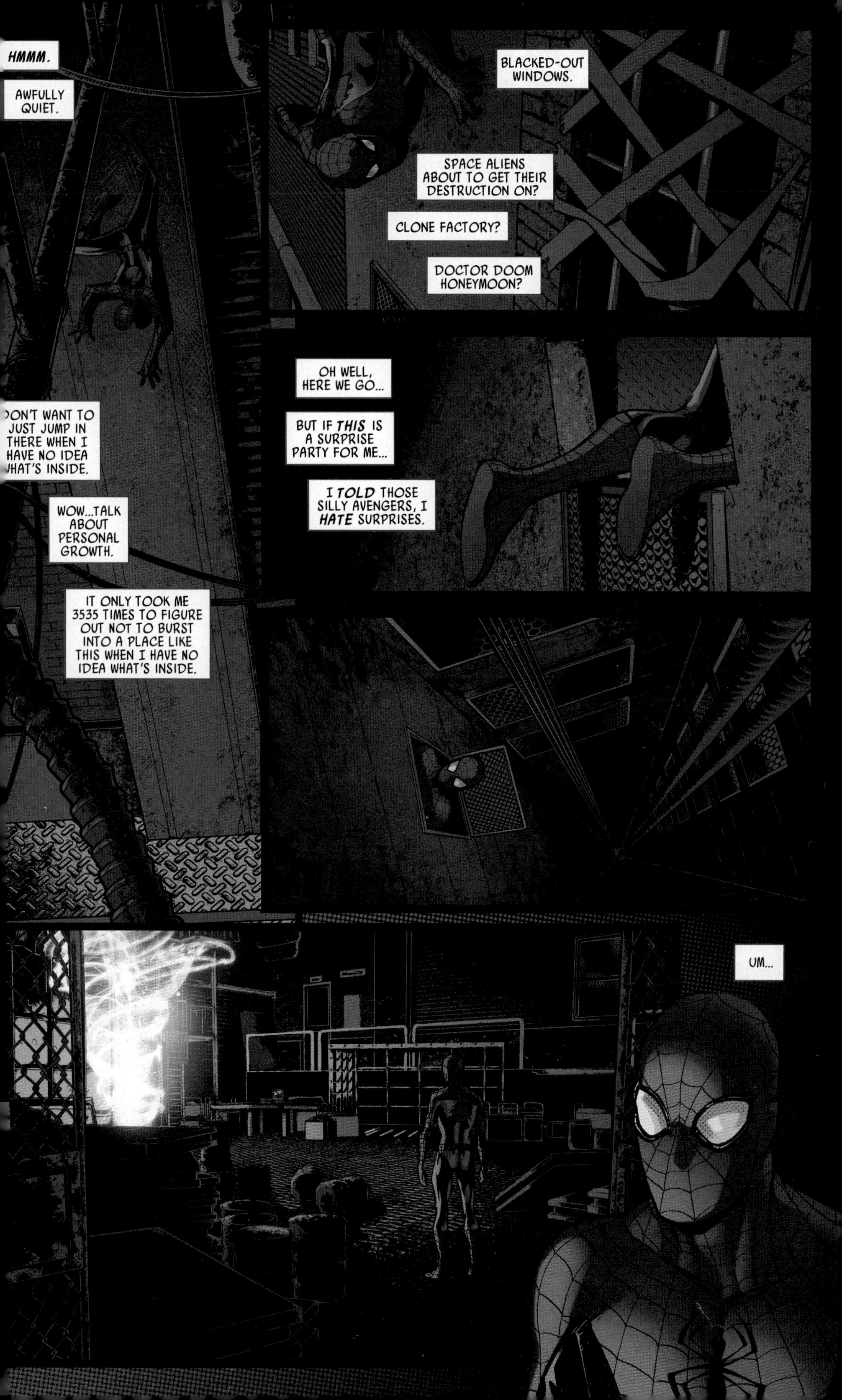
HMMM.
AWFULLY QUIET.
BLACKED-OUT WINDOWS.
SPACE ALIENS ABOUT TO GET THEIR DESTRUCTION ON?
CLONE FACTORY?
DOCTOR DOOM HONEYMOON?
DON'T WANT TO JUST JUMP IN THERE WHEN I HAVE NO IDEA WHAT'S INSIDE.
WOW...TALK ABOUT PERSONAL GROWTH.
IT ONLY TOOK ME 3535 TIMES TO FIGURE OUT NOT TO BURST INTO A PLACE LIKE THIS WHEN I HAVE NO IDEA WHAT'S INSIDE.
OH WELL, HERE WE GO...
BUT IF THIS IS A SURPRISE PARTY FOR ME...
I TOLD THOSE SILLY AVENGERS, I HATE SURPRISES.
UM...

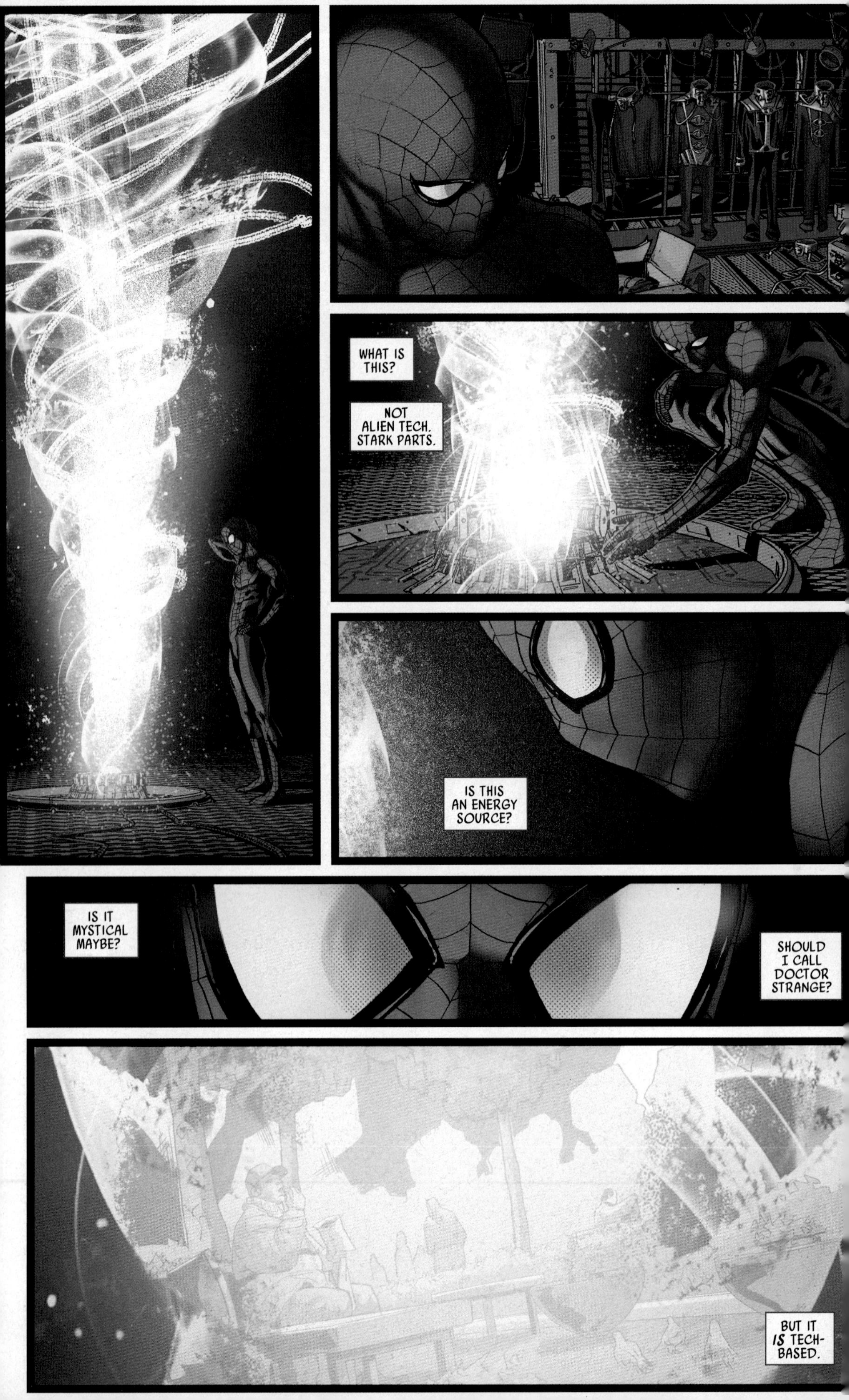
WHAT IS THIS?
NOT ALIEN TECH. STARK PARTS.
IS THIS AN ENERGY SOURCE?
IS IT MYSTICAL MAYBE?
SHOULD I CALL DOCTOR STRANGE?
BUT IT *IS* TECH-BASED.

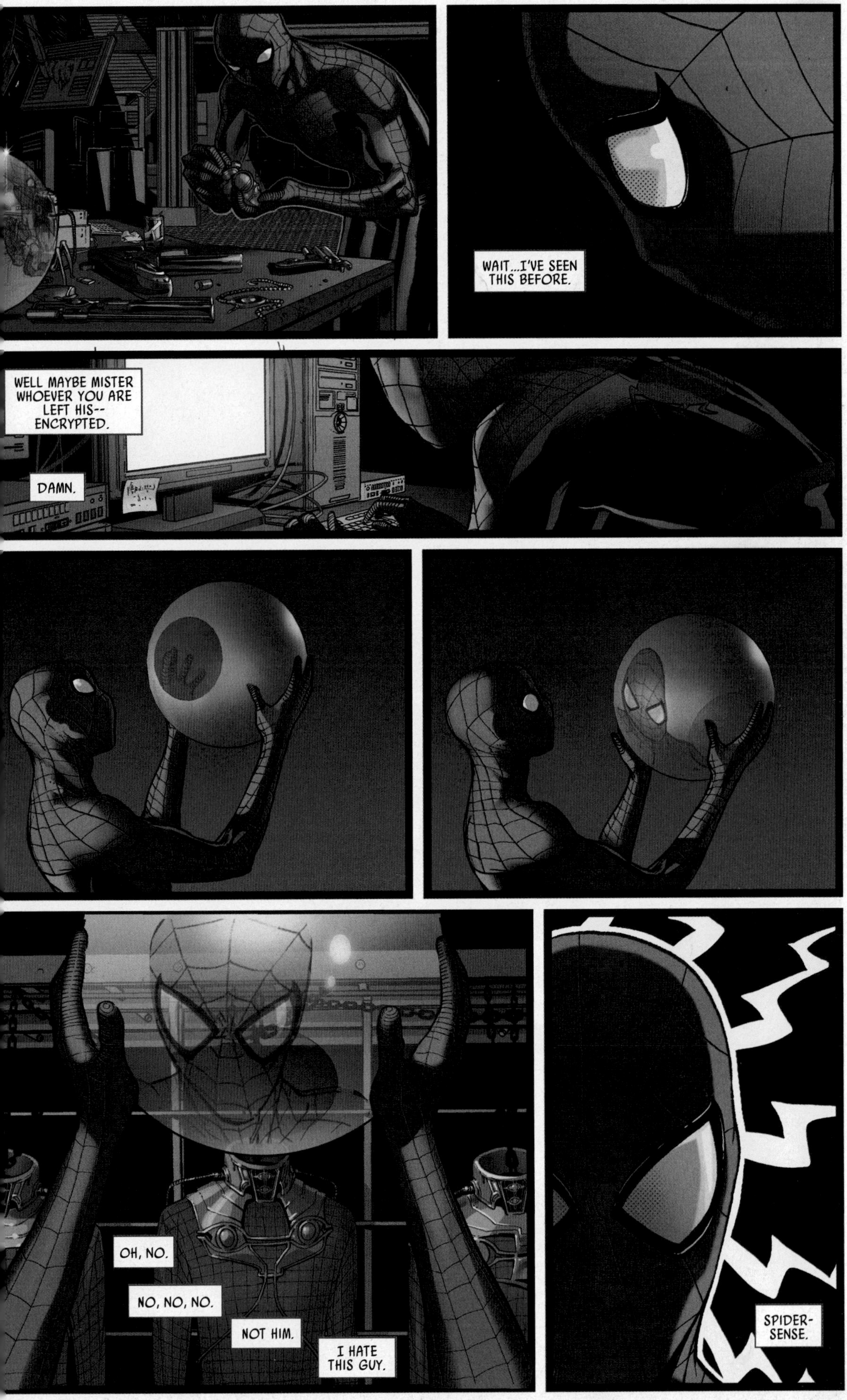
WAIT...I'VE SEEN THIS BEFORE.
WELL MAYBE MISTER WHOEVER YOU ARE LEFT HIS-- ENCRYPTED.
DAMN.
OH, NO.
NO, NO, NO.
NOT HIM.
I HATE THIS GUY.
SPIDER-SENSE.

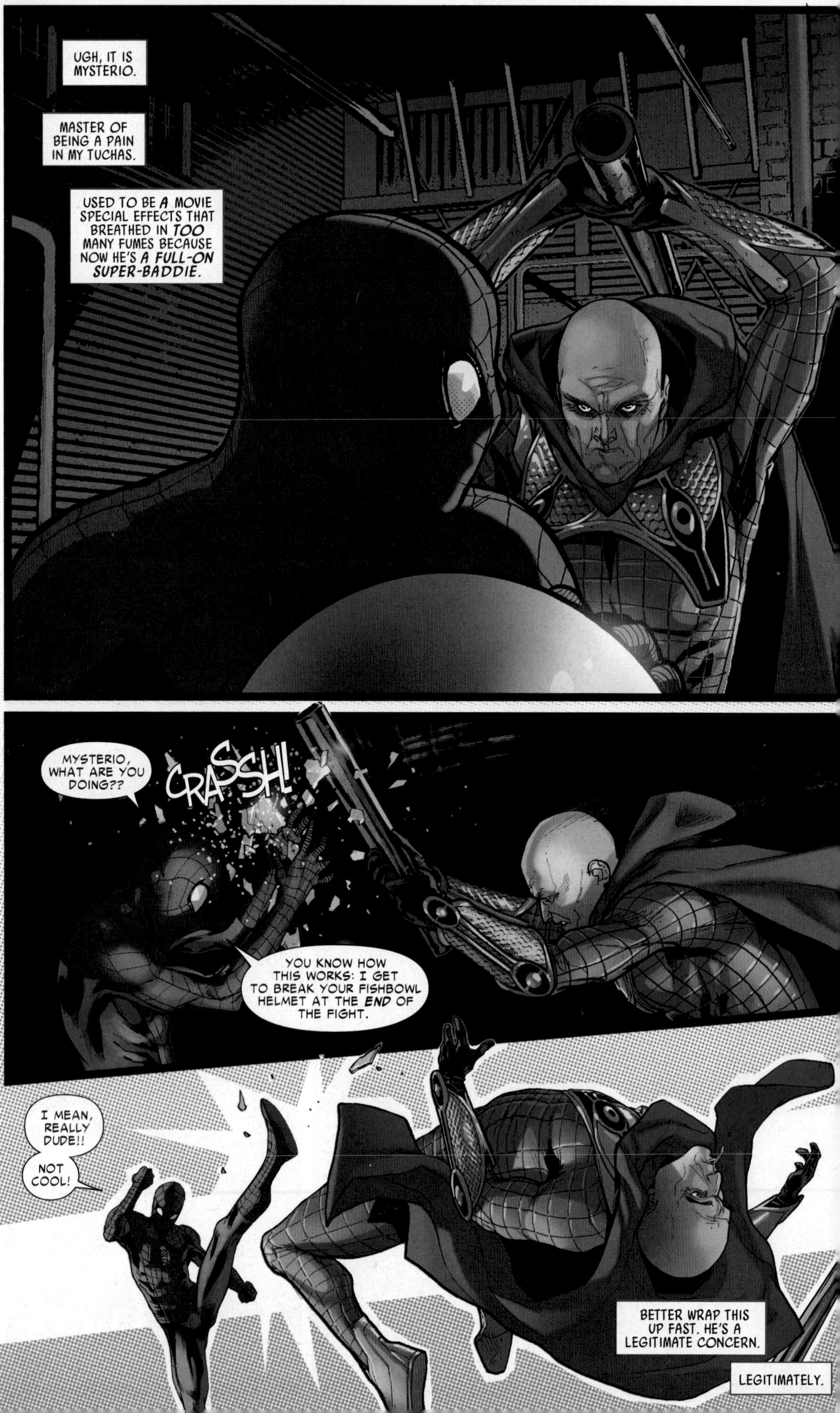
UGH, IT IS MYSTERIO.
MASTER OF BEING A PAIN IN MY TUCHAS.
USED TO BE A MOVIE SPECIAL EFFECTS THAT BREATHED IN TOO MANY FUMES BECAUSE NOW HE'S A FULL-ON SUPER-BADDIE.
MYSTERIO, WHAT ARE YOU DOING??
CRASSH!
YOU KNOW HOW THIS WORKS: I GET TO BREAK YOUR FISHBOWL HELMET AT THE END OF THE FIGHT.
I MEAN, REALLY DUDE!!
NOT COOL!
BETTER WRAP THIS UP FAST. HE'S A LEGITIMATE CONCERN.
LEGITIMATELY.

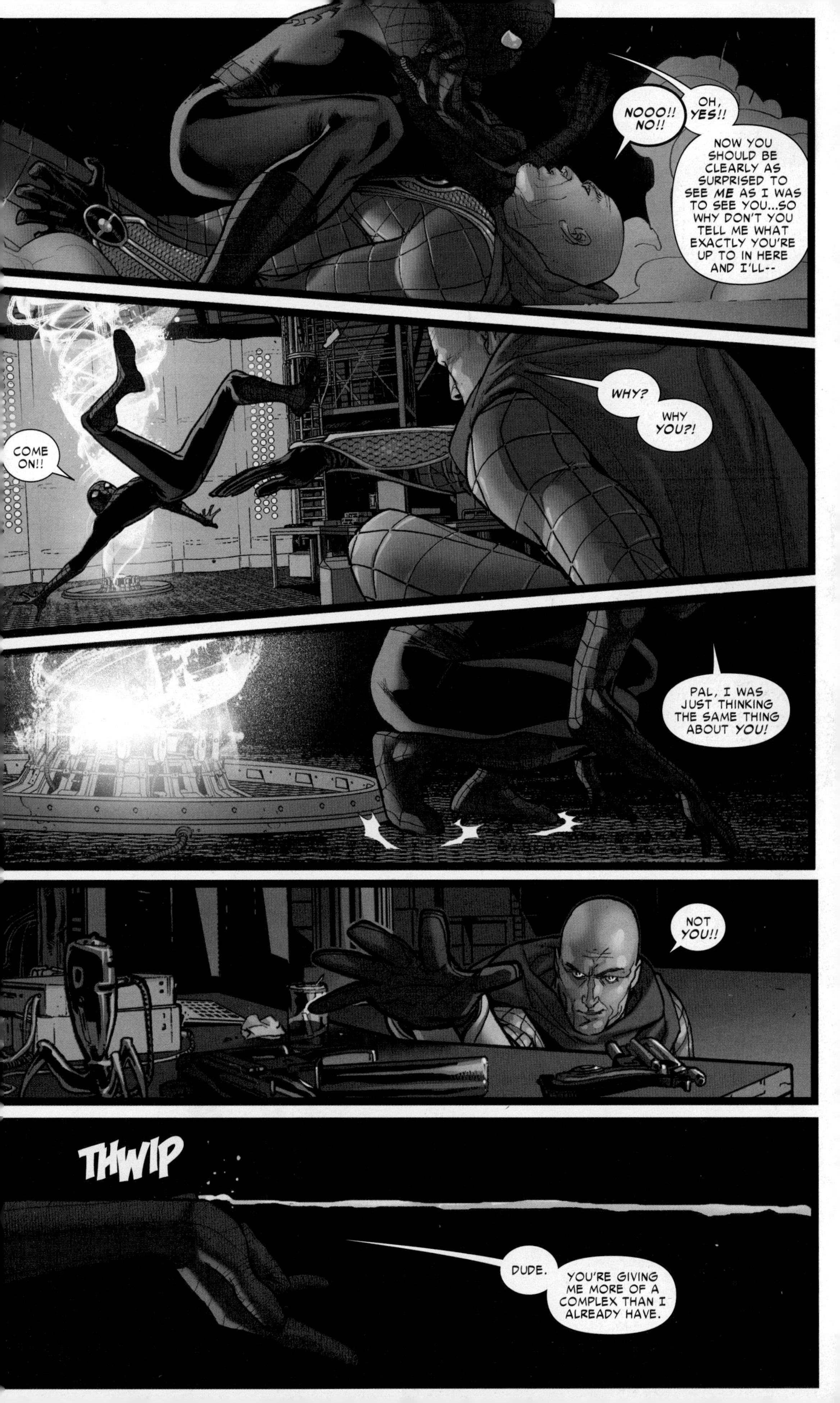
NOOO!! NO!!
OH, YES!!
NOW YOU SHOULD BE CLEARLY AS SURPRISED TO SEE ME AS I WAS TO SEE YOU...SO WHY DON'T YOU TELL ME WHAT EXACTLY YOU'RE UP TO IN HERE AND I'LL--
WHY?
WHY YOU?!
COME ON!!
PAL, I WAS JUST THINKING THE SAME THING ABOUT YOU!
NOT YOU!!
THWIP
DUDE.
YOU'RE GIVING ME MORE OF A COMPLEX THAN I ALREADY HAVE.

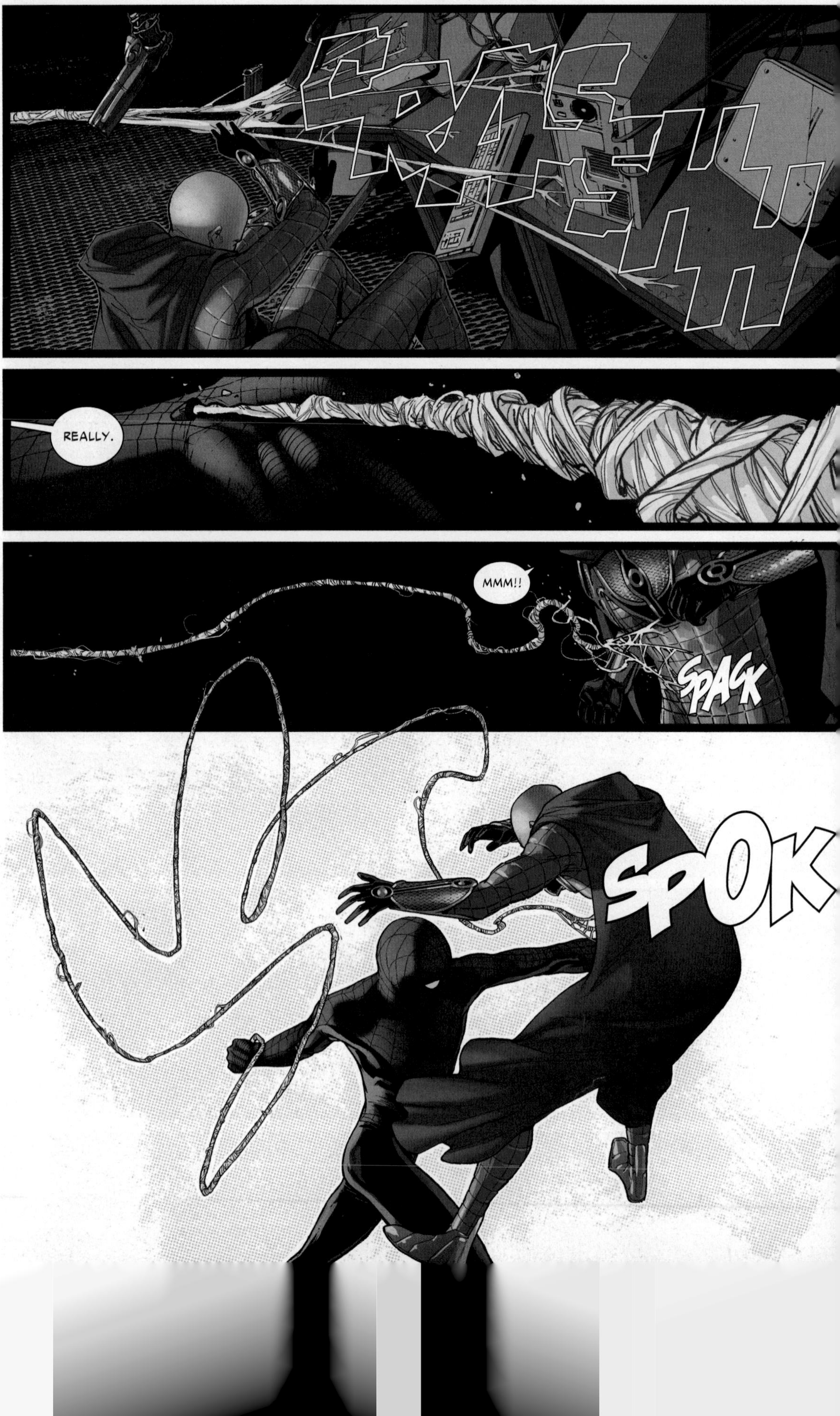
REALLY.
MMM!!
SPACK
SPOK

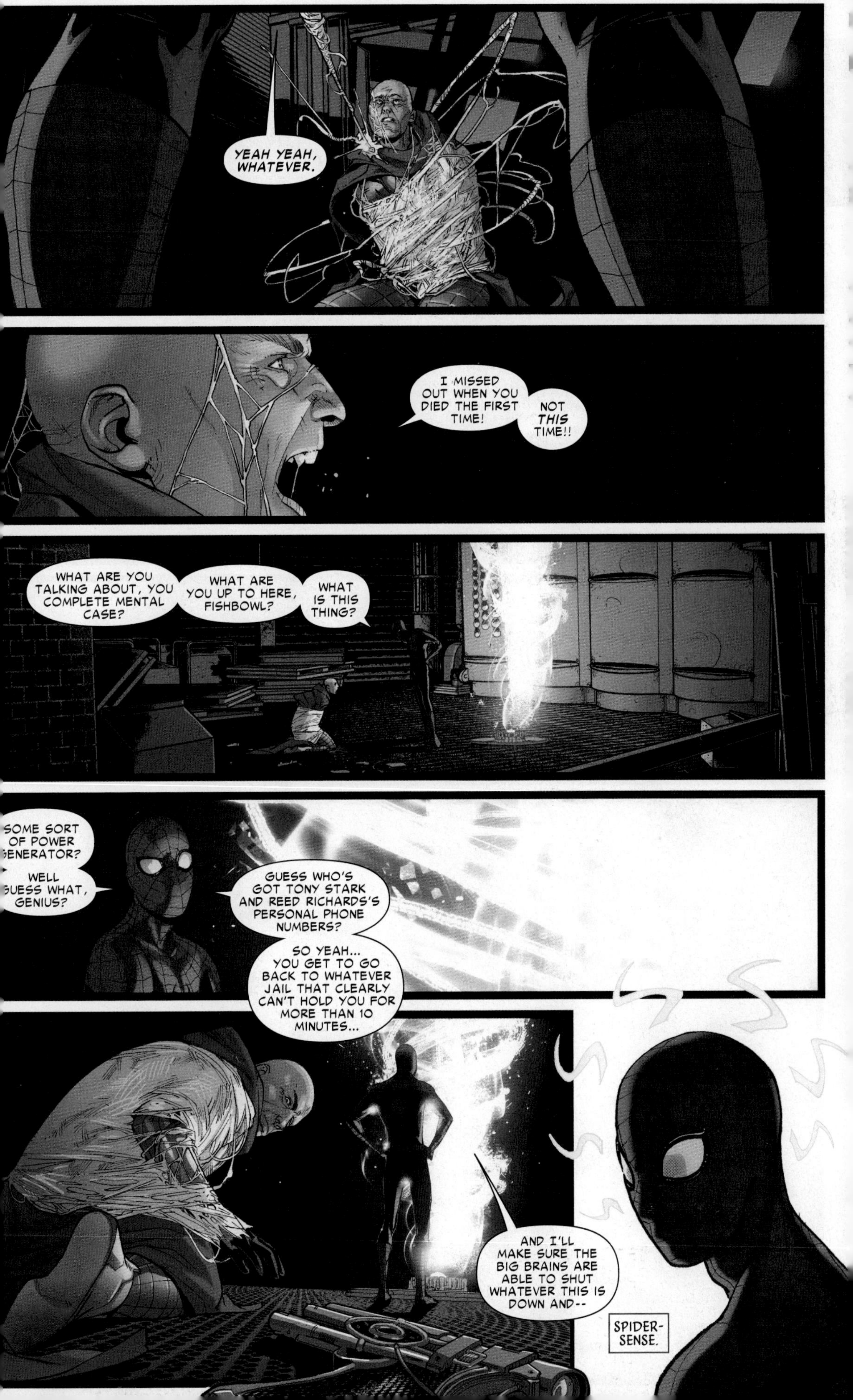
YEAH YEAH, WHATEVER.
I MISSED OUT WHEN YOU DIED THE FIRST TIME!
NOT *THIS* TIME!!
WHAT ARE YOU TALKING ABOUT, YOU COMPLETE MENTAL CASE?
WHAT ARE YOU UP TO HERE, FISHBOWL?
WHAT IS THIS THING?
SOME SORT OF POWER GENERATOR?
WELL GUESS WHAT, GENIUS?
GUESS WHO'S GOT TONY STARK AND REED RICHARDS'S PERSONAL PHONE NUMBERS?
SO YEAH... YOU GET TO GO BACK TO WHATEVER JAIL THAT CLEARLY CAN'T HOLD YOU FOR MORE THAN 10 MINUTES...
AND I'LL MAKE SURE THE BIG BRAINS ARE ABLE TO SHUT WHATEVER THIS IS DOWN AND--
SPIDER-SENSE.

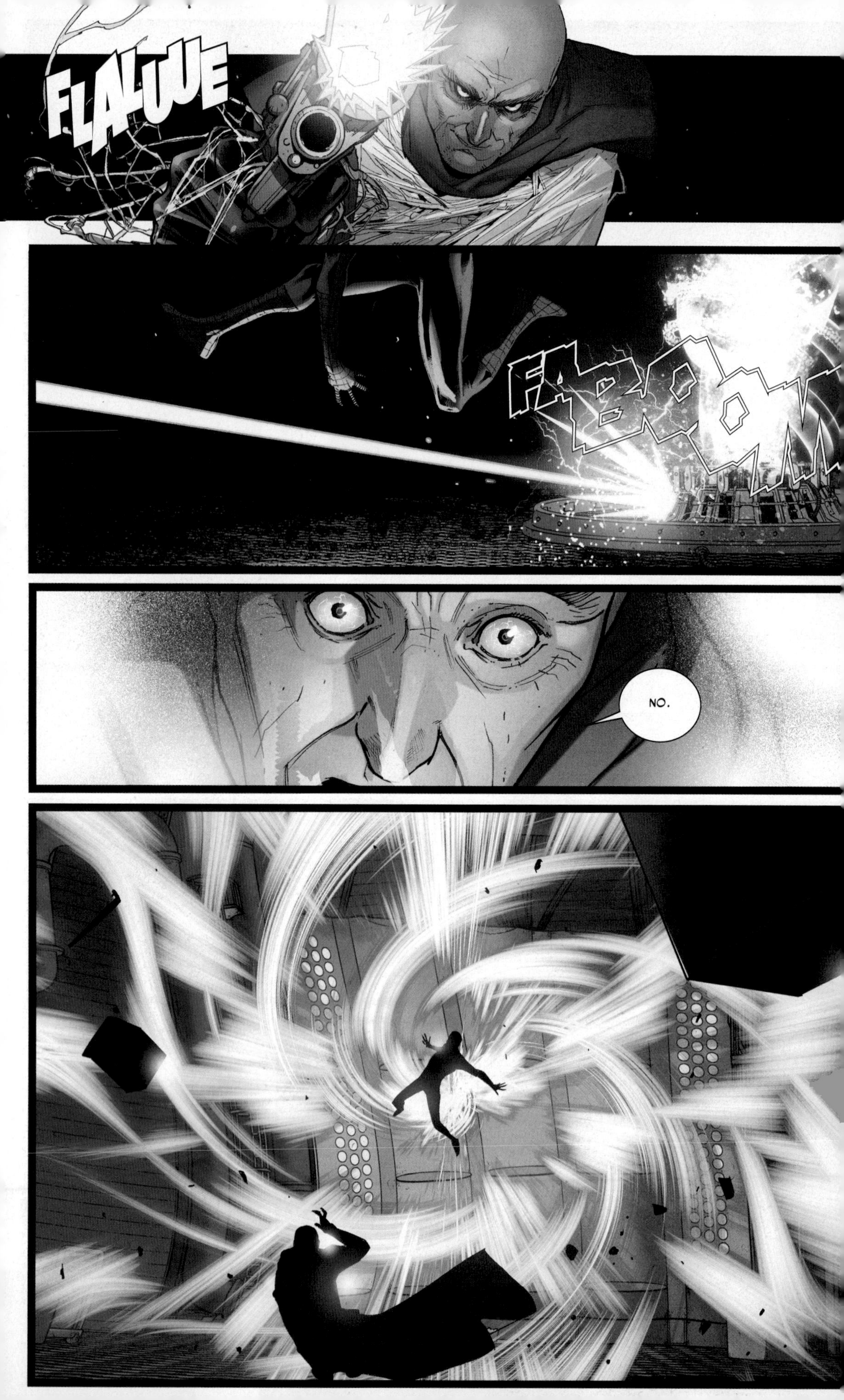
FLALUUE
FABOOM
NO.

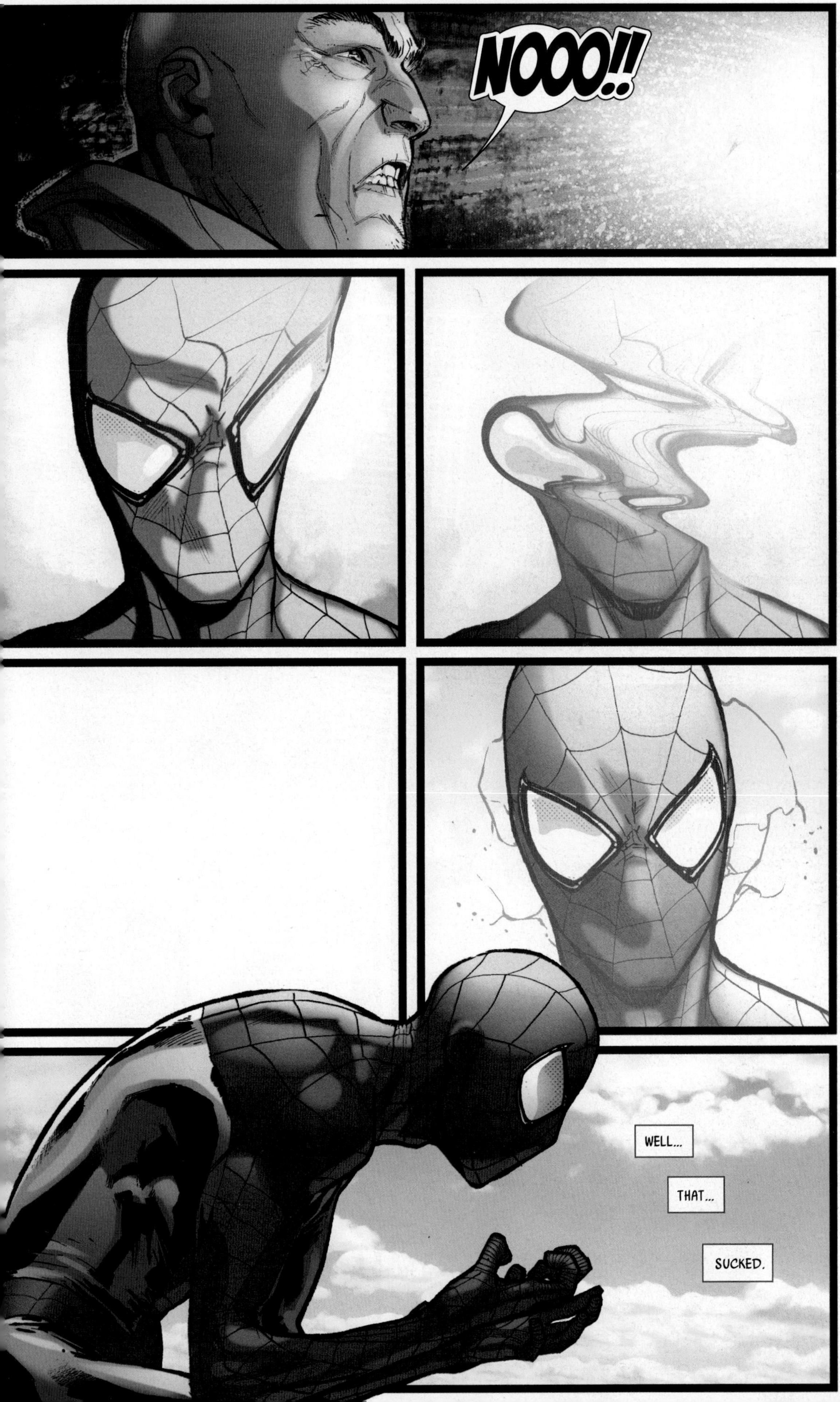
NOOO!!
WELL...
THAT...
SUCKED.

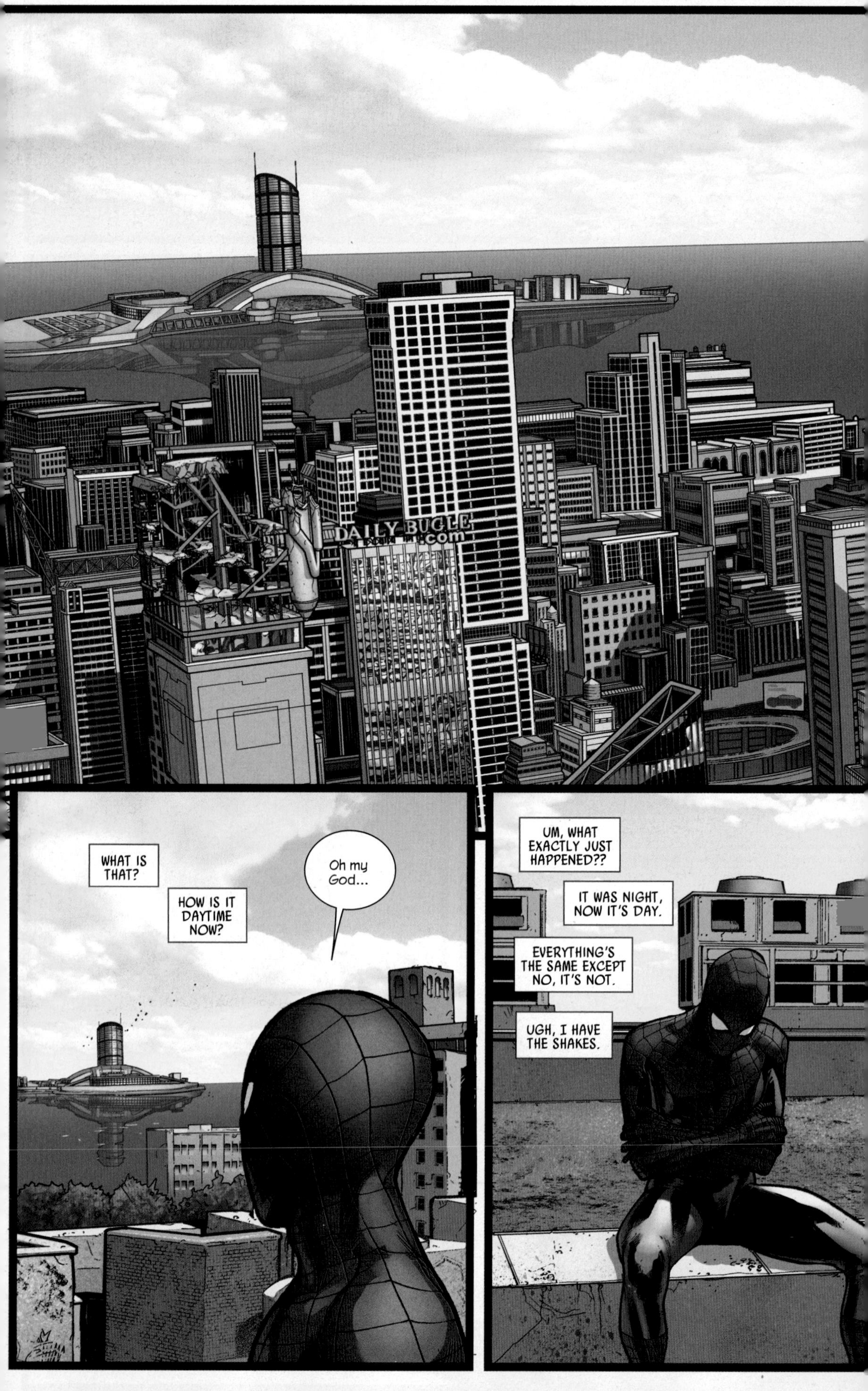
DAILY BUGLE .com
WHAT IS THAT?
HOW IS IT DAYTIME NOW?
Oh my God...
UM, WHAT EXACTLY JUST HAPPENED??
IT WAS NIGHT, NOW IT'S DAY.
EVERYTHING'S THE SAME EXCEPT NO, IT'S NOT.
UGH, I HAVE THE SHAKES.

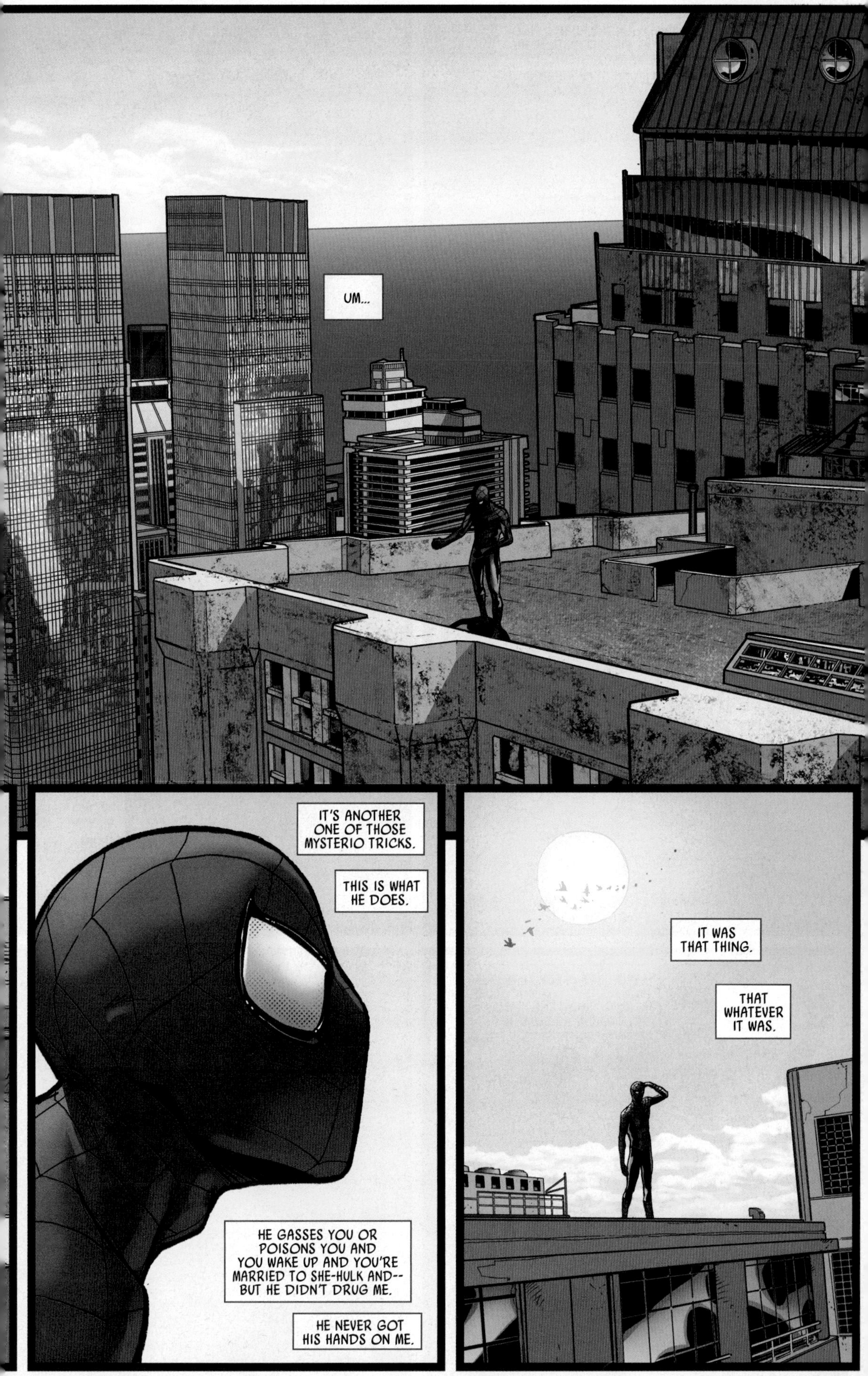
UM...
IT'S ANOTHER ONE OF THOSE MYSTERIO TRICKS.
THIS IS WHAT HE DOES.
HE GASSES YOU OR POISONS YOU AND YOU WAKE UP AND YOU'RE MARRIED TO SHE-HULK AND-- BUT HE DIDN'T DRUG ME.
HE NEVER GOT HIS HANDS ON ME.
IT WAS THAT THING.
THAT WHATEVER IT WAS.

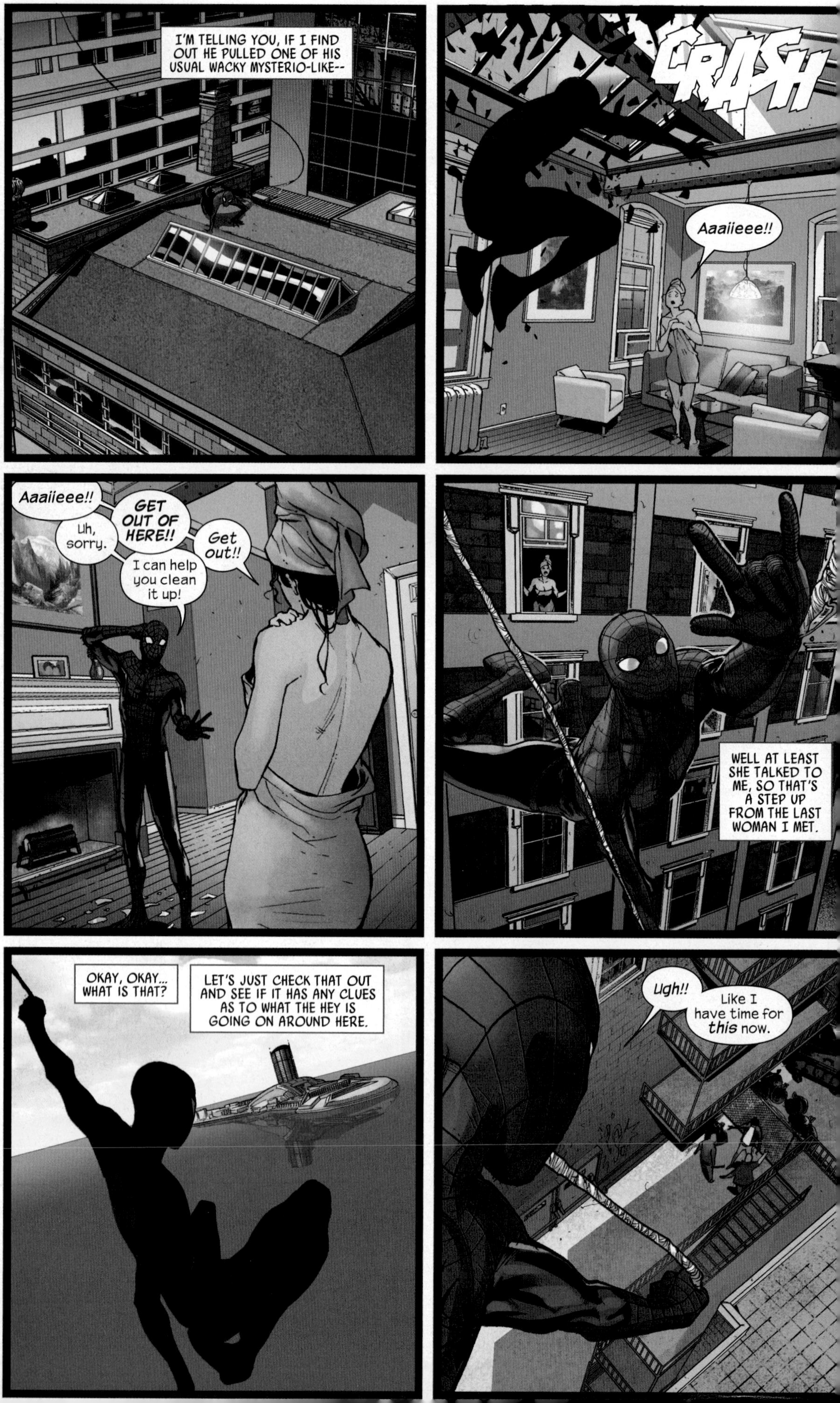
I'M TELLING YOU, IF I FIND OUT HE PULLED ONE OF HIS USUAL WACKY MYSTERIO-LIKE--
CRASH
Aaaiieee!!
Aaaiieee!!
Uh, sorry.
GET OUT OF HERE!!
I can help you clean it up!
Get out!!
WELL AT LEAST SHE TALKED TO ME, SO THAT'S A STEP UP FROM THE LAST WOMAN I MET.
OKAY, OKAY... WHAT IS THAT?
LET'S JUST CHECK THAT OUT AND SEE IF IT HAS ANY CLUES AS TO WHAT THE HEY IS GOING ON AROUND HERE.
Ugh!!
Like I have time for *this* now.

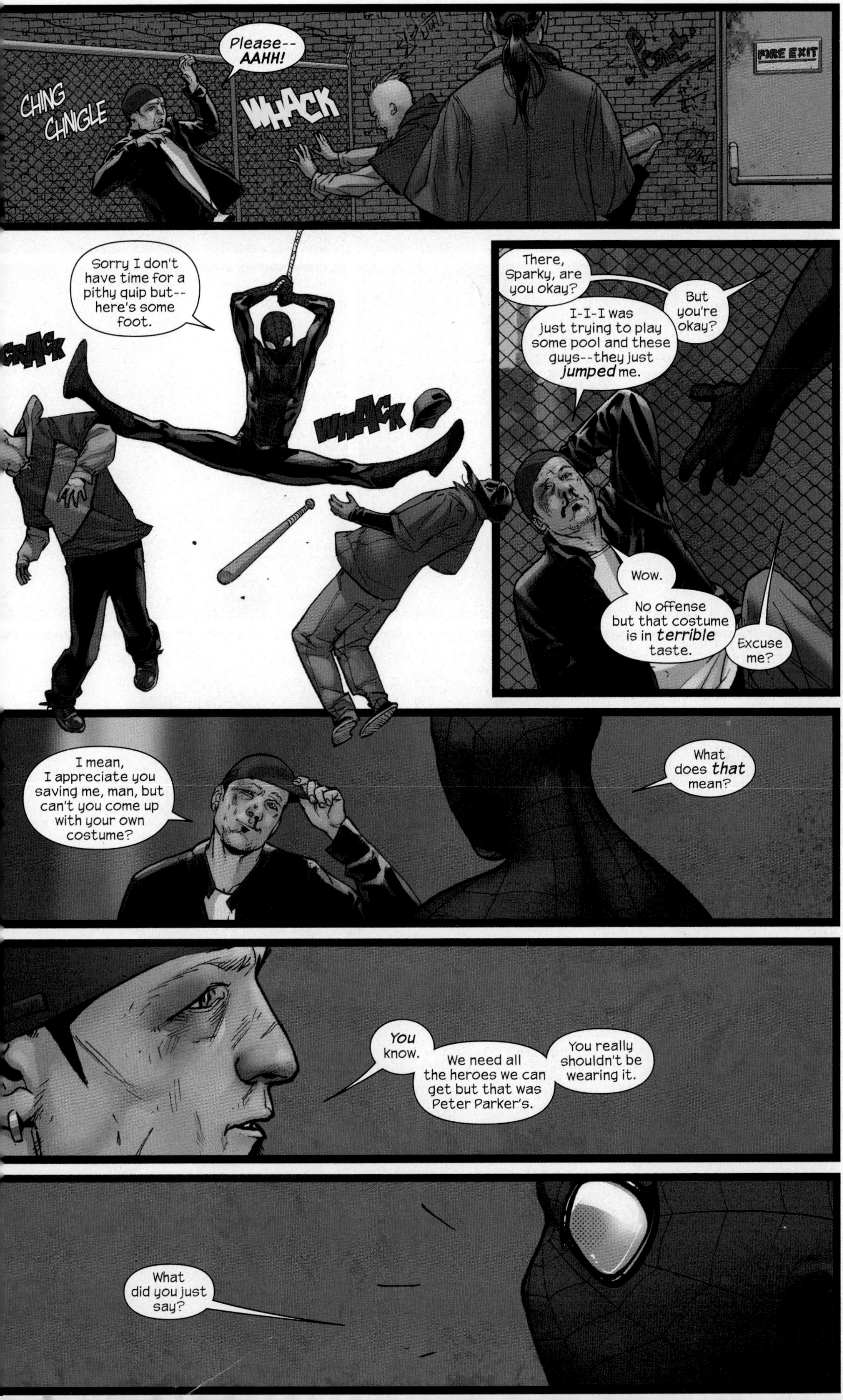
Please--
AAHH!
CHING
CHNIGLE
WHACK
Sorry I don't have time for a pithy quip but-- here's some foot.
CRACK
WHACK
There, Sparky, are you okay?
But you're okay?
I-I-I was just trying to play some pool and these guys--they just *jumped* me.
Wow.
No offense but that costume is in *terrible* taste.
Excuse me?
I mean, I appreciate you saving me, man, but can't you come up with your own costume?
What does *that* mean?
You know.
We need all the heroes we can get but that was Peter Parker's.
You really shouldn't be wearing it.
What did you just say?

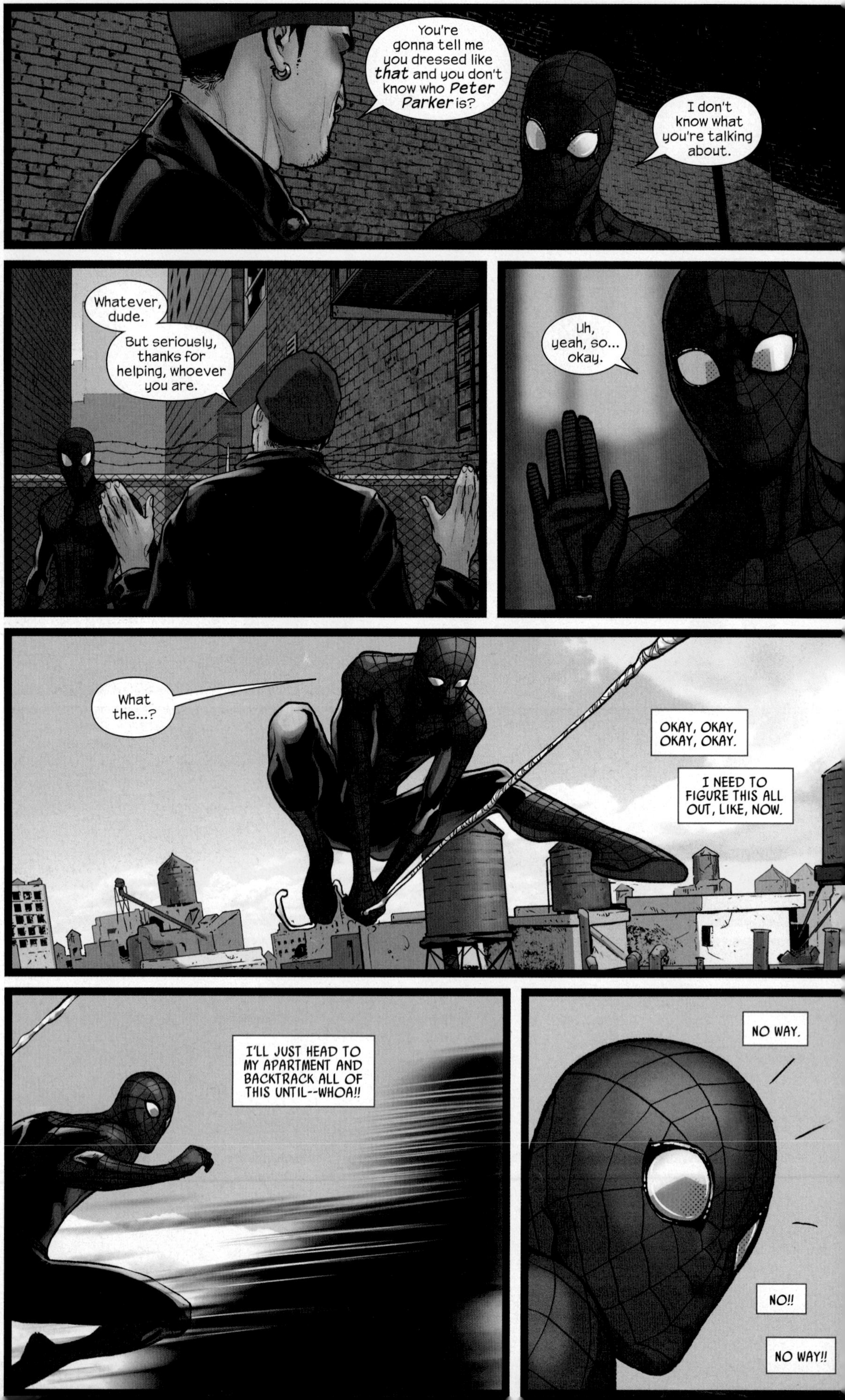

You're gonna tell me you dressed like *that* and you don't know who *Peter Parker* is?
I don't know what you're talking about.
Whatever, dude.
But seriously, thanks for helping, whoever you are.
Uh, yeah, so... okay.
What the...?
OKAY, OKAY, OKAY, OKAY.
I NEED TO FIGURE THIS ALL OUT, LIKE, NOW.
I'LL JUST HEAD TO MY APARTMENT AND BACKTRACK ALL OF THIS UNTIL--WHOA!!
NO WAY.
NO!!
NO WAY!!

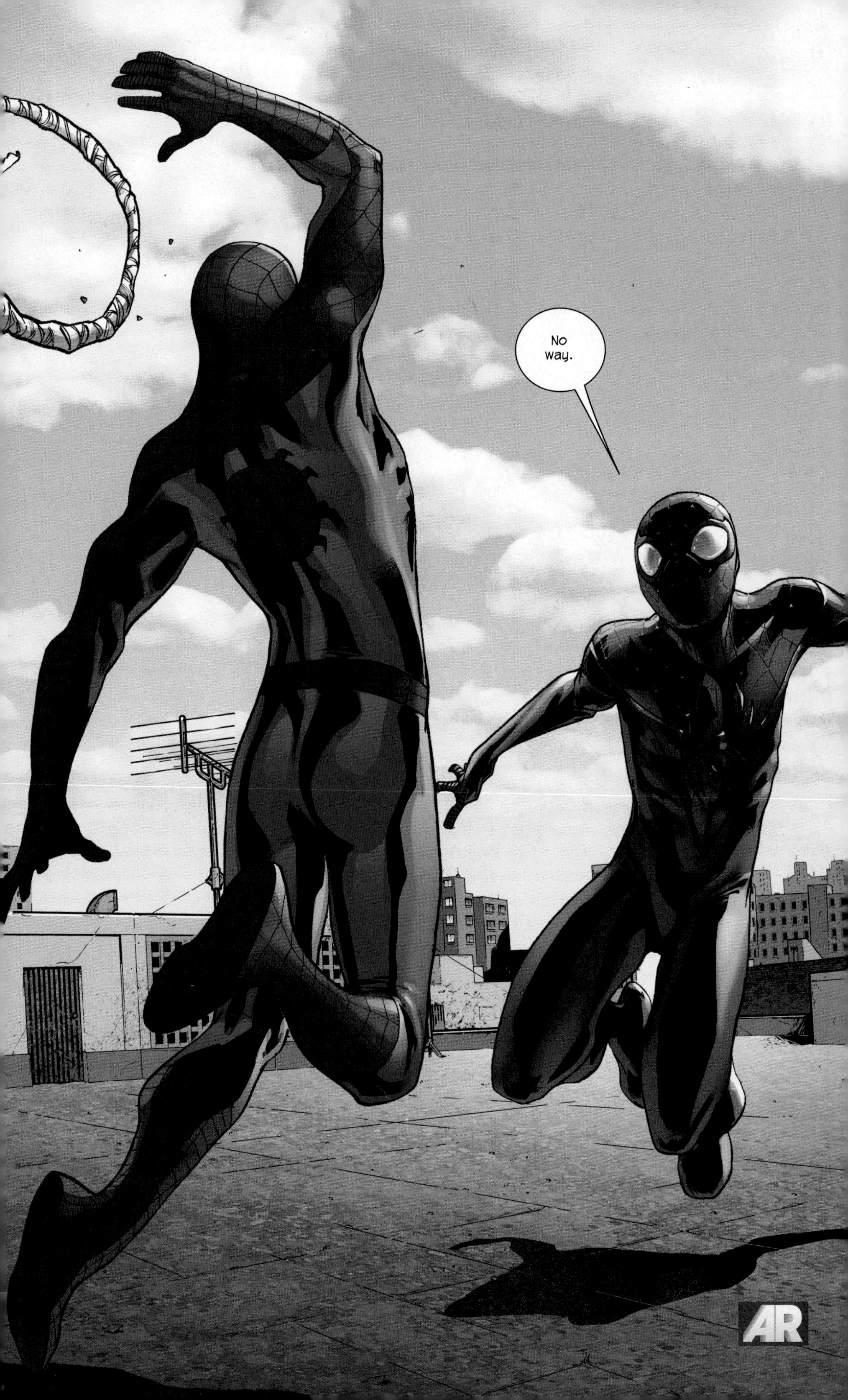
No way.

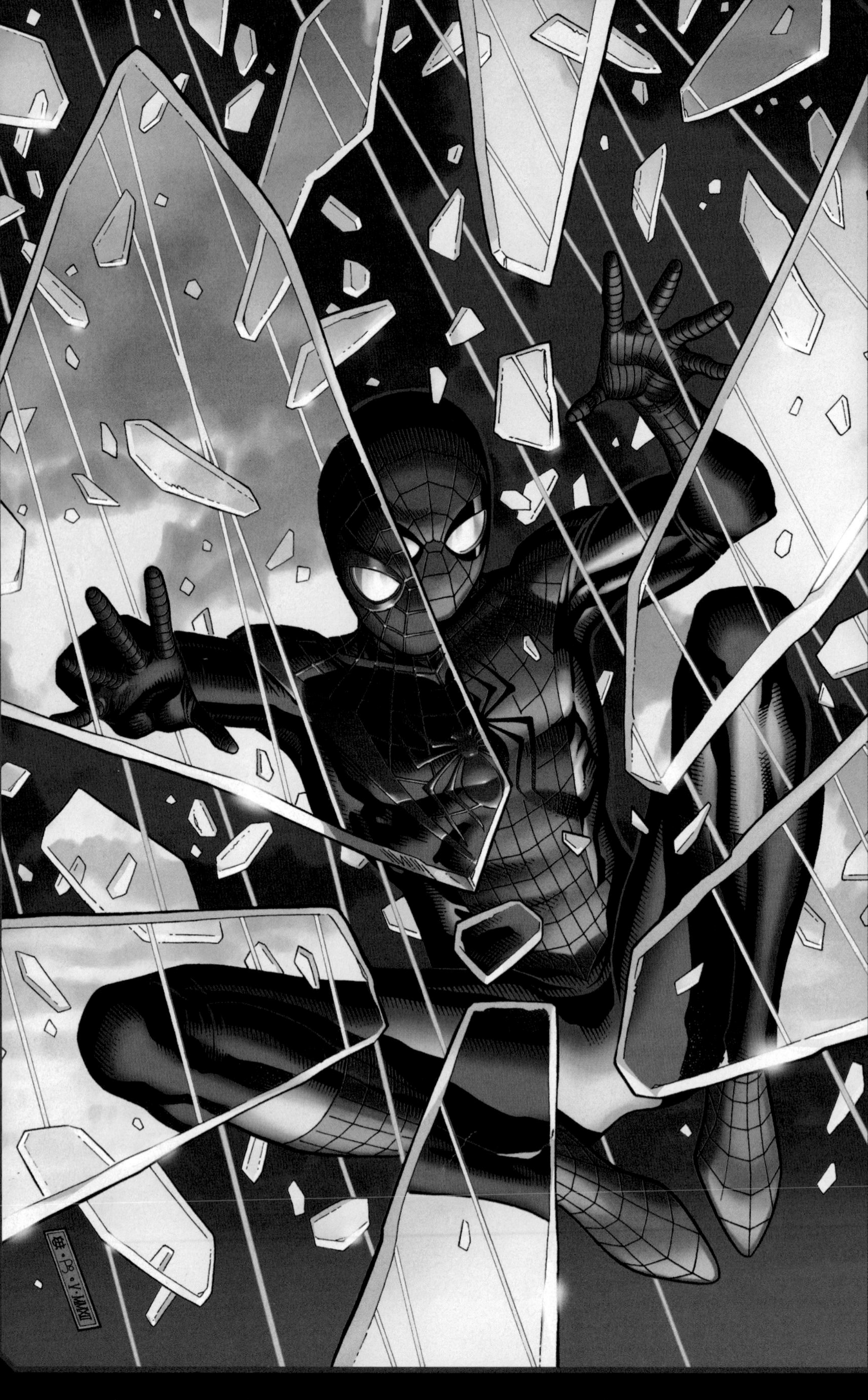

SPIDER-MEN #2

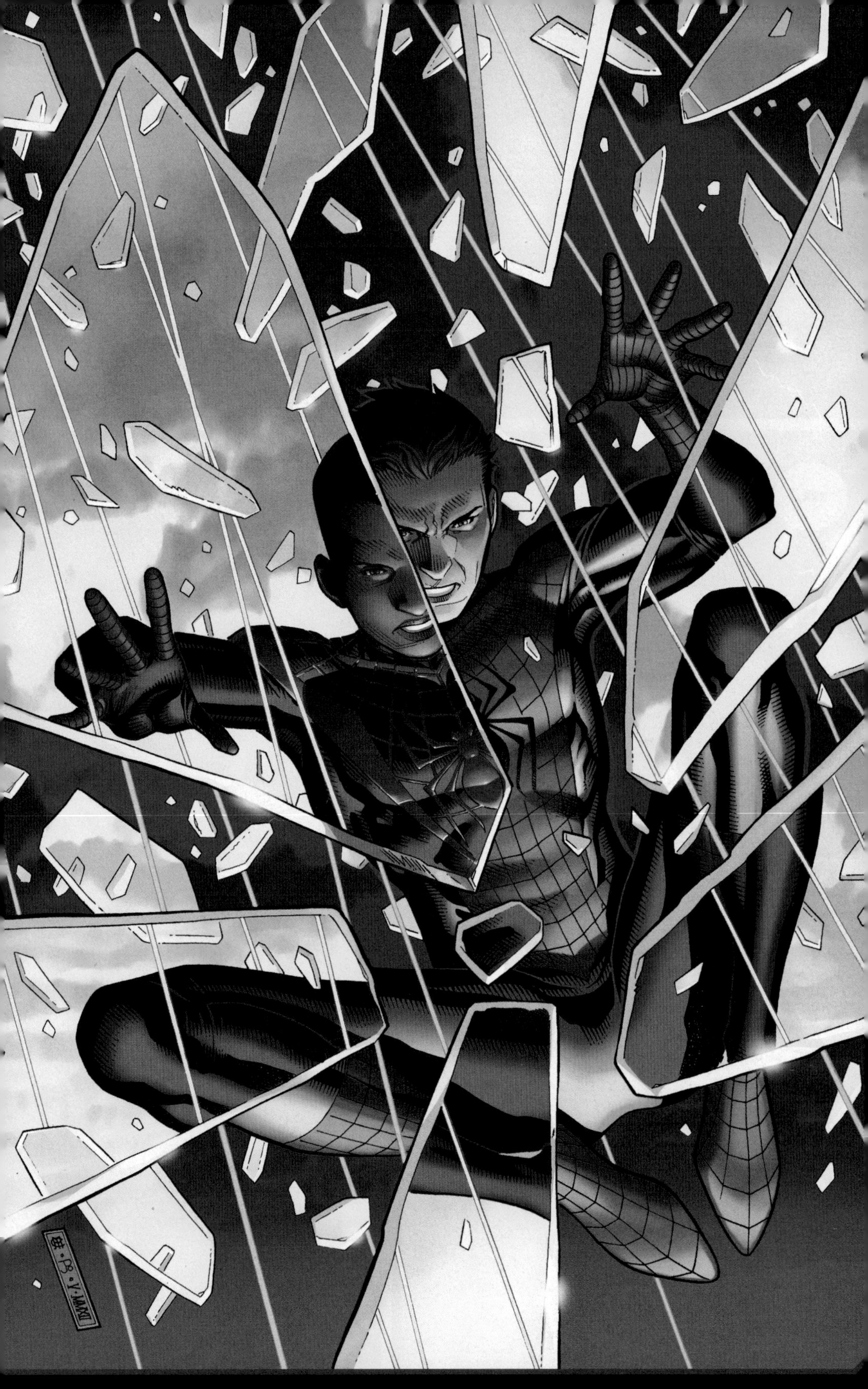

SPIDER-MEN #2 2ND PRINTING VARIANT BY JIM CHEUNG & JUSTIN PONSOR

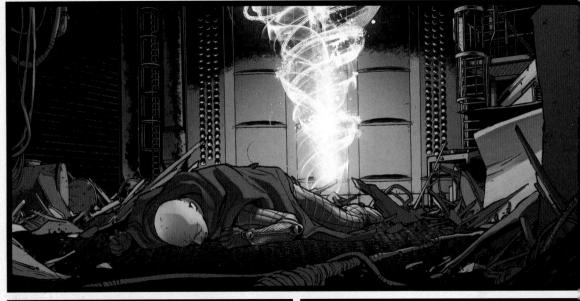

RRR...

OH NO!!

OH NO NO NO!!

HE DIDN'T. HE DID.

WHY SPIDER-MAN?

WHY IS IT ALWAYS SPIDER-MAN?

SHOW ME, SHOW ME...

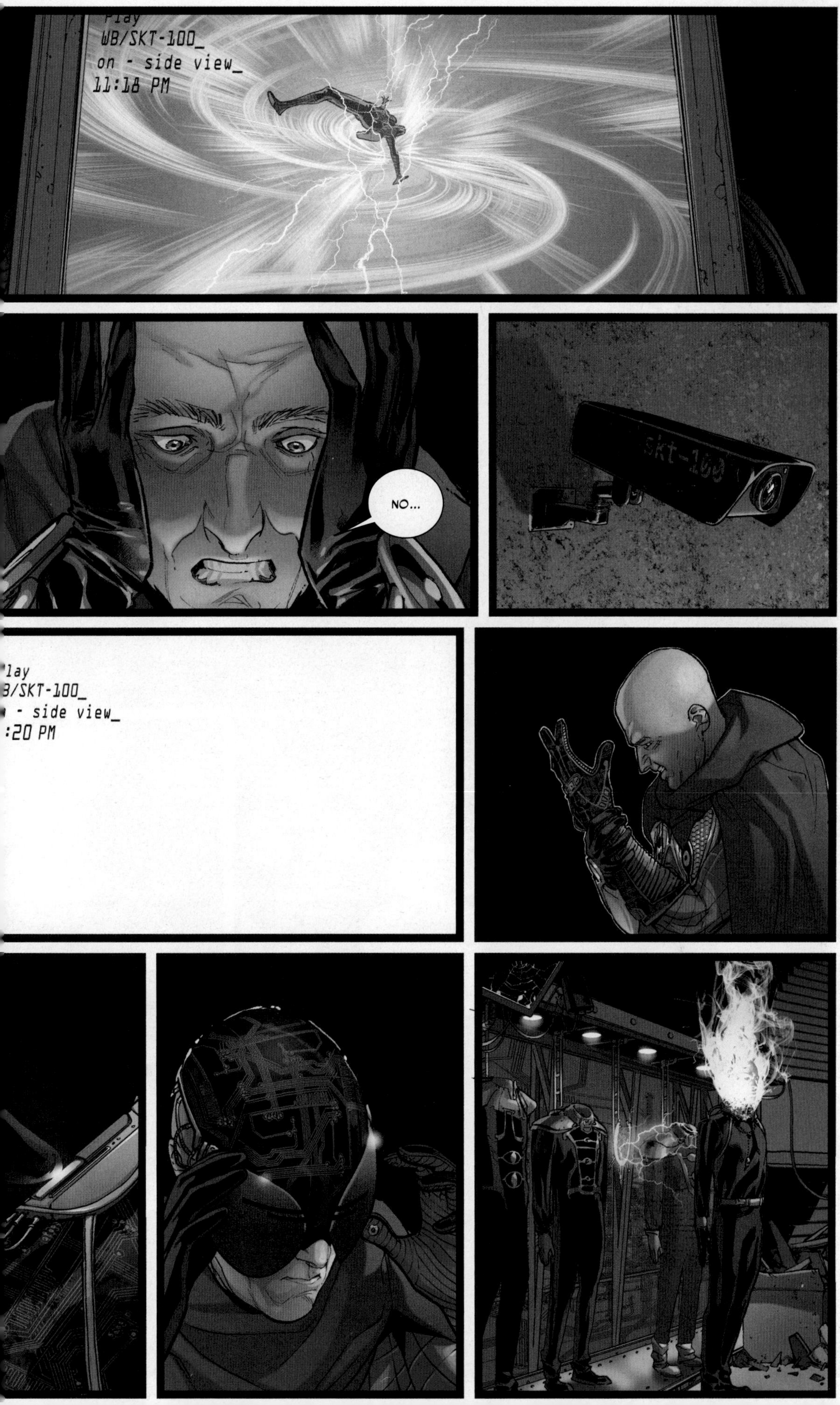
Play
WB/SKT-100_
on - side view_
11:18 PM
NO...
skt-100
lay
B/SKT-100_
- side view_
:20 PM

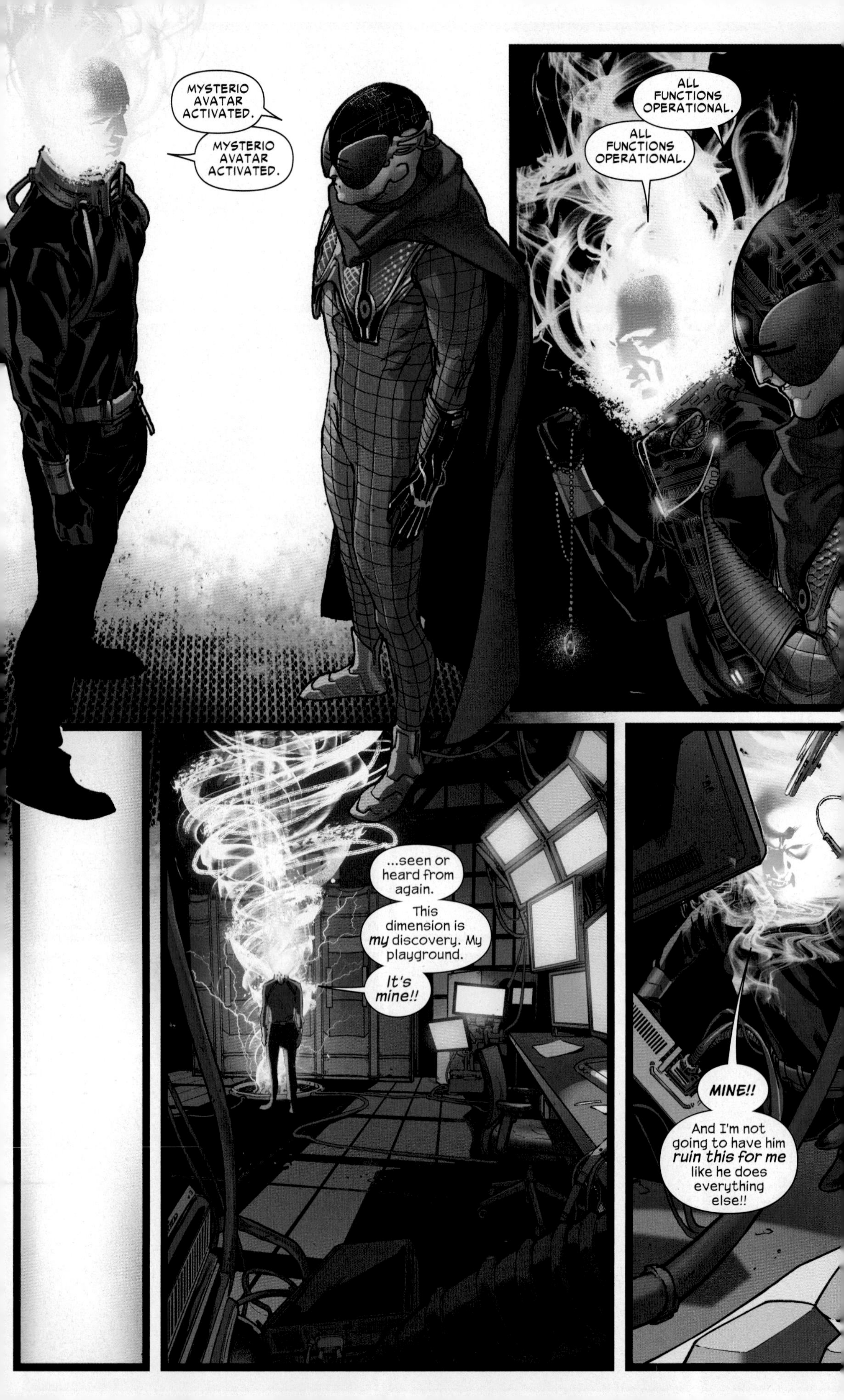
MYSTERIO AVATAR ACTIVATED.
MYSTERIO AVATAR ACTIVATED.
ALL FUNCTIONS OPERATIONAL.
ALL FUNCTIONS OPERATIONAL.
...seen or heard from again.
This dimension is *my* discovery. My playground.
It's mine!!
MINE!!
And I'm not going to have him ***ruin this for me*** like he does everything else!!

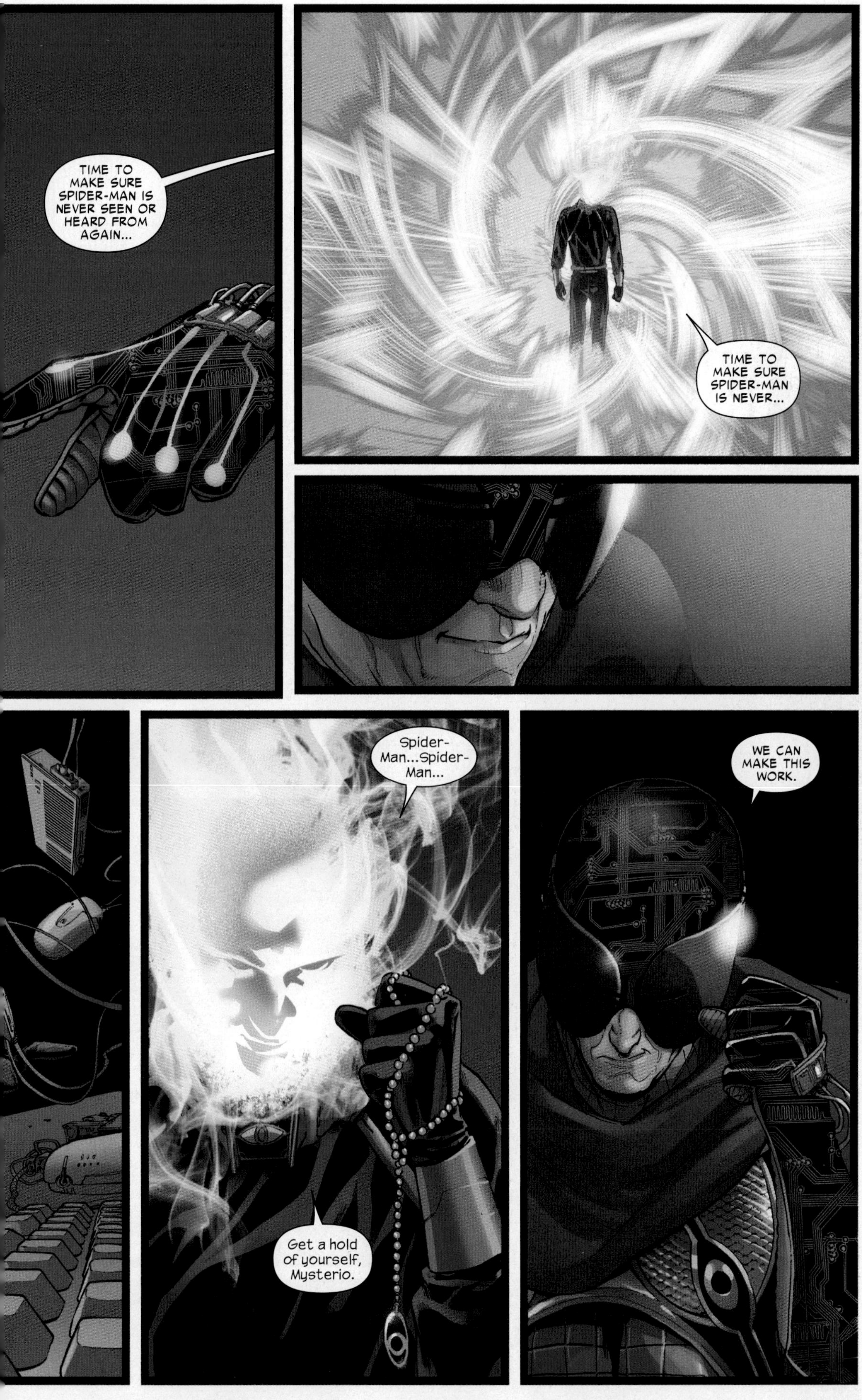
TIME TO MAKE SURE SPIDER-MAN IS NEVER SEEN OR HEARD FROM AGAIN...
TIME TO MAKE SURE SPIDER-MAN IS NEVER...
Spider-Man...Spider-Man...
Get a hold of yourself, Mysterio.
WE CAN MAKE THIS WORK.

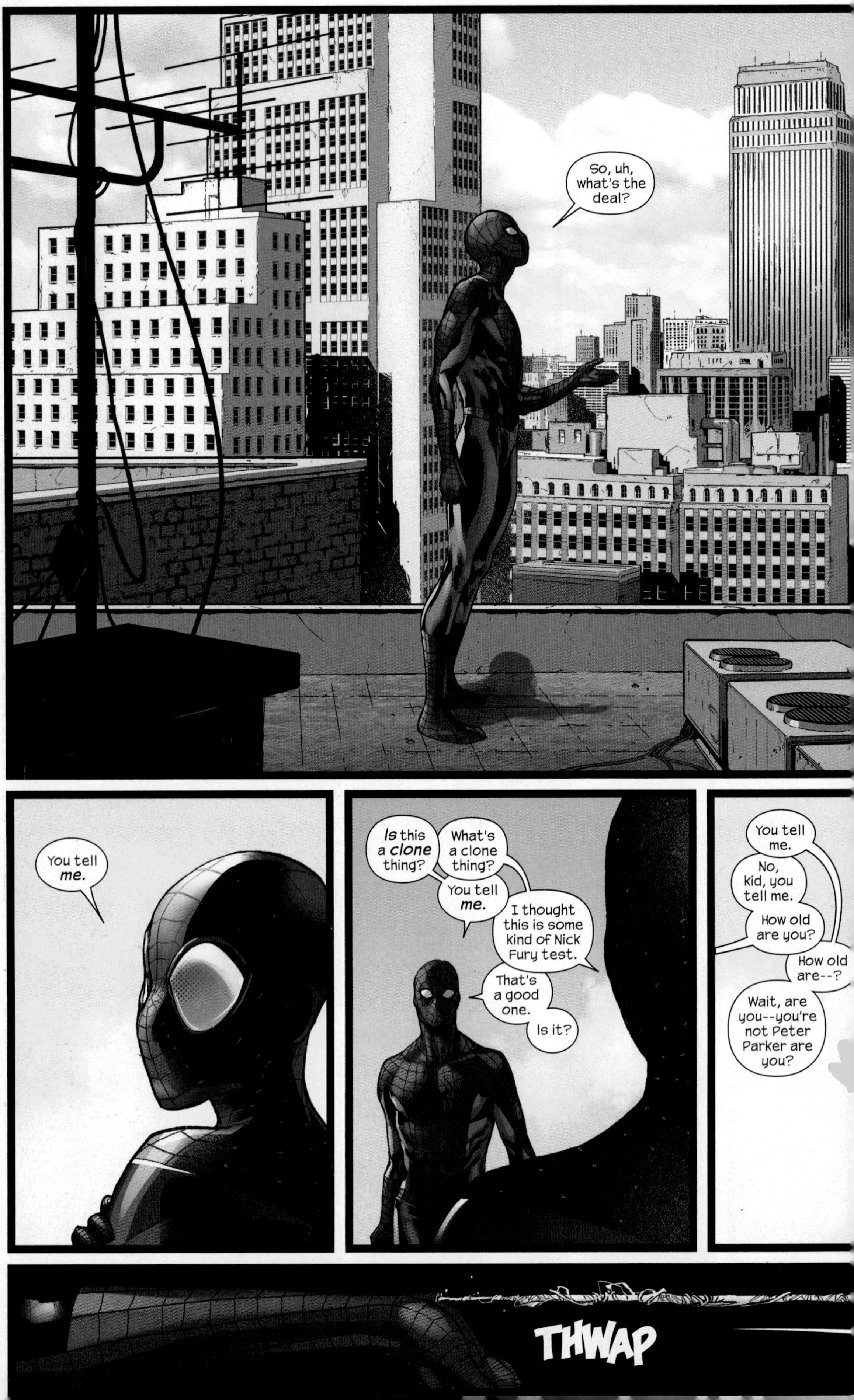
So, uh, what's the deal?
You tell *me.*
Is this a ***clone*** thing?
What's a clone thing?
You tell *me.*
I thought this is some kind of Nick Fury test.
That's a good one.
Is it?
You tell me.
No, kid, you tell me.
How old are you?
How old are--?
Wait, are you--you're not Peter Parker are you?
THWAP

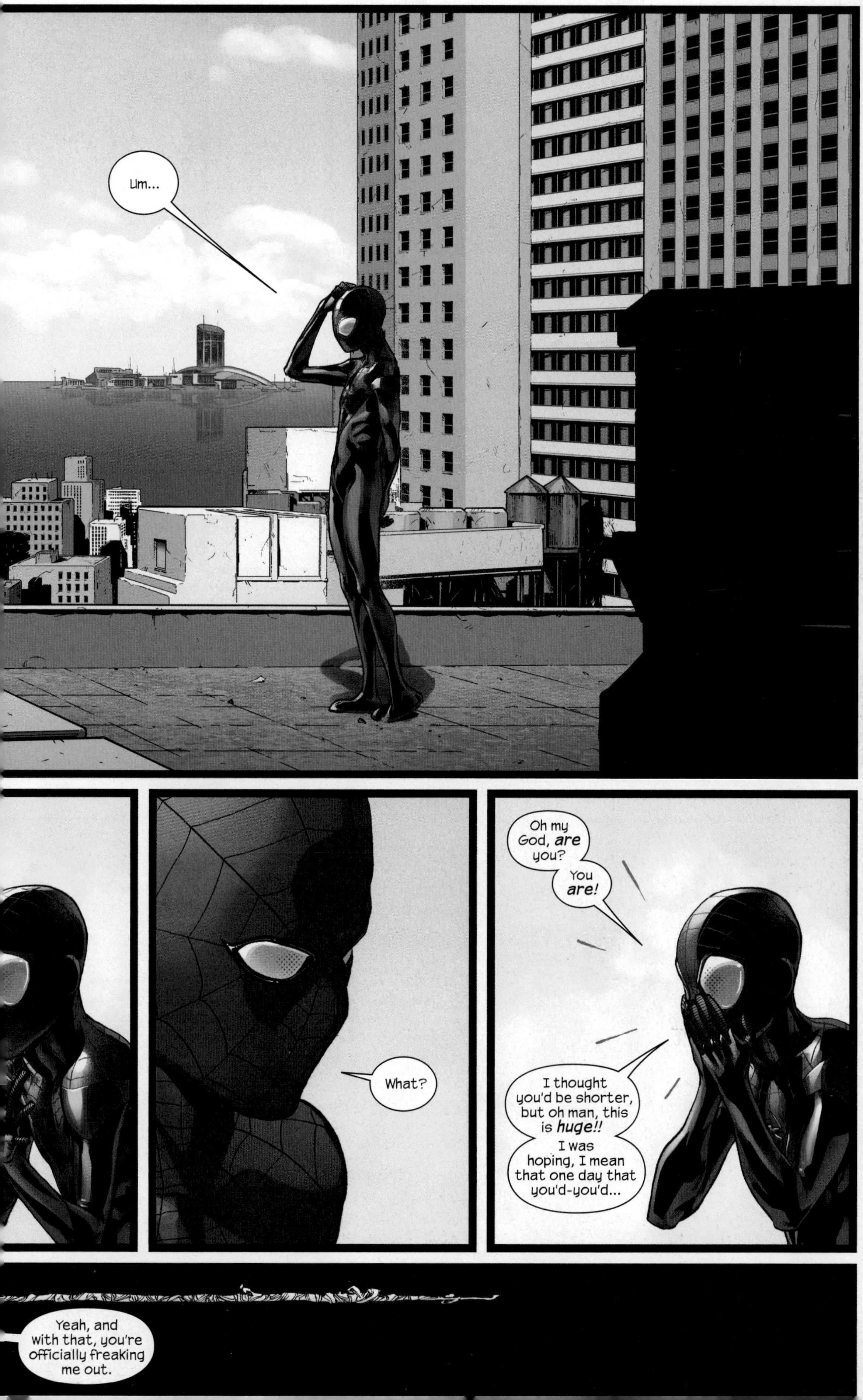
Um...
What?
Oh my God, are you?
You are!
I thought you'd be shorter, but oh man, this is huge!!
I was hoping, I mean that one day that you'd-you'd...
Yeah, and with that, you're officially freaking me out.

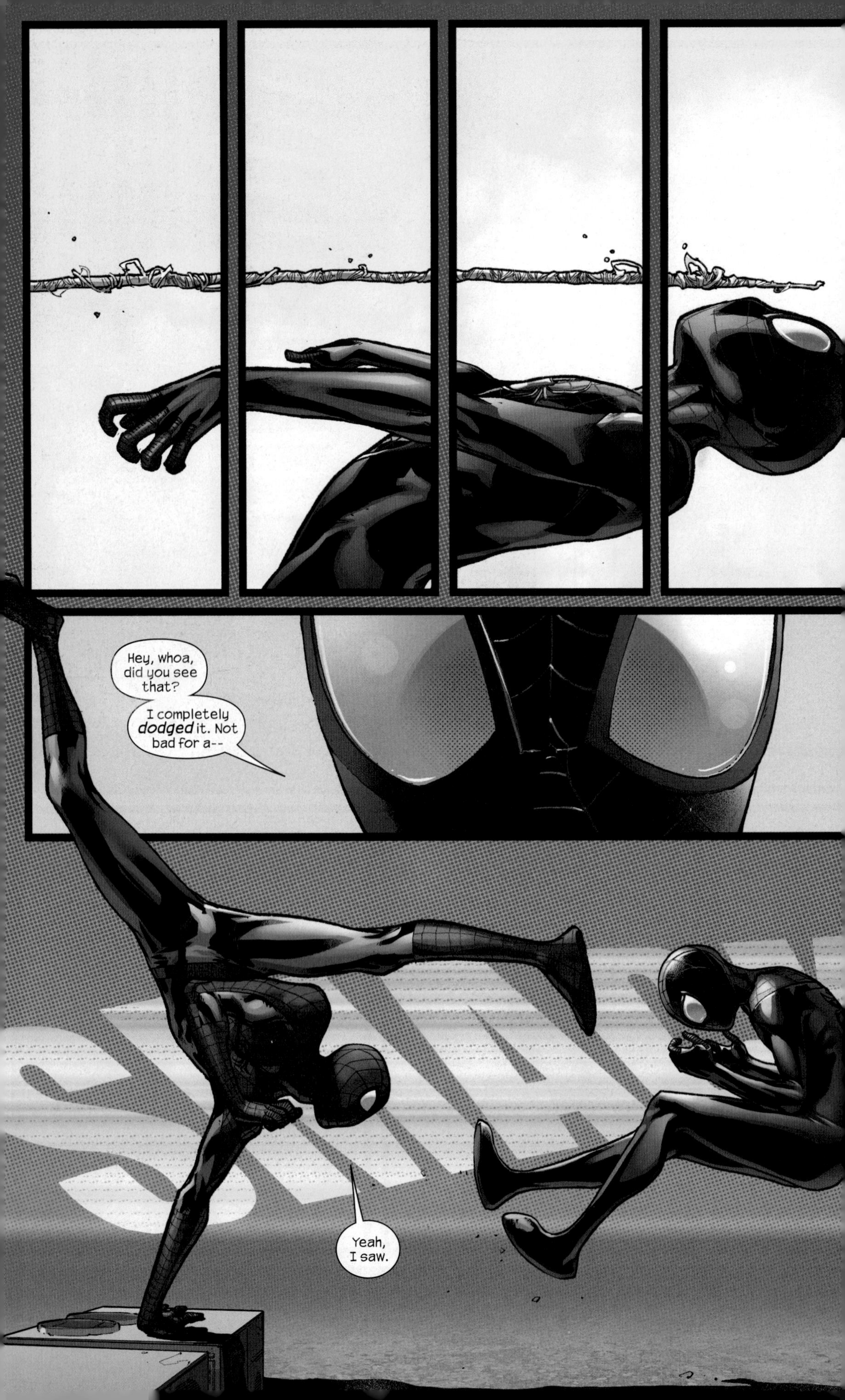
Hey, whoa, did you see that?
I completely *dodged* it. Not bad for a--
Yeah, I saw.

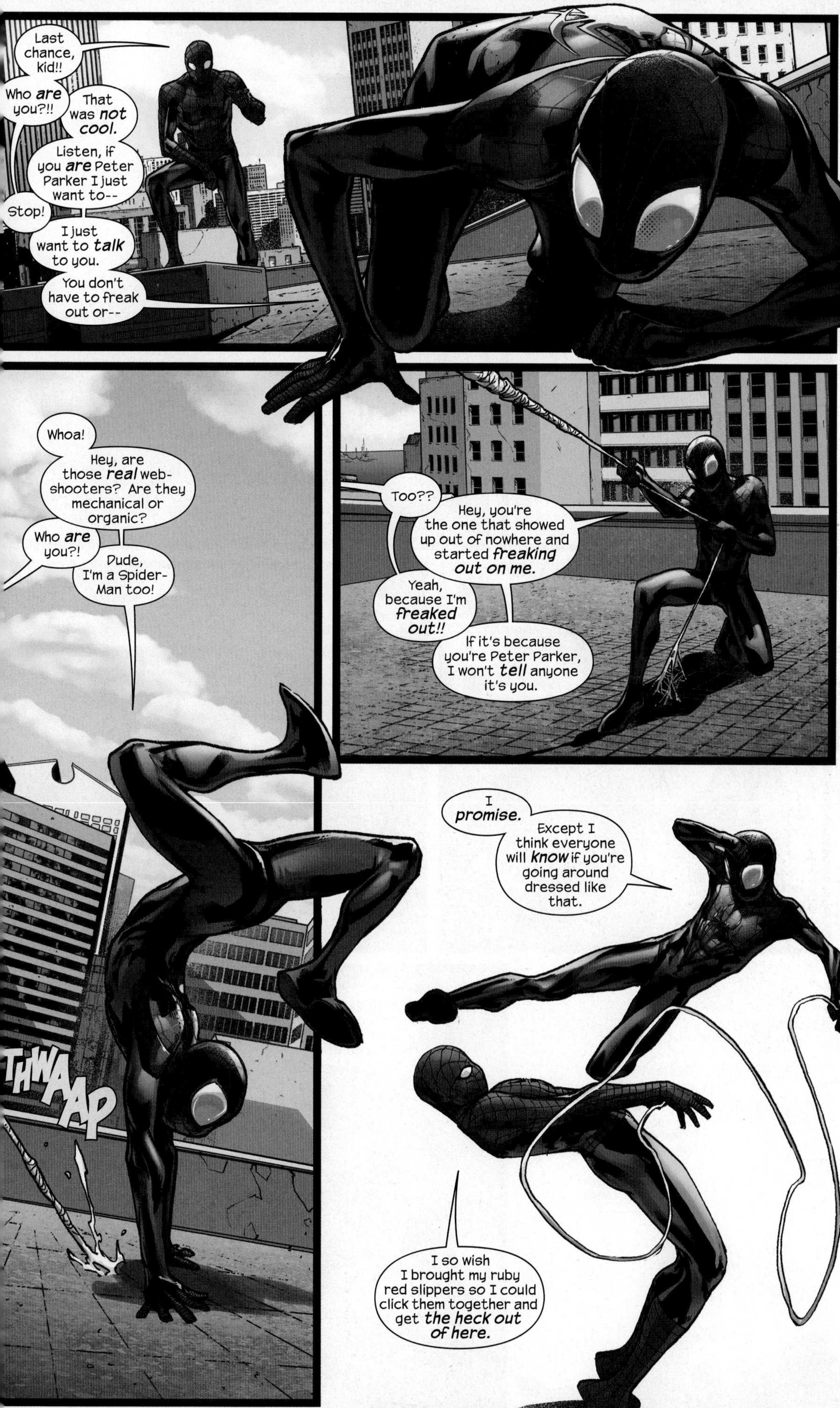

Last chance, kid!!
Who are you?!!
That was not cool.
Listen, if you are Peter Parker I just want to--
Stop!
I just want to talk to you.
You don't have to freak out or--
Whoa!
Hey, are those real web-shooters? Are they mechanical or organic?
Who are you?!
Dude, I'm a Spider-Man too!
Too??
Hey, you're the one that showed up out of nowhere and started freaking out on me.
Yeah, because I'm freaked out!!
If it's because you're Peter Parker, I won't tell anyone it's you.
THWAAAP
I promise.
Except I think everyone will know if you're going around dressed like that.
I so wish I brought my ruby red slippers so I could click them together and get the heck out of here.

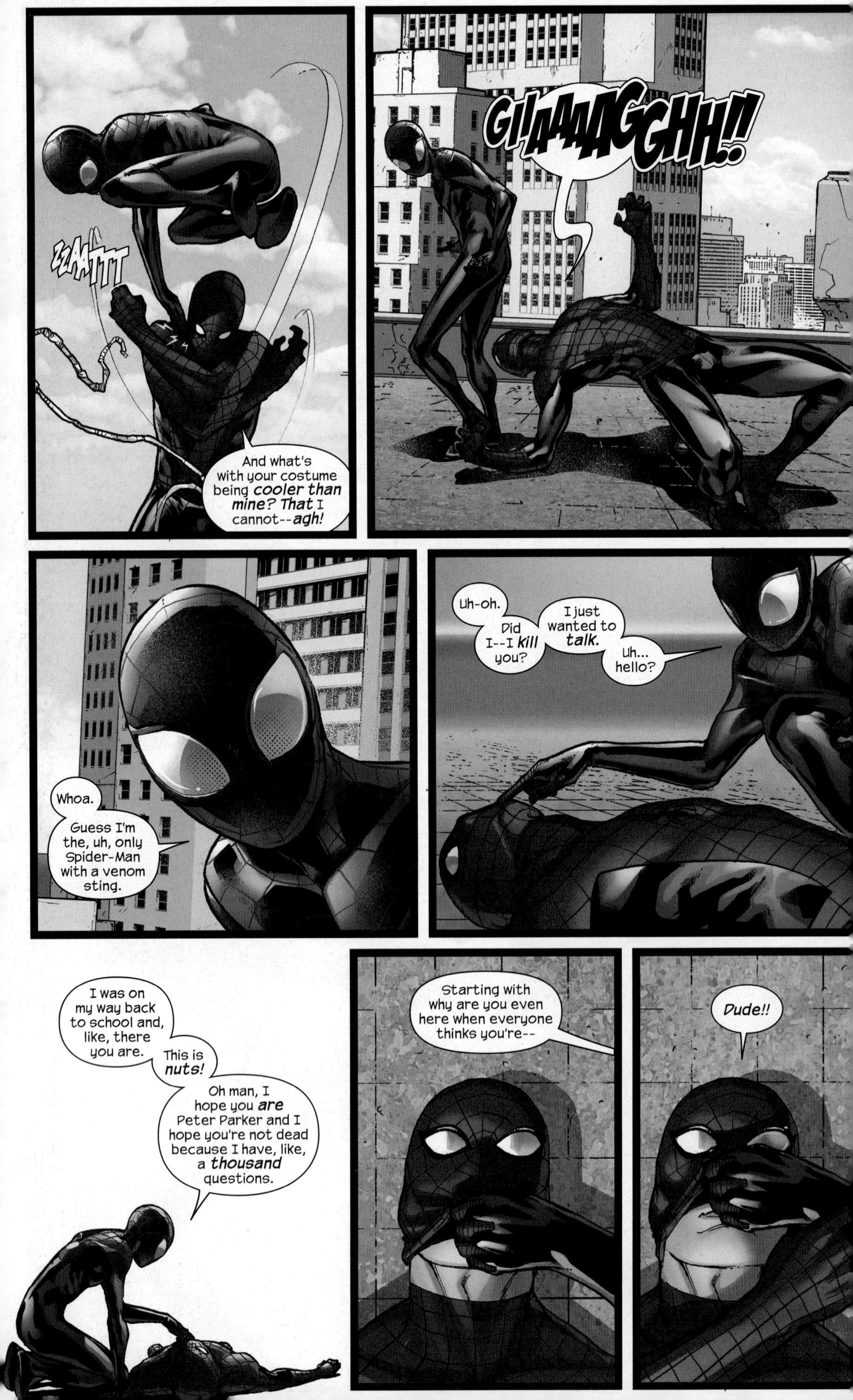
ZZAATTT
And what's with your costume being *cooler than mine? That* I cannot--*agh!*
GIIAAAAAGGHH!!
Whoa.
Guess I'm the, uh, only Spider-Man with a venom sting.
Uh-oh.
Did I--I *kill* you?
I just wanted to *talk.*
Uh... hello?
I was on my way back to school and, like, there you are.
This is *nuts!*
Oh man, I hope you *are* Peter Parker and I hope you're not dead because I have, like, a *thousand* questions.
Starting with why are you even here when everyone thinks you're--
Dude!!

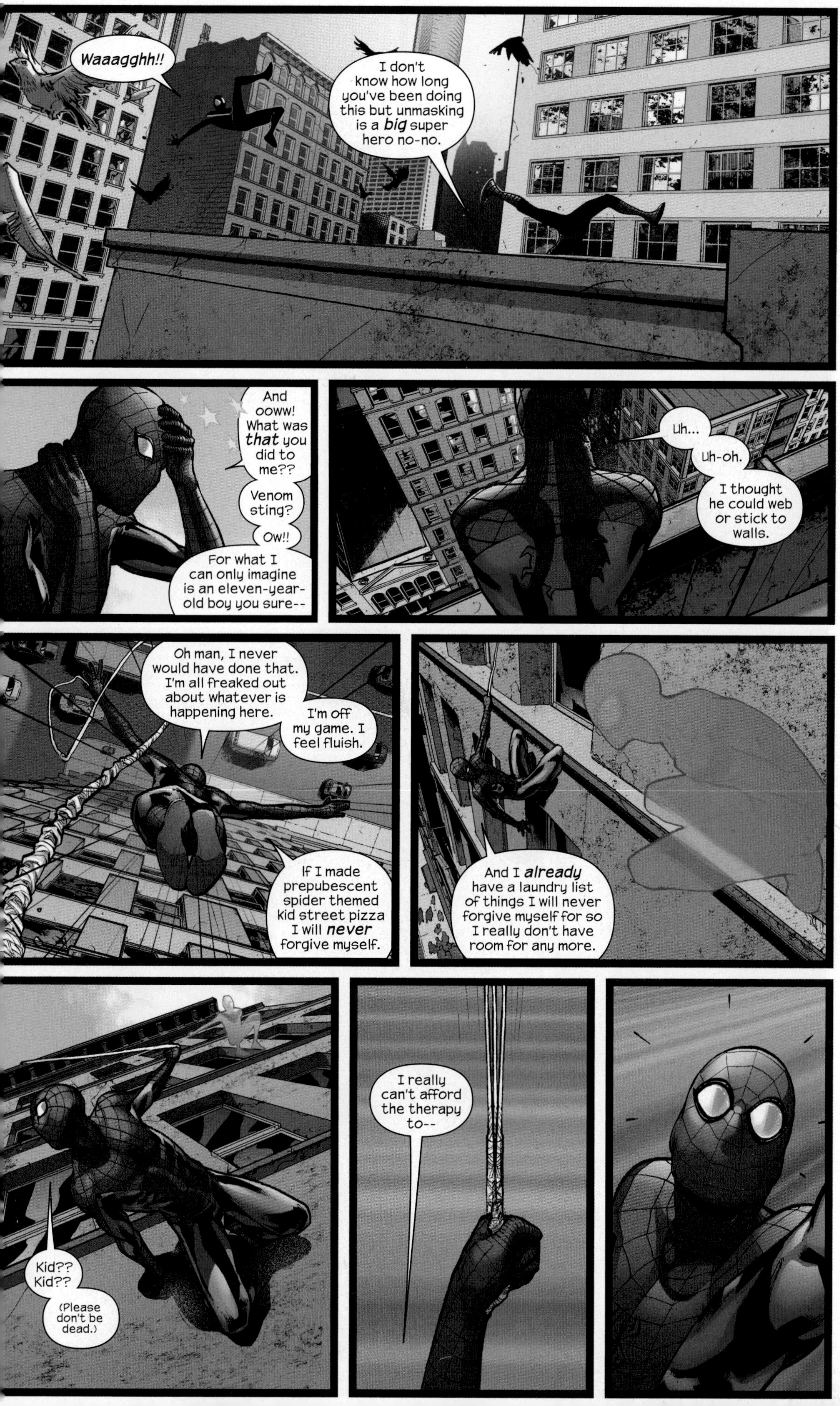
Waaagghh!!
I don't know how long you've been doing this but unmasking is a big super hero no-no.
And ooww! What was that you did to me??
Venom sting?
Ow!!
For what I can only imagine is an eleven-year-old boy you sure--
Uh...
Uh-oh.
I thought he could web or stick to walls.
Oh man, I never would have done that. I'm all freaked out about whatever is happening here.
I'm off my game. I feel fluish.
If I made prepubescent spider themed kid street pizza I will never forgive myself.
And I already have a laundry list of things I will never forgive myself for so I really don't have room for any more.
Kid?? Kid??
(Please don't be dead.)
I really can't afford the therapy to--

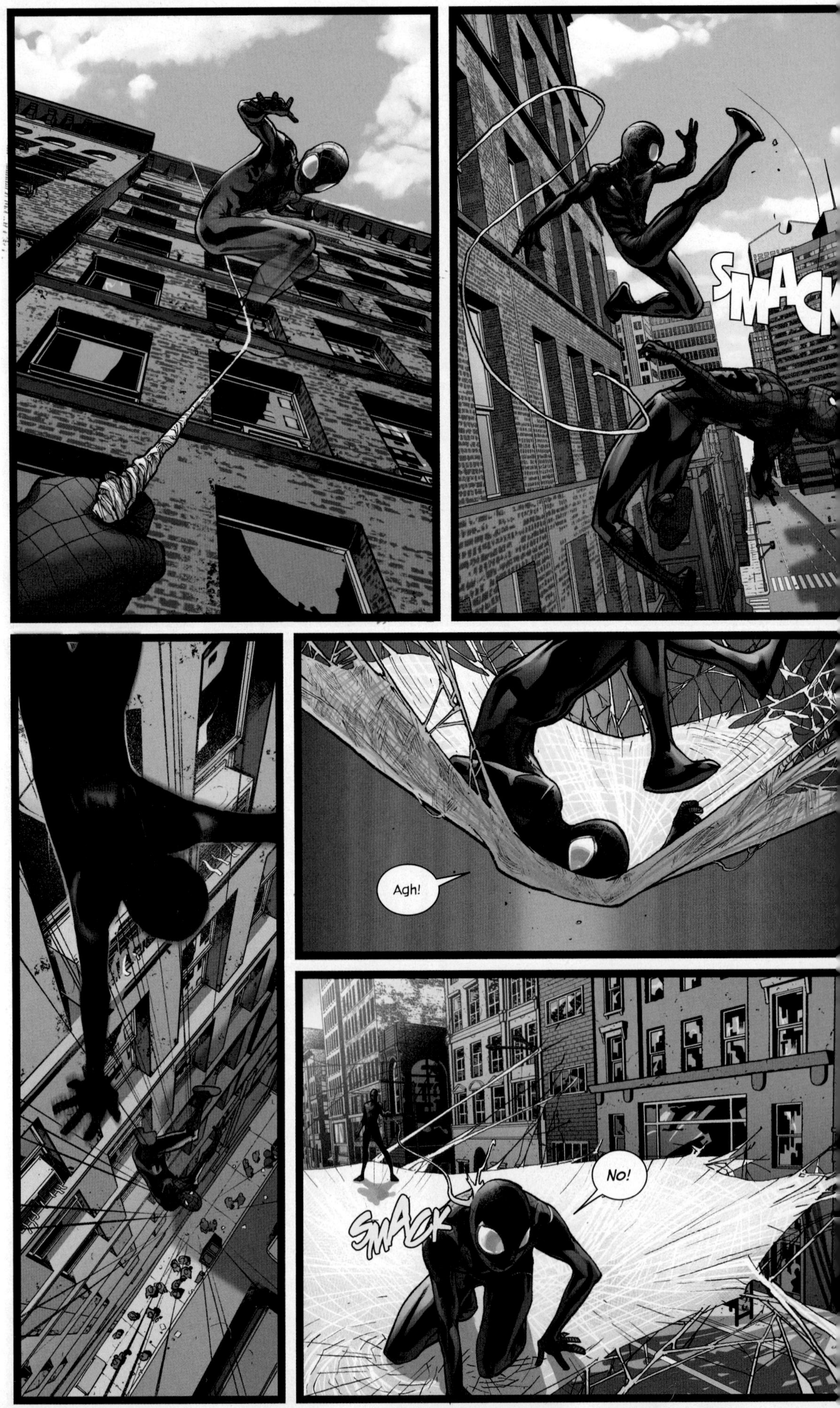
SMACK
Agh!
No!
SMACK

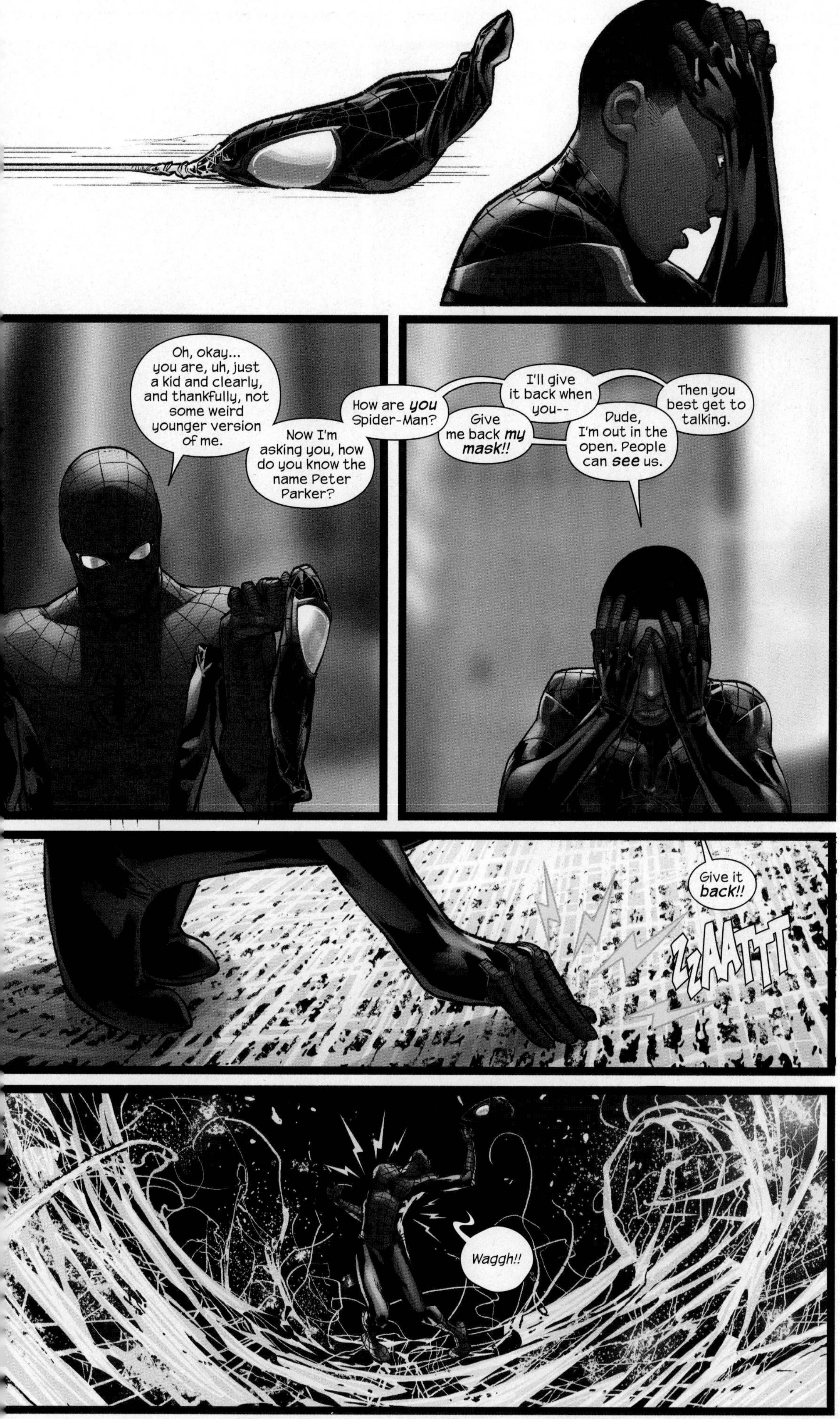
Oh, okay... you are, uh, just a kid and clearly, and thankfully, not some weird younger version of me.
Now I'm asking you, how do you know the name Peter Parker?
How are *you* Spider-Man?
Give me back *my mask!!*
I'll give it back when you--
Dude, I'm out in the open. People can *see* us.
Then you best get to talking.
Give it *back!!*
ZZAATTT
Waggh!!

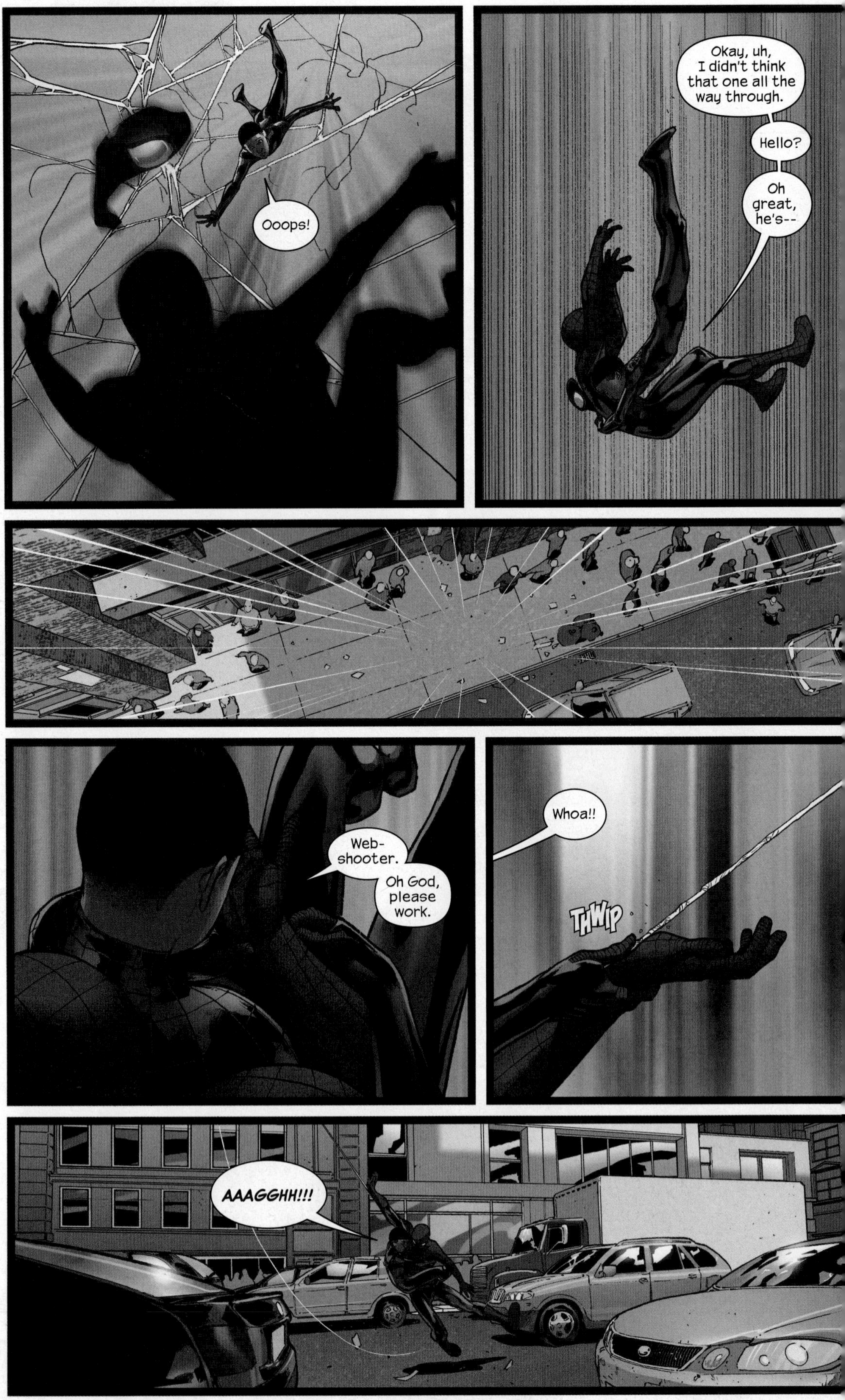
Ooops!
Okay, uh, I didn't think that one all the way through.
Hello?
Oh great, he's--
Web-shooter.
Oh God, please work.
Whoa!!
THWIP
AAAGGHH!!!

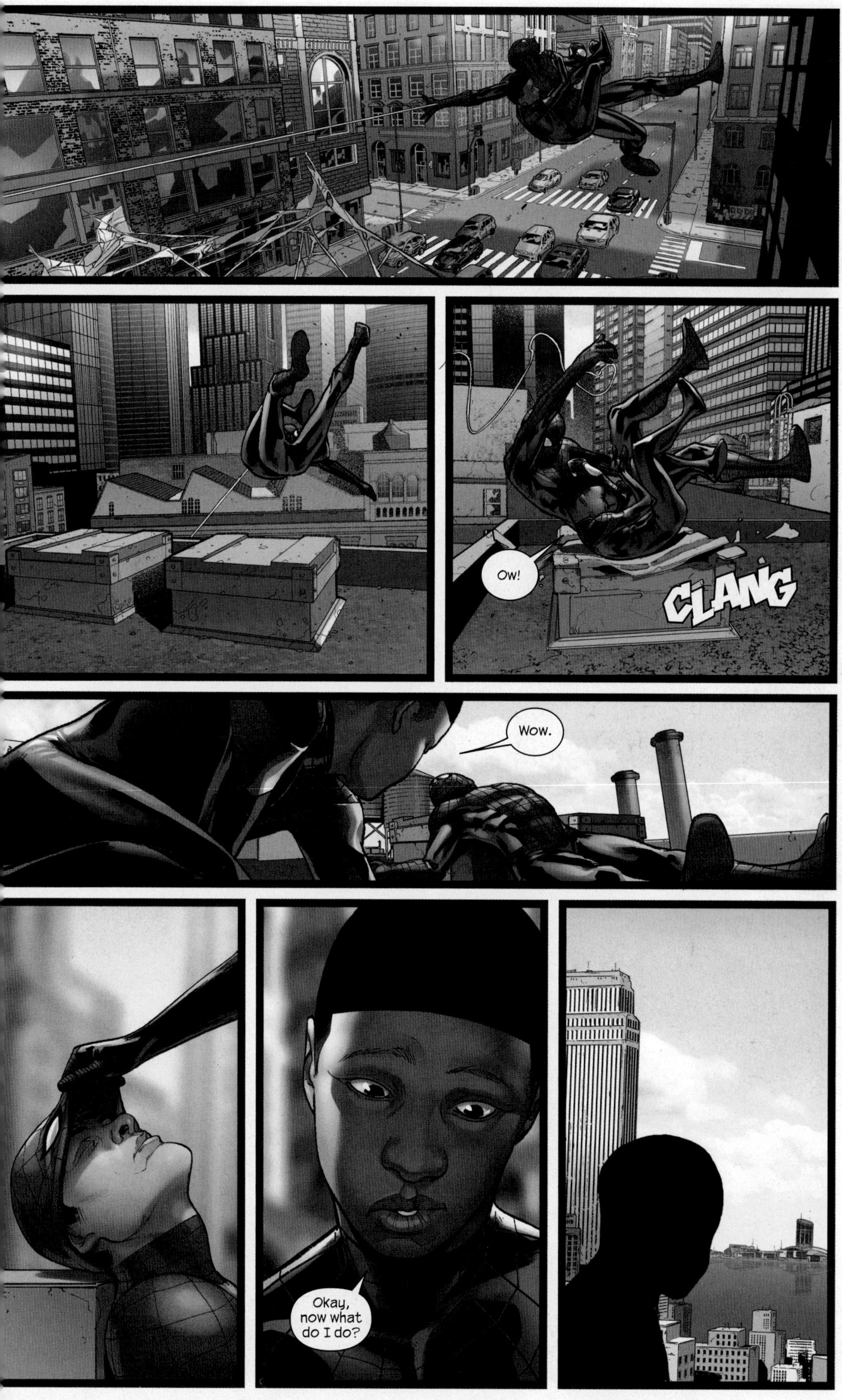
Ow!
CLANG
Wow.
Okay, now what do I do?

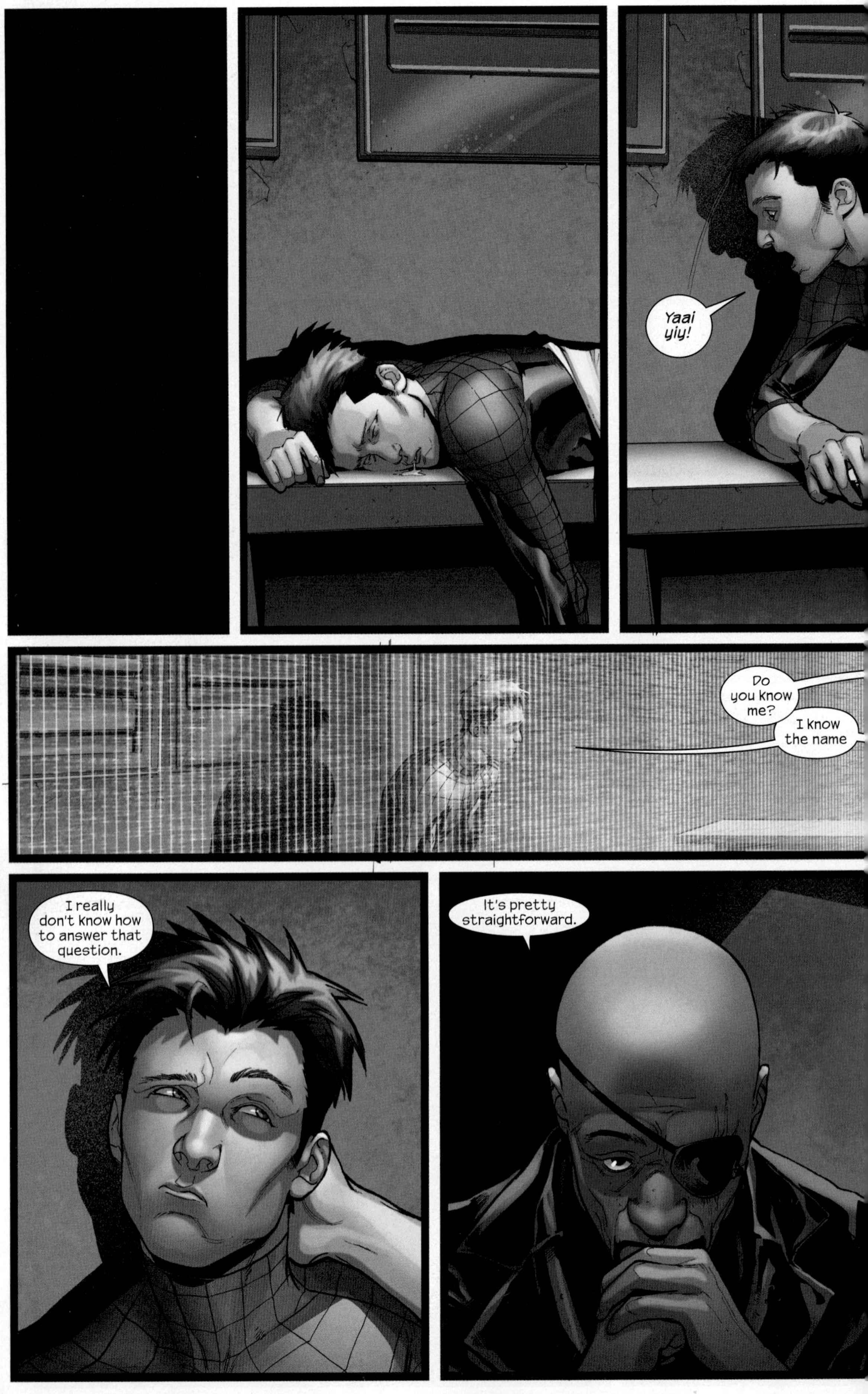
Yaai yiy!
Do you know me?
I know the name
I really don't know how to answer that question.
It's pretty straightforward.

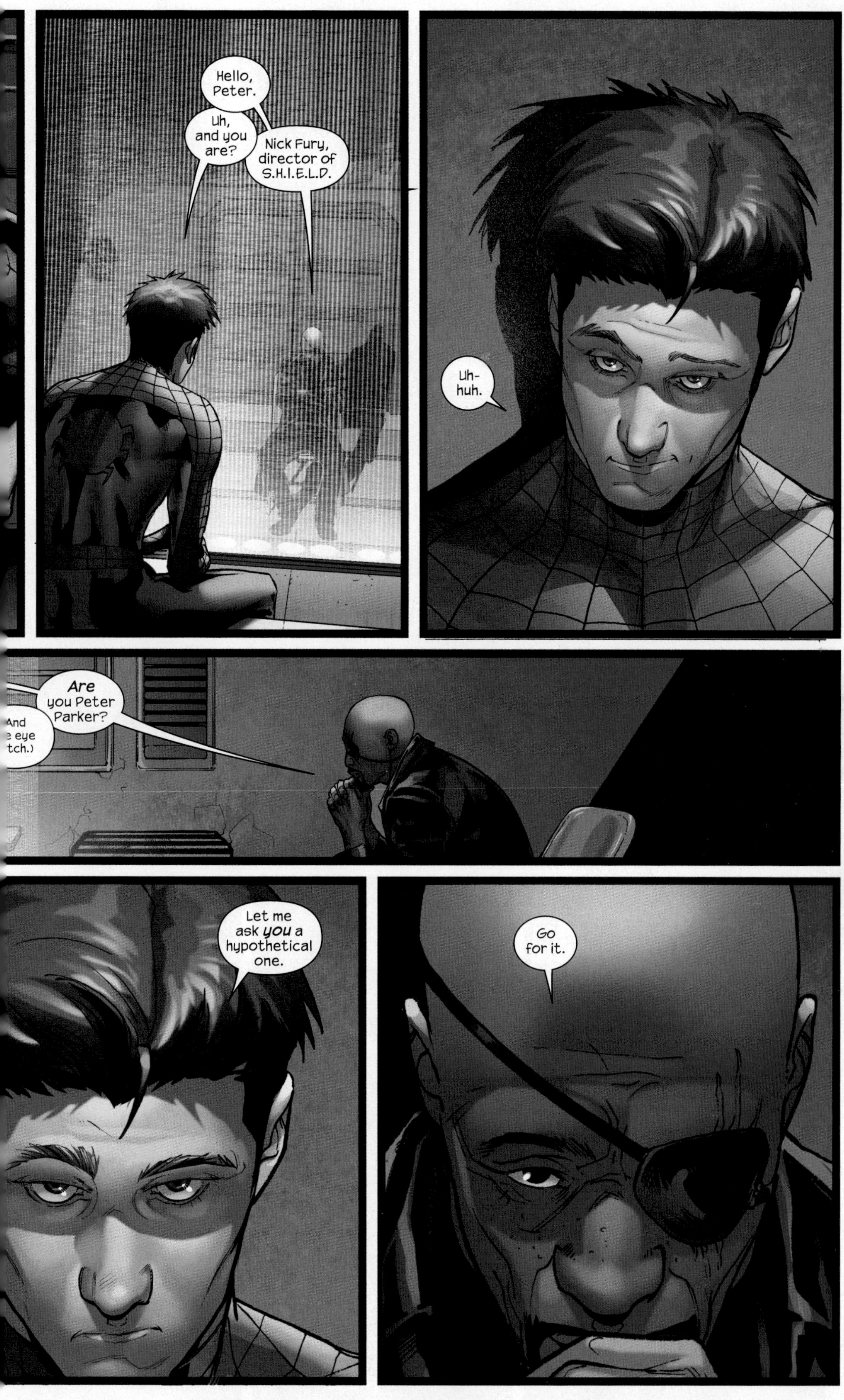
Hello, Peter.
Uh, and you are?
Nick Fury, director of S.H.I.E.L.D.
Uh-huh.
Are you Peter Parker?
And
e eye
tch.)
Let me ask *you* a hypothetical one.
Go for it.

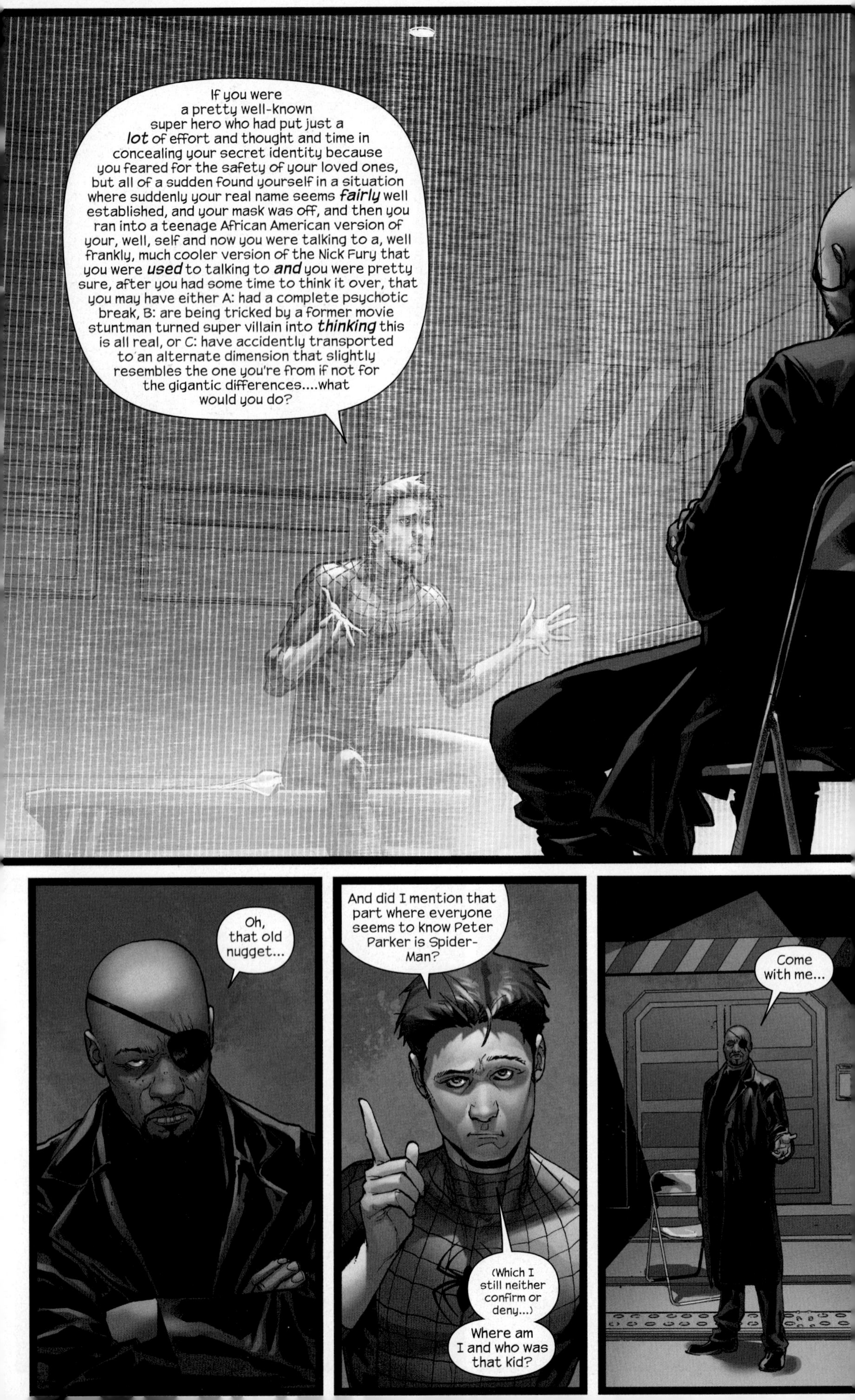
If you were a pretty well-known super hero who had put just a *lot* of effort and thought and time in concealing your secret identity because you feared for the safety of your loved ones, but all of a sudden found yourself in a situation where suddenly your real name seems *fairly* well established, and your mask was off, and then you ran into a teenage African American version of your, well, self and now you were talking to a, well frankly, much cooler version of the Nick Fury that you were *used* to talking to *and* you were pretty sure, after you had some time to think it over, that you may have either A: had a complete psychotic break, B: are being tricked by a former movie stuntman turned super villain into *thinking* this is all real, or C: have accidently transported to an alternate dimension that slightly resembles the one you're from if not for the gigantic differences....what would you do?
Oh, that old nugget...
And did I mention that part where everyone seems to know Peter Parker is Spider-Man?
(Which I still neither confirm or deny...)
Where am I and who was that kid?
Come with me...

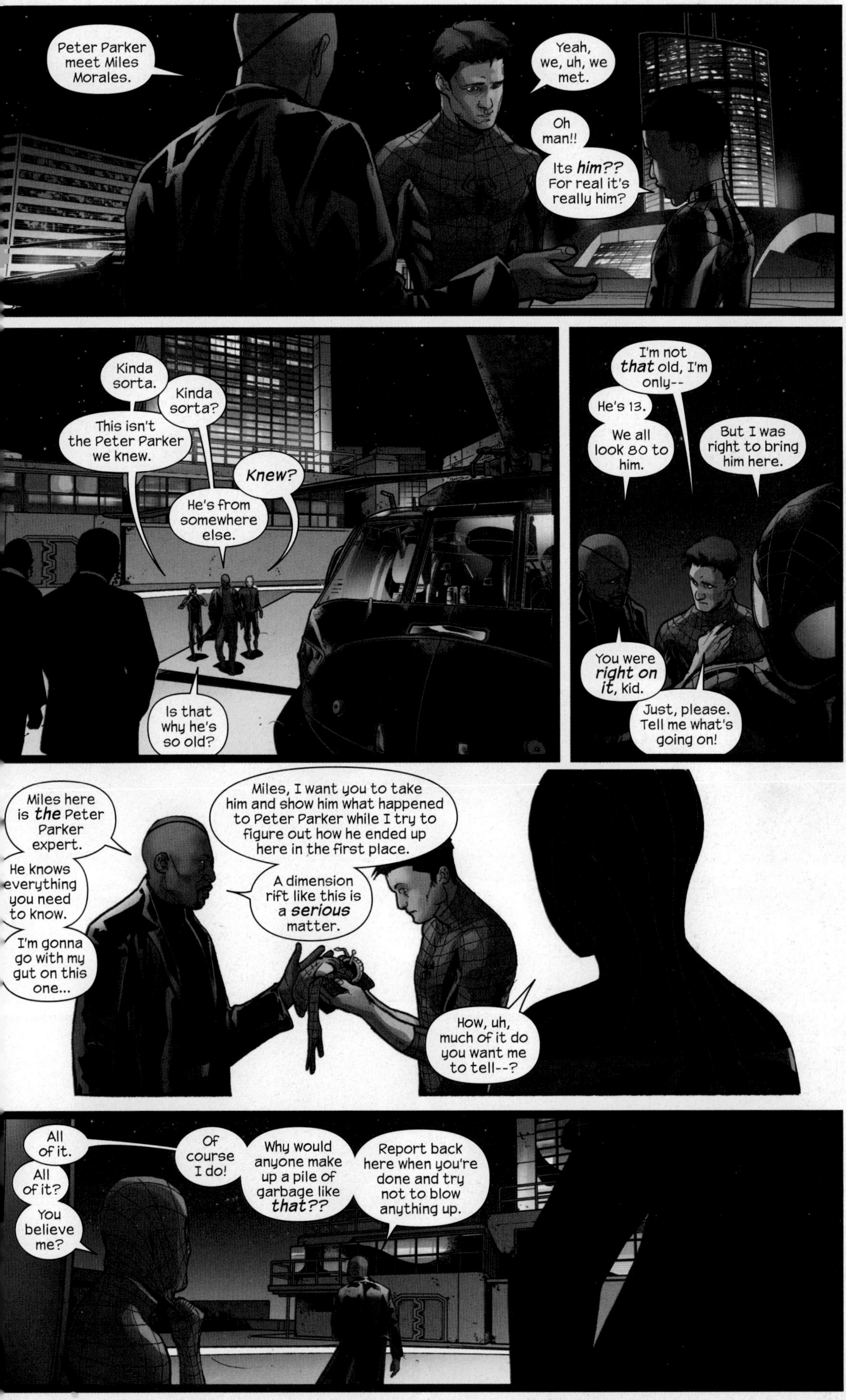

Peter Parker meet Miles Morales.
Yeah, we, uh, we met.
Oh man!!
Its *him??* For real it's really him?
Kinda sorta.
Kinda sorta?
This isn't the Peter Parker we knew.
Knew?
He's from somewhere else.
Is that why he's so old?
I'm not *that* old, I'm only--
He's 13.
We all look 80 to him.
But I was right to bring him here.
You were *right on it*, kid.
Just, please. Tell me what's going on!
Miles here is *the* Peter Parker expert.
He knows everything you need to know.
I'm gonna go with my gut on this one...
Miles, I want you to take him and show him what happened to Peter Parker while I try to figure out how he ended up here in the first place.
A dimension rift like this is a *serious* matter.
How, uh, much of it do you want me to tell--?
All of it.
All of it?
You believe me?
Of course I do!
Why would anyone make up a pile of garbage like *that??*
Report back here when you're done and try not to blow anything up.

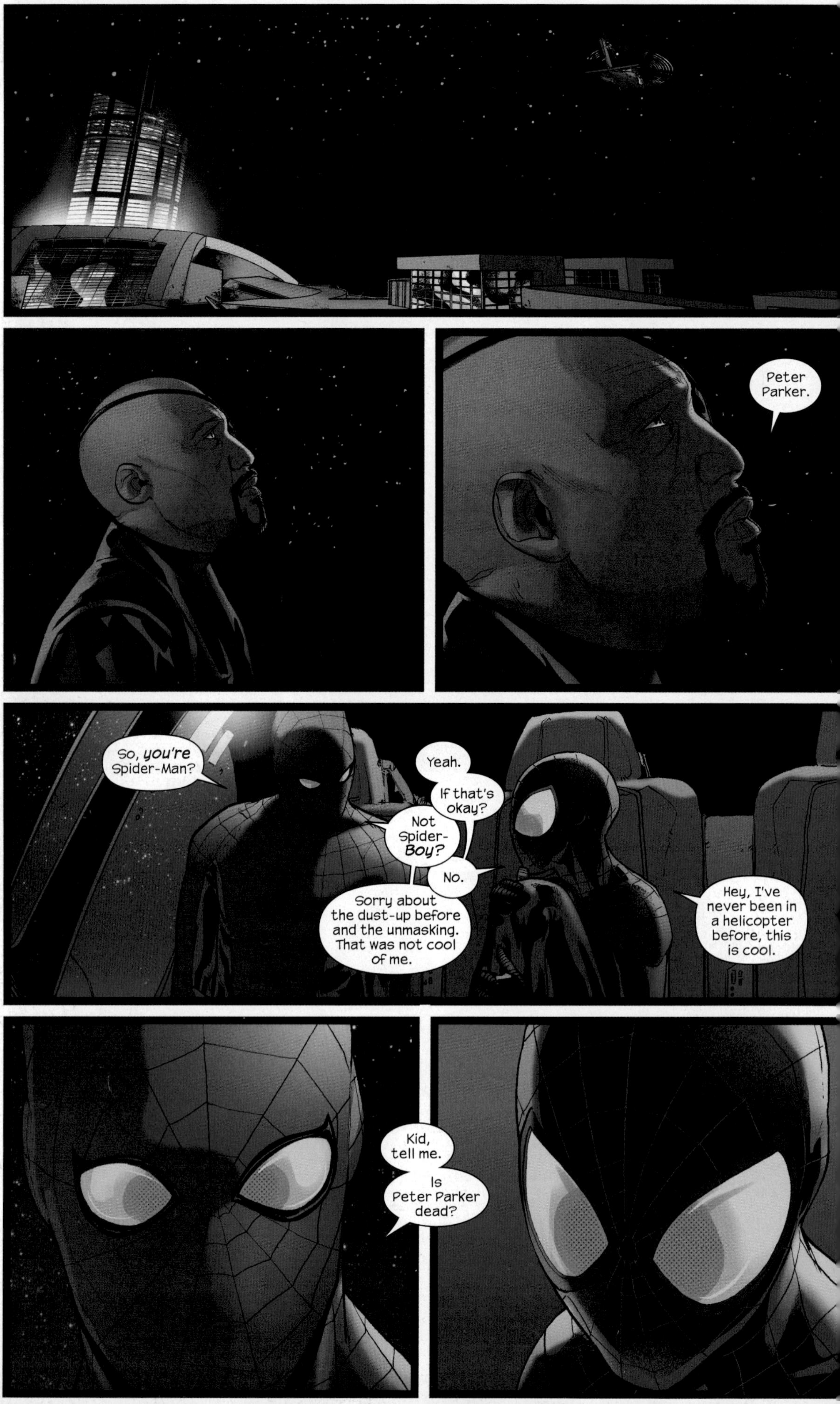
Peter Parker.
So, you're Spider-Man?
Yeah.
If that's okay?
Not Spider-Boy?
No.
Sorry about the dust-up before and the unmasking. That was not cool of me.
Hey, I've never been in a helicopter before, this is cool.
Kid, tell me.
Is Peter Parker dead?

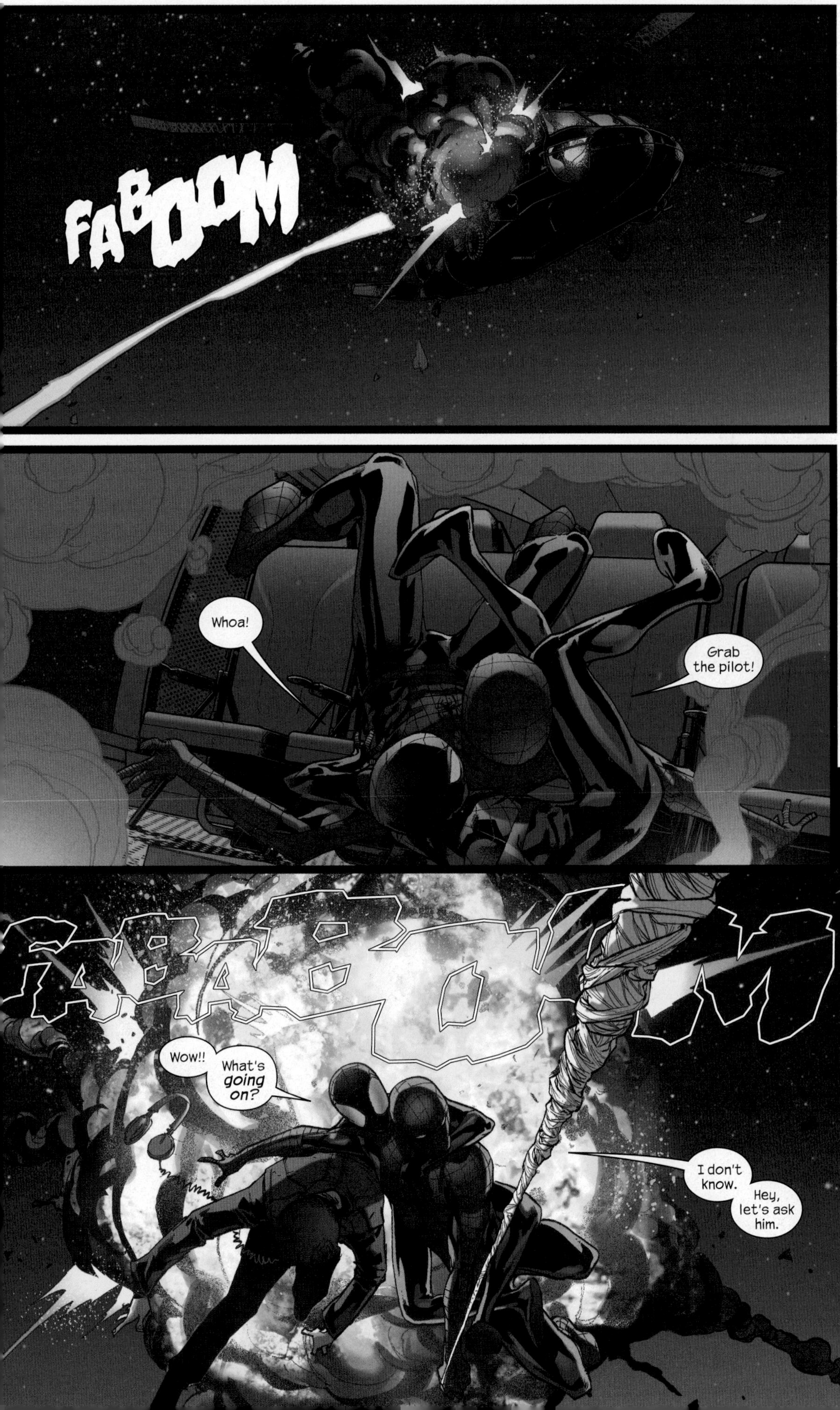
FABOOM
Whoa!
Grab the pilot!
FABOOM
Wow!!
What's going on?
I don't know.
Hey, let's ask him.

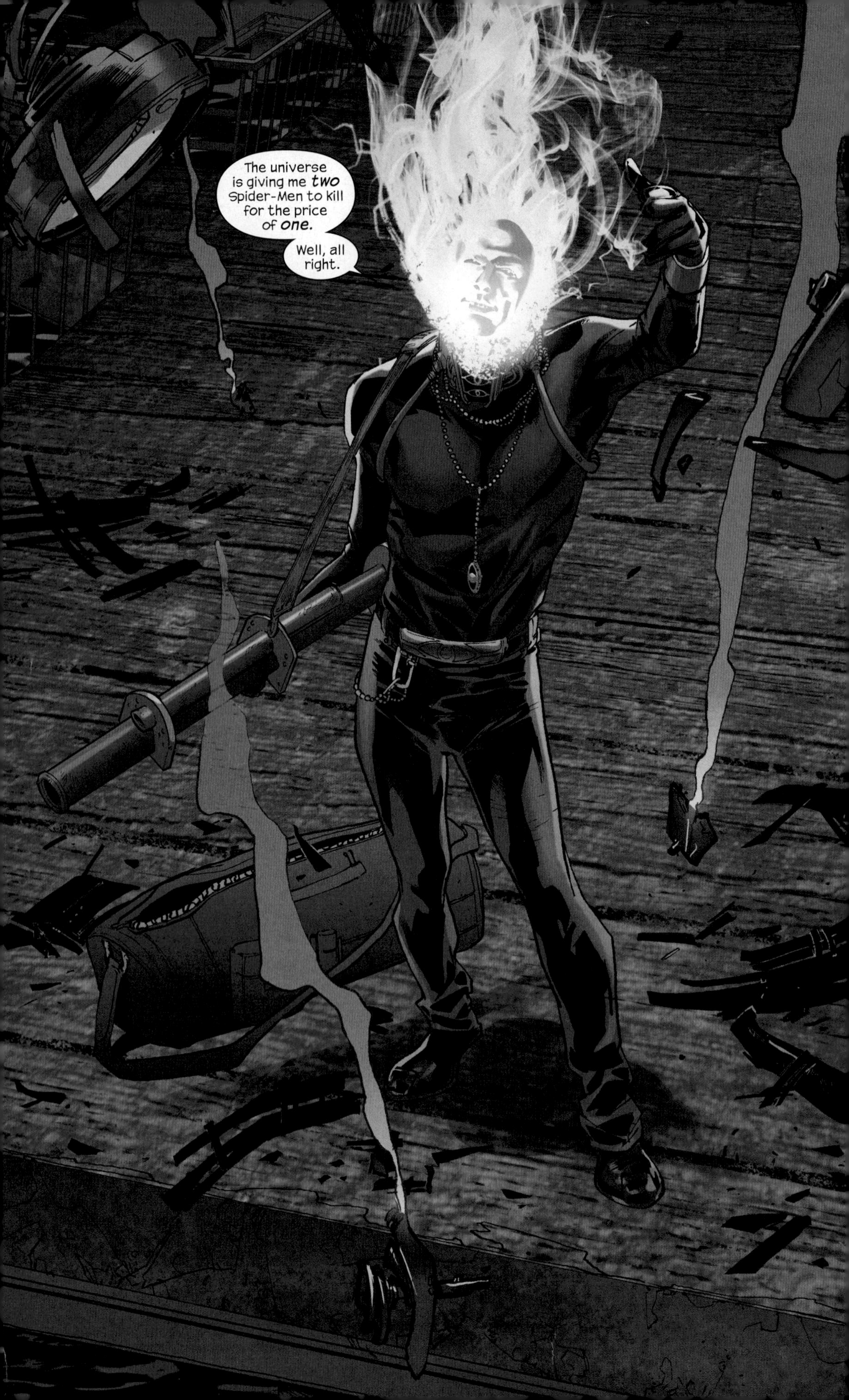
The universe is giving me *two* Spider-Men to kill for the price of *one.*
Well, all right.

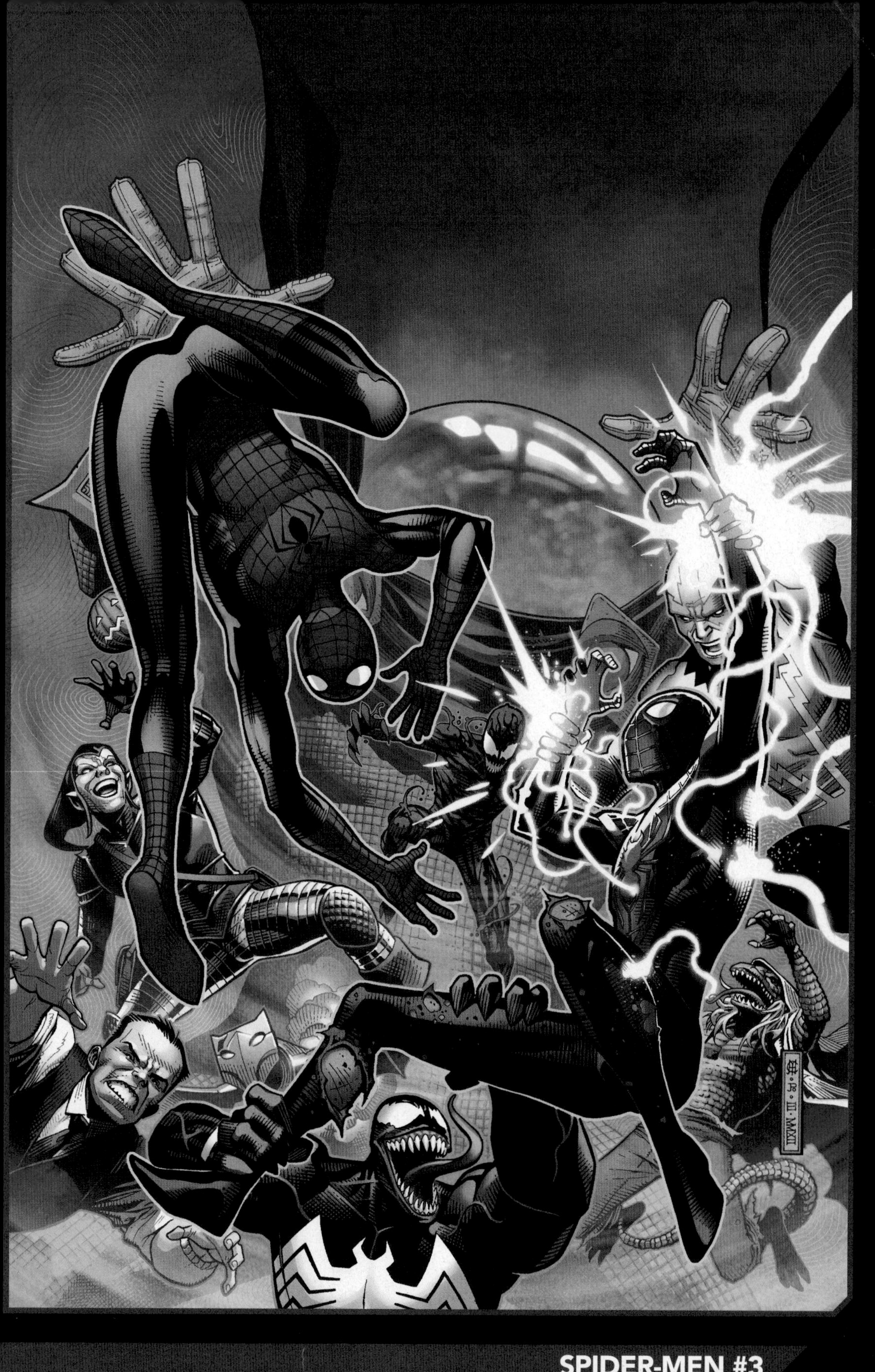

SPIDER-MEN #3

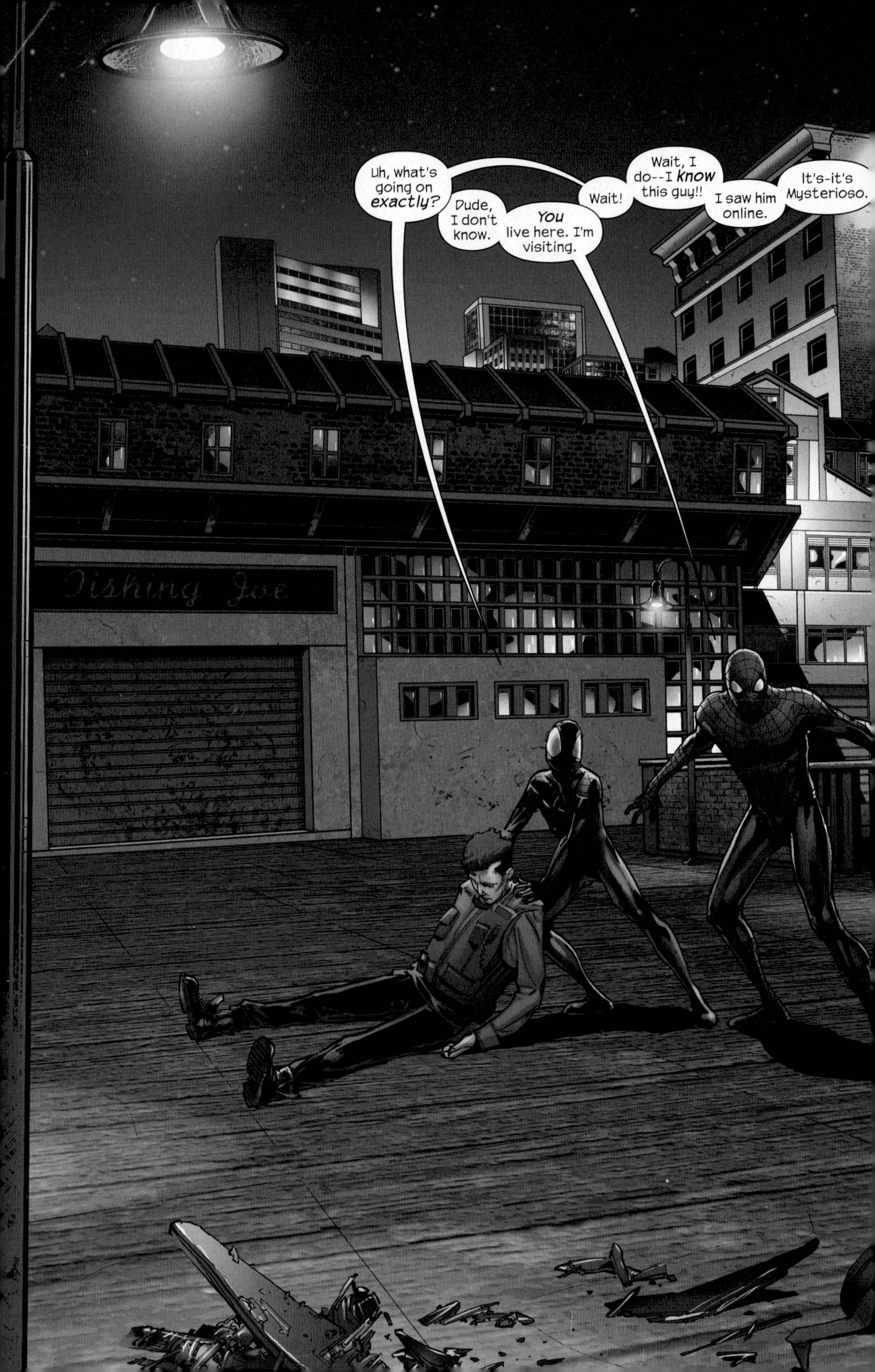
Uh, what's going on *exactly?*
Dude, I don't know.
You live here. I'm visiting.
Wait!
Wait, I do--I **know** this guy!!
I saw him online.
It's-it's Mysterioso.
Fishing Joe

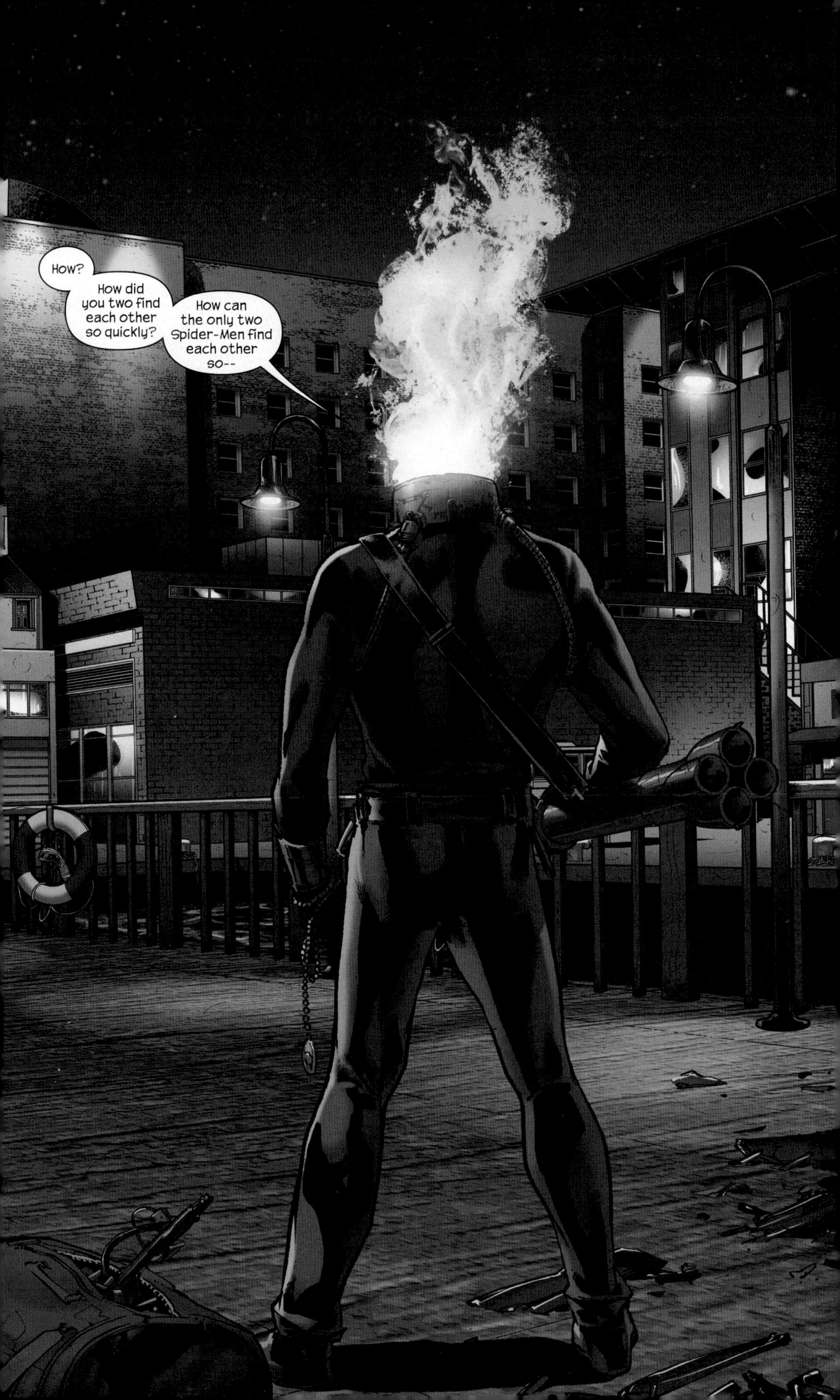

How?
How did you two find each other so quickly?
How can the only two Spider-Men find each other so--

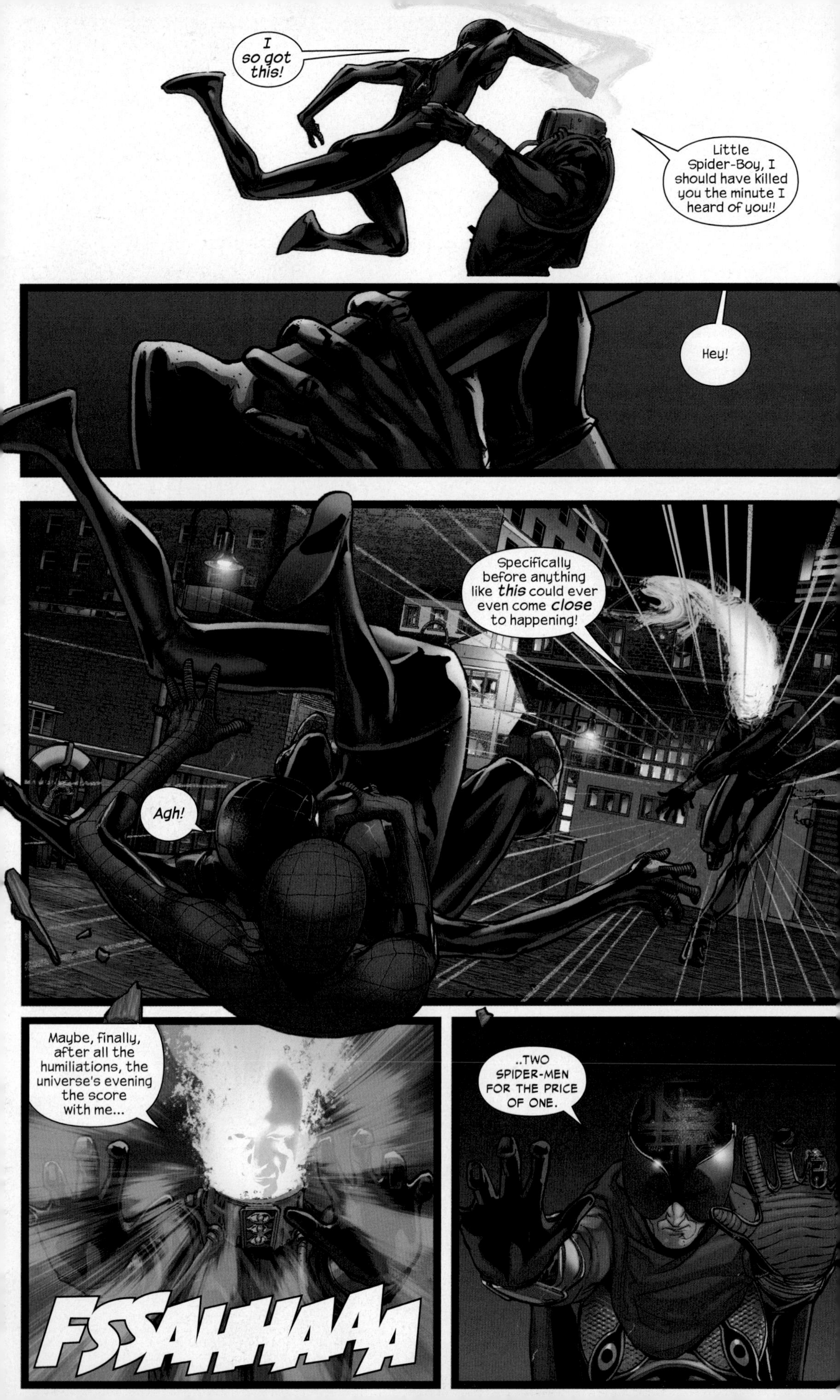

I so got this!
Little Spider-Boy, I should have killed you the minute I heard of you!!
Hey!
Specifically before anything like *this* could ever even come *close* to happening!
Agh!
Maybe, finally, after all the humiliations, the universe's evening the score with me...
FSSAHHAAA
..TWO SPIDER-MEN FOR THE PRICE OF ONE.

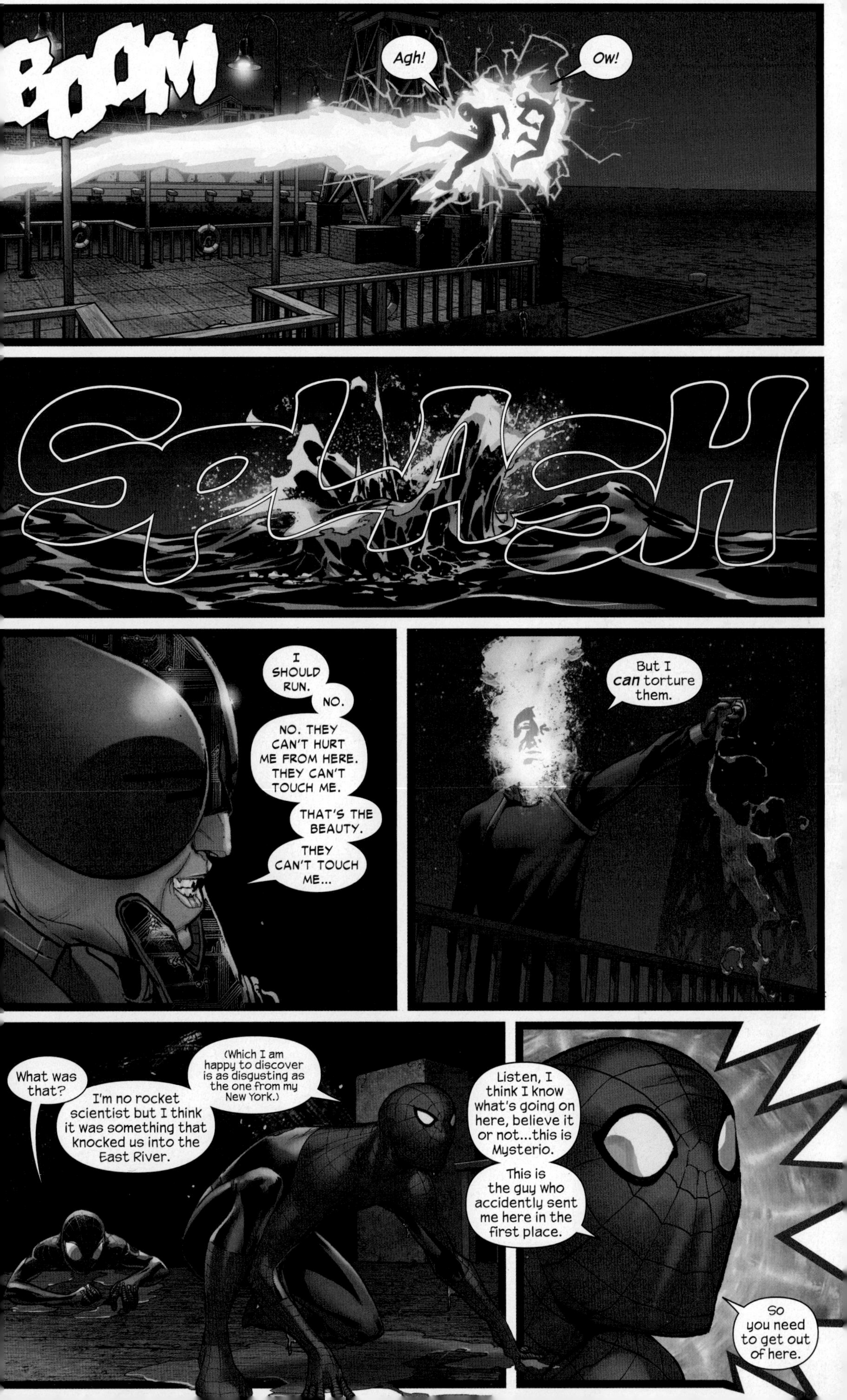
BOOM
Agh!
Ow!
SPLASH
I SHOULD RUN.
NO.
NO. THEY CAN'T HURT ME FROM HERE. THEY CAN'T TOUCH ME.
THAT'S THE BEAUTY.
THEY CAN'T TOUCH ME...
But I can torture them.
What was that?
I'm no rocket scientist but I think it was something that knocked us into the East River.
(Which I am happy to discover is as disgusting as the one from my New York.)
Listen, I think I know what's going on here, believe it or not...this is Mysterio.
This is the guy who accidently sent me here in the first place.
So you need to get out of here.

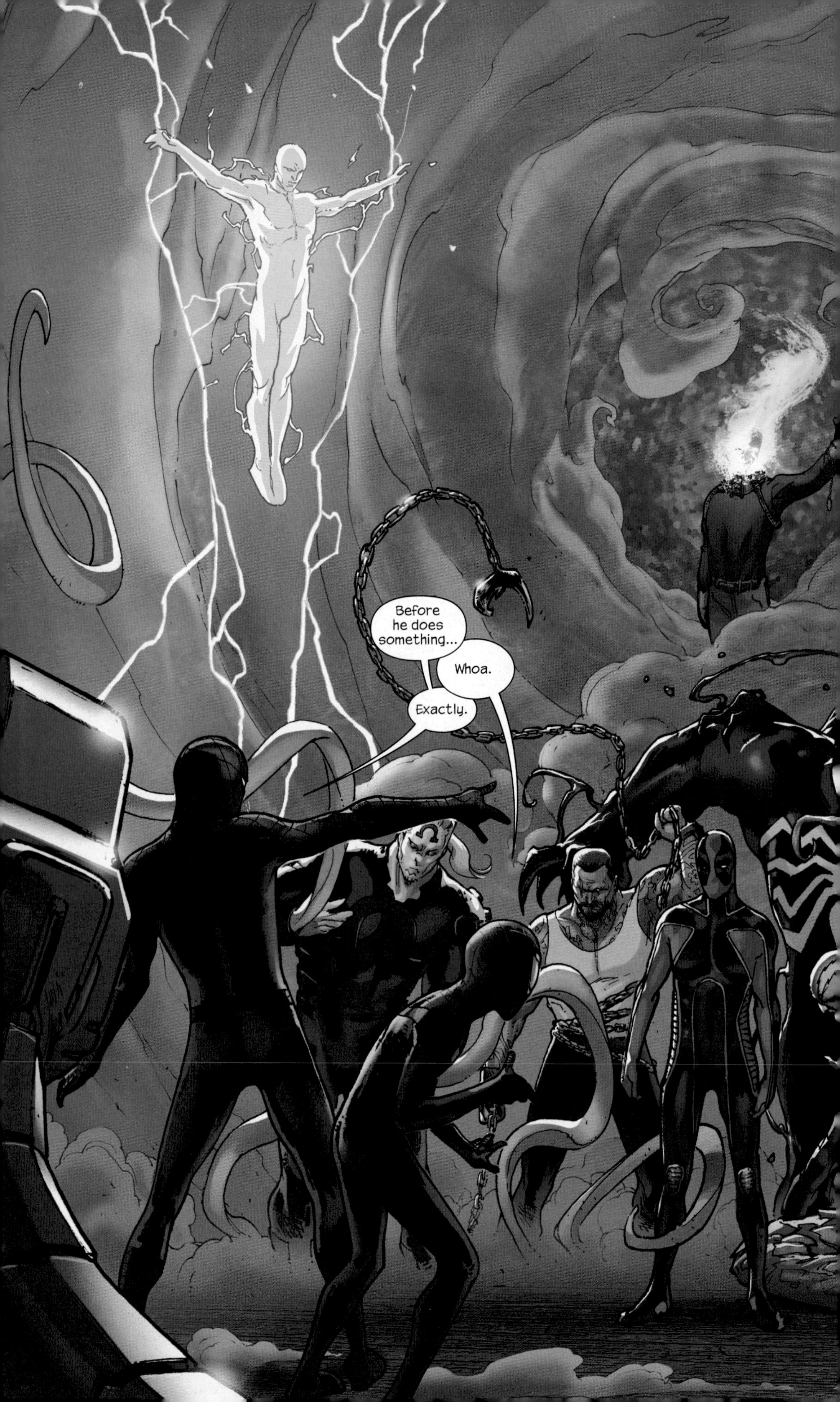
Before he does something...
Whoa.
Exactly.

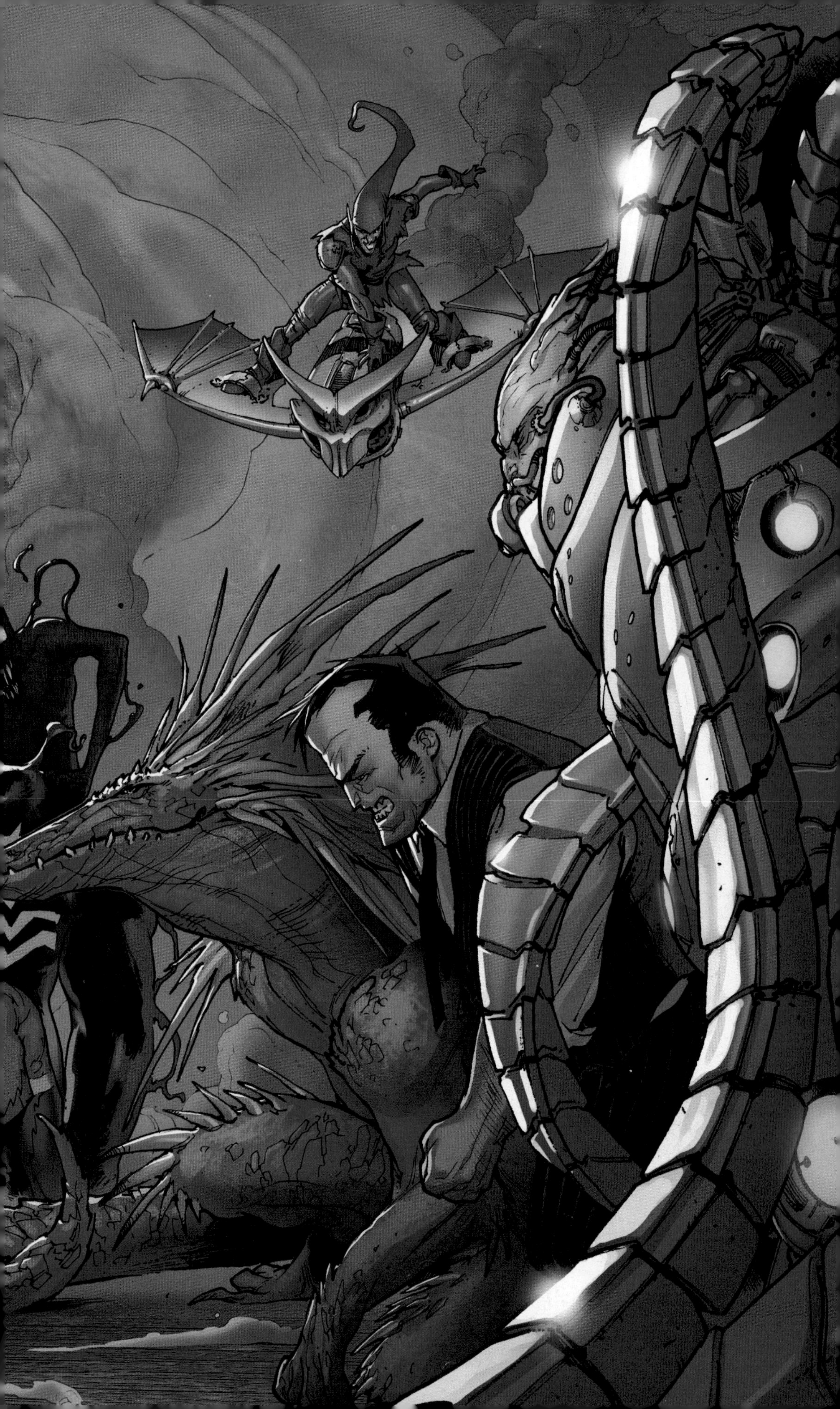

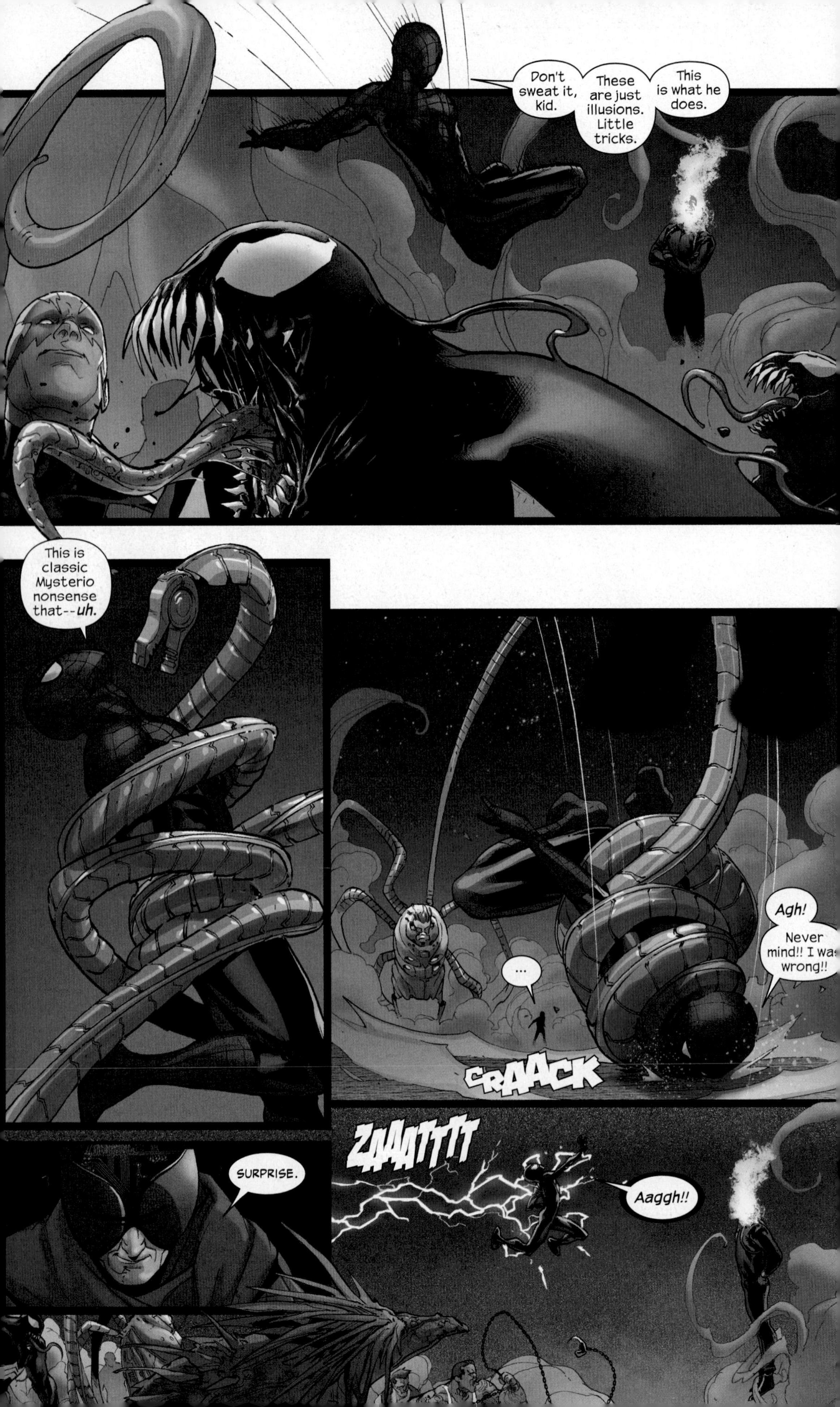
Don't sweat it, kid.
These are just illusions. Little tricks.
This is what he does.
This is classic Mysterio nonsense that--*uh.*
...
Agh!
Never mind!! I wa wrong!!
CRAACK
SURPRISE.
ZAAATTTT
Aaggh!!

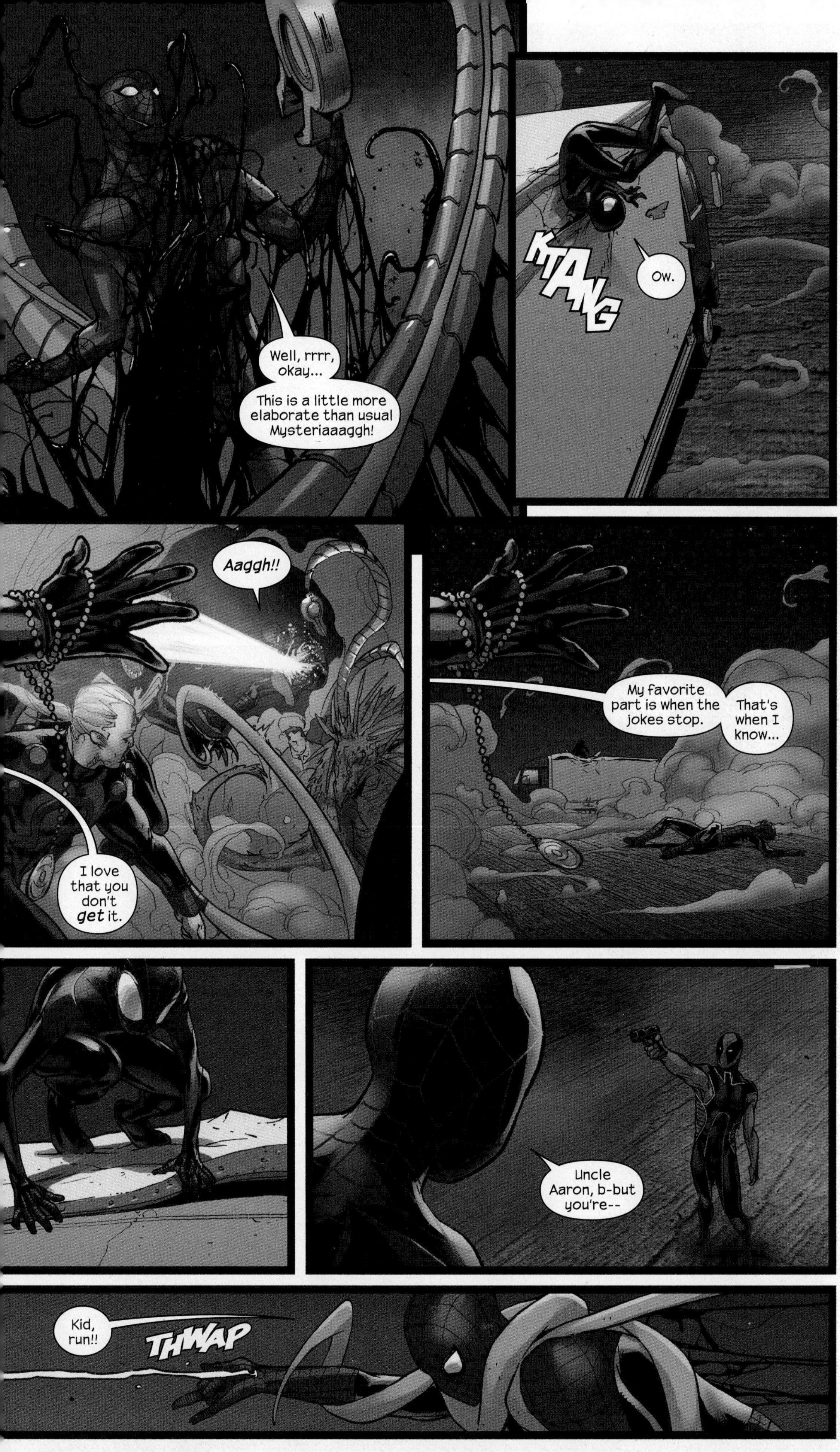
Well, rrrr, okay...
This is a little more elaborate than usual Mysteriaaaggh!
KTANG
Ow.
Aaggh!!
I love that you don't *get* it.
My favorite part is when the jokes stop.
That's when I know...
Uncle Aaron, b-but you're--
Kid, run!!
THWAP

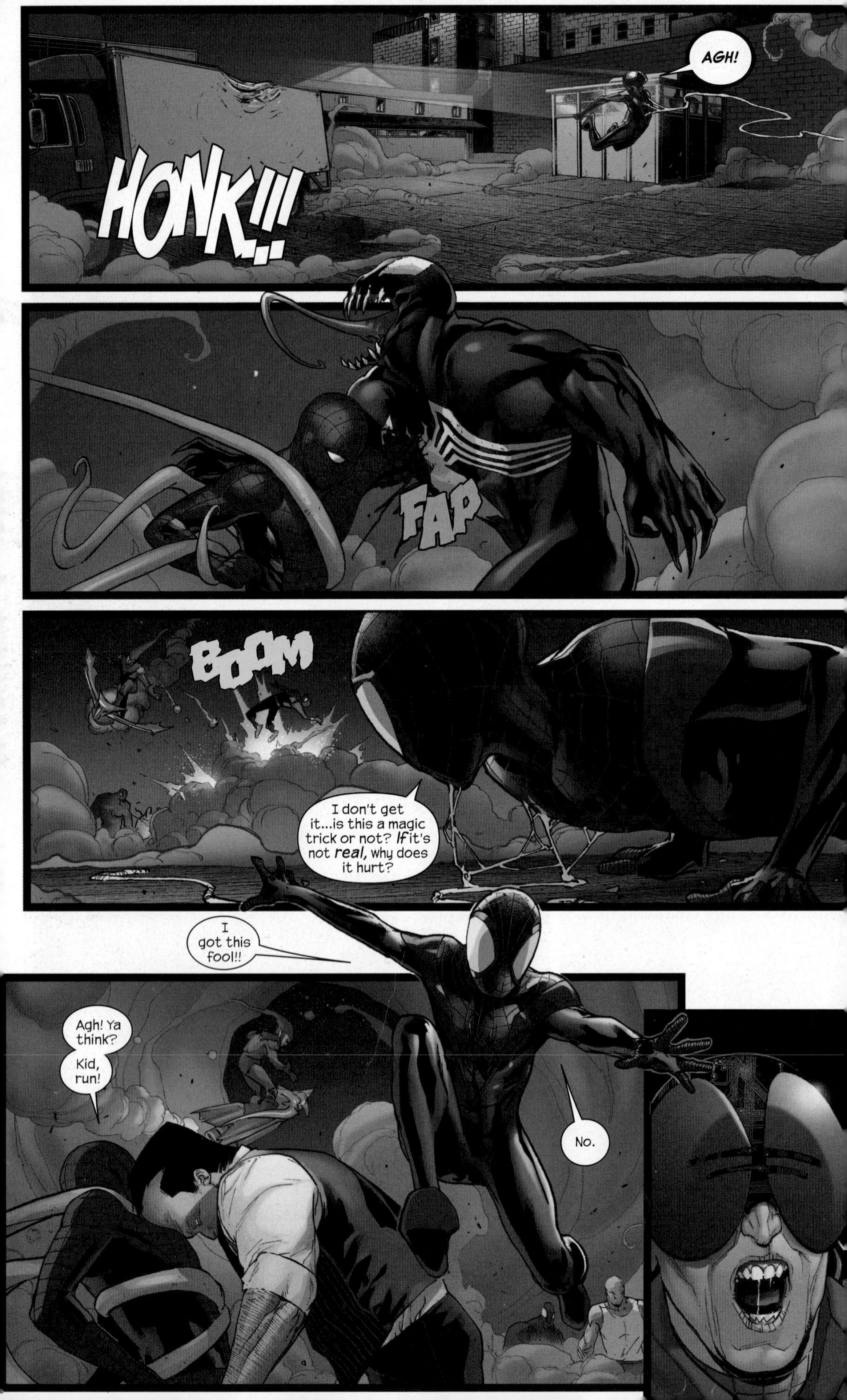
AGH!
HONK!!!
FAP
BOOM
I don't get it...is this a magic trick or not? *If* it's not *real,* why does it hurt?
I got this fool!!
Agh! Ya think?
Kid, run!
No.

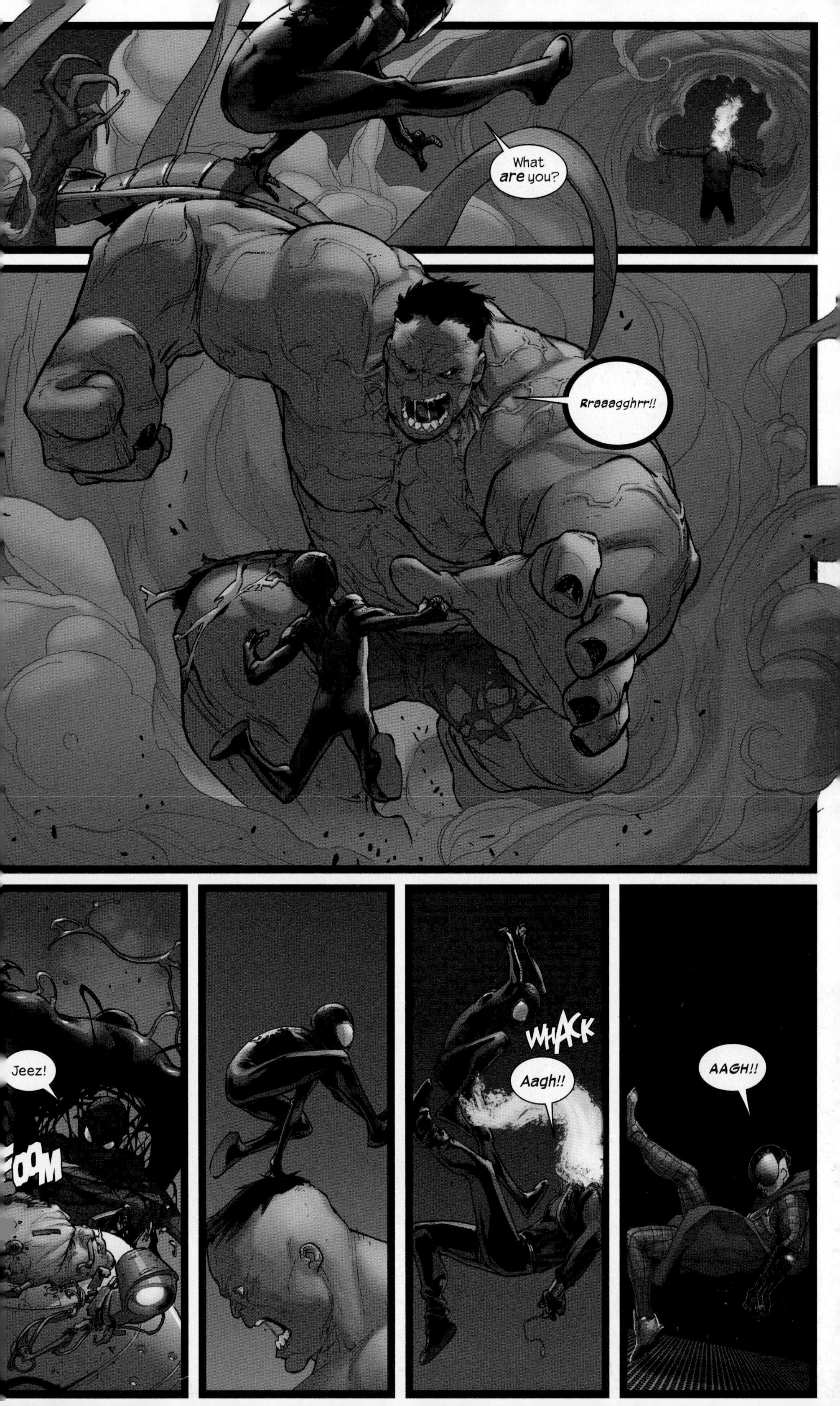
What are you?
Rraaagghrr!!
Jeez!
FOOM
WHACK
Aagh!!
AAGH!!

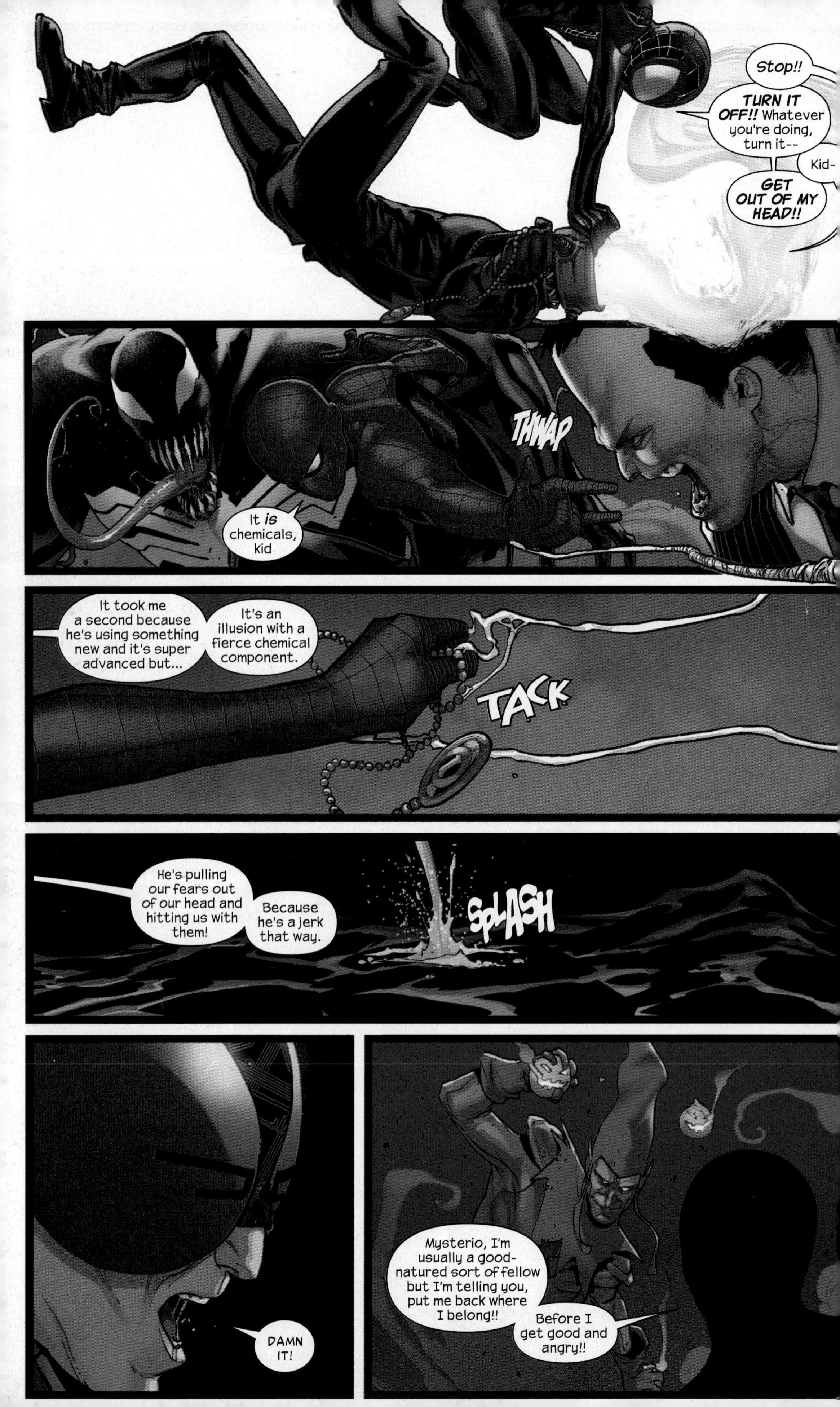
Stop!!
TURN IT OFF!! Whatever you're doing, turn it--
Kid-
GET OUT OF MY HEAD!!
THWAP
It is chemicals, kid
It took me a second because he's using something new and it's super advanced but...
It's an illusion with a fierce chemical component.
TACK
He's pulling our fears out of our head and hitting us with them!
Because he's a jerk that way.
SPLASH
DAMN IT!
Mysterio, I'm usually a good-natured sort of fellow but I'm telling you, put me back where I belong!!
Before I get good and angry!!

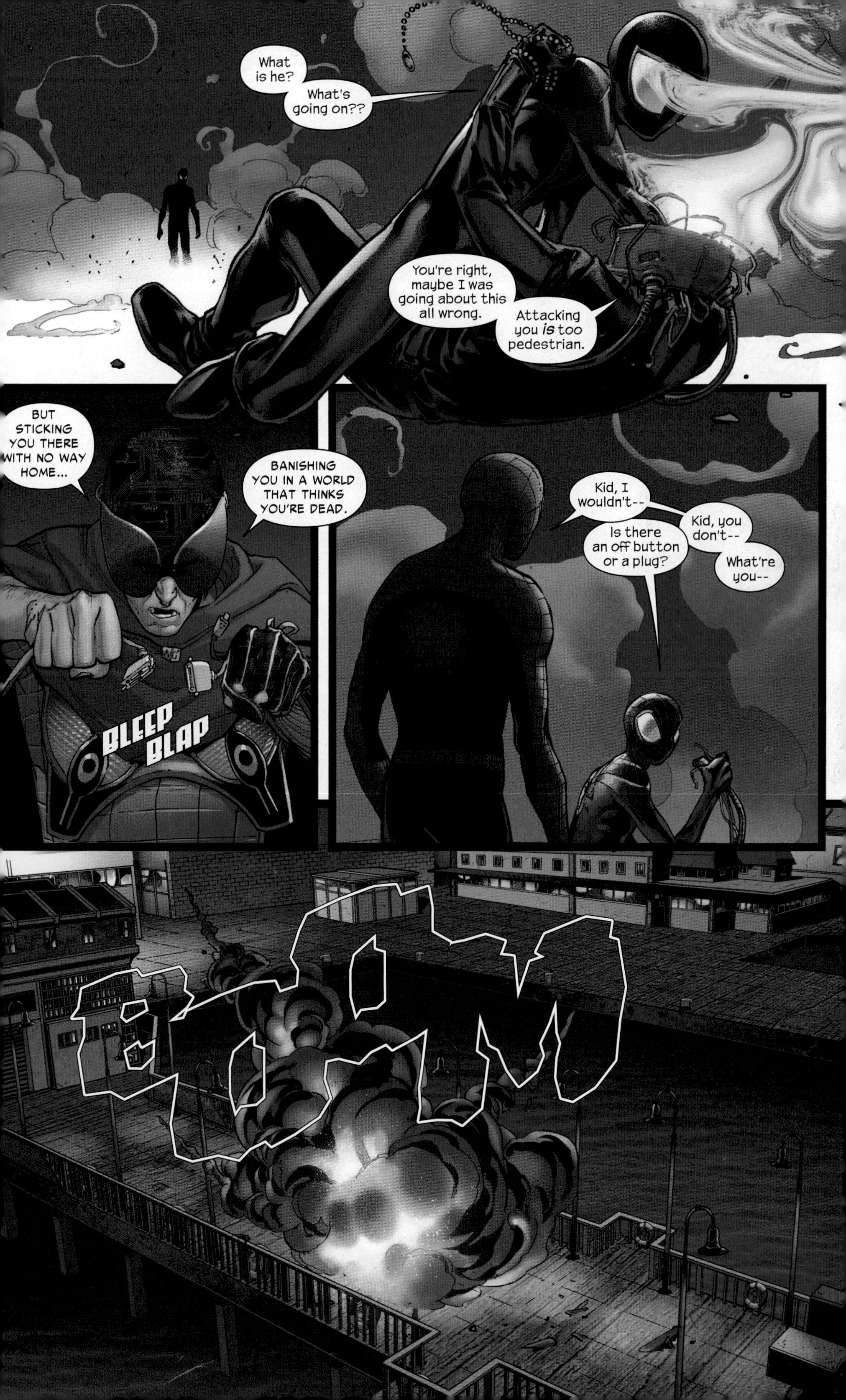

What is he?
What's going on??
You're right, maybe I was going about this all wrong.
Attacking you *is* too pedestrian.
BUT STICKING YOU THERE WITH NO WAY HOME...
BANISHING YOU IN A WORLD THAT THINKS YOU'RE DEAD.
BLEEP
BLAP
Kid, I wouldn't--
Is there an off button or a plug?
Kid, you don't--
What're you--
BOOM

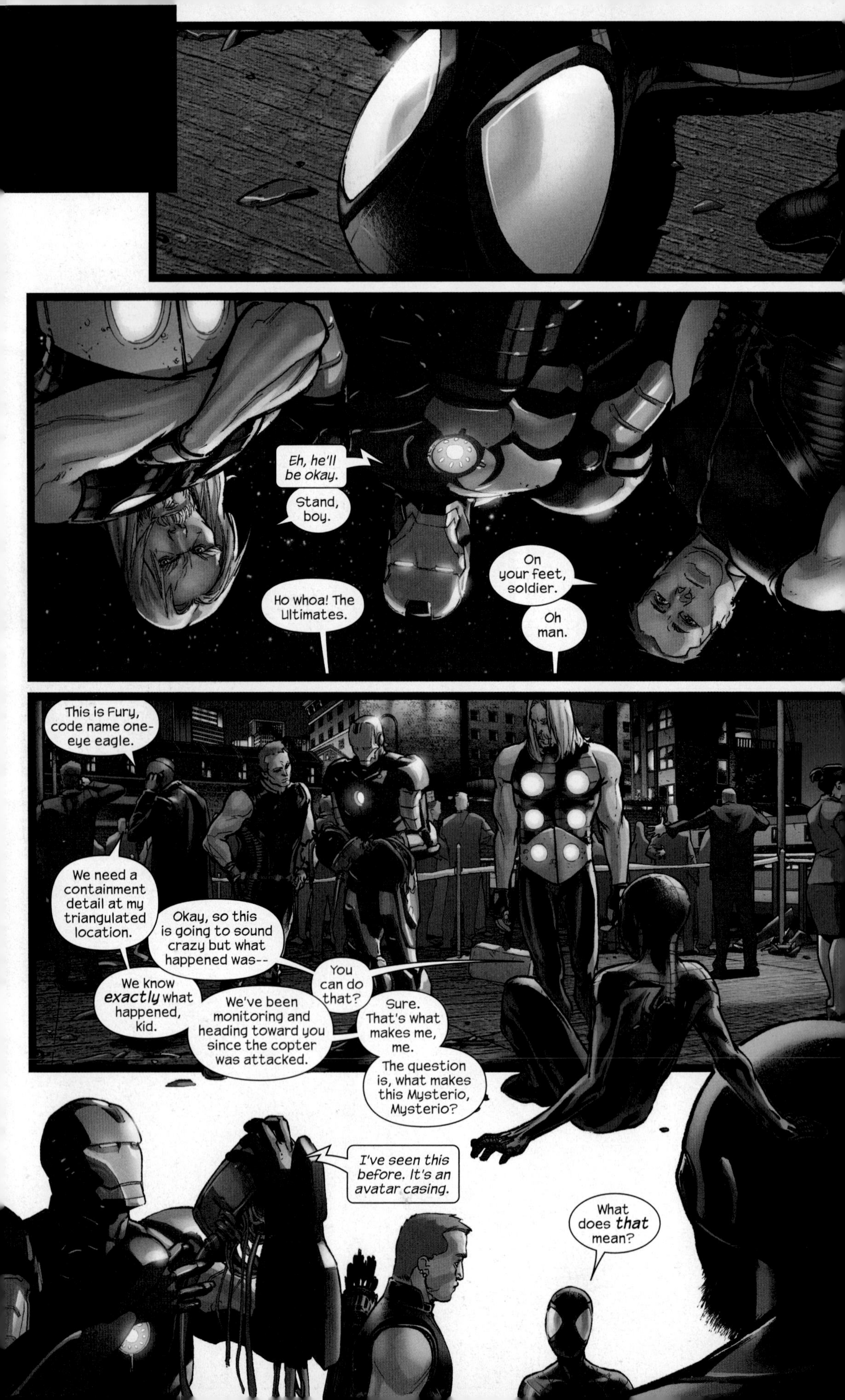
Eh, he'll be okay.
Stand, boy.
Ho whoa! The Ultimates.
On your feet, soldier.
Oh man.
This is Fury, code name one-eye eagle.
We need a containment detail at my triangulated location.
Okay, so this is going to sound crazy but what happened was--
We know *exactly* what happened, kid.
We've been monitoring and heading toward you since the copter was attacked.
You can do that?
Sure. That's what makes me, me.
The question is, what makes this Mysterio, Mysterio?
I've seen this before. It's an avatar casing.
What does *that* mean?

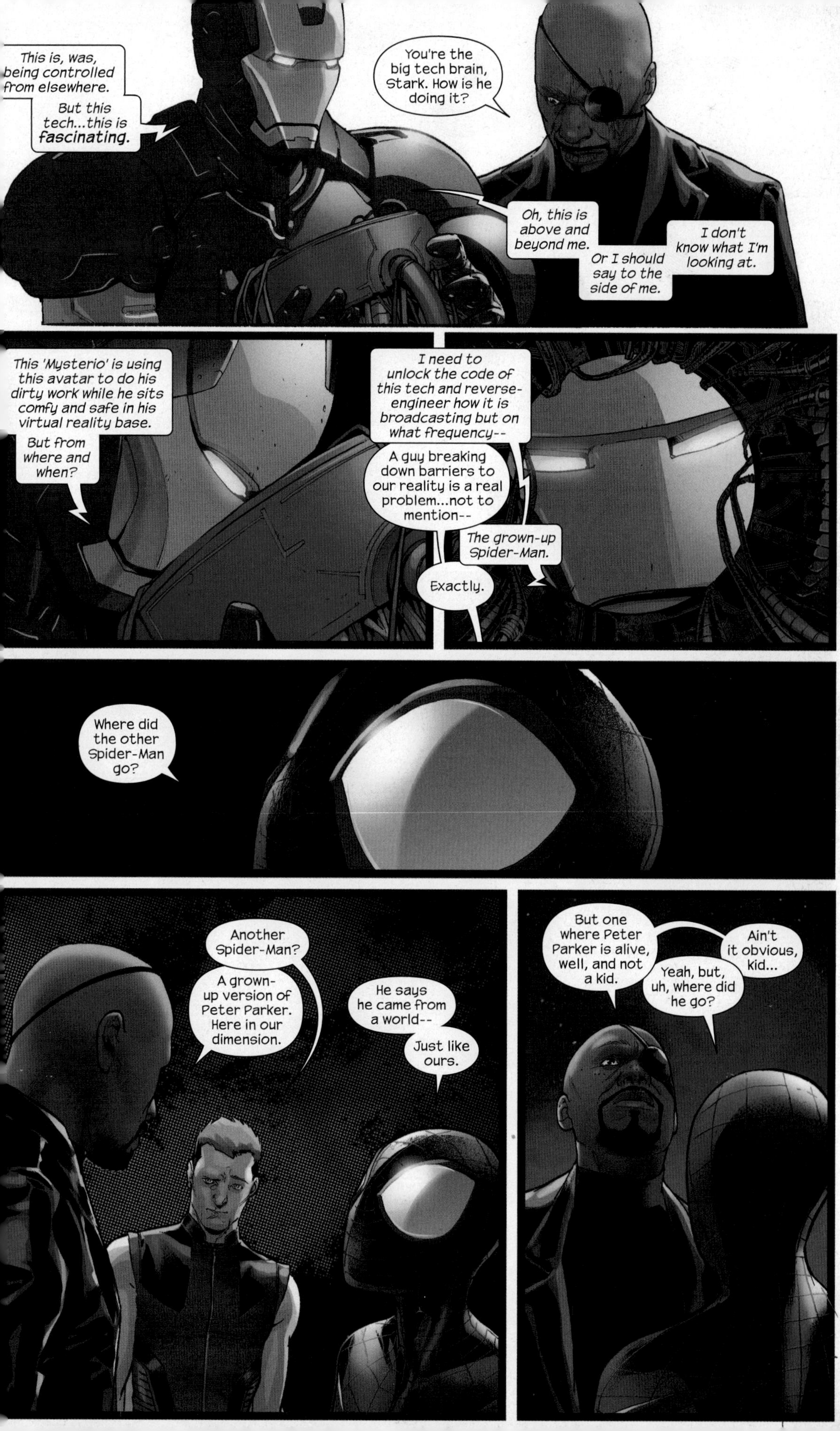

This is, was, being controlled from elsewhere.
But this tech...this is fascinating.
You're the big tech brain, Stark. How is he doing it?
Oh, this is above and beyond me.
Or I should say to the side of me.
I don't know what I'm looking at.
This 'Mysterio' is using this avatar to do his dirty work while he sits comfy and safe in his virtual reality base.
But from where and when?
I need to unlock the code of this tech and reverse-engineer how it is broadcasting but on what frequency--
A guy breaking down barriers to our reality is a real problem...not to mention--
The grown-up Spider-Man.
Exactly.
Where did the other Spider-Man go?
Another Spider-Man?
A grown-up version of Peter Parker. Here in our dimension.
He says he came from a world--
Just like ours.
But one where Peter Parker is alive, well, and not a kid.
Ain't it obvious, kid...
Yeah, but, uh, where did he go?

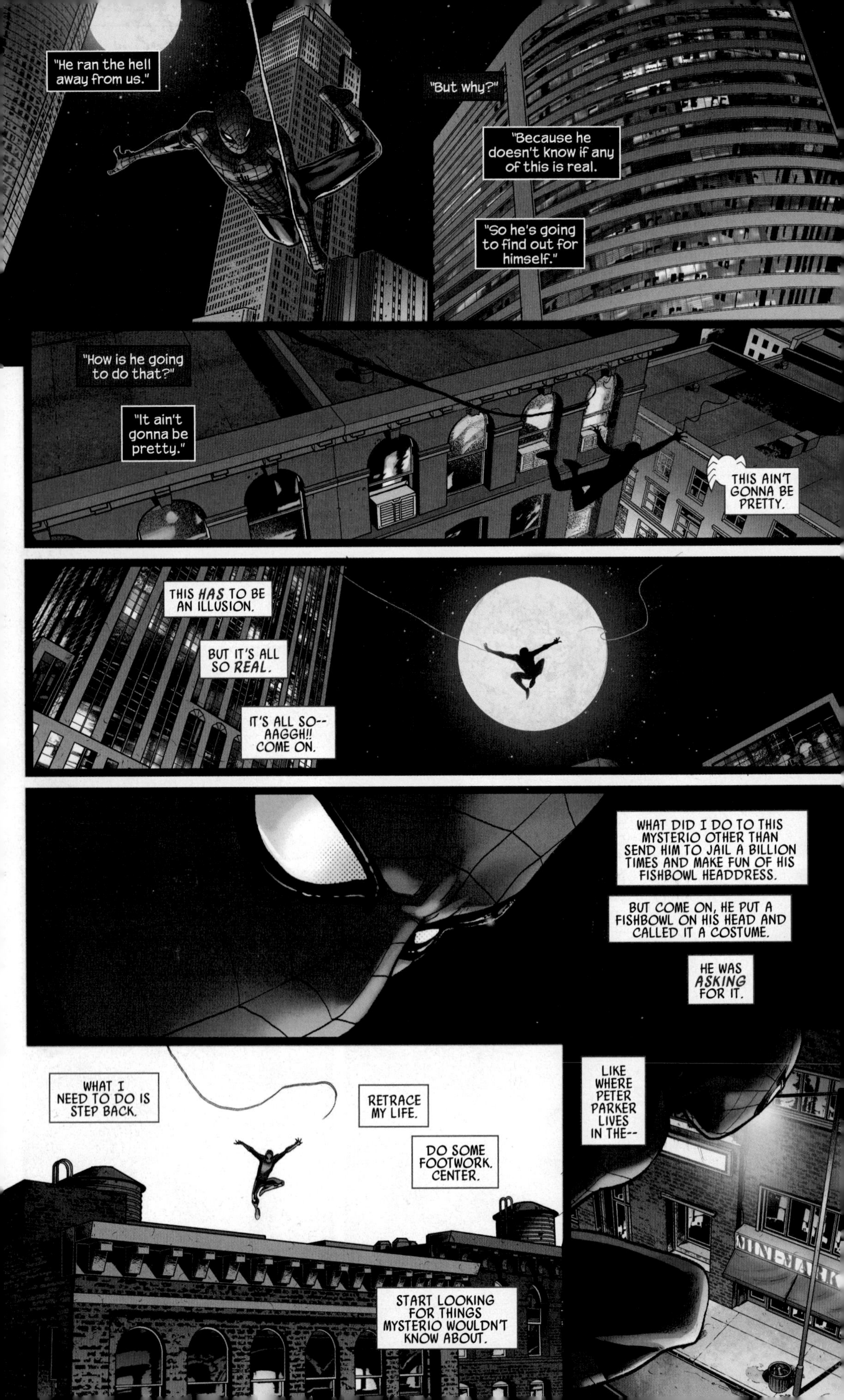
"He ran the hell away from us."
"But why?"
"Because he doesn't know if any of this is real.
"So he's going to find out for himself."
"How is he going to do that?"
"It ain't gonna be pretty."
THIS AIN'T GONNA BE PRETTY.
THIS HAS TO BE AN ILLUSION.
BUT IT'S ALL SO REAL.
IT'S ALL SO-- AAGGH!! COME ON.
WHAT DID I DO TO THIS MYSTERIO OTHER THAN SEND HIM TO JAIL A BILLION TIMES AND MAKE FUN OF HIS FISHBOWL HEADDRESS.
BUT COME ON, HE PUT A FISHBOWL ON HIS HEAD AND CALLED IT A COSTUME.
HE WAS ASKING FOR IT.
WHAT I NEED TO DO IS STEP BACK.
RETRACE MY LIFE.
DO SOME FOOTWORK. CENTER.
START LOOKING FOR THINGS MYSTERIO WOULDN'T KNOW ABOUT.
LIKE WHERE PETER PARKER LIVES IN THE--

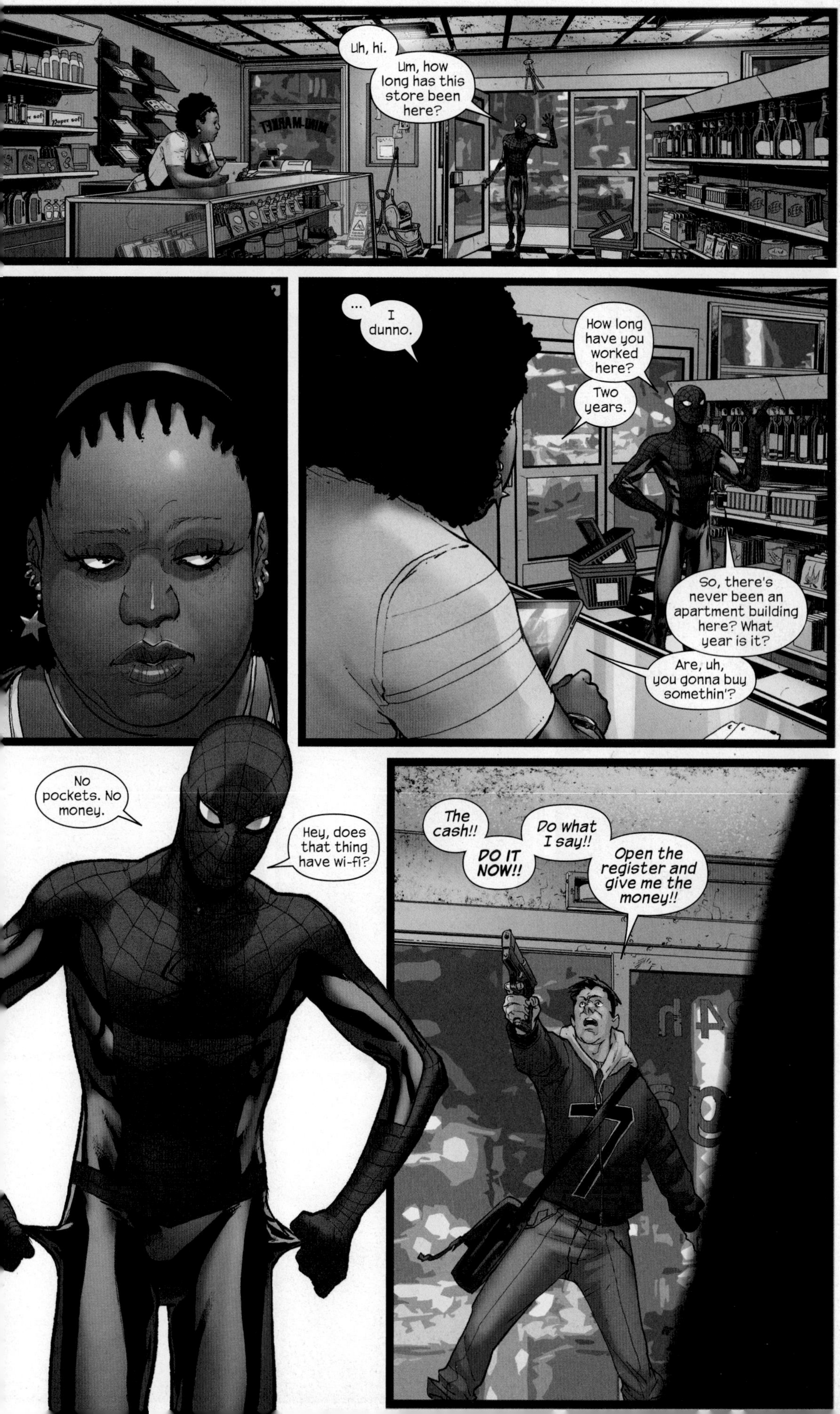

MINI-MARKET
Uh, hi.
Um, how long has this store been here?
... I dunno.
How long have you worked here?
Two years.
So, there's never been an apartment building here? What year is it?
Are, uh, you gonna buy somethin'?
No pockets. No money.
Hey, does that thing have wi-fi?
The cash!!
DO IT NOW!!
Do what I say!!
Open the register and give me the money!!

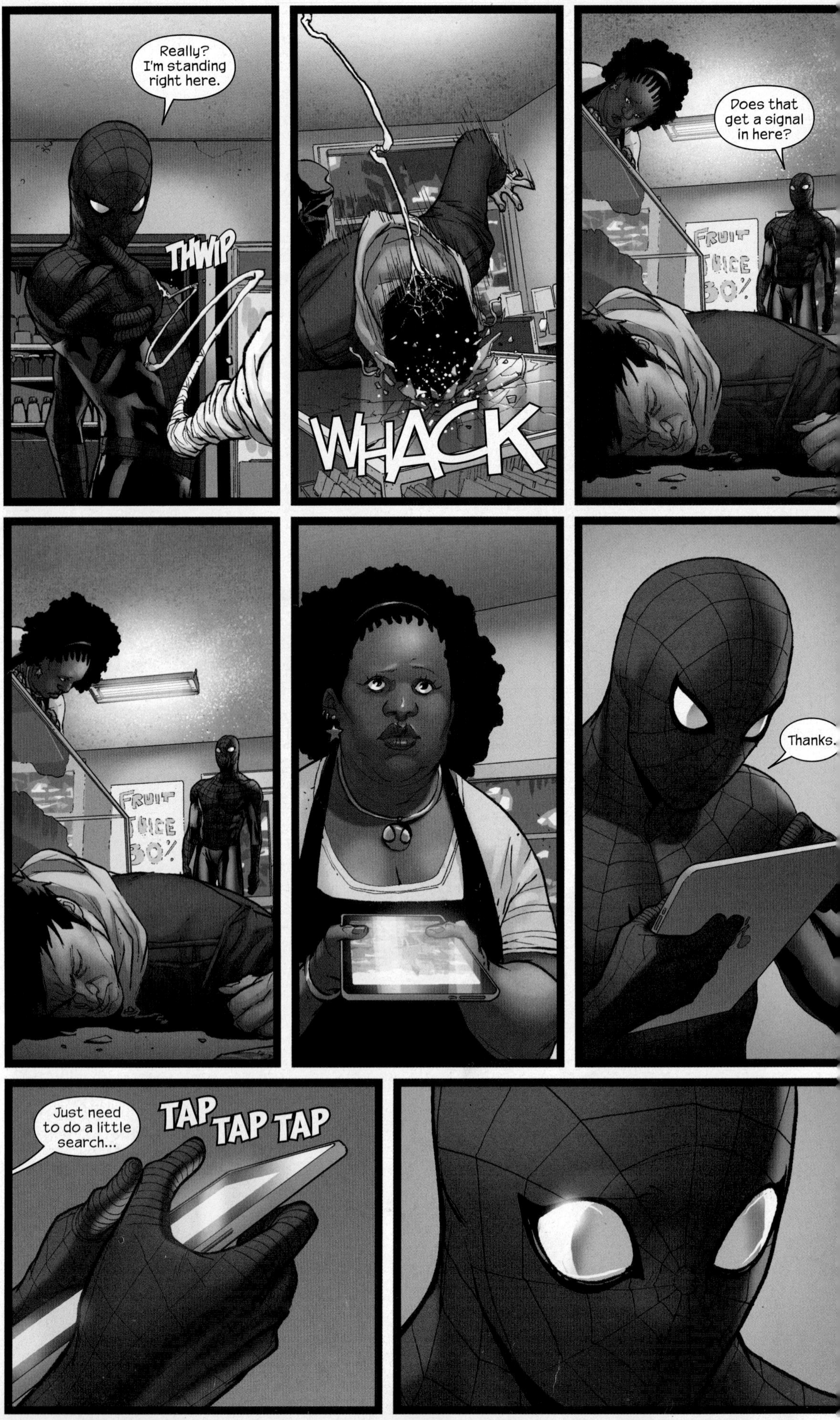
Really? I'm standing right here.
THWIP
WHACK
Does that get a signal in here?
FRUIT JUICE 80%
FRUIT JUICE 80%
Thanks.
Just need to do a little search...
TAP TAP TAP TAP

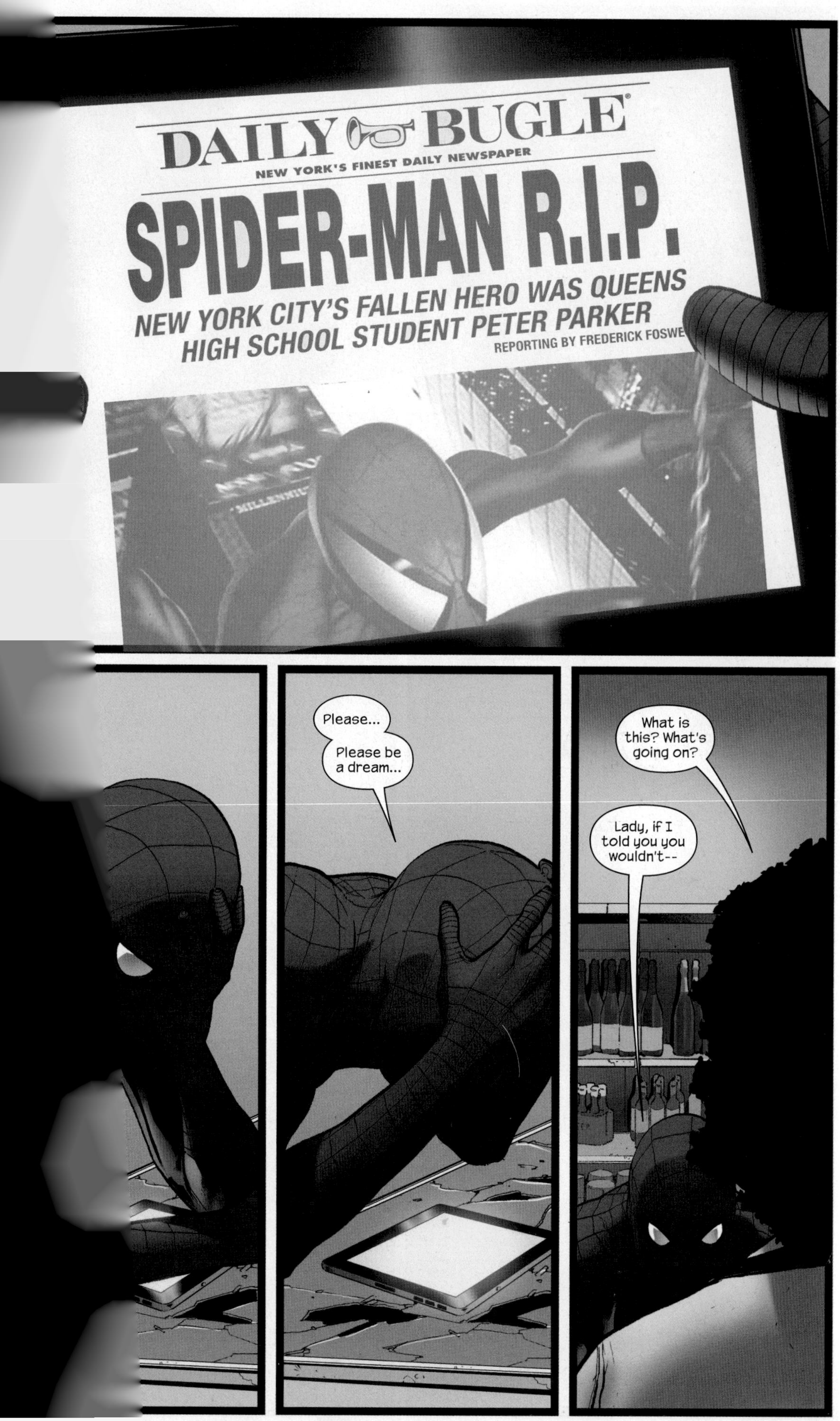
DAILY BUGLE
NEW YORK'S FINEST DAILY NEWSPAPER
SPIDER-MAN R.I.P.
NEW YORK CITY'S FALLEN HERO WAS QUEENS HIGH SCHOOL STUDENT PETER PARKER
REPORTING BY FREDERICK FOSWE
Please...
Please be a dream...
What is this? What's going on?
Lady, if I told you you wouldn't--

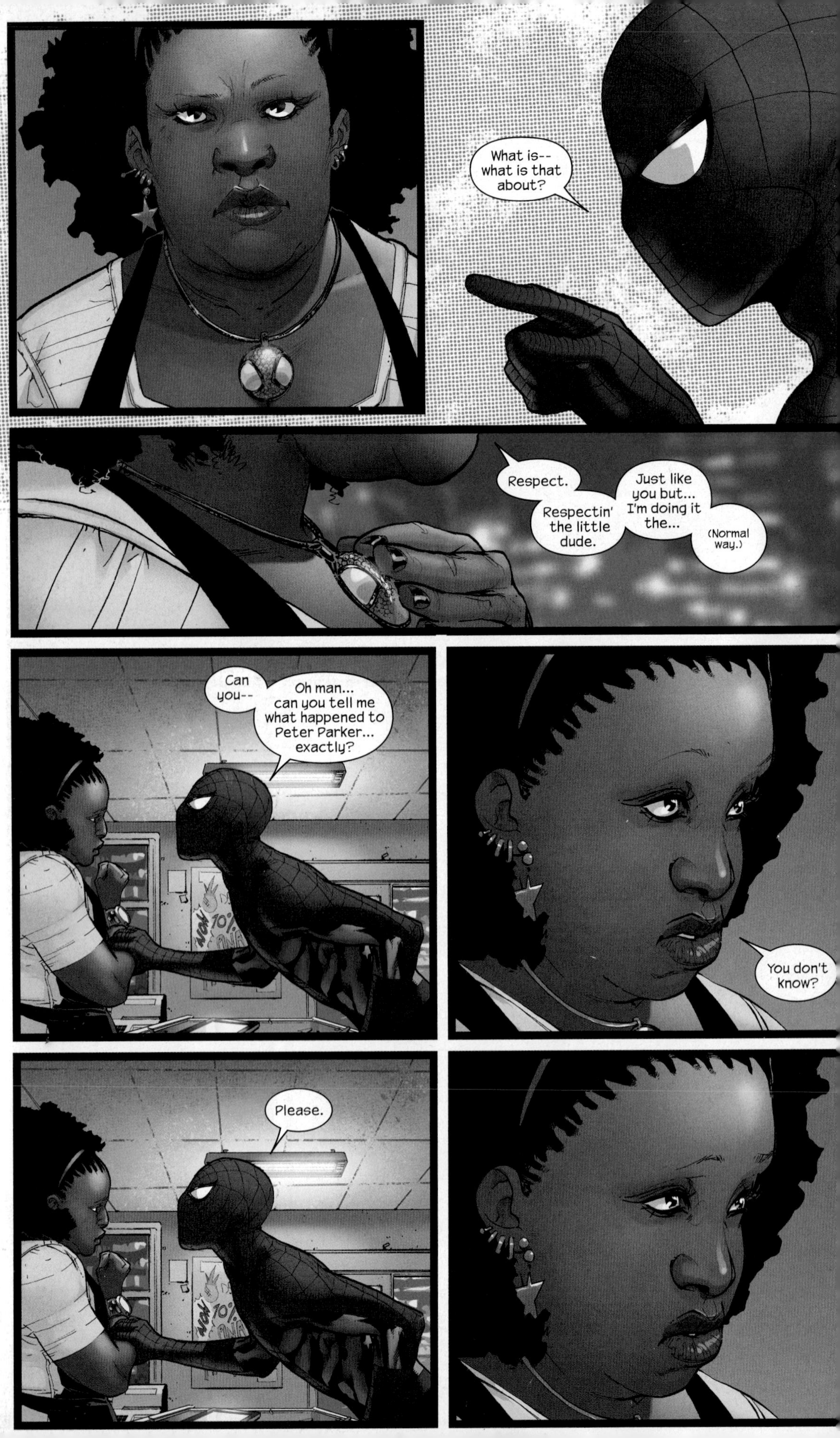

What is--
what is that
about?
Respect.
Respectin'
the little
dude.
Just like
you but...
I'm doing it
the...
(Normal
way.)
Can
you--
Oh man...
can you tell me
what happened to
Peter Parker...
exactly?
You don't
know?
Please.

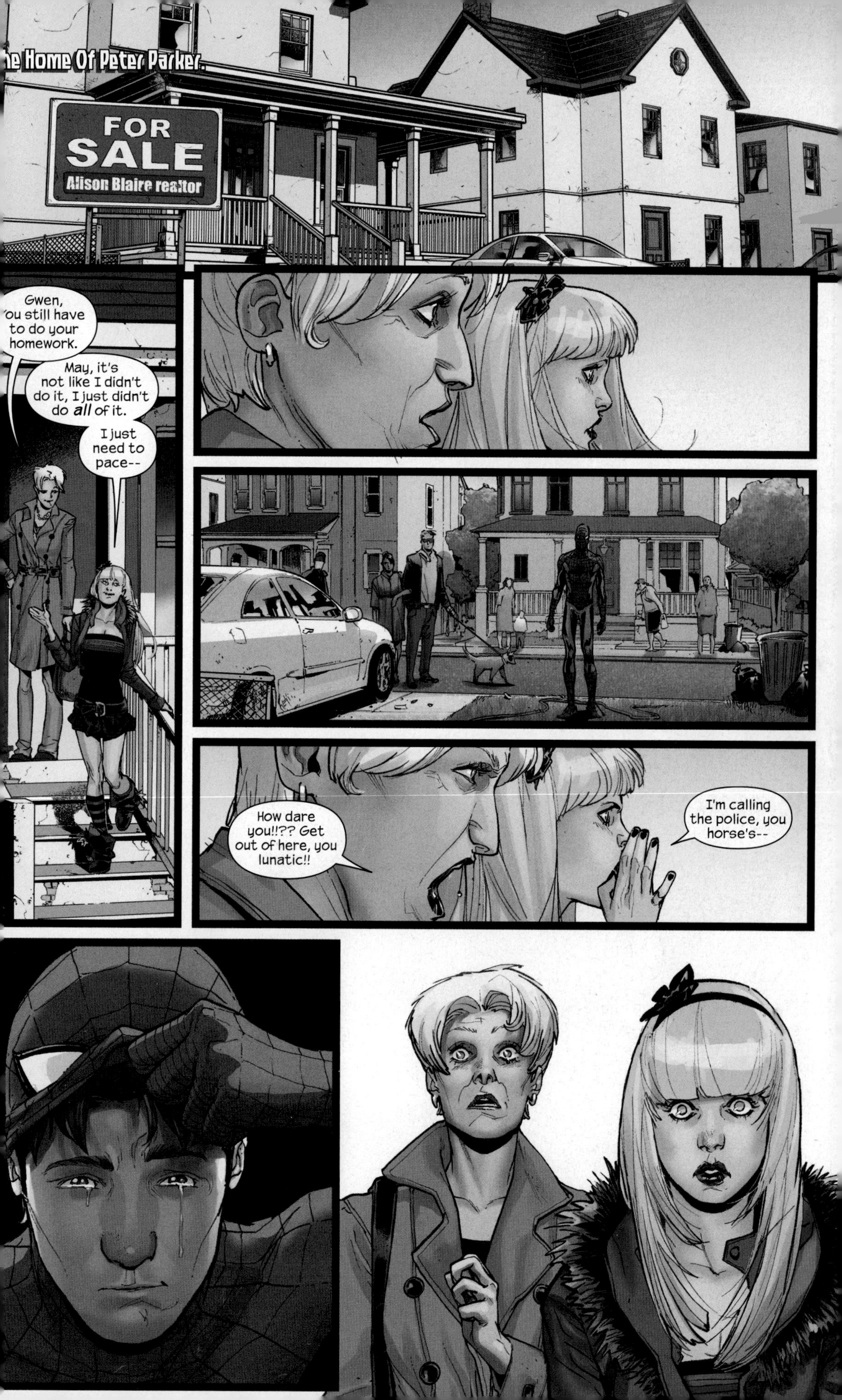
he Home Of Peter Parker.
FOR SALE
Alison Blaire realtor
Gwen, ou still have to do your homework.
May, it's not like I didn't do it, I just didn't do *all* of it.
I just need to pace--
How dare you!!?? Get out of here, you lunatic!!
I'm calling the police, you horse's--

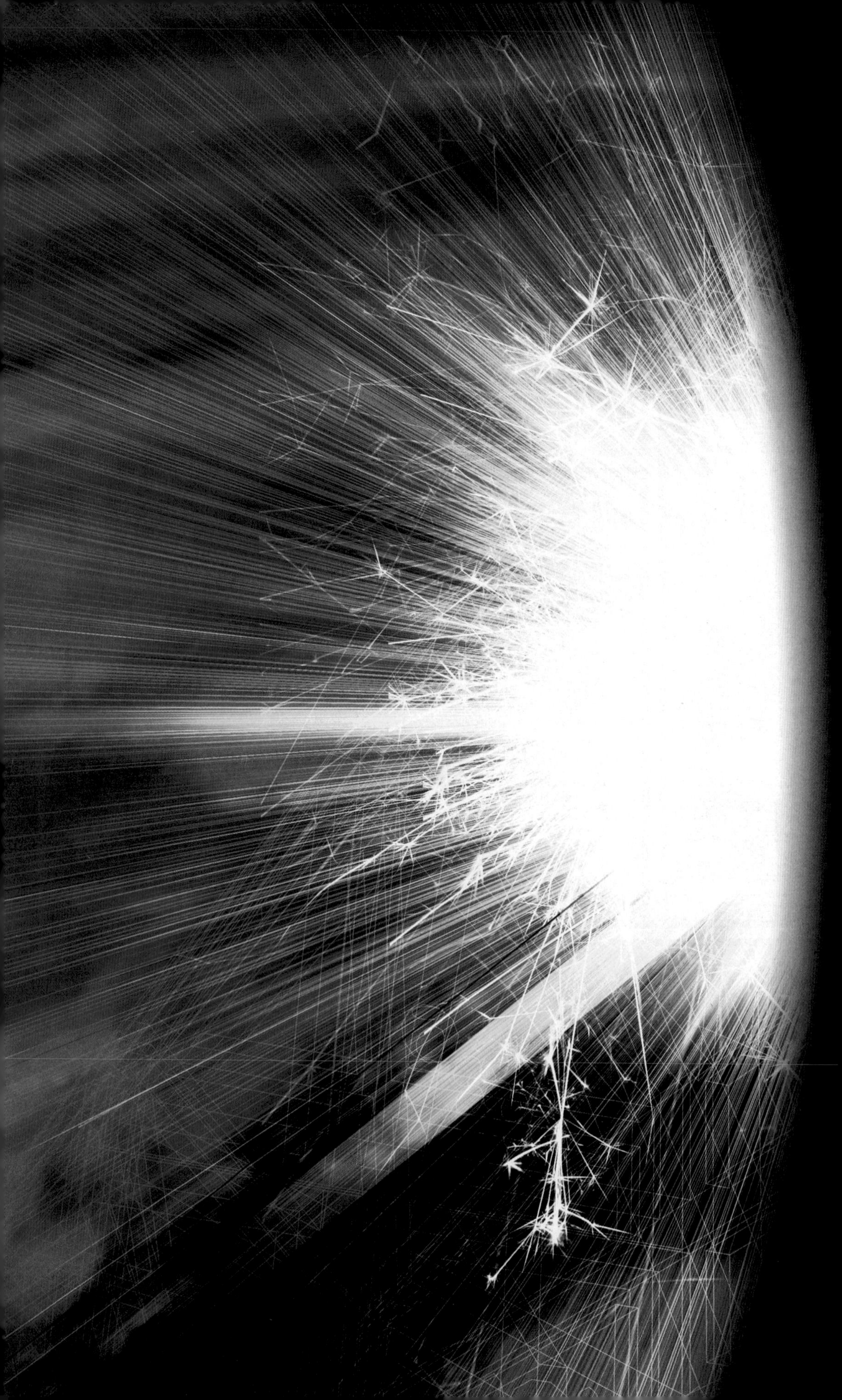

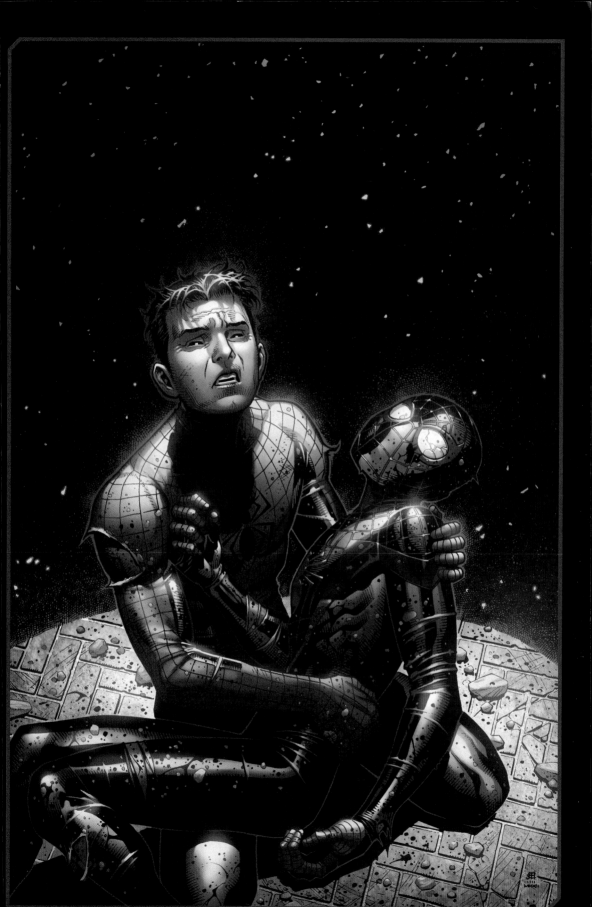

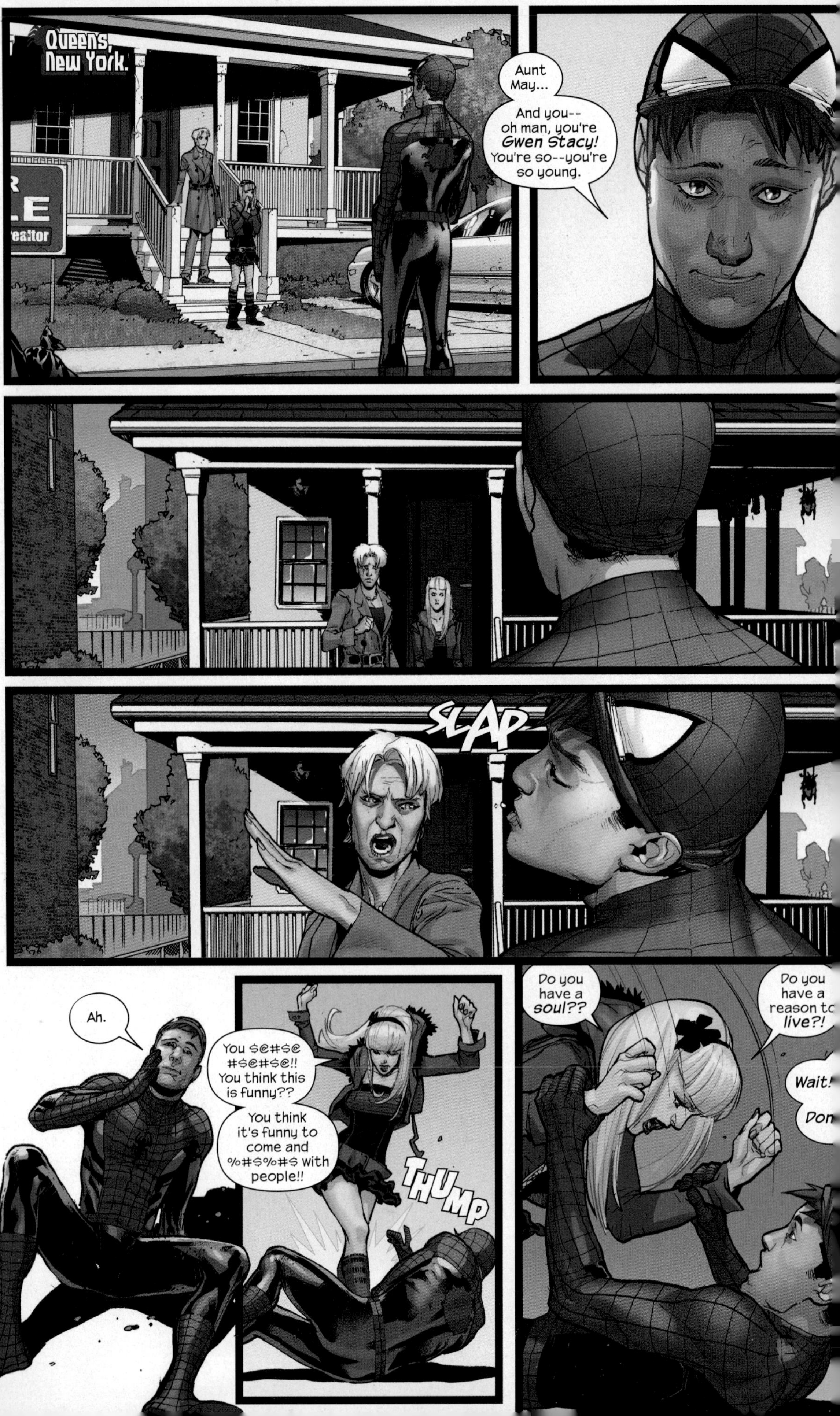
Queens, New York.
Aunt May...
And you-- oh man, you're Gwen Stacy! You're so--you're so young.
SLAP
Ah.
You $@#$@ #$@#$@!! You think this is funny??
You think it's funny to come and %#$%#$ with people!!
THUMP
Do you have a soul??
Do you have a reason to live?!
Wait!

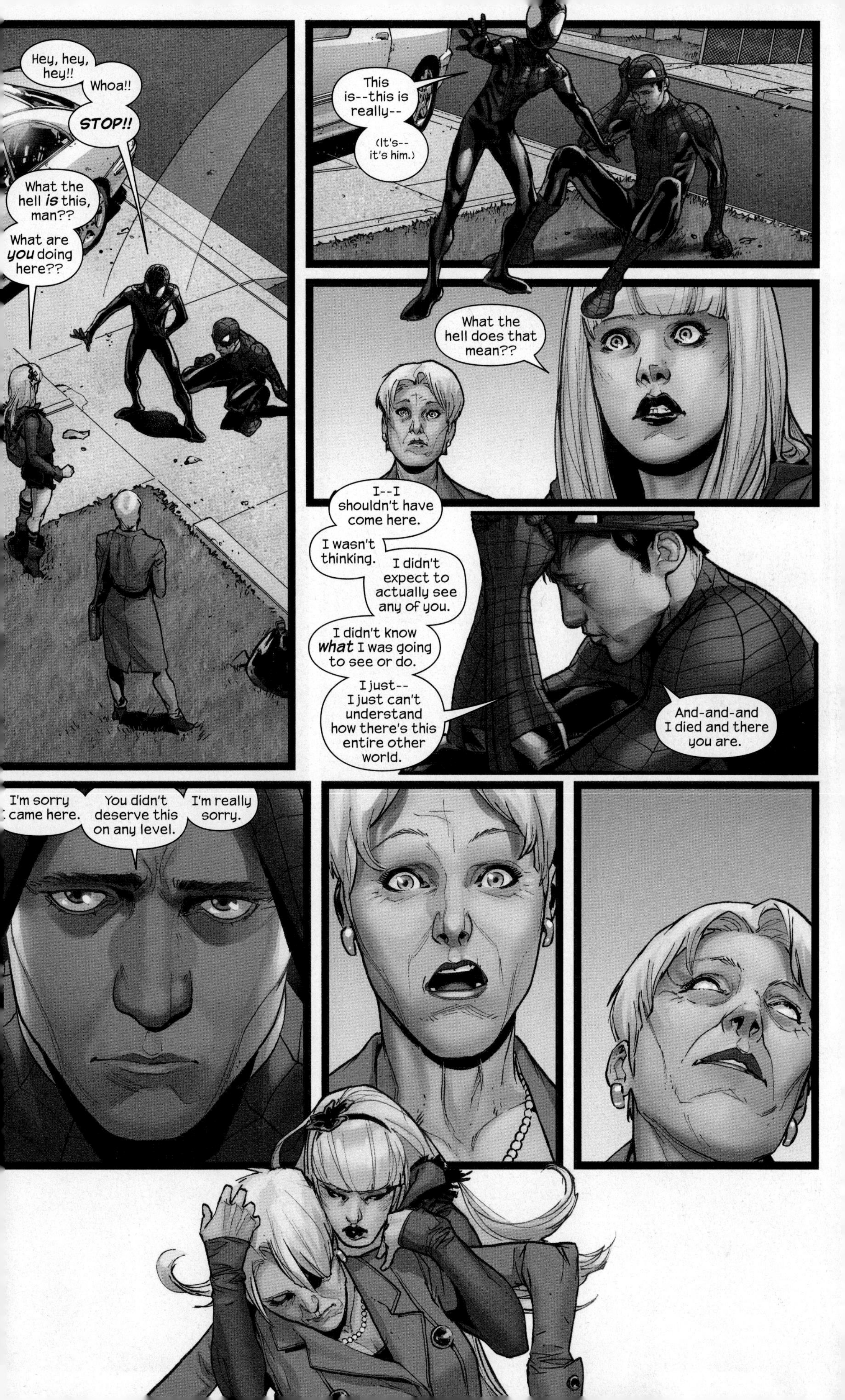
Hey, hey, hey!!
Whoa!!
STOP!!
What the hell *is* this, man??
What are *you* doing here??
This is--this is really--
(It's-- it's him.)
What the hell does that mean??
I--I shouldn't have come here.
I wasn't thinking.
I didn't expect to actually see any of you.
I didn't know *what* I was going to see or do.
I just-- I just can't understand how there's this entire other world.
And-and-and I died and there you are.
I'm sorry I came here.
You didn't deserve this on any level.
I'm really sorry.

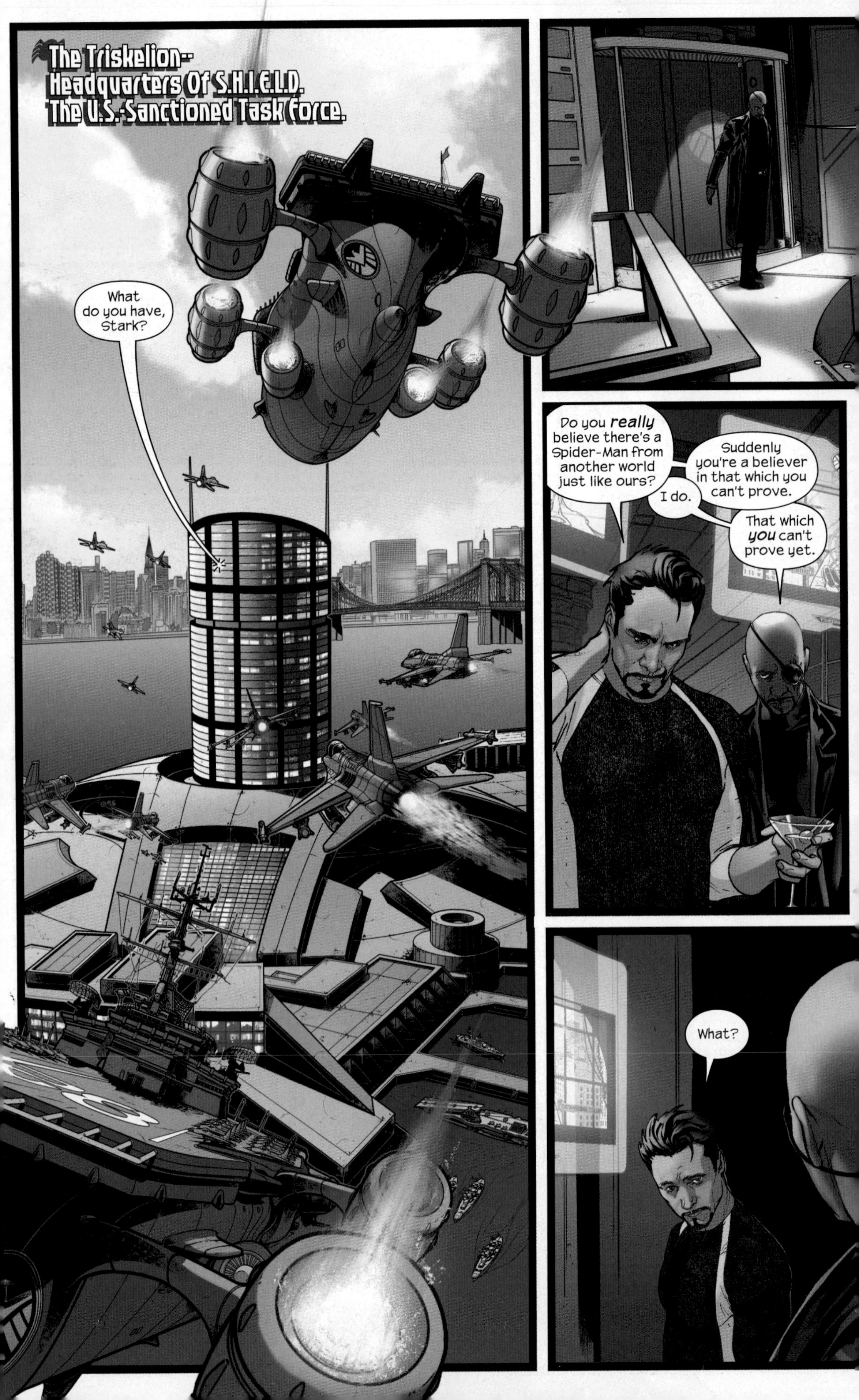
The Triskelion--
Headquarters Of S.H.I.E.L.D.
The U.S.-Sanctioned Task Force.
What do you have, Stark?
Do you really believe there's a Spider-Man from another world just like ours?
I do.
Suddenly you're a believer in that which you can't prove.
That which you can't prove yet.
What?

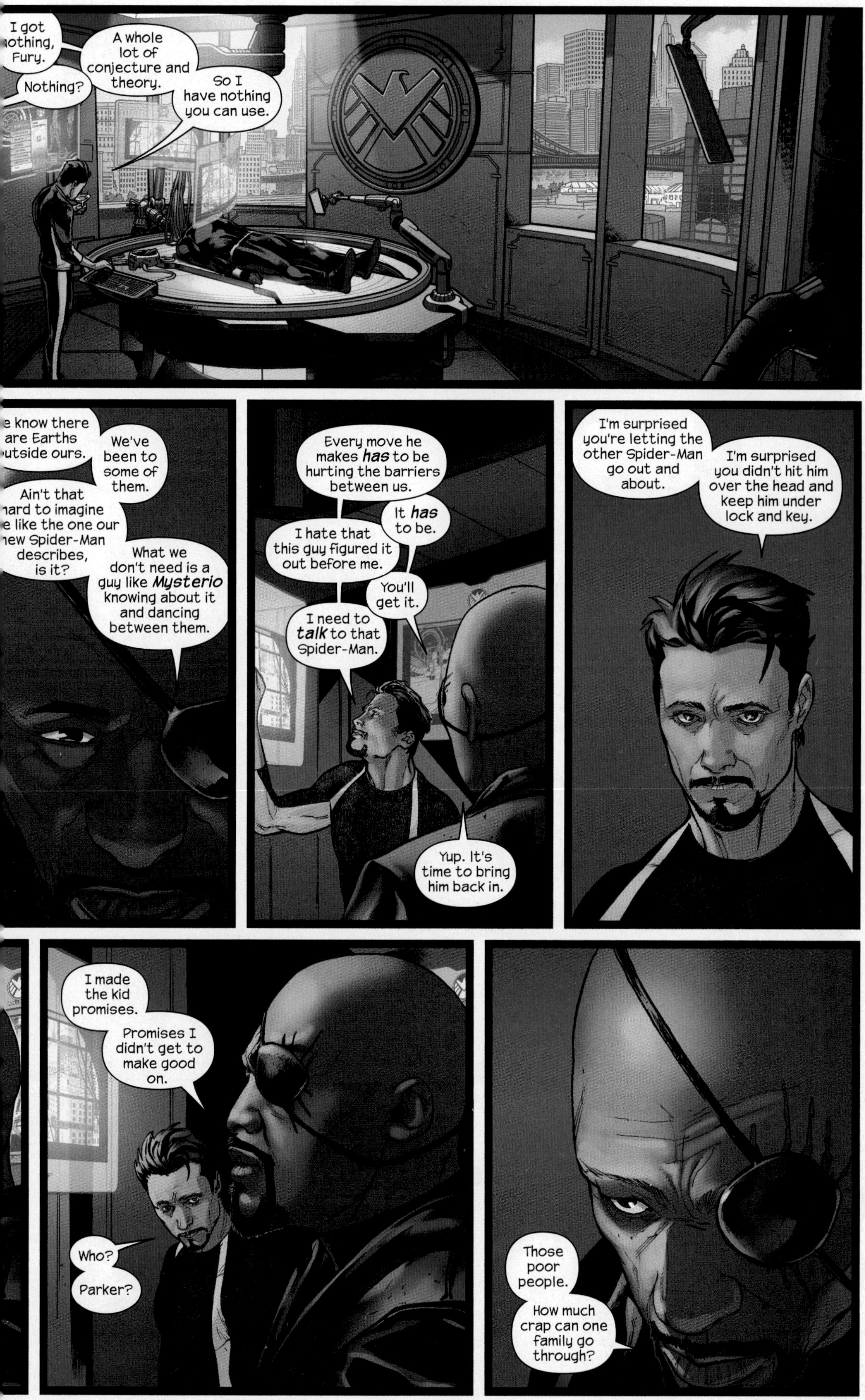
I got othing, Fury.
Nothing?
A whole lot of conjecture and theory.
So I have nothing you can use.
e know there are Earths utside ours.
We've been to some of them.
Ain't that hard to imagine e like the one our new Spider-Man describes, is it?
What we don't need is a guy like *Mysterio* knowing about it and dancing between them.
Every move he makes *has* to be hurting the barriers between us.
It *has* to be.
I hate that this guy figured it out before me.
You'll get it.
I need to *talk* to that Spider-Man.
Yup. It's time to bring him back in.
I'm surprised you're letting the other Spider-Man go out and about.
I'm surprised you didn't hit him over the head and keep him under lock and key.
I made the kid promises.
Promises I didn't get to make good on.
Who?
Parker?
Those poor people.
How much crap can one family go through?

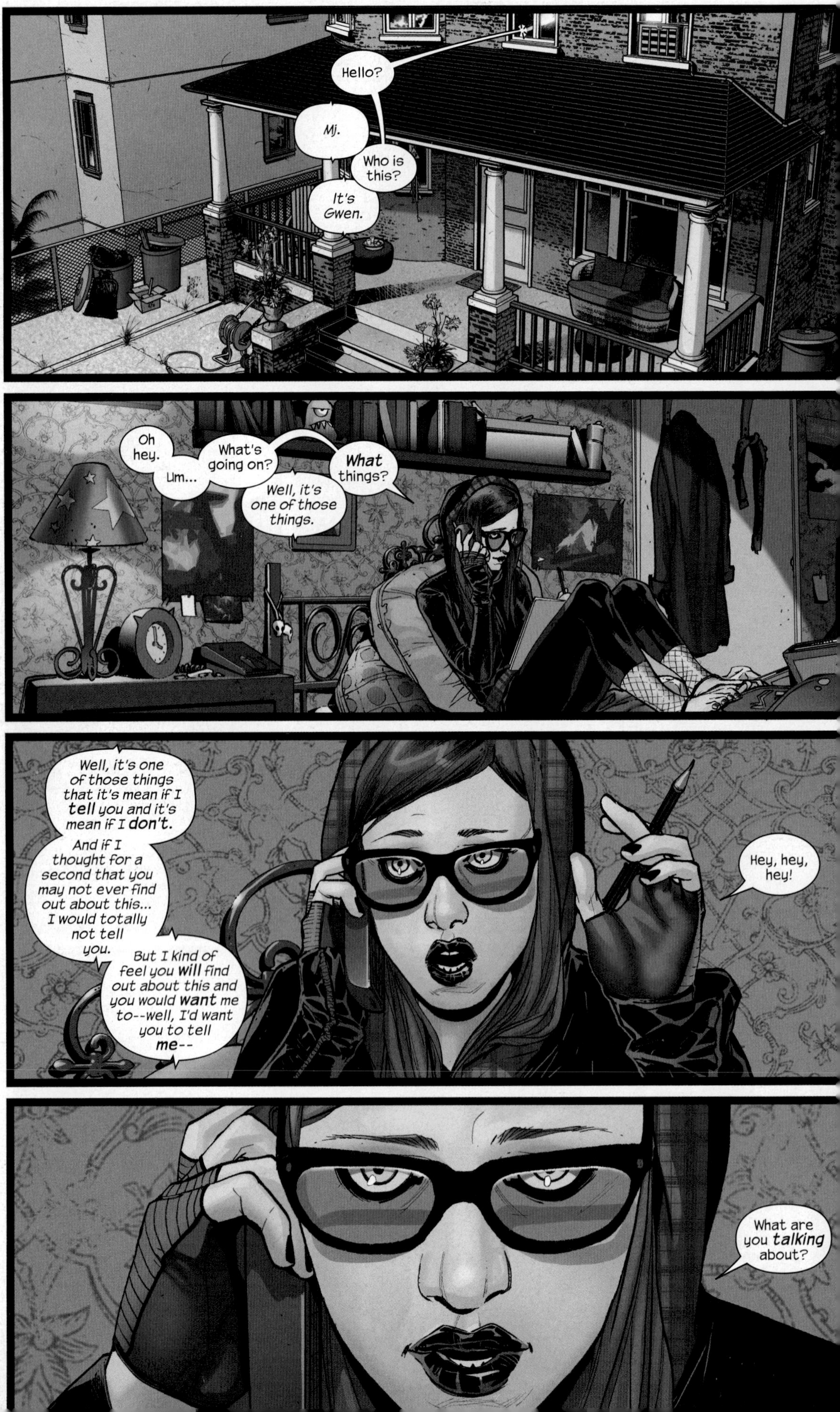
Hello?
Mj.
Who is this?
It's Gwen.
Oh hey.
Um...
What's going on?
Well, it's one of those things.
What things?
Well, it's one of those things that it's mean if I tell you and it's mean if I don't.
And if I thought for a second that you may not ever find out about this... I would totally not tell you.
But I kind of feel you will find out about this and you would want me to--well, I'd want you to tell me--
Hey, hey, hey!
What are you talking about?

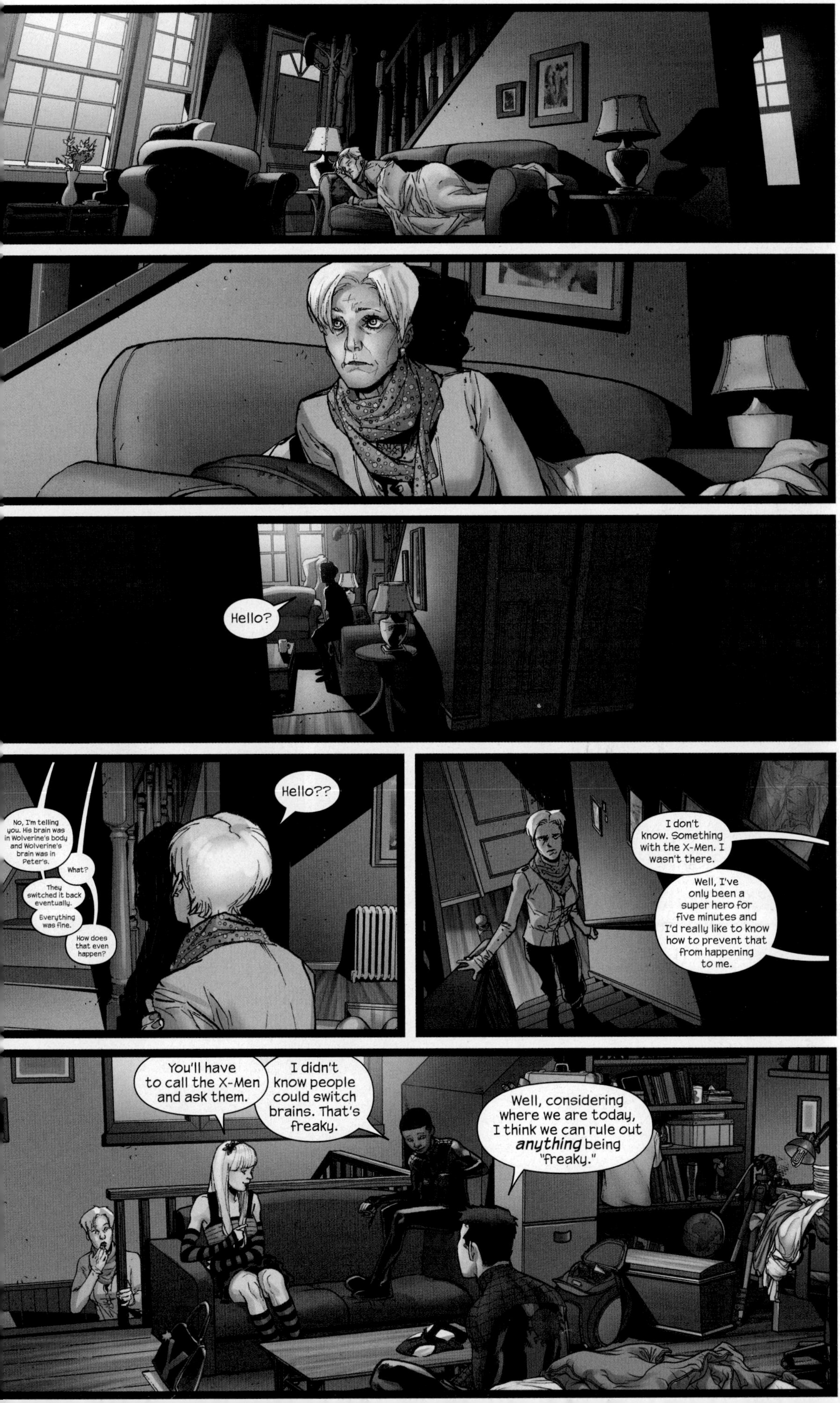
Hello?
Hello??
No, I'm telling you. His brain was in Wolverine's body and Wolverine's brain was in Peter's.
What?
They switched it back eventually.
Everything was fine.
How does that even happen?
I don't know. Something with the X-Men. I wasn't there.
Well, I've only been a super hero for five minutes and I'd really like to know how to prevent that from happening to me.
You'll have to call the X-Men and ask them.
I didn't know people could switch brains. That's freaky.
Well, considering where we are today, I think we can rule out *anything* being "freaky."

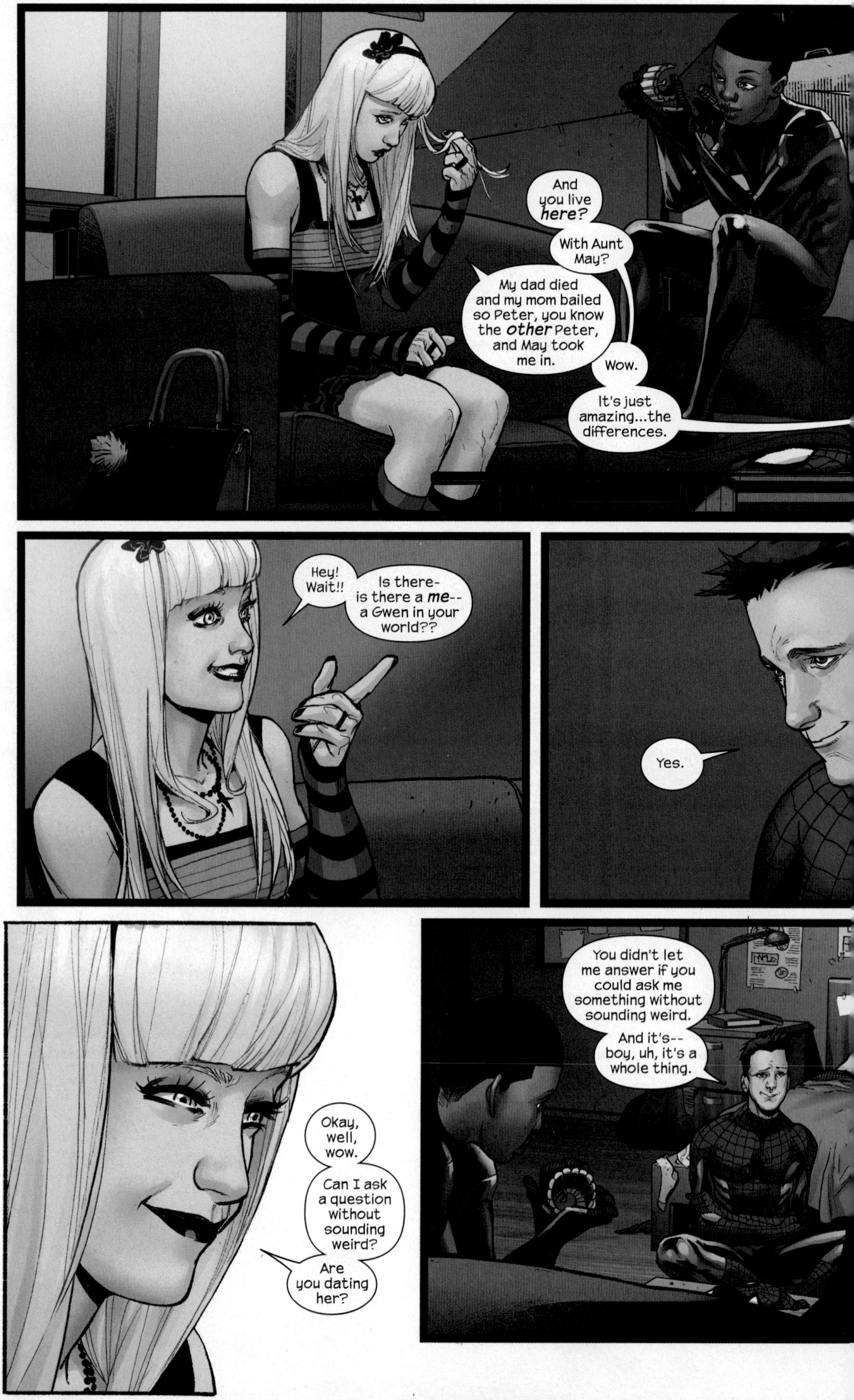

And you live *here*?
With Aunt May?
My dad died and my mom bailed so Peter, you know the *other* Peter, and May took me in.
Wow.
It's just amazing...the differences.
Hey! Wait!!
Is there- is there a *me*-- a Gwen in your world??
Yes.
Okay, well, wow.
Can I ask a question without sounding weird?
Are you dating her?
You didn't let me answer if you could ask me something without sounding weird.
And it's-- boy, uh, it's a whole thing.

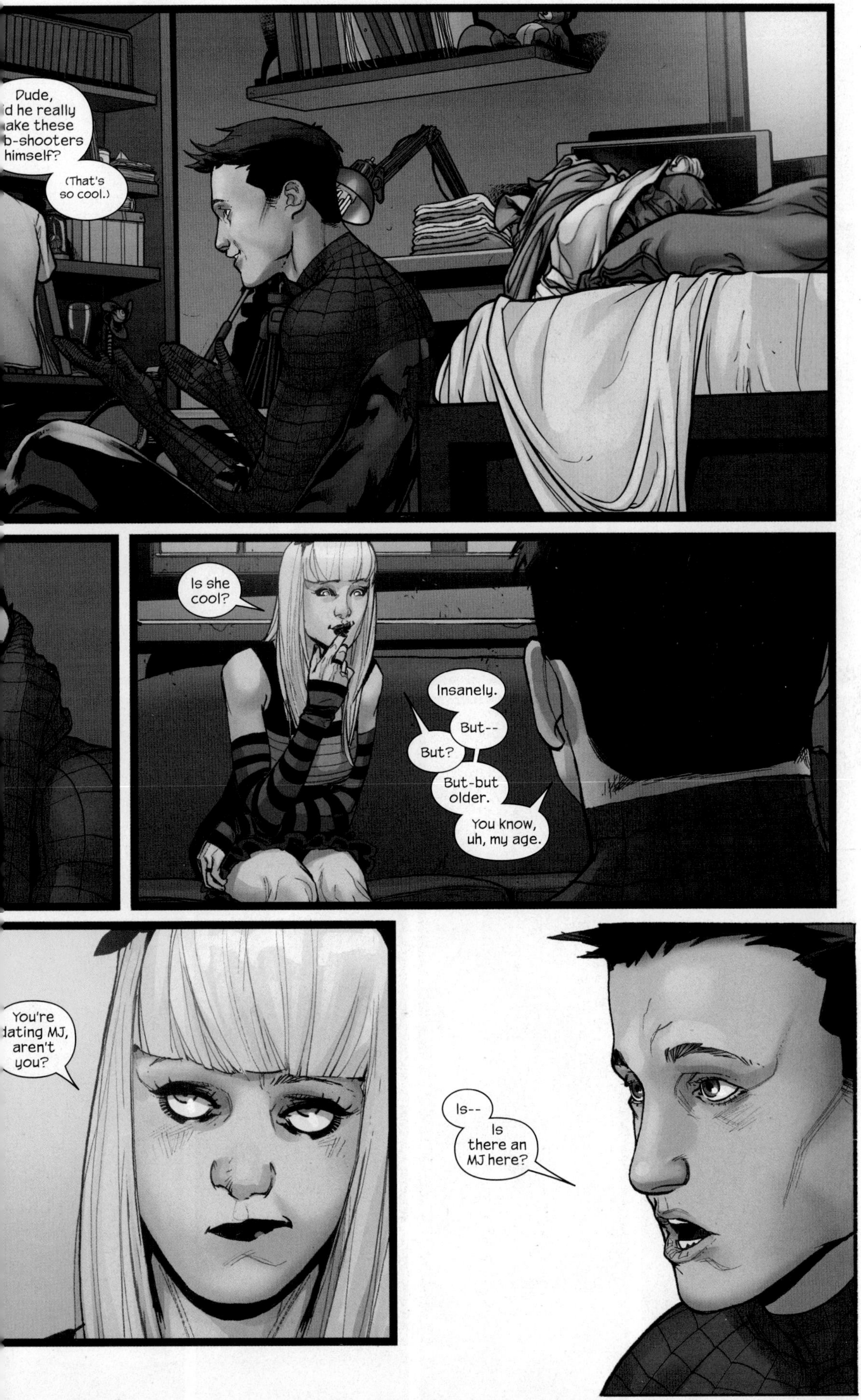
Dude,
d he really
ake these
b-shooters
himself?
(That's
so cool.)
Is she
cool?
Insanely.
But--
But?
But-but
older.
You know,
uh, my age.
You're
dating MJ,
aren't
you?
Is--
Is
there an
MJ here?

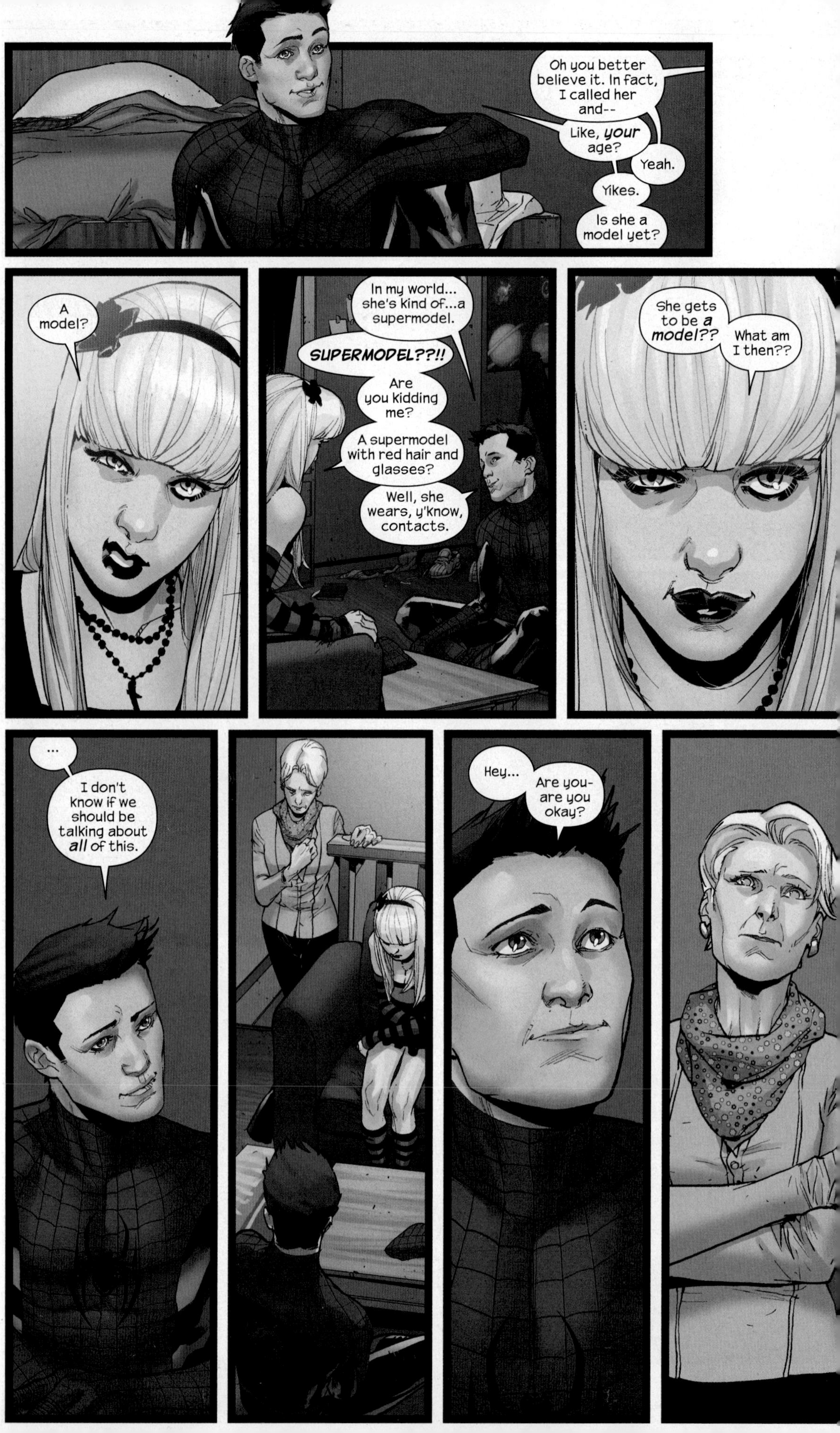

Oh you better believe it. In fact, I called her and--
Like, *your* age?
Yeah.
Yikes.
Is she a model yet?
A model?
In my world... she's kind of...a supermodel.
SUPERMODEL??!!
Are you kidding me?
A supermodel with red hair and glasses?
Well, she wears, y'know, contacts.
She gets to be *a model??*
What am I then??
...
I don't know if we should be talking about *all* of this.
Hey...
Are you- are you okay?

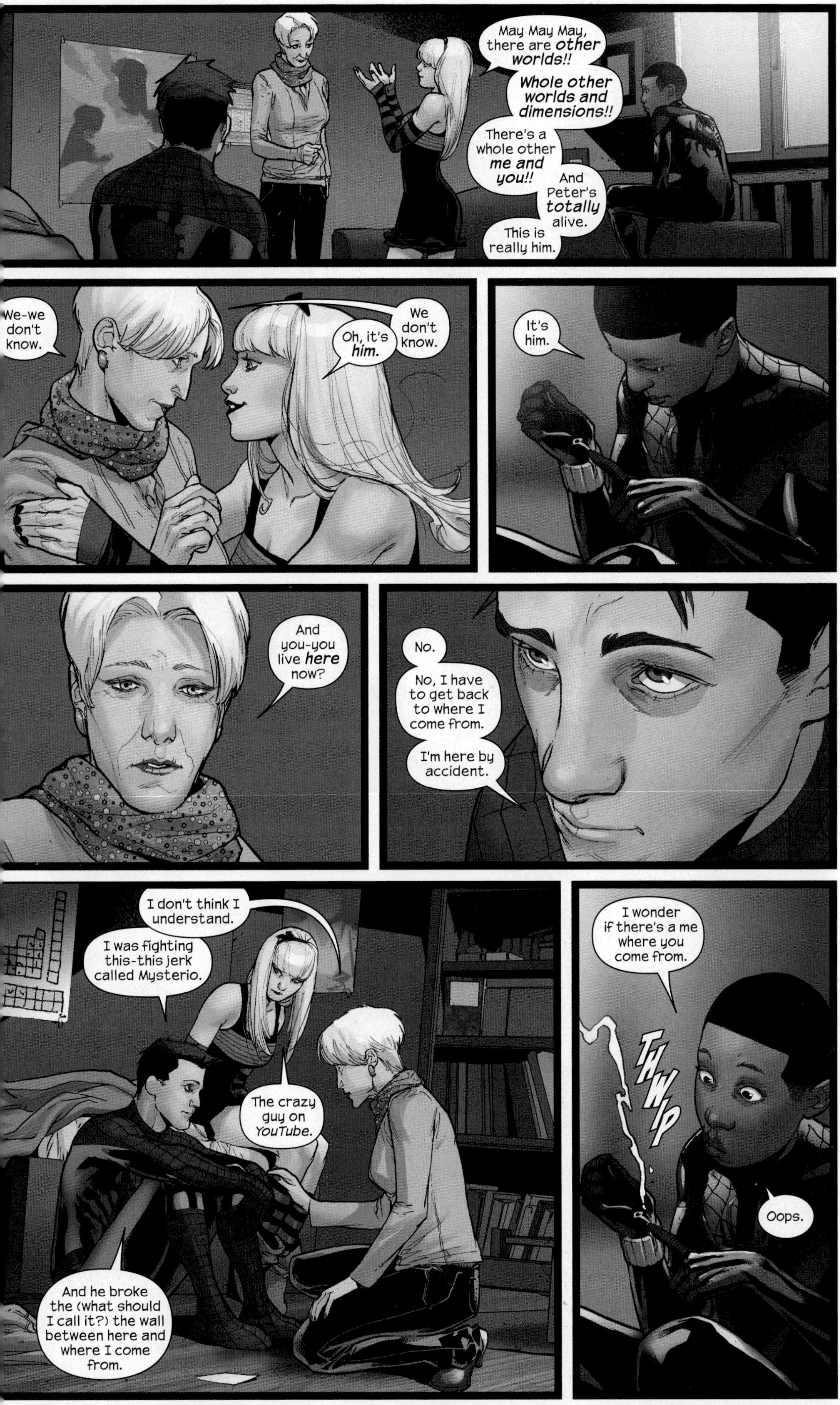
May May May, there are *other worlds!!*
Whole other worlds and dimensions!!
There's a whole other *me and you!!*
And Peter's *totally* alive.
This is really him.
We-we don't know.
We don't know.
Oh, it's *him.*
It's him.
And you-you live *here* now?
No.
No, I have to get back to where I come from.
I'm here by accident.
I don't think I understand.
I was fighting this-this jerk called Mysterio.
The crazy guy on YouTube.
And he broke the (what should I call it?) the wall between here and where I come from.
I wonder if there's a me where you come from.
THWIP
Oops.

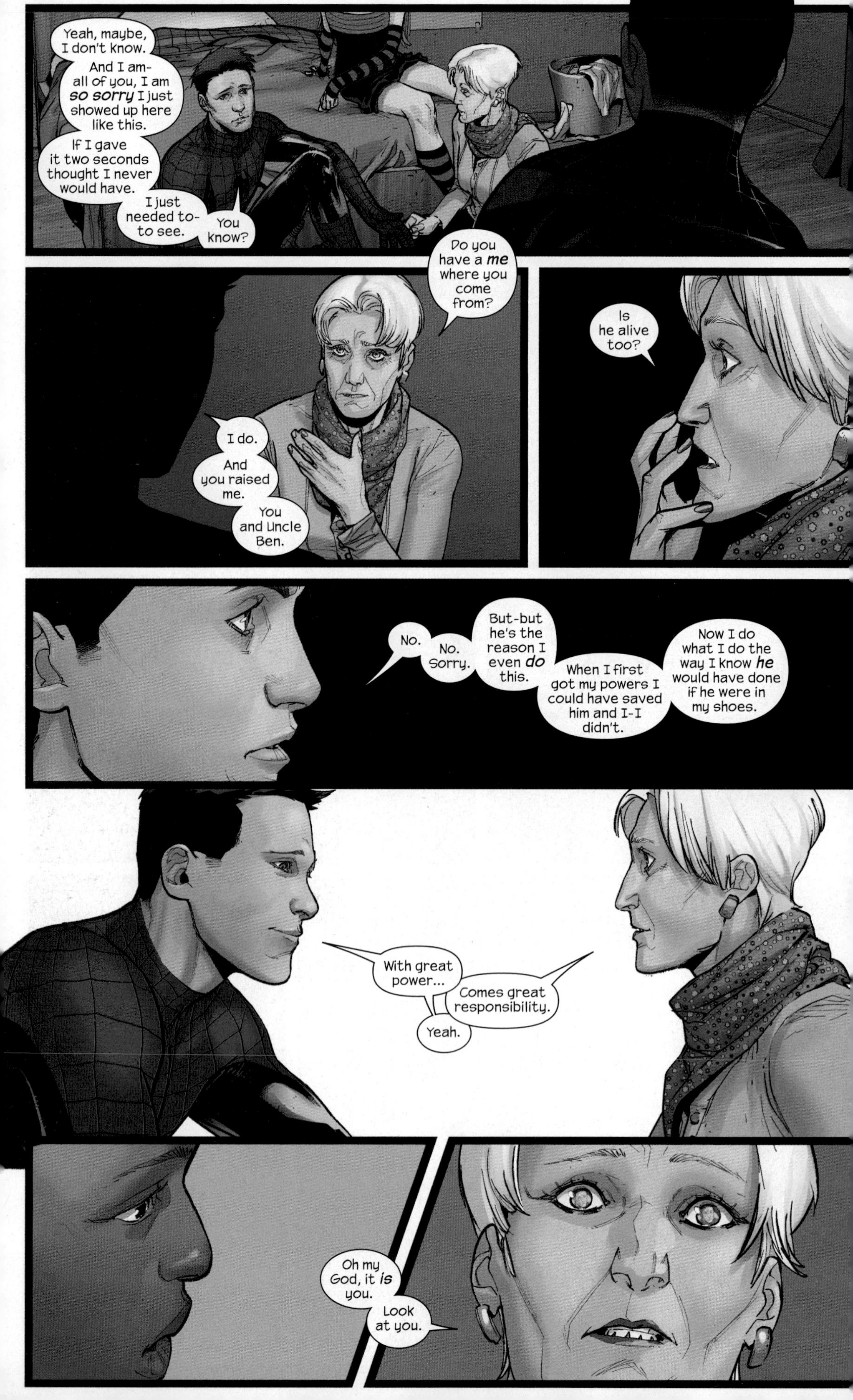
Yeah, maybe, I don't know.
And I am- all of you, I am *so sorry* I just showed up here like this.
If I gave it two seconds thought I never would have.
I just needed to- to see.
You know?
Do you have a *me* where you come from?
I do.
And you raised me.
You and Uncle Ben.
Is he alive too?
No.
No. Sorry.
But-but he's the reason I even *do* this.
When I first got my powers I could have saved him and I-I didn't.
Now I do what I do the way I know *he* would have done if he were in my shoes.
With great power...
Comes great responsibility.
Yeah.
Oh my God, it *is* you.
Look at you.

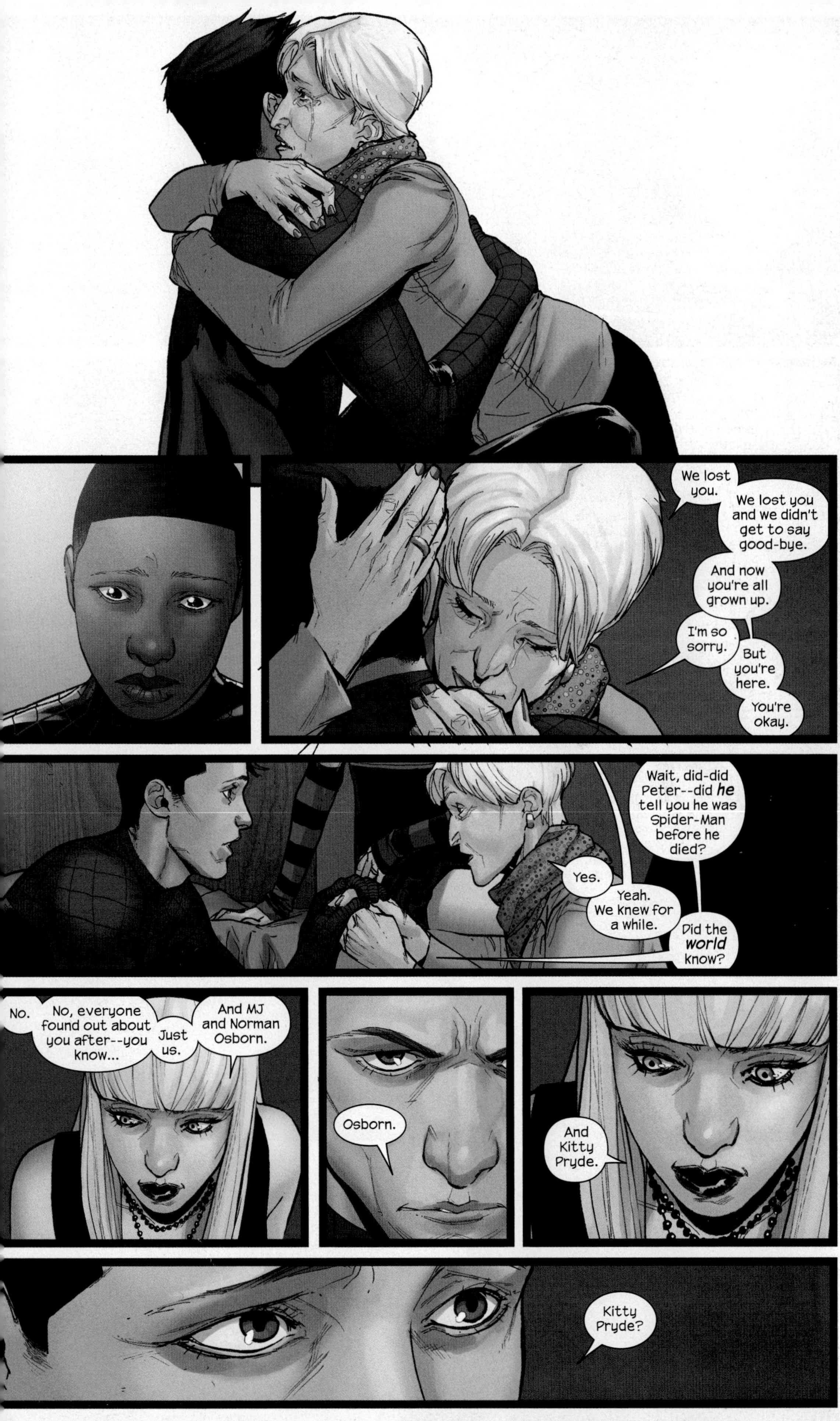
We lost you.
We lost you and we didn't get to say good-bye.
And now you're all grown up.
I'm so sorry.
But you're here.
You're okay.
Wait, did-did Peter--did he tell you he was Spider-Man before he died?
Yes.
Yeah. We knew for a while.
Did the world know?
No.
No, everyone found out about you after--you know...
Just us.
And MJ and Norman Osborn.
Osborn.
And Kitty Pryde.
Kitty Pryde?

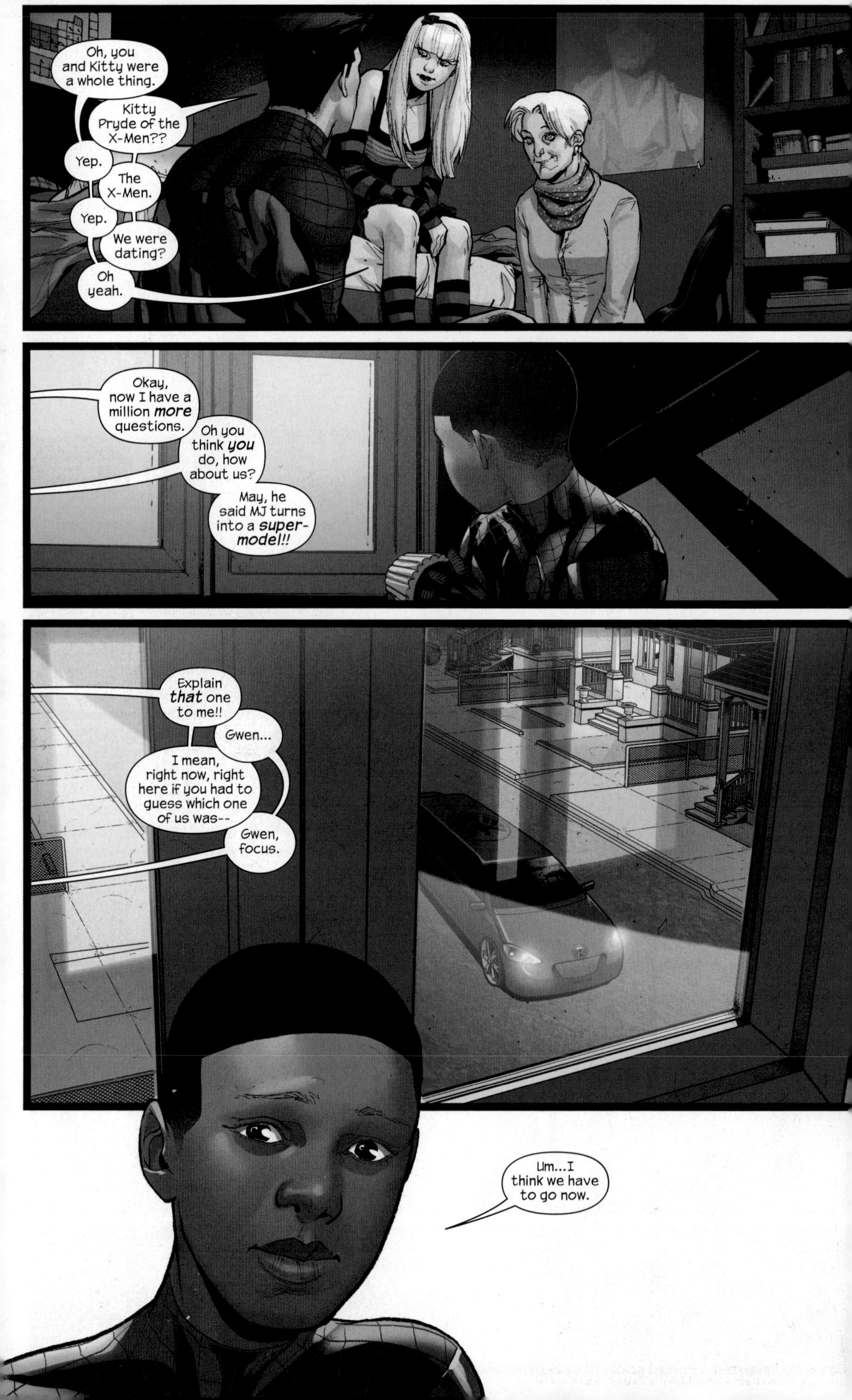
Oh, you and Kitty were a whole thing.
Kitty Pryde of the X-Men??
Yep.
The X-Men.
Yep.
We were dating?
Oh yeah.
Okay, now I have a million *more* questions.
Oh you think *you* do, how about us?
May, he said MJ turns into a *super-model*!!
Explain *that* one to me!!
Gwen...
I mean, right now, right here if you had to guess which one of us was--
Gwen, focus.
Um...I think we have to go now.

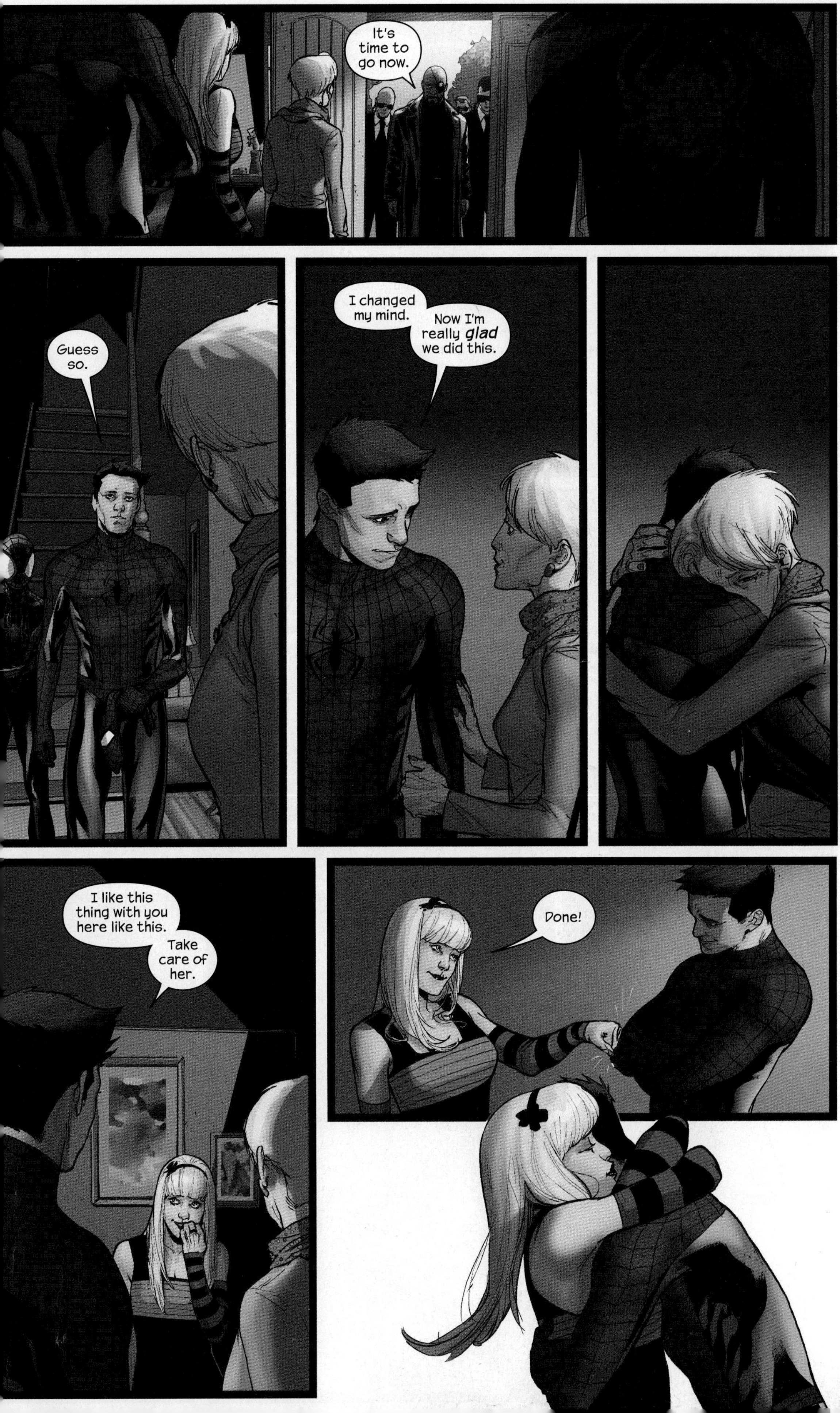
It's time to go now.
Guess so.
I changed my mind.
Now I'm really *glad* we did this.
I like this thing with you here like this.
Take care of her.
Done!

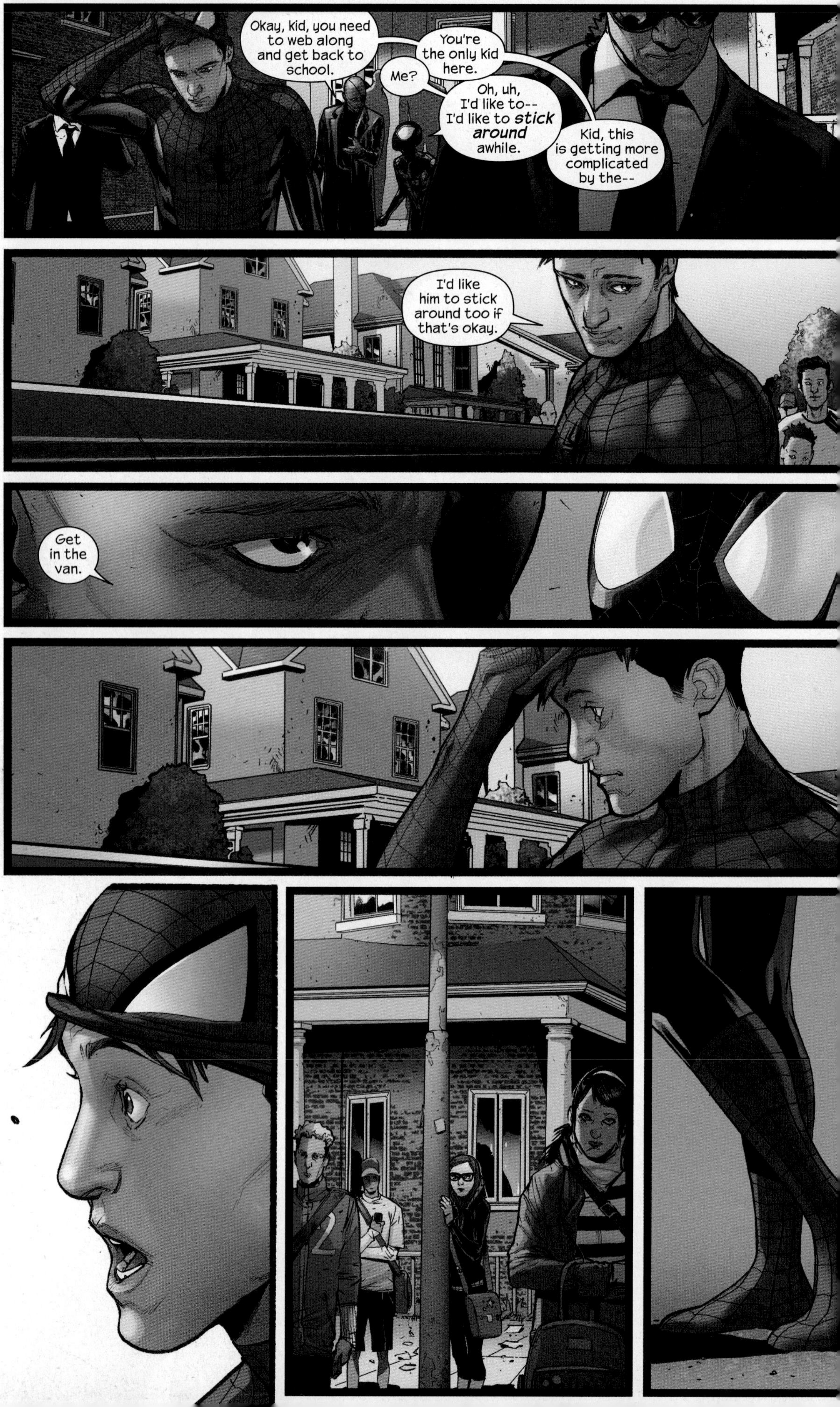
Okay, kid, you need to web along and get back to school.
Me?
You're the only kid here.
Oh, uh, I'd like to-- I'd like to stick around awhile.
Kid, this is getting more complicated by the--
I'd like him to stick around too if that's okay.
Get in the van.

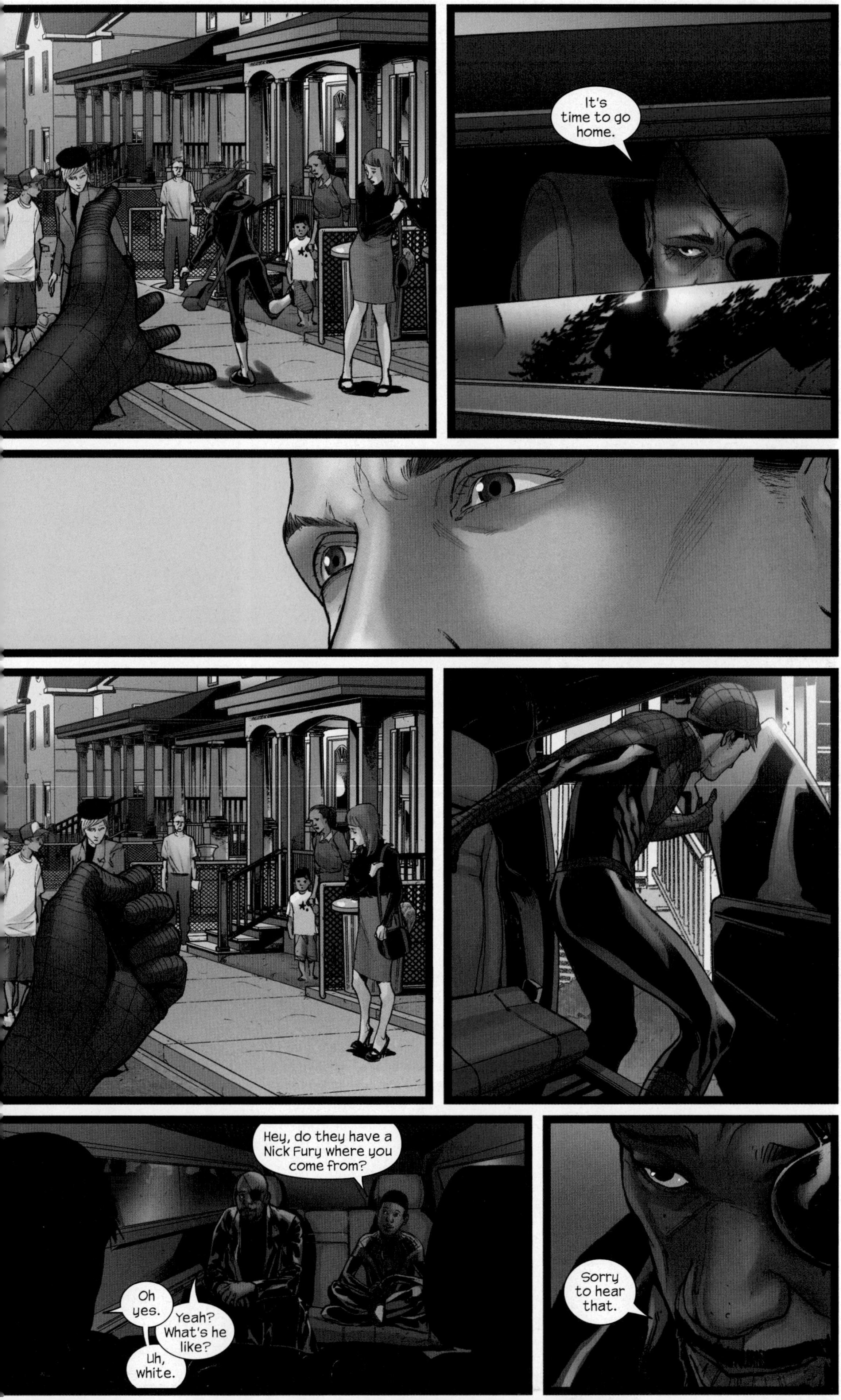
It's time to go home.
Hey, do they have a Nick Fury where you come from?
Oh yes.
Yeah? What's he like?
Uh, white.
Sorry to hear that.

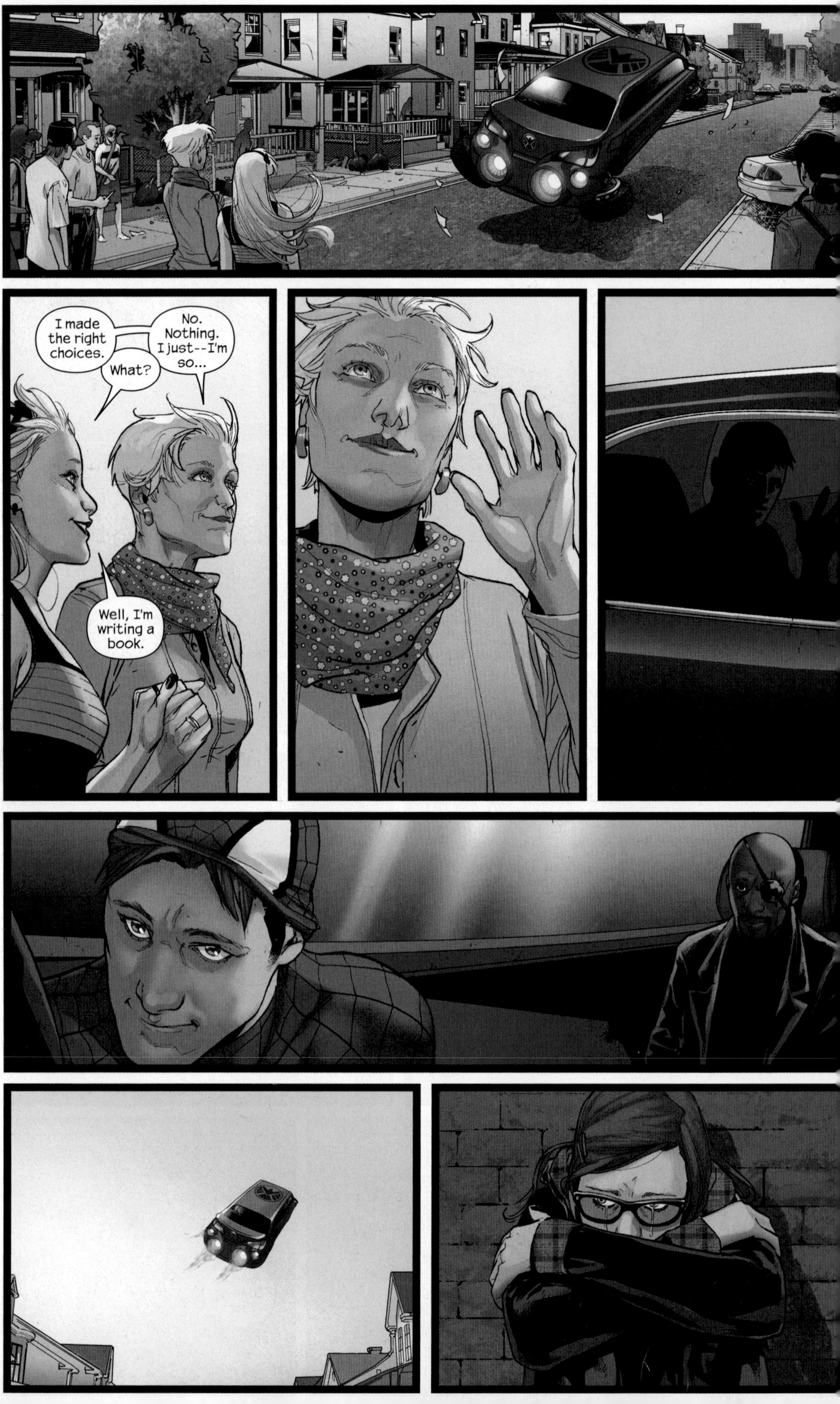
I made the right choices.
What?
No. Nothing. I just--I'm so...
Well, I'm writing a book.

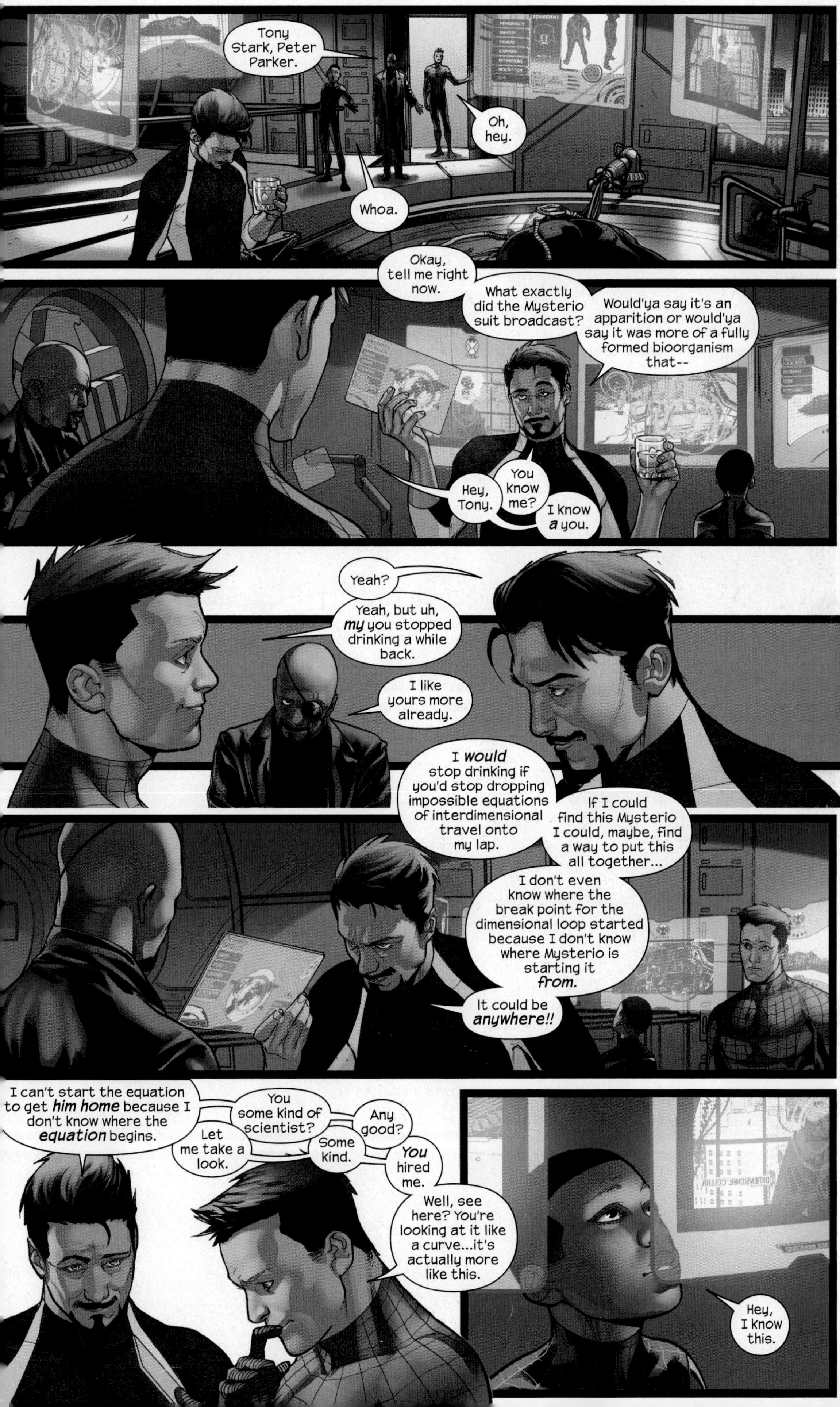
Tony Stark, Peter Parker.
Oh, hey.
Whoa.
Okay, tell me right now.
What exactly did the Mysterio suit broadcast?
Would'ya say it's an apparition or would'ya say it was more of a fully formed bioorganism that--
Hey, Tony.
You know me?
I know *a* you.
Yeah?
Yeah, but uh, *my* you stopped drinking a while back.
I like yours more already.
I *would* stop drinking if you'd stop dropping impossible equations of interdimensional travel onto my lap.
If I could find this Mysterio I could, maybe, find a way to put this all together...
I don't even know where the break point for the dimensional loop started because I don't know where Mysterio is starting it *from.*
It could be *anywhere!!*
I can't start the equation to get *him home* because I don't know where the *equation* begins.
Let me take a look.
You some kind of scientist?
Some kind.
Any good?
You hired me.
Well, see here? You're looking at it like a curve...it's actually more like this.
Hey, I know this.

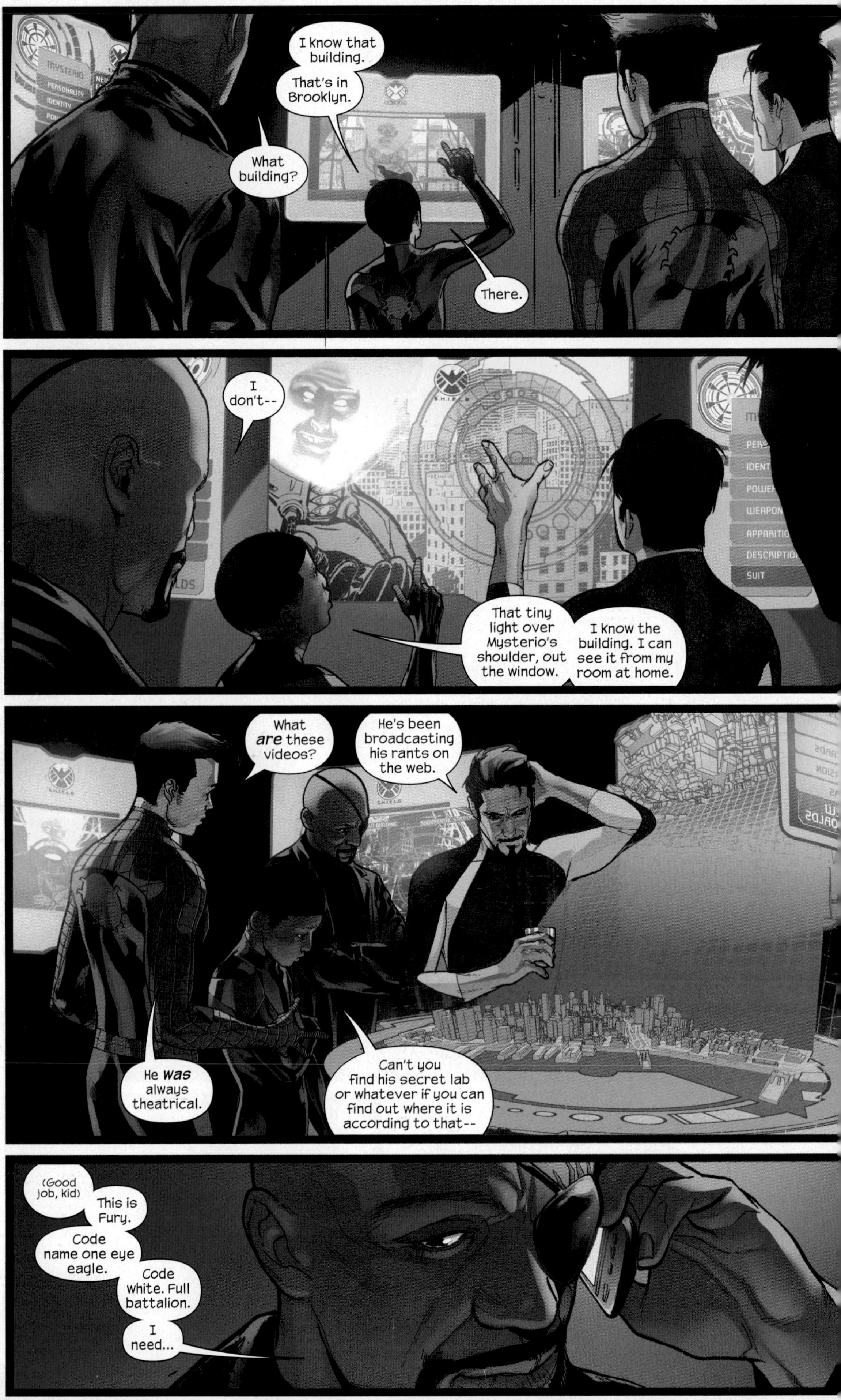

I know that building.
That's in Brooklyn.
What building?
There.
I don't--
That tiny light over Mysterio's shoulder, out the window.
I know the building. I can see it from my room at home.
What *are* these videos?
He's been broadcasting his rants on the web.
He *was* always theatrical.
Can't you find his secret lab or whatever if you can find out where it is according to that--
(Good job, kid)
This is Fury.
Code name one eye eagle.
Code white. Full battalion.
I need...

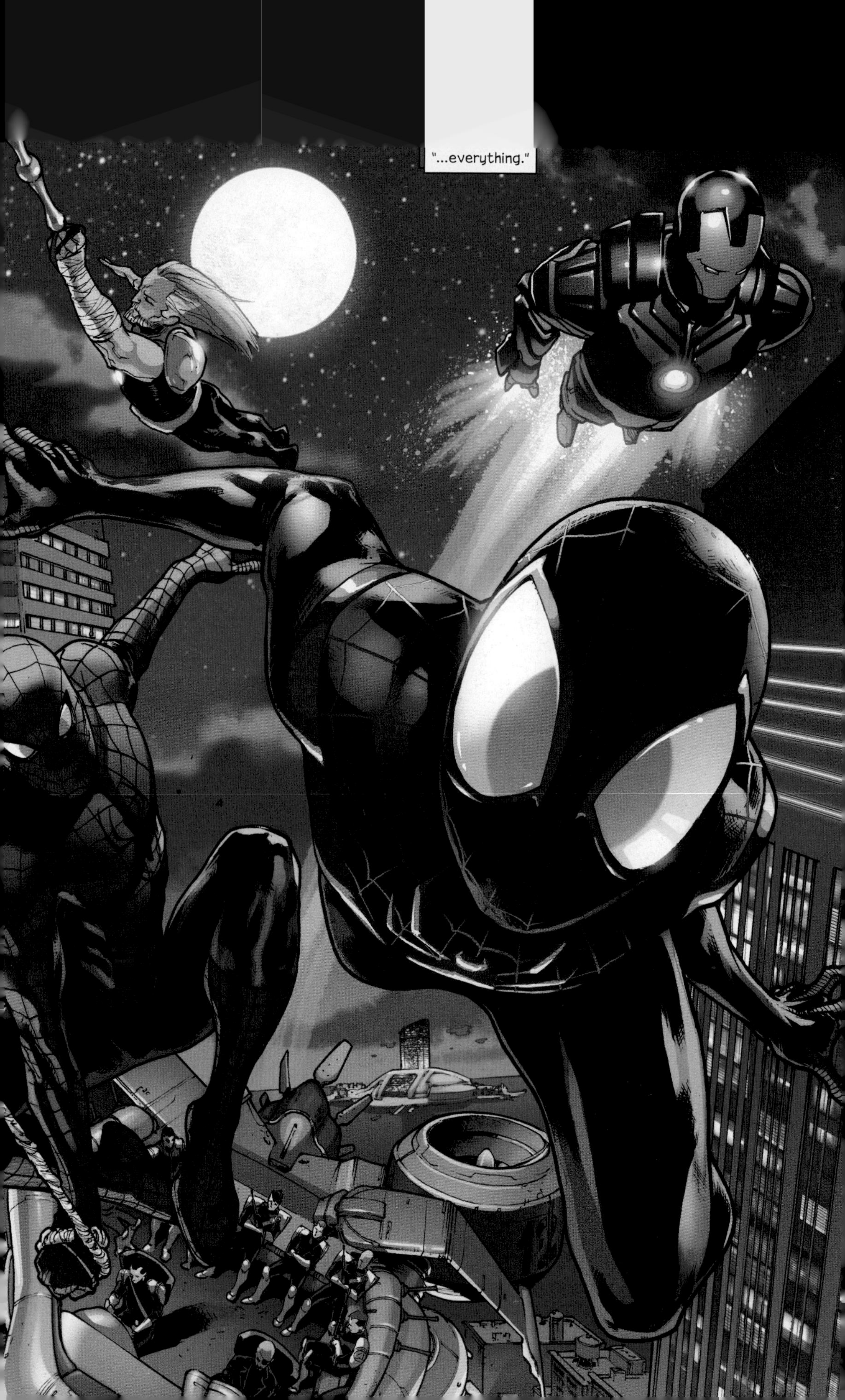
"...everything."

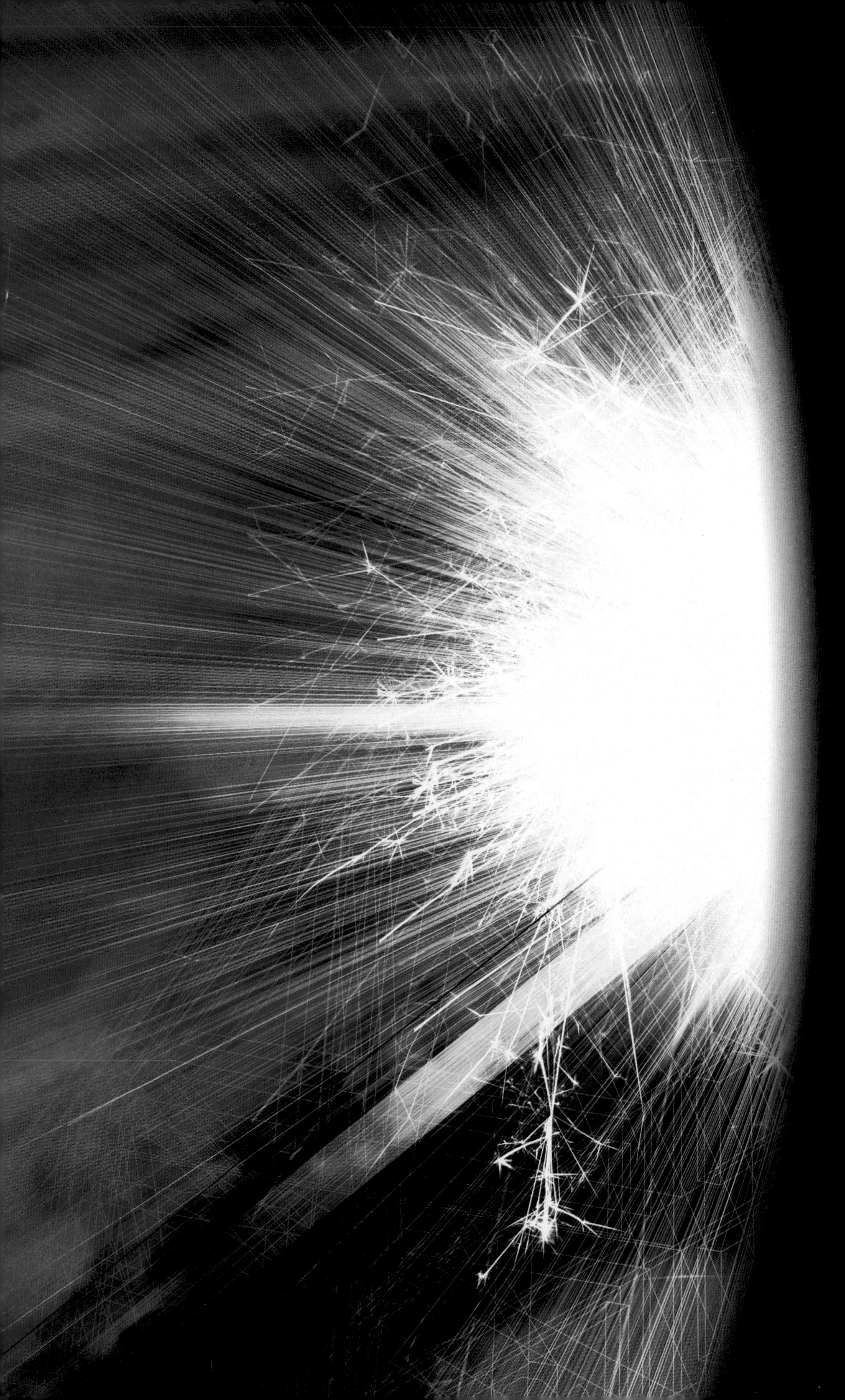

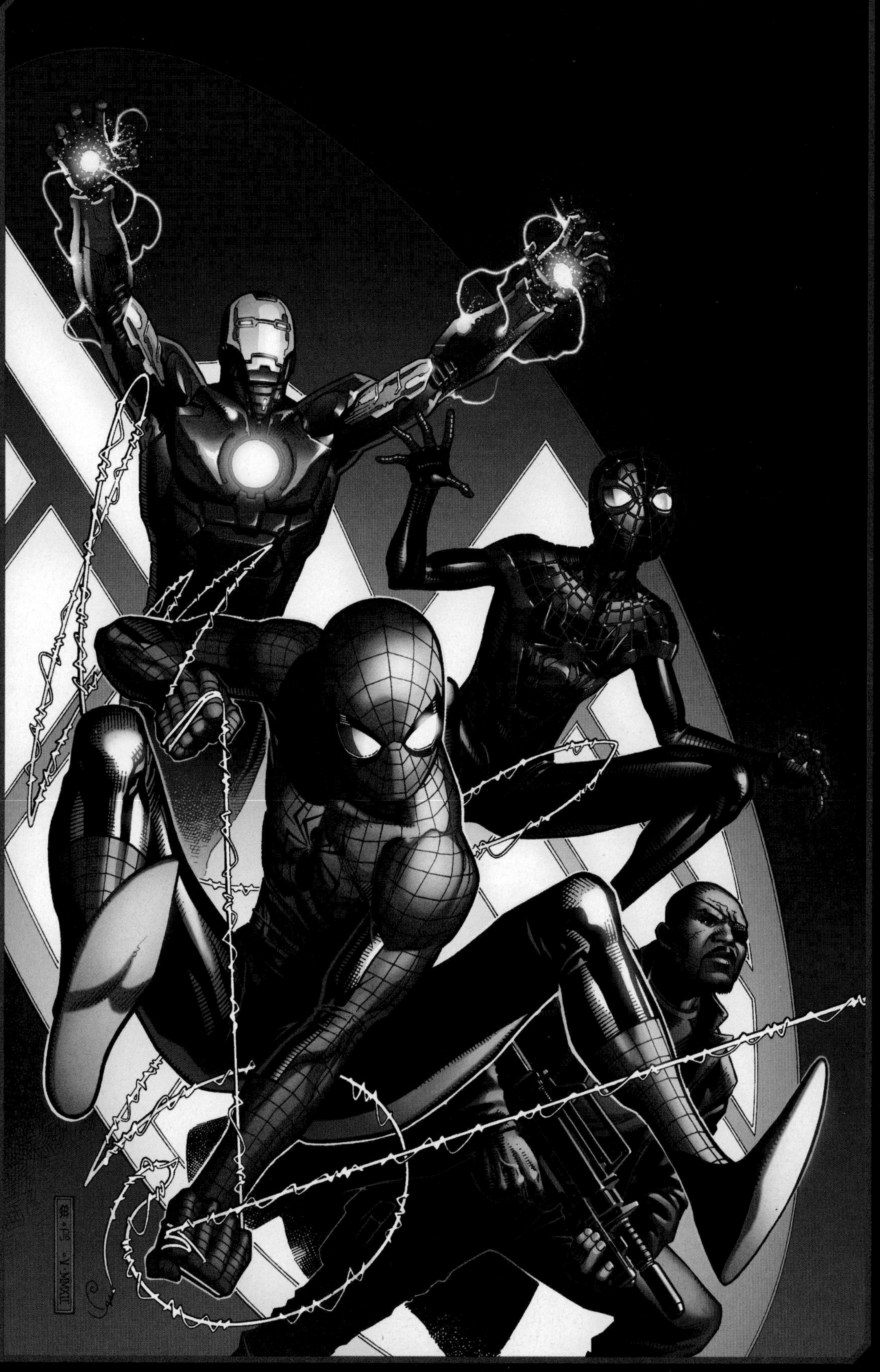

SPIDER-MEN #5

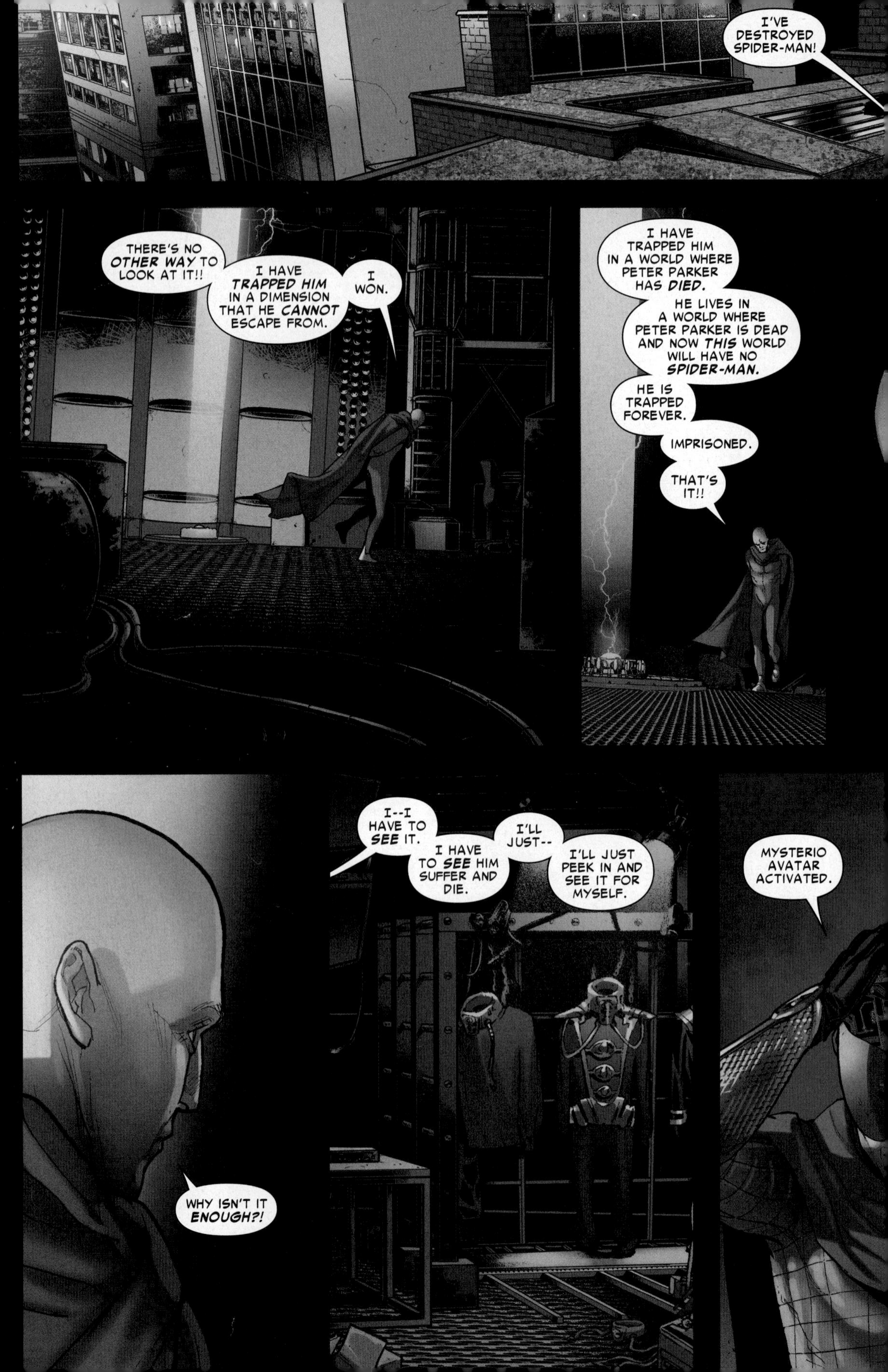
I'VE DESTROYED SPIDER-MAN!
THERE'S NO OTHER WAY TO LOOK AT IT!!
I HAVE TRAPPED HIM IN A DIMENSION THAT HE CANNOT ESCAPE FROM.
I WON.
I HAVE TRAPPED HIM IN A WORLD WHERE PETER PARKER HAS DIED.
HE LIVES IN A WORLD WHERE PETER PARKER IS DEAD AND NOW THIS WORLD WILL HAVE NO SPIDER-MAN.
HE IS TRAPPED FOREVER.
IMPRISONED.
THAT'S IT!!
WHY ISN'T IT ENOUGH?!
I--I HAVE TO SEE IT.
I HAVE TO SEE HIM SUFFER AND DIE.
I'LL JUST--
I'LL JUST PEEK IN AND SEE IT FOR MYSELF.
MYSTERIO AVATAR ACTIVATED.

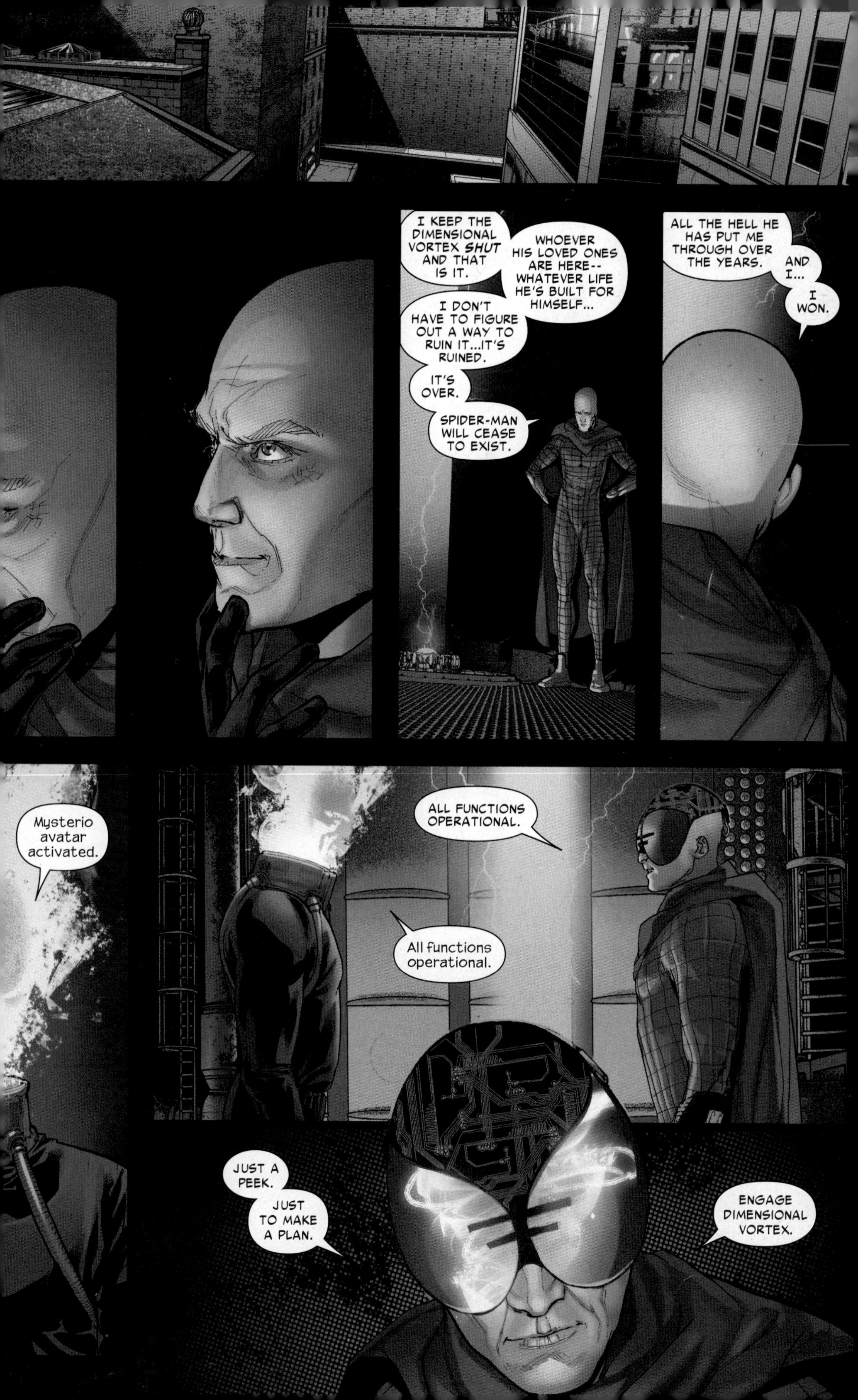
I KEEP THE DIMENSIONAL VORTEX SHUT AND THAT IS IT.
WHOEVER HIS LOVED ONES ARE HERE-- WHATEVER LIFE HE'S BUILT FOR HIMSELF...
I DON'T HAVE TO FIGURE OUT A WAY TO RUIN IT...IT'S RUINED.
IT'S OVER.
SPIDER-MAN WILL CEASE TO EXIST.
ALL THE HELL HE HAS PUT ME THROUGH OVER THE YEARS.
AND I...
I WON.
Mysterio avatar activated.
ALL FUNCTIONS OPERATIONAL.
All functions operational.
JUST A PEEK.
JUST TO MAKE A PLAN.
ENGAGE DIMENSIONAL VORTEX.

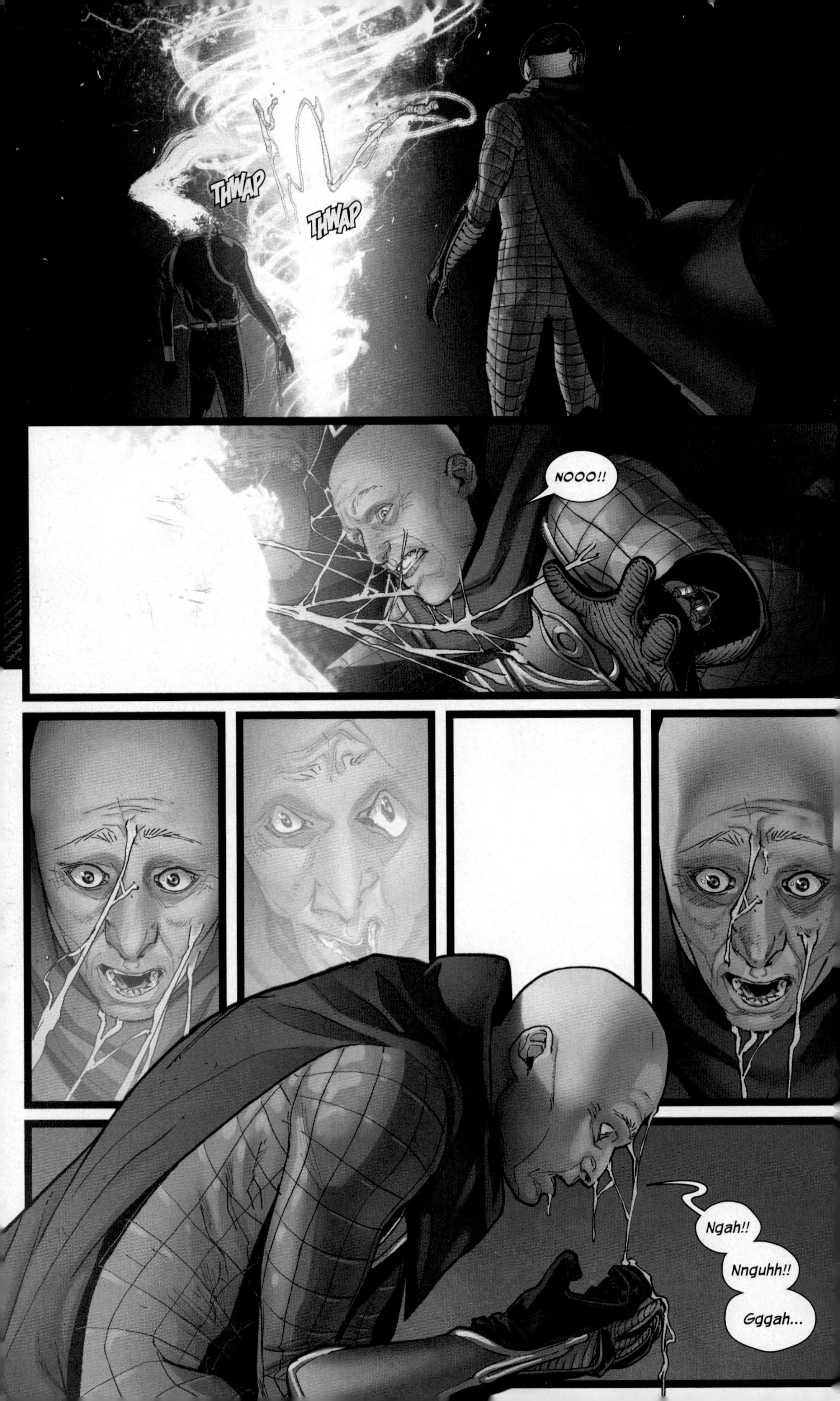
THWAP
THWAP
NOOO!!
Ngah!!
Nnguhh!!
Gggah...

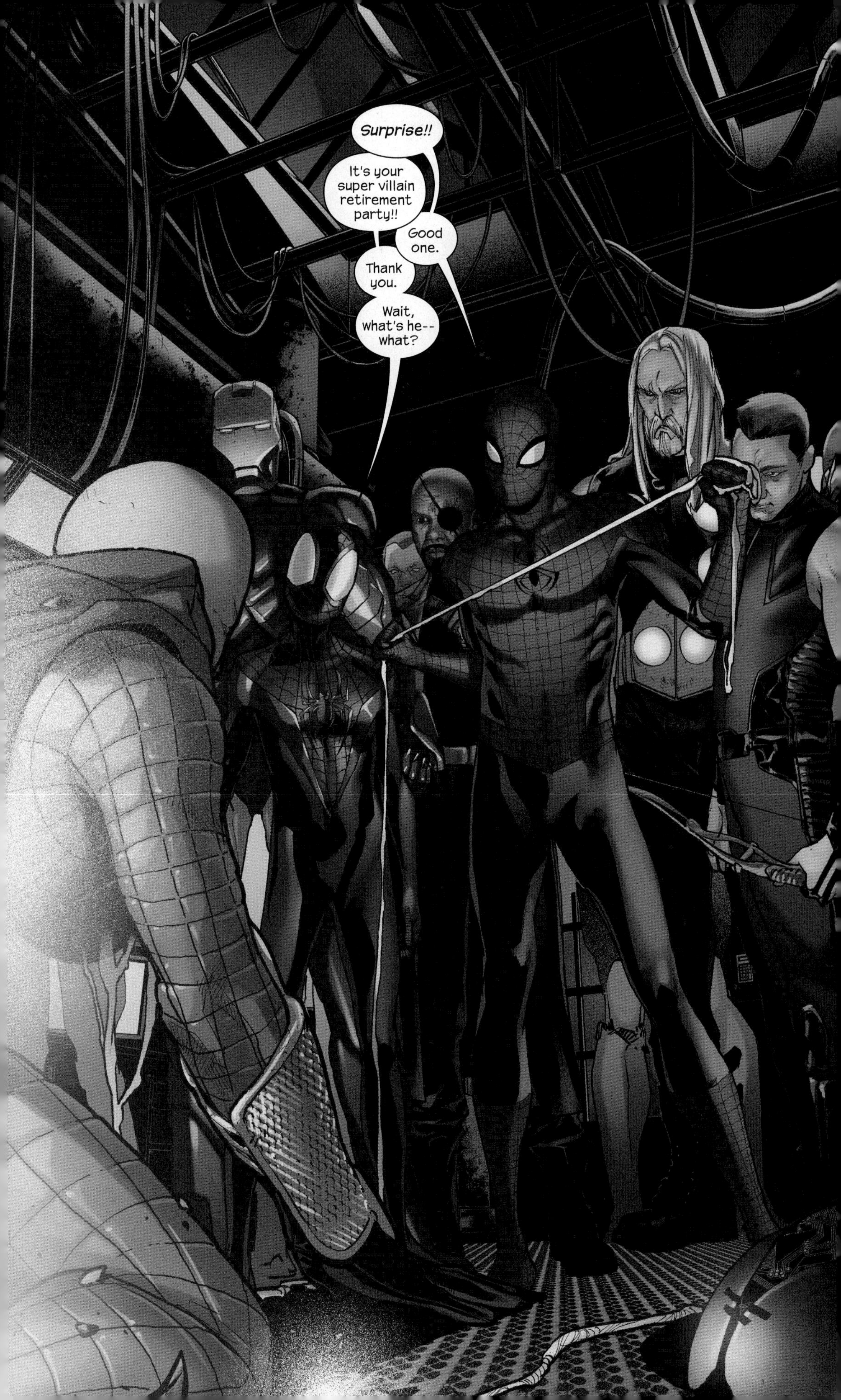
Surprise!!
It's your super villain retirement party!!
Good one.
Thank you.
Wait, what's he-- what?

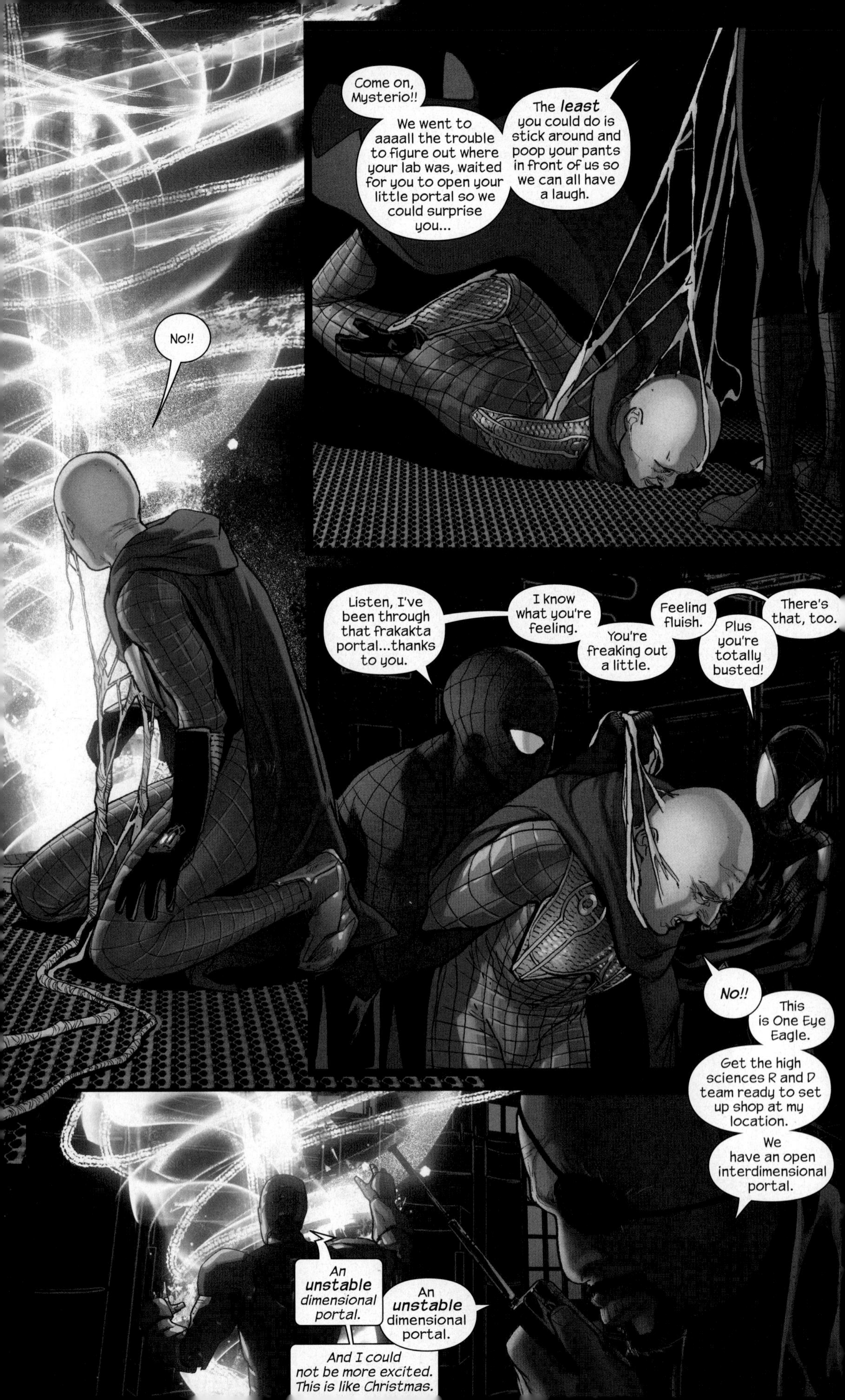
Come on, Mysterio!!
We went to aaaall the trouble to figure out where your lab was, waited for you to open your little portal so we could surprise you...
The *least* you could do is stick around and poop your pants in front of us so we can all have a laugh.
No!!
Listen, I've been through that frakakta portal...thanks to you.
I know what you're feeling.
You're freaking out a little.
Feeling fluish.
Plus you're totally busted!
There's that, too.
No!!
This is One Eye Eagle.
Get the high sciences R and D team ready to set up shop at my location.
We have an open interdimensional portal.
An ***unstable*** *dimensional portal.*
An ***unstable*** dimensional portal.
And I could not be more excited. This is like Christmas.

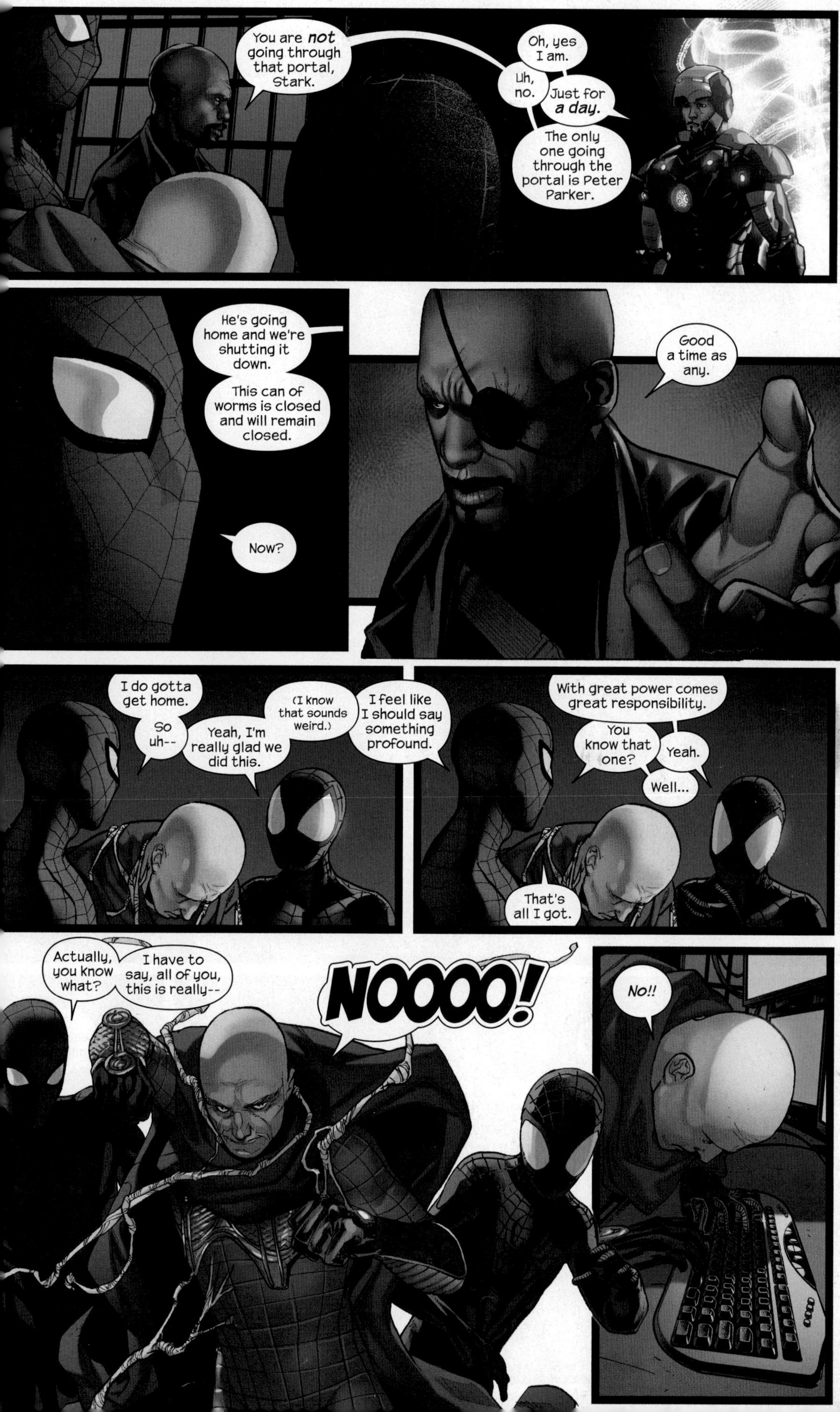
You are not going through that portal, Stark.
Oh, yes I am.
Uh, no.
Just for a day.
The only one going through the portal is Peter Parker.
He's going home and we're shutting it down.
This can of worms is closed and will remain closed.
Good a time as any.
Now?
I do gotta get home.
So uh--
Yeah, I'm really glad we did this.
(I know that sounds weird.)
I feel like I should say something profound.
With great power comes great responsibility.
You know that one?
Yeah.
Well...
That's all I got.
Actually, you know what?
I have to say, all of you, this is really--
NOOOO!
No!!

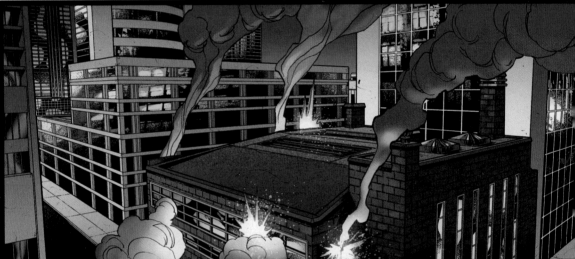

I'm ten steps *ahead* of you!!

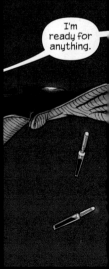

I'm ready for anything.

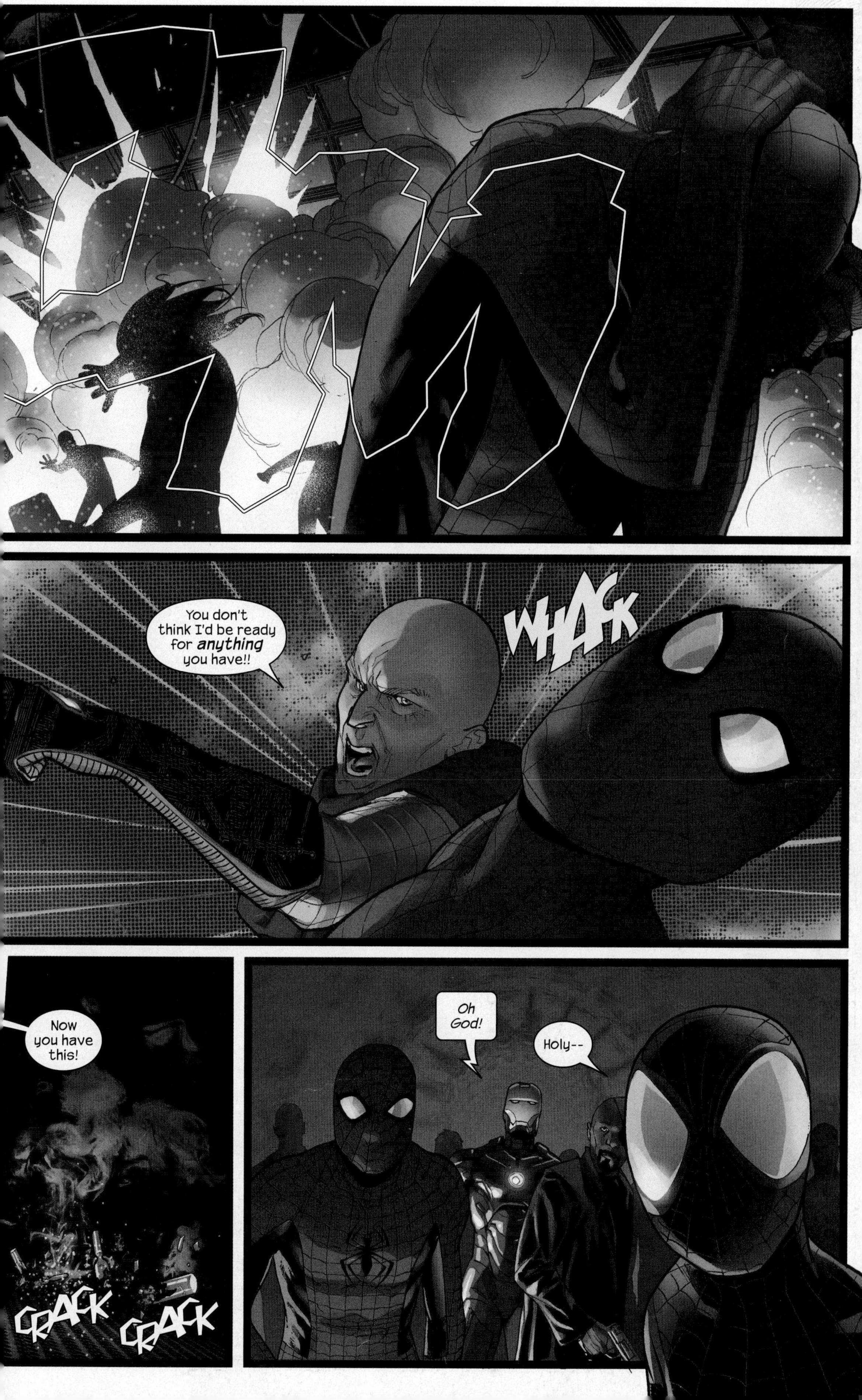
You don't think I'd be ready for *anything* you have!!
WHACK
Now you have this!
CRACK
CRACK
Oh God!
Holy--

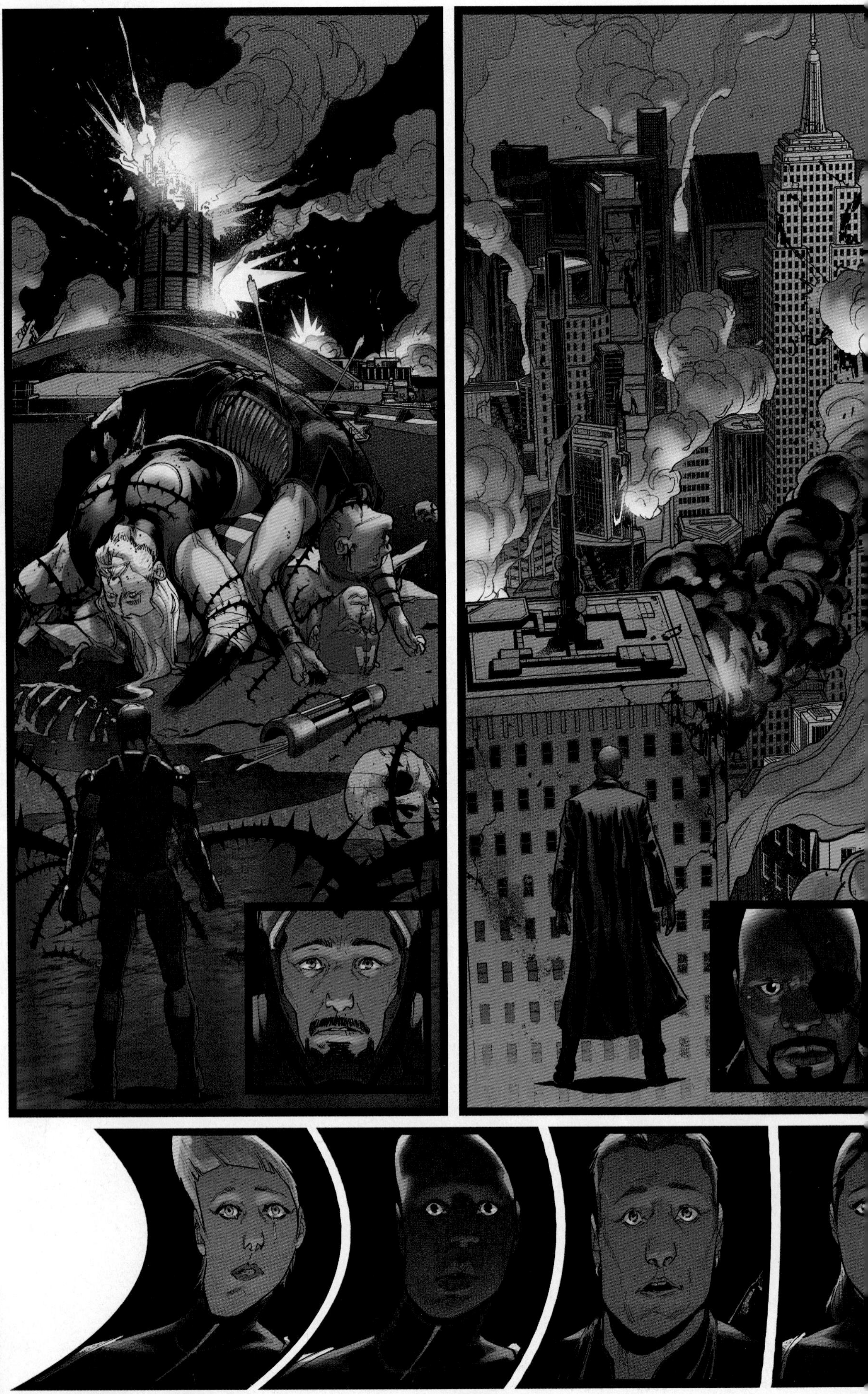

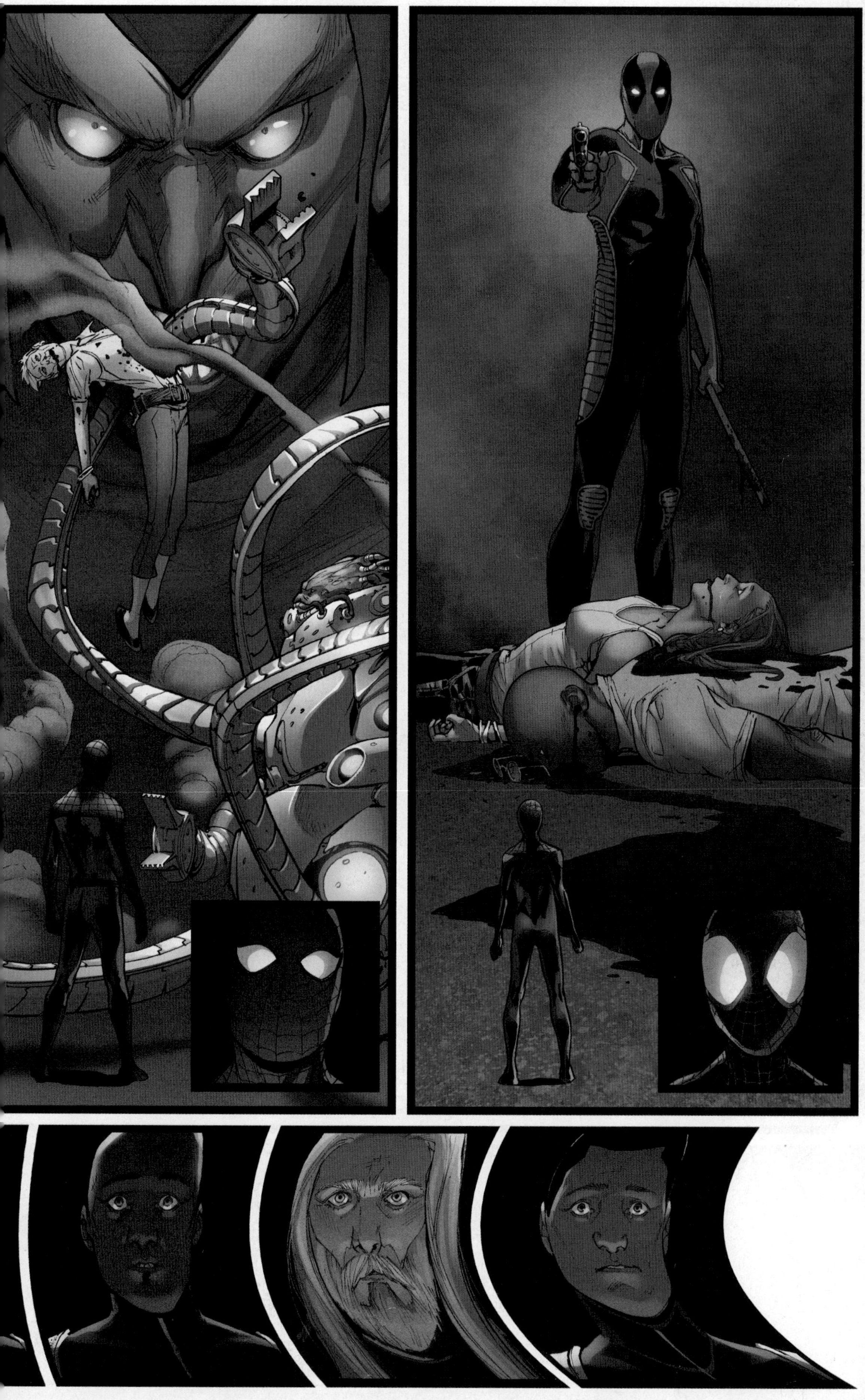

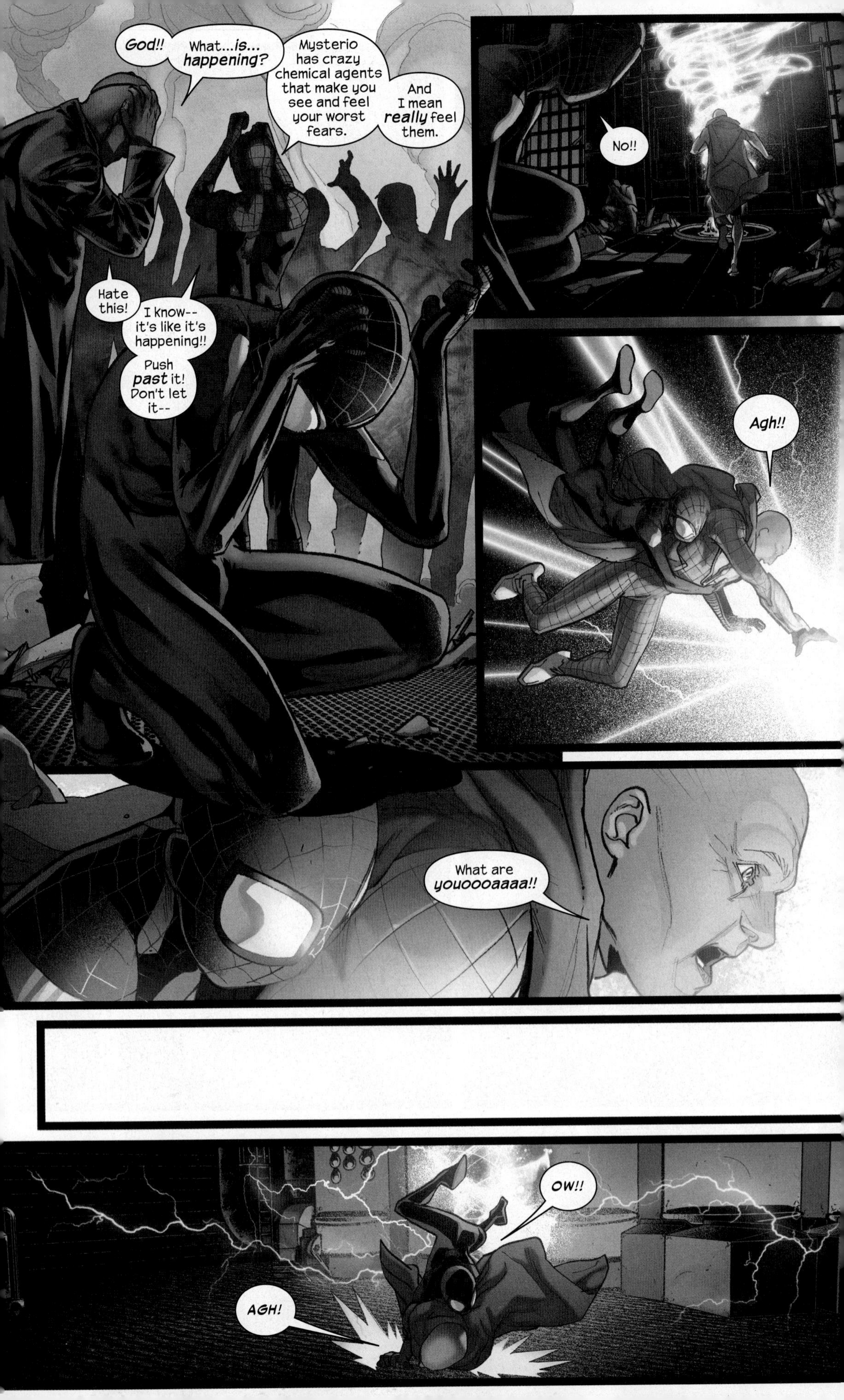
God!!
What...is... happening?
Mysterio has crazy chemical agents that make you see and feel your worst fears.
And I mean really feel them.
No!!
Hate this!
I know-- it's like it's happening!!
Push past it! Don't let it--
Agh!!
What are youoooaaaa!!
OW!!
AGH!

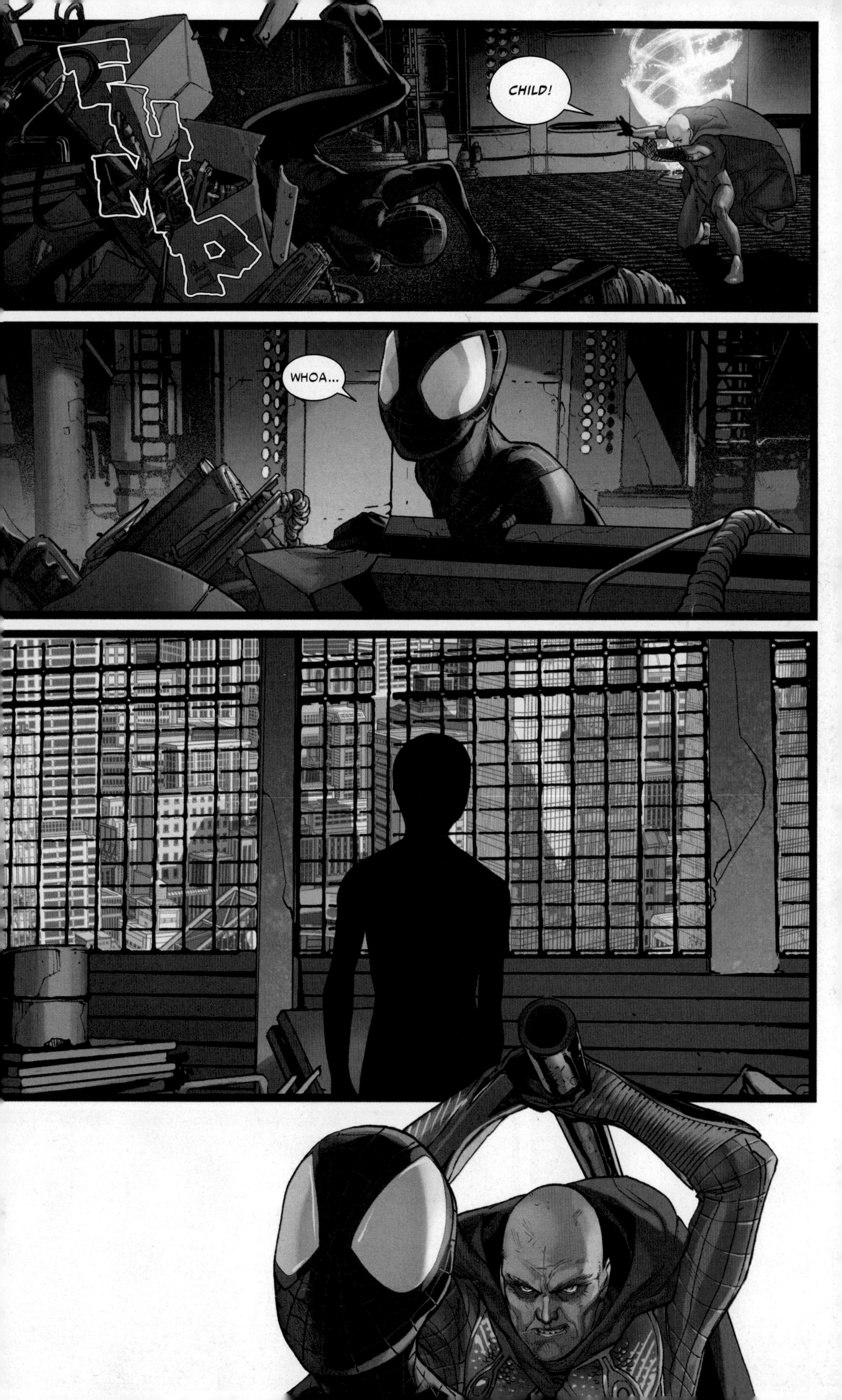

THUMP
CHILD!
WHOA...

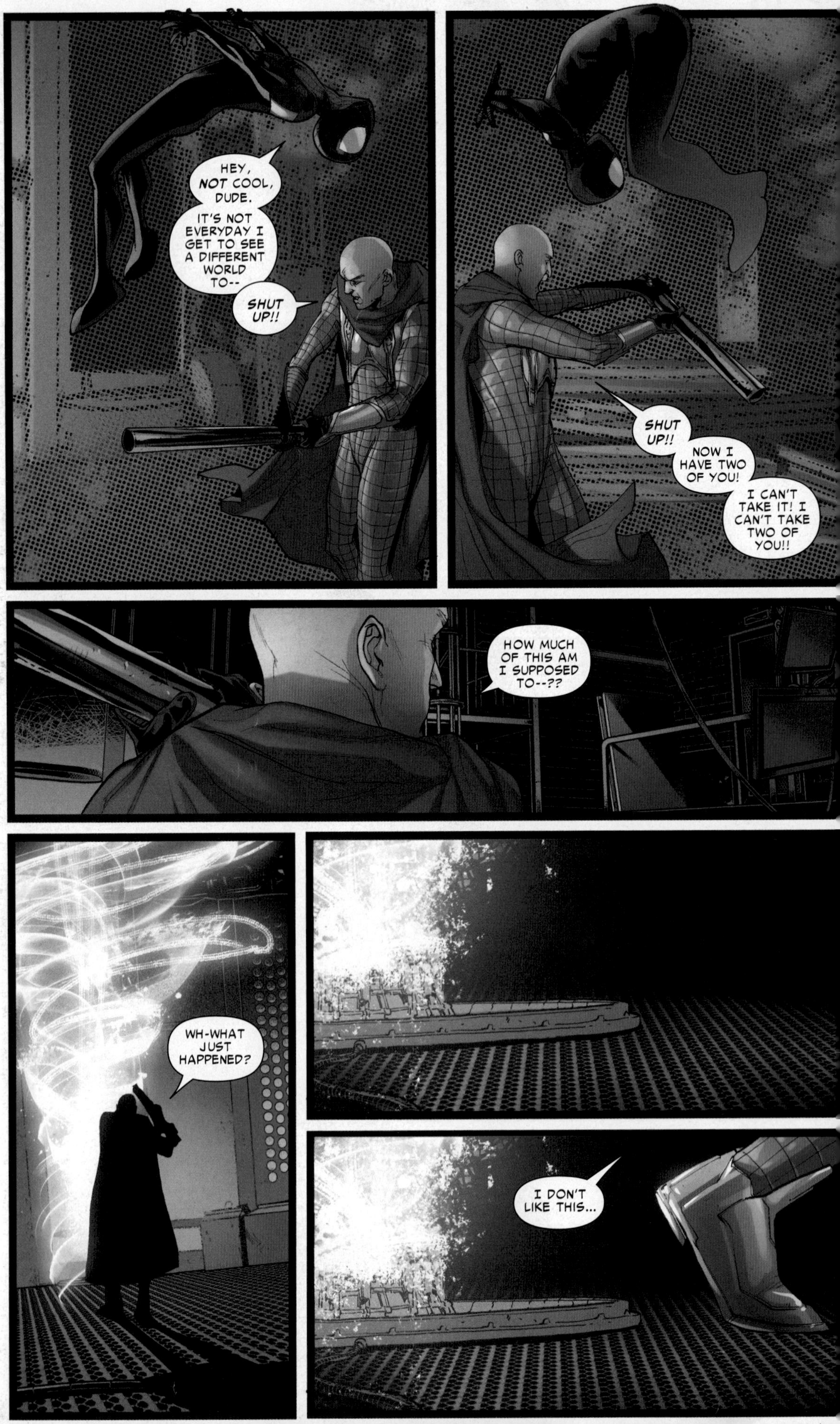
HEY, NOT COOL, DUDE.
IT'S NOT EVERYDAY I GET TO SEE A DIFFERENT WORLD TO--
SHUT UP!!
SHUT UP!!
NOW I HAVE TWO OF YOU!
I CAN'T TAKE IT! I CAN'T TAKE TWO OF YOU!!
HOW MUCH OF THIS AM I SUPPOSED TO--??
WH-WHAT JUST HAPPENED?
I DON'T LIKE THIS...

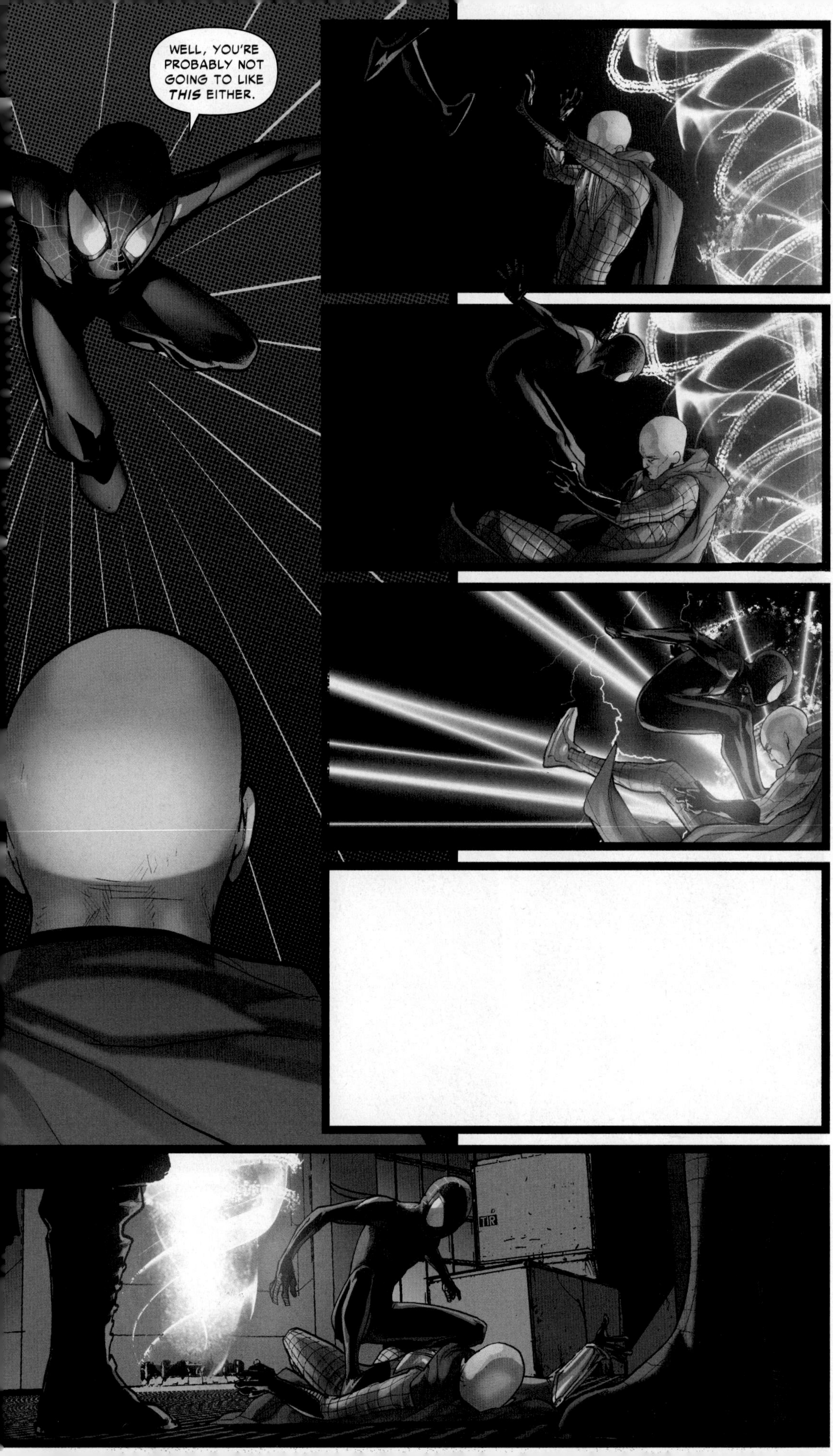
WELL, YOU'RE PROBABLY NOT GOING TO LIKE *THIS* EITHER.
TIR

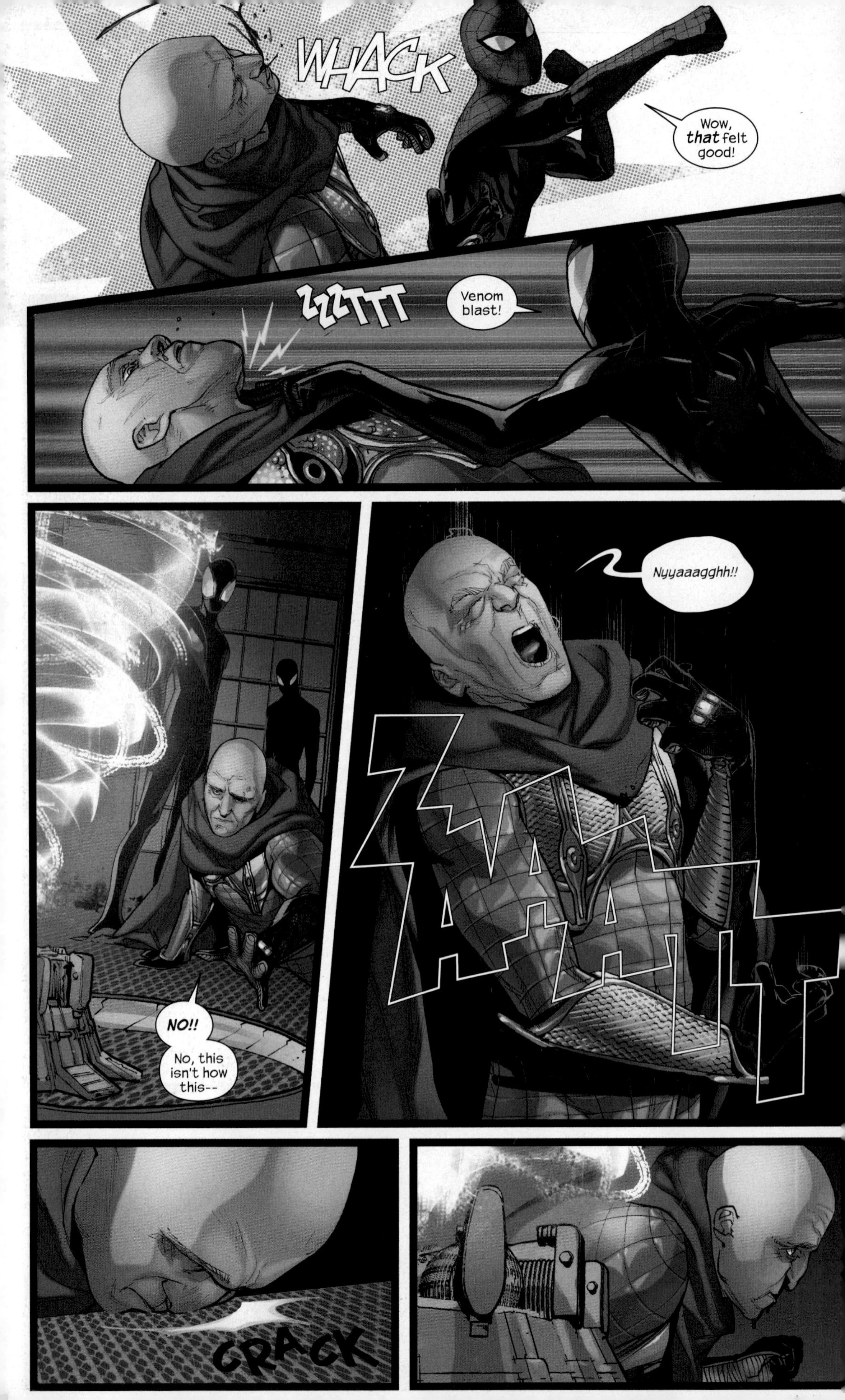
WHACK
Wow, that felt good!
ZZZTTT
Venom blast!
NO!!
No, this isn't how this--
Nyyaaagghh!!
ZAAAAT
CRACK

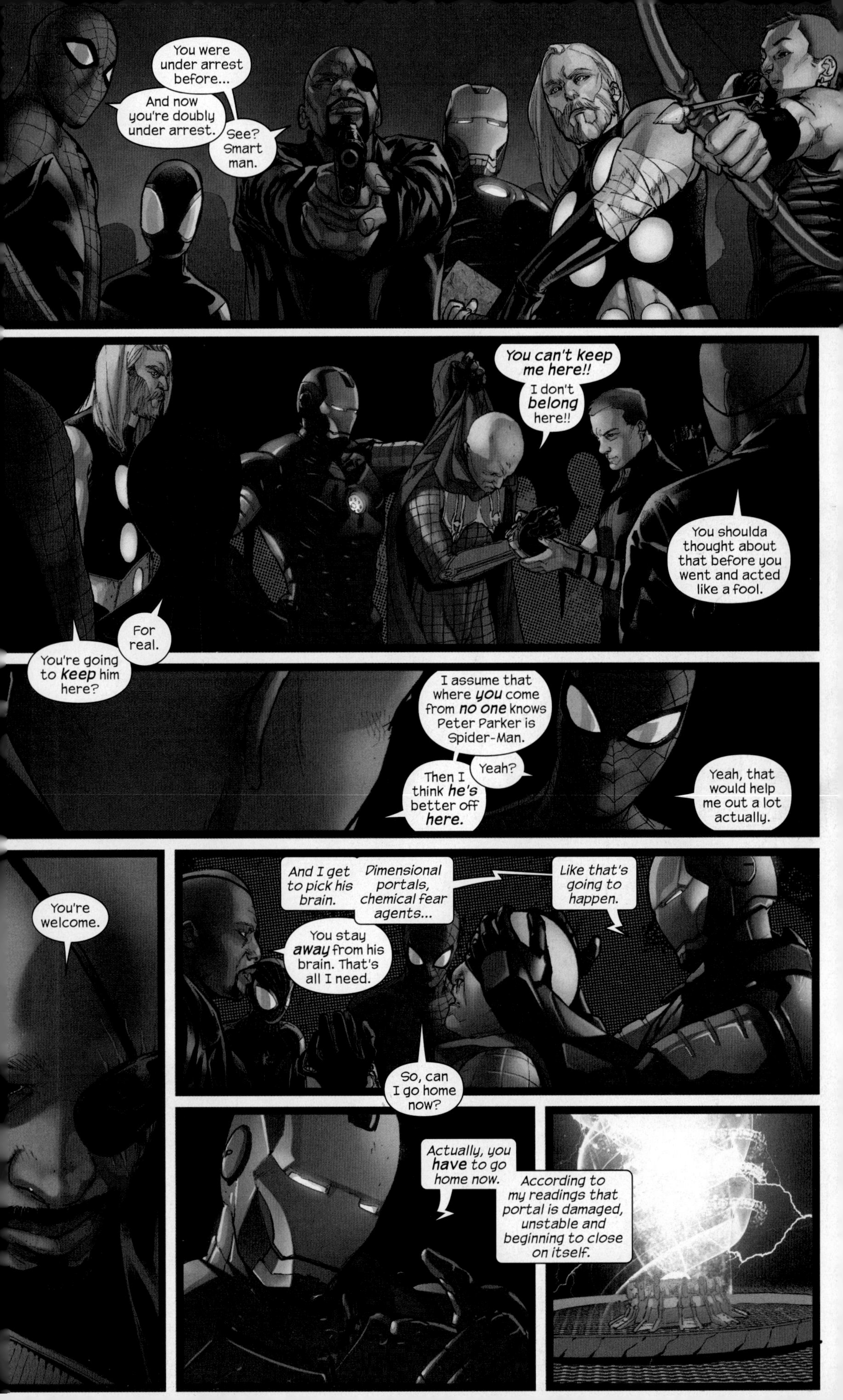
You were under arrest before...
And now you're doubly under arrest.
See? Smart man.
You can't keep me here!!
I don't belong here!!
You shoulda thought about that before you went and acted like a fool.
For real.
You're going to keep him here?
I assume that where you come from no one knows Peter Parker is Spider-Man.
Yeah?
Then I think he's better off here.
Yeah, that would help me out a lot actually.
You're welcome.
And I get to pick his brain.
Dimensional portals, chemical fear agents...
Like that's going to happen.
You stay away from his brain. That's all I need.
So, can I go home now?
Actually, you have to go home now.
According to my readings that portal is damaged, unstable and beginning to close on itself.

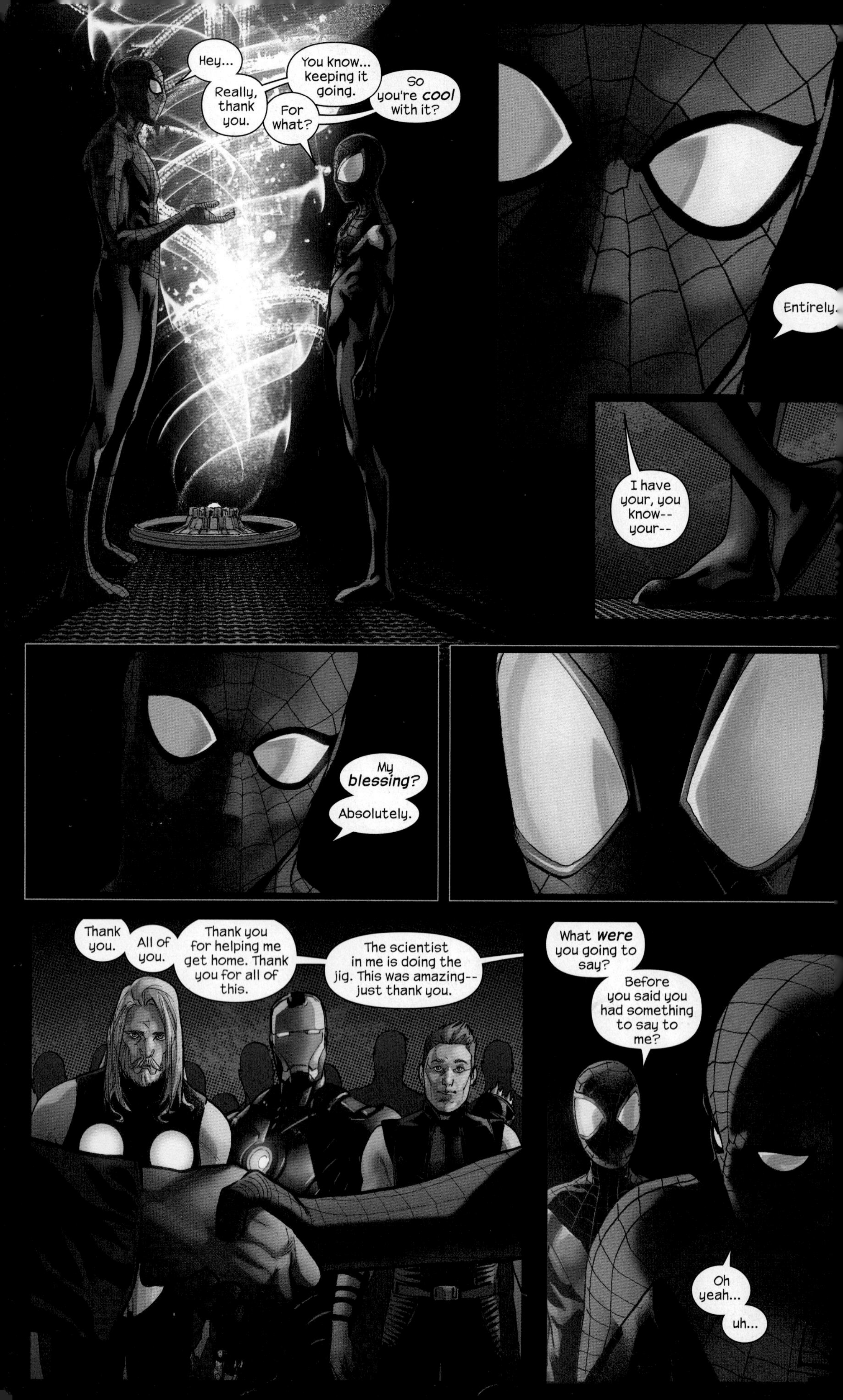
Hey...
Really, thank you.
You know... keeping it going.
For what?
So you're *cool* with it?
Entirely.
I have your, you know-- your--
My *blessing*?
Absolutely.
Thank you.
All of you.
Thank you for helping me get home. Thank you for all of this.
The scientist in me is doing the jig. This was amazing-- just thank you.
What *were* you going to say?
Before you said you had something to say to me?
Oh yeah...
uh...

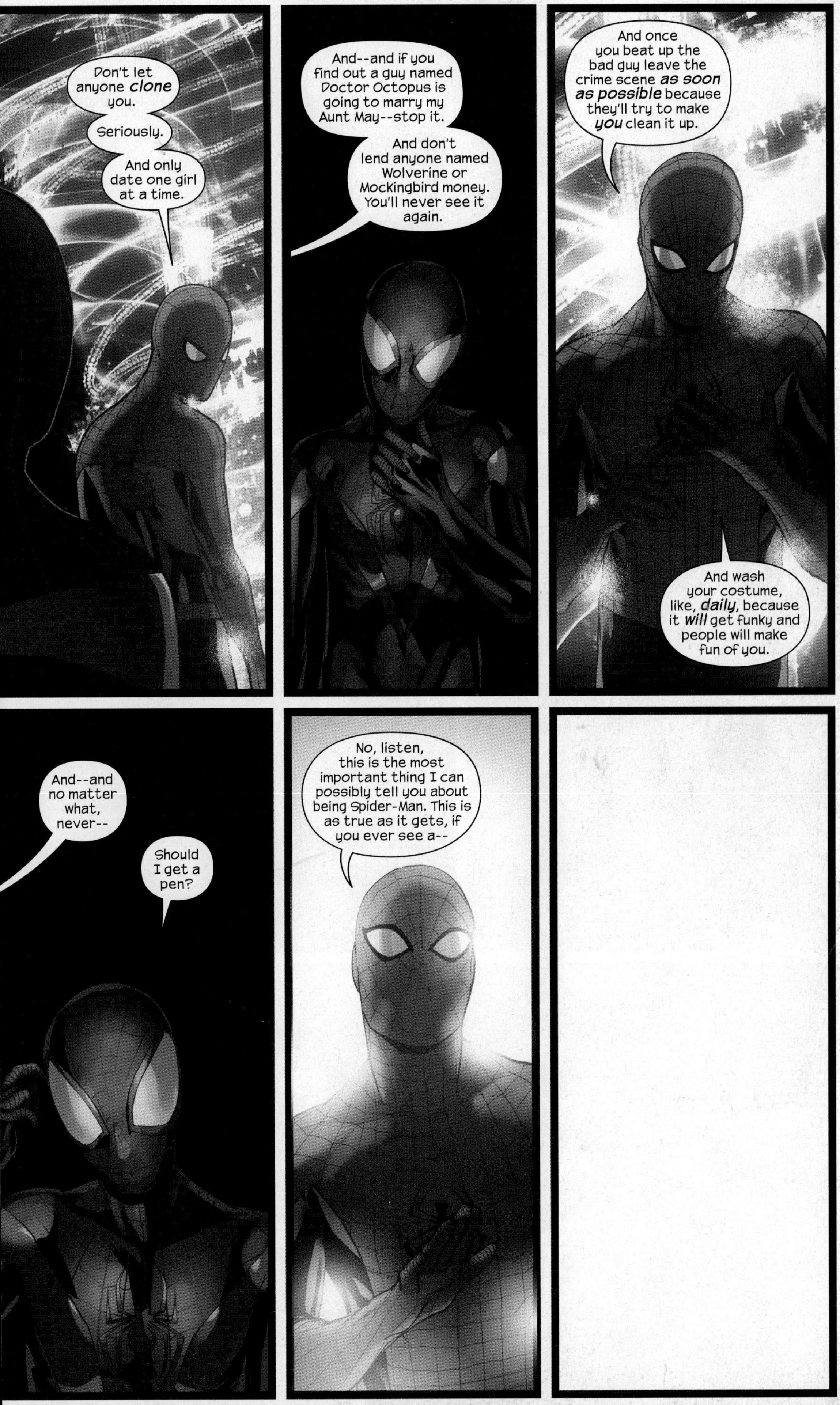
Don't let anyone clone you.
Seriously.
And only date one girl at a time.
And--and if you find out a guy named Doctor Octopus is going to marry my Aunt May--stop it.
And don't lend anyone named Wolverine or Mockingbird money. You'll never see it again.
And once you beat up the bad guy leave the crime scene as soon as possible because they'll try to make you clean it up.
And wash your costume, like, daily, because it will get funky and people will make fun of you.
And--and no matter what, never--
Should I get a pen?
No, listen, this is the most important thing I can possibly tell you about being Spider-Man. This is as true as it gets, if you ever see a--

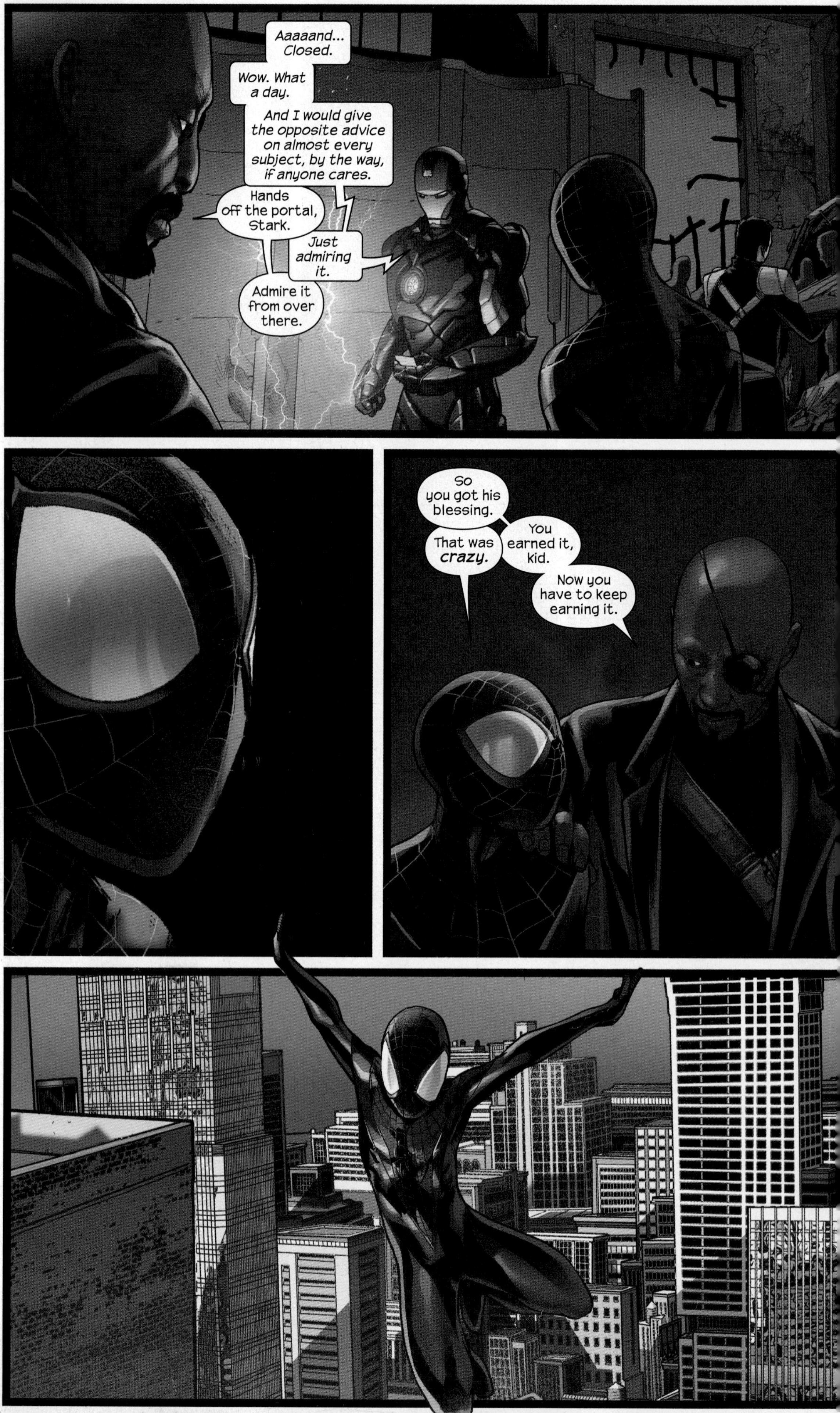
Aaaaand... Closed.
Wow. What a day.
And I would give the opposite advice on almost every subject, by the way, if anyone cares.
Hands off the portal, Stark.
Just admiring it.
Admire it from over there.
So you got his blessing.
That was *crazy.*
You earned it, kid.
Now you have to keep earning it.

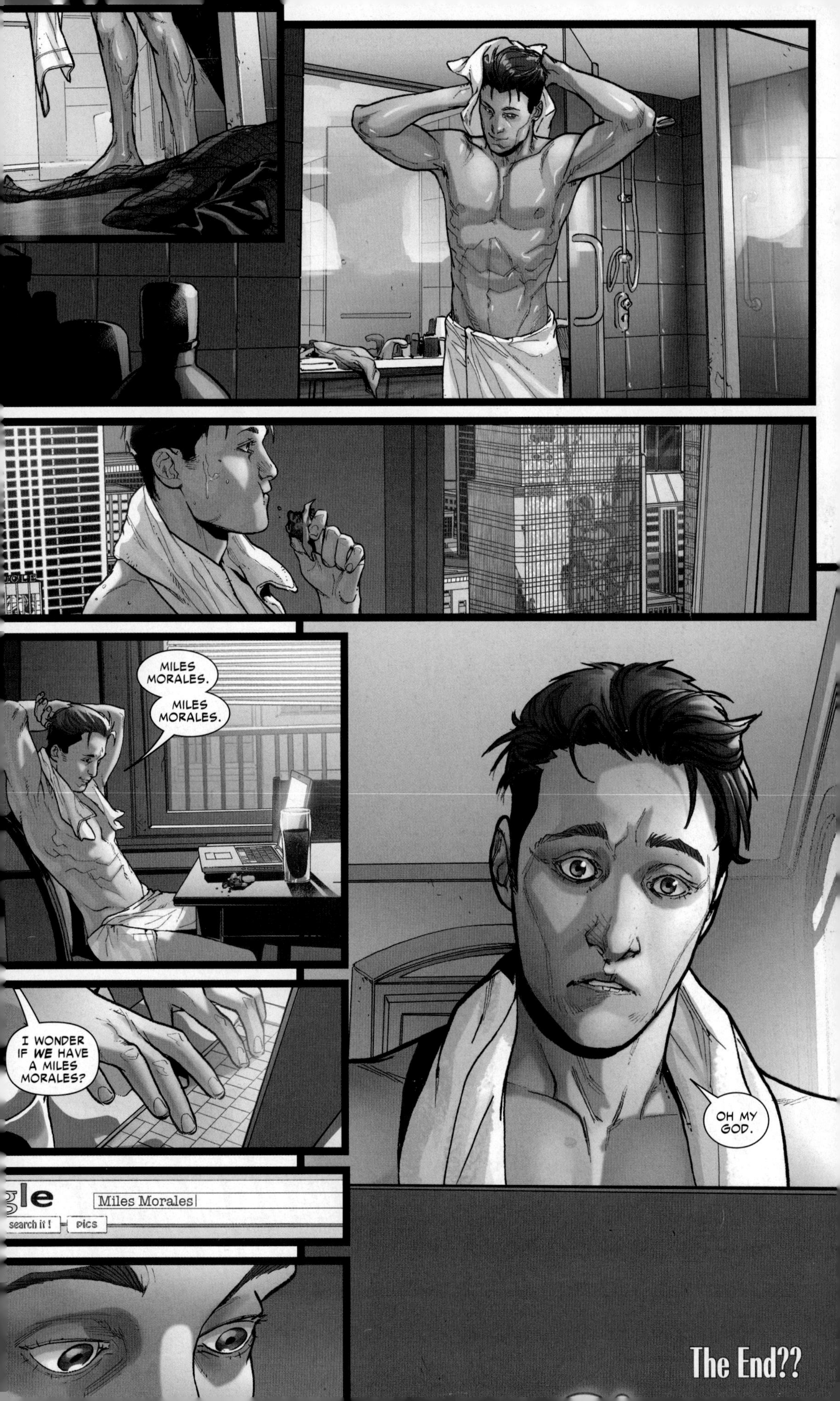
MILES MORALES.
MILES MORALES.
I WONDER IF WE HAVE A MILES MORALES?
gle
Miles Morales
search it !
pics
OH MY GOD.
The End??

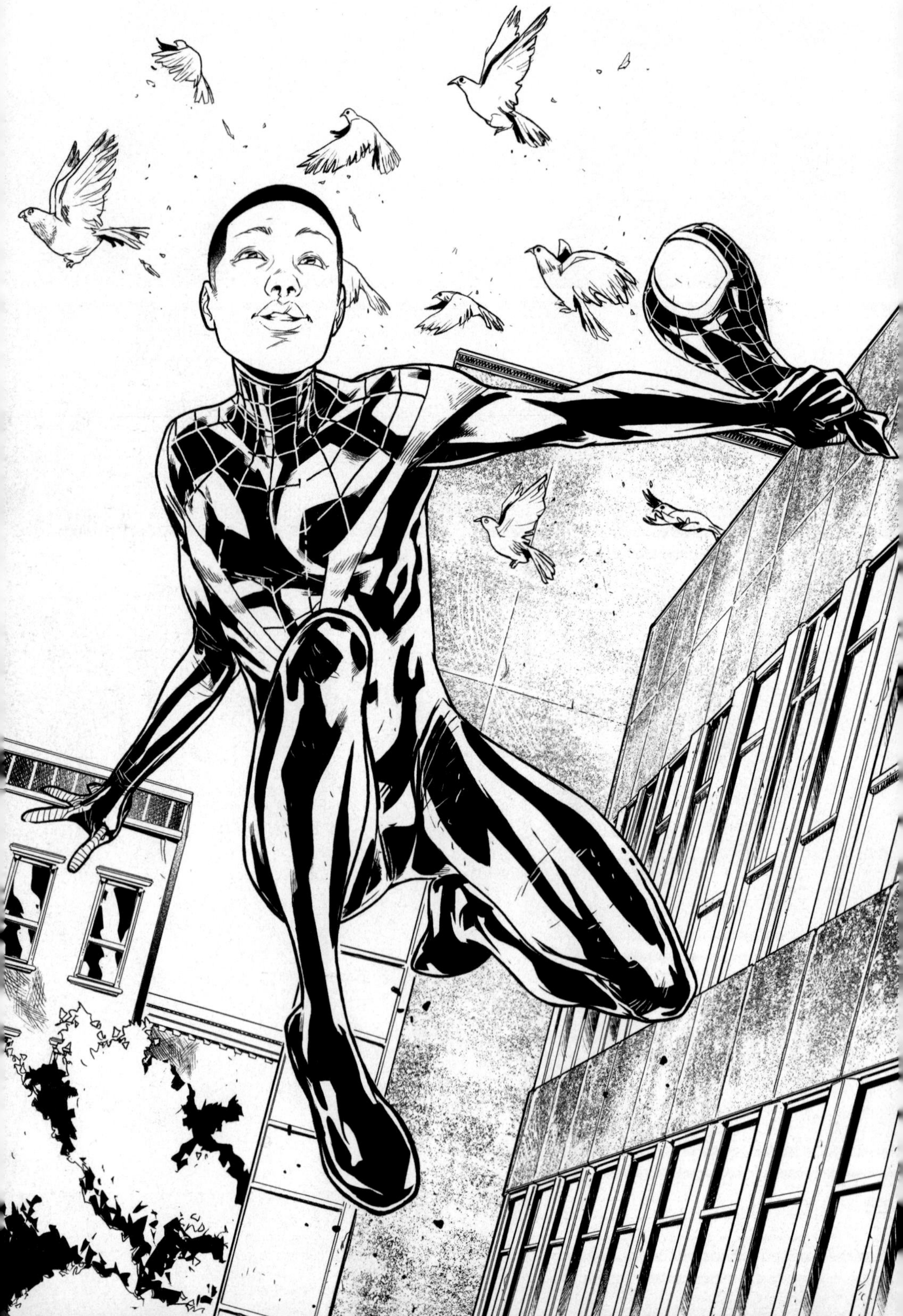

ULTIMATE COMICS SPIDER-MAN #1 SKETCH VARIANT BY SARA PICHELLI

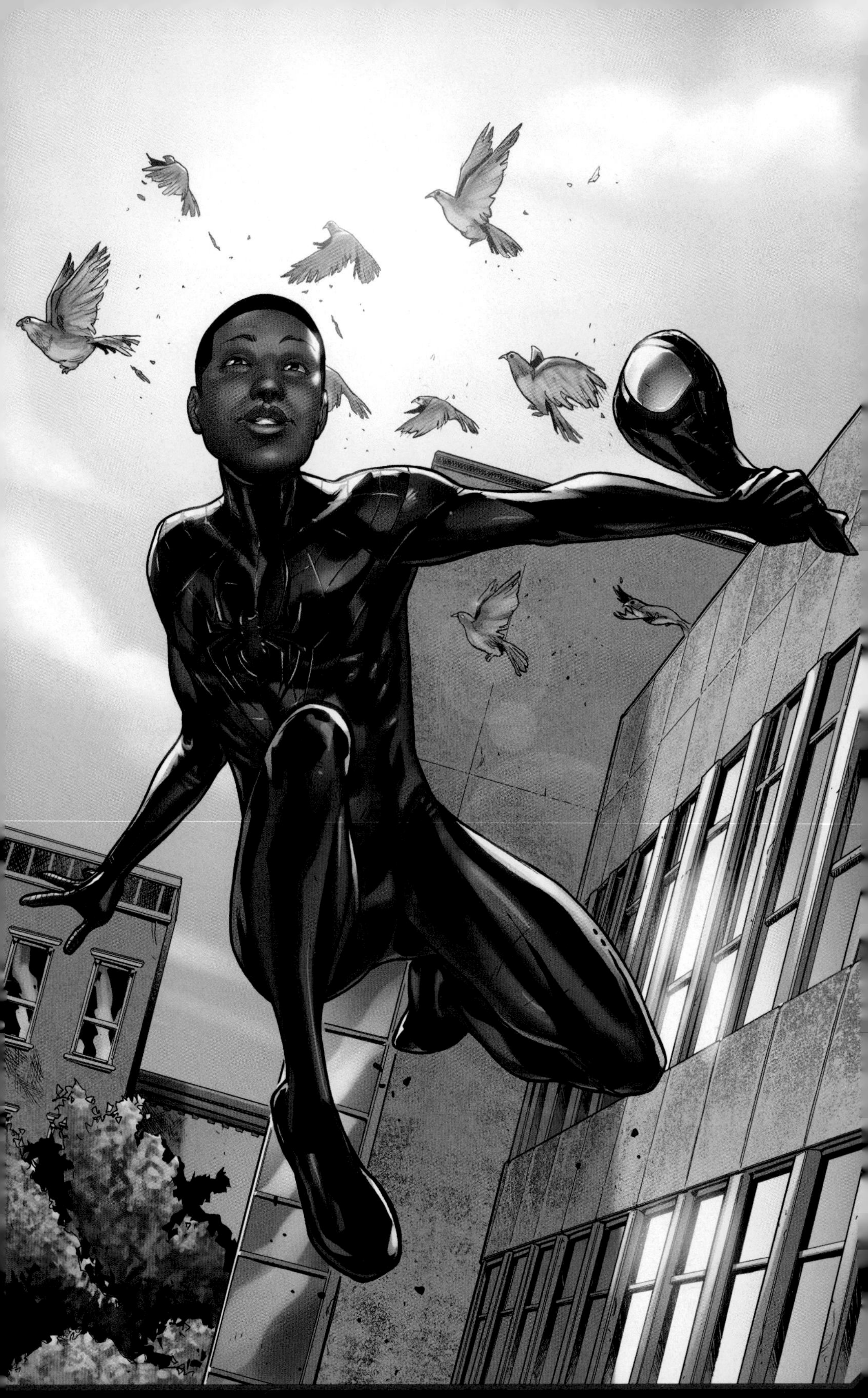

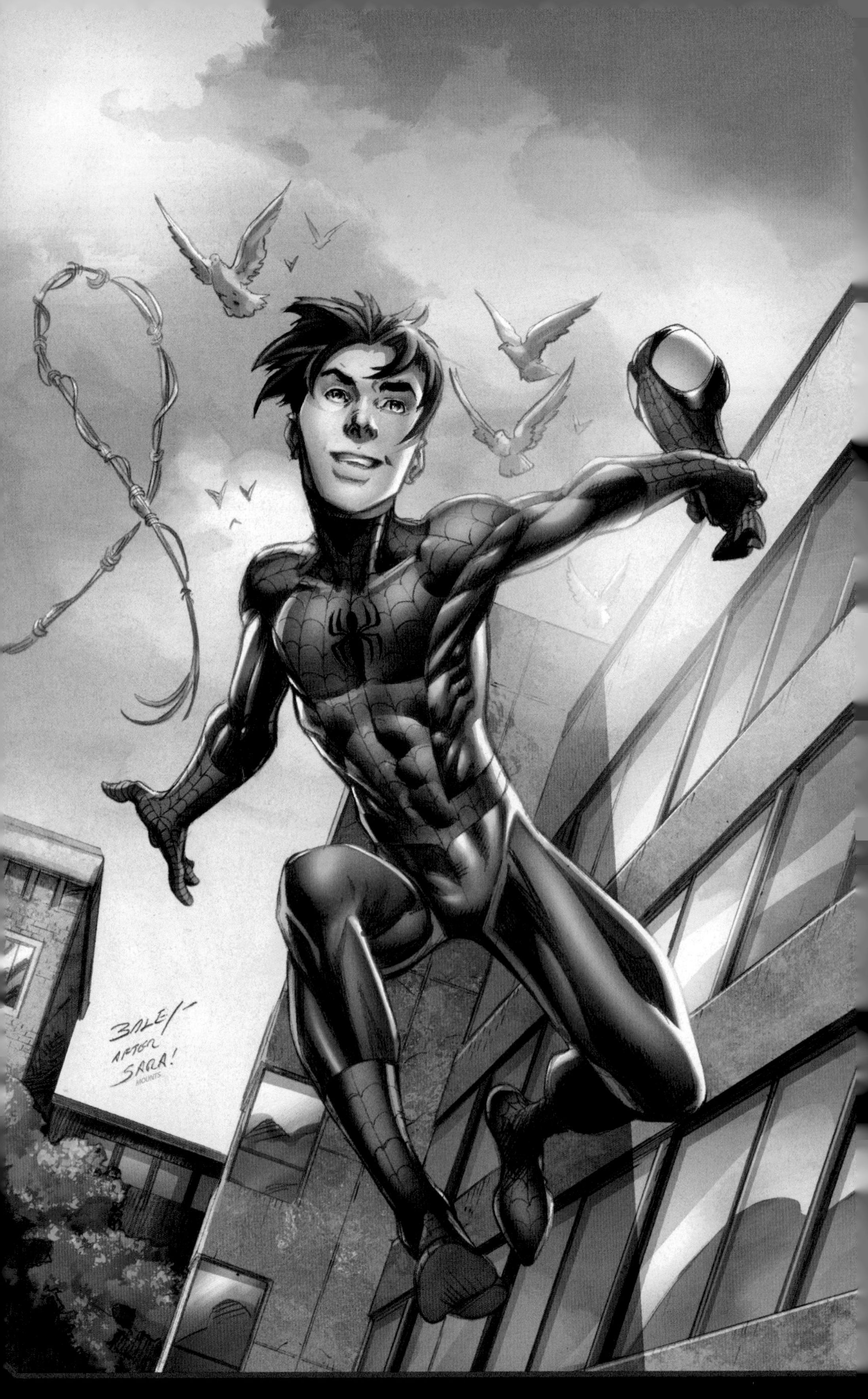
BAGLEY
AFTER
SARA!
MOUNTS

ULTIMATE COMICS SPIDER-MAN #6 VARIANT BY MARK BAGLEY

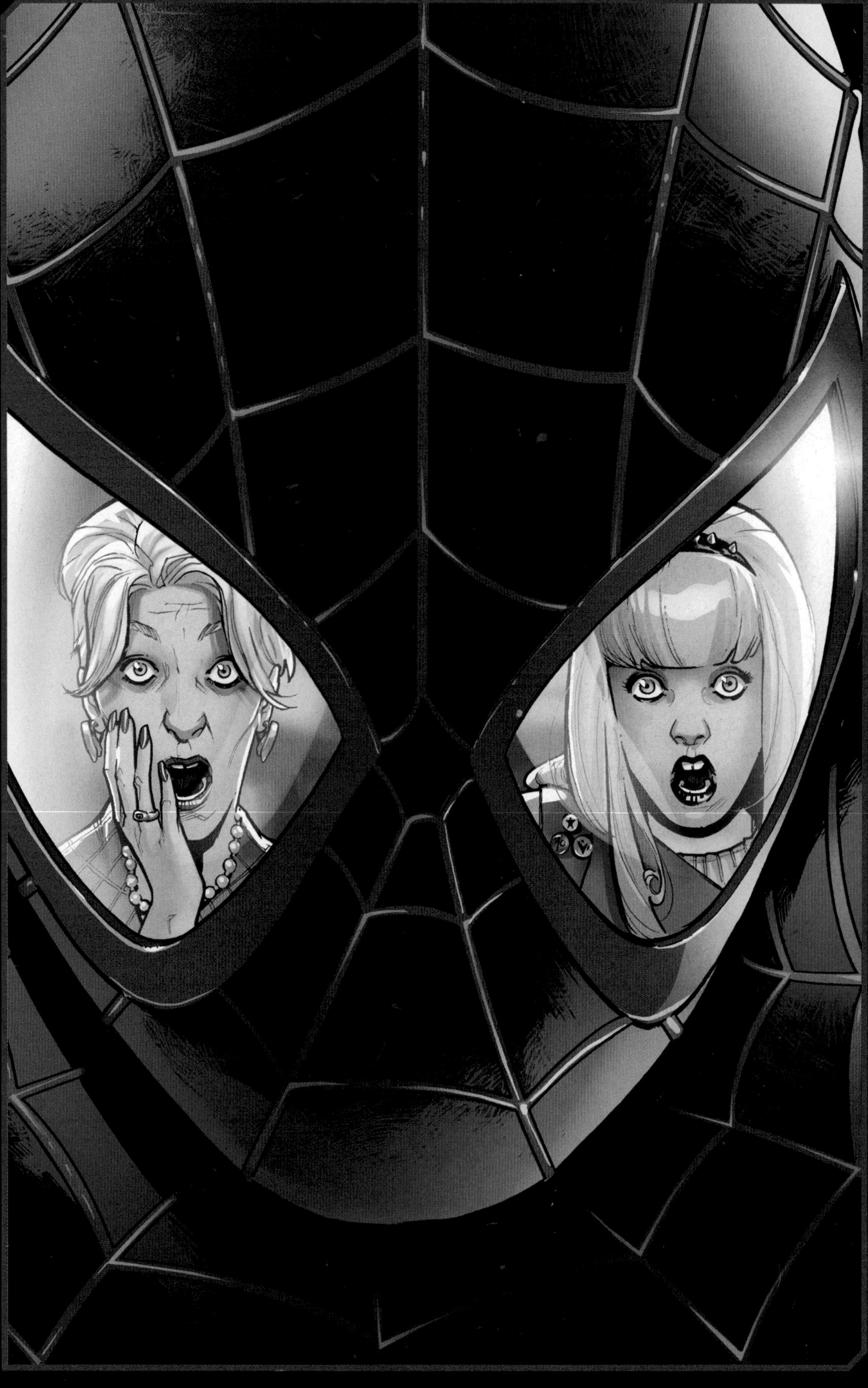

ULTIMATE COMICS SPIDER-MAN #8 VARIANT BY SARA PICHELLI & JUSTIN PONSOR

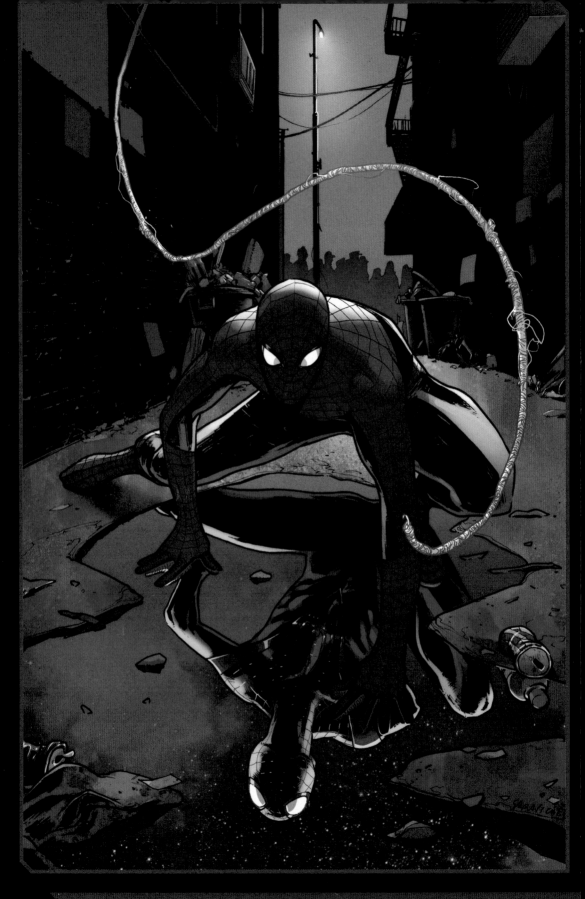

SPIDER-MEN #1 VARIANT BY SARA PICHELLI & JUSTIN PONSOR

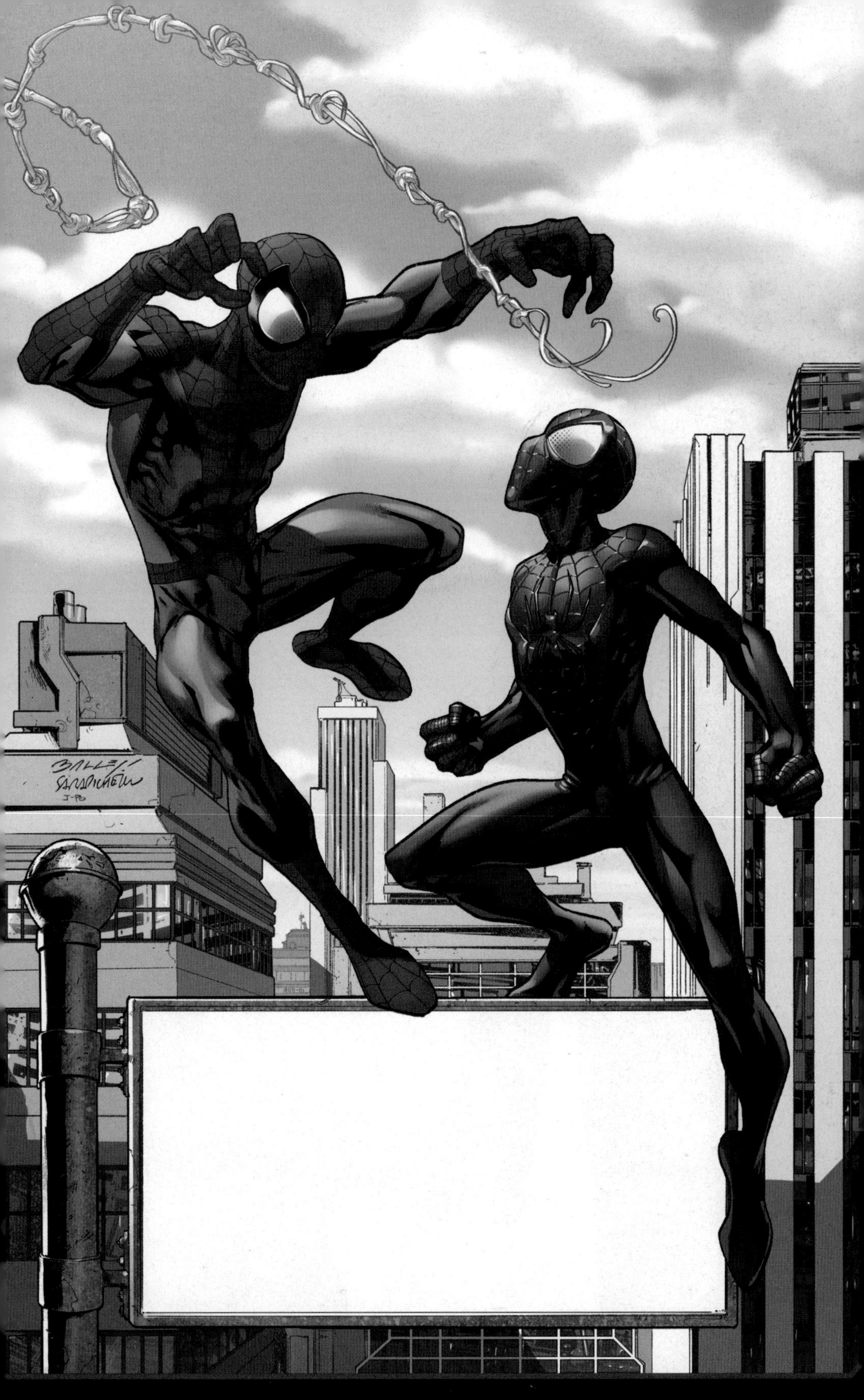

SPIDER-MEN #1 RETAILER VARIANT BY MARK BAGLEY, SARA PICHELLI & JUSTIN PONSOR

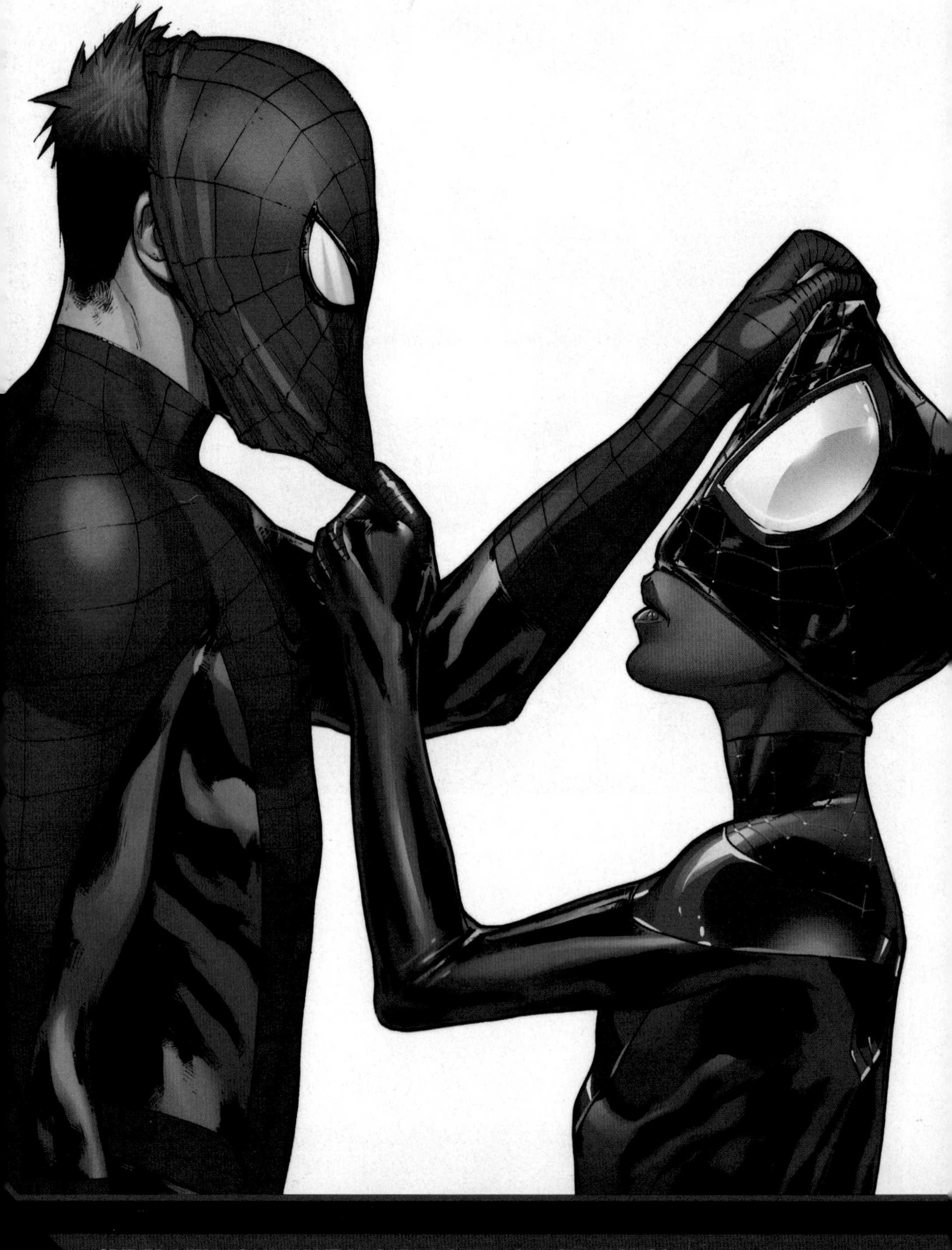

SPIDER-MEN #2 VARIANT BY SARA PICHELLI & JUSTIN PONSOR

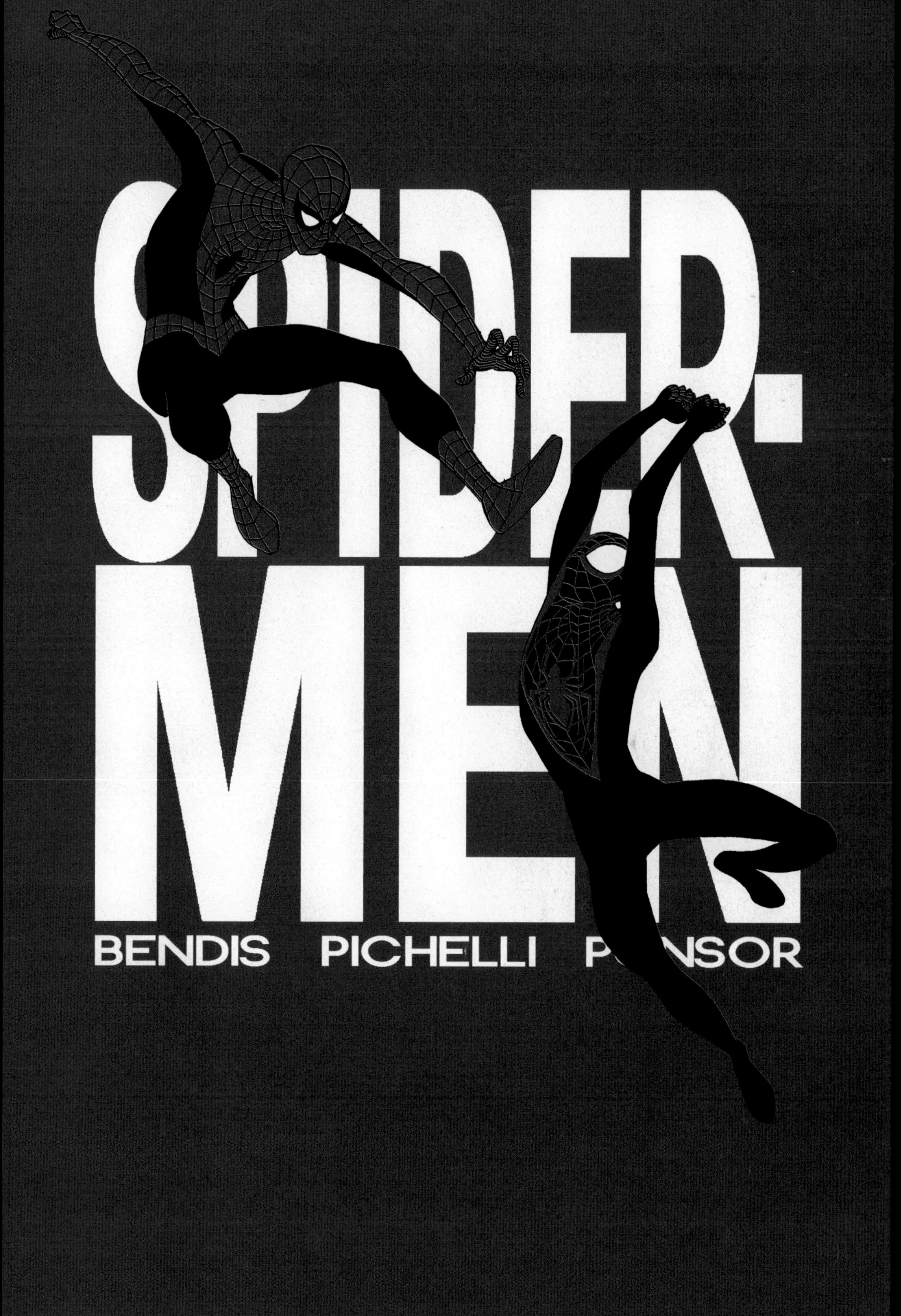
SPIDER-
MEN
BENDIS PICHELLI PONSOR

SPIDER-MEN #2 VARIANT BY MARCOS MARTIN

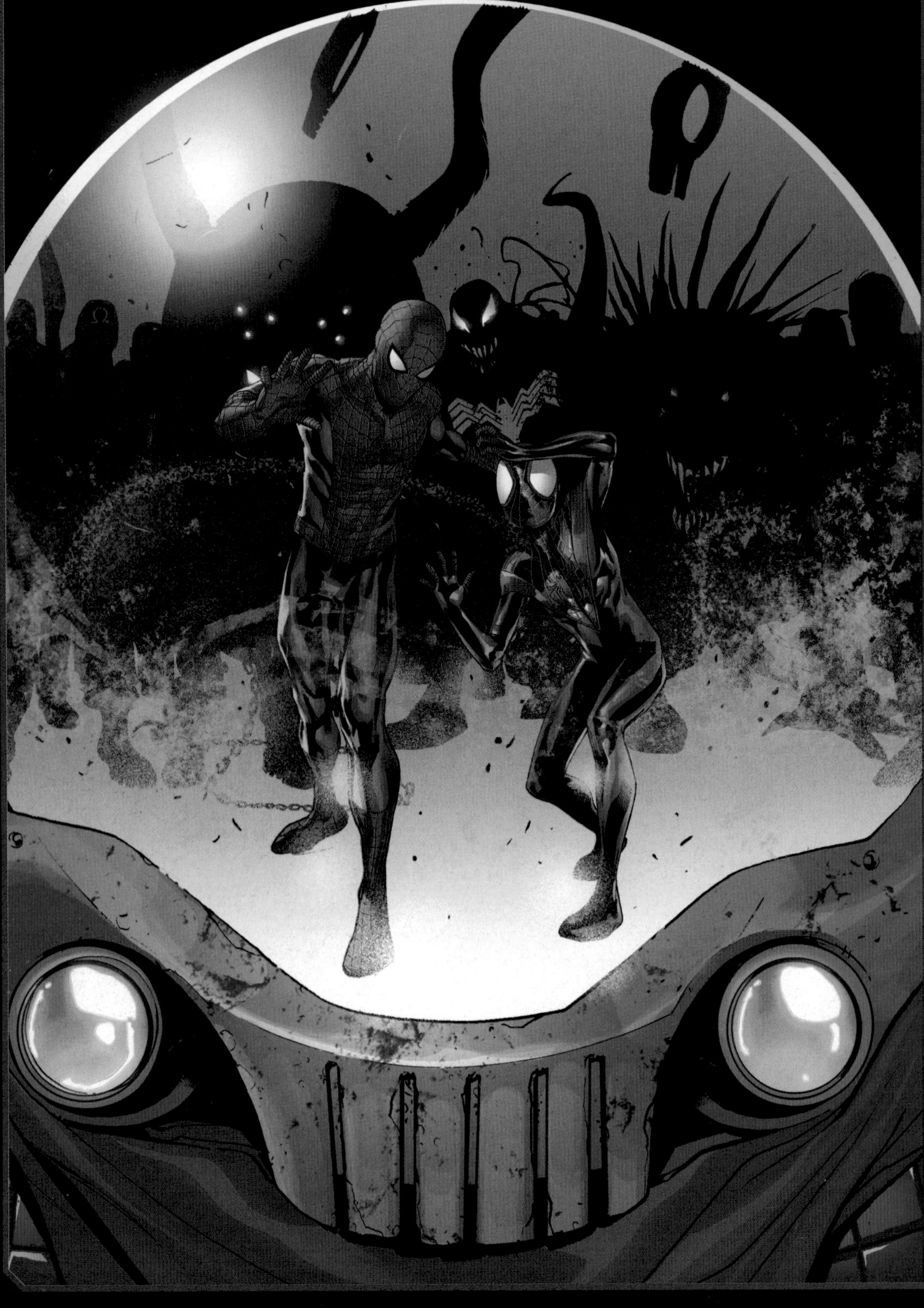

SPIDER-MEN #3 VARIANT BY SARA PICHELLI & RAIN BEREDO

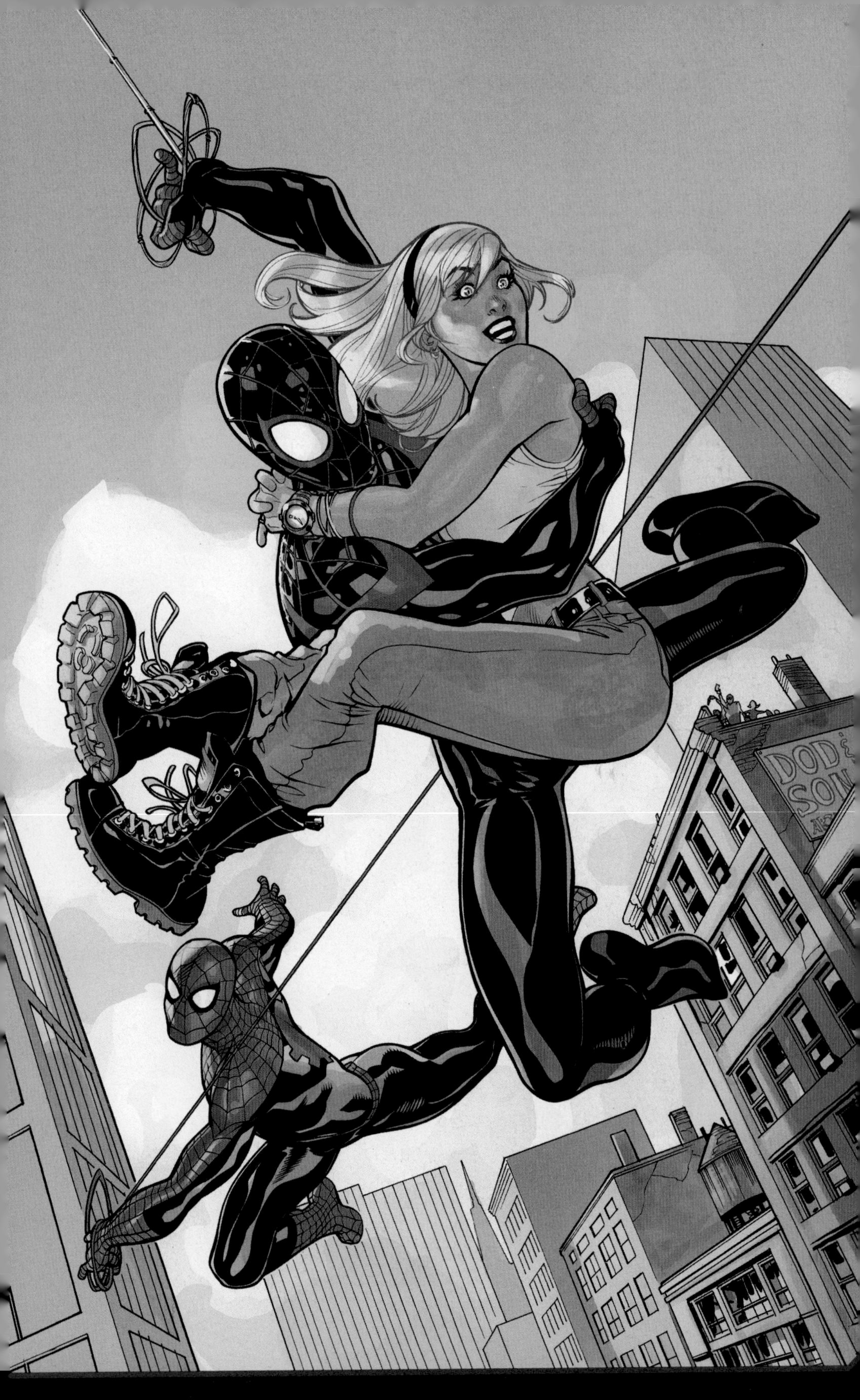

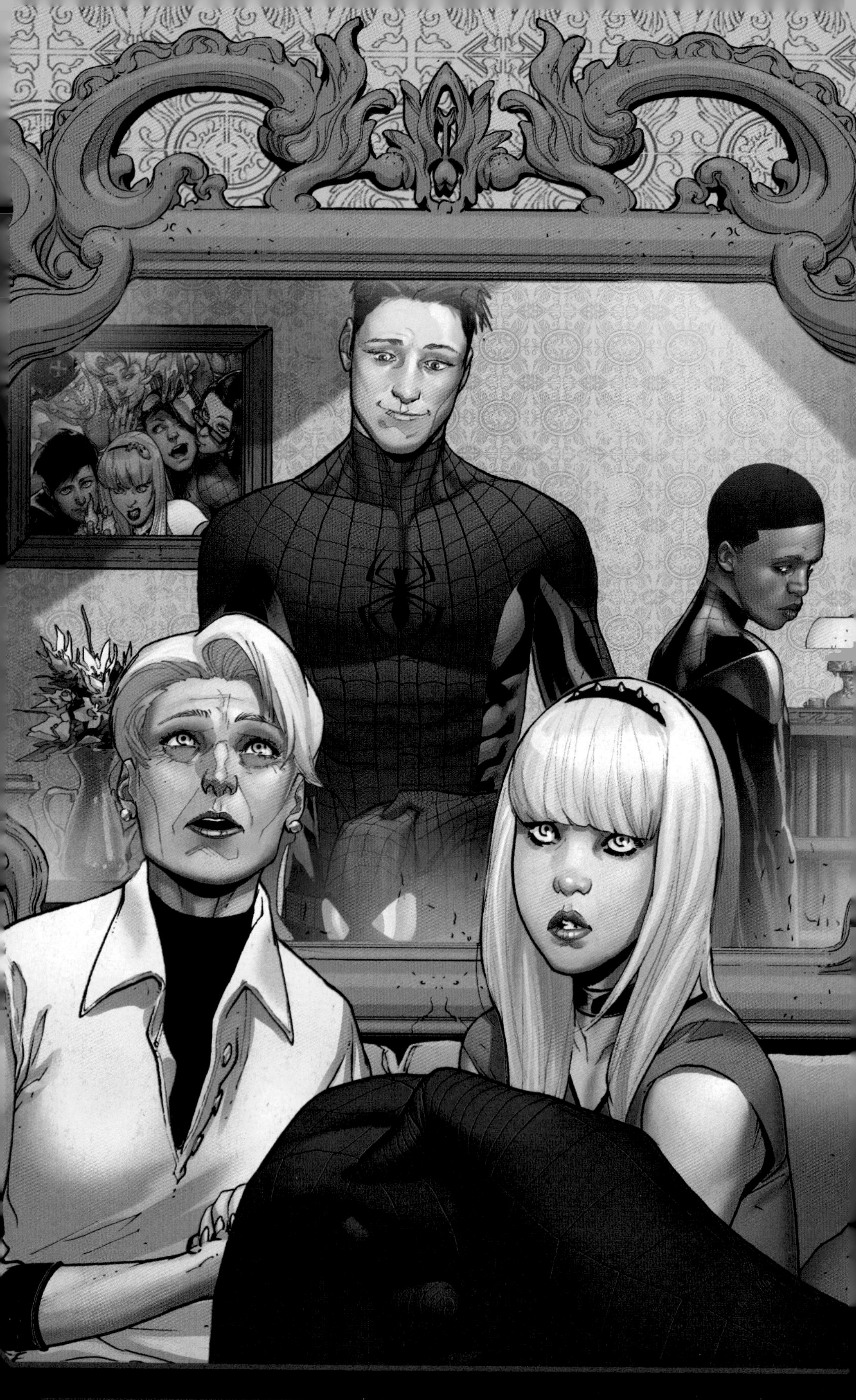

SPIDER-MEN #4 VARIANT BY SARA PICHELLI & JUSTIN PONSOR

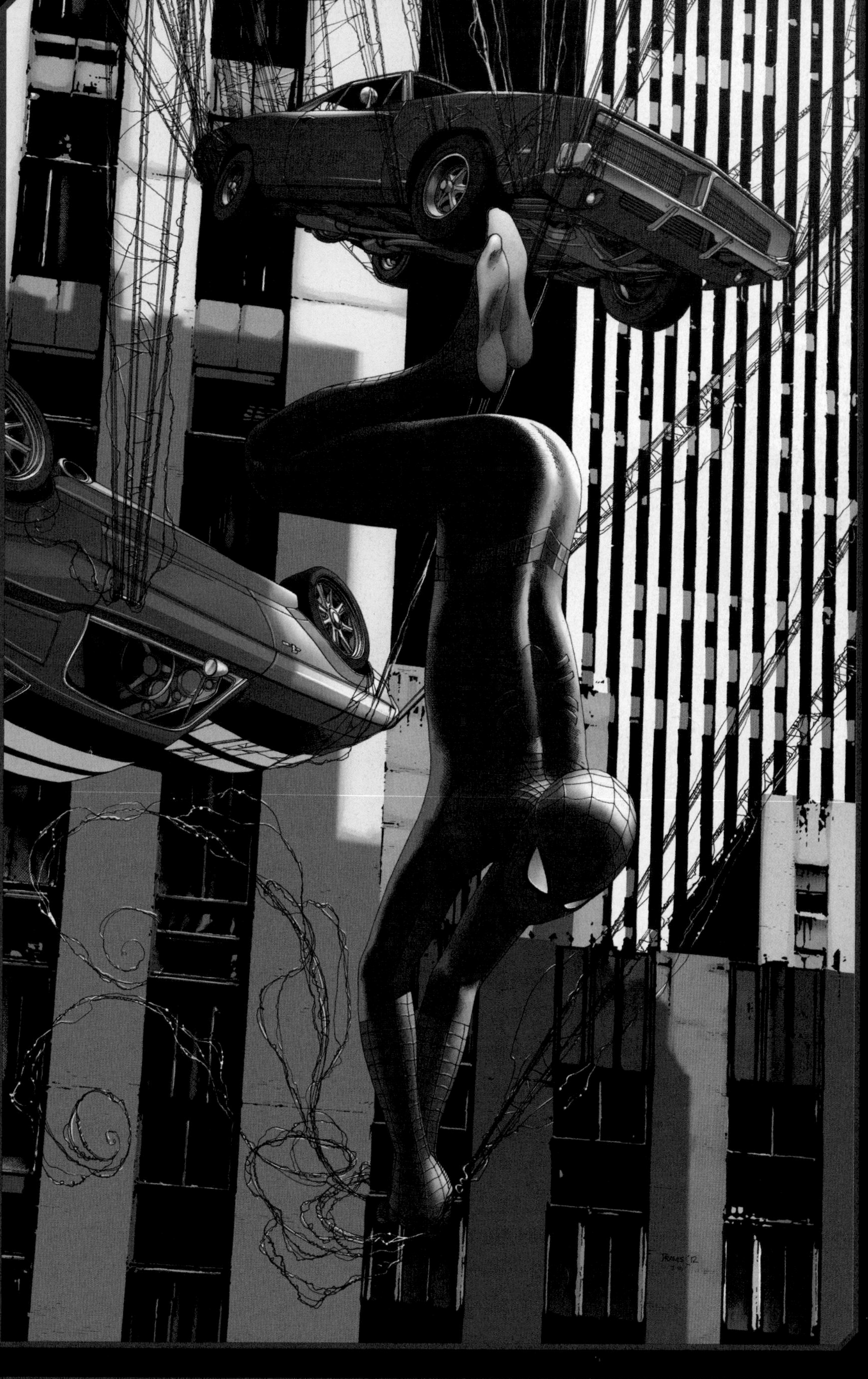

SPIDER-MEN #5 VARIANT BY TRAVIS CHAREST

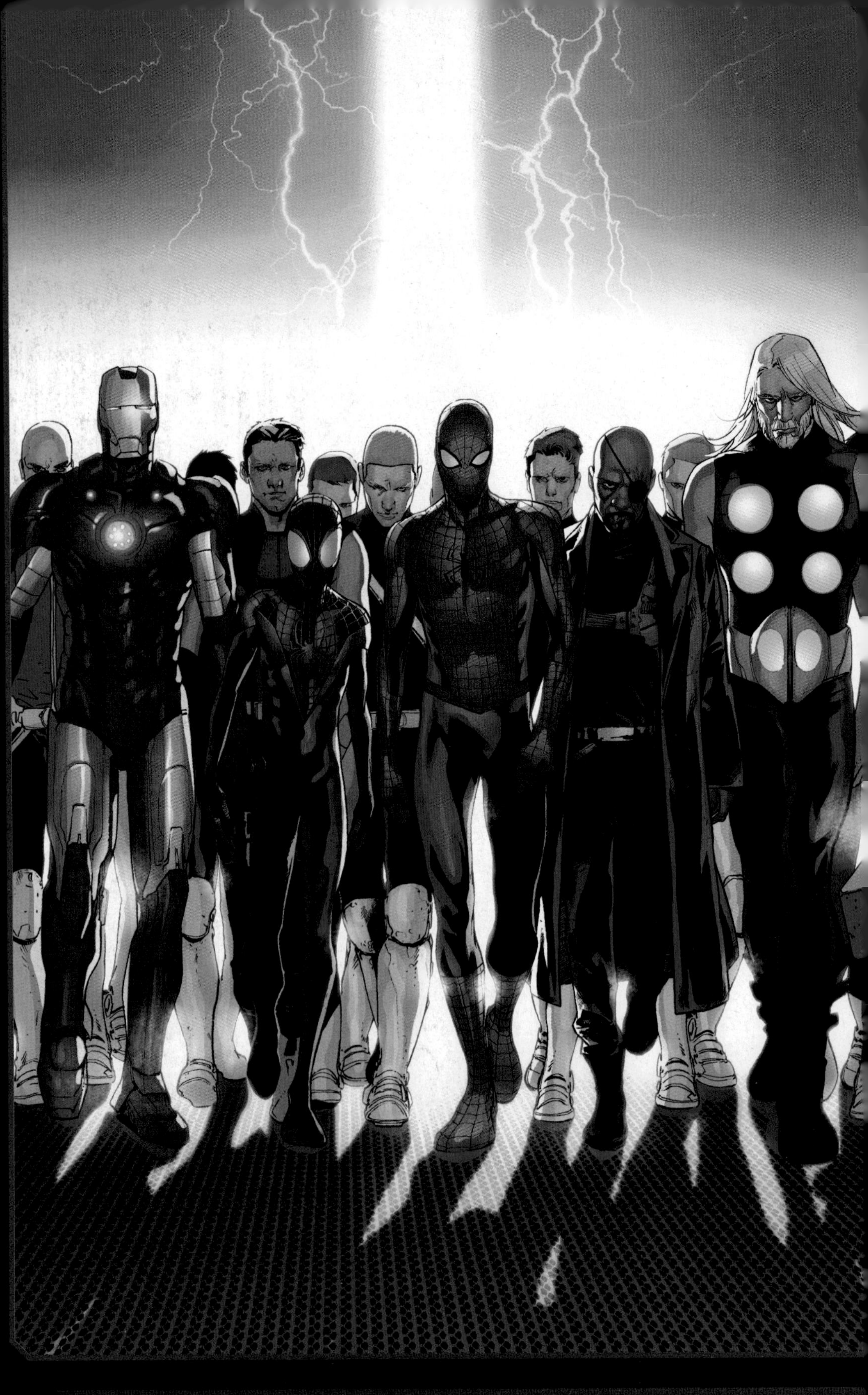

SPIDER-MEN #5 VARIANT BY SARA PICHELLI & RAIN BEREDO

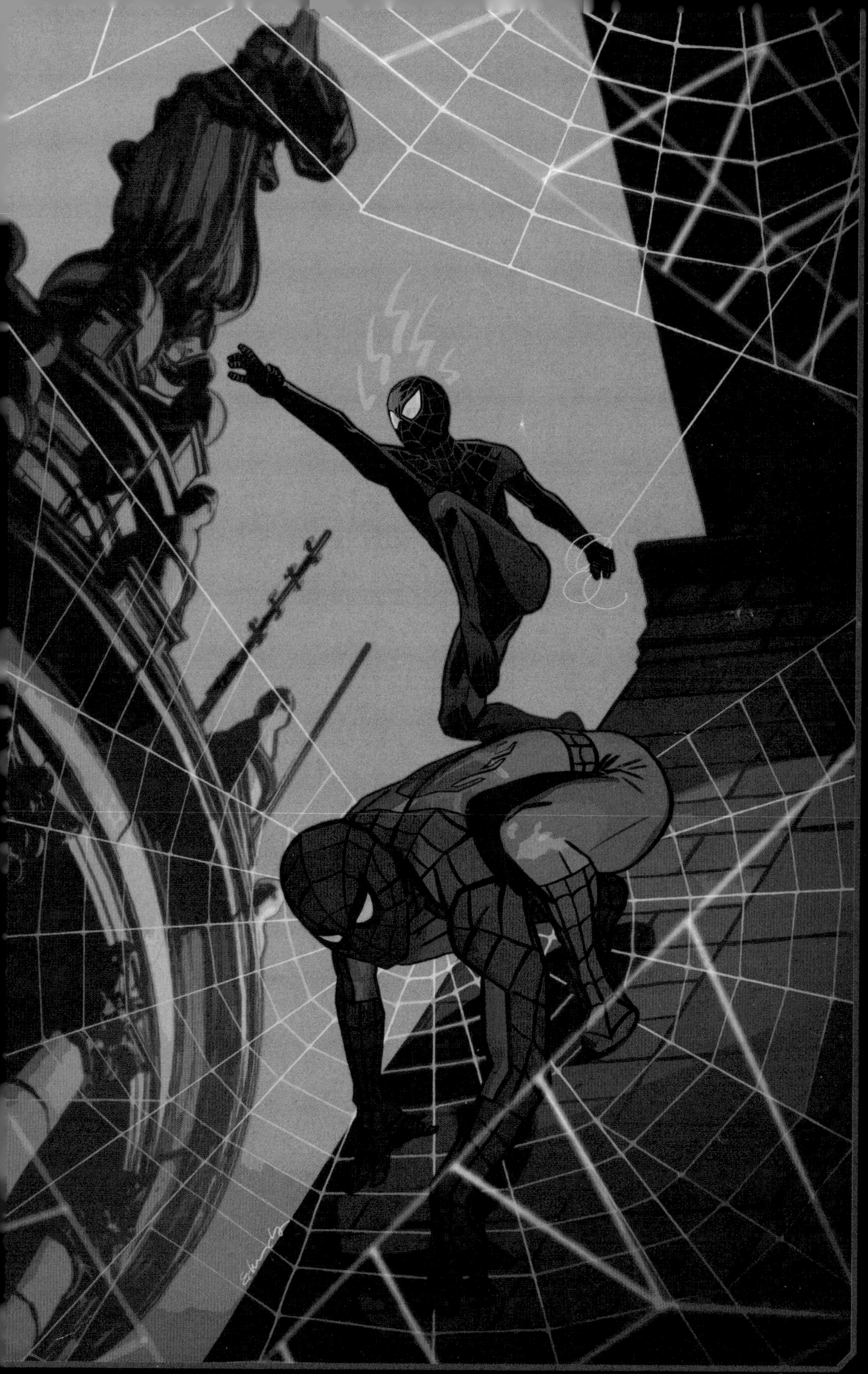

SPIDER-MEN #5 VARIANT BY TOMMY LEE EDWARDS

A
B
C
D
E

SPIDER-MEN #1 COVER PROCESS BY JIM CHEUNG

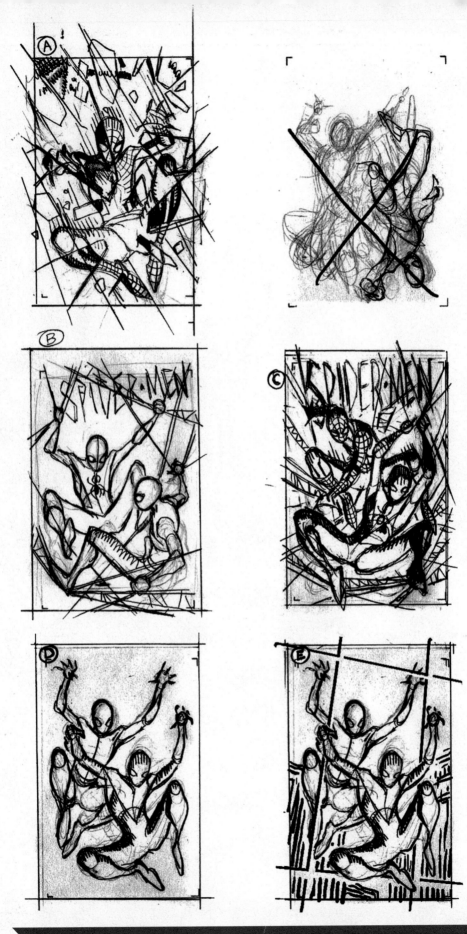

SPIDER-MEN ONE COVER CHEUNG

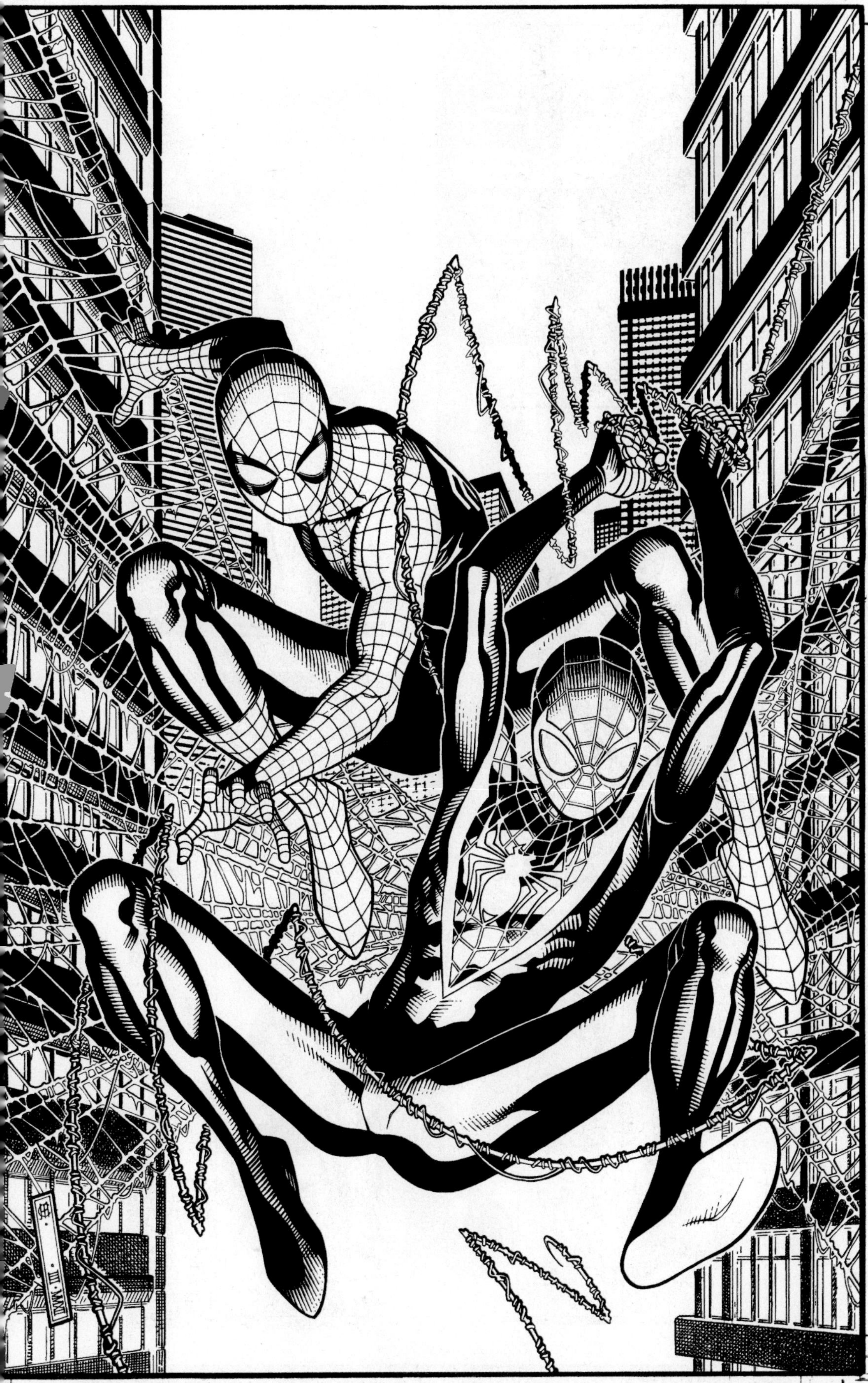

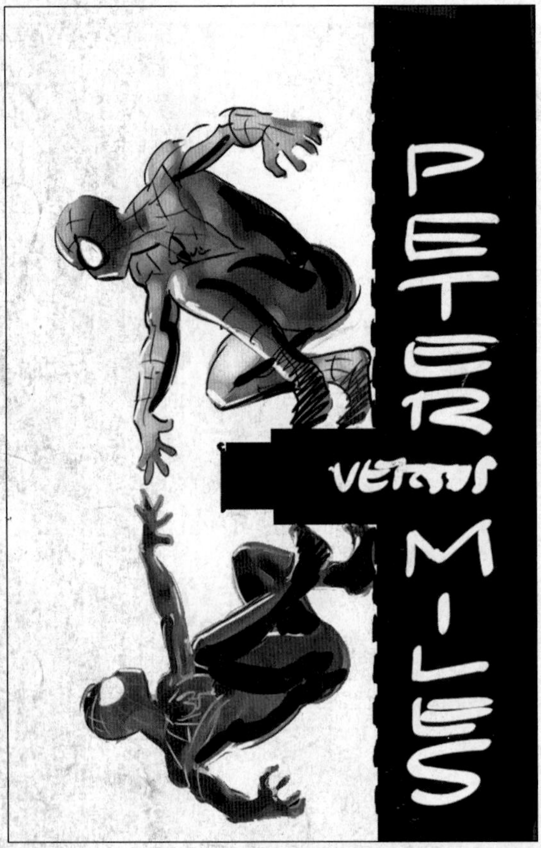
PETER
versus
MILES

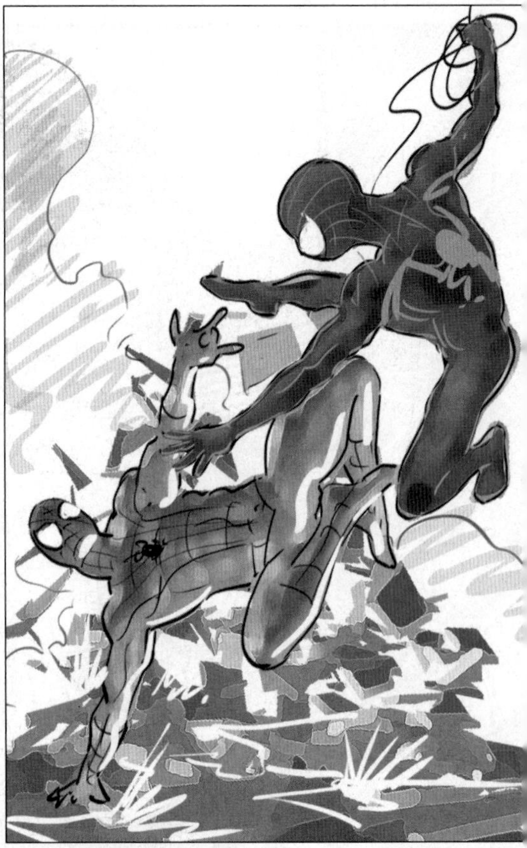

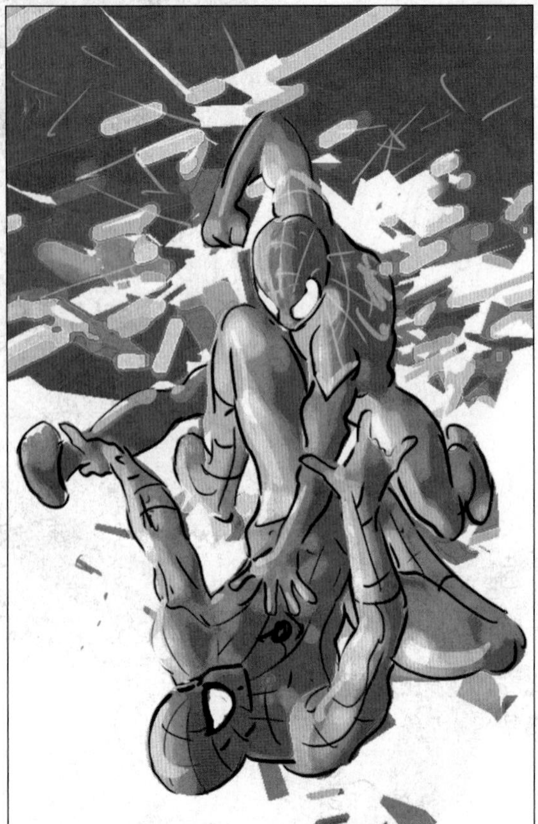

SPIDER-MEN #4 VARIANT COVER PROCESS BY MIKE DEODATO

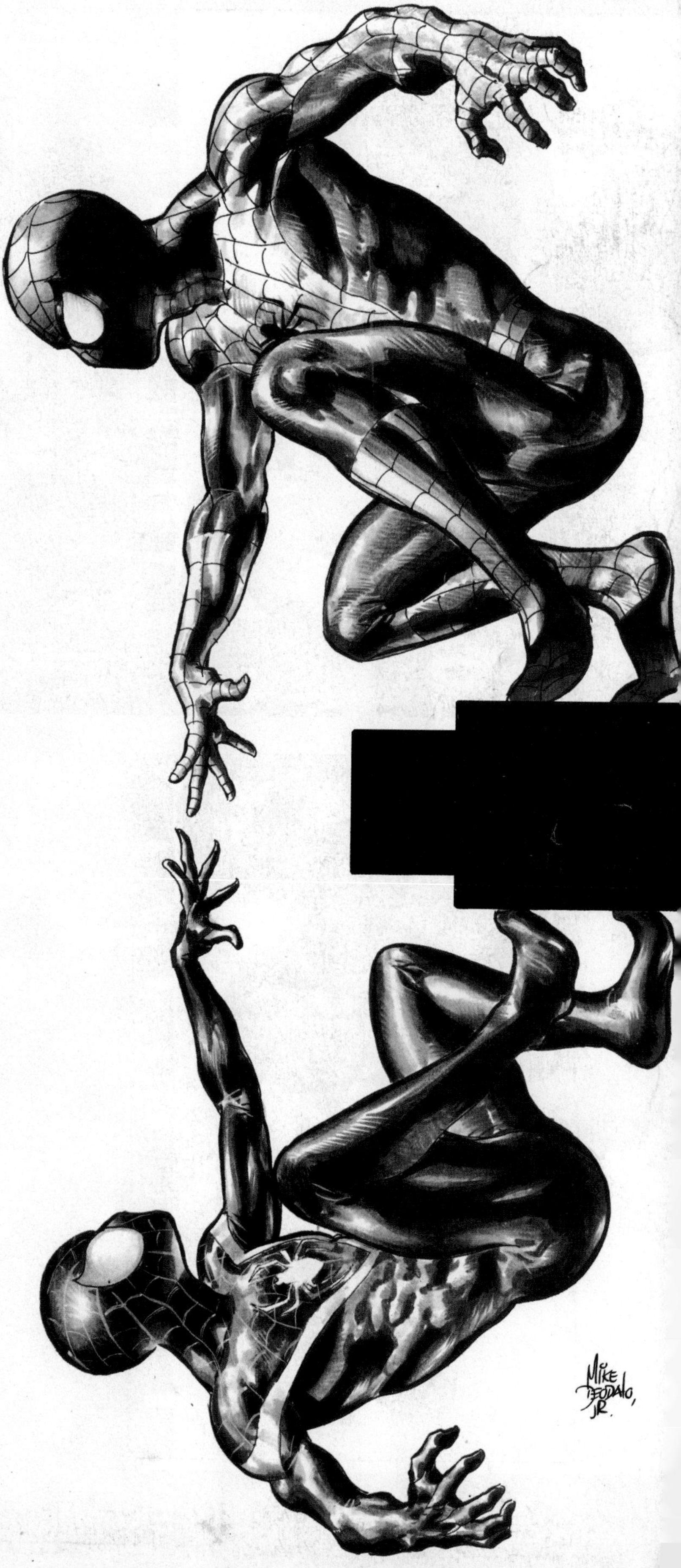
MIKE DEODATO, JR.

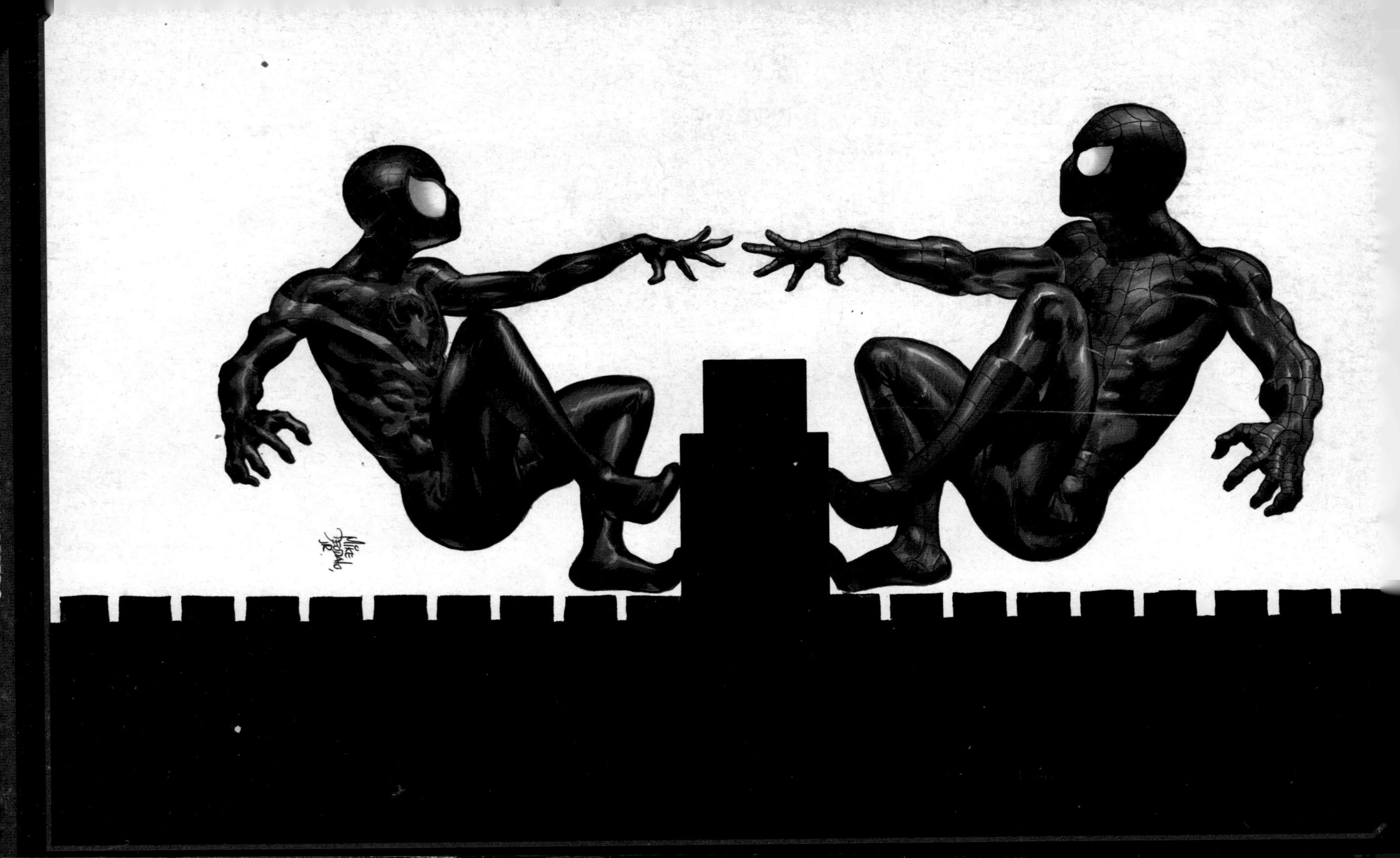
Mike Deodato, Jr.